ENGINEERING EDUCATION AND RESEARCH USING MATLAB

Edited by **Ali H. Assi**

Engineering Education and Research Using MATLAB
Edited by Ali H. Assi

Published by InTech
Janeza Trdine 9, 51000 Rijeka, Croatia

Publishing Process Manager Davor Vidic

Technical Editor Teodora Smiljanic

Cover Designer InTech Design Team

Additional hard copies can be obtained from orders@intechopen.com

Engineering Education and Research Using MATLAB, Edited by Ali H. Assi
p. cm.
ISBN 978-953-307-656-0

Meet the editor

Dr. Ali H. Assi received his Ph.D. degree in Electrical Engineering from Ecole Polytechnique De Montreal. In January 1998, he joined Texas Instruments in Ottawa, where he worked as an ASIC Applications engineer. In June 1999, Dr. Assi moved to Texas Instruments in Dallas as senior ASIC design engineer. In September 2000, he joined the Department of Electrical Engineering at the American University of Beirut (AUB) as a lecturer. In September 2001, Dr. Assi joined the Department of Electrical Engineering at the United Arab Emirates University (UAEU) as an assistant professor. He is currently an associate professor and his research interests include VLSI/CAD and Mixed-Signal Analog/Digital circuits design, Renewable Energy, and Photovoltaics/Solar cells. He published more than 80 scientific articles in peer-reviewed books, journals, and conference proceedings where MATLAB was one of the many engineering tools used in his research. Dr. Assi is a senior member of the IEEE.

Contents

Preface

MATLAB is a software package used primarily in the field of engineering for signal processing, numerical data analysis, modeling, programming, simulation, and computer graphic visualization. In the last few years, it has become widely accepted as an efficient tool, and, therefore, its use has significantly increased in scientific communities and academic institutions. MATLAB has proven itself to be very useful and important for education and research, hence the title of this book. It has become very popular for various reason - these include being programmable, well developed, well tested, compact, extensible, and compatible with many operating systems.

This book consists of 20 chapters presenting research works using MATLAB tools. The chapters were written by researchers recognized as experts and users of MATLAB. Chapters include techniques for programming and developing Graphical User Interfaces (GUIs), dynamic systems, electric machines, signal and image processing, power electronics, mixed signal circuits, genetic programming, digital watermarking, control systems, time-series regression modeling, and artificial neural networks.

The task of completing this book and its chapters was accomplished thanks to the support and contribution of the authors, who spent a lot of effort and time on this project. Thanks go equally to the editorial board and the team of InTech for the excellent work in making the revisions of chapters smooth and accurate.

Ali Hussein Assi
United Arab Emirates University
United Arab Emirates

1

Modeling and Simulation of Multiphase Machines in the Matlab/Simulink Environment

Alberto Tessarolo
University of Trieste
Italy

1. Introduction

Multiphase machines are AC machines characterized by a stator winding composed of a generic number n of phases. In today's electric drive and power generation technology, multiphase machines play an important role for the benefits they bring compared to traditional three-phase ones (Levi, 2008; Levi et al., 2007). Such benefits have been widely highlighted by existing literature (Levi et al., 2007) and are mainly related to: an increased fault tolerance; higher power ratings achieved through power segmentation; enhanced performance in terms of efficiency and torque ripple.

The use of multiphase machines is spreading both in small-power safety-critical applications as well as in very high-power industrial drives (Tessarolo et al., 2010), in electric-propulsion drives (Castellan et al., 2007) and power generation systems (Sulligoi et al., 2010).

Regardless of whether they are used as motors or generators, multiphase electrical machines are almost always connected to power electronics systems (inverters for motors, rectifiers for generators), which interface them to the electric grid (Sulligoi et al., 2010; Castellan et al. 2008). Therefore, if the dynamic behaviour of a multiphase machine is to be predicted through simulations in the design and development stage, it is essential to do this by means of system-level simulations, where not only the electric machine is included, but also the power electronics and control systems that interact with it. Such a system-level simulation approach makes it difficult to use Finite-Element (FE) methods due to the complexity of the domain to be modelled and to the well-known computational heaviness of time-stepping FE simulations. Conversely, lumped-parameter models, to be implemented in the Matlab/Simulink environment, may provide designers with a powerful mean of analysis and investigation, provided that all the system components to be studied are modelled with an adequate level of accuracy and completeness.

As concerns power electronics systems usually interfaced to multiphase machines, whether operating as motors or generators, the Matlab/Simulink environment offers wide and complete libraries where the designer can find reliable pre-defined blocks (for electronic switches, snubbers, diodes, etc.) to be used in building the application-related apparatus models. The same pertains to control and regulation blocks, which can be built up directly based on their transfer functions and logics.

A possible criticality can be encountered when it comes to build the multiphase machine model. In fact, no predefined blocks are presently available in the Matlab/Simulink environment for this purpose. On the other side, building a dedicated user-defined machine

model for any specific multiphase arrangement may require a non-trivial work due to the wide variety of multiphase schemes (in terms of phase number and distribution) and due to the several different modelling approaches which can be derived from the current literature on the subject (Levi et al., 2007).
Based on the above premises, this Chapter aims at providing Matlab/Simulink users, interested in simulating electromechanical systems where multiphase machines are involved, with some general modelling and implementation strategies which enable them to treat all the multiphase machine schemes of practical interest in a unified manner.
The Chapter is organized so as to sequentially cover the topics listed below:

- Qualitative description of the various stator multiphase arrangements for multiphase machines.
- Introduction of Vector-Space Decomposition as a method for a unified treatment of the mentioned multiphase schemes.
- Implementation of the VSD-based model in the Matlab-Simulink environment.
- Application examples.

2. Variety, modelling and representation of multiphase winding schemes

There is a large variety of multiphase machines depending on:

1. The number of phases n constituting the stator winding;
2. The way in which the n phases are physically arranged;
3. The kind of rotor (which may be of squired-cage, permanent-magnet, reluctance, assisted-reluctance type as well as in ordinary three-phase machines).

As concerns phase arrangement, for instance, the n phases may be distributed symmetrically around the stator circumference with a phase shift of $360/n$ electrical degrees, as it happens in five-phase (Pereira et al., 2006) and seven-phase (Figueroa et al., 2006) symmetrical machines (Fig. 1a).
Otherwise, the n phases (with n necessarily being an integer multiple of 3) may be grouped into N three-phase sets, displaced by $60/N$ electrical degrees apart: this is the case of the so called split-phase winding configurations (Levi et al., 2007; Tessarolo et al., 2010) (Fig. 1b).
Finally, more complicated solutions can be also implemented, such as in the propulsion motor described by Terrein et al., 2004, where n=15 stator phases are grouped into three five-phase sets.

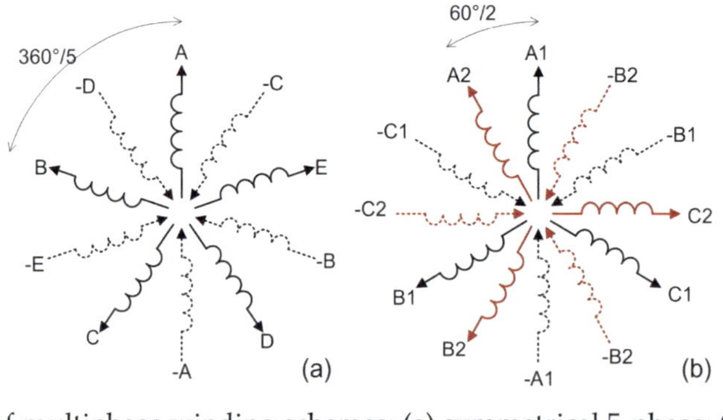

Fig. 1. Examples of multiphase winding schemes: (a) symmetrical 5-phase; (b) split-phase double-star

2.1 Graphical representation convention

The graphical representation of the winding scheme used in Fig. 1 is quite conventional and widespread. However, for the sake of clarity it can be better understood referring to Fig. 2 and Fig. 3, where such graphical representation is shown aside the physical phase arrangement in the case of a concentrated winding machine (the same pertains to distributed windings, of course). It can be seen that each coil group of the phase is represented by an arrow pointing in the direction of the magnetic field which would originate if the coil group carried a positive current. Coil groups shifted by 180 electrical degrees are represented by arrows of different line styles (solid and dashed).

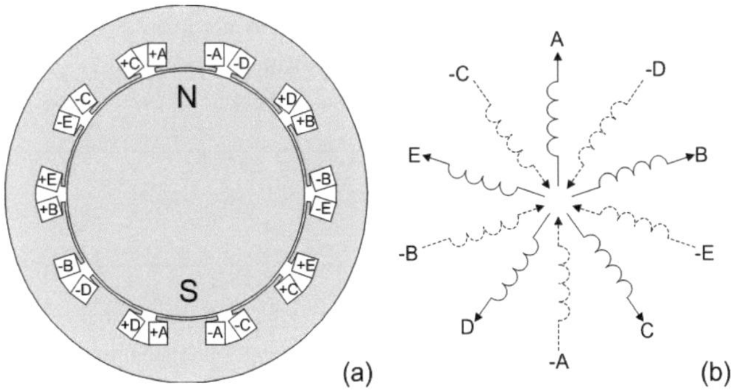

Fig. 2. Example of a two-pole 5-phase electric machine where each phase has coil groups shifted by π electrical radians

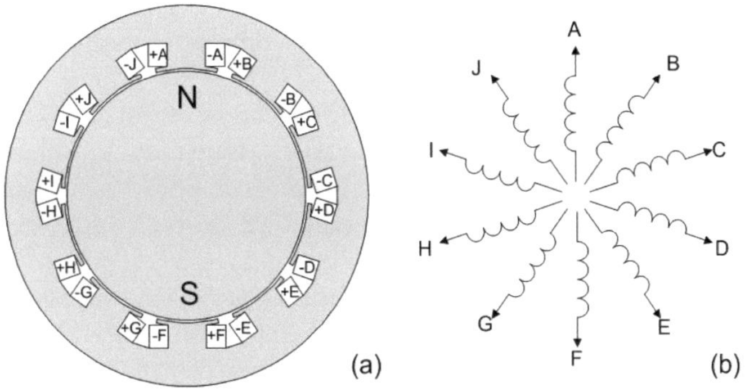

Fig. 3. Example of a two-pole 10-phase electric machine where each phase is not composed of coil groups shifted by π electrical radians. (a) Physical winding topology; (b) conventional winding representation

2.2 Modeling assumptions

In modelling the various types of multiphase machines, the following usual assumptions with be made in the rest of the Chapter:

1. Magnetic saturation is neglected, so inductances are assumed as constant.
2. It is assumed that the air-gap width of the machine can be modelled as a constant plus a sinusoidal function whose period equals a pole pitch.
3. All the n phases are geometrically identical except for their angular displacement, hence electrical machines with fractional slot windings are not covered.

4. Each phase is composed of identical coil groups (or phase belts) shifted by π electrical radians apart (as in the 5-phase example shown in Fig. 2); in other words, each phase has one coil group per pole. Conversely, such winding topologies as that shown in Fig. 3 (one phase belt per pole pair) and are not covered.

It is noticed that the assumption made in point 4 is not importantly restrictive, since such winding schemes as that shown in Fig. 3 are very rarely used in practice as they give rise to important even-order space harmonics in the air-gap (Klingshirn, 1983).

3. Multiphase machine modelling through Vector-Space Decomposition

The purpose of this Section is to propose a VSD method which applies to both symmetrical and asymmetrical n-phase winding schemes, for whatever integer n greater than 3. To do this, we propose that the VSD transformation should consist of two cascaded steps (Fig. 4):

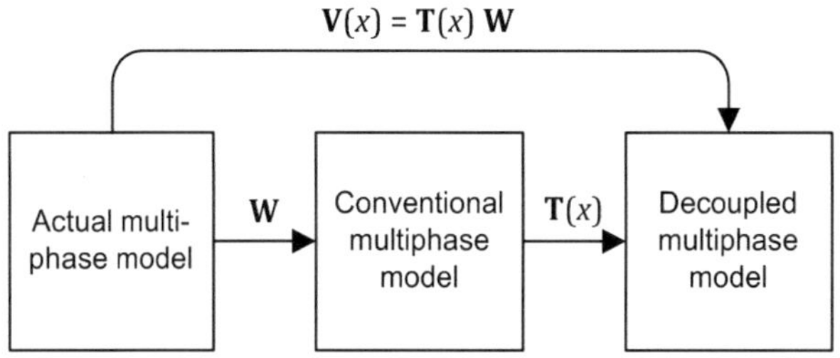

Fig. 4. Two-step transformation for the VSD of a generic multiphase model

1. The first is a merely geometrical transformation (**W**) capable of mapping the actual winding structure into a conventional one; the precise meaning of this "mapping" operation will be clarified next.
2. The second is a decoupling transformation [represented by matrix $\mathbf{T}(x)$ where x is the rotor position] to be applied to the conventional machine model. Such transformation is meant to project machine variables onto a set of mutually orthogonal subspaces.

The overall VSD transformation $\mathbf{V}(x)=\mathbf{T}(x)\mathbf{W}$ will then result from combining the two transformations. The advantage of this approach is that the properly called VSD theory can be developed only for the conventional multiphase model (thereby making abstraction of the particular phase arrangement of the actual machine), instead of tailoring VSD procedures on any particular multiphase winding topology that may occur in practice.

3.1 Selection of the conventional multiphase model

The question arises as to which multiphase model is the most suitable for being chosen as "conventional". A natural answer would be the symmetrical n-phase winding scheme with $2\pi/n$ phase progression, which is considered by Figueroa et al., 2006. With such a choice, the theory proposed in by Figueroa et al., 2006 could be in fact used to build the VSD transformation $\mathbf{V}(x)$. The problem which would occur with this choice, however, would be the lack of generality. In fact, there would be some n-phase schemes of practical importance which could not be mapped into an equivalent symmetrical winding with $2\pi/n$ phase progression through any transformation **W**. For instance, this would happen for any split-phase (multiple-star) windings composed of an even number of phases. The concept is illustrated in Fig. 5a-b; the figure shows how a triple-star winding can be certainly mapped into a symmetrical 9-phase scheme with $2\pi/9$ phase progression (through a transformation $\mathbf{W}'_{3\times3}$ mapping phase A1 into A, phase A2 into -F, phase A3 into B, etc.), while a dual-star winding (Fig. 5c) cannot be mapped into any 6-phase scheme with $2\pi/6$ phase progression, just because there does not exist a 6-phase scheme with $2\pi/6$ phase progression.

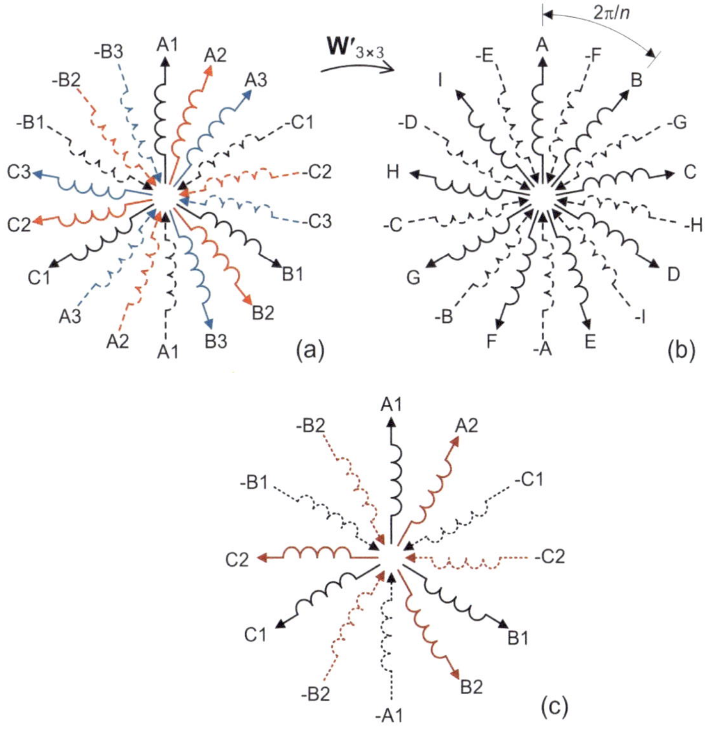

Fig. 5. Mapping of a triple-star winding (a) into a symmetrical 9-phase scheme with $2\pi/9$ phase progression (b); a dual-star winding (c) cannot be mapped into any symmetrical 6-phase scheme with $2\pi/6$ phase progression

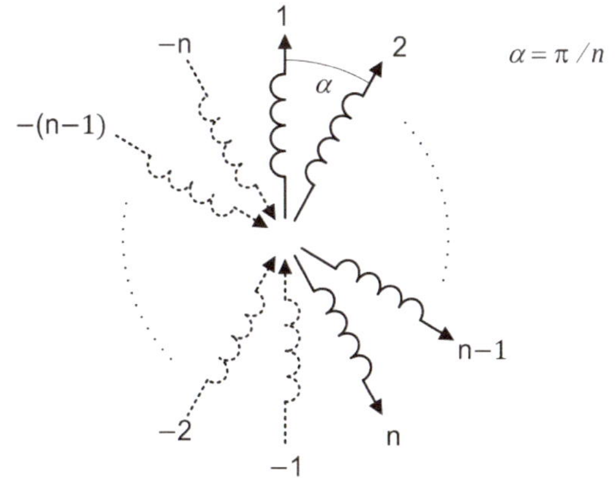

Fig. 6. Conventional arrangement for an n-phase winding

In order to overcome the above limitation, a different choice of the conventional multiphase scheme is made. The conventional n-phase winding arrangement selected for the purpose is shown in Fig. 6 and entails n phases numbered from 0 to n−1 and sequentially arranged over a pole span with a phase progression angle.

$$\alpha = \pi / n \tag{1}$$

With such a choice, any n-phase winding (whether symmetrical or asymmetrical, with even or odd phase count) can be mapped into a conventional n-phase arrangement such as that in Fig. 6 by means of a geometrical transformation **W**, built as detailed in the next Section.

3.2 Geometrical transformation into conventional winding scheme

By geometrical transformation we mean a sequence of phase permutations and reversals capable of reducing the actual winding scheme into an equivalent one having the conventional structure shown in Fig. 6. The principle is illustrated in Fig. 7 with the examples of a symmetrical 5-phase winding (a) and of an asymmetrical 6-phase (dual star) winding (c) to be mapped into their corresponding conventional arrangements respectively through transformations $\mathbf{W}_5$ and $\mathbf{W}_{2\times3}$.

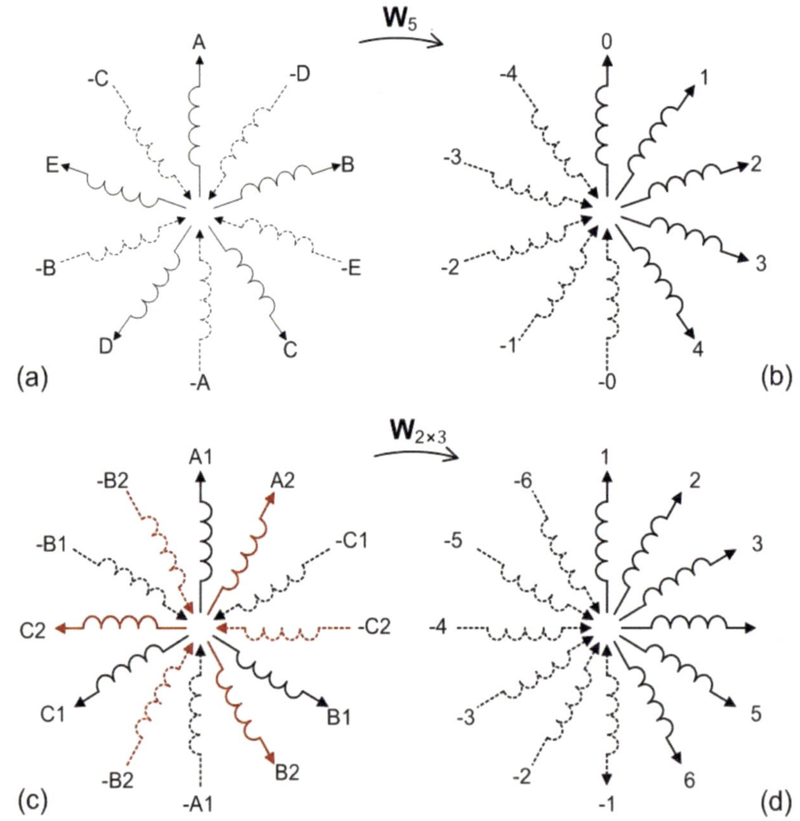

Fig. 7. Geometrical transformation into conventional phase arrangement

Let us suppose that the phase variables are arranged in vector form as per (2) and (3) respectively for the 5-phase and the dual star case and as per (4) for the conventional winding schemes:

$$\mathbf{y}_{A..E} = \begin{pmatrix} y_A & y_B & y_C & y_D & y_E \end{pmatrix}^t \tag{2}$$

$$\mathbf{y}_{2\times ABC} = \begin{pmatrix} y_{A1} & y_{A2} & y_{B1} & y_{B2} & y_{C1} & y_{C2} \end{pmatrix}^t \tag{3}$$

$$\mathbf{y}_n = \begin{pmatrix} y_0 & y_1 & y_2 & \cdots & y_{n-1} \end{pmatrix}^t \tag{4}$$

where y indicates a generic phase variable, such as a current, voltage or flux linkage and superscript t indicates transposition. It can be easily seen that the following relationships must hold for the windings (a), (c) to be respectively equivalent to windings (b), (d) in Fig. 7:

$$\mathbf{y}_5 = \mathbf{W}_5 \mathbf{y}_{A..E}, \quad \mathbf{W}_5 = \begin{pmatrix} 1 & 0 & 0 & 0 & 0 \\ 0 & 0 & 0 & -1 & 0 \\ 0 & 1 & 0 & 0 & 0 \\ 0 & 0 & 0 & 0 & -1 \\ 0 & 0 & 1 & 0 & 0 \end{pmatrix} \tag{5}$$

$$\mathbf{y}_6 = \mathbf{W}_{2\times 3} \mathbf{y}_{2\times ABC}, \quad \mathbf{W}_{2\times 3} = \begin{pmatrix} 1 & 0 & 0 & 0 & 0 & 0 \\ 0 & 0 & 0 & 1 & 0 & 0 \\ 0 & 0 & -1 & 0 & 0 & 0 \\ 0 & 0 & 0 & 0 & 0 & -1 \\ 0 & 1 & 0 & 0 & 0 & 0 \\ 0 & 0 & 0 & 0 & 1 & 0 \end{pmatrix} \tag{6}$$

3.2.1 General transformation for symmetrical *n*-phase configurations

Let us now consider the general case of a symmetrical n-phase winding with $2\pi/n$ phase progression (see Fig. 1a and Fig. 5b as examples); it can be mapped into a conventional phase arrangement through the geometrical transformation $\mathbf{W}_n$ defined as:

$$\{\mathbf{W}_n\}_{i,j} = \begin{cases} 1 & \text{if } 2j - i = 0 \\ -1 & \text{if } |2j - i| = n \\ 0 & \text{otherwise} \end{cases} \qquad i,j = 0, \ldots, n-1; \tag{7}$$

The formal proof of (7) is omitted for the sake of brevity as the formula can be easily checked on a case-by-case basis.

3.2.2 General transformation for asymmetrical (split-phase) configurations

Let us consider the general case of an asymmetrical (or split-phase) winding composed of N m-phase stars shifted by $2\pi/(mN)$ stars (Fig. 5a shows an example with m=3 and N=3, Fig. 1b with m=3 and N=2). Such a winding can be mapped into a conventional mN-phase arrangement through the geometrical transformation given by:

$$\left\{\mathbf{W}_{N\times m}\right\}_{i,j} = \begin{cases} 1 & \text{if } i - \mathrm{trunc}\left(j/m\right) - 2N\,\mathrm{mod}(j,m) = 0 \\ -1 & \text{if } \left|i - \mathrm{trunc}\left(j/m\right) - 2N\,\mathrm{mod}(j,m)\right| = mN \\ 0 & \text{otherwise} \end{cases} \qquad i,j = 0,\ldots,mN-1\,; \tag{8}$$

The formula can be easily checked to hold on a case-by-case basis.

3.3 Machine model in conventional multiphase variables

In the previous Section it has been shown how any multiphase scheme can be mapped into an equivalent one having a "conventional" phase arrangement and the suitable variable transformation matrices to be applied for this purpose have been presented. Therefore, it is not restrictive to suppose, in the following, that stator phases are distributed according to the conventional scheme. Hereinafter we shall present the form that the machine model equations take in this case.

The stator voltage equation in matrix form is given by:

$$\mathbf{v}_s = \mathbf{R}_s\mathbf{i}_s + \frac{d}{dt}\boldsymbol{\varphi}_s + \mathbf{e}_s \tag{9}$$

where phase variables are (superscript t denotes transposition):

$$\mathbf{v}_s = \begin{pmatrix} v_0 & v_1 & \cdots & v_{n-2} & v_{n-1} \end{pmatrix}^t \tag{10}$$

$$\mathbf{i}_s = \begin{pmatrix} i_0 & i_1 & \cdots & i_{n-2} & i_{n-1} \end{pmatrix}^t \tag{11}$$

$$\boldsymbol{\varphi}_s = \begin{pmatrix} \varphi_0 & \varphi_1 & \cdots & \varphi_{n-2} & \varphi_{n-1} \end{pmatrix}^t \tag{12}$$

$$\mathbf{e}_s = \begin{pmatrix} e_0 & e_1 & \cdots & e_{n-2} & e_{n-1} \end{pmatrix}^t \tag{13}$$

The symbol x_k, with $x \in \{v, i, \varphi, e\}$ and $k \in \{0, 1,\ldots, n-1\}$ represents the kth phase voltage (v), current (i), flux linkage (φ) or e.m.f. due to the rotor (e). The resistance matrix **R** is the $n\times n$ diagonal matrix having all its diagonal elements equal to phase resistance r:

$$\mathbf{R}_s = \begin{pmatrix} r & 0 & & 0 \\ 0 & r & & 0 \\ & & \ddots & \\ 0 & 0 & & r \end{pmatrix} \tag{14}$$

Phase flux linkage and current vectors are linked by the stator inductance matrix **L** which, for salient-pole machines, is a function of the rotor position x.

$$\boldsymbol{\varphi}_s = \mathbf{L}_s\left(x\right)\mathbf{i}_s \tag{15}$$

The stator inductance matrix is assumed to be composed of a leakage inductance term $\mathbf{L}_s^{(l)}$, not dependent on rotor position, and of an air-gap inductance term $\mathbf{L}_s^{(ag)}\left(x\right)$:

$$\mathbf{L}_s(x) = \mathbf{L}_s^{(l)} + \mathbf{L}_s^{(ag)}(x) \tag{16}$$

Substitution of (16) into (9) gives:

$$\mathbf{v}_s = \mathbf{R}_s\mathbf{i}_s + \frac{d}{dt}(\mathbf{L}_s\mathbf{i}_s) + \mathbf{e}_s = \mathbf{R}_s\mathbf{i}_s + \left(\frac{d}{dt}\mathbf{L}_s\right)\mathbf{i}_s + \mathbf{L}_s\frac{d}{dt}\mathbf{i}_s + \mathbf{e}_s \tag{17}$$

It is easy to show (Tessarolo, 2010) that the leakage inductance matrix has the following structure.

$$\mathbf{L}_s^{(l)} = \begin{pmatrix} \ell_0 & \ell_1 & \ell_2 & & -\ell_3 & -\ell_2 & -\ell_1 \\ \ell_1 & \ell_0 & \ell_1 & \cdots & -\ell_4 & -\ell_3 & -\ell_2 \\ \ell_2 & \ell_1 & \ell_0 & & -\ell_5 & -\ell_4 & -\ell_3 \\ & \vdots & & & & \vdots & \\ -\ell_3 & -\ell_4 & -\ell_5 & & \ell_0 & \ell_1 & \ell_2 \\ -\ell_2 & -\ell_3 & -\ell_4 & \cdots & \ell_1 & \ell_0 & \ell_1 \\ -\ell_1 & -\ell_2 & -\ell_3 & & \ell_2 & \ell_1 & \ell_0 \end{pmatrix} \tag{18}$$

Based on the assumptions listed in 2.2, the air-gap inductance matrix can be written as:

$$\mathbf{L}_s^{(ag)} = \frac{L_{md} + L_{mq}}{2}\mathbf{\Gamma}_1 + \frac{L_{md} - L_{mq}}{2}\left[\mathbf{\Gamma}_2\cos(2x) + \mathbf{\Gamma}_3\sin(2x)\right] \tag{19}$$

where:

$$\mathbf{\Gamma}_1 = \begin{pmatrix} 1 & \cos(\alpha) & \cos(2\alpha) & \cos(3\alpha) & \\ \cos(\alpha) & \cos(2\alpha) & \cos(3\alpha) & & \\ \cos(2\alpha) & \cos(3\alpha) & & & \\ \cos(3\alpha) & & & \iddots & \\ & & & & \end{pmatrix} \tag{20}$$

$$\mathbf{\Gamma}_2 = \begin{pmatrix} 1 & \cos(\alpha) & \cos(2\alpha) & \cos(3\alpha) & \\ \cos(\alpha) & 1 & \cos(\alpha) & \cos(2\alpha) & \\ \cos(2\alpha) & \cos(\alpha) & 1 & \cos(\alpha) & \\ \cos(3\alpha) & \cos(2\alpha) & \cos(\alpha) & 1 & \\ & & & & \ddots \end{pmatrix} \tag{21}$$

$$\mathbf{\Gamma}_3 = \begin{pmatrix} 1 & \sin(\alpha) & \sin(2\alpha) & \sin(3\alpha) & \\ \sin(\alpha) & 1 & \sin(\alpha) & \sin(2\alpha) & \\ \sin(2\alpha) & \sin(\alpha) & 1 & \sin(\alpha) & \\ \sin(3\alpha) & \sin(2\alpha) & \sin(\alpha) & 1 & \\ & & & & \ddots \end{pmatrix} \tag{22}$$

Equations (19)-(22) directly descend from the expression of the mutual inductance (due to air-gap flux) between two phases of indices "i" and "j" (Tessarolo et al., 2009):

$$\left[\mathbf{L}_s^{(ag)}\right]_{i,j} = \frac{L_{md}+L_{mq}}{2}\cos\left[(i-j)\alpha\right] + \frac{L_{md}-L_{mq}}{2}\cos\left[2\left(x-\frac{i+j}{2}\alpha\right)\right] \tag{23}$$

3.4 VFD transformation matrix

The problem with the machine model expressed in multiphase variables is that stator model matrices are not constant in presence of rotor saliency ($L_{md} \neq L_{mq}$), as shown by (23). Furthermore, it would be desirable that model variables become constant during sinusoidal steady-state operation. Additionally, the model written as per 3.2 contains quite involved inductance matrix structure and is thereby little suitable for implementation. Finally, a simple expression for the machine torque cannot be derived from the model formulated as per 3.2.

Vector-Space Decomposition (VSD) is a modelling technique which enables one to significantly simplify the machine equations (Levi et al., 2007) and finally yields a model structure (including diagonal matrices) which is simple to implement numerically. VSD, as proposed in this Chapter, is based on using a variable transformation **T** which maps the conventional multiphase vector variables (10)-(13) into "orhtonormal" vector coordinates (denoted with subscript dq in the following) as per (24). Model matrices are accordingly transformed as per (25).

$$\mathbf{v}_{dq} = \mathbf{T}(x)\mathbf{v}_s,\ \mathbf{i}_{dq} = \mathbf{T}(x)\mathbf{i}_s,\ \boldsymbol{\varphi}_{dq} = \mathbf{T}(x)\boldsymbol{\varphi}_s,\ \mathbf{e}_{dq} = \mathbf{T}(x)\mathbf{e}_s \tag{24}$$

The transformation matrix $\mathbf{T}(x)$ proposed here to accomplish the VSD is given by:

$$\mathbf{T}(x) = \mathbf{P}(x)\mathbf{C} \tag{25}$$

where:

$$\mathbf{P}(x) = \left(\begin{array}{cc|cc|cc|c} \cos(\omega x) & \sin(\omega x) & 0 & 0 & 0 & 0 & \\ -\sin(\omega x) & \cos(\omega x) & 0 & 0 & 0 & 0 & \\ \hline 0 & 0 & \cos(3\omega x) & \sin(3\omega x) & 0 & 0 & \\ 0 & 0 & -\sin(3\omega x) & \cos(3\omega x) & 0 & 0 & \\ \hline 0 & 0 & 0 & 0 & \cos(5\omega x) & \sin(5\omega x) & \\ 0 & 0 & 0 & 0 & -\sin(5\omega x) & \cos(5\omega x) & \\ \hline & & & & & & \ddots \end{array}\right) \tag{26}$$

$$\mathbf{C} = \sqrt{\frac{2}{n}}\left(\begin{array}{cccccc} 1 & \cos(\alpha) & \cos(2\alpha) & \cos(3\alpha) & \cdots & \cos\left[(n-1)\alpha\right] \\ 0 & \sin(\alpha) & \sin(2\alpha) & \sin(3\alpha) & \cdots & \sin\left[(n-1)\alpha\right] \\ \hline 1 & \cos(3\alpha) & \cos(6\alpha) & \cos(9\alpha) & \cdots & \cos\left[3(n-1)\alpha\right] \\ 0 & \sin(3\alpha) & \sin(6\alpha) & \sin(9\alpha) & \cdots & \sin\left[3(n-1)\alpha\right] \\ \hline 1 & \cos(5\alpha) & \cos(10\alpha) & \cos(15\alpha) & \cdots & \cos\left[5(n-1)\alpha\right] \\ 0 & \sin(5\alpha) & \sin(10\alpha) & \sin(10\alpha) & \cdots & \sin\left[5(n-1)\alpha\right] \\ \hline \vdots & \vdots & \vdots & \vdots & & \vdots \end{array}\right) \tag{27}$$

We notice that the proposed matrices do not coincide either with those used by Figueroa et al., 2006, or with those mentioned in Levi et al., 2007, but are specifically design to treat an n-phase machine with conventional multiphase arrangement (Tessarolo, 2009).

3.5 Machine model in transformed coordinates

In this Section, the transformation $\mathbf{T}(x)$ defined above will be applied to the model of the n-phase salient-pole machine whose model in conventional multiphase coordinates has been established in 3.2.

By applying transformation $\mathbf{T}(x)$ to model variables as per (24) and matrices (16) and (16) we obtain the transformed model matrices (marked by subscript dq) below:

$$\mathbf{R}_{dq} = \mathbf{T}(x)\mathbf{R}_s\mathbf{T}(x)^t = \mathbf{T}(x)(r\mathbf{I})\mathbf{T}(x)^t = r\mathbf{T}(x)\mathbf{T}(x)^t = r\mathbf{I} = \mathbf{R}_s \tag{28}$$

$$\mathbf{L}_{dq} = \mathbf{L}_{dq}^{(l)} + \mathbf{L}_{dq}^{(ag)} = \mathbf{T}(x)\mathbf{L}_s(x)\mathbf{T}(x)^t = \mathbf{T}(x)\mathbf{L}_{dq}^{(l)}\mathbf{T}(x)^t + \mathbf{T}(x)\mathbf{L}_{dq}^{(l)}\mathbf{T}(x)^t \tag{29}$$

More precisely, the transformed leakage inductance matrix takes the diagonal form (Tessarolo, 2009):

$$\mathbf{L}_{dq}^{(l)} = \mathbf{T}(x)\mathbf{L}_{dq}^{(l)}\mathbf{T}(x)^t = \begin{pmatrix} \lambda_1 & 0 & 0 & 0 & 0 & 0 & \\ 0 & \lambda_1 & 0 & 0 & 0 & 0 & \\ 0 & 0 & \lambda_3 & 0 & 0 & 0 & \\ 0 & 0 & 0 & \lambda_3 & 0 & 0 & \ddots \\ 0 & 0 & 0 & 0 & \lambda_5 & 0 & \\ 0 & 0 & 0 & 0 & 0 & \lambda_5 & \\ & & & \ddots & & & \ddots \end{pmatrix} \tag{30}$$

where:

$$\lambda_h = \ell_0 + 2\sum_{k=0}^{n-1} \ell_k \cos(kh\alpha) \tag{31}$$

for h = 1, 3, 5, ... is the harmonic inductance of the machine of order h (Tessarolo, 2009).
The air-gap inductance matrix becomes:

$$\begin{aligned} \mathbf{L}_{dq}^{(ag)} &= \mathbf{T}(x)\mathbf{L}_{dq}^{(ag)}\mathbf{T}(x)^t = \frac{L_{md}+L_{mq}}{2}\mathbf{T}(x)\mathbf{\Gamma}_1\mathbf{T}(x)^t \\ &+ \frac{L_{md}-L_{mq}}{2}\left[\mathbf{T}(x)\mathbf{\Gamma}_2\mathbf{T}(x)^t\cos(2x) + \mathbf{T}(x)\mathbf{\Gamma}_3\mathbf{T}(x)^t\sin(2x)\right] \\ &= n\begin{pmatrix} L_{md} & 0 & 0 & 0 & \\ 0 & L_{mq} & 0 & 0 & \\ 0 & 0 & 0 & 0 & \\ 0 & 0 & 0 & 0 & \\ & & & & \ddots \end{pmatrix} \end{aligned} \tag{32}$$

The overall inductance matrix in transformed coordinates is then the diagonal matrix below:

$$\mathbf{L}_{dq}=\begin{pmatrix} nL_{md}+\lambda_1 & 0 & 0 & 0 & 0 & 0 & \\ 0 & nL_{md}+\lambda_1 & 0 & 0 & 0 & 0 & \\ 0 & 0 & \lambda_3 & 0 & 0 & 0 & \\ 0 & 0 & 0 & \lambda_3 & 0 & 0 & \ddots \\ 0 & 0 & 0 & 0 & \lambda_5 & 0 & \\ 0 & 0 & 0 & 0 & 0 & \lambda_5 & \\ & & & \ddots & & & \ddots \end{pmatrix} \tag{33}$$

Using (24), the relationship (15) between the flux linkage and current vectors becomes:

$$\boldsymbol{\varphi}_s=\mathbf{T}(x)^t\boldsymbol{\varphi}_{dq}=\mathbf{L}_s(x)\mathbf{T}(x)^t\,\mathbf{i}_{dq} \quad\Rightarrow\quad \boldsymbol{\varphi}_{dq}=\mathbf{T}(x)\mathbf{L}_s(x)\mathbf{T}(x)^t\,\mathbf{i}_{dq} \tag{34}$$

which, in virtue of (29), gives:

$$\boldsymbol{\varphi}_{dq}=\mathbf{L}_{dq}\,\mathbf{i}_{dq} \tag{35}$$

Using the above relationships, the stator voltage equation (9) becomes:

$$\begin{aligned}\mathbf{v}_s&=\mathbf{T}(x)^t\,\mathbf{v}_{dq}=\mathbf{R}_s\mathbf{T}(x)^t\mathbf{i}_{dq}+\frac{d}{dt}\left[\mathbf{T}(x)^t\boldsymbol{\varphi}_{dq}\right]+\mathbf{e}_s\\ &=\mathbf{R}_s\mathbf{T}(x)^t\mathbf{i}_{dq}+\frac{d}{dt}\left[\mathbf{T}(x)^t\mathbf{L}_{dq}\mathbf{i}_{dq}\right]+\mathbf{e}_s\\ &=\mathbf{R}_s\mathbf{T}(x)^t\mathbf{i}_{dq}+\left[\frac{d}{dt}\mathbf{T}(x)^t\right]\left[\mathbf{L}_{dq}\mathbf{i}_{dq}\right]+\mathbf{T}(x)^t\frac{d}{dt}\left[\mathbf{L}_{dq}\mathbf{i}_{dq}\right]+\mathbf{e}_s\\ &=\mathbf{R}_s\mathbf{T}(x)^t\mathbf{i}_{dq}+\left[\frac{d}{dt}\mathbf{T}(x)^t\right]\left[\mathbf{L}_{dq}\mathbf{i}_{dq}\right]+\mathbf{T}(x)^t\mathbf{L}_{dq}\frac{d}{dt}\mathbf{i}_{dq}+\mathbf{e}_s\end{aligned} \tag{36}$$

It is important to remark that in the last passage of (37), we have used the fact that L_{dq}, given by (34), is time-invariant, i.e.

$$\tfrac{d}{dt}\mathbf{L}_{dq}=\mathbf{0} \tag{37}$$

so that it is correct to write:

$$\tfrac{d}{dt}\left[\mathbf{L}_{dq}\mathbf{i}_{dq}\right]=\left[\tfrac{d}{dt}\mathbf{L}_{dq}\right]\mathbf{i}_{dq}+\mathbf{L}_{dq}\tfrac{d}{dt}\mathbf{i}_{dq}=\mathbf{L}_{dq}\tfrac{d}{dt}\mathbf{i}_{dq} \tag{38}$$

If we left-multiply (37) by $\mathbf{T}(x)$ we obtain:

$$\begin{aligned}\mathbf{T}(x)\mathbf{v}_s&=\mathbf{v}_{dq}=\mathbf{T}(x)\mathbf{R}_s\mathbf{T}(x)^t\mathbf{i}_{dq}+\mathbf{T}(x)\left[\frac{d}{dt}\mathbf{T}(x)^t\right]\mathbf{L}_{dq}\mathbf{i}_{dq}+\mathbf{L}_{dq}\frac{d}{dt}\mathbf{i}_{dq}+\mathbf{T}(x)\mathbf{e}_{dq}\\ &=\mathbf{R}_{dq}\mathbf{i}_{dq}+\mathbf{T}(x)\left[\frac{dx}{dt}\frac{d}{dx}\mathbf{T}(x)^t\right]\mathbf{L}_{dq}\mathbf{i}_{dq}+\mathbf{L}_{dq}\frac{d}{dt}\mathbf{i}_{dq}+\mathbf{e}_{dq}\\ &=\mathbf{R}_{dq}\mathbf{i}_{dq}+\omega\mathbf{T}(x)\left[\frac{d}{dx}\mathbf{T}(x)^t\right]\mathbf{L}_{dq}\mathbf{i}_{dq}+\mathbf{L}_{dq}\frac{d}{dt}\mathbf{i}_{dq}+\mathbf{e}_{dq}\end{aligned} \tag{39}$$

where the rotor speed in electrical radians per second has been introduced:

$$\omega = \frac{dx}{dt} \tag{40}$$

The product $\mathbf{T}(x)\left[\frac{d}{dx}\mathbf{T}(x)^t\right]$ in (40) can be expanded using (25) as follows:

$$\begin{aligned}\mathbf{T}(x)\left[\frac{d}{dx}\mathbf{T}(x)^t\right] &= \mathbf{P}(x)\mathbf{C}\left[\frac{d}{dx}\mathbf{C}^t\mathbf{P}(x)^t\right] = \mathbf{P}(x)\mathbf{C}\left\{\left(\frac{d}{dx}\mathbf{C}^t\right)\mathbf{P}(x)^t + \mathbf{C}^t\left[\frac{d}{dx}\mathbf{P}(x)^t\right]\right\} \\ &= \mathbf{P}(x)\mathbf{C}\,\mathbf{C}^t\left[\frac{d}{dx}\mathbf{P}(x)^t\right] = \mathbf{P}(x)\left[\frac{d}{dx}\mathbf{P}(x)^t\right] = \mathbf{P}(x)\left[\frac{d}{dx}\mathbf{P}(x)\right]^t\end{aligned} \tag{41}$$

where we have used identities $\mathbf{C}\,\mathbf{C}^t = \mathbf{I}$ and $\frac{d}{dx}\mathbf{C} = \mathbf{0}$.
Considering the structure (26) of **P**(x), the product $\mathbf{P}(x)\left[\frac{d}{dx}\mathbf{P}(x)\right]^t$ can be expanded as:

$$\mathbf{P}(x)\left[\tfrac{d}{dx}\mathbf{P}(x)\right]^t = \left(\begin{array}{cc|cc|cc|c} 0 & -1 & 0 & 0 & 0 & 0 & \\ 1 & 0 & 0 & 0 & 0 & 0 & \\ \hline 0 & 0 & 0 & -3 & 0 & 0 & \\ 0 & 0 & 3 & 0 & 0 & 0 & \\ \hline 0 & 0 & 0 & 0 & 0 & -5 & \\ 0 & 0 & 0 & 0 & 5 & 0 & \\ \hline & & & & & & \ddots \end{array}\right) = \mathbf{J} \tag{42}$$

The final expression for the machine voltage equation in orthonormal coordinates is then:

$$\mathbf{v}_{dq} = \mathbf{R}_{dq}\mathbf{i}_{dq} + \omega\mathbf{J}\mathbf{L}_{dq}\mathbf{i}_{dq} + \mathbf{L}_{dq}\frac{d}{dt}\mathbf{i}_{dq} + \mathbf{e}_{dq} \tag{43}$$

which is formally identical to the transformed voltage equation of a three-phase synchronous machine in the rotor dq reference frame.
From (44) a simple expression for the machine electromagnetic torque can be also derived. In fact, if we left-multiply both sides of (44) by $\mathbf{i}_{dq}{}^t$ we obtain:

$$\mathbf{i}_{dq}{}^t\mathbf{v}_{dq} = \mathbf{i}_{dq}{}^t\mathbf{R}_{dq}\mathbf{i}_{dq} + \omega\mathbf{i}_{dq}{}^t\mathbf{J}\mathbf{L}_{dq}\mathbf{i}_{dq} + \mathbf{i}_{dq}{}^t\mathbf{L}_{dq}\frac{d}{dt}\mathbf{i}_{dq} + \mathbf{i}_{dq}{}^t\mathbf{e}_{dq}\,. \tag{44}$$

Using (10), (11), (24), we can write the left-hand side member of (45) as follows:

$$\mathbf{i}_{dq}{}^t\mathbf{v}_{dq} = \left[\mathbf{T}(x)\mathbf{i}_s\right]^t\mathbf{T}(x)\mathbf{v}_s = \mathbf{i}_s{}^t\mathbf{T}(x)^t\mathbf{T}(x)\mathbf{v}_s = \mathbf{i}_s{}^t\mathbf{v}_s = \sum_{k=0}^{n-1} v_k i_k = p_e \tag{45}$$

where p_e is the instantaneous electrical power entering machine terminals; using (14) and (28), the term $\mathbf{i}_{dq}{}^t\mathbf{R}_{dq}\mathbf{i}_{dq}$ can be written as:

$$\mathbf{i}_{dq}{}^t\mathbf{R}_{dq}\mathbf{i}_{dq}{}^t = r\,\mathbf{i}_{dq}{}^t\mathbf{i}_{dq}{}^t = \sum_{k=0}^{n-1} r i_k{}^2 = p_j \tag{46}$$

where p_j is the total amount of joule losses in stator phases; finally, the term $\mathbf{i}_{dq}{}^t\mathbf{L}_{dq}\frac{d}{dt}\mathbf{i}_{dq}$ can be written as:

$$\mathbf{i}_{dq}{}^t\mathbf{L}_{dq}\frac{d}{dt}\mathbf{i}_{dq} = \frac{d}{dt}w_{mag} = \frac{d}{dt}\left(\frac{1}{2}\mathbf{i}_{dq}{}^t\mathbf{L}_{dq}\mathbf{i}_{dq}\right) = p_{mag} \tag{47}$$

where p_{mag} is the amount of power used to change the magnetic energy $w_{mag} = \frac{1}{2}\mathbf{i}_{dq}{}^t\mathbf{L}_{dq}\mathbf{i}_{dq}$ stored in machine magnetic circuits. As a result of (46)-(48), equation (45) becomes:

$$p_e = p_j + p_{mag} + p_m\,. \tag{48}$$

where

$$p_m = \omega\mathbf{i}_{dq}{}^t\mathbf{J}\mathbf{L}_{dq}\mathbf{i}_{dq} + \mathbf{i}_{dq}{}^t\mathbf{e}_{dq}\,. \tag{49}$$

is the part of the power converted into mechanical power. Then, the power p_m can be also written in terms of electromagnetic machine torque T_{em} and mechanical rotor speed ω_m:

$$p_m = T_{em}\,\omega_m = T_{em}\frac{\omega}{p}\,. \tag{50}$$

where p is the number of pole pairs. By equalling (50) and (51) one obtains the expression for the electromagnetic torque:

$$T_{em} = p\mathbf{i}_{dq}{}^t\mathbf{J}\mathbf{L}_{dq}\mathbf{i}_{dq} + \frac{p}{\omega}\mathbf{i}_{dq}{}^t\mathbf{e}_{dq} \tag{51}$$

where the first term represents the reluctance torque component (due to rotor saliency and acting even in absence of rotor MMF) and the second term represents the torque component due to the interaction between stator and rotor magneto-motive force fields.
The electromagnetic torque (52) is to be used along with the externally-applied torque T_{ext} in the mechanical differential equation which governs the shaft speed dynamics:

$$T_{em} - T_{ext} = J\frac{d\omega_m}{dt} + B\omega_m \tag{52}$$

where J is the rotor moment of inertia, B is the viscous friction coefficient and ω_m is mechanical rotor speed, equal to ω/p.

4. VSD model implementation in the Matlab/Simulink environment

The mathematical modelling of the multiphase machines described above is suitable for a modular, scalable and flexible implementation in the Matlab/Simulink environment.
A block scheme which can be used for this purpose is provided in Fig. 8, where the particular case of a multiphase synchronous machine with wound-field rotor is considered. Of course, the same scheme holds in case of induction machines as well as for Permanent Magnet (PM) or reluctance synchronous machines, provided that the field voltage input is removed or properly replaced.

The overall system comprises a "Simulink domain", where the multiphase machine model is implemented, and a "SimPowerSystems domain" where the power electronics connected to the machine is modelled.

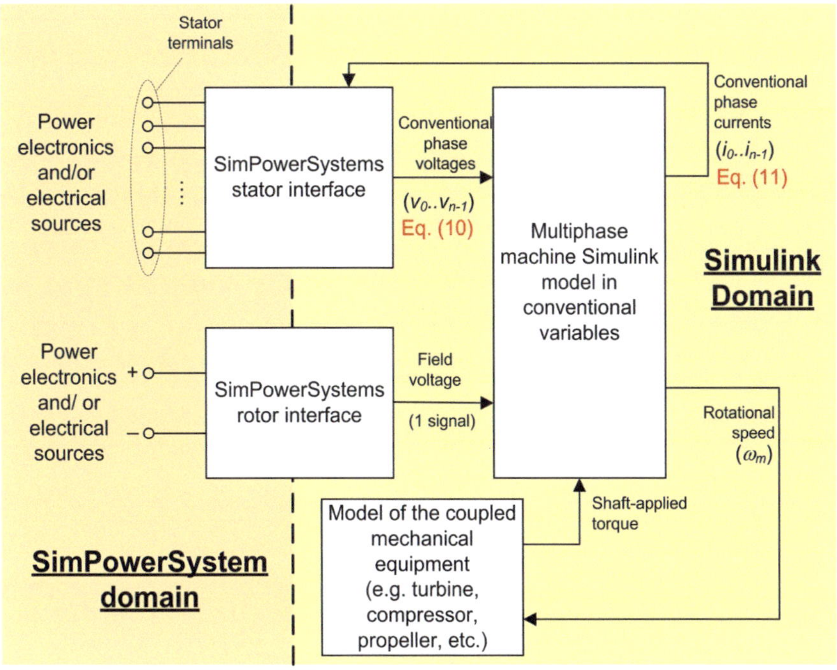

Fig. 8. Block scheme of the Simulink implementation of the multiphase machine model

4.1 Implementation of multiphase machine model in conventional phase variables

The core of the system represented in Fig. 8 is constituted by the "Multiphase machine Simulink model in conventional variables" block, whose detailed structure is depicted in Fig. 9. It implements the differential equations of the machine under the hypothesis that stator phases are geometrically arranged according to the "conventional" n-phase scheme discussed in 3.1. Therefore, the mathematical model implemented is the one described in Section 3.2 of this Chapter. The choice of using conventional variables makes the block independent of the phase arrangement and on the phase number.

In order to be implemented using phase currents as state variables, the stator voltage equation (44) is rewritten in the following form:

$$\frac{d}{dt}\mathbf{i}_{dq} = -\mathbf{L}_{dq}^{-1}\left(\mathbf{R}_{dq} + \omega\mathbf{J}\mathbf{L}_{dq}\right)\mathbf{i}_{dq} + \mathbf{L}_{dq}^{-1}\left(\mathbf{v}_{dq} - \mathbf{e}_{dq}\right) \tag{53}$$

This differential equation directly maps into the block scheme shown in Fig. 9.

As to the torque equation, it is implemented according to (52) as it does not involve any dynamics. Finally, the mechanical equation (53) is rewritten for implementation as:

$$\frac{d\omega_m}{dt} = \frac{1}{J}\left(T_{em} - T_{ext}\right) - \frac{B}{J}\omega_m \tag{54}$$

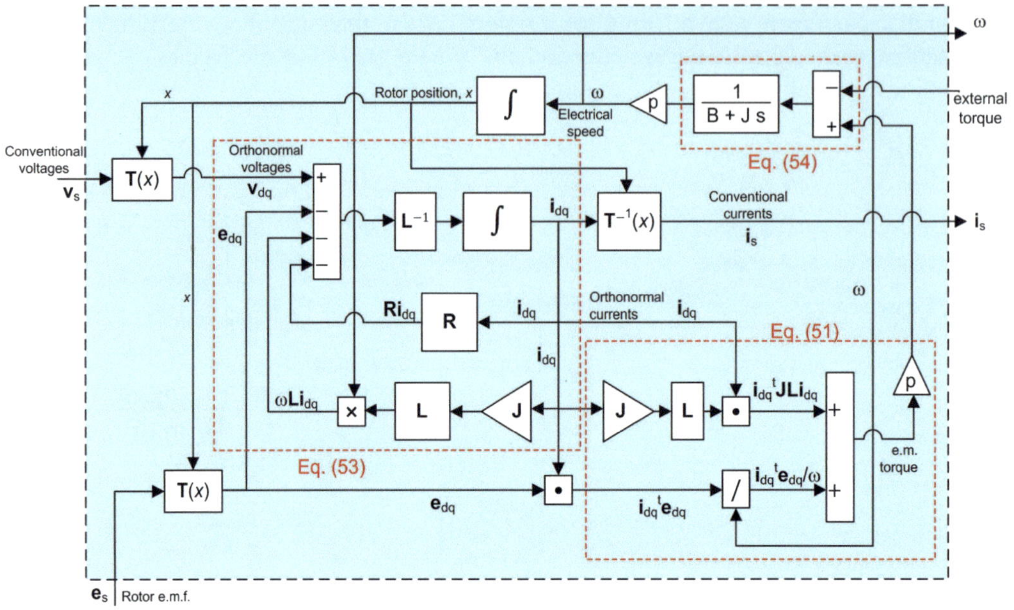

Fig. 9. Internal structure of the model "Multiphase machine Simulink model in conventional variables"

Beside implementing equations (52), (54) and (55), the block scheme in Fig. 4 includes the variable transformation $\mathbf{T}(x)$, defined by (25)-(27), between the conventional multiphase variable vectors (10)-(11) and the orthonormal coordinate vectors (24).

4.2 Interface with external blocks

The machine block shown in Fig. 9 accepts "conventional voltages" $\mathbf{v}_s$ as inputs and provides "conventional currents" $\mathbf{i}_s$ as outputs. The actual machine phases, however, are not arranged according to the conventional multiphase scheme assumed for unification purposes as per 3.1. Therefore, for the machine block to communicate with external blocks, it is necessary to "reorder" or "permute" conventional variable vectors to obtain the vectors of the physical (or natural) phase voltages and currents.

Moreover, external blocks interfaced with the machine model are often representative of power electronics equipment since it is very unusual that a multiphase machine is directly connected to the grid or to passive loads. Power electronics blocks, used to simulate inverters or converters, are generally built using SimPowerSystems library items.

As a result, the "stator interface" block appearing in Fig. 8 is added to perform these two tasks (the internal block structure is shown in Fig. 10):

1. Machine variable transformation between "conventional" and "natural" coordinate systems.
2. Conversion of machine phase voltages and currents from plain Simulink signals into SimPowerSystems bus attributes.

The former task is performed by means of the permutation matrices $\mathbf{W}$ introduced in 3.1 and 3.2.

The latter task is performed making use of one ideal current generator block and one voltage measurement block per machine phase. More precisely, the voltage across each machine phase is measured and used to build the natural phase voltage vector, which will be then transformed into the conventional phase voltage vector through matrix **W**. The natural phase currents which come from the machine model, instead, are imposed to flow across their relative phase bus by means of the ideal current generators.

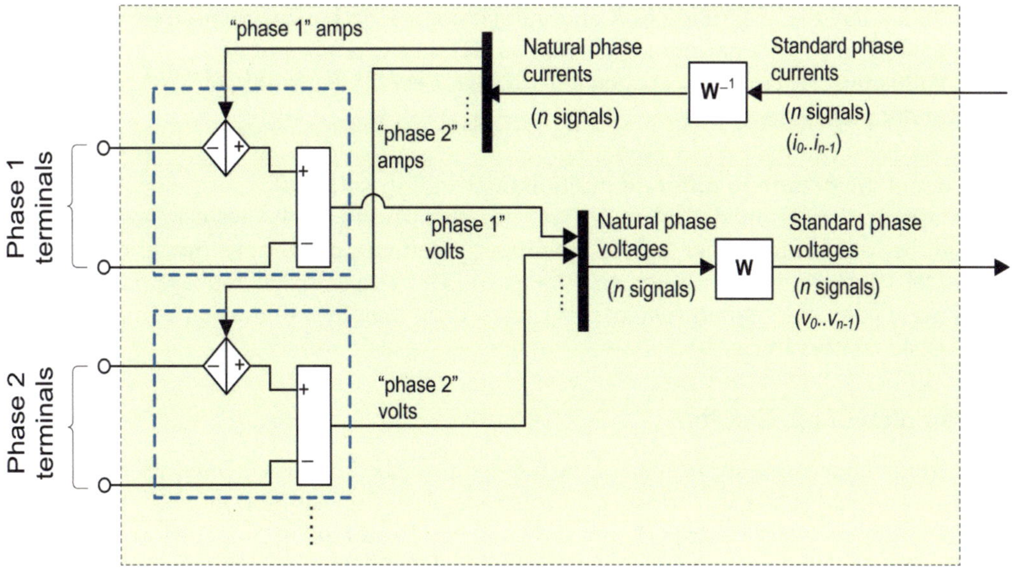

Fig. 10. Internal structure of the stator interface block

4.3 Model parameterization, initialization and adaptation to different multiphase machines

The advantage of the multiphase machine model implementation presented in this Chapter is that it can be easily parametrized and initialized so as to adapt it to simulate various kinds of multiphase machines, differing by the number and geometrical arrangement of the phases.

4.3.1 Parametrization

The input parameters which the user has to define, as far as the stator portion of the model is concerned, are the following:

a. The number of phases
b. The phase arrangement, to be chosen among the types described in Section 2. Typically: n-phase symmetrical or asymmetrical, in the latter case specifying the number N of winding sections and the number m of phases per section.
c. The phase resistance r, to be used to build the diagonal resistance matrix **R** as per (28).
d. The phase harmonic inductances (31), to build the diagonal transformed inductance matrix (30).

4.3.2 Initialization

The initialization can be performed through a Matlab script run only once at the beginning of the simulation. The script performs the following tasks:

a. It assigns the permutation matrices **W** in the stator interface blocks (Fig. 10). Permutation matrices are selected and defined as per 3.2.1 and 3.2.2 depending on the phase number and arrangement specified as an input;
b. It defines the variable transformation matrix **T**(x) as per (25) depending only on the number of phases;
c. It builds the diagonal matrices **R** and inductance matrix **L** using respectively the phase resistance and stator harmonic inductances (31) specified as input data;
d. It builds the constant block-diagonal matrix J as per (43) depending only on the number of stator phases.

4.3.3 Model adaptation to different multiphase winding schemes

The adaptation of the model to implement different winding schemes can be essentially done in the initialization stage simply by properly defining the various model matrices as the model structure essentially remains the same. Of course, for an n-phase machine, we shall have n pairs of terminals (one pair per phase) and thereby n of the blocks marked with blue dashed contour in Fig. 10.

5. Examples of application

To illustrate the possible application of the method described in this Chapter, we next report the case of a dual-star and a triple-star synchronous machines (the dual and triple three-phase winding schemes are respectively shown in Fig. 1b and in Fig. 5a). The former (2 MW, 1200 V, 6300 rpm) is operated as a motor fed by two Load-Commutated Inverters (Castellan et al., 2008), the latter (20 kVA, 720 V, 3000 V) is operated as a driven generator with its stator terminals in short circuit. Both machines are simulated using the same Matlab/Simulink model, described in Section 3, adapted to the two cases by a different initialization of its matrices [**W**, **C**, **P**(x)] as reported below.
Provided that natural phase variables are arranged in vector form as follows

$$\mathbf{y}_{2\times ABC} = \begin{pmatrix} y_{A1} & y_{A2} & y_{B1} & y_{B2} & y_{C1} & y_{C2} \end{pmatrix}^t, \tag{55}$$

$$\mathbf{y}_{3\times ABC} = \begin{pmatrix} y_{A1} & y_{B1} & y_{C1} & y_{A2} & y_{B2} & y_{C2} & y_{A3} & y_{B3} & y_{C3} \end{pmatrix}^t, \tag{56}$$

the permutation matrices in the two cases are given by (58) and (59) and the transformation matrices **C** and **P**(x), used to build **T**(x)=**P**(x)**C**, are given by (60)-(63).
The Matlab/Simulink models used for the simulations are shown in Fig. 11 and Fig. 12, where the yellow block represents the same model differently initialized to represent the two different machines (shown in Fig. 13).

$$\mathbf{W}_{2\times 3} = \begin{pmatrix} 1 & 0 & 0 & 0 & 0 & 0 \\ 0 & 0 & 0 & 1 & 0 & 0 \\ 0 & 0 & -1 & 0 & 0 & 0 \\ 0 & 0 & 0 & 0 & 0 & -1 \\ 0 & 1 & 0 & 0 & 0 & 0 \\ 0 & 0 & 0 & 0 & 1 & 0 \end{pmatrix}, \tag{57}$$

$$\mathbf{W}_{3\times3} = \begin{pmatrix} 1 & 0 & 0 & 0 & 0 & 0 & 0 & 0 & 0 \\ 0 & 0 & 0 & 1 & 0 & 0 & 0 & 0 & 0 \\ 0 & 0 & 0 & 0 & 0 & 0 & 1 & 0 & 0 \\ 0 & 0 & -1 & 0 & 0 & 0 & 0 & 0 & 0 \\ 0 & 0 & 0 & 0 & 0 & -1 & 0 & 0 & 0 \\ 0 & 0 & 0 & 0 & 0 & 0 & 0 & 0 & -1 \\ 0 & 1 & 0 & 0 & 0 & 0 & 0 & 0 & 0 \\ 0 & 0 & 0 & 0 & 1 & 0 & 0 & 0 & 0 \\ 0 & 0 & 0 & 0 & 0 & 0 & 0 & 1 & 0 \end{pmatrix}, \tag{58}$$

$$\mathbf{C}_6 = \sqrt{\frac{2}{6}} \begin{pmatrix} 1 & \cos(\alpha_6) & \cos(2\alpha_6) & \cos(3\alpha_6) & \cos(4\alpha_6) & \cos(5\alpha_6) \\ 0 & \sin(\alpha_6) & \sin(2\alpha_6) & \sin(3\alpha_6) & \sin(4\alpha_6) & \sin(5\alpha_6) \\ 1 & \cos(3\alpha_6) & \cos(6\alpha_6) & \cos(9\alpha_6) & \cos(12\alpha_6) & \cos(15\alpha_6) \\ 0 & \sin(3\alpha_6) & \sin(6\alpha_6) & \sin(9\alpha_6) & \sin(12\alpha_6) & \sin(15\alpha_6) \\ 1 & \cos(5\alpha_6) & \cos(10\alpha_6) & \cos(15\alpha_6) & \cos(20\alpha_6) & \cos(25\alpha_6) \\ 0 & \sin(5\alpha_6) & \sin(10\alpha_6) & \sin(15\alpha_6) & \sin(20\alpha_6) & \sin(25\alpha_6) \end{pmatrix} \tag{59}$$

$$\mathbf{C}_9 = \sqrt{\frac{2}{9}} \begin{pmatrix} 1 & \cos(\alpha_9) & \cos(2\alpha_9) & \cdots & \cos(8\alpha_9) & \cos(9\alpha_9) \\ 0 & \sin(\alpha_9) & \sin(2\alpha_9) & \cdots & \sin(8\alpha_9) & \sin(9\alpha_9) \\ 1 & \cos(3\alpha_9) & \cos(6\alpha_9) & \cdots & \cos(24\alpha_9) & \cos(27\alpha_9) \\ 0 & \sin(3\alpha_9) & \sin(6\alpha_9) & \cdots & \sin(24\alpha_9) & \sin(27\alpha_9) \\ 1 & \cos(5\alpha_9) & \cos(10\alpha_9) & \cdots & \cos(40\alpha_9) & \cos(45\alpha_9) \\ 0 & \sin(5\alpha_9) & \sin(10\alpha_9) & \cdots & \sin(40\alpha_9) & \sin(45\alpha_9) \\ 1 & \cos(7\alpha_9) & \cos(14\alpha_9) & \cdots & \cos(56\alpha_9) & \cos(63\alpha_9) \\ 0 & \sin(7\alpha_9) & \sin(14\alpha_9) & \cdots & \sin(56\alpha_9) & \sin(63\alpha_9) \\ \frac{1}{\sqrt{2}} & \frac{1}{\sqrt{2}}\cos(9\alpha_9) & \frac{1}{\sqrt{2}}\cos(18\alpha_9) & & \frac{1}{\sqrt{2}}\cos(72\alpha_9) & \frac{1}{\sqrt{2}}\cos(81\alpha_9) \end{pmatrix} \tag{60}$$

$$\mathbf{P}_6(x) = \begin{pmatrix} \cos(x) & \sin(x) & 0 & 0 & 0 & 0 \\ -\sin(x) & \cos(x) & 0 & 0 & 0 & 0 \\ 0 & 0 & \cos(3x) & \sin(3x) & 0 & 0 \\ 0 & 0 & -\sin(3x) & \cos(3x) & 0 & 0 \\ 0 & 0 & 0 & 0 & \cos(5x) & \sin(5x) \\ 0 & 0 & 0 & 0 & -\sin(5x) & \cos(5x) \end{pmatrix} \tag{61}$$

$$\mathbf{P}_9(x) = \begin{pmatrix} \cos(x) & \sin(x) & 0 & 0 & 0 & 0 & 0 & 0 & 0 \\ -\sin(x) & \cos(x) & 0 & 0 & 0 & 0 & 0 & 0 & 0 \\ 0 & 0 & \cos(3x) & \sin(3x) & 0 & 0 & 0 & 0 & 0 \\ 0 & 0 & -\sin(3x) & \cos(3x) & 0 & 0 & 0 & 0 & 0 \\ 0 & 0 & 0 & 0 & \cos(5x) & \sin(5x) & 0 & 0 & 0 \\ 0 & 0 & 0 & 0 & -\sin(5x) & \cos(5x) & 0 & 0 & 0 \\ 0 & 0 & 0 & 0 & 0 & 0 & \cos(7x) & \sin(7x) & 0 \\ 0 & 0 & 0 & 0 & 0 & 0 & -\sin(7x) & \cos(7x) & 0 \\ 0 & 0 & 0 & 0 & 0 & 0 & 0 & 0 & 1 \end{pmatrix} \tag{62}$$

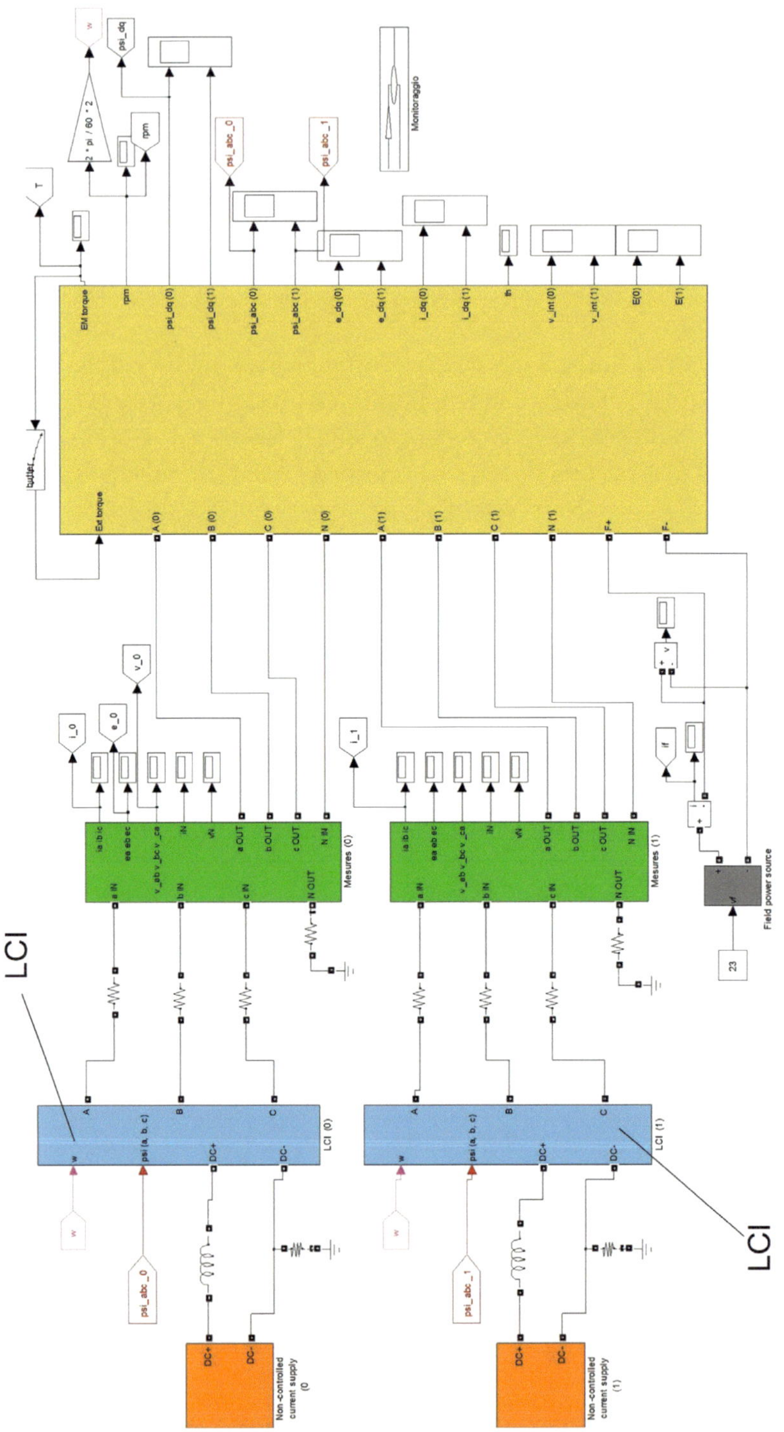

Fig. 11. Matlab/Simulink model for the simulation of a dual-star synchronous machine supplied by two Load-Commutated Inverters

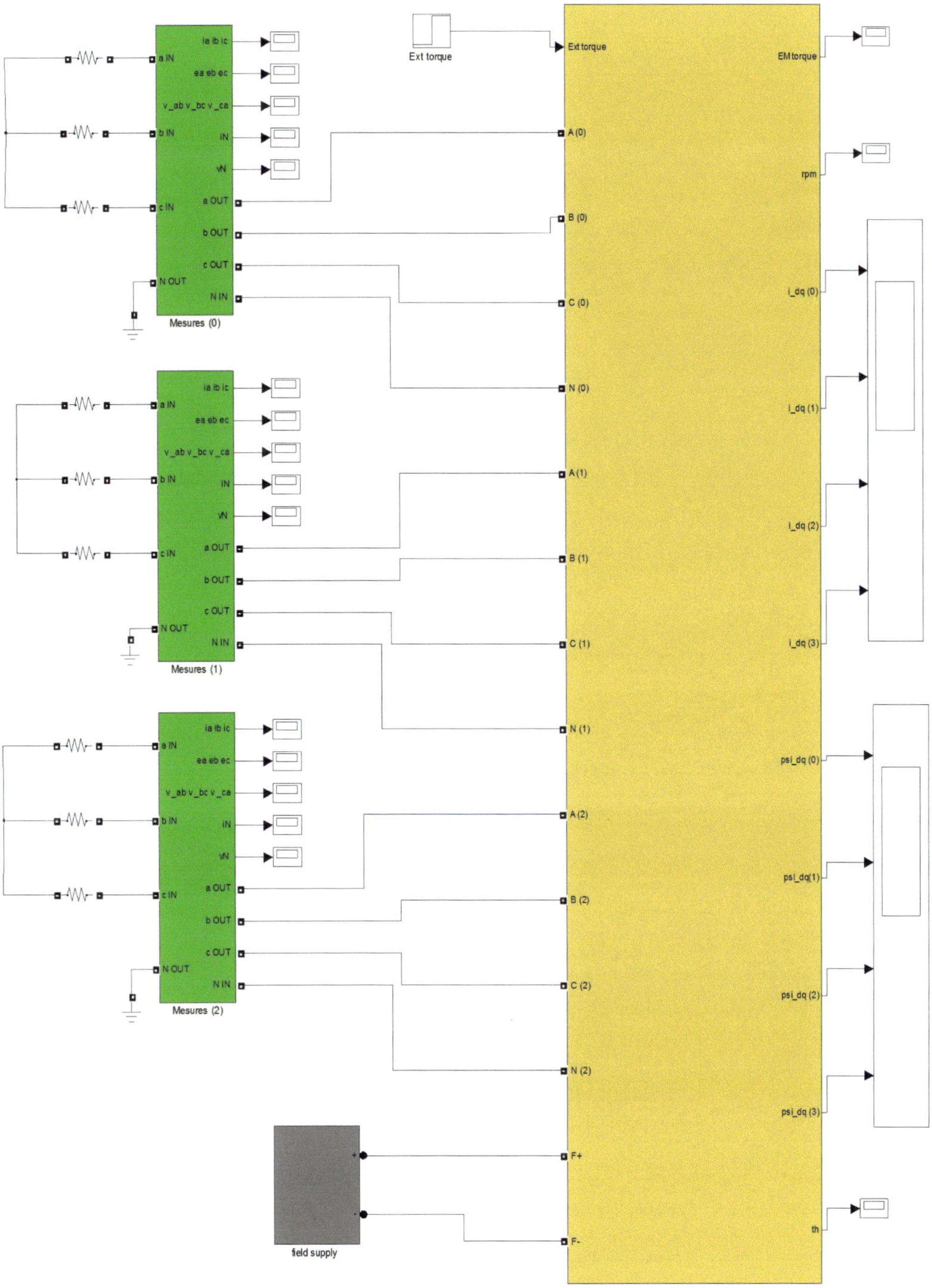

Fig. 12. Matlab/Simulink model for the simulation of a triple-star synchronous machine operating as a driven generator with short-circuited stator terminals

(a) (b)

Fig. 13. (a) Dual-star synchronous motor (2 MW, 1200V, 6300 rpm) to be fed from two LCIs. (b) Triple-star synchronous generator driven with short-circuit stator terminals

Simulation results, compared with measurements, for the dual- and triple-star machine are reported in Fig. 14 and Fig. 15, showing a good accordance in all the operating conditions

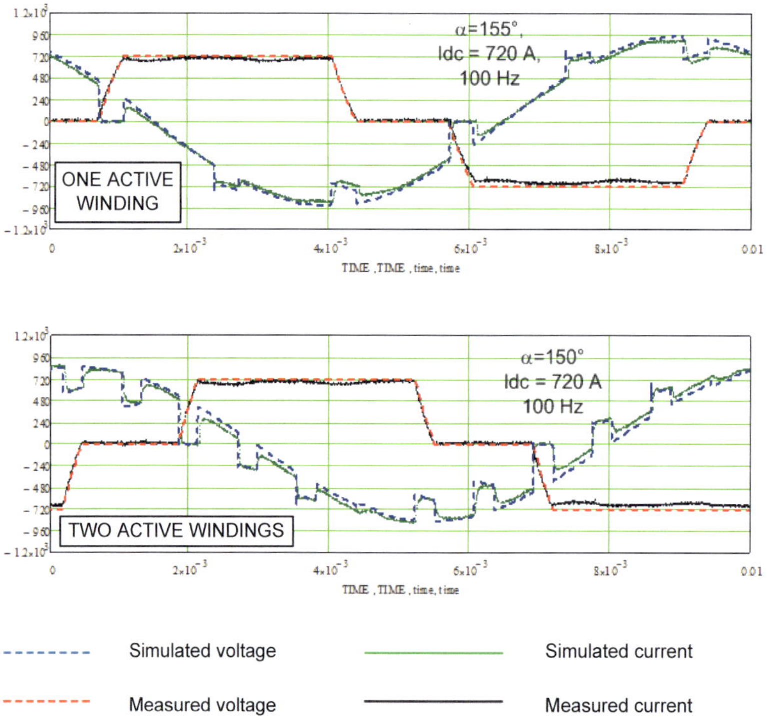

Fig. 14. Comparison between simulated and measured voltages and currents for the dual-star synchronous motor under LCI supply in case of both active windings and one single active winding

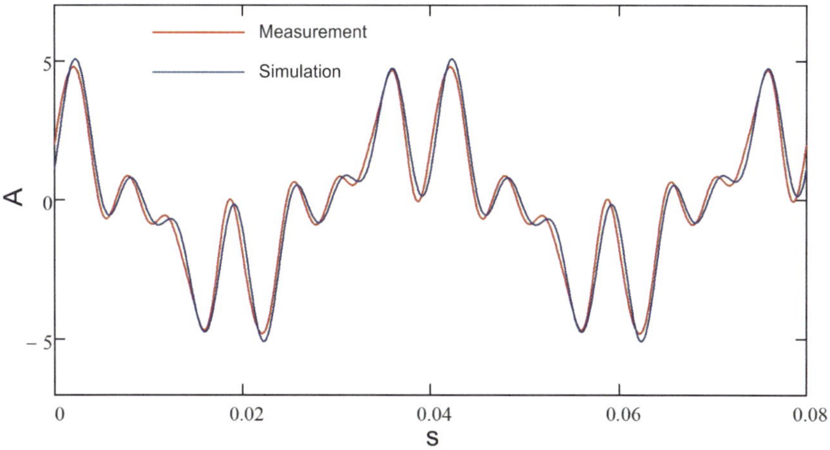

Fig. 15. Comparison between simulated and measured short-circuit current in a triple-star generator driven with short-circuited stator terminals

A further application examples of the methodology described in this Chapter can found in Tessarolo et al., 2009, where the same synchronous machine model used for the two simulation cases reported in this Section has been employed to simulate a symmetrical five-phase synchronous motor fed by a five-phase Load Commutated Inverter.

6. References

E. Levi, "Multiphase electric machines for variable-speed applications", IEEE Trans. on Industrial Electronics, vol. 55, May 2008, pp. 1893-1909.

E. Levi, R. Bojoi, F. Profumo, H.A. Tolyat, S. Williamson, "Multiphase induction motor drives - a technology status review", Electric Power Application, IET, 2007, July 2007, vol. 1, pp. 489-516.

A. Tessarolo, G. Zocco, C. Tonello, "Design and testing of a 45-MW 100-Hz quadruple-star synchronous motor for a liquefied natural gas turbo-compressor drive", International Symposium on Power Electronics, Electrical Drives, Automation and Motion, SPEEDAM 2010, 14-16 June 2010, Pisa, Italy, pp. 1754-1761.

S. Castellan, R. Menis, M. Pigani, G. Sulligoi, A. Tessarolo, "Modeling and simulation of electric propulsion systems for all-electric cruise liners", IEEE Electric Ship Technologies Symposium, IEEE ESTS 2007, 21-23 May 2007, Arlington, VA, USA, pp. 60-64.

G. Sulligoi, A. Tessarolo, V. Benucci, M. Baret, A. Rebora, A. Taffone, "Modeling, simulation and experimental validation of a generation system for Medium-Voltage DC Integrated Power Systems", IEEE Electric Ship Technologies Symposium, 2009, ESTS 2009, 20-22 April 2009, Baltimora, US, pp. 129- 134.

S. Castellan, G. Sulligoi, A. Tessarolo, "Comparative performance analysis of VSI-fed and CSI-fed supply solutions for high power multi-phase synchronous motor drives", International Symposium on Power Electronics, Electrical Drives, Automation and Motion, SPEEDAM 2008, 11-13 June 2008, Ischia, Italy, pp. 854-859.

L.A. Pereira, C. C. Scharlau, L.F.A. Pereira, J.F. Haffner, "General model of a five-phase induction machine allowing for harmonics in the air-gap", *IEEE Trans. on Energy Conversion*, vol. 21, issue 4, Dec. 2006, pp. 891-899.

J. Figueroa, J. Cros, P. Viarouge, "Generalized Transformations for Polyphase Phase-Modulated Motors", *IEEE Transactions On Energy Conversion*, vol. 21, June 2006, pp. 332-341.

F. Terrein, S. Siala, P. Noy, "Multiphase induction motor sensorless control for electric ship propulsion", *IEE Power Electronics, Machines and Drives Conference*, PEMD 2004, pp. 556-561.

E.A. Klingshirn, "High phase order induction motors–Part I–Description and theoretical considerations", *IEEE Trans. on Power Apparatus and Systems*, Jan. 1983, vol. PAS-102, pp. 47-53.

A. Tessarolo, "On the modeling of poly-phase electric machines through Vector-Space Decomposition: theoretical considerations", *International Conference on Power Engineering, Energy and Electrical Drives, POWERENG 2009*, 18-20 March 2009, Lisbon, Portugal, 18-20 March 2009, pp. 519-523.

A. Tessarolo, S. Castellan, R. Menis, "Analysis and simulation of a novel Load-Commutated Inverter drive based on a five-phase synchronous motor", *European Conference on Power Electronics and Applications, 2009, EPE '09*, 8-10 Sept. 2009, Barcelona, Spain, CD-ROM paper.

2

De-Noising Audio Signals Using MATLAB Wavelets Toolbox

Adrian E. Villanueva- Luna[1], Alberto Jaramillo-Nuñez[1], Daniel Sanchez-Lucero[1], Carlos M. Ortiz-Lima[1], J. Gabriel Aguilar-Soto[1], Aaron Flores-Gil[2] and Manuel May-Alarcon[2]
[1]*Instituto Nacional de Astrofisica, Optica y Electronica (INAOE)*
[2]*Universidad Autonoma del Carmen (UNACAR)*
Mexico

1. Introduction

Based on the fact that noise and distortion are the main factors that limit the capacity of data transmission in telecommunications and that they also affect the accuracy of the results in the signal measurement systems, whereas, modeling and removing noise and distortions are at the core of theoretical and practical considerations in communications and signal processing. Another important issue here is that, noise reduction and distortion removal are major problems in applications such as; cellular mobile communication, speech recognition, image processing, medical signal processing, radar, sonar, and any other application where the desired signals cannot be isolated from noise and distortion.

The use of wavelets in the field of de-noising audio signals is relatively new, the use of this technique has been increasing over the past 20 years. One way to think about wavelets matches the way how our eyes perceive the world when they are faced to different distances. In the real world, a forest can be seen from many different perspectives; they are, in fact, different scales of resolution. From the window of an airplane, for instance, the forest cover appears as a solid green roof. From the window of a car, the green roof gets transformed into individual trees, and if we leave the car and approach to the forest, we can gradually see details such as the trees branches and leaves. If we had a magnifying glass, we could see a dew drop on the tip of a leaf. As we get closer to even smaller scales, we can discover details that we had not seen before. On the other hand, if we tried to do the same thing with a photograph, we would be completely frustrated. If we enlarged the picture "closer" to a tree, we would only be able to see a blurred tree image; we would not be able to spot neither the branch, nor the leaf, and it would be impossible to spot the dew drop. Although our eyes can see on many scales of resolution, the camera can only display one at a time.

In this chapter, we introduce the reader to a way to reduce noise in an audio signal by using wavelet transforms. We developed this technique by using the wavelet tool in MATLAB. A Simulink is used to acquire an audio signal and we use it to convert the signal to a digital format so it can be processed. Finally, a Graphical User Interface Development Environment (GUIDE) is used to create a graphical user interface. The reader can go through this chapter systematically, from the theory to the implementation of the noise reduction technique.

We will introduce in the first place the basic theory of an audio signal, the noise treatment fundamentals and principles of the wavelets theory. Then, we will present the development of noise reduction when using wavelet functions in MATLAB. In the foreground, we will demonstrate the usefulness of wavelets to reduce noise in a model system where Gaussian noise is inserted to an audio signal. In the following sections, we will present a practical example of noise reduction in a sinusoidal signal that has been generated in the MATLAB, which it is followed by an example with a real audio signal captured via Simulink. Finally, the graphic noise reduction model using GUIDE will be shown.

2. Basic audio theory

Sound is the vibration of an elastic medium, whether gaseous, liquid or solid. These vibrations are a type of mechanical wave that has the capability to stimulate human ear and to create a sound sensation in the brain. In air, sound is transmitted due to pressure variations at a rate of change that is called frequency. The difference between the extreme values of pressure represents its amplitude. Pressure variations in the range of 20 Hz to 20 kHz produce the sound which is audible to the human ear and this is more receptive when it is between 1 kHz to 4 kHz. In physical terms, the sound is a longitudinal wave that travels through the air due to vibration of the molecules. Similar to light, sound waves can be reflected, absorbed, diffracted, or refracted.
Audio signals, which represent longitudinal variations of pressure in a medium, are converted into electrical signals by piezoelectric transducers. Transducers convert the energy of a mechanical displacement into an electrical signal, either voltage or current. The main advantage of converting an audio signal into an electrical signal is that the signal can now be processed. An example is an analog signal obtained from the transducer that can be converted into an encoded digital data stream by using an analog-digital converter (ADC) and constitutes digital processing of analog signals. Alternatively, if a digital-analog converter (DAC) is applied to a digital data stream, the audio signal transmits through an amplifier and a speaker. The process is show schematically in Figure 1, which identifies the important steps in digital audio processing.

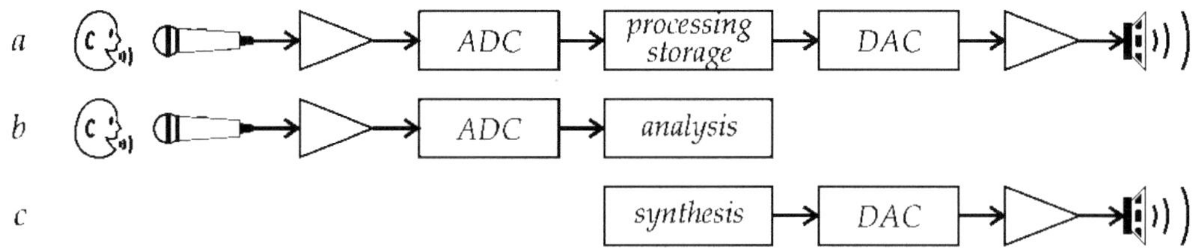

Fig. 1. Shows the process of digital processing of three types of audio signal. Part (*a*) represents a complete digital audio processing comprising (from left to right) a microphone, amplifier, ADC, digital processing material, DAC, amplifying section and speaker; an audio recognition system in (*b*), and a set of audio synthesis (*c*)

2.1 Recording audio signals in Simulink/MATLAB

Once in the digital domain, these signals can be processed, transmitted or stored. We found that the Audio Device block in Simulink enables experimentation and processing of digital signals. The From Audio Device block reads audio data from an audio device in real time.

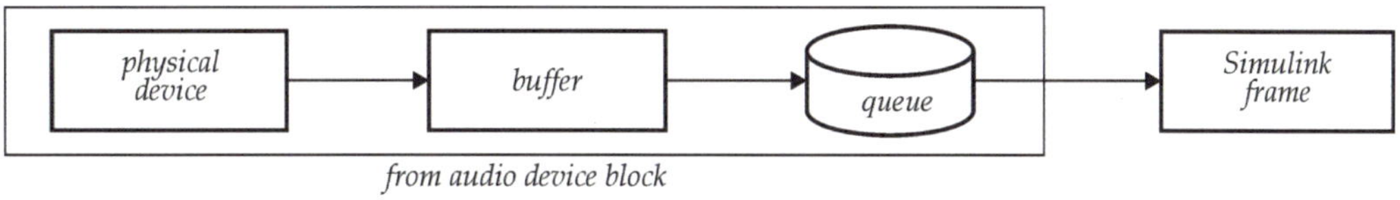

Fig. 2. Shows the process identifies the main steps in a digital audio processing system based in Simulink software

The From Audio Device block buffers the data from the audio device by means of using the process illustrated by Figure 2. We selected the block MATLAB Simulink audio and multimedia file block in order to save the audio acquired by a given time. Figure 3 shows the From Audio Device GUI, where we selected a 5 second queue period. At the start of the simulation, the audio device writes input data to a buffer. When the buffer is full, the From Audio Device block writes the contents of the buffer to the queue. The size of this queue can be specified in the queue duration (seconds) parameter. As the audio device appends audio data to the bottom of the queue, the From Audio Device block pulls data from the top of the queue to fill the Simulink frame. We used this file to make our de-noise method using wavelets.

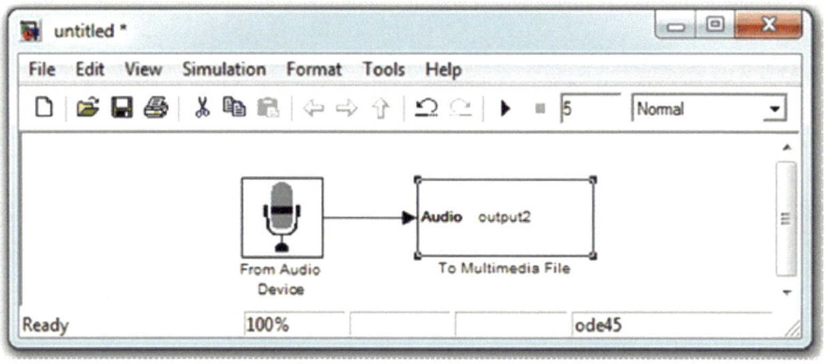

Fig. 3. Shows block diagram of audio acquire

We used the *wavread* function. It loads a: WAVE file specified by the string filename, returning the sampled data in *y*. If the filename does not include an extension, *wavread* appends a .wav extension. Example code is: *[x,Fs,nbits]= wavread('filename') where the function returns the filename with* the number of bits per sample (nbits).

```
[x,Fs,nbits]= wavread ('voice');
y = awgn(x,10,'measured');
```

For example, *wavwrite(y,Fs,'filename')* writes the data stored in the variable *y* to a WAVE file called 'filename'. The data have a sample rate, Fs, in Hz and is assumed 16-bit.

```
wavwrite(y,Fs,'noisyvoice')
wavwrite(xd,Fs,'voice5')
```

3. Basic noise theory

Noise is defined as an unwanted signal that interferes with the communication or measurement of another signal. A noise itself is an information-bearing signal that conveys information regarding the sources of the noise and the environment in which it propagates.

There are many types and sources of noise or distortions and they include:
1. *Electronic noise* such as thermal noise and shot noise,
2. *Acoustic noise* emanating from moving, vibrating or colliding sources such as revolving machines, moving vehicles, keyboard clicks, wind and rain,
3. *Electromagnetic noise* that can interfere with the transmission and reception of voice, image and data over the radio-frequency spectrum,
4. *Electrostatic noise* generated by the presence of a voltage,
5. *Communication channel* distortion and fading and
6. *Quantization noise* and lost data packets due to network congestion.

Signal distortion is the term often used to describe a systematic undesirable change in a signal and refers to changes in a signal from the non-ideal characteristics of the communication channel, signal fading reverberations, echo, and multipath reflections and missing samples. Depending on its frequency, spectrum or time characteristics, a noise process is further classified into several categories:
1. *White noise*: purely random noise has an impulse autocorrelation function and a flat power spectrum. White noise theoretically contains all frequencies in equal power.
2. *Band-limited white noise*: Similar to white noise, this is a noise with a flat power spectrum and a limited bandwidth that usually covers the limited spectrum of the device or the signal of interest. The autocorrelation of this noise is sinc-shaped.
3. *Narrowband noise*: It is a noise process with a narrow bandwidth such as 50/60 Hz from the electricity supply.
4. *Coloured noise*: It is non-white noise or any wideband noise whose spectrum has a non-flat shape. Examples are pink noise, brown noise and autoregressive noise.
5. *Impulsive noise*: Consists of short-duration pulses of random amplitude, time of occurrence and duration.
6. *Transient noise pulses*: Consist of relatively long duration noise pulses such as clicks, burst noise etc.

3.1 Signal to noise ratio

The signal-to-noise ratio (*SNR*) is commonly used to assess the effect of noise on a signal. This measurement is based on an additive noise model, where the quantized signal $xq[n]$ is a superposition of the unquantized, undistorted signal $x[n]$ and the additive quantization error $e[n]$. The ratio between the signal powers of $x[n]$ and $e[n]$ defines the *SNR*. To capture the wide range of potential *SNR* values and to consider the logarithmic perception of loudness in humans, *SNR* generally given in a logarithmic scale, in decibels (dB)

$$SNR_{dB} = 10 * \log_{10} \frac{\sigma_x^2}{\sigma_e^2}, \tag{1}$$

Where, σ2x and σ^2_e are the powers of $x[n]$, and $e[n]$, respectively. Specifically for the assessment of quantization noise, *SNR* is often labeled as the signal to quantization-noise ratio (SQNR).

3.2 White noise

Shown in Figure 4, white noise is defined as an uncorrelated random noise process with equal power at all frequencies. Random noise has the same power at all frequencies in the range of ∞ it would necessarily need to have infinite power, and it is therefore an only a theoretical concept. However, a band-limited noise process with a flat spectrum covering the frequency range of a band-limited communication system is practically considered a white noise process.

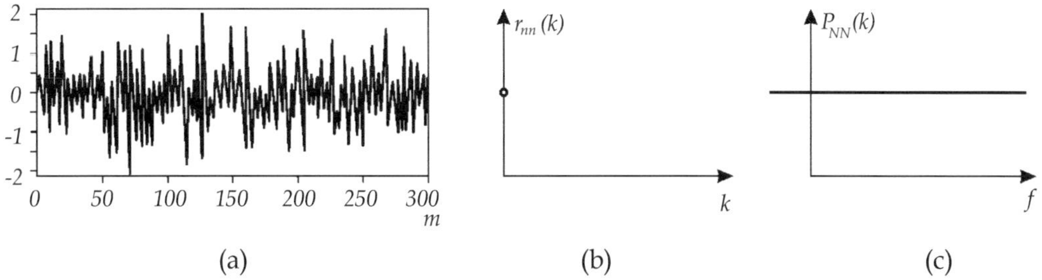

Fig. 4. Shows an illustration of (a) white noise time-domain signal, (b) its autocorrelation function is a delta function, and (c) its power spectrum is a constant function of frequency

3.3 Additive White Gaussian Noise Model (AWGN)

In classical communication theory, it assumed that the noise is a stationary additive white Gaussian (AWGN) process. Although for some problems this is a valid assumption and leads to mathematically convenient and useful solutions, in practice, the noise is often time-varying, correlated and non-Gaussian. This is particularly true for impulsive-type noise and for acoustic noise, which is non-stationary and non-Gaussian and hence cannot be modeled using the AWGN assumption.

3.4 Adding noise using MATLAB

How to do it with MATLAB: In the Communication Toolbox in MATLAB is possible to find the function *awgn*. This function means adding Gaussian white noise to signal.

Syntax
y = awgn(x,snr)
y = awgn(x,snr,'measured')

y = awgn(x,snr) adds white Gaussian noise to the vector signal *x*. The scalar *SNR* specifies the signal-to-noise ratio per sample, in dB. If x is complex, *awgn* adds complex noise. This syntax assumes that the power of *x* is 0 dBW.
y = awgn(x,snr,'measured') is the same as *y = awgn(x,snr)*, except that *awgn* measures the power of *x* before adding noise.
Figure 5 shows one example of how to add white noise to the sinusoidal signal using the communication toolbox of MATLAB. We generate the interval of the signal (k), considering some frequency (w), then we generate a sinusoidal function with these parameters, considering this function with the *x* vector. Now we generate a Gaussian white noise and add to the sinusoidal function and plot.

```
k = 0:9.0703e-005:5;
w=500*pi;
h=w.*k;
x = sin(h); % Create sinus signal.
y = awgn(x,10,'measured'); % Add white Gaussian noise.
figure(1)
plot(k,y)
```

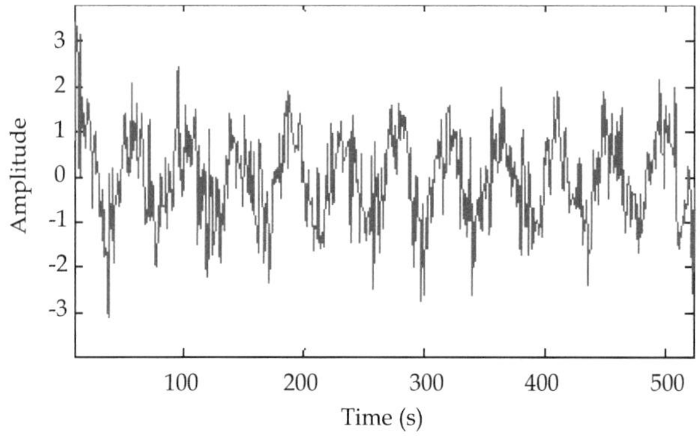

Fig. 5. Shows adding Gaussian white noise to sine signal

4. Wavelets theory

Wavelets are used in a variety of fields including physics, medicine, biology and statistics. Among the applications in the field of physics, there is the removal of noise from signals containing information. There are different ways to reduce noise in audio. (Johnson et al., 2007) demonstrated the application of the Bionic Wavelet Transform (BWT), an adaptive wavelet transform derived from a non-linear auditory model of the cochlea, to enhance speech signal. (Bahoura & Rouat, 2006) proposed a new speech enhancement method based on time and scale adaptation of wavelet thresholds. (Ching-Ta & Hsiao-Chuan Wang, 2003 & 2007) proposed a method based on critical-band decomposition, which converts a noisy signal into wavelet coefficients (WCs), and enhanced the WCs by subtracting a threshold from noisy WCs in each subband. Additionally, they proposed a gain factor in each wavelet subband subject to a perceptual constraint. (Visser et al., 2003) has presented a new speech enhancement scheme by spatial integration and temporal signal processing methods for robust speech recognition in noisy environments. It further de-noised by exploiting differences in temporal speech and noise statistics in a wavelet filter bank. (Képesia & Weruaga, 2006) proposed new method for time-frequency analysis of speech signals. The analysis basis of the proposed Short-Time Fan-Chirp Transform (FChT) defined univocally by the analysis window length and by the frequency variation rate, that parameter predicted from the last computed spectral segments. (Li et al., 2008) proposed an audio de-noising algorithm based on adaptive wavelet soft-threshold, based on the gain factor of linear filter system in the wavelet domain and the wavelet coefficients teager energy operator in order to progress the effect of the content-based songs retrieval system. (Dong et al., 2008) has proposed a speech de-noising algorithm for white noise environment based on perceptual weighting filter, which united the spectrum subtraction and adopted auditory perception properties in the traditional Wiener filter. (Shankar & Duraiswamy, 2010) proposed an audio de-noising technique based on biorthogonal wavelet transformation.

Wavelets are characterized by scale and position, and are useful in analyzing variations in signals and images in terms of scale and position. Because of the fact that the wavelet size can vary, it has advantage over the classical signal processing transformations to simultaneously process time and frequency data. The general relationship between wavelet scales and frequency is to roughly match the scale. At low scale, compressed wavelets are used. They correspond to fast-changing details, that is, to a high frequency. At high scale,

the wavelets are stretched. They correspond to slow changing features, that is, to a low frequency.
The wavelet only has a time domain representation as the wavelet function ψ (*t*). The mother wavelet is scaled (or dilated) by a factor of *a* and translated (or shifted) by a factor of *b* to give

$$\psi_{a,b}(t) = \frac{1}{\sqrt{|a|}}\psi\left(\frac{t-b}{a}\right). \tag{2}$$

Wavelets are defined by the wavelet function ψ (*t*) (i.e. the mother wavelet) and scaling function φ (*t*) (also called father wavelet) in the time domain. The wavelet function is in effect a band-pass filter and scaling it for each level halves its bandwidth. This creates the problem that in order to cover the entire spectrum, an infinite number of levels would be required. The scaling function filters the lowest level of the transform and ensures that the entire spectrum is covered. For a wavelet with compact support, φ (*t*) can be considered finite in length and is equivalent to the scaling filter *g*.
Wavelets can be scaled and copied (known as "daughter wavelets") of a finite-length or fast-decaying oscillating waveform (known as the "mother wavelet"). Wavelet transforms have advantages over traditional Fourier transforms for representing functions that have discontinuities and sharp peaks, and for accurately deconstructing and reconstructing finite, non-periodic and/or non-stationary signals.
Wavelet transforms are classified into two broad groups: discrete wavelet transforms (DWTs) and continuous wavelet transforms (CWTs). Note that both DWT and CWT are continuous-time (analog) transforms and can represent continuous-time (analog) signals. CWTs operate over every possible scale and translation whereas DWTs use a specific subset of scale and translation values or representation grid. When wavelet-functions coefficients are expressed as z-transform, then the number of zeros at π corresponds to the number of vanishing moments. S, o *p* zeros in π means *p* vanishing moments.
Having *p* vanishing moments means that wavelet-coefficients for *p-th* order polynomial will be zero. That is, any polynomial signal up to order *p-1* can be represented completely in scaling space. In theory, more vanishing moments meaning that scaling function can represent more signals that are complex accurately, *p* which it is also called as the accuracy of the wavelet.
Daubechies wavelets are a family of orthogonal wavelets defining a discrete wavelet transform and they are characterized by a maximal number of vanishing moments for some given support. With each wavelet type of this class, a scaling function (also called father wavelet) generates an orthogonal multi-resolution analysis.
In general the Daubechies wavelets are chosen to have the highest number *A* of vanishing moments, (this does not imply the best smoothness) for given support width *N=2A*, and between the 2^{A-1} possible solutions the number one is chosen whose scaling filter has extreme phase. The wavelet transform is also easy to put into practice by using the fast wavelet transform. Daubechies wavelets are widely used in solving a broad range of problems, e.g. self-similarity properties of a signal or fractal problems, signal discontinuities, etc.
Coiflets are discrete wavelets designed by Ingrid Daubechies, at the request of Ronald Coifman, to have scaling functions with vanishing moments. The wavelet is near symmetric

their wavelet functions have $N/3$ vanishing moments and scaling functions $N/3-1$, they are used in many applications using Calderón-Zygmund Operators.
Db 10 and Db 9 are asymmetric, orthogonal and biorthogonal, Coif 5 is near symmetric, orthogonal and biorthogonal. Figure 6 shows the scale and wavelet function of Coiflet 5, Daubechies 9 and 10.

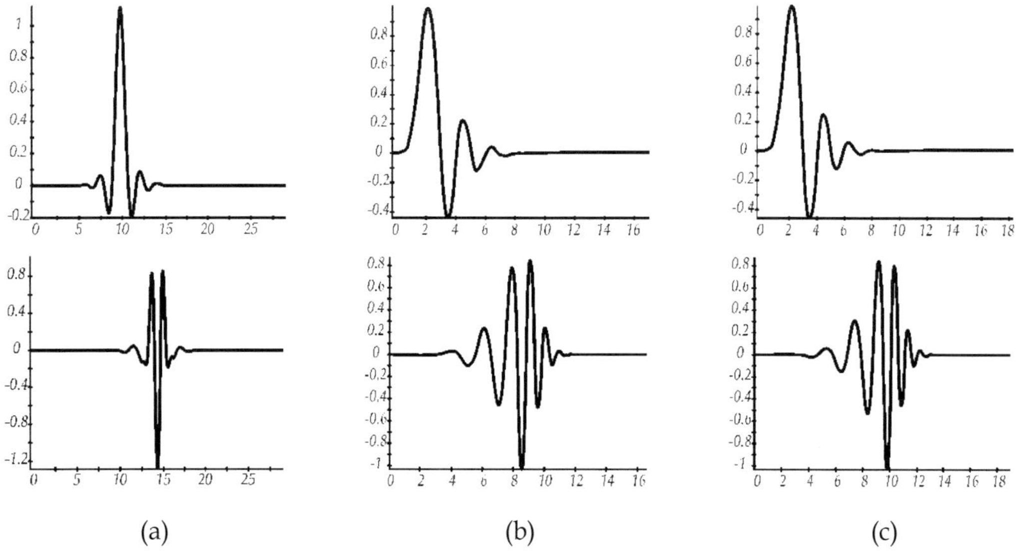

Fig. 6. Shows the scale function (left) and wavelet function (right) of (a) Coiflet 5, (b) Daubechies 9 and (c) Daubechies 10

4.1 One stage filtering: Approximations and details

For many signals, the low-frequency content is the most important part because it gives to the signal its identity. The high-frequency content, on the other hand, imparts nuance. Consider the human voice. If high-frequency components are removed, the voice sounds different, but the words are still audible and clearly recognized. However, if enough low-frequency components are removed, the resulting audio signal is not clear. In wavelet analysis, approximations are the high-scale, low-frequency components and the details are the low-scale, high-frequency components of the signal. Figure 7 shows the steps for signal decomposition.

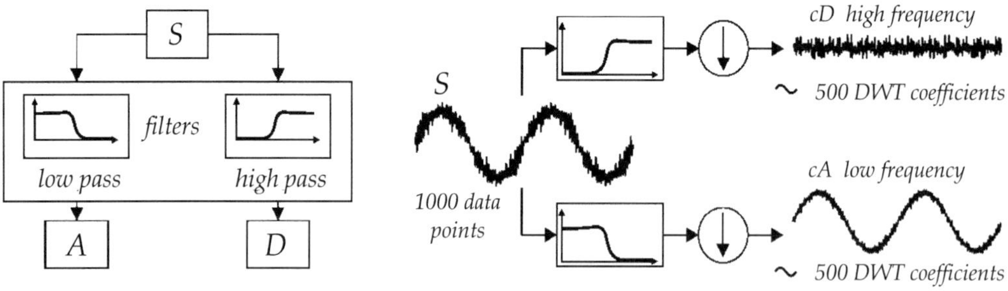

Fig. 7. Show the way to decompose a signal

4.2 Multiple-level decomposition

The decomposition process can be iterated, with successive approximations being decomposed in turn, so that one signal is broken down into many lower resolution components. This is called the wavelet decomposition tree that is shown on figure 8.

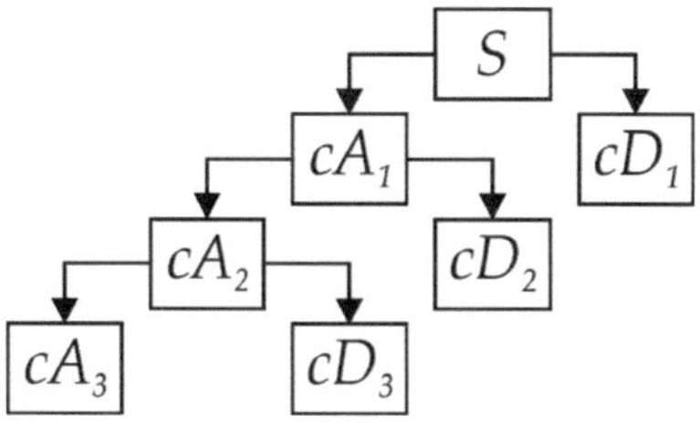

Fig. 8. Shows the process of performing, the multiple decomposition, which it is called wavelet decomposition tree

4.3 Number of levels

Since the analysis process is iterative, in theory it can be continued indefinitely. Realistically, the decomposition can proceed only until the individual details consist of a single sample or pixel. Moreover, the processes include selecting a suitable number of levels based on the nature of the signal, or on a suitable criterion such as *entropy*.

4.4 Wavelet reconstruction

Discrete wavelet transform can be used to analyze, or decompose, signals and images in a process called decomposition or analysis. Conversely, reconstruction or synthesis is the process of assembling hose components back into the original signal without loss of information. While being this transformation, it is desirable to establish its investment, i.e. to return to the original signal from the output tree. This methodology follows reasoning in the opposite direction, i.e. from the coefficients while depending on the number of levels and considering the high frequency (H') and low (L') bands that must be obtained from the reconstructed signal S, shown in figure 9. The mathematical manipulation that affects synthesis is called: the *inverse discrete wavelet transforms* (IDWT). In order to synthesize a signal by using Wavelet Toolbox software, we reconstruct it from the wavelet coefficients.

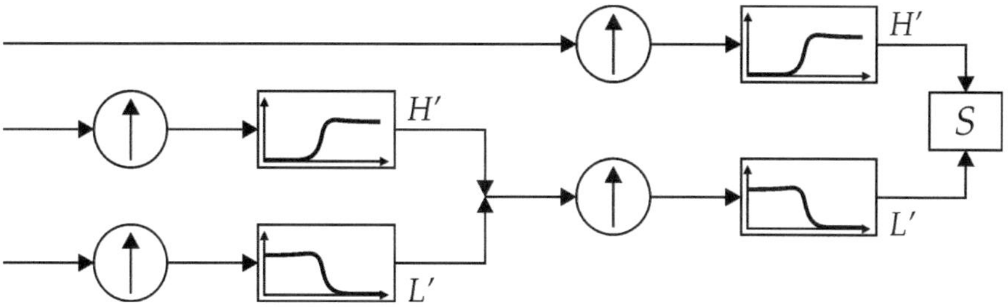

Fig. 9. Show how to reconstruct a signal using wavelets

4.5 Wavelet using MATLAB

We will describe a simple method for wavelet transform of a given signal. You must choose a wavelet function, which is the mother wavelet, as well as determining the value of the

signal wavelet scale, using the command *wname*. In this example we use a wavelet *coif5* level 10.
wname = 'coif5'; lev = 10;

In most of the signals of low frequency components that give the signal most of its information, while the high frequency components are responsible for incorporating particular features, that is why we subdivide the components of a signal into two categories: approaches (low frequencies) and details (high frequencies). To perform this decomposition the *wpdec* command is used which is responsible for creating a tree that consists of a vector in this case it is the signal to break down "*y*" the level to be decomposed *lev = 10* and the type of wavelet used, which in this case is coiflet 5 and it is stored as a tree in the *tree* variable:
tree = wpdec(y,lev,wname);

We generate the coefficients of the decomposition of the signal using the *wpcoef* command where needed as the variable information and the number of tree node that has a better performance in the tree that was generated, which in this case is two.
det1 = wpcoef(tree,2);

We determine noise threshold by using *wpbmpen* command that returns a global threshold *THR* for de-noising. *THR* obtained by a wavelet packet coefficients selection rule by means of using a penalization method provided by Birge-Massart. T (in our case tree) is a wavelet packet tree corresponding to the wavelet packet decomposition of the signal or image to be de-noised. *SIGMA* is the standard deviation of the zero mean Gaussian white noise in the de-noising model. *alpha* is a tuning parameter for the penalty term, which must be a real number greater than 1. The sparsity of the wavelet packet representation of the de-noised signal or image grows with *alpha*. Typically *alpha* = 2.
sigma = median(abs(det1))/0.6745;
alpha = 2;
thr = wpbmpen(tree,sigma,alpha);

We use command *wpdencmp* that performs a de-noising or compression process of a signal, when using wavelet packet. The ideas and the procedures for de-noising and compression by using wavelet packet decomposition are the same as those used in the wavelets framework. *Wpdencmp (TREE,SORH,CRIT,PAR,KEEPAPP)* has the same output arguments, using the same options as above, but which were obtained directly from the input wavelet packet tree decomposition *TREE* of the signal to be de-noised or compressed. *SORH* (*'s' or 'h'*) stands for soft or hard thresholding. Best decomposition performed using entropy criterion defined by string *CRIT* and parameter *PAR*. Threshold parameter is also PAR. In addition, if *CRIT* = *'nobest'* no optimization is done, and the current decomposition is thresholded. If *KEEPAPP= 1*, approximation coefficients cannot be thresholded; otherwise, they can be:
keepapp = 1;
xd = wpdencmp(tree,'s','nobest',thr,keepapp);

All those parameters help us to de-noise our signals by using wavelets.

5. Sine signal example

With MATLAB, it is possible to process noisy signals containing certain information, such as an audio one, in order to reduce the quantity of noise contained in it. Non-periodicity characterizes an audio signal, which is composed by a large number of different frequencies signals. This feature allows the use of conventional methods such as digital filters to eliminate noise mixed into the signal.

In this section, we will introduce the treatment of noise in audio signals by using wavelet transforms, which are included as a tool in MATLAB. To do this we will start by using a sine wave signal, which is periodic and presents a well-known behavior.

First, it is necessary to define the time interval *k*, and to define the angular frequency *w*.

```
k = 0:9.0703e-005:5;
w=500*pi;
```

The variable *h* represents the argument of the sine function *x* in the next two instructions

```
h=w.*k;
x = sin(h);
```

Once we have defined the signal to be treated *x*, it is necessary to generate the noise source in order to be mixed with the original signal. One of the most common sources of noise is Gaussian white noise, which contains all frequencies. Thus to generate white Gaussian noise we use the *awgn* instruction described in section 3.4.

```
y = awgn(x,0,'measured');
wname = 'coif5'; lev = 10;
tree = wpdec(y,lev,wname);
det1 = wpcoef(tree,2);
sigma = median(abs(det1))/0.6745;
alpha = 2;
thr = wpbmpen(tree,sigma,alpha);
keepapp = 1;
xd = wpdencmp(tree,'s','nobest',thr,keepapp);
```

Correlation between both signals, original and filtered one, is the parameter to compare them. We used the command *crosscorr*, which computes and plots the sample cross-correlation function *XCF* between two univariate, stochastic time series. To plot the *XCF* sequence without the confidence bounds, set nSTDs = 0.

```
D=crosscorr(x,xd);
Finally, we plot three figures.
figure(1)
plot(k,xd)
hold on
plot(k,y,'k')
hold on
plot(k,x,'g')
legend('Denoise signal','Signal with AWGN','Original signal');
figure(2)
plot(z,D)
legend('Correlation @ 0');
```

The sinusoidal waveform *x* represents the signal to which is added white Gaussian noise; this will subsequently be reduced to recover the sine wave.

We evaluate three wavelets families, Symlets 2 to 8, Daubechies 2 to 10 and Coiflet 1 to 5 by using the program presented above. Our results show that Coiflet 5 and Daubechies 9 and 10 are the best options for better de-noised in our signals. We choose cross correlation to evaluate the best performance; the cross correlation number that we select is the maximum at zero. Figure 10 shows the original signal sinus waveform. Part (*b*) is an extension of two periods of part (*a*). We choose a frequency of 250 Hz due to voice is in that range.

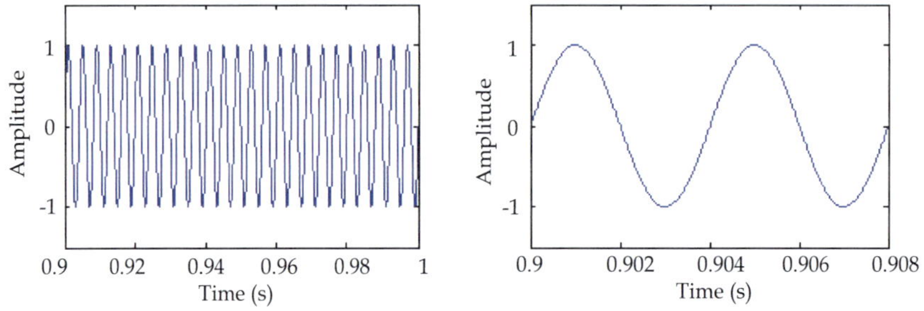

Fig. 10. Shows original sinus waveform. The right one shows a zoom view of left figure

We add white Gaussian noise to sine waveform represented in Figure 11 and the resulting graph is the plot shown in Figure 11. We set *SNR* to *AWGN=10*

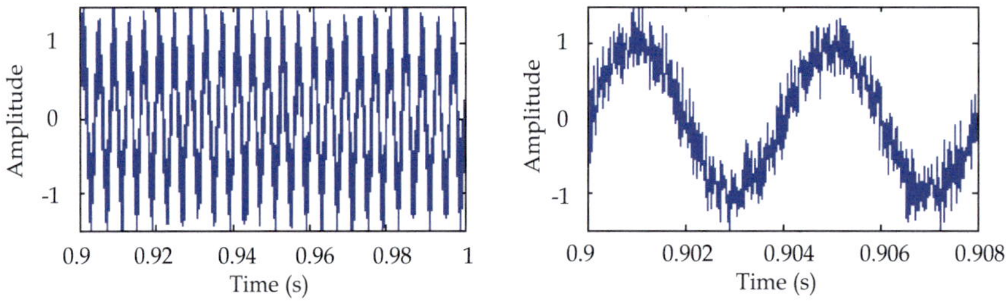

Fig. 11. Shows sine waveform with *AWGN=10.*

After running the program, we find the cross correlation *D* between original signal and signal de-noise. Figure 12 presents the result

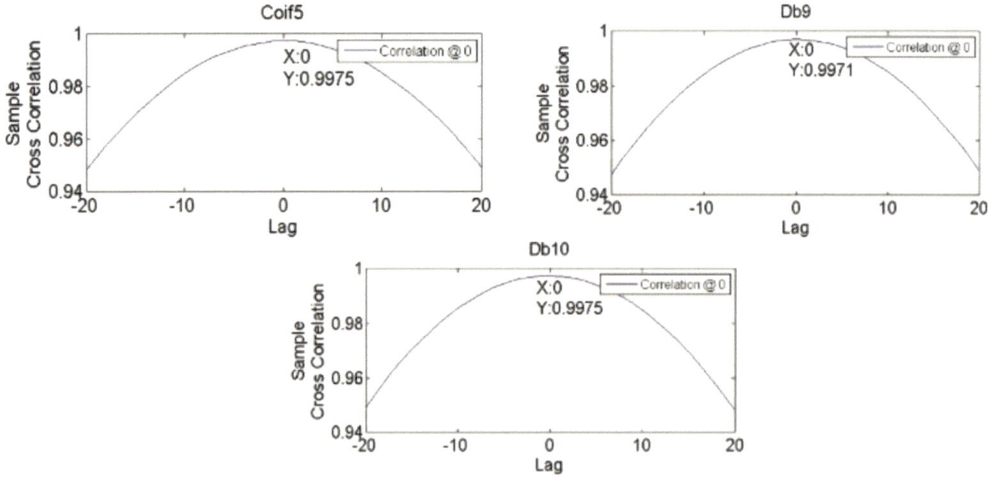

Fig. 12. Shows cross correlation of original signal and signal de-noise

Figure 13 shows the plot of a signal after its processing method using Coiflet 5.

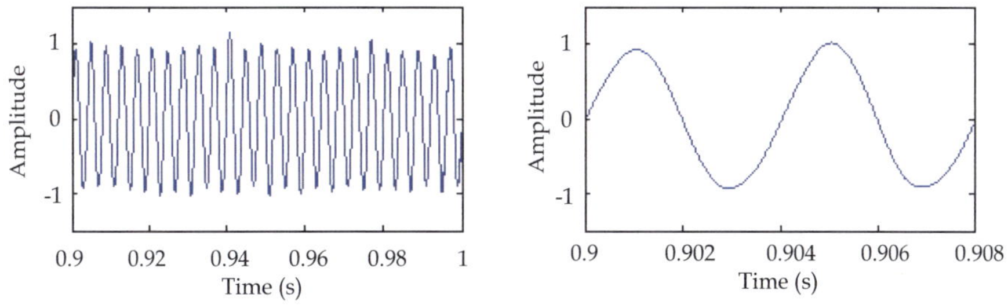

Fig. 13. Shows signal after processing method of de-noise using Coiflet 5

Evaluation of the resultant waveform *xd* presented in Figure 14 is compared with the original sine function *x* form Figure 11 gives numbers higher than 99% as presented in Figure 13. These results support the reliability of the proposed method for de-noising.

6. Audio signal example

As it has been described in section 2.1, to obtain an audio signal, we select the audio block and we connect it to the multimedia file block. This information is saved in a user-specified file with extension .wav and then we use the program to extract this information and process it with wavelets *coif5*, *db9* and *db10*. Figure 14 shows the original audio signal, audio signal with noise and the recovered signal using the wavelet *coif5*. Figure 15 shows the best correlation using the above wavelets.

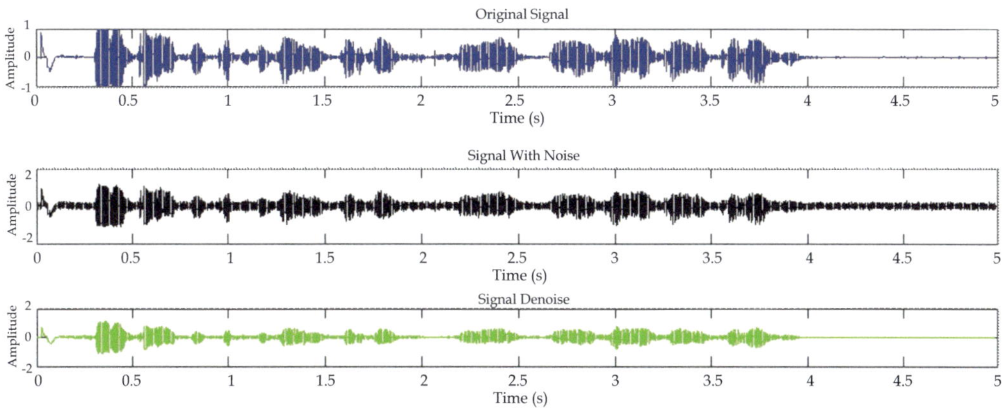

Fig. 14. Shows original audio signal, audio signal with noise and the recovered signal

To make the signal processing we use the next code:

```
clc,close all,clear all
 k = 0:9.0703e-005:5;
 w=500*pi;
 h=w.*k;
 [x,Fs,nbits]= wavread ('voice');
 y = awgn(x,10,'measured'); % Add white Gaussian noise.
```

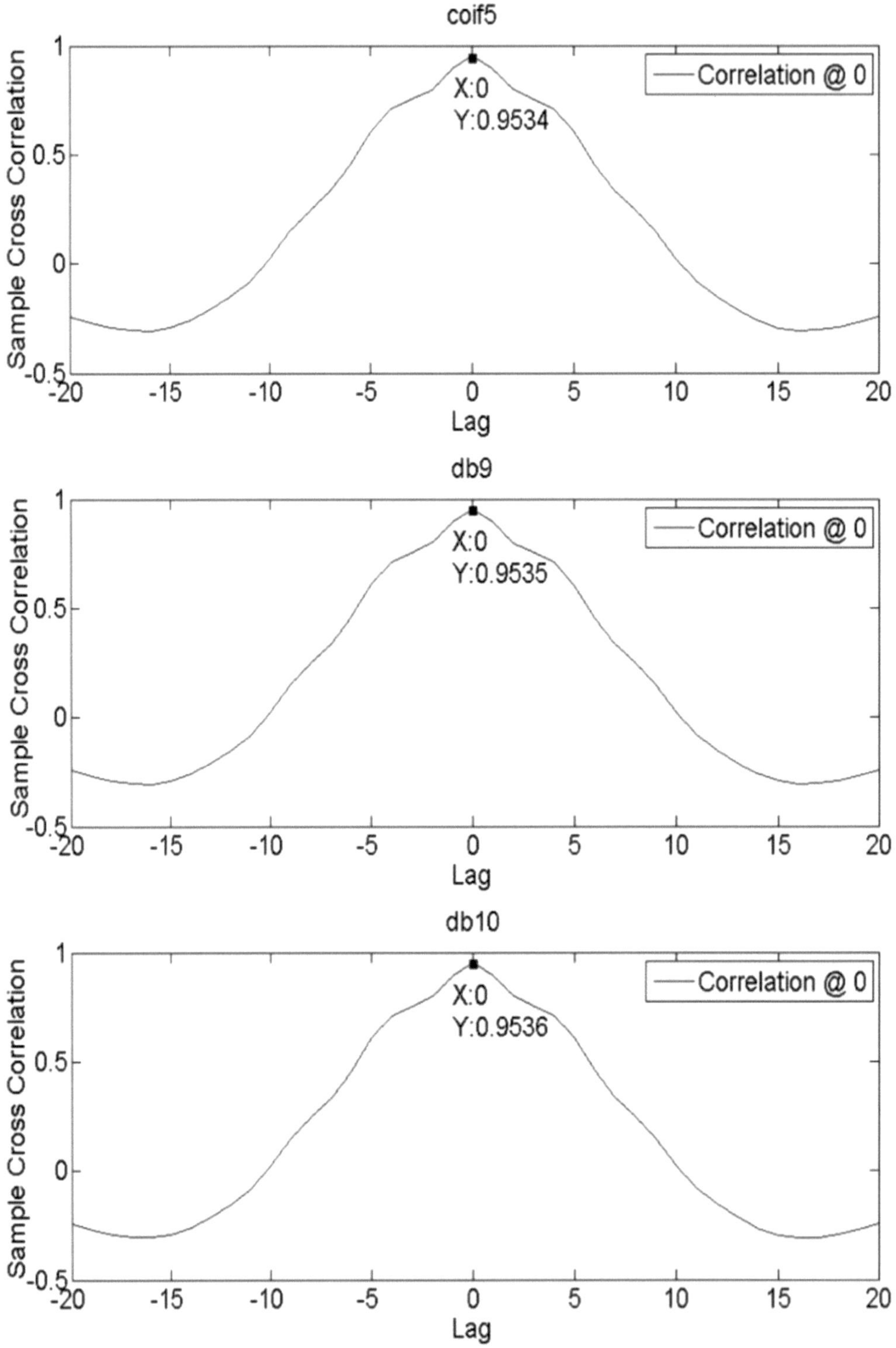

Fig. 15. Shows cross-correlation for determine the best result after noise reduction

```
wavwrite(y,Fs,'noisyvoice')
wname = 'coif5'; lev = 10;
tree = wpdec(y,lev,wname);
det1 = wpcoef(tree,2014);
 sigma = median(abs(det1))/0.6745;
alpha = 1.8;
thr = wpbmpen(tree,sigma,alpha)
keepapp = 1;
xd = wpdencmp(tree,'s','nobest',thr,keepapp);
D=crosscorr(x,y);
 z=-20:1:20;
 figure(1)
subplot(311)
plot(k,x)
xlabel('time')
ylabel('Amplitude')
title('original signal');
subplot(312)
plot(k,y,'k')
xlabel('time')
ylabel('Amplitude')
title('signal with noise');
subplot(313)
plot(k,xd,'g')
xlabel('time')
ylabel('Amplitude')
title('signal denoise');
figure(2)
plot(z,D)
title('coif5')
legend('Correlation @ 0');
wavwrite(xd,Fs,'voice5')
```

In signal processing, analogue-to-digital converters also suffer linearity errors, they add noise, distortion, and introduces quantization error due to the precision of their voltage sampling process. The result of all this is a computerized sequence of samples that may not be as closely related to the real-world sound as you might expect. Do not be surprised when high-precision analysis or measurements are unrepeatable due to noise, or if delicate changes made to a sampled audio signal are undetectable to the naked ear upon replay.

7. Graphical Interface using GUIDE

For better understanding of the content of this chapter, we have developed a graphical interface, only in the case of a sine wave. We used GUIDE of MATLAB to build this interface, you need pop-up menu, slider, edit text, four push button and four graphics (axes), after all that is placed in your figure you need to program each item. Figure 16 shows how all of this should be seen.

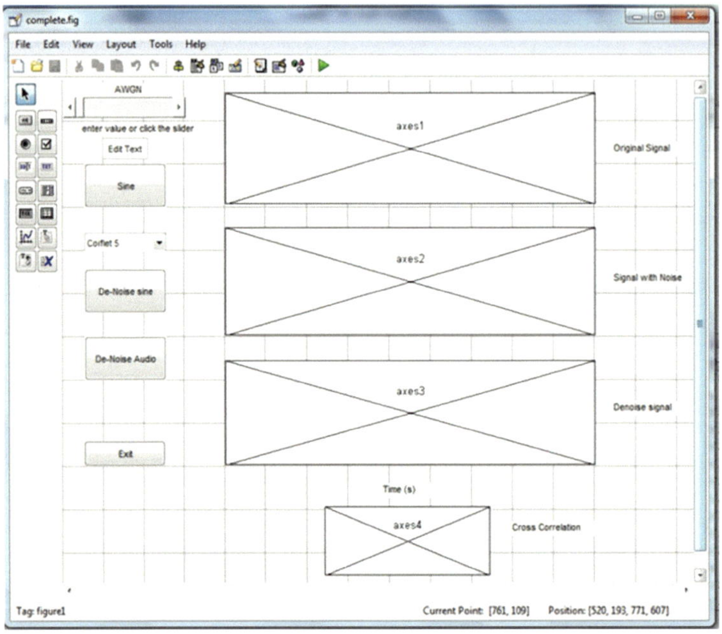

Fig. 16. Shows graphical interface using GUIDE

First you need to configure axes, you do this by double clicking on the graphic, this will show you an inspector on figure 17, you need to change *nextplot from replace to replacechildren* that means to remove all child objects when *HandleVisibility* property is set to an on function and then to reset figure *NextPlot* property to an add function. To set axes limits you need to change *Xlimit* from 0.20 to 0.24, and in our case, *Ylimit* from -1 to 1.

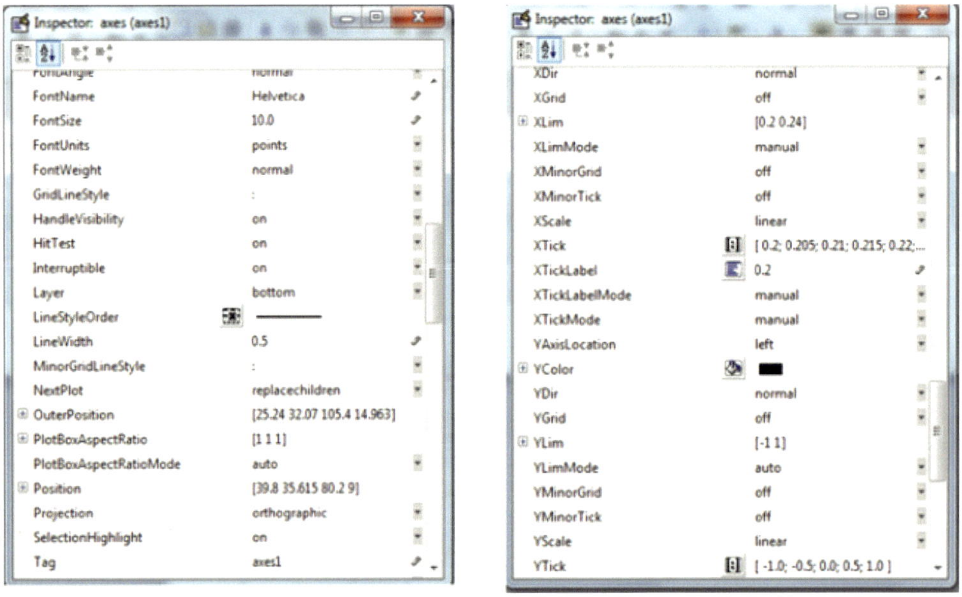

Fig. 17. Shows configurations of axes using inspector

In our case, a slider is coupled to an edit text component so that: The edit text displays the current value of the slider. The user can enter a value into the edit text box and cause the slider to update to that value. Both components update the appropriate model parameters when activated by the user. Our slider is called *AWGN* (average white generator noise) and it is from 0 to 10 *SNR*.

```
function complete_OpeningFcn(hObject, eventdata, handles, varargin)
% Choose default command line output for example5
handles.output = hObject;
 clc
% initalize error count and use edit1 object's userdata to store it.
data.number_errors = 0;
set(handles.edit1,'UserData',data)
% Update handles structure
guidata(hObject, handles);
% --- Executes on slider movement.
function slider1_Callback(hObject, eventdata, handles)
set(handles.edit1,'String',...
  num2str(get(hObject,'Value')));
% --- Executes during object creation, after setting all properties.
function slider1_CreateFcn(hObject, eventdata, handles)
function edit1_Callback(hObject, eventdata, handles)
val = str2double(get(hObject,'String'));
% Determine whether val is a number between 0 and 10.
if isnumeric(val) && length(val)==10 && ...
  val >= get(handles.slider1,'min') && ...
  val <= get(handles.slider1,'max')
  set(handles.slider1,'Value',val);
else
% Retrieve and increment the error count.
% Error count is in the edit text UserData,
% so we already have its handle.
  data = get(hObject,'UserData');
  data.number_errors = data.number_errors+1;
% Save the changes.
  set(hObject,'UserData',data);
% Display new total.
  set(hObject,'String',...
  ['You have entered an invalid entry ',...
   num2str(data.number_errors),' times.']);
   % Restore focus to the edit text box after error
  uicontrol(hObject)
end
% --- Executes during object creation, after setting all properties.
function edit1_CreateFcn(hObject, eventdata, handles)
if ispc && isequal(get(hObject,'BackgroundColor'),
get(0,'defaultUicontrolBackgroundColor'))
   set(hObject,'BackgroundColor','white');
end
```

In the case of the pushbutton 1 that is called sine, and if it only shows sine signal and signal with noise, it needs to be programmed as follow

```
% --- Executes on button press in pushbutton1.
function pushbutton1_Callback(hObject, eventdata, handles)
 k =(0:9.0703e-005:5);
 w=500*pi;
 h=w.*k;
 x = sin(h);
 f=get(handles.slider1,'Value');
 y = awgn(x,f,'measured');
 D=crosscorr(x,y);
 z=-20:1:20;
  plot(handles.axes1,k,x)
  plot(handles.axes2,k,y)
  plot(handles.axes3,z,D)
```

For programming, push button 2, called de-noise sine, this button performs all the processing method, which was described previously. It is necessary to write all this code

```
% --- Executes on button press in pushbutton2.
function pushbutton2_Callback(hObject, eventdata, handles)
menu= get(handles.popupmenu1,'Value');
switch menu
   case 1  %case 1: coiflet 5
 % example3 code
 k =(0:9.0703e-005:5);
 w=500*pi;
 h=w.*k;
 x = sin(h);
 f=get(handles.slider1,'Value');
 y = awgn(x,f,'measured');
wname = 'coif5'; lev = 10; %  wavelet that need to change!
tree = wpdec(y,lev,wname);
det1 = wpcoef(tree,2);
sigma = median(abs(det1))/0.6745;
alpha = 2;
thr =wpbmpen(tree,sigma,alpha);
keepapp = 1;
xd = wpdencmp(tree,'s','nobest',thr,keepapp);
D=crosscorr(x,xd);
z=-20:1:20;
  plot(handles.axes1,k,x)
  plot(handles.axes2,k,y)
  plot(handles.axes3,k,xd)
    set(gca,'XLim',[ 0.2,  0.24], ...
      'YLim',[-1 1]);
  plot(handles.axes4,z,D)
   case 2     %case2 Daubechies 10
```

```
·% example3 code
  case 3    %Case 3: Daubechies 9
·% example3 code
End
```

For programing push button 3, called de-noise audio, this button performs all processing method, which was described previously. It is necessary to write all this code

```
 % --- Executes on button press in pushbutton3.
function pushbutton3_Callback(hObject, eventdata, handles)
menu= get(handles.popupmenu1,'Value');
switch menu
  case 1                                              %case 1: Coiflet 5
·% example4 code
 k = 0:9.0703e-005:5;
 w=500*pi;
 h=w.*k;
 [x,Fs,nbits]= wavread ('voice');
 f=get(handles.slider1,'Value');
 y = awgn(x,f,'measured');
 wavwrite(y,Fs,'noisyvoice')
wname = 'coif5'; lev = 10;
tree = wpdec(y,lev,wname);
det1 = wpcoef(tree,2);
sigma = median(abs(det1))/0.6745;
alpha = 2;
thr =wpbmpen(tree,sigma,alpha);
keepapp = 1;
xd = wpdencmp(tree,'s','nobest',thr,keepapp);
D=crosscorr(x,xd);
z=-20:1:20;
 plot(handles.axes1,k,x)
 plot(handles.axes2,k,y)
 plot(handles.axes3,k,xd)
 plot(handles.axes4,z,D)
case 2    %case2 Daubechies 10
·% example4 code
  case 3    %Case 3: Daubechies 9
·% example4 code
end
```

For programing push button 4 called exit

```
% --- Executes on button press in pushbutton4.
function pushbutton3_Callback(hObject, eventdata, handles)
close all
```

Figure 18 (left) shows *AWGN 1*, and it plots original signal, in this case sine, and signal with noise, cross correlation between them. Figure 18 (right) shows sine after de-noise and cross correlation between the original signal and the de-noised.

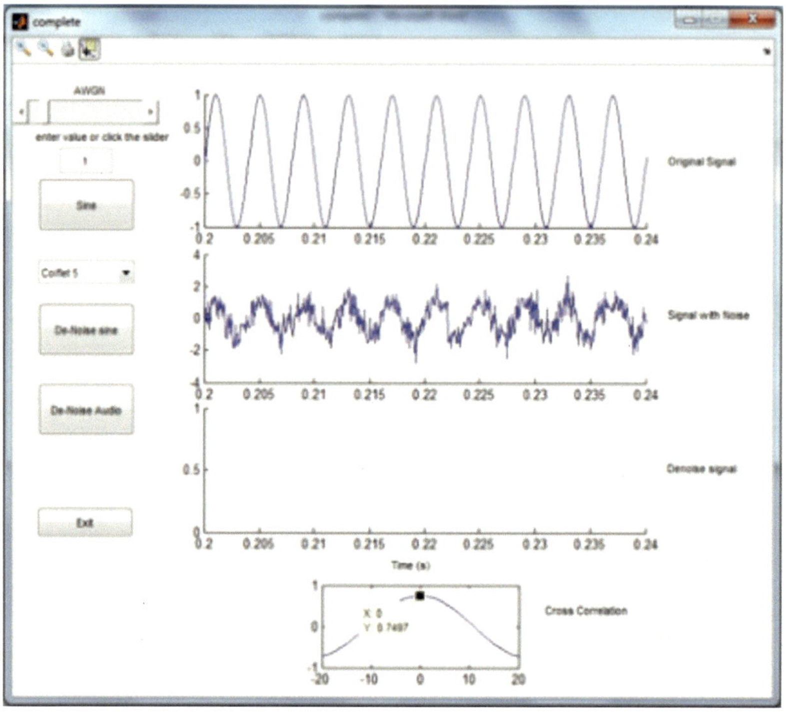

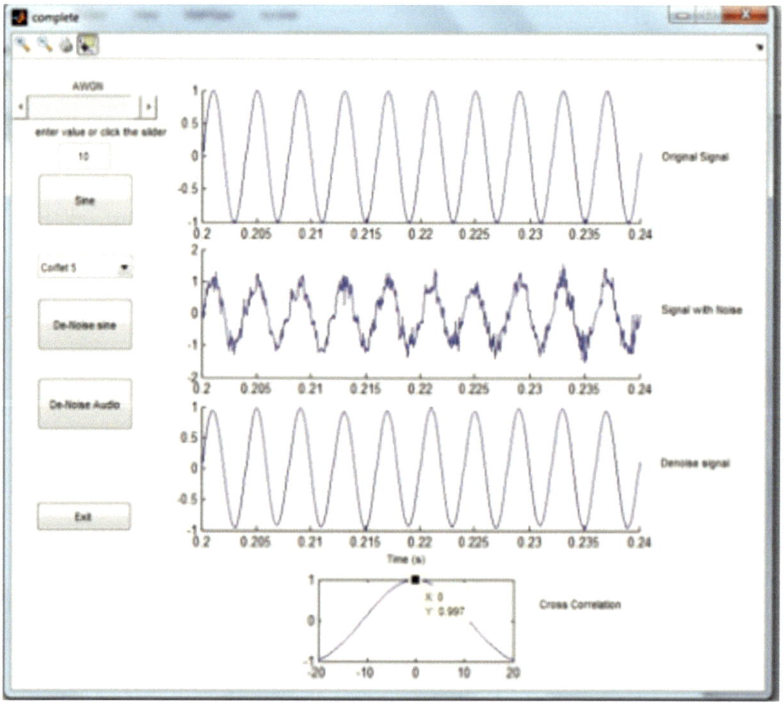

Fig. 18. (up) *AWGN* at 1 *SNR* with a correlation of 0.7497 and (down) sine after de-noise with *SNR* of 10 and correlation of 0.997

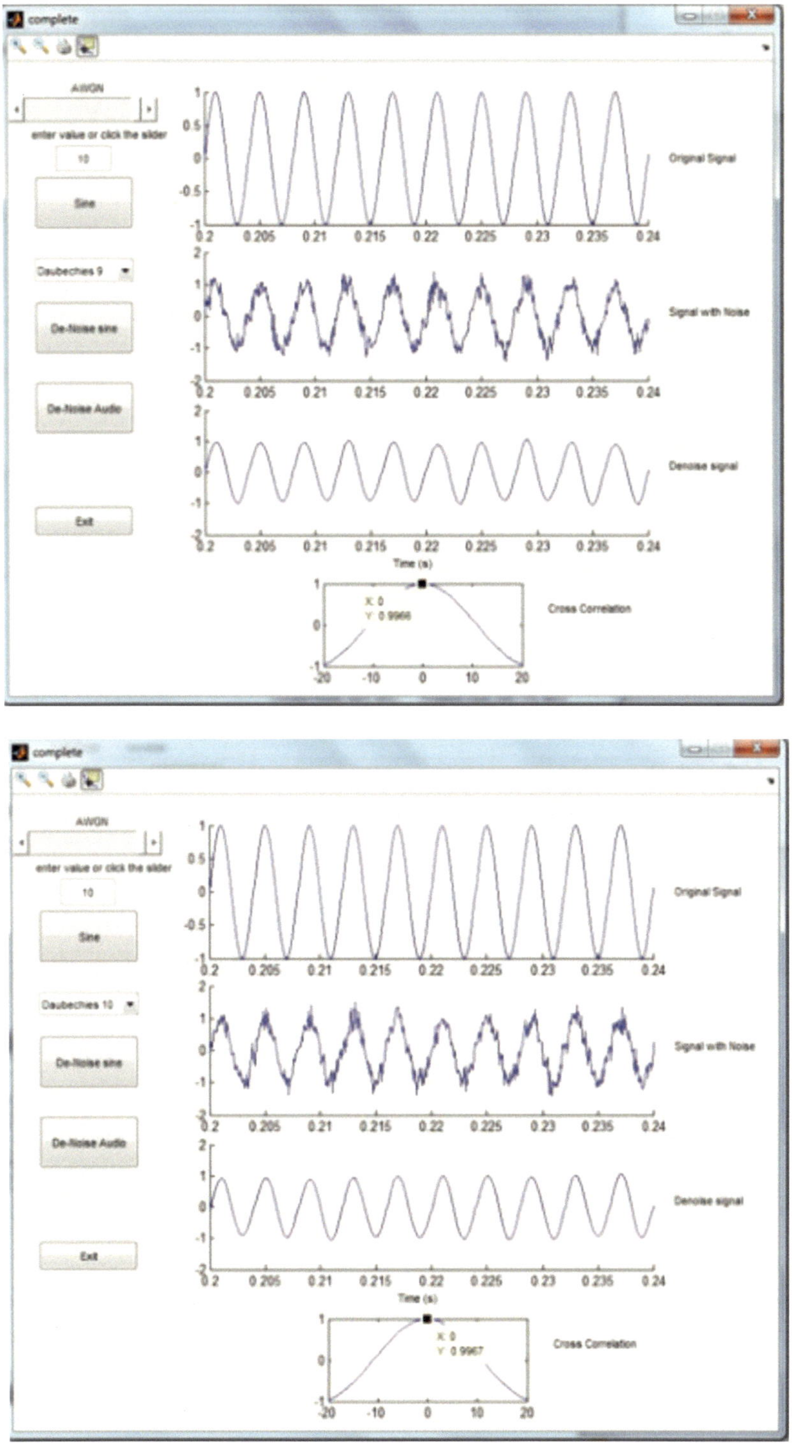

Fig. 19. (up). *AWGN* at 10 *SNR* with a correlation of 0.9966 after de-noise using Daubechies 9 and (down) *AWGN* at 10 *SNR* with a correlation of 0.9967 after de-noise using Daubechies 10

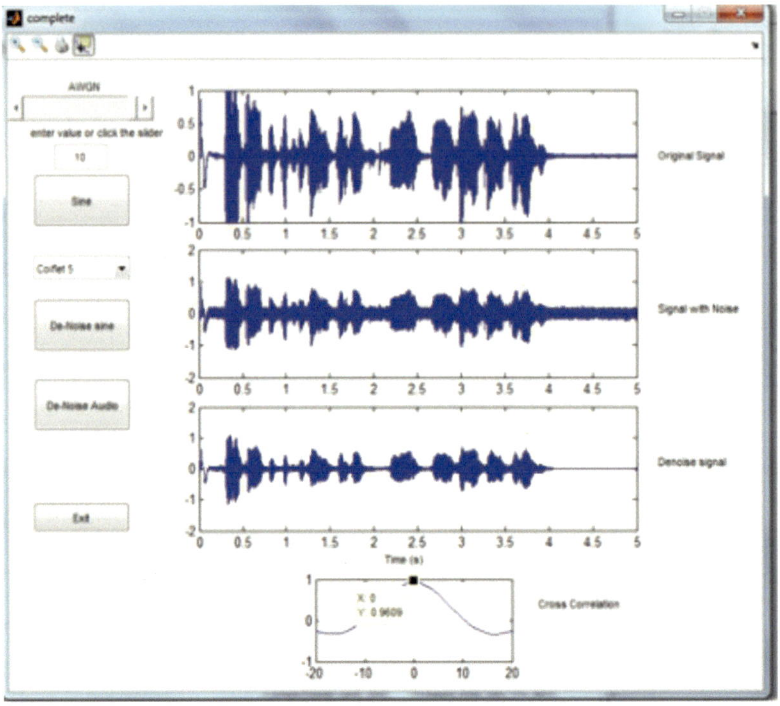

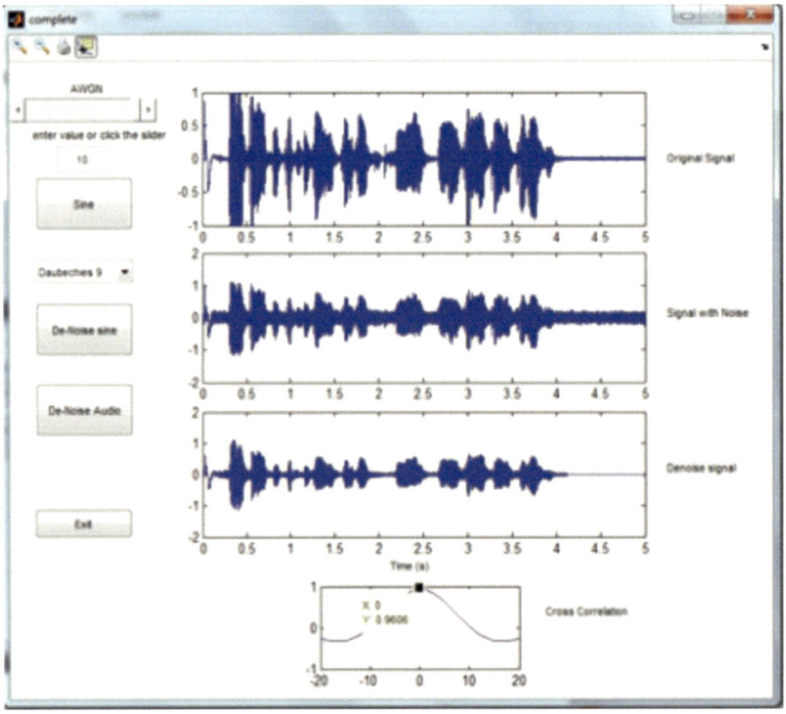

Fig. 20. (up). *AWGN* at 10 *SNR* with a correlation of 0.9609 after de-noise using Coiflet 5 and (down) *AWGN* at 10 *SNR* with a correlation of 0.9606 after de-noise using Daubechies 9

Figure 19 shows de-noise of sine with noise using *AWGN* of 10, using Daubechies 9 and 10, this wavelets show a better performance that any others. Figure 20 shows behavior of Coiflet 5 and Daubechies 9 using *AWGN* of 10 adding to audio signal.
In this section, it was described how to build a graphical interface using MATLAB code that was developed to de-noised sine and audio signals. This interface helps to be able to visualize the results obtained throughout this chapter, in addition to make it accessible to the user.

8. Conclusions

We provide a practical approach in how to put into practice wavelets in noisy audio data to improve clarity and signal retrieval. Since there are no books that show the code for a graphical interface with audio processing using wavelets, this chapter presents MATLAB code to reduce the Gaussian white noise in periodic signals (sine function) and in audio signals (composed of several frequencies) using wavelet analysis. We compared different wavelet families: Symlets, Daubechies and Coiflets, and we used cross-correlation to determine the best fit between an original signal and the processed one. By using Coiflet 5, Daubechies 9 and 10 we obtained the best result because they have a higher correlation at zero. Our signal processing technique recovers signal with a correlation higher than 99%. In analysis for audio signal with added Gaussian white noise, while using the technique we obtained a recovered signal with a correlation of 95%. This analysis is very useful to help the reader understand the know how in removing noise from a signal by using wavelets. Therefore, when a signal shows a periodic signal extraction from noise, it will be satisfactory. The graphical interface presented in the last section was performed while using GUIDE this one gives the readers a guideline to develop their own projects in MATLAB.

9. Acknowledges

The authors would like to thank Dr. Karen Esmonde-White for her helpful review and comments of this chapter. AEVL would like to thanks to Fundacion Pablo Garcia for help and support.

Apendix A: Five steps to a continuous Wavelet Transform

Here are the five steps of an easy recipe for creating a Continuous Wavelet Transform (CWT), see Figure A:

1. Take a wavelet and compare it to a section at the start of the original signal.
2. Calculate a number C, that represents how closely correlated the wavelet is with this section of the signal. The larger the number C is in absolute value, the more the similarity appears. If the signal energy and the wavelet energy are equal to one, C may be interpreted as a correlation coefficient. Note that, in general, the signal energy does not equal one and the CWT coefficients are not directly interpretable as correlation coefficients. Therefore, the CWT coefficients are different when you compute the CWT for the same signal by using different wavelets.
3. Shift the wavelet to the right and repeat steps 1 and 2 until you have covered the whole signal.
4. Scale (stretch) the wavelet and repeat steps 1 through 3.
5. Repeat steps 1 through 4 for all scales.

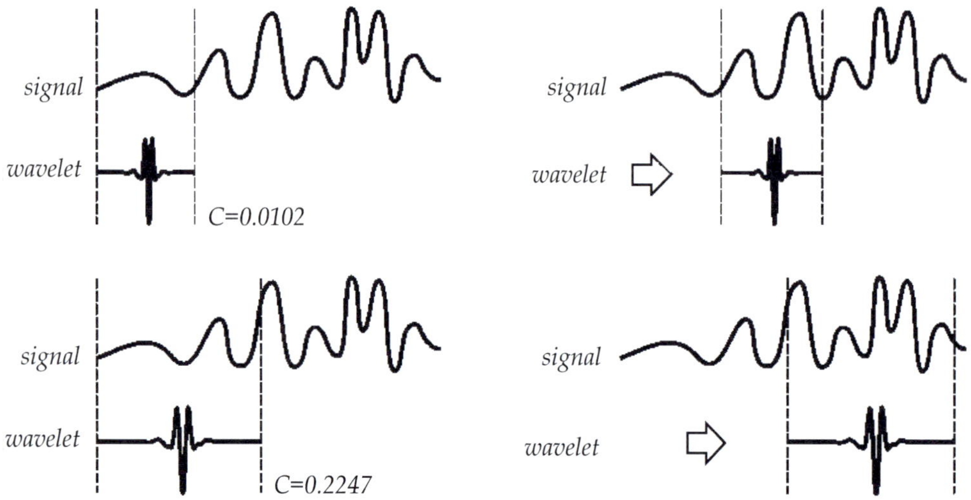

Fig. A. Shows recipe for creating a CWT

Appendix B: User Interface MATLAB code

In this appendix, it shows the complete code to develop the GUI using the GUIDE of MATLAB, and develops it as an example using a sine wave signal, which is added a certain level of noise and signal is shown graphically also recovered as the ratio correlation between the original signal and recovered signal.

```
function varargout = complete(varargin)
% Begin initialization code - DO NOT EDIT
gui_Singleton = 1;
gui_State = struct('gui_Name',       mfilename, ...
                   'gui_Singleton',  gui_Singleton, ...
                   'gui_OpeningFcn', @complete_OpeningFcn, ...
                   'gui_OutputFcn',  @complete_OutputFcn, ...
                   'gui_LayoutFcn',  [] , ...
                   'gui_Callback',   []);
if nargin && ischar(varargin{1})
   gui_State.gui_Callback = str2func(varargin{1});
end
if nargout
   [varargout{1:nargout}] = gui_mainfcn(gui_State, varargin{:});
else
   gui_mainfcn(gui_State, varargin{:});
end
% End initialization code - DO NOT EDIT
% --- Executes just before complete is made visible.
function complete_OpeningFcn(hObject, eventdata, handles, varargin)
handles.output = hObject;
clc
% Initalize error count and use edittext1 object's userdata to store it.
```

```
data.number_errors = 0;
set(handles.edit1,'UserData',data)
% Update handles structure
guidata(hObject, handles);
% --- Outputs from this function are returned to the command line.
function varargout = complete_OutputFcn(hObject, eventdata, handles)
% Get default command line output from handles structure
varargout{1} = handles.output;
% --- Executes on button press in pushbutton1.
function pushbutton1_Callback(hObject, eventdata, handles)
 k =(0:9.0703e-005:5);
 w=500*pi;
 h=w.*k;
 x = sin(h);
 f=get(handles.slider1,'Value');
 y = awgn(x,f,'measured');
 D=crosscorr(x,y);
 z=-20:1:20;
 plot(handles.axes1,k,x)
 plot(handles.axes2,k,y)
 plot(handles.axes4,z,D)
% --- Executes on button press in pushbutton2.
function pushbutton2_Callback(hObject, eventdata, handles)
menu= get(handles.popupmenu1,'Value');
switch menu
  case 1                                          %case 1: Coiflet 5
 k =(0:9.0703e-005:5);
 w=500*pi;
 h=w.*k;
 x = sin(h);
 f=get(handles.slider1,'Value');
 y = awgn(x,f,'measured');
 wname = 'coif5'; lev = 10;
 tree = wpdec(y,lev,wname);
 det1 = wpcoef(tree,2);
 sigma = median(abs(det1))/0.6745;
 alpha = 2;
 thr =wpbmpen(tree,sigma,alpha);
 keepapp = 1;
 xd = wpdencmp(tree,'s','nobest',thr,keepapp);
 D=crosscorr(x,xd);
 z=-20:1:20;
  plot(handles.axes1,k,x)
  plot(handles.axes2,k,y)
  plot(handles.axes3,k,xd)
    set(gca,'XLim',[ 0.2,  0.24], ...
      'YLim',[-1 1]);
```

```
 plot(handles.axes4,z,D)
  case 2                                        %Case2 Daubechies 10
k =(0:9.0703e-005:5);
w=500*pi;
h=w.*k;
x = sin(h);
f=get(handles.slider1,'Value');
y = awgn(x,f,'measured');
wname = 'db10'; lev = 10;
tree = wpdec(y,lev,wname);
det1 = wpcoef(tree,2);
sigma = median(abs(det1))/0.6745;
alpha = 2;
thr =wpbmpen(tree,sigma,alpha);
keepapp = 1;
xd = wpdencmp(tree,'s','nobest',thr,keepapp);
D=crosscorr(x,xd);
z=-20:1:20;
 plot(handles.axes1,k,x)
 plot(handles.axes2,k,y)
 plot(handles.axes3,k,xd)
    set(gca,'XLim',[ 0.2,  0.24], ...
     'YLim',[-1.1 1.1]);
 plot(handles.axes4,z,D)
  case 3                                        %Case 3: Daubechies 9
k =(0:9.0703e-005:5);
w=500*pi;
h=w.*k;
x = sin(h);
f=get(handles.slider1,'Value');
y = awgn(x,f,'measured');
wname = 'db9'; lev = 10;
tree = wpdec(y,lev,wname);
det1 = wpcoef(tree,2);
sigma = median(abs(det1))/0.6745;
alpha = 2;
thr =wpbmpen(tree,sigma,alpha);
keepapp = 1;
xd = wpdencmp(tree,'s','nobest',thr,keepapp);
D=crosscorr(x,xd);
z=-20:1:20;
 plot(handles.axes1,k,x)
 plot(handles.axes2,k,y)
 plot(handles.axes3,k,xd)
 plot(handles.axes4,z,D)
end
```

```
% --- Executes on button press in pushbutton3.
function pushbutton3_Callback(hObject, eventdata, handles)
menu= get(handles.popupmenu1,'Value');
switch menu
  case 1                                    %case 1: coiflet 5
 k = 0:9.0703e-005:5;
 w=500*pi;
 h=w.*k;
 [x,Fs,nbits]= wavread ('voice');
 f=gethandles.slider1,'Value');
 y = awgn(x,f,'measured');
 wavwrite(y,Fs,'noisyvoice')
 wname = 'coif5'; lev = 10;
 tree = wpdec(y,lev,wname);
 det1 = wpcoef(tree,2);
 sigma = median(abs(det1))/0.6745;
 alpha = 2;
 thr =wpbmpen(tree,sigma,alpha);
 keepapp = 1;
 xd = wpdencmp(tree,'s','nobest',thr,keepapp);
 D=crosscorr(x,xd);
 z=-20:1:20;
  plot(handles.axes1,k,x)
  plot(handles.axes2,k,y)
  plot(handles.axes3,k,xd)
  plot(handles.axes4,z,D)
  case 2                                    %case 2 Daubechies 10
 k = 0:9.0703e-005:5;
 w=500*pi;
 h=w.*k;
 [x,Fs,nbits]= wavread ('voice');
 f=get(handles.slider1,'Value');
 y = awgn(x,f,'measured');
 wavwrite(y,Fs,'noisyvoice')
 wname = 'db10'; lev = 10;
 tree = wpdec(y,lev,wname);
 det1 = wpcoef(tree,2);
 sigma = median(abs(det1))/0.6745;
 alpha = 2;
 thr =wpbmpen(tree,sigma,alpha);
 keepapp = 1;
 xd = wpdencmp(tree,'s','nobest',thr,keepapp);
 D=crosscorr(x,xd);
 z=-20:1:20;
  plot(handles.axes1,k,x)
  plot(handles.axes2,k,y)
  plot(handles.axes3,k,xd)
```

```
 plot(handles.axes4,z,D)
  case 3                                          %Case 3: Daubechies 9
k = 0:9.0703e-005:5;
w=500*pi;
h=w.*k;
[x,Fs,nbits]= wavread ('voice');
f=get(handles.slider1,'Value');
y = awgn(x,f,'measured');
wavwrite(y,Fs,'noisyvoice')
wname = 'db9'; lev = 10;
tree = wpdec(y,lev,wname);
det1 = wpcoef(tree,2);
sigma = median(abs(det1))/0.6745;
alpha = 2;
thr =wpbmpen(tree,sigma,alpha);
keepapp = 1;
xd = wpdencmp(tree,'s','nobest',thr,keepapp);
D=crosscorr(x,xd);
z=-20:1:20;
 plot(handles.axes1,k,x)
 plot(handles.axes2,k,y)
 plot(handles.axes3,k,xd)
 plot(handles.axes4,z,D)
end
% --- Executes on slider movement.
function slider1_Callback(hObject, eventdata, handles)
set(handles.edit1,'String',...
  num2str(get(hObject,'Value')));
% --- Executes during object creation, after setting all properties.
function slider1_CreateFcn(hObject, eventdata, handles)
if isequal(get(hObject,'BackgroundColor'), get(0,'defaultUicontrolBackgroundColor'))
   set(hObject,'BackgroundColor',[.9 .9 .9]);
end
function edit1_Callback(hObject, eventdata, handles)
val = str2double(get(hObject,'String'));
% Determine whether val is a number between 0 and 1.
if isnumeric(val) && length(val)==10 && ...
  val >= get(handles.slider1,'min') && ...
  val <= get(handles.slider1,'max')
  set(handles.slider1,'Value',val);
else
% Retrieve and increment the error count.
% Error count is in the edit text UserData,
% so we already have its handle.
  data = get(hObject,'UserData');
  data.number_errors = data.number_errors+10;
```

```
% Save the changes.
  set(hObject,'UserData',data);
% Display new total.
  set(hObject,'String',...
  ['You have entered an invalid entry ',...
   num2str(data.number_errors),' times.']);
  % Restore focus to the edit text box after error
  uicontrol(hObject)
end
% --- Executes during object creation, after setting all properties.
function edit1_CreateFcn(hObject, eventdata, handles)
if ispc && isequal(get(hObject,'BackgroundColor'),
get(0,'defaultUicontrolBackgroundColor'))
   set(hObject,'BackgroundColor','white');
end
% --- Executes on selection change in popupmenu1.
function popupmenu1_Callback(hObject, eventdata, handles)
% --- Executes during object creation, after setting all properties.
function popupmenu1_CreateFcn(hObject, eventdata, handles)
if ispc && isequal(get(hObject,'BackgroundColor'),
get(0,'defaultUicontrolBackgroundColor'))
   set(hObject,'BackgroundColor','white');
end
% --- Executes on button press in pushbutton4.
function pushbutton4_Callback(hObject, eventdata, handles)
close all
```

10. References

Abbate A, Decusatis C. M, Das P. K. (2002). Wavelets and subbands: fundamentals and applications, ISBN 0-8176-4136-X, Birkhauser, Boston, USA.

Bahoura M & Rouat J, (2006). Wavelet speech enhancement based on time-scale adaptation, Speech Communication, Vol. 48, No. 12, pp: 1620-1637. ISSN: 0167-6393.

Davis, G, M, (2002). 'Noise Reduction in Speech Applications, CRC Press LLC, ISBN 0-8493-0949-2, USA.

Dong E & Pu X. (2008). Speech denoising based on perceptual weighting filter, Proceedings of 9th IEE International Conference on Signal Processing, pp: 705-708, October 26-29, Beijing. Print ISBN: 978-1-4244-2178-7.

Gold, B. & Morgan, N. (1999) Speech and audio signal processing: processing and perception of apeech, and music, John Wiley & Sons, INC., ISBN: 0-471-35154-7, New York, USA.

Johnson M. T, Yuan X and Ren Y, (2007). Speech Signal Enhancement through Adaptive Wavelet Thresholding, Speech Communications, Vol. 49, No. 2, pp: 123-133, ISSN: 0167-6393.

Képesia M & Weruaga L. (2006). Adaptive chirp-based time-frequency analysis of speech signals, Speech Communication, Vol. 48, No. 5, pp: 474-492. ISSN: 0167-6393.

Li N & Zhou M. (2008). Audio Denoising Algorithm Based on Adaptive Wavelet Soft-Threshold of Gain Factor and Teager Energy Operator, Proceedings of IEEE International Conference on Computer Science and Software Engineering, Vol. 1, pp: 787-790. Print ISBN: 978-0-7695-3336-0.

Mcloughlin I (2009). Applied Speech and Audio Processing With MATLAB Examples, Cambridge University Press, ISBN-13 978-0-521-51954-0, UK.

Minkoff, J. (2002). Signal Processing Fundamentals and Applications for Communications and Sensing Systems, ARTECH HOUSE, INC., ISBN 1-58053-360-4, USA.

Shankar B. J & Duraiswamy K. (2010). Wavelet-Based Block Matching Process: An Efficient Audio Denoising Technique,European Journal of Scientific Research, Vol.48 No.1, pp.16-28. ISSN 1450-216X.

Tuzlukov, V. P. (2002). Signal processing noise, CRC Press LLC, ISBN 0-8493-1025-3,USA.

Vaseghi, S. V. (2008), Advanced Digital Signal Processing and Noise Reduction, fourth edition, John Wiley & Sons Ltd., ISBN 978-0-470-75406-1 (H/B), United Kingdom.

Visser E, Otsuka M & Lee T W. (2003). A spatio-temporal speech enhancement scheme for robust speech recognition in noisy environments, Speech Communication, Vol. 41, No. 2-3, pp: 393-407. ISSN: 0167-6393.

Wang C T& Wang H. G, (2003). Enhancement of single channel speech based on masking property and wavelet transform, Speech Communication, Vol. 41, No 2-3, pp: 409-427. ISSN: 0167-6393.

Wang C T& Wang H. G (2007). Speech enhancement using hybrid gain factor in critical-band-wavelet-packet transform, Digital Signal Processing, Vol. 17, No. 1, pp: 172-188. ISSN: 1051-2004.

3

A Matlab® Approach for Implementing Control Algorithms in Real-Time: RTWT

Andres Hernandez, Adrian Chavarro and Robin De Keyser
Ghent University, Dep. Electrical energy, Systems and Automation, Technologiepark 913, B-9052 Gent, Belgium

1. Introduction

The literature about real-time systems presents digital control or computer controlled systems as one of its most important practical applications. However, it is very difficult to find in these textbooks real-time control aspects (Gambier, 2005). It seems to be more natural that these applications should be treated as part of digital control courses. In spite of that, control system literature rarely includes extensively the real-time subject and it does normally not pay much attention to real-time implementation aspects. Nevertheless, in practice there is the requirement for the design of control algorithms which run in the specified time without detriment to quality and functionality.

Thanks to the improvement in some software products, new control algorithms can be designed and tested in real life practical applications very quickly with excellent quality, giving a new optic to the control engineering courses. Software like Matlab/Simulink with its RTW (Real Time Workshop) and the RTWT (Real Time Windows Target) give us the opportunity to work from an easy interface and produce good results, while one deals with time-critical applications.

This chapter attempts to give a guide for the implementation of real-time control systems, using the RTWT toolbox, as a practical tool for students in control engineering. A digital PID controller will be tested in a real-life application (Hernandez *et al.*, 2011), in order to present a description of the implementation procedure.

The outline of the paper is as follows: a brief introduction to the application problem is depicted in the next section. Definitions and characteristics of real-time systems are described in Section 3. Section 4 treats the implementation of real-time controllers using RTWT in Matlab®. Section 5 is devoted to the configuration of RTWT for our specific application as an example, including some experimental results. Final conclusions are drawn in the last section.

2. Application description: Lungs function test

Non-invasive lung function tests are broadly used for assessing respiratory mechanics (Northrop, 2002; Oostveen *et al.*, 2003). Contrary to the forced maneuvers from patient side and special training for the technical medical staff necessary in spirometry and in body plethysmography (Pellegrino *et al.*, 2005), the technique of superimposing air pressure

oscillations is simple and requires minimal cooperation from the patient, during tidal breathing (Oostveen *et al.*, 2003). Among the air pressure oscillation techniques for lung function testing, the most popular one is that of Forced Oscillation Technique (FOT). FOT uses a multisine signal to excite the respiratory mechanical properties over a wide range of frequencies, usually between 4-48Hz (Oostveen *et al.*, 2003).
Using measurements of air pressure and air flow, it is possible to extract information regarding the human respiratory input impedance. However this is a linear approximation of a nonlinear system, hence the output will depend on the input's amplitude and frequency (Schoukens & Pintelon, 2001). It is therefore important to ensure that the desired signal to be applied at the patient's mouth will be delivered by the lung function testing device, without introducing distortions and nonlinear effects. Hence, a closed loop control system is necessary, to continuously monitor and correct the errors between the desired input signal and the one delivered by the device at the patient's mouth.
In practice, in order to send a sinusoidal signal of 50 Hz it is necessary to have a sample rate of at least 500 Hz, which means 10 samples per sinusoid period. The corresponding sampling time is 0.002 seconds, which can be delivered by the DAQcard 6024E used in this application. In this particular example, it is not possible to work with Matlab running in normal operation, because the delay for calculations in the closed loop is about 14ms, much higher than the desired sample rate. A solution to overcome this limitation consists in using RTWT to assign some resources of the system exclusively for this task, ensuring the desired sampling time.

3. Definitions and characteristics: Real-time systems

Nowadays, thanks to the computational and graphical power of modern computers, more flexible control systems including higher-level functions and advanced algorithms can be implemented successfully in real systems. Furthermore, most current complex control systems could not be implemented without the application of digital hardware; moreover these systems now contain not only physical components but also algorithms, which must be programmed, i.e. software is now included in the control loop. This leads to new aspects to take into account by designing control systems.
When one builds a control algorithm in any programming language, one normally assumes that sampling is uniform, periodic and synchronous. However, that is not realistic since the control algorithm also consumes some time producing a control or feedback delay (control or feedback latency), i.e. a delay between a sampling instant and the instant at which a control-signal value is applied to the actuator. Also the computational time of control algorithms can change from one sampling instant to other (e.g. hybrid controller with controller switching mechanism, event based controllers, adaptive controllers with on-line parameter update, etc.). This variation in the delay is called control jitter (according to the IEEE, jitter is "the time-related abrupt, spurious variation in the duration of any specified related interval") (Gambier, 2005)
It is important to clarify also some other aspects about the meaning of 'real-time', although it is a vast field and therefore a complete discussion about the topic is outside the scope of this document. Fast computing aims at getting the results as quickly as possible, while real-time computing aims at getting the results at a prescribed point of time within defined time tolerances. This idea explains how real-time is not just for fast systems, but for any control loop where a task must be achieved in a specific time.

4. Implementation of real-time controllers using RTWT[1]

4.1 Overview on RTWT

Real-Time Windows Target™ rapid prototyping software is a PC solution for prototyping and testing real-time systems. Real-Time Windows Target software uses a single computer as a host and target. On this computer, you use the MATLAB® environment, Simulink® software, and Stateflow® software (optional) to create models using Simulink blocks and Stateflow diagrams.

After creating a model and simulating it using Simulink software in *normal mode*, you can generate executable code using RTW and your C/C++ compiler. Then you can run your application in real time with Simulink in *external mode*.

Integration between Simulink external mode and Real-Time Windows Target software allows you to use your Simulink model as a graphical user interface for

- *Signal visualization* – Use the same Simulink Scope blocks that you use to visualize signals during a non-real-time simulation to visualize signals while running a real-time application.
- *Parameter tuning* – Use the Block Parameter dialog boxes to change parameters in your application while it is running in real time.

Typical uses for Real-Time Windows Target applications include

- *Real-time control* – Create a prototype of automotive, computer peripheral, and instrumentation control systems.
- *Real-time hardware-in-the-loop simulation* – Create a prototype of controllers connected to a physical plant. For example, the physical plant could be an automotive engine. Create a prototype of a plant connected to an actual controller. For example, the prototyped plant could be an aircraft engine.
- *Education* – Teach concepts and procedures for modelling, simulating, testing real-time systems, and iterating designs

4.2 Real time kernel

Real-Time Windows Target software uses a small real-time kernel to ensure a deterministic sampling rate in the application. The real-time kernel runs at CPU ring zero (privileged or kernel mode) and uses the PC clock as its primary source of time. Some important aspects regarding the kernel operation includes:

- *Timer interrupt* – The kernel intercepts the interrupt from the PC clock before the Windows® operating system receives it. The kernel then uses the interrupt to trigger the execution of the compiled model. As a result, the kernel is able to give the real-time application the highest priority available. To achieve precise sampling, the kernel reprograms the PC clock to a higher frequency. Because the PC clock is also the primary source of time for the Windows operating system, the kernel sends a timer interrupt to the operating system at the original interrupt rate.
- *Scheduler* – RTWT lets you to work with a single sample rate or with multiple/different sampling rates in your model. Each sampling rate is defined like a task and is clocked by a simple scheduler that runs the executable. The maximum

---

[1] Parts of the text has been subtracted from the "Real-Time Windows Target User's Guide", Copyright 1999 by The MathWorks, Inc. http://www.mathworks.com/products/rtwt/

number of tasks is 32, and faster tasks have higher priorities than slower tasks. For example, a faster task can interrupt a slower task.

- *Communication with hardware* – The kernel interfaces and communicates with I/O hardware using I/O driver blocks, and it checks for proper installation of the I/O board. If the board has been properly installed, the drivers allow your real-time application to run.
- *Simulink external mode* – Communication between Simulink software and the real-time application is through the Simulink external mode interface module. This module talks directly to the real-time kernel, and is used to start the real-time application, change parameters, and retrieve scope data.

  Opening a dialog box for a source block causes simulation to pause. While simulation is paused, you can edit the parameter values. You must close the dialog box to have the changes take effect and allow simulation to continue.

4.3 System concepts

Non-real time simulation

When you run your Simulink model using *normal mode*, Simulink software uses a computed time vector to step your model. After the outputs are computed for a given time value, the Simulink software immediately repeats the computations for the next time value. This process is repeated until it reaches the stop time.

Because this computed time vector is not connected to a hardware clock, the outputs are calculated in non-real-time as fast as your computer can run. The time to run a simulation can differ significantly from real time.

Real time execution

For real-time execution on your PC, you must use Simulink *external mode*, Real-Time Workshop code generation software, Real-Time Windows Target software, and a C/C++ compiler, to produce an executable that the kernel can run in real time. This real-time application uses the initial parameters available from your Simulink model at the time of code generation.

If you use continuous-time components in your model and create code with RTW code generation software, you must use a fixed-step integration algorithm. Based on your selected sample rate, RTWT software uses interrupts to step your application in real time at the proper rate. With each new interrupt, the executable computes all of the block outputs from your model.

Development process

With Real-Time Windows Target rapid prototyping software, one can use a desktop PC with the MATLAB environment, Simulink software, Real-Time Workshop code generation software, and Real-Time Windows Target software to:

1. *Design a control system* – Use the MATLAB environment and Control System Toolbox™ software to design and select the system coefficients for your controller.
2. *Create a Simulink model* – Use Simulink blocks to graphically model your physical system.
3. *Run a simulation in non-real time* – Check the behavior of your model before you create a real-time application. For example, you can check the stability of your model.

4. *Create a real-time application* – Real-Time Workshop code generation software creates C code from your Simulink model. The C/C++ compiler compiles the C code to an executable that runs with the Real-Time Windows Target kernel.
5. *Run an application in real time* – Your PC is the target computer to run the real-time application.
6. *Analyze and visualize signal data* – Use MATLAB functions to plot data saved to the MATLAB workspace or a disk.

Simulink external mode

External mode requires a communication interface to pass external parameters. On the receiving end, the same communications protocol must be used to accept new parameter values and insert them in the proper memory locations for use by the real-time application. In some Real-Time Workshop targets such as Tornado/VME targets, the communications interface uses TCP/IP protocol. In the case of a Real-Time Windows Target application, the host computer also serves as the target computer. Therefore, only a virtual device driver is needed to exchange parameters between the MATLAB environment, Simulink memory space, and memory that is accessible by the real-time application.

Signal acquisition – You can capture and display signals from your real-time application while it is running. Signal data is retrieved from the real-time application and displayed in the same Simulink Scope blocks you used for simulating your model.

Parameter tuning – You can change parameters in your Simulink block diagram and have the new parameters passed automatically to the real-time application. Simulink external mode changes parameters in your real-time application while it is running in real time.

Data buffer and transferring data

At each sample interval of the real-time application, Simulink software stores contiguous data points in memory until a data buffer is filled. Once the data buffer is filled, Simulink software suspends data capture while the data is transferred back to the MATLAB environment through Simulink external mode. Your real-time application, however, continues to run. Transfer of data is less critical than maintaining deterministic real-time updates at the selected sample interval. Therefore, data transfer runs at a lower priority in the remaining CPU time after model computations are performed while waiting for another interrupt to trigger the next model update.

Data captured within one buffer is contiguous. When a buffer of data has been transferred, it is immediately plotted in a Simulink Scope block, or it can be saved directly to a MAT-file using the data archiving feature of the Simulink external mode.

With data archiving, each buffer of data can be saved to its own MAT-file. The MAT-file names can be automatically incremented, allowing you to capture and automatically store many data buffers. Although points within a buffer are contiguous, the time required to transfer data back to the Simulink software forces an intermission for data collection until the entire buffer has been transferred and may result in lost sample points between data buffers.

4.4 Installation of the software RTWT

Once Matlab® is installed all Real-Time Windows Target software is copied onto your hard drive, but the Real-Time Windows Target kernel is not automatically installed into the operating system. You must install the kernel before you can run a Real-Time Windows

Target application. Installing the kernel configures it to start running in the background each time you start your computer. The kernel installation is done in the workspace by typing:

```
>> rtwintgt – install
```

You can also use the command **rtwintgt -setup** to install the kernel. The MATLAB Command Window displays one of these messages:

```
>> You are going to install the Real-Time Windows Target kernel.
Do you want to proceed? [y] :
```

or:

```
>> There is a different version of the Real-Time Windows Target kernel installed.
Do you want to update to the current version? [y] :
```

Type **y** to continue installing the kernel, or **n** to cancel installation without making any change. If you type **y**, the MATLAB environment installs the kernel and displays the message:

```
>> The Real-Time Windows Target kernel has been successfully installed.
```

If a message appears asking you to restart your computer, do so before attempting to use the kernel, or your Real-Time Windows Target model will not run correctly. After installing the kernel, verify that it was correctly installed by typing:

```
>> rtwho
```

The MATLAB Command Window should display a message that shows the kernel version number, followed by performance, timeslice, and other information.

```
>>Real Time Windows Target version 1.00 (C) The MathWorks, Inc. 1994-2010
Running on Multiprocessor APIC computer
MATLAB performance = 98.5%
Kernel timeslice period = 0.999 ms
```

Matlab specifies the performance of the running application on the actual PC and the used sampling time. It is desirable to execute your applications near 100% performance, is not recommended to use values of performance near to 50% because the switching execution time will decrease in the real time windows target in order to attend other programs in the Operative system.

Once the kernel is installed, you can leave it installed. The kernel remains idle after you have installed it, which allows the Windows operating system to control the execution of any standard Windows based application, including Internet browsers, word processors, the MATLAB environment, and so on. The kernel becomes active when you begin execution of your model, and becomes idle again after model execution completes.

The Real-Time Windows Target requires a C compiler which is not included in the installation in MATLAB. To choose the compiler to use it is necessary to type the following command in the workspace:

```
>> mex -setup
```

The following dialog will appear:

>> Would you like mex to locate installed compilers [y]/n? y

Select a compiler:

[1] Intel Visual Fortran 9.1 (with Microsoft Visual C++ 2005 linker) in
C:\Program Files\Intel\Compiler\Fortran\9.1
[2] Lcc-win32 C 2.4.1 in C:\PROGRA~1\MATLAB\R2007b\sys\lcc
[3] Microsoft Visual C++ 2005 in
C:\Program Files\Microsoft Visual Studio 8
[0] None

After you choose your compiler for instance, Compiler: 2, the following dialog will appear:

>> Please verify your choices:
Compiler: Lcc-win32 C 2.4.1
Location: C:\PROGRA~1\MATLAB\R2007b\sys\lcc
>> Are these correct?([y]/n): y
Done . . .

After you confirm your choice typing *y* the process finish it. You can use any PC-compatible computer that runs Microsoft® Windows XP 32-bit, or Microsoft Windows Vista ™ 32-bit. Your computer can be a desktop, laptop, or notebook PC.

4.5 Hardware I/O boards

Real-Time Windows Target applications use standard and inexpensive I/O boards for PC-compatible computers. When running your models in real time, RTWT captures the sampled data from one or more input channels, uses the data as inputs to your block diagram model, immediately processes the data, and sends it back to the outside world through an output channel on your I/O board.
Real-Time Windows Target software provides a custom Simulink block library. The I/O driver block library contains universal drivers for supported I/O boards. These universal blocks are configured to operate with the library of supported drivers. This allows easy location of driver blocks and easy configuration of I/O boards. You drag and drop an universal I/O driver block from the I/O library the same way as you would from a standard Simulink block library. And you connect an I/O driver block to your model just as you would connect any standard Simulink block.
You create a real-time application in the same way as you create any other Simulink model, by using standard blocks and C-code S-functions. You can add input and output devices to your Simulink model by using the I/O driver blocks from the **rtwinlib** library provided with the Real-Time Windows Target software. This library contains the blocks depicted in figure 1.
The Real-Time Windows Target software provides driver blocks for more than 200 I/O boards. These driver blocks connect the physical world to your real-time application:

- Sensors and actuators are connected to I/O boards.
- I/O boards convert voltages to numerical values and numerical values to voltages.
- Numerical values are read from or written to I/O boards by the I/O drivers.

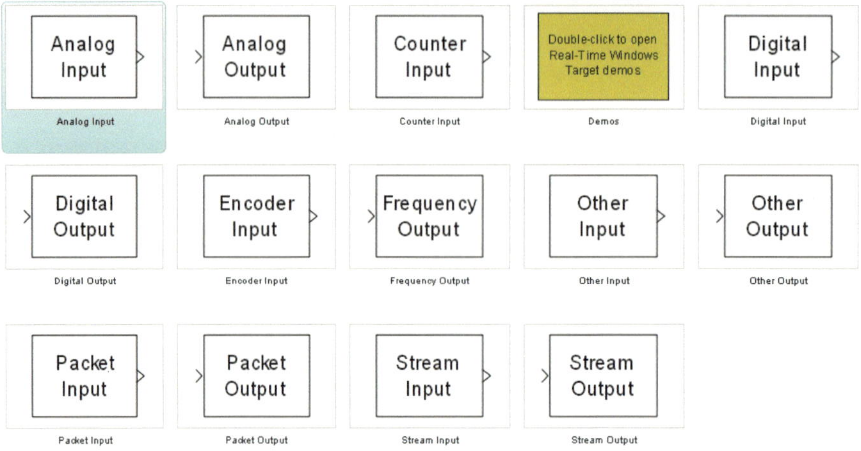

Fig. 1. Library Real Time Windows Target

5. Application of the real-time control in a lung function test device

By following the procedure described in section 4.3 the Simulink scheme will be implemented and configured. The computer characteristics used in this example are: Intel core duo processor of 1.73 GHz with 3Gb of RAM , Windows Xp 32 Bits, and expressCard to PCMCIA adapter.

5.1 Implementing the simulink model

The communication between the computer running Matlab and the FOT device is made by using the National Instruments DAQCard 6024E (which is recognized by Matlab and supported for real time applications). The corresponding Simulink model was developed in order to send and receive signals to/from the real FOT system, as depicted in figure 2.

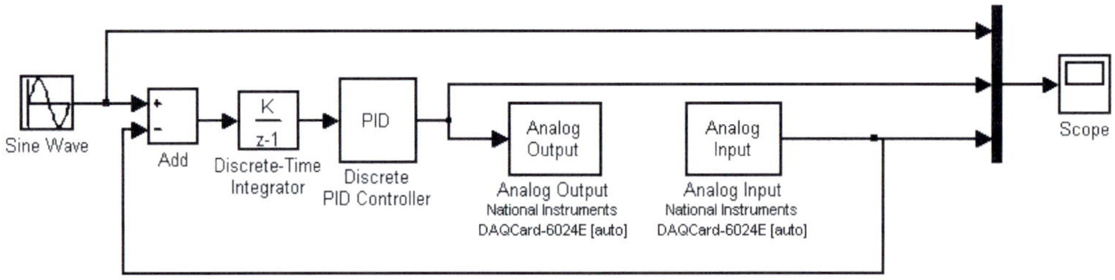

Fig. 2. Simulink model for the RTWT application

At this point it is recommendable to create a new folder in your current directory, because the compilation procedure creates several files and this will let you work in an orderly manner.
In this application our interest is to test a discrete PID controller; its parameters have been previously tuned, and its design will not be presented in detail.

Configuration of the simulation parameters

Once the model has been created, we must set the simulation parameters. By pressing the combination of keys '*Ctrl+E*' the configuration parameters window will appear (figure 3).

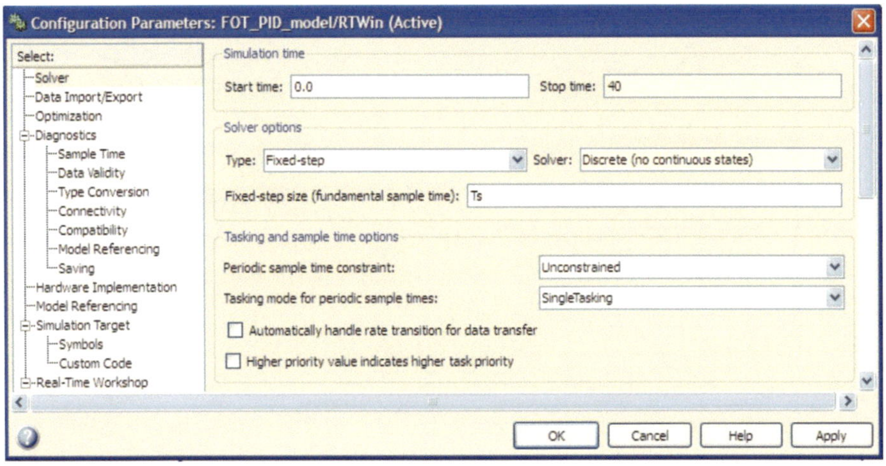

Fig. 3. Solver configuration

The first parameter to configure is the solver. We can choose the stop time of the simulation, between a fixed value or to run indefinitely by typing 'inf'. In this application a stop time of 40s was chose. In the solver options you can choose between variable or fixed step, in this application what we want is to guarantee a fixed sampling time, hence, we choose the type 'Fixed-step' and as solver the 'discrete (no continuous states)'.

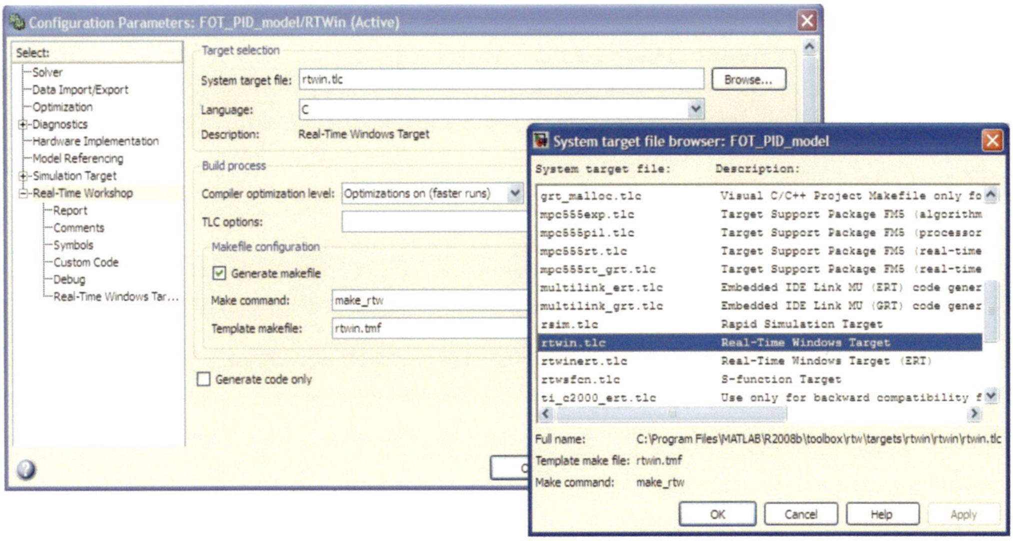

Fig. 4. Configuration System Target

The next step is to configure the target, for this we must select the option 'Real-time Workshop' as presented in figure 4. The first option to select is the system target file, there are several options available when we press the 'Browse' button, however we must select 'rtwin.tlc' which is the Real-Time Windows Target. The language can be selected as C or C++, we choose C language by default. We accept these changes and return to our model in Simulink. At this point we can choose the simulation as external mode, as depicted in Figure 5. Remember to save your model by pressing the keys 'ctrl+S'

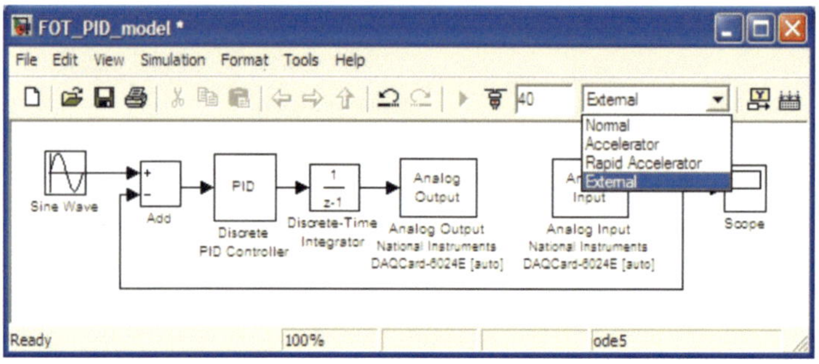

Fig. 5. Configuring the simulation in External mode

Configuring the analog input and output

After our simulation parameters has been configured, then we can continue with the process interfacing. By double clicking in the analog output block in our Simulink model, the configuration window will appear as depicted in Figure 6. In this window we must select our hardware board, in this case the National Instruments acquisition board DAQCard-6024E. The sampling time is selected as *'Ts'*, which can be previously defined in the workspace as *Ts*=0.002. In this step also the output range can be configured, which is in our case from -10 V to 10 V. Some initial and final values can be established at this point, for the cases when we need that the DAQ board remains with some value after the simulation stops. It is possible to test our hardware to verify that there are not communication problems between Simulink and our external hardware. By pressing the *'Board Setup'* button a new window will appear, and by pressing the *'Test'* Button we can test all the inputs and outputs available in our board. To configure the analog input the same procedure must be followed, the only difference is that you'll not find the 'initial' and 'final' value parameters available in the analog output.

Discrete PID configuration

For this application we have tuned the parameters of a PID controller by means of the KCR algorithm (Hernandez *et al*, 2010); this procedure will not be described here, because our interest is to present how to use the Real-Time Windows Target toolbox.
The discrete PID controller used in this work can be found in the: SimPowerSystems/Extra Library/Discrete Control Blocks/Discrete PID Controller (Figure 7). This block implements a discrete PID controller, where the *Kp*, *Ki*, *Kd* and sampling time *Ts* parameters can be configured. There are also some other options available, e.g. the time constant for the derivative action or the constraints in the output, which have been selected as 1000 and [-1 1] respectively.

Scope configuration to display and save data

Until now, the simulation parameters, PID and I/O have been configured; nevertheless, another important issue to solve is how to save the data on our hard disk. By double clicking

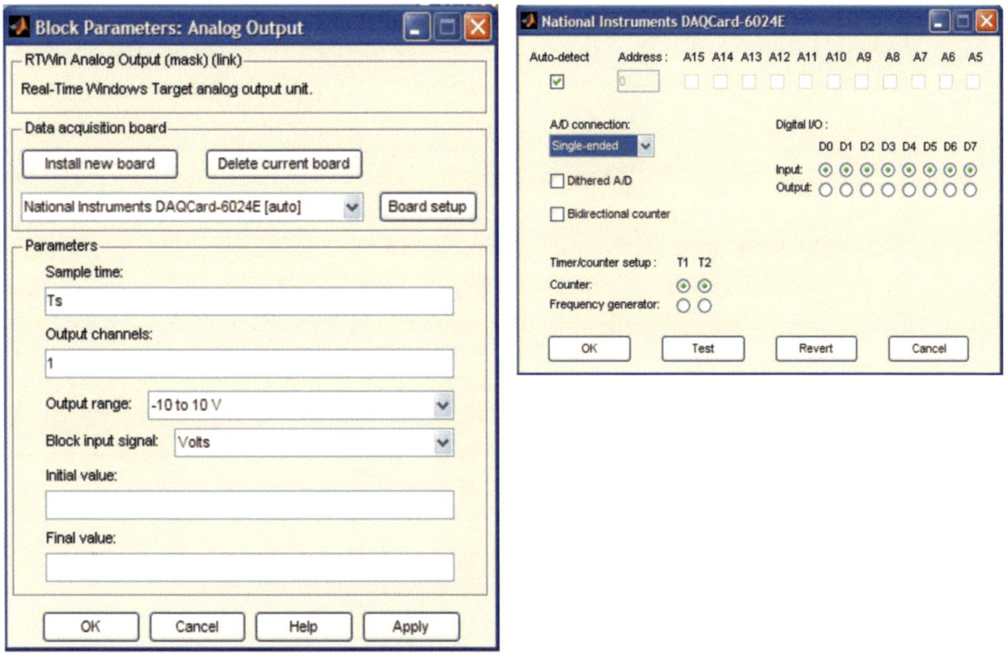

Fig. 6. Configuration window Analog input/output

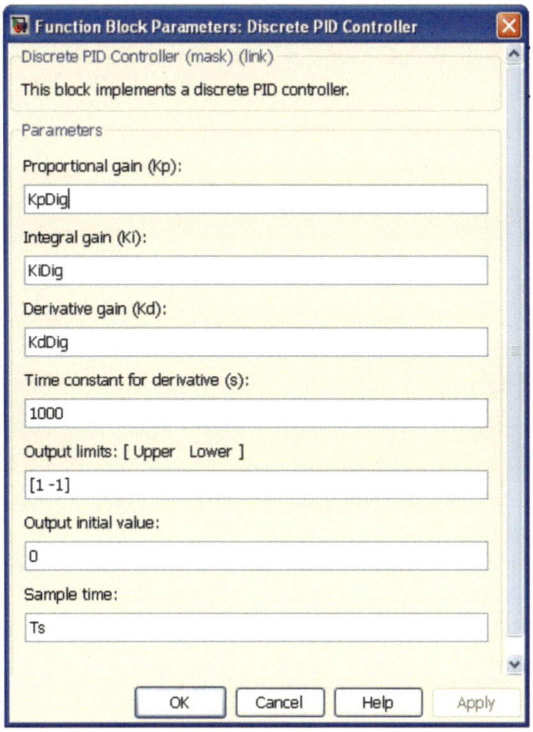

Fig. 7. Configuration Window Discrete PID

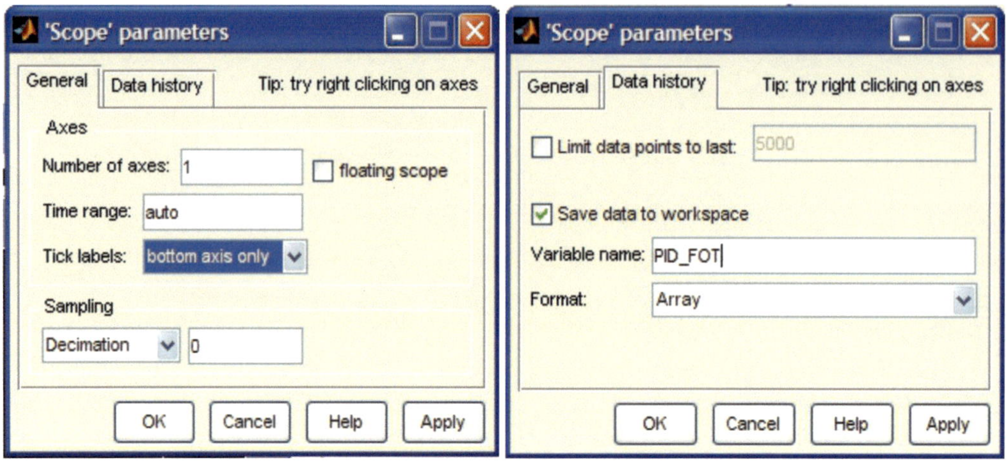

Fig. 8. Scope Configuration Window to display and save the data

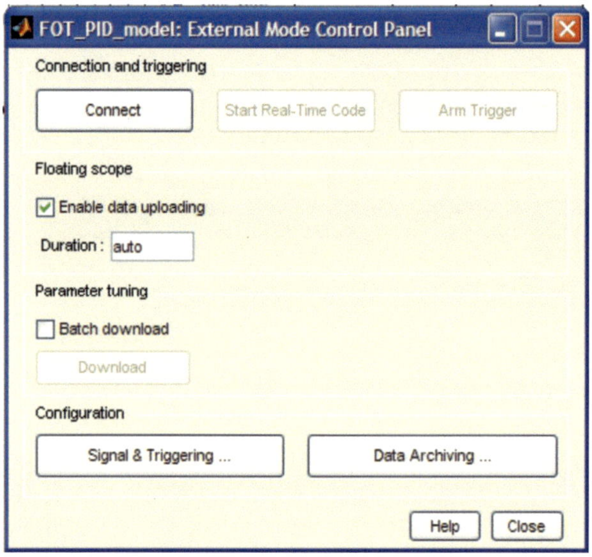

Fig. 9. External mode control panel

in the scope a new window will appear, there, the sampling will be chosen as '*Decimation*'=0, this is done to consider this block as an analog block because the triggering will not be done by this block. By selecting the next tap '*Data history*' (Figure 8-right), we must avoid to limit the data points and instead of this, we select save data to workspace. We type a name for the variable we want to save and then we choose array as data format and we press '*ok*' in all the windows.

Going back to our Simulink model, we choose in the toolbar the option Tools/External Mode Control Panel, a new window will appear as depicted in Figure 9.

The first step is to press the '*Signal & Triggering*' button; in this new window we must configure the trigger as '*manual*' and the mode in '*normal*'. The duration is the number of samples that you are going to simulate. A very important detail when we choose this value

is to know how much our sampling time is, how long our simulation will be and that Real-Time Windows Target takes zero as an extra value. By taking this into account it is possible to see that in 40s at 2ms sampling time, we need to save 2000 samples, however, taking into account the sample at time zero, finally we choose 2001 as parameter.
After choosing the signal and trigger options, we press the '*Data Archiving*' button; in this new window we have to enable '*archiving*' and then type de directory where we want to save our data and the name of the file (Figure 10). If we have more than one variable to save then an array will be saved in this address with the name we chose, the first column is always the time vector and the next columns each one of our variables. In this application we have used a mux block to put all the measured variables into one scope (see Figure 2), however it is also possible to have one scope for each variable.

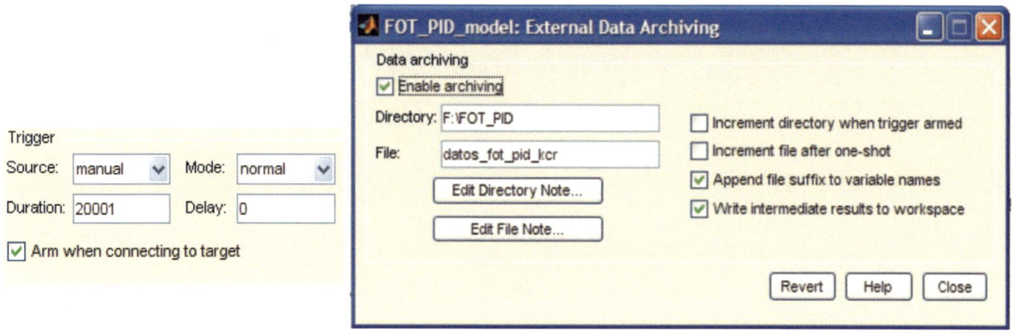

Fig. 10. External Signal & Triggering and External Data Archiving configuration window

Once the simulink model has been configured, then it has to be saved to accept all the changes and then compilate it, by using the combination of keys *ctrl+B*.
Once all procedures have been completed, then we can press the button '*Connect to Target*' and then '*Start Simulation*', to run the simulation as depicted in figure 11.

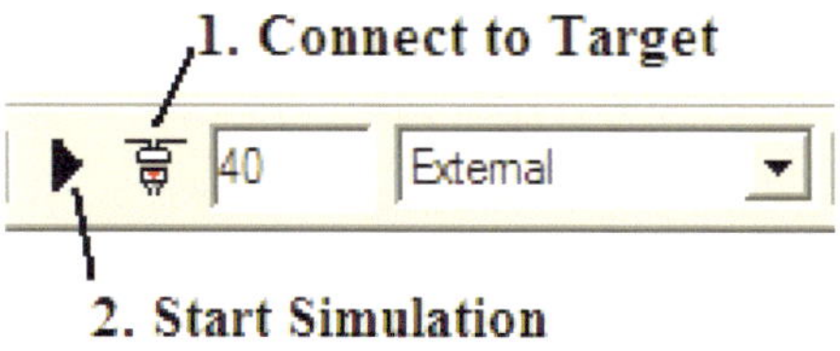

Fig. 11. Run simulation

5.2 Experimental results

By using the hardware and software described in section 4, it is possible to do the open loop and closed loop identification using the Chirp-TFA algorithm (Ionescu C., *et al.*, 2010). Some results are given by means of Bode plots in Figure 12. It can be observed that the bandwidth (frequency at -3dB) of the system is about 45Hz.
In order to be able to follow a reference signal in a closed loop it is necessary that the magnitude of the closed loop remains around 0dB and the phase around 0° in the frequency-range of interest. From the Bode plot in Figure 12-right for the closed loop, we can observe that the results are in agreement with the expected bandwidth, and that the controller

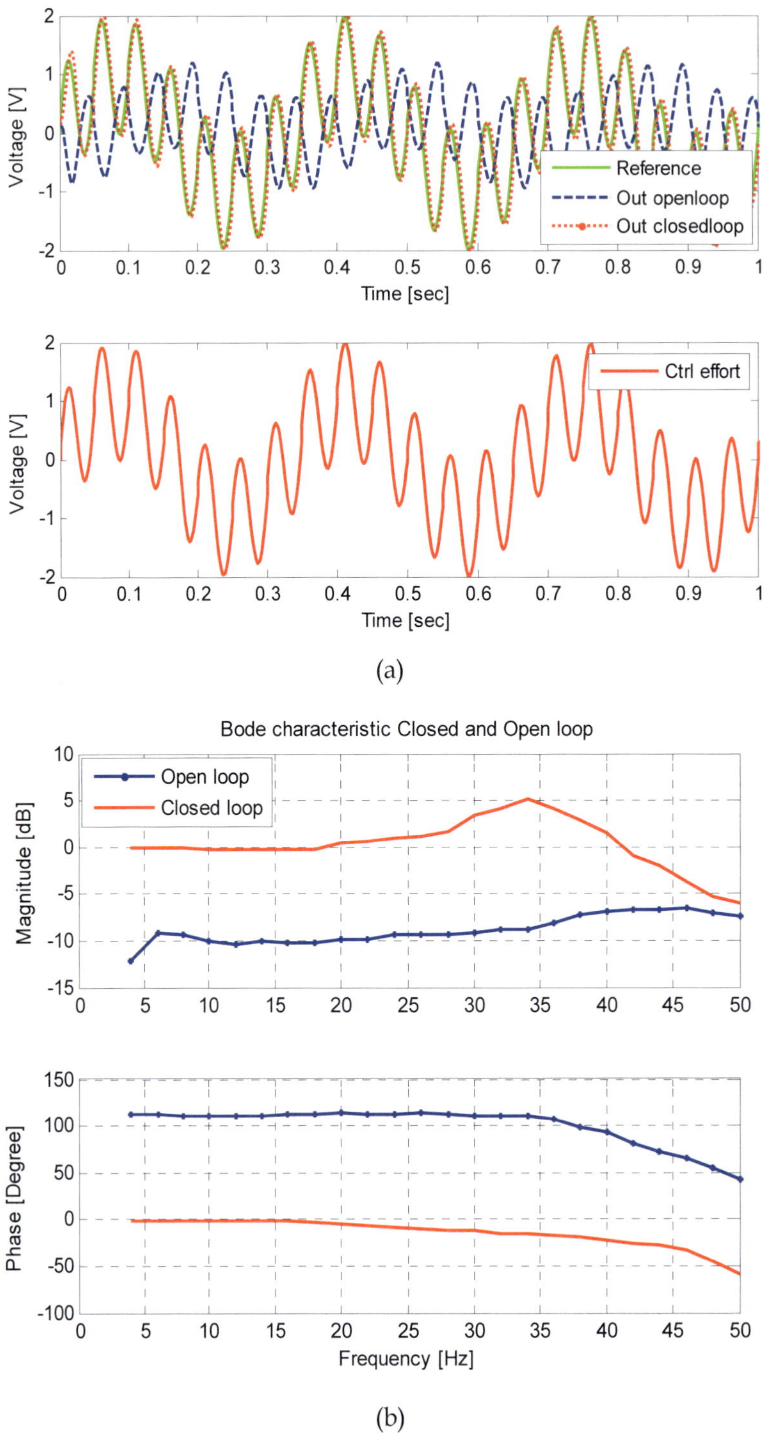

Fig. 12. Open and Closed loop characteristics. a) Performance in time. b) Performance in frequency

performs satisfactorily. This result is also visible when a comparison in time domain between open loop and closed loop is done. The controller avoids distortions and nonlinear effects at the output of the lung function device; the desired signal will be successfully delivered at the patient's mouth as depicted in Figure 12-left.

6. Conclusions

In this work an interactive and effective tool to design control loops in real-time has been presented. A real system was used as an example to discuss the importance of real-time, and clarify some fundamental aspects about the meaning of real time in control. An introduction to real-time control from an educational and practical point of view has been given. Some well-known misconceptions coming from the control system community were discussed. The relevance of the real-time implementation has been exposed by implementing the closed loop control of a medical device for lung function testing.

Although Real-Time Windows Target is a good tool to run control algorithms over a higher priority than just using a typical m-file algorithm, this tool has two drawbacks: as this is still a tool running over Windows, complex algorithms could cause that it cannot ensure a fast sampling time, because it depends on the PC characteristics and its performance. Secondly, although points within a buffer are contiguous, the time required to transfer data back to the Simulink software forces an intermission for data collection until the entire buffer has been transferred and may result in lost sample points between data buffers.

7. References

Dixon W., Dawson D., Costic B., de Queiroz M., "A MATLAB-based Control Systems Laboratory Experience for Undergraduate Students: toward Standardization and Shared Resources", *IEEE Transactions on Education*, Vol. 45, No. 3, 2002

Gambier A., "Real-time Control Systems: a Tutorial", Automation Laboratory, B6 23-29, EG. Bauteil C, University of Mannheim, 68131 Mannheim, Germany, 2005

Hernandez A. , De Keyser R., Ionescu C., "Application of a novel PID Autotuner to a lung function testing device, in *Proc. of the Int. Conf. on Biomedical Electronics and Devices (BIODEVICES 2011)*, Rome, Italy, 55-61, 2011

Ionescu C., Robayo F., De Keyser R., Naumovic M., "The Fequency Response Analyse revisited", in *Proc. of the IEEE 18th Mediterranean Conference on Control and Automation*, Marrakesh, Marocco, 1441-1446, 2010

Northrop R., "Non-invasive measurements and devices for diagnosis", CRC Press, 2002

Oostveen E., Macleod D., Lorino H., Farré R., Hantos Z., Desager K., Marchal F., "The forced oscillation technique in clinical practice: methodology, recommendations and future developments", *European Respiratory Journal*, 22: 1026-1041, 2003

Pellegrino R., Viegi G., Brusasco V., Crapo R., Burgos F., Casaburi R., Coates A., van der Grinten C.P.M., Gustafsson P., Hankinson J., Jensen R., Johnson D.C., McKay R., Miller M.R., Navajas D., Pedersen O.F., Wanger J., "Interpretative Strategies for Lung Function Tests". *European Respiratory Journal*, 26: 948-968, 2005

"Real-Time Windows Target User's Guide", The MathWorks Inc. http://www.mathworks.com/products/rtwt/, 1999

Schoukens J., Pintelon R., "System Identification: a Frequency-domain Approach", (IEEE Press, 2001)

4

MatLab in Model-Based Design for Power Electronics Systems

Adriano Carvalho and Maria Teresa Outeiro
Institute of Systems and Robotics, University of Porto
Portugal

1. Introduction

This chapter's main goal is to show how MatLab can be very useful when applied in the model-based design of dynamic systems, especially in the domain of power electronics systems. Two cases will be described that are encountered in energy conversion: i) a slip energy recovery (SER) system and ii) a power electronic converter for a fuel cell (FC) based energy generation system. In both cases, the energy handled in the process needs to be controlled and optimized in order to increase the efficiency of the systems. The chapter explains how MatLab/Simulink, with its toolboxes, is well adapted to solve the issues of defining the design requirements, at developing different components' models for the physical evolution processes and, through the combination of various sub-systems, how it enables engineers to verify that the overall performance satisfies the requirements. Considering the aspects mentioned above, the chapter will illustrate how a simple PC can be used to test any power system and through the analysis of simulation results, manufacturing companies can reduce the amount of experimental tests and thus save lots of money.
For each case study some details of the requirements and implementation are discussed and validation results are presented in order to conclude on the advantages of modelling processes using the MatLab/Simulink. In fact, at designing electrical engineering systems that require accurate models of components and sub-systems, MatLab/Simulink is shown to be an accurate design tool and useful for implementation and rapid prototyping.
In the first case, a brief explanation about the circuit's configuration of a SER system is presented and its control implementation in MatLab/Simulink are done. The SER system presents some problems associated with the operation of the power electronics converter, namely its effects on the electromagnetic torque. To analyze these effects, the model of the system implemented in MatLab/Simulink supports the harmonic study, with several special features. The oscillations of the electromagnetic torque are explained by considering the interaction between the stator and the rotor fundamental and harmonic currents. The simulation results show a strong disturbance in the electromagnetic torque in the steady state, caused by the power converter operation. To reduce this disturbance, and consequently to increase the mechanical life of the motor, an appropriate DC link coil is shown to be useful.
The presentation of the second case illustrates how MatLab/Simulink can be used when undertaking an accurate design of electrical generation systems based on hydrogen. The behaviour of PEM fuel cells is dependent on so many parameters, so obtaining an accurate

model of a PEM fuel cell, including dynamical behaviour, becomes essential to design electrical power generation based on fuel cells.
For that purpose, a mathematical model of a PEM fuel cell system developed in MatLab/Simulink is explained and the accuracy demonstrated. However, the difficulties emerge in the lack of manufacturer data about the exact values of the parameters needed for modelling it. The method adopted in order to determine the optimum set of parameters is the simulated annealing (SA) optimization algorithm, which proves to be well adapted to satisfy the goal of a fast convergence to establish the right values for the cell parameters.
In fact, optimization is a key task in modelling almost all-modern technology. Optimization forms the basis for modelling and computational analysis, design of experiments and the associated statistical analysis of the data.
The results carried out with a DC-DC power electronics converter appropriate to optimize the real point operation of a FC show that the MatLab model is appropriate to be applied in designing electrical generation systems.
For each case study presented, the simulation results are compared with experimental data obtained from commercial systems.

2. Slip energy recovery (SER) system

A slip energy recovery system is designed over a well-known control method of motor speed, which increases efficiency by returning the slip power back to the energy source system. However, this system presents some inconveniences, for example, low power factor, extra losses, harmonic current generation and electromagnetic torque oscillation. As a consequence, electromechanical vibrations are generated, which can cause motor failure and therefore, a need for motor rewinding and/or replacement.
Operation of power electronic converters typically is cause of current and voltage harmonics, either on the mains side and or on the motor side, and these harmonics' components are transferred from one side to the other. Particularly, in a slip energy recovery system, harmonics are produced not only by the rectifier, but also by the inverter and motor through the DC link.
This kind of analysis is not new, indeed, some authors have already studied similar problems. The following must be referred to: A. Mayer (1982) presented a complete study of a hiposynchronous converter cascade system, including the effects of the torque oscillation on the motor and the effects of harmonics in the mains. J. Brown and B. Jones (1986) developed and presented an analytical model for the analysis of performance of the Kramer drive system during transients. But in the present study, the system configuration is changed to overcome some of the remaining issues. The developed model is validated through the analysis and comparison of the results obtained in four types of different inverter thyristor bridges, with the same motor, diode bridge, and smoothing inductance. It is firstly concluded that it is better to adopt controlled flywheeling rather than the normal fully controlled technique for single-phase recovery bridge. Secondly, a 3-phase controlled flywheeling bridge gives the best machine performance, but at the expense of higher distortion in the supply currents than in the case with a fully controlled bridge. Results for stator current and voltage, rotor current and voltage, rectified current and electromagnetic torque are compared.
R. Hanna (1989) presented some techniques for reduction of the harmonic content produced by adjustable speed drives. After a brief presentation of the main harmonic sources, the

need to comply with harmonic standard IEEE 519 - 1982 is discussed. The effects of harmonics on static devices and on electrical machines are examined and some techniques for their reduction are given. E. Akpinar and P. Pillay (1992) developed a model to predict the detailed operation of a slip energy recovery drive system in the transient and in the steady state system. They adopted a hybrid model which retains the actual rotor phase variables, but transforms the stator. They concluded that measurement and simulation results showed a good compromise. Y. Baghzouz (1992) introduced a method to evaluate the harmonics of currents and voltages of the SER system. The harmonic components were determined from closed form expressions that were functions of the numerical values of the distorted waveforms. The non-periodic nature of the stator currents and the existence of harmonics in the rotor currents and voltages for several speeds of operation were also presented. L. Refoufi and P. Pillay (1994) analyzed the impact of the system in terms of harmonic generation, with a chopper-controlled SER induction motor drive. They studied in detail the waveforms of the supply, stator and recovery currents, for different values of speed and analyzed the respective harmonic spectrum. The simulation and experimental results showed good agreement. W. Zakaria et al. (1996) developed a model of machine with a double-circuit in the rotor, one being delta connected and the other star connected, these two windings fed a 12-pulse diode bridge rectifier, in order to reduce the time harmonics in the machine. The simulation and experimental results showed a significant reduction of the current harmonics injected into the network and a significant reduction in the pulsating torque. A. Dell'Aquila et al. (1998) developed a method for the analysis of harmonic currents of the line side produced by variable speed induction motor drives. They developed a method to reproduce the distorted current waveforms injected by the drive system into the grid. G. Marques and P. Verdelho (2000) presented a circuit configuration that included a boost-chopper to connect the diode rectifier bridge to the dc-link voltage imposed by a voltage source inverter. To solve the drawbacks caused by the harmonics introduced by the rotor rectifier, they presented two different solutions. Despite its simplicity, this system presented good performance. A comparison between the phase-control and SPWM techniques showed that the SPWM is advantageous with regard to the phase-control technique.

M. N. Eskander et al. (2001) presented a comparison between two inverter topologies for application in industrial drives. They presented the analysis of the steady-state characteristics of slip energy recovery drives, employing: a three-phase thyristor bridge inverter (topology 'A') and a three single-phase bridge inverter operating in the flywheeling mode (topology 'B') dealing with the waveforms of voltages and currents of the stator, rotor, DC link, inverter output and recovery transformer output. The results indicated that the power factor of the system employing inverter topology 'B' was higher than that of inverter topology 'A'. Therefore, the results encourage adopting the inverter topology 'B', in spite of the relatively more complex requirements of its control circuit. J. Faiz et al. (2001) studied the harmonics and performance of a slip energy recovery induction motor drive, based on the hybrid model dqabc. The sinusoidal pulse-with modulation (SPWM) control technique was used to improve the power factor of the drive and to weaken the injected low order harmonics into the supply. With the PWM technique, self-commutated switches (GTO or IGBT) replace the inverter thyristors and the inverter may operate with a zero reactive power. N. Hoshi et al. (1983) undertook a study of a slip power recovery system having sinusoidal rotor currents. The proposed system uses a PWM boost rectifier as a substitute for a diode rectifier and a boost chopper in a conventional compact type slip power recovery system.

Therefore, with the incentives for energy-economy, a cement plant company decided to recuperate energy from the rotor of an induction motor that powered a big-blower. Instead of the conventional diode bridge, DC coil, thyristor inverter and adapter transformer, a set consisting of a thyristor bridge, no DC coil, thyristor inverter and an adapter transformer were selected. This presentation serves to present and discuss the particularities of the detailed model implemented in MatLab/Simulink. In the model, the motor, the transformer, and mechanical load parameters, are estimated by the experimental data provided by each manufacturer. Then, a three-phase transient model is modelled and simulated.

2.1 Circuit configuration

Fig.1 shows the circuit configuration of the SER system, without the DC link coil, used in this study, with particular emphasis on the control system, represented by the S1 and S2 subtractors and NR and IR regulators. Besides the control system, the circuit is composed of: 1) a three-phase feedback transformer, represented by the Dd0 box; 2) the asynchronous motor M, fed through the stator by the three-phase mains RST; 3) the rotor windings, which are connected to the thyristor bridge SR1; 4) SR1 and SR2, which are the 6-pulse, 3-phase thyristor bridge rectifier and the 3-phase thyristor bridge inverter, respectively; 5) system components TG, IM and UM, which are used to measure the speed, current and voltage, necessary to the system control.

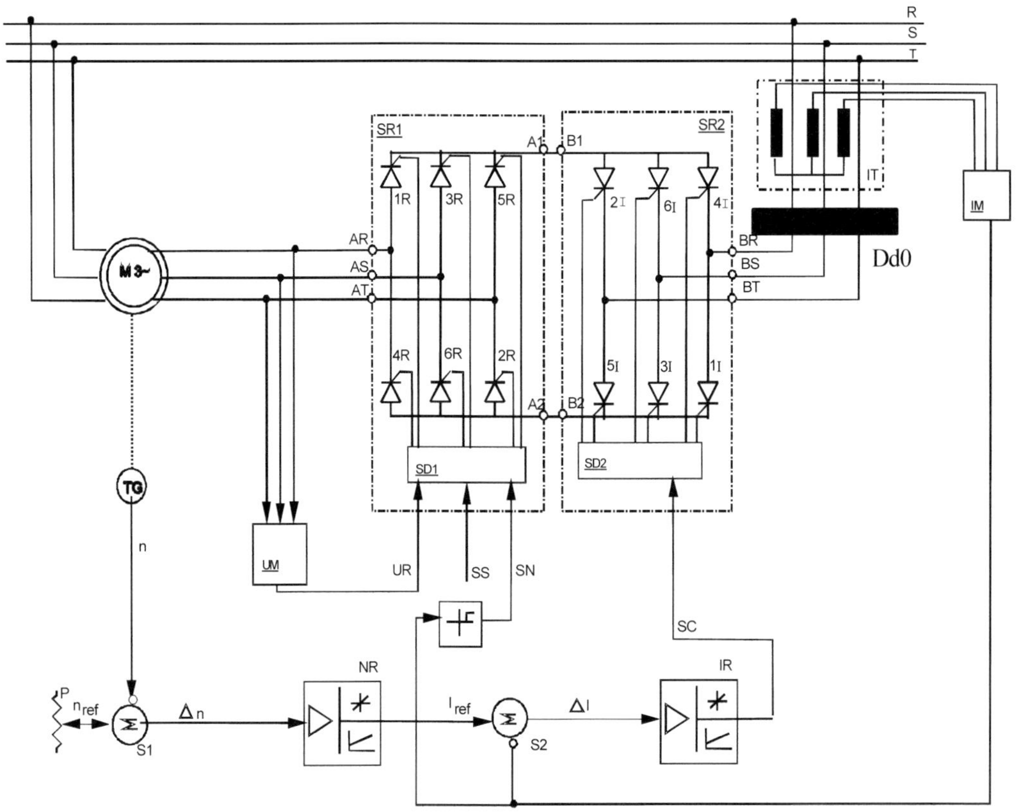

Fig. 1. Circuit configuration of the SER system

2.2 Model implemented in MatLab/Simulink

The model of the induction-motor is made in the PSB library. In this model, the rotor is referred to the stator. The adapter transformer is modelled with tree linear single-phase transformer models, also available in the PSB library. The converter is modelled with two thyristor bridges and no DC coil. It has the following main modules shown in Fig. 2: mains (M), asynchronous motor (AM), adapter transformer YgY0 (AT), starter rheostat (RS), rectifier bridge (SR1=RB), inverter bridge (SR2=IB), inverter adapter transformer (IAT), circulation-current-controller (CCC), mechanical load (blower - ML), rotor slip frequency calculator (RSFC), rotor voltages adaptive filter (RVAF), rectifier pulse generator (RPG), main voltage signal filter (MVSF), inverter pulse generator (IPG), rectifier controller (RC), inverter controller (IC) and inverter activation controller (IAC). Next, a general description of the system is presented.

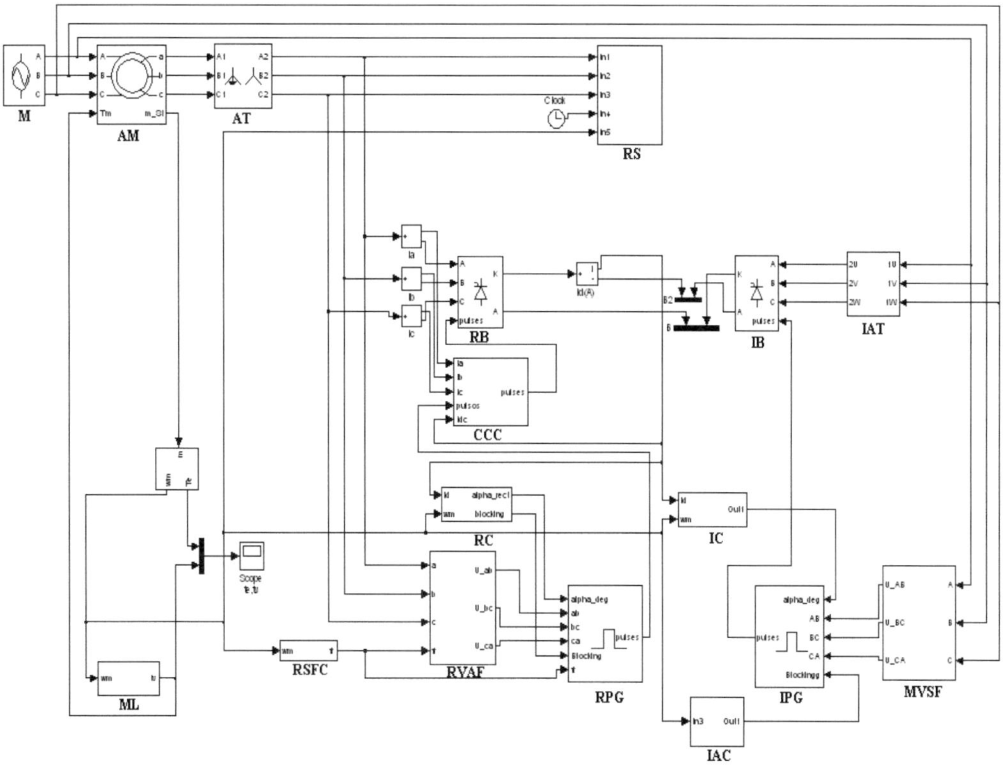

Fig. 2. Model of the SER system implemented in MatLab/Simulink

2.2.1 General description

The rotor voltages are measured and with the slip frequency are the inputs of the adaptive filter (RVAF) that consists of a specially designed phase-locked 3-phase generator outputting three voltages with the successive 120° phase shift and phases locked with the corresponding unfiltered rotor voltages. The amplitudes of the generated voltages are limited in order to obtain a more stable system. These voltages, V_ab, V_bc and V_ca, are inputs to the rectifier pulse generator. In this pulse generator, V_ab, V_bc and V_ca, are

processed in order to obtain the zero–crossing positive-going instants and a time-delay is computed according to the running values of the slip frequency and delay angle computed by the rectifier controller (RC). With these values of time, they are generated pulses, to be applied to the thyristors if they do not cause difficulties.
The circulation-current-controller module (CCC) detects the occurrence of circulation current if it occurs and, in this case, blocks the ignition of the adequate thyristor in order to go out of the circulation current mode.
The inverter controller (IC) and the rectifier controller (RC) have a rectified bridge current (Id) as input. The rectifier controller (RC) uses it for overcurrent protection, the inverter controller (IC) for imposing the current level of Id, in normal operation. Some details of the implementation of the various modules are presented below.

2.2.2 Pulse generation of the 3-phase inverter bridge

The pulse-generator of the 3-phase inverter bridge is based on the classical method applied for line-commutated converters, because the mains voltages are almost perfect with the particularity of the IGBTs pulses blocked during system startup.

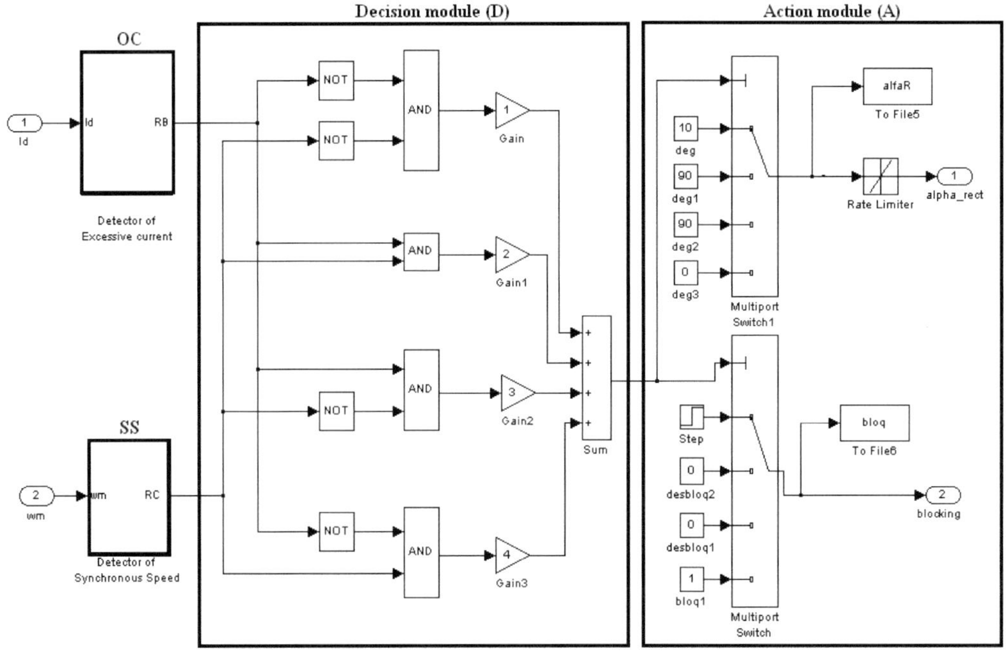

Fig. 3. Control of rectifier bridge - module RC

2.2.3 Rectifier controller (RC)

The control of the rectifier bridge (RB), one of the main difficulties, is implemented considering that the system may operate in one of the following modes:

1. Normal operation, corresponding to the state variable A at high level.
2. Overcurrent operation, corresponding to the state variable B at high level.
3. Synchronous-speed operation, corresponding to the state variable C at high level.
4. Operation to avoid the presence of circulating currents in the cascade.

The control of the 3-phase rectifier is a more complex problem because the rotor voltages are not sinusoidal ones and have a low-frequency component proportional to the slip, which varies with the rotating speed. The difficulty increases because there is no DC link, therefore the voltage step due to the inverter appears directly in the rotor terminal voltages.
Fig. 3 shows the details of the rectifier controller module (RC) that contains four sub-modules. Input Id is used for detecting overcurrent operation and input wm is used to detect if speed is inside the narrow band centred in the synchronous speed. The action to be taken is dependent on the output of the decision module (D).

1) Action module (A)

In normal asynchronous operation the output of D is 1, the action to take is to force αR to be 10°, using a rate limiter and the unblocking of the pulses after a delay of 0.8s, during rheostat system startup. In asynchronous mode with overcurrent, the output of the sum block is 3 and αR is forced to 90° using a rate limiter and the pulses are unblocked. This action tends to lower the DC current, if speed is inside the speed band and there is no overcurrent, the output of the sum block is 4, the action to take is to block the pulses and force αR to 0° using a rate limiter. Finally, if the speed is inside the speed band and there is overcurrent, the output of the sum block is 2, the action to take is to unblock the pulses and force αR to be 90° using a rate limiter.

2) Decision module (D)

Considering the operating modes 1, 2 and 3 described above, and using Boolean algebra, a table can be built, whose state variables set (A, B and C) may be in one of $2^3 = 8$ different states.
Logic variable A at high level corresponds to the sub-synchronous normal mode. Logic variable B at high level corresponds to the overcurrent mode. Logic variable C at high level corresponds to the synchronous mode. The oversynchronous mode is not considered in this implementation. Table 1 presents the eight possible theoretical combinations; some of them do not occur in practice. Considering only the practical combinations, it may be verified that $A = \overline{B + C}$.

State Variable Values			Actions to be performed
A	B	C	
1	1	1	This combination of states is not verified in practice
1	1	0	This combination of states is not verified in practice
1	0	1	This combination of states is not verified in practice
1	0	0	(a) ==> $\alpha_R \cong 10$½
0	1	1	(b) ==> $\alpha_R \cong 90^{\circ} \wedge$ Unblock pulses to the rectifier bridge
0	1	0	(c) ==> $\alpha_R \cong 90$½
0	0	1	(d) ==> Block pulses to the rectifier bridge
0	0	0	This combination of states is not verified in practice

Table 1. State and actions to be performed by the decision module

3) Overcurrent module (OC)

Fig. 4 shows the overcurrent module where the DC current, in SI units, is reduced to a per-unit system using a base current of 983A. The result is passed through a low pass filter, with a time constant of 1.1ms, to reduce the oscillations. The output of this filter is compared with a per-unit maximum allowed overcurrent (2pu) and the difference is transformed into a logic level using a hysteretic comparator (Relay B), with ±0.01pu limits. When the output of the overcurrent module is equal to one, it indicates 'overcurrent'.

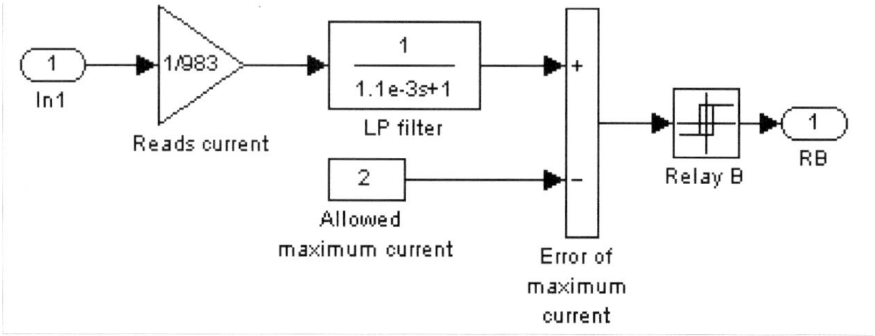

Fig. 4. Overcurrent module

4) Synchronous speed module (SS)

In the detector of synchronous speed module presented in Fig. 3 above the speed wm, in radmec/s is reduced to a per-unit system, using a base speed of (3/100pi) radmec/s. The result is passed to a low-pass filter with time constant 1.1ms. The output of this filter is compared with a per-unit speed of 0.99pu and the difference is transformed into a long level using a hysteretic comparator (Relay C) with 0pu limits. When the output of the synchronous-speed module is equal to one, it indicates 'synchronous-speed'.

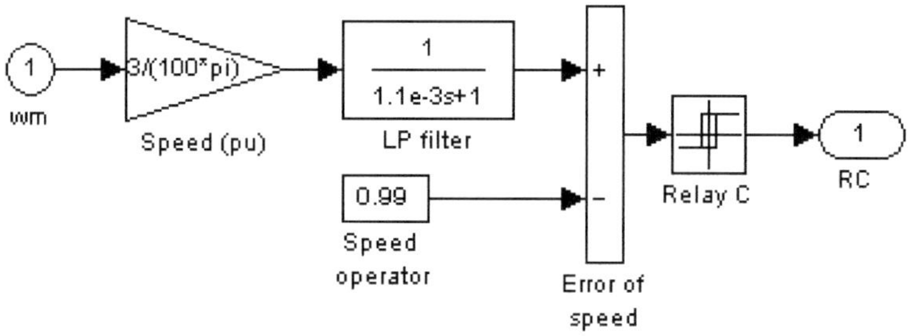

Fig. 5. Synchronous speed module

2.2.4 Circulation current controller (CCC)

As shown in Fig. 2, the implementation of the circulation current controller module, the sub-systems of which are presented in Fig. 6a) and Fig. 6b), has inputs such as the rotor currents ia, ib and ic (A), the rectified current Id (A) and the pulses sent by the RPG module. The objective of this module is to send the pulses to the rectifier bridge-RB.

In order to minimize the problem of the circulating-current, this module must implement some actions such as:

1st Action: Detection of the currents' state of conduction of each thyristor.

To know the values of the instantaneous current of each of the six thyristors rectifier, the rotor currents were measured and processed by hysteretic components.

2nd Action: Detection of critical states using AND blocks.

Critical situations occur only with more than two thyristors conducting. Therefore, it suffices to take action with three thyristors conducting (123, 234, 345..., and 612). Table 2 presents these cases and the actions to be taken, that is: with thyristors 456 conducting, the

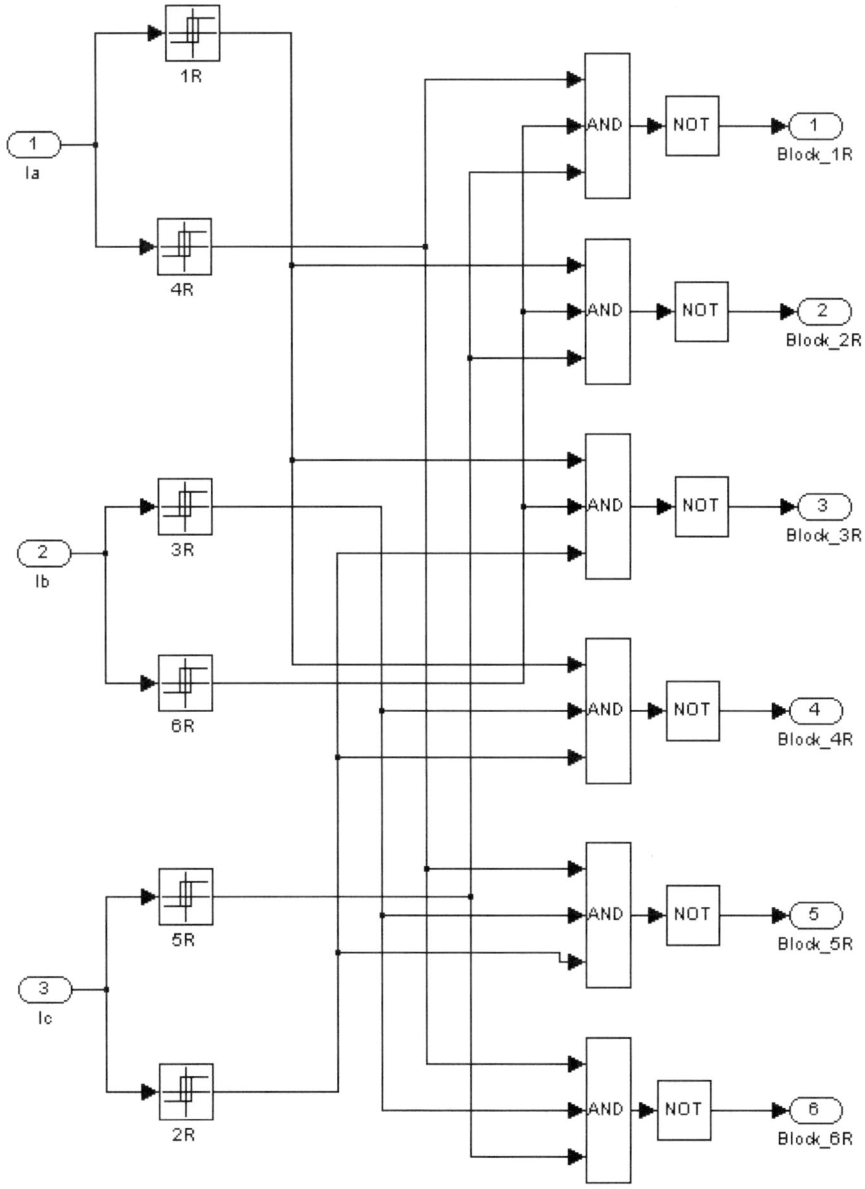

(a)

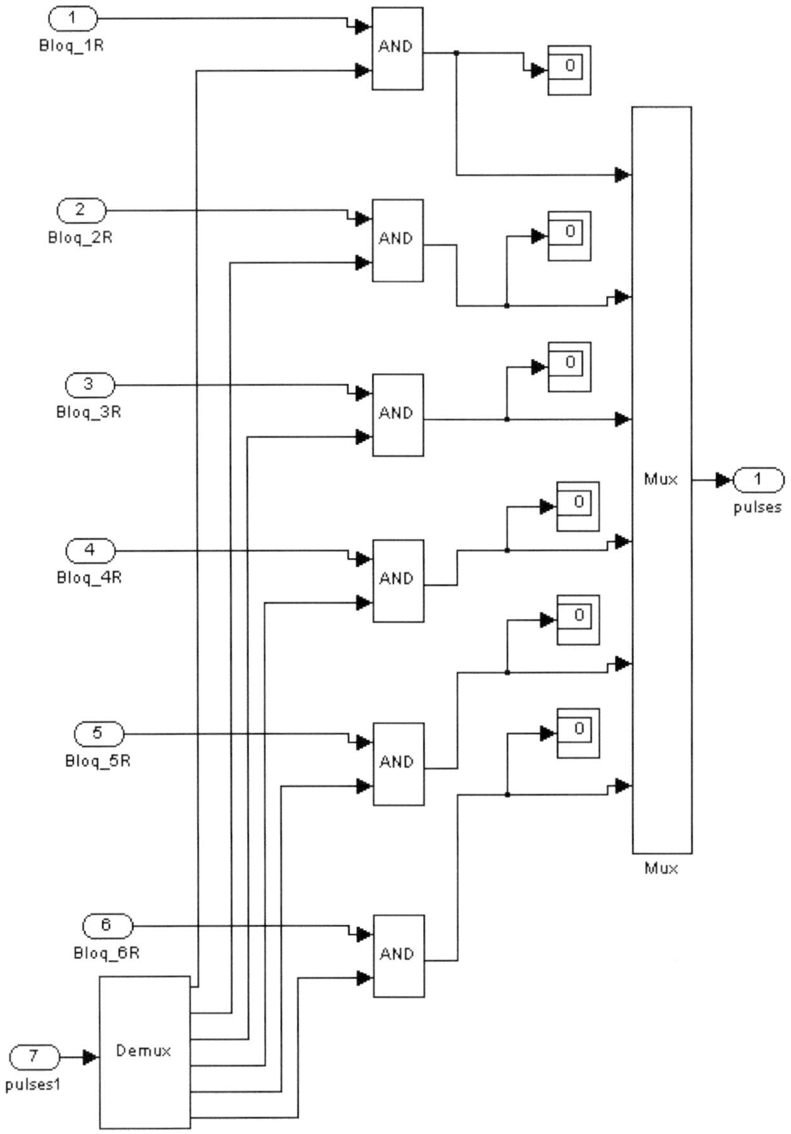

(b)

Fig. 6. Sub-systems of the module CCC: a) Deblocking signal module (DSM), b) Output logic module (OLM)

non-safe condition occurs if thyristor 1 starts conducting. To stop this occurrence the blocking of pulses for thyristor 1 is activated. A similar procedure is taken for the other five possible cases.
3rd Action: Blocking of pulses (sent by the RPG) to the thyristor in each instance, to short-circuit the rectifier bridge (RB).
The module of circulation current controller performs the all-necessary calculations, using AND operators to process the outputs of the DSM and RPG, for each thyristor.

Critical state				Thyristor to	Deblocking signal for each thyristor					
Topology	Ia	Ib	Ic	be blocked	1	2	3	4	5	6
456	-	-	+	(1R)	0	1	1	1	1	1
561	+	-	+	(2R)	1	0	1	1	1	1
612	+	-	-	(3R)	1	1	0	1	1	1
123	+	+	-	(4R)	1	1	1	0	1	1
234	-	+	-	(5R)	1	1	1	1	0	1
345	-	+	+	(6R)	1	1	1	1	1	0

Table 2. Critical states and preventive actions

2.2.5 Inverter controller (IC)

As shown in Fig. 2, the inverter controller module inputs are the mechanical-speed (wm) and the DC link current (Id). This module contains two sub-modules in cascade such as the speed regulator (SR) and the DC current regulator (CR) as presented in the Fig. 7 below. The module SR sends the reference value of the current to the CR module, which in turn determines the value of the inverter angle, αI.

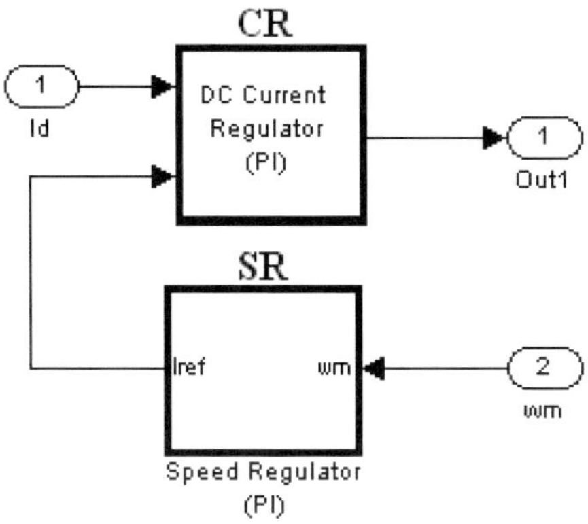

Fig. 7. Inverter controller sub-modules

1) Speed regulator (SR)

The speed regulator sub-module is presented in Fig. 8 and the speed *wm* as the input (in radmec/s). This is processed by two paths: (a) In path1, *wm* is reduced to a per-unit value, using as base speed the synchronous mechanical speed, then the per-unit value *wmpu* is

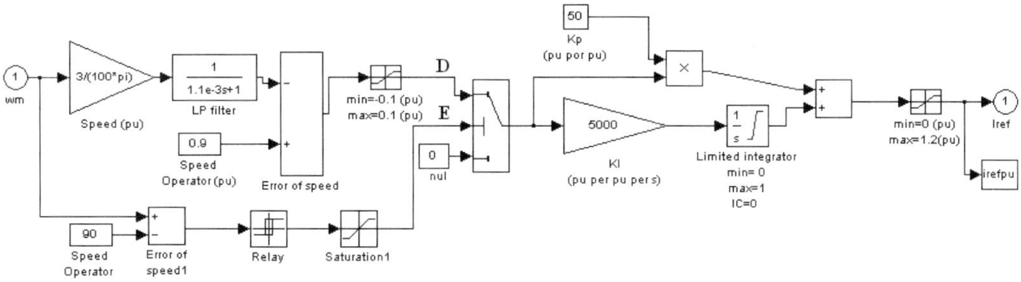

Fig. 8. Speed regulator module

passed through a low-pass filter, with a time constant of 1.1ms and compared with the per-unit reference speed in order to obtain the filtered error speed. This error is applied to a limiter with limits ±0.1pu. The output of this limiter is the signal D, the per-unit filtered and limiter speed error, which is active during most of the time. (b) Through the path2 the instantaneous speed is compared with the reference of 90radmec/s. The control signal E is used to select the input value of the PI controller. Then the main purpose of this module is to send a reference current (in pu units) to the DC current regulator module.

2) DC current regulator (CR)

The DC current regulator module is presented in Fig. 9 below. It has the DC current Id(A) and reference current iref(pu) as inputs. The DC current is reduced to a per-unit value, using a base-current of 982.43A. The per-unit value is passed through a low-pass filter with a 1.1ms time constant. The output of this filter is compared with irefpu and applied to a limited PI controller if time is higher than 0.8s. Between 0 and 0.8s, the controller input of the PI is zero, keeping the αI value constant. This action minimizes the initial transients due to the inverter.

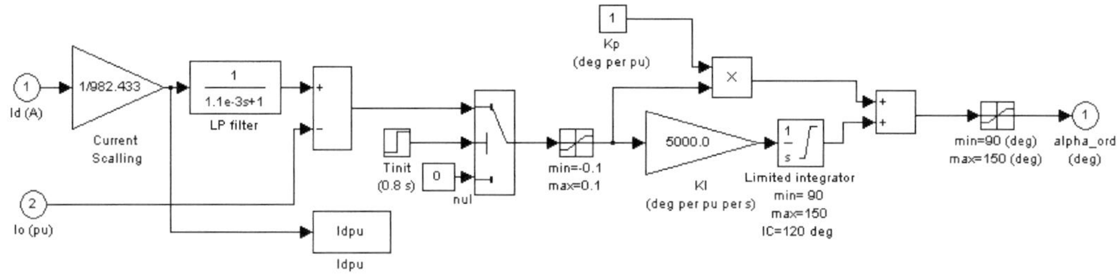

Fig. 9. DC current regulator module

2.2.6 Starter rheostat (RS)

During startup of the system, the two bridges are blocked and the rotor starting current passes through a liquid rheostat. This liquid rheostat is a time-dependent resistance as can be seen in Fig. 10. To model the variable resistance, the rotor currents were measured and the measurements were used to command a voltage-controlled-source, which in turn gives the values of the resistors R1, R2 and R3, as presented in Fig. 11. It was considered that the

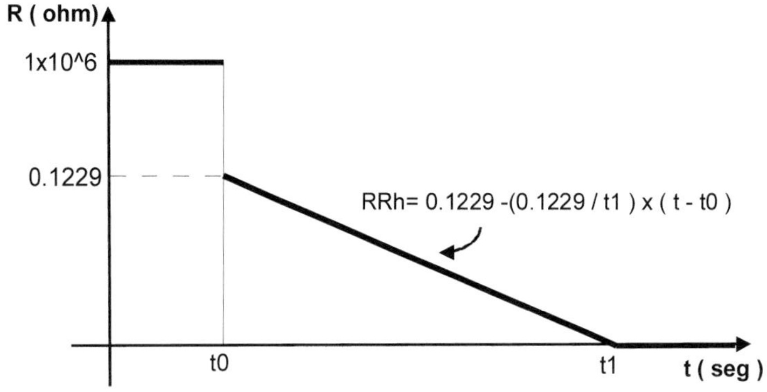

Fig. 10. Starter-rheostat

resistance decays linearly from 0.1229 to zero during the time interval of t0 to t1, being equal to 1MΩ during the time interval between zero and t0, and again equal to 1MΩ when either some starter time has elapsed or if the speed exceeds 30π radmec/s.

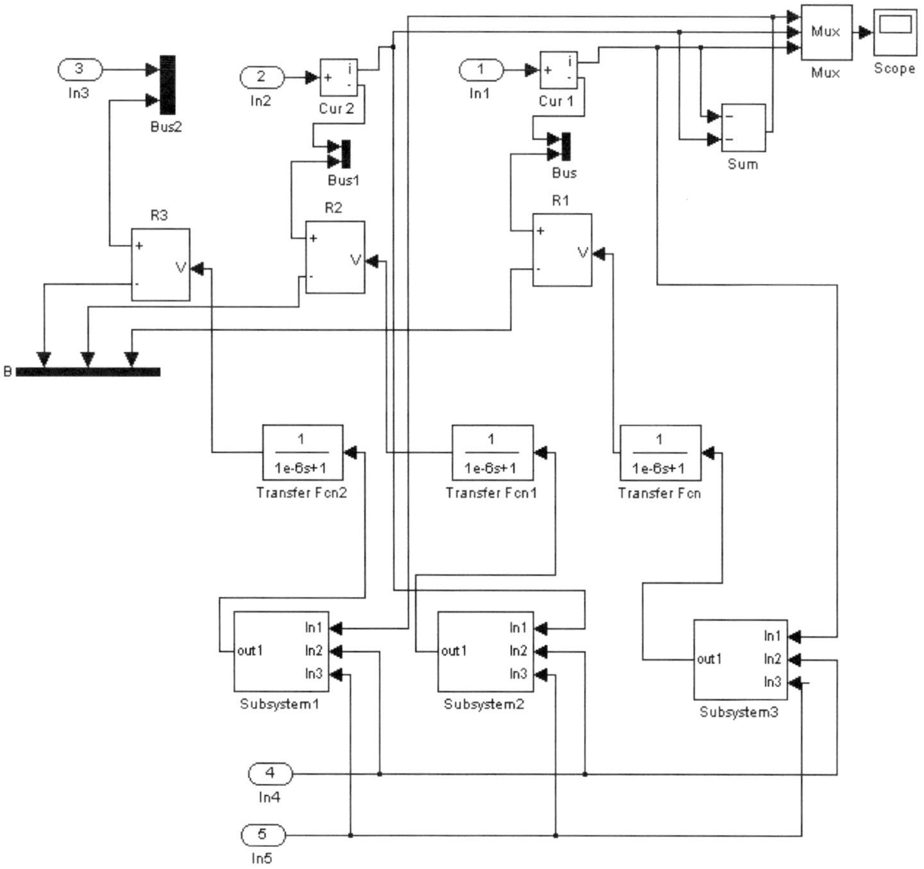

Fig. 11. Starter-rheostat module

2.3 Simulation results

The simulation results are obtained considering the following parameters and conditions: integration method; ode23tb [stiff/TR-BDF2], step variable with a maximum value of 2e-4; absolute and relative tolerances of 10e-3; reference speed of 30π radmec/s and interval of time simulation of 0-10 seconds. The variations of the angles of the inverter and rectifier bridges are respectively: $90^{\circ} < \alpha_I < 150^{\circ}$ and $5^{\circ} < \alpha_R < 90^{\circ}$.

2.3.1 Electromagnetic and mechanical torques

The electromagnetic torque is measured directly from the block model of the three-phase asynchronous machine selected in the library of MatLab/Simulink software. The S.I. unit parameter is selected. All the stator and rotor quantities are referred to in the rotor reference frame (qd frame). Considering an electrical system with these conditions, the electromagnetic torque is given by Eq. 1. In this equation p corresponds to the number of pole pairs, φ_{ds} and

φ_{qs} are the stator d and q axis fluxes respectively, and ids and iqs are the d and q axis stator currents respectively.

$$Tem = 1.5p(\varphi_{ds}i_{qs} - \varphi_{qs}i_{ds}) \tag{1}$$

Some Simulink blocks implement the mechanical load torque. The characterization of the load torque took into account the information supplied by the manufacturer, namely: the inertia moment (J) = 142.50 kg.m2, the rated speed (NN) = 985 r.p.m and the rated torque (TN) = 1405 kg.m. The information is transformed to the S.I. units and a curve fitting led to the Eq. 2 below where wm corresponded to the mechanical speed. This equation is only valid for the positive speed.

$$Tvent = 206{,}745 - 1{,}50325 \times 3 \times wm + 0{,}146636 \times (3 \times wm)^2 + 1447{,}22 \times e^{-\left(\frac{3\times wm}{11{,}75}\right)} \tag{2}$$

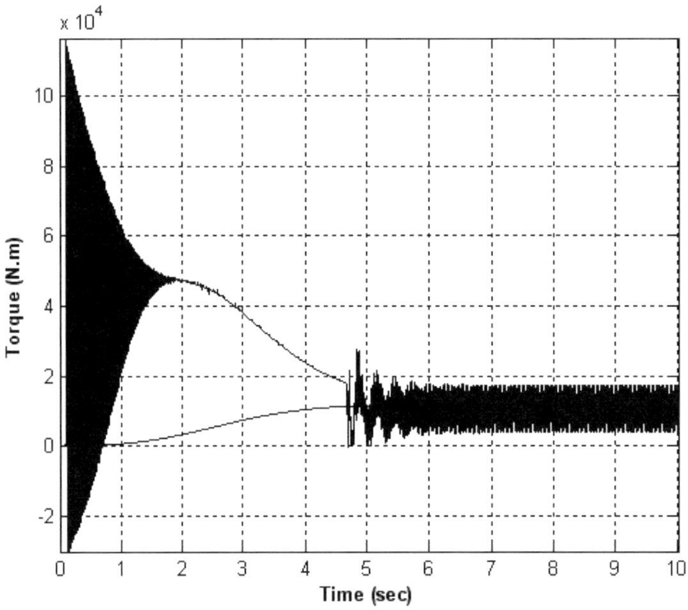

Fig. 12. Electromagnetic and load torques

2.4 Harmonic analysis

The harmonic analysis of the system is based on a programme developed for the effect, with several features, namely: the capability to analyse a large range of frequencies (until 2500Hz or more) and high resolution of the plots. The results for the stator current, the rotor current and the electromagnetic torque are presented below in Fig. 13 a) and b), Fig. 14 a) and b), and Fig. 15 a) and b), respectively. These figures show the signal amplitude versus frequency modulus. In order to obtain the maximum information concerning the spectrum of the variable, a logarithmic y-axis scale is adopted. The Discrete Fourier Transform (DFT) was used in this study and its module coefficients a0, ak and bk were calculated. A total of 10000 samples were used in the calculations.

2.4.1 Rotor current, ir

In steady state behaviour, a non-quality factor can be defined such as NQFir=(ir_{max}-ir_{min})/(ir_{max}+ir_{min}) which corresponds to the distortion of the waveform of the rotor current. Without inductance in the DC link coil, this corresponds to a 0.4628 value and if an inductance of 10mH is used in the DC link coil, the value decays to 0.062. The spectrum of the harmonic components of the rotor currents due to the six-pulse rectifier (SR1) and to the DC side average value, appear at frequencies given by the Eq. 3, in which k=0, 1, 2, 3.

$$f_{r,h}^{R} = |1 \pm 6k| s f_{ms} \tag{3}$$

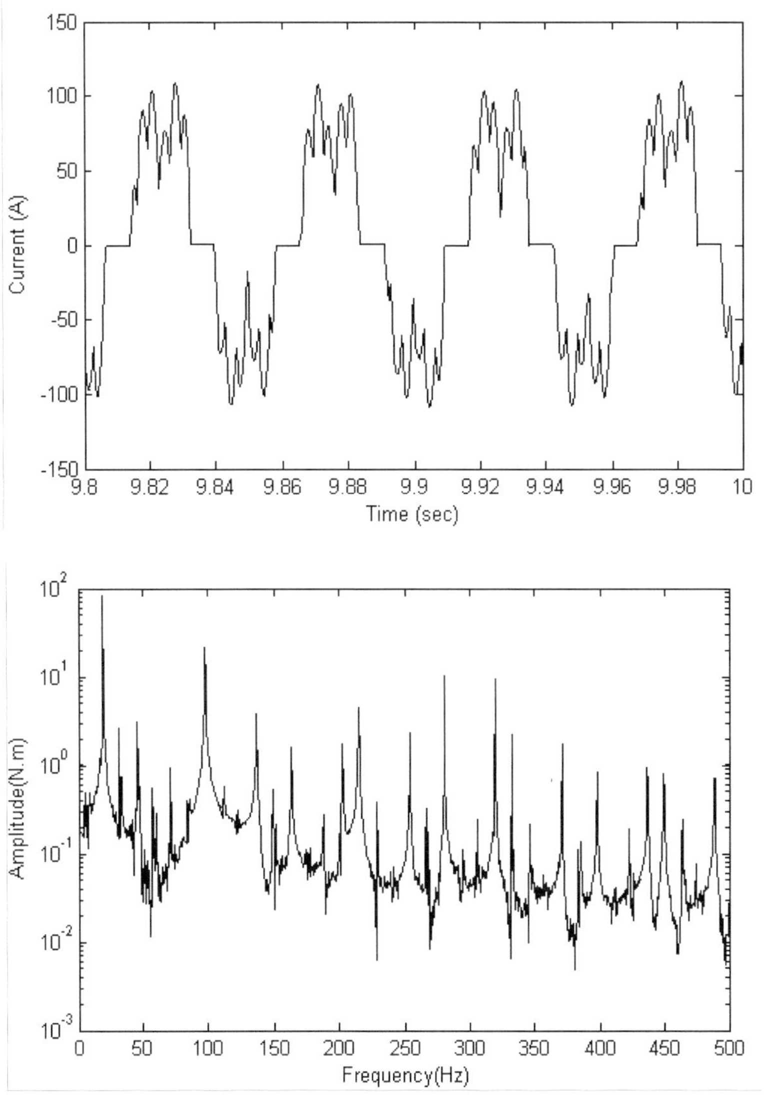

Fig. 13. a) Rotor current referred to the stator in steady state and the frequency spectrum without inductance L - the rotor slip in the case is 0.3906

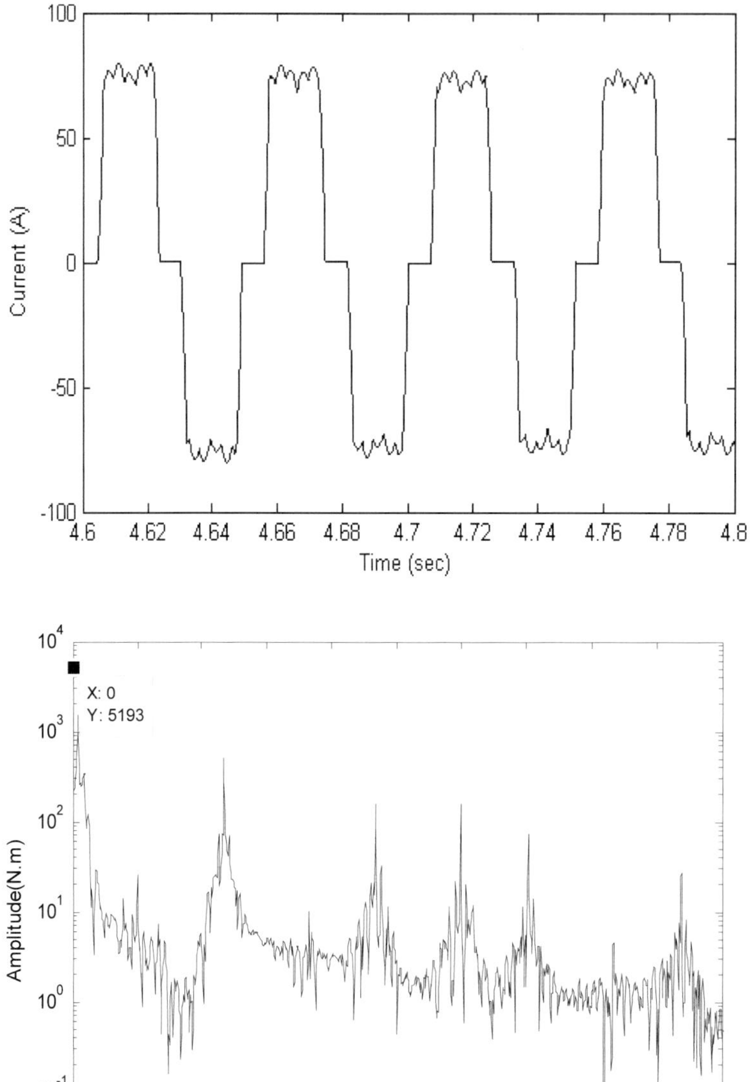

Fig. 13. b) Rotor current referred to the stator in steady state and the frequency spectrum with an inductance L of 10mH - the rotor slip in the case is 0.3906

Considering the Eq. 3, for k=0 and the slip s=0.3906, the fundamental rotor frequency is equal to 19.53Hz. Then the 5th, 7th, 11th and 13th harmonic orders appears in the rotor current and are equal to -97.66Hz, +136.7Hz, -214.8Hz and +253.89Hz, respectively. As it can be observed by the rotor current spectrums of Fig. 13 a) and Fig. 13 b) and by the Table 3, the rotor current frequencies reflect the DC current frequencies with two side-bands of the

fundamental rotor frequency, which is 19.53Hz. The harmonic components, due to the six-pulse inverter that appear on the DC current at frequencies multiples of 300Hz, appear also in the rotor currents with two side-bands of m300Hz±19.53Hz, which for m=1 corresponds to the frequencies of 285.47Hz and 319.53Hz, respectively.
The DC current distortion introduced by the six-pulse inverter is reflected on the rotor currents, resulting in the appearance of additional harmonics, given by Eq. 4, with k=0, 1, 2, 3,... and m=0, 1, 2, 3,...

$$f_{r,h}^{R} = |1 \pm 6k| sf_{ms} \pm 6mf_{ms} = \left(|1 \pm 6k| s \pm 6m \right) f_{ms} \tag{4}$$

Observing the rotor figures presented above and by comparison of the amplitude values of Table 3, for different values of inductance L in the DC link coil, it is possible to conclude that the value of the inductance of the DC link coil affects directly the ripple of the waveform of the rotor current, which is reflected in the values of amplitude of the frequency spectrum.

Frequency (Hz)	Amplitude of rotor current (A)			
	Without L	With L=1mH	With L=5mH	With L=10mH
+19.53	82.16	81.33	81.17	79.7
-97.66	21.52	17.92	14.35	14.49
+136.71	3.8	4.436	5.7	7.26
-214.83	4.5	4.69	5.2	3.1
+253.89	12.3	3.1	2	2.9
-280.47	10.5	6.3	1	1.2
+319.53	9.3	5.5	-	1.1

Table 3. Frequencies and amplitudes of the rotor current referred to the stator for phase a and for slip=0.3906

2.4.2 Stator current, is

It was observed that in a steady state the peak-to-peak value of the stator current is not greatly affected by the value of the inductance placed on the DC link coil.
A DC component of the rotor current establishes a rotating magnetic field in the air gap and induces voltages in the stator winding at frequency given by Eq. 5, where s is the slip and fms is the fundamental frequency. For s=0.3906 and fms=50Hz, this corresponds to a 30.47Hz with positive sequence.
Similarly, a rotor current frequency fr manifests itself in the stator current frequencies of (fr+fm) with fr>0, for positive sequence rotor currents, and fr<0, for negative sequence rotor currents. Adding the effect of motor speed to the rotor current frequencies, the reflected stator frequencies are given by Eq. 5, with k=0,1,2,3,....

$$f_{r,h}^{R} = |fr + fm| = |(1 \pm 6k) sf_{ms} + (1 - s) f_{ms}| = |1 \pm 6ks| f_{ms} \tag{5}$$

Adding the effect of rotor side-band frequencies due to the inverter harmonics, the frequencies of the induced harmonics present in the stator, considering these two effects are given by Eq. 6, with k,m=0, 1, 2, 3. This equation will be reduced to the Eq. 5 if m = 0.

$$f_{r,h} = |1 \pm 6ks \pm 6m| f_{ms} \tag{6}$$

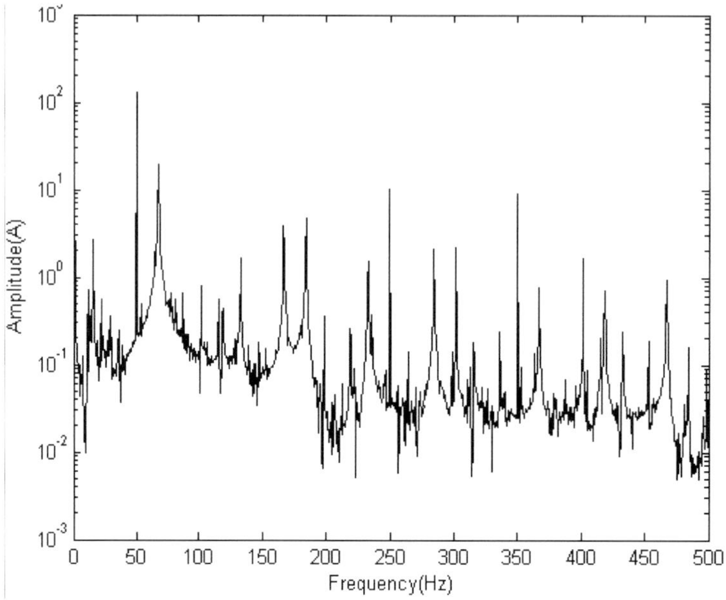

(a)

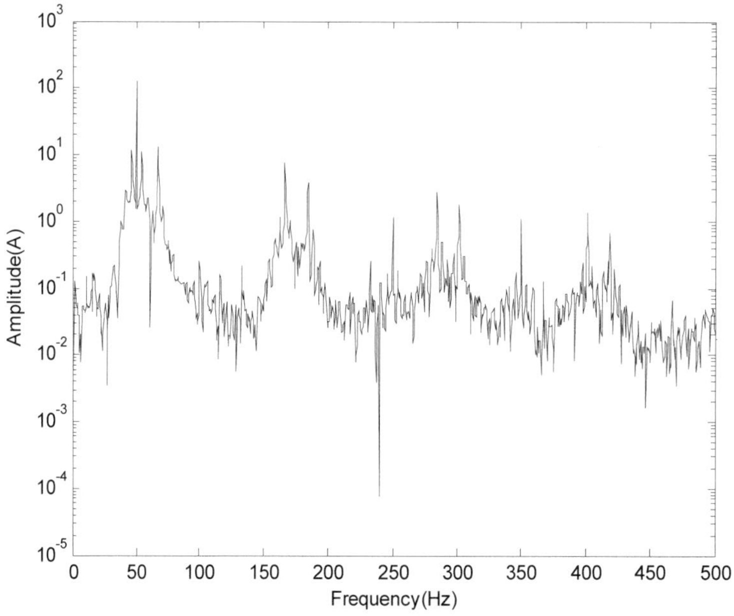

(b)

Fig. 14. Frequency spectrum of the stator current for a rotor slip=0.3906, (a) without inductance L and, (b) with an inductance of 10mH

Figs. 14a) and 14b) show the spectrum of the stator current and Table 4 corresponds to the amplitude of the frequencies. By Eq. 6, if s=0.3906 and k=0, the fundamental frequency will be equal to 50Hz.

Frequency (Hz)	Amplitude of stator current (A)			
	Without L	With L=1mH	With L=5mH	With L=10mH
50	130.5	129.6	129	127.2
-67.19	19.5	18	12.8	13.2
+167.18	6.5	-	6.2	7.55
-250	10.1	9.2	2.36	1.18
+350	9.1	9	2	1.12

Table 4. Frequencies and amplitudes of stator current in phase A, for a slip=0.3906

By Eq. 7, if k=1 and m=0, the 5th and 7th harmonic orders of the rotor current appear in the stator at frequencies modules of |-97.66 +30.47|=67.19Hz and |+136.7 +30.47| = 167.1Hz. If k=2 and m=0, the 11th and 13th harmonics of the rotor current appear in the stator at frequencies of module 184.36 Hz and 284.36Hz. If k=0 and m≠0, Eq. 6 gives the frequency effect due to the inverter harmonics. The 300Hz of the inverter referred to the stator introduces two side-band frequencies module of 250Hz, 289Hz, 310.9Hz and 350Hz, given from equation $\left|\pm 300 + 30.47 \pm 19.53\right|$.
The peaks presented in the stator frequency module, which corresponds to the rotor frequencies of 285.47Hz and 319.53Hz, are the 250Hz and 350Hz peaks, respectively.

2.4.3 Electromagnetic torque, tem

Figs. 15 a) and 15 b) show the spectrum of the harmonics of the electromagnetic torque, considering two situations without and with an inductance of 10 mH. The harmonics presented in the spectrum of the electromagnetic torque can be explained considering the interaction of the magnetomotive forces (mmf) between the stator and the rotor currents, in its fundamental and harmonic components. The Eq. 7 below is used for the calculation of the electromagnetic torque.

$$\Gamma_{em} = \frac{3}{2} \times p \times L_{sr} \left(i_{qs} i_{dr} - i_{ds} i_{qr} \right) \tag{7}$$

Each component spectrum of the electromagnetic torque is due to the interaction between a sinusoidal component of the stator current and a sinusoidal component of the rotor current as is described by the Eq. 8 following:

$$\Gamma_{em} = k \times \left(\cos(w_s)t \right) \times \left(\cos(w_r + w_m)t \right) \tag{8}$$

By rearranging the Eq. 8 above, this can be presented in the new form of Eq. 9, where k and k1 are constants, ws is the angular speed of the stator currents, wr is the angular speed of the rotor currents, wm is the mechanical speed in radelec/s, fs and fr are the stator and the rotor current frequencies and fm=(1-s).fs is the mechanical frequency in electrical Hertz. The values of ws and wr can be either positive or negative depending on the positive or negative characteristics of the sequence.

$$\Gamma_{em} = \frac{k1}{2} \times \left[\cos\left(f_s - fr - fm\right)t - \varphi + \cos\left(f_s + fr + fm\right)t + \varphi \right] \tag{9}$$

The frequency components of the electromagnetic torque presented in Figs. 15 a) and 15 b) are for the slip=0.3906. As can be observed, with an inductance placed in the DC link, the spectrum presented is cleaner and has lower amplitude values when compared to the situation without the inductance L.

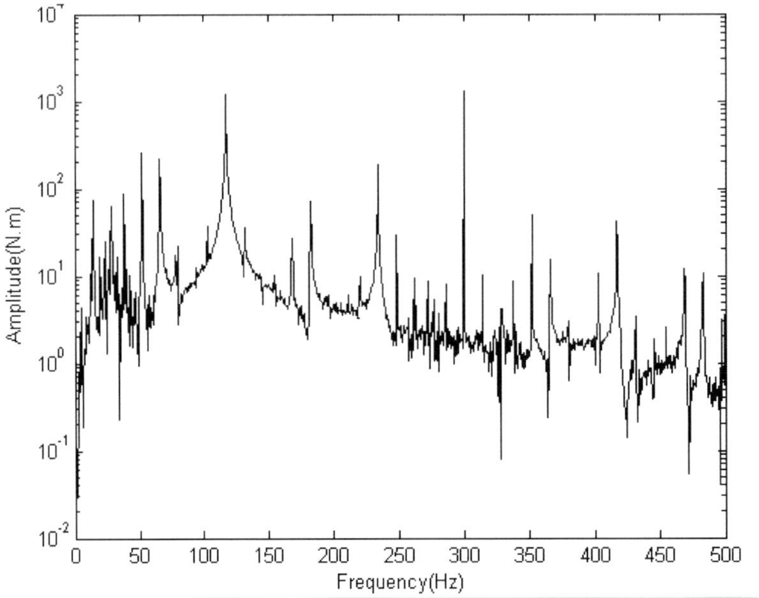

(a)

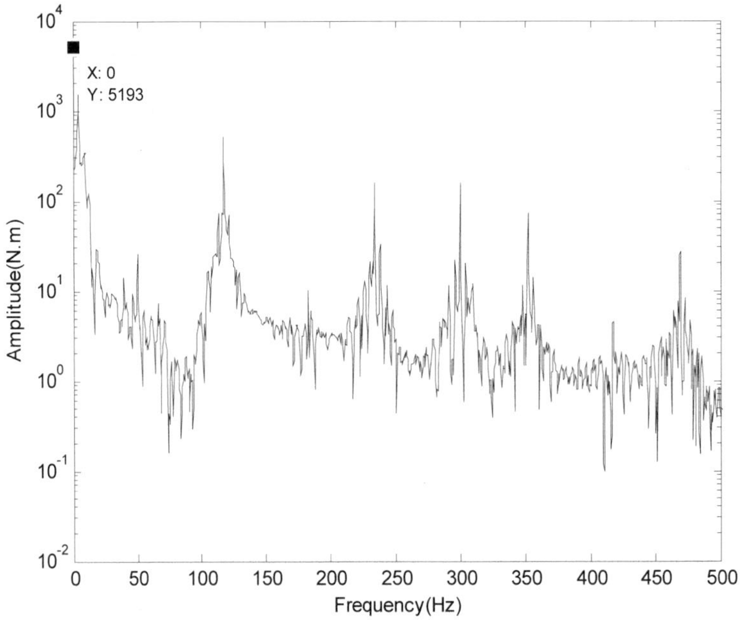

(b)

Fig. 15. Frequency spectrum of the electromagnetic torque for slip=0.3906, a) without inductance L and, b) with an inductance of 10mH

Table 5 shows the spectral components and correspondent amplitude values considering that the torque is higher than 10N.m. As shown in Figs. 15 a) and 15 b), and then reflected by the table, the most relevant peaks of the electromagnetic torque appear for frequencies multiples of 117 Hz and at 300Hz.

Frequency Modulus (Hz)	Amplitude of torque components (N.m)			
	Without L	With L=1mH	With L=5mH	With L=10mH
0	5294	5292	5281	5193
14	75.16	4883-	68.56	-
28	62.05	-	-	-
37.5	87.64	44.07	12.26	-
51.5	254.2	91.21	18	25.5
65.5	218.7	74.72	-	7.3
79.5	21.73	-	-	-
117	1223	804.3	504	513.4
169	23.52	14.29	-	-
183	70.12	34.8	13.5	10.12
234.5	186.1	165.8	200	160.6
248.5	29.46	-	-	-
300	1287	775.7	300	156.4
351.5	50.26	66.99	85.86	75.28
365	15.56	-	-	-
417	41.75	22.72	-	4.5
468.5	-	17.12	29.82	26

Table 5. Frequencies and amplitudes of the electromagnetic torque

Table 5 also shows that the amplitudes of the components decrease for the most relevant frequencies, if the DC link inductance increases.

As examples, it appears that with the 300 Hz component of the electromagnetic torque, the amplitude varies between 1287N.m for L=0mH to 156.4N.m for L=10mH and the amplitude of the electromagnetic torque, 117Hz changes its value from 1223N.m for L=0mH to 513.4N.m for L=10mH.

2.5 Experimental results

Although the main objective of this study did not focus on the power quality of the energy provided by the network, in order to evaluate the effects caused in this, by the system under analysis i.e. by the SER system, some experimental measurements were taken in the voltage busbars of 60kV and 6KV and also the voltage busbar that feeds directly the SER system. It was verified, however, that in any of the situations analyzed, only the fundamental frequency component of 50Hz is present. The current measured on the busbar of the SER system shows a waveform whose spectrum has the fundamental component of 50Hz and its multiples. Figs. 16 and 17 show the experimental results concerning the current waveforms for the rotor and the stator.

The information relating to the harmonic spectrum of these variables is presented using linear scales in both x and y-axis. Due to the low plot resolution (just 256 points) used by the experimental equipment, the results do not show the detailed information that is obtained in simulation (with 10000 points). The experimental results were obtained for slip = 0.3906 and are in accordance with the simulation ones for the same conditions of the SER system operation.

2.5.1 Experimental rotor current, ir

Figs. 16 a) and 16 b) show the rotor current and correspondent spectrum for the slip=0.3906, the correspondent fundamental rotor frequency is 19.53Hz. The harmonic components introduced by the six-pulse rectifier converter, due to the DC side average value, are reflected on the rotor currents at frequencies given by the Eq. 3.
The frequency of 19.53Hz (100%) is obtained when k is equal to zero in Eq. 3. The harmonics of 5th, 7th and 11th orders are also present in the spectrum and predicted by the equation. They correspond to the frequencies of 97.66Hz (26.8%), 136.71Hz and 214.83Hz, respectively.
As it is observed, the harmonic components, due to the six-pulse inverter that appear in the DC current at frequencies multiples of 300Hz, also appear in the spectrum of the rotor currents with two side-bands of 300Hz ± 19.53Hz. These correspond to the 280.47Hz and 319.53Hz peak frequencies in the spectrum of Fig. 16 b), respectively.

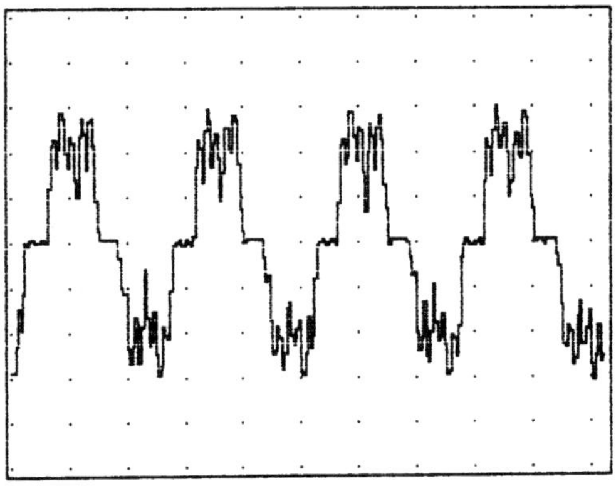

X Scale: 20ms/div, Y Scale: 100mV/div,
X Resol: 25# /div, Y Resol: 25# /div, X size: 256.

(a)

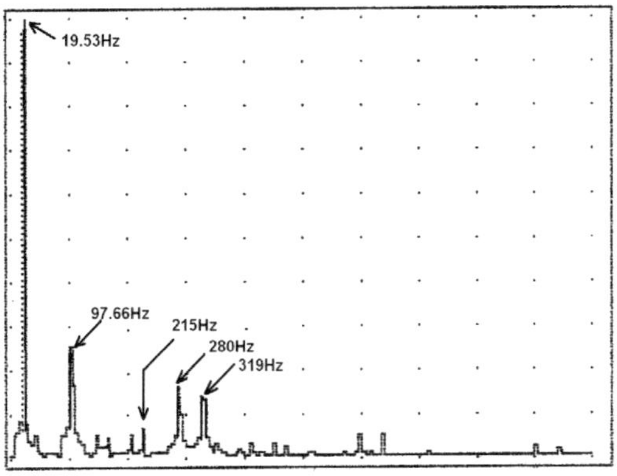

X Scale: 97.7 Hz/div, Y Scale: 10 %/div,
X Resol: 20 # /div, Y Resol: 25 # /div, X size: 200

(b)

Fig. 16. Rotor current for slip=0.3906, with relevant peaks at frequencies of 19.53Hz (100%), the signalised, 97.66 Hz (26.8%), 136.71 Hz, 253.89 Hz, 280.47 Hz and 319.53 Hz

2.5.2 Experimental stator current, is

Figs. 17 a) and 17 b) show the stator current and correspondent spectrum for the slip=0.3906. By the Eq. 5 and Eq. 6 presented above, the analysis of the spectrum of Fig. 17 shows that: 1) the 50Hz fundamental frequency can be obtained when k is equal to zero in equation 5, 2) the 5th and 7th harmonics of the rotor current appear in the stator at frequencies of |-97.66 +30.47|=+67.19Hz and |+136.71 +30.47| = 167.18Hz, which correspond to using k equal to one and m equal to zero in equation 6, 3) the 11th harmonic of the rotor current appears in the stator at frequencies of |-214.83 +30.47|=184.36Hz.

The effects of the inverter harmonics on the stator current were obtained by Eq. 6 with k = 0. The highest peaks of the stator frequency are the 250Hz and the 350Hz corresponding to the rotating fields established by the rotor frequencies of 280.47Hz and 319.53Hz.

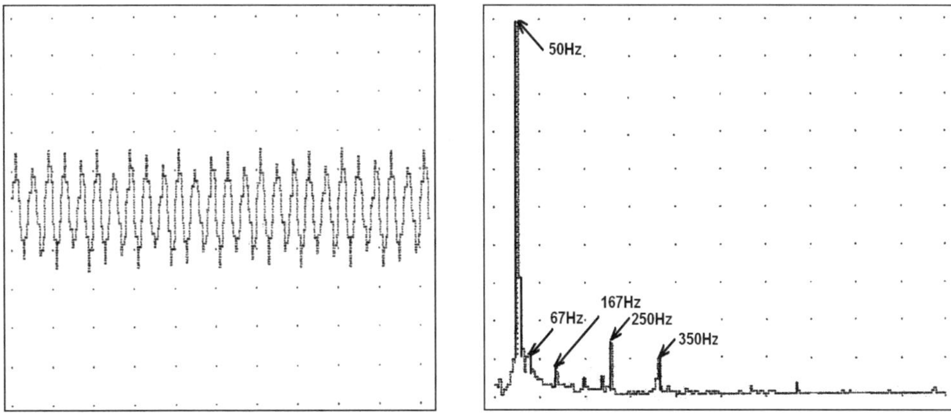

X Scale: 50ms/div, Y Scale: 100mV/div,
X Resol: 25# /div, Y Resol: 25# /div, X size: 256.

(a)

X Scale: 97.5 Hz/div, Y Scale: 10 %/div,
X Resol: 20 # /div, Y Resol: 25 # /div, X size: 200

(b)

Fig. 17. Stator current for slip=0.3906, with relevant peaks at frequencies of 50Hz (100%), 250 Hz (13.6%) and 350 Hz (9.6%)

2.6 Conclusions

With this case study it was shown in a simple but clear form that the MatLab tools could meet all the requirements of implementing a particular and rather complex power electronics system such as the SER. The implementation of the SER system in MatLab has allowed a better understanding of the same and, in addition, has provided the answers necessary to act in conformity with the results. The implementation of the control and the characterization of the various elements of the system were presented in detail according to the strategy imposed by the commercial system. It should be noted that when this study was undertaken, the SER system was operating in a cement plant.
The control strategy implemented allows the elimination of the circulation current of the system and for the harmonic analysis, a MatLab programme is developed for the effect, with several features, namely: the capability to analyze a large range of frequencies and high resolution. Some results for the stator current, the rotor current and the electromagnetic torque were presented. These results show the existence of strong components of high frequency on the stator and rotor currents. The oscillations presented in the electromagnetic torque were explained by considering the interaction between the stator and the rotor fundamental and harmonic currents. Considering the effect of the inductance of the DC link coil, it affects directly the ripple of the waveform of the rotor current, which is reflected in the values of amplitude of the frequency spectrum.

3. Power electronic converter for a fuel cell (FC) system

Power electronic converters in general and the DC-DC converters in particular are of very high importance in the performance and the efficiency of fuel cell (FC) processes based on energy generation systems. The control of the operation point of the PEM fuel cell requires appropriate use of static power electronic converters, capable of providing accurate support to the control methods. Hence, the main objective of applying converters with fuel cells is to obtain maximum efficiency using the easiest and correct control strategies, taking into account requirements like cost, efficiency, ripple current and stable operation under transient load conditions.

There are two main possible converter topologies which can be utilized in order to meet the objective: a DC-DC converter together with a DC-AC and a DC-AC interfacing directly with the FC to the grid. A specific application must be considered in order to select the best topology. Usually the DC-DC converter is put between the fuel cell and the inverter which performs two functions: 1) acts as the DC isolation for the inverter; and 2) produces sufficient voltage for the inverter input so that the required magnitude of the AC voltage can be produced.

The inverter can be single-phase or three-phase depending on the utility connection. Some typical structures of the electrical fuel cell system are presented in Figs. 18, 19 and 20 below.

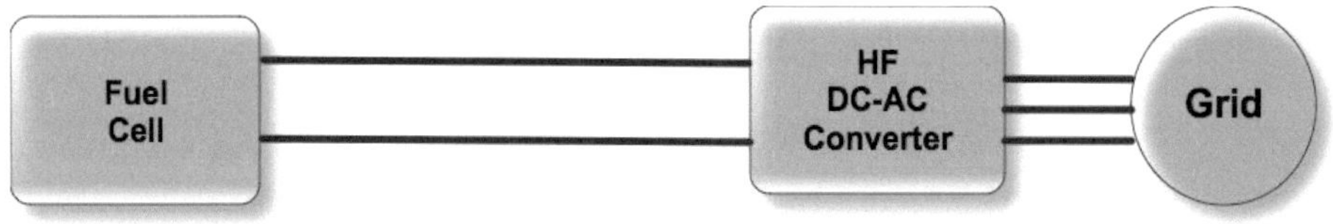

Fig. 18. A typical FC configuration with a DC-AC converter interfacing directly to the grid

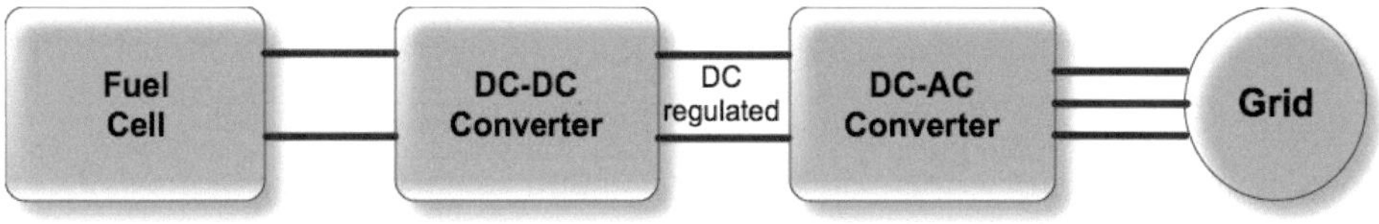

Fig. 19. A typical FC configuration with a DC-DC and a DC-AC converter

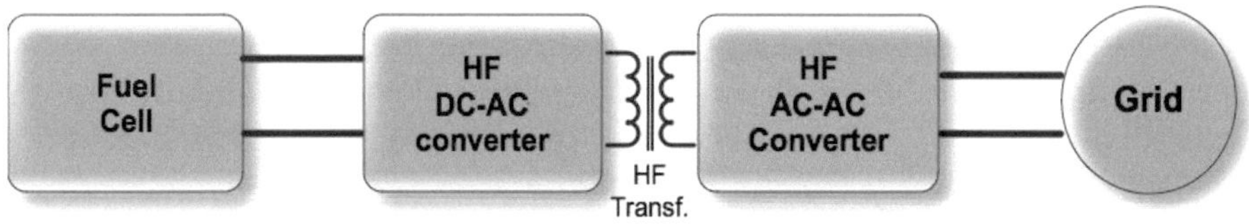

Fig. 20. A typical FC configuration with a DC-AC and an AC-AC converter

3.1 Requirements and selection of the converter topology

The main requirements considered for selecting the converter topology are as follows:

- Control of output voltage according to a given reference,
- Deliver current with little ripple and harmonic distortion,
- High efficiency in the whole operating range,
- Proper operation in all conditions,
- Incorporated filtering and storing possibilities,
- Low cost.

Basically, the DC-DC converter can be a current-fed or a voltage-fed type. A current-fed DC–DC converter requires less input filtering to minimize the high frequency current ripple drawn by the fuel cell because the inductor is placed at the input. Then, after an analysis and comparison of various topologies, a full-bridge resonant inverter, followed by an HF transformer and rectifier, composes the power scheme selected to our application. Additionally, two low-pass filters are inserted, one on the primary side is used to protect the fuel cell ripple-current and another on the secondary side is used to improve the quality of the energy supplied by the power system. The next sessions give some characteristics of the series-resonant topology, which are necessary for its design.

3.2 Model of the converter in MatLab/Simulink

A modular power scheme of the DC-DC converter and its implementation in MatLab/Simulink is presented in Fig. 21. The operation of this converter can be described as follows: the voltage supplied by the fuel cell stack, which is typically low (29V - 42V), must be converted to a high and constant level, in our case, for 400VDC in order to be used to generate power to the grid through an inverter. The HF transformer is a step-up voltage transformer, which also serves as galvanic isolation between the high and low voltage levels of the circuits. The resonant converter with its LC series resonant circuit gives the sinusoidal waveforms of voltage and current in the primary side of the transformer. Selecting appropriate values for the L and C elements, the resonant frequency of the circuit is established. Then, the DC voltage of the fuel cell is firstly inverted in the primary side of the HF transformer, being rectified on the secondary side. The LC filter in the primary side allows protecting the PEM fuel cell from the ripple current and voltage produced by the converter, and also allows the storage of energy in the DC bus. The LC filter in the secondary allows reducing the ripple current and ripple voltage to the load, respectively.

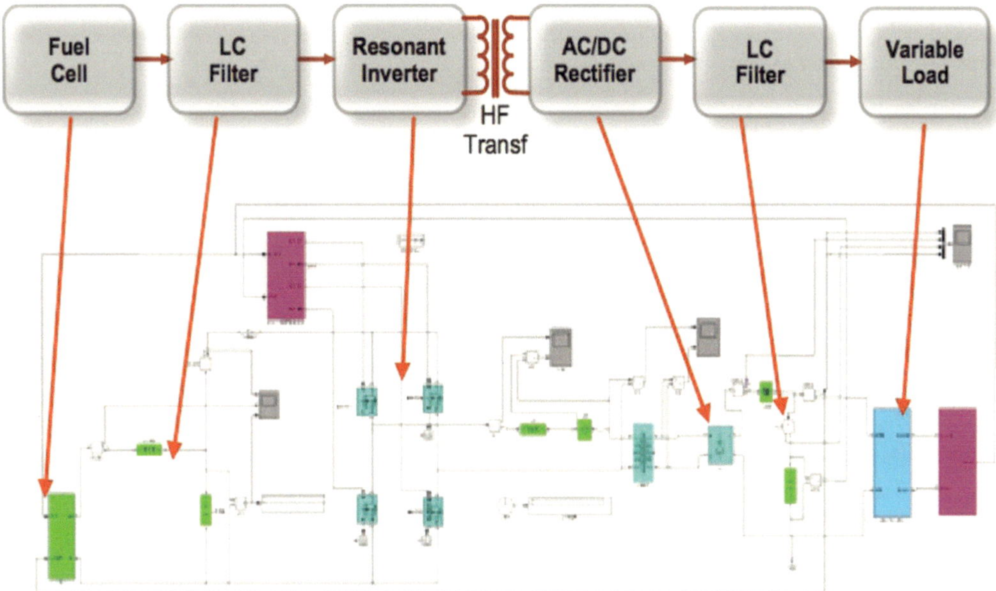

Fig. 21. The power electronic converter implemented in MatLab/Simulink

3.2.1 Control structure

The control structure implemented in MatLab/Simulink corresponds to the modular scheme represented in Fig. 22, which is presented and described considering two parts.

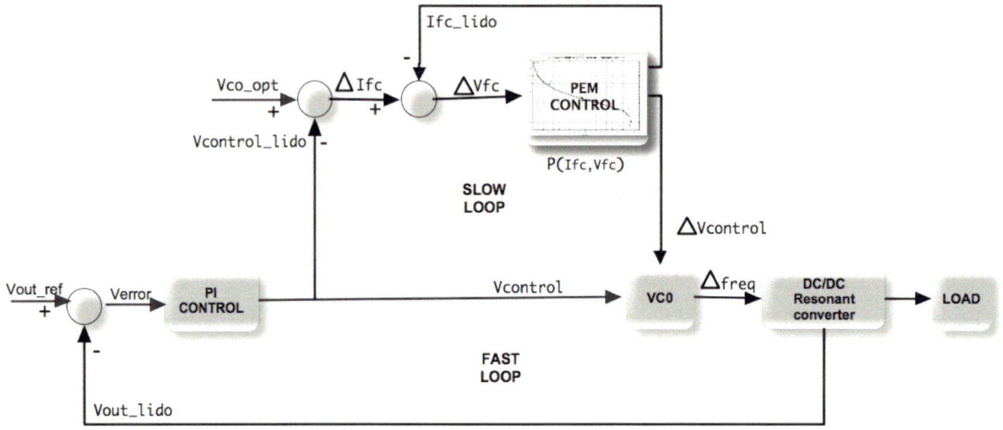

Fig. 22. Modular scheme of the control structure selected

3.2.2 Voltage controller

The voltage control sub-system is implemented in MatLab/Simulink as represented in Fig. 23

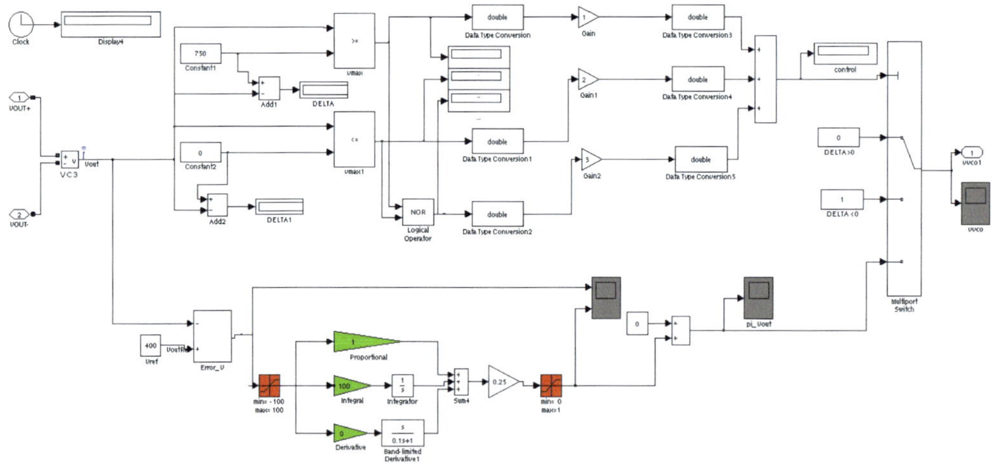

Fig. 23. Voltage control sub-system of the converter

Explanation of the voltage control sub-system

The voltage control sub-system of the converter allows limiting the maximum and minimum values for the output voltage i.e. the control output signal, Vcontrol, is always equal to zero (0), if Vout> = 750V(Selector #1), on the other side is always equal to one (1), if Vout = 0V (Selector #2). Otherwise, the control module works according to the main goal for which it was designed, that is, through a PI controller and regardless of the type and amount of load applied to the power system, it keeps the converter output voltage at 400V (Selector #3). This works as follows: the value of the output voltage (Vout) of the converter is obtained and compared with the reference value; an error signal is produced and processed by the P - proportional I -integral controller producing a reference signal of voltage control (Vcontrol). The proportional term responds immediately to the error voltage yet typically cannot achieve the required set-point accuracy without an unacceptably large gain. On the other hand, the integral term yields an error zero in steady state for a constant set-point and enables the rejection of disturbances.

3.2.3 Frequency controller

The frequency control sub-system implemented in MatLab/Simulink is represented in Fig. 24.

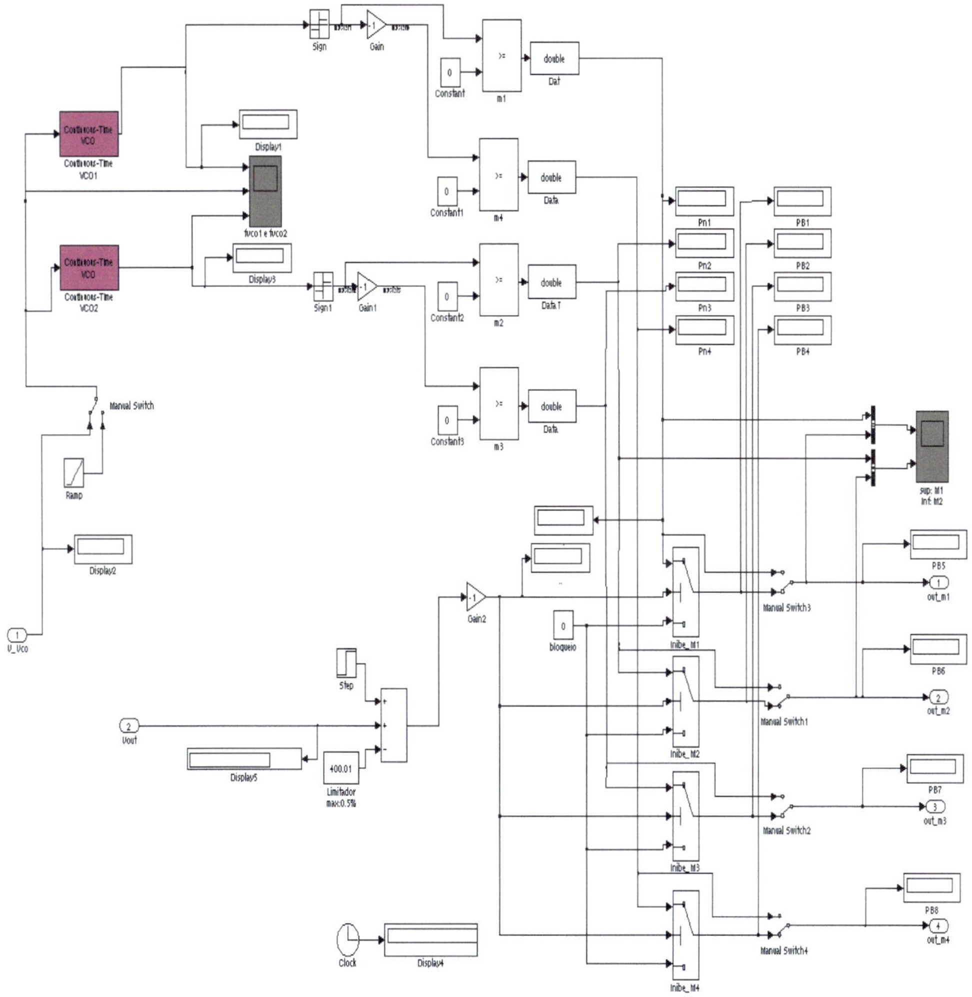

Fig. 24. Frequency control sub-system of the converter

Explanation of the frequency control sub-system

The frequency control sub-system allows the generation of the four gate signals to the resonant inverter bridge, which changes accordingly to the signal reference. Once the input signal is known, interpreted as a voltage (VCOref), established by the PI controllers, the continues-time VCO generates a sinusoidal signal whose frequency shifts from the Quiescent frequency parameter (fc) with a sensitivity to the input parameter (kc) and amplitude Ac. The inverter topology is a full-bridge; then four output signals need to be generated by this sub-system, one for each transistor respectively (Mi, i =1,2,3,4). They are synchronized by φ, which is the initial phase parameter and assumes zero or π value in the case. Parameterization of the voltage control oscillator blocks are shown in Fig. 25 according to the Eq. 10.

$$y(t) = A_C \times \cos\left(2\pi f_c + 2\pi k_c \int_0^t u(\tau)d\tau + \varphi\right) \tag{10}$$

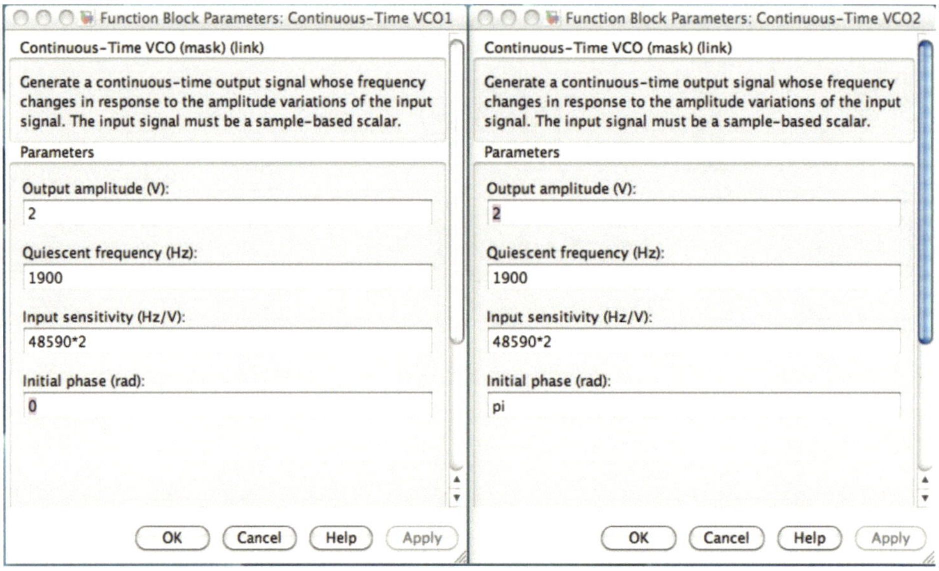

Fig. 25. Parameterization of the two voltage control oscillator blocks

3.3 PEM Controller

While the voltage-controller is responsible for controlling the output voltage of the converter, the PEM-controller is responsible for controlling the operation of the PEM, keeping it in its optimal operation point. This controller works as follows; once characterized an operation point of the PEM, for certain load conditions and constant output voltage (maintained by the voltage-controller), assuming for example that is point P in Fig. 26, the PEM-loop has the task of improving the performance of the system, defining a new point P ' or P'' that best optimizes the PEM performance, i.e. which maximizes the energy produced with minimum consumption of hydrogen. The algorithm of control that satisfies these conditions of operation is represented by the flowchart of Fig. 27 and its descriptive explanation are further given through the summary presented in the table below:

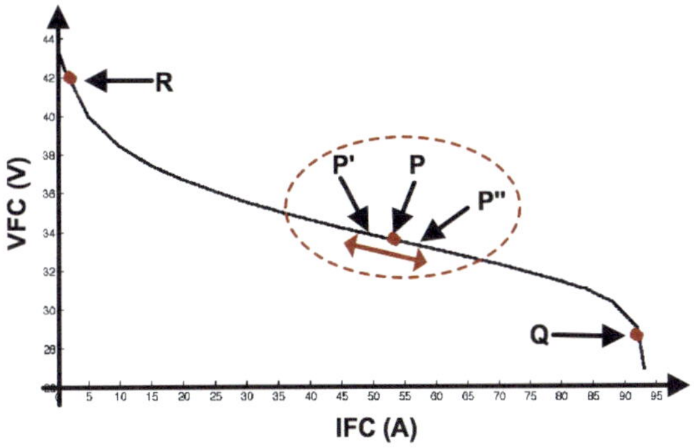

Fig. 26. Output characteristic of the PEM

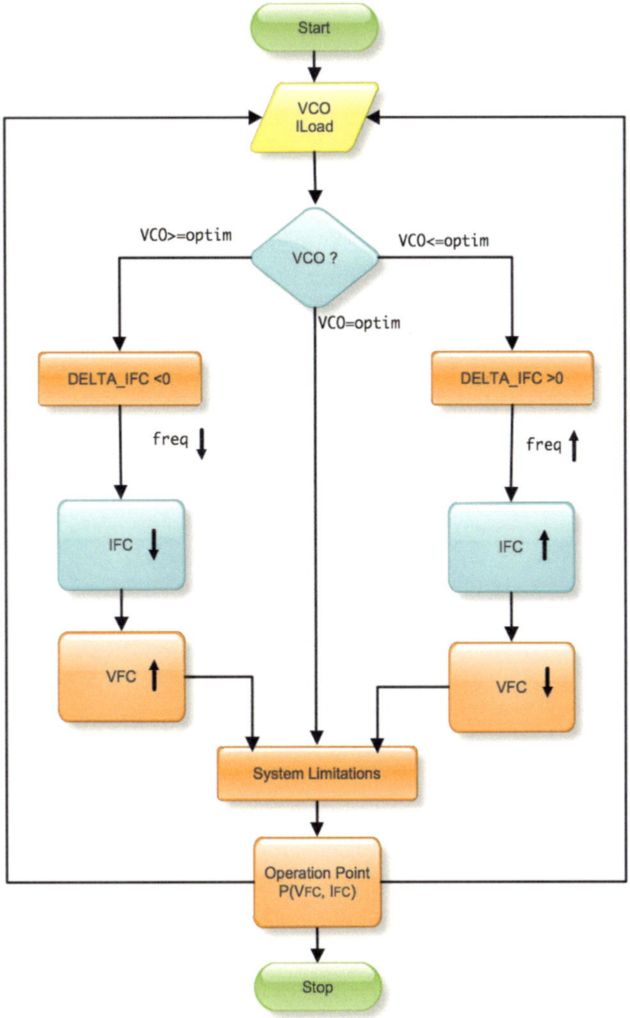

Fig. 27. Flowchart of PEM controller

3.3.1 Flowchart explanation

While the voltage-loop is responsible of control-ling the output voltage of the converter, the PEM-loop is responsible of controlling the operation of the PEM, keeping it in its optimal operation point. This controller is implemented in MatLab/Simulink and works as follows; once characterized an operation point of the PEM, assuming for example that is point P in Fig. 26, the PEM-loop has the task of improving the performance of the system, defining a new point P' or P'' that best optimizes the PEM performance, i.e. introducing small perturbations in the system thus leading the cell to operate under conditions of maximum efficiency of the PEM, in other words, providing maximum power with minimal consumption of hydrogen.
However, a minimum consumption of hydrogen means the operation of the PEM with minimum current, i.e. IFC minimum and VFC maximum, just in the sense of P' of the output characteristic of the PEM, as exemplified in the graph above.
A lowering of the current cell implies a lowering of the operating frequency of the resonant converter, so the search condition from the point of optimum operation of PEM requires the lowering of the resonant frequency of the converter. Once you find the optimum for the present conditions of load, the resonant converter is operating at a frequency that is also the minimum frequency that ensures the load conditions imposed on the system. The process is repeated whenever there is a variation of the conditions imposed by the load. The actions to be performed by the PEM controller considering a particular condition of operation of the converter are summarized in Table 6.

3.3.2 PEM controller in MatLab/Simulink

As shown in Fig. 28 below, the implementation in MatLab/Simulink of the PEM controller previously explained is a cascade of various sub-systems, such as in a first step a sub-system generates a DELTA value. Once known, the value of DELTA, a new sub-system, generates a voltage reference value (Vcontrol), according to the current value of IFC. The term of IFC expressed by Eq. 13 takes into account the load conditions; the fact is that the power transferred from the PEM to the load has no losses and the output voltage must be kept always constant and equal to 400VDC. The DELTA value is reduced by a factor of 0.25 as shown in Fig. 28. Finally, there is a sub-system to control the output voltage VFC acting under the control algorithm previously explained.

$$PFC = Pout + PLoss \text{ and } PLoss \approx 0 \quad (11)$$

$$VFC \times IFC = Iout \times 400 \quad (12)$$

$$IFC = \frac{Iout \times 400}{VFC} \quad (13)$$

3.3.3 DELTA sub-system in MatLab/Simulink

The sub-system DELTA and the corresponding parameterization of function relay are implemented in MatLab/Simulink as shown in Fig. 29 and Fig. 30.

Explanation of the DELTA system

For each module that produces a specific DELTA, the following methodology is used:

a. VCO is compared with the lower limit value of the relay,
b. VCO is compared with the upper limit value of the relay (the top line that enters in the comparator limit value).

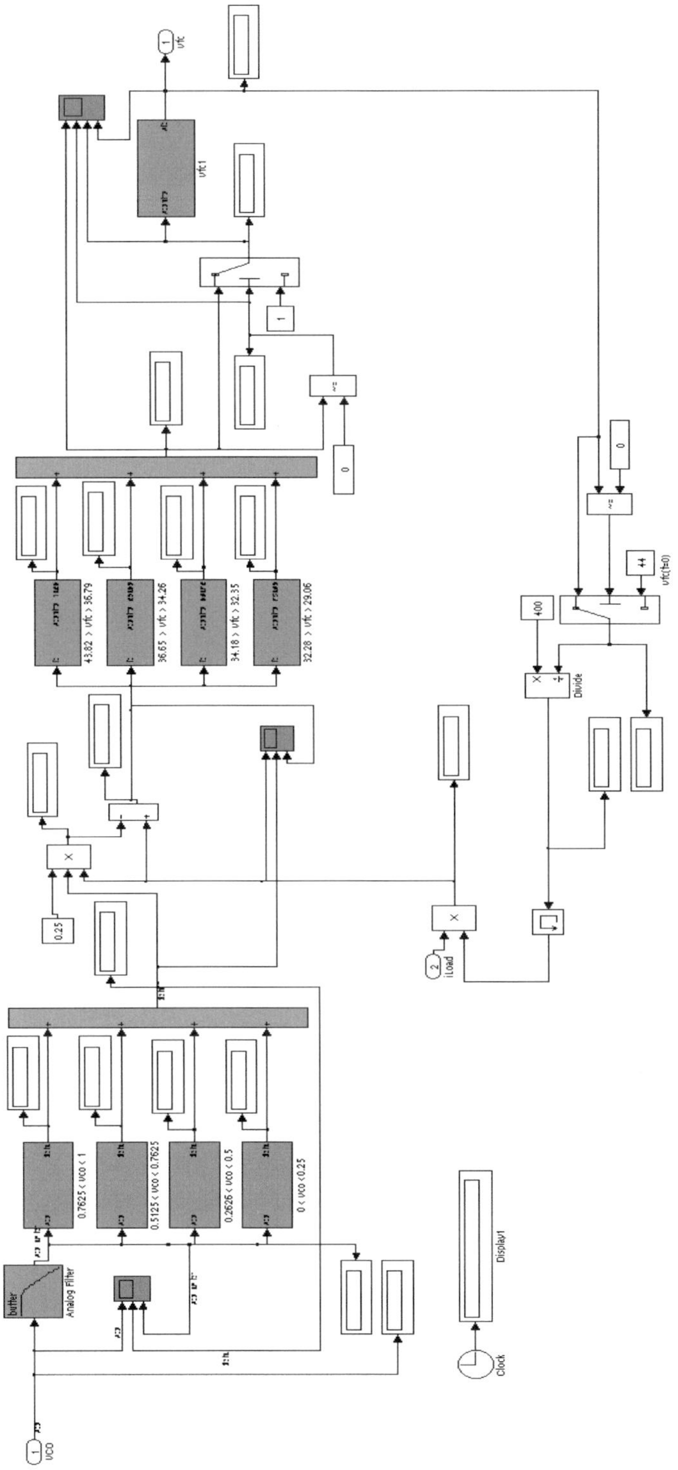

Fig. 28. PEM controller implemented in MatLab/Simulink

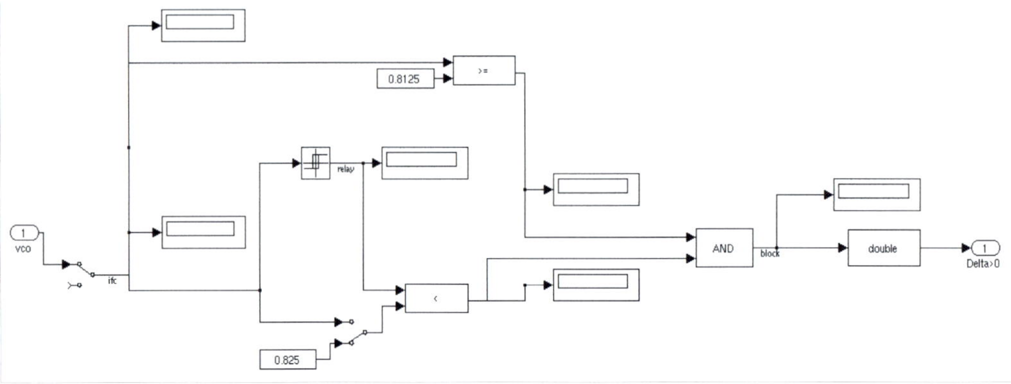

Fig. 29. DELTA sub-system in MatLab/Simulink

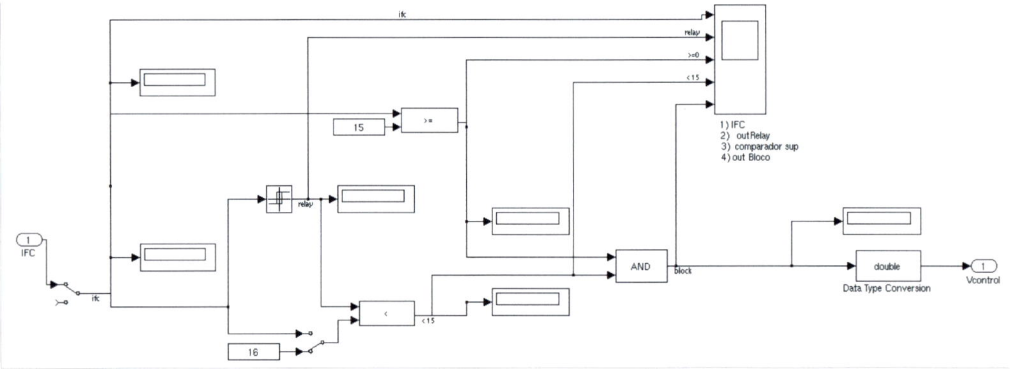

Fig. 30. Voltage control in MatLab/Simulink

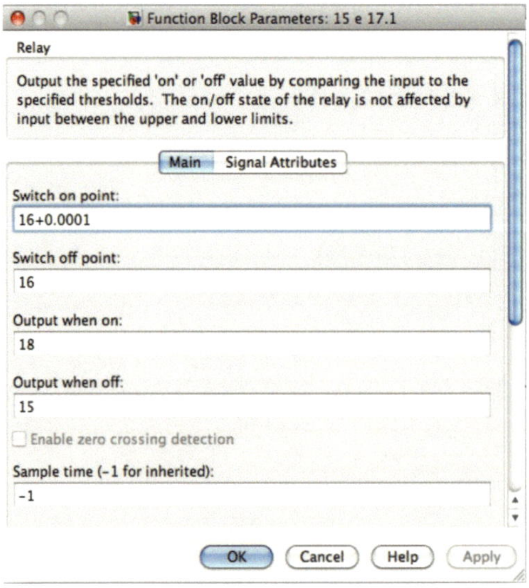

Fig. 31. Parameterization of relay function in Vcontrol

The upper limit of each module of the sub-system DELTA is determined by the function 'relay' whose output is determined according to the following conditions.

i. The lower value VCO to reach the ceiling value of the relay,
ii. The higher value since the relay changes state (with VCO greater than the upper value of the relay),
iii. The output relay again put on the lower value of output relay when VCO back down and reach the lower limit value. From this moment, the relay output (value upper/lower) is defined by this cycle - then turns to step i) and the cycle repeats.

This methodology is applied for the overall DELTA steps, as an example, if the natural limit is 0.825, the relay has the limits > 0.825 and ≤ 1. When VCO goes up to 0.825, the output of relay is 0.825, and in this case there is a condition of equality. Above 0.825, VCO is greater and the relay function goes to the 2nd block.

In the next internals of time, the current continues to rise and when it reaches the 1 value or other value may be higher it happens a singular situation, i.e. in either case in which VCO is 'exactly' equal to 1 is on the 1st block, leaving in the next block, because the voltage in the 1st block is greater. With these conditions, an increase of VCO happens.

3.3.4 Voltage control sub-system in MatLab/Simulink

The sub-system Vcontrol and the corresponding parameterization of function relay are implemented in MatLab/Simulink as shown in Fig. 30 and Fig. 31.

Explanation of the Vcontrol sub-system

For each module that produces a specific Vcontrol, the following methodology is used:

a. IFC is compared with the lower value of the relay,
b. IFC is compared with the upper limit value of the relay (the top line that enters in the comparator limit value).

The upper limit of each module of the sub-system Vcontrol is determined by the function 'relay' whose output is determined according to the following conditions.

i. The lower value IFC to reach the ceiling value of the relay,
ii. The higher value since the relay changes state (with IFC greater than the upper value of the relay),
iii. The output relay again put on the lower value of output relay when IFC back down and reach the lower limit value. From this moment, the relay output (value upper/lower) is defined by this cycle - then turns to step i) and the cycle repeats.

This methodology is applied for the overall Vcontrol (92 steps), as an example, if the natural limit is 15A. The relay has the limits >15A and ≤ 16A. When IFC goes up to 15A, the output of relay is 15 and in this case there is a condition of equality. Above 15A, IFC is greater and the relay function goes to the 2nd block.

In the next internals of time, the current continues to rise and when it reaches the 16A (or other value ... may be higher) a singular situation happens, i.e. in either case in which IFC is 'exactly' equal to 16A on the 1st block, leaving in the next block, because the voltage in the 1st block is greater. With these conditions, an increase of IFC happens.

3.4 Simulation results

The following parameter conditions were implemented in test simulations of the converter.
Simulation method: ode23t (Stiff/ Trapezoidal)

Tolerances: 1e-3 (Rel.) 1e-6 (Abs.)
Max step size: 1e-5
Initial output voltage of capacitor = 400.1V
Voltage control: kp=1, ki= 100
Quiescent frequency parameter (fc):1900Hz
Sensitivity to the input parameter (kc):45100Hz

3.4.1 Analysis of the static behaviour of the PEM

The analysis of the static behaviour of the PEM fuel cell is done for some variables that better characterizes its performance, namely, its polarisation plot Vfc =f(Ifc) and power delivery as function of the load supplied to the NEXA system. The voltage varies between 45V and 22V approximately, while current varies from 5 to 45A. The efficiency of this stack is around 22% - 33%.

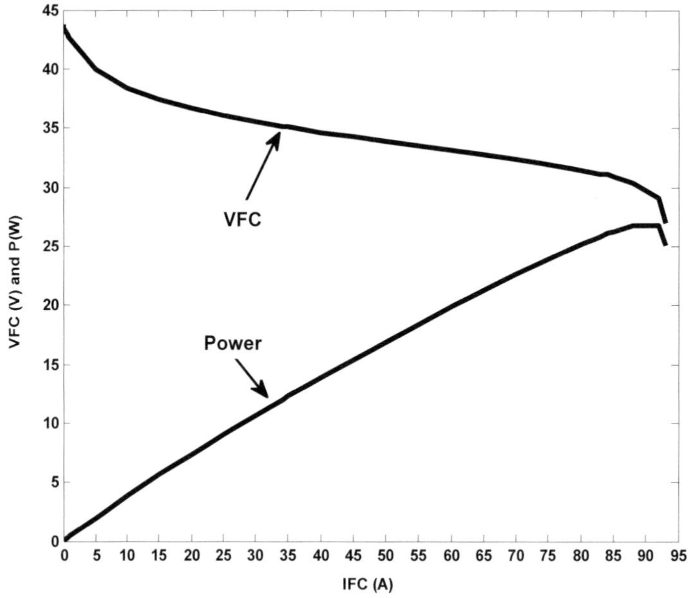

Fig. 32. Voltage and power variables function of the load for the NEXA PEM

3.4.2 Analysis of the dynamic behaviour of the PEM

The analysis of the dynamic behaviour of the PEM fuel cell is done for several variables, which better characterizes its behaviour. The results presented correspond to the NEXA system. Fig. 33 illustrates the influence of the temperature on its polarization curve. As can be seen, in normal operation the losses experienced by the fuel cell are converted into heat, the stack temperature will increase or decrease respectively to the power delivered, therefore, as the temperature affects the performance of the PEM fuel cell, this needs to be analyzed in detail. So, three levels of temperature operation were considered for this study (40ºC, 50°C and 60ºC). Fig. 33 clearly shows that an increase in temperature decreases the value of output voltage and consequently the efficiency of the fuel cell.
The dynamic behaviour of the PEM fuel cell is also affected by capacitor value, as can be observed in Fig. 34. If there is a decrease in the fuel cell current, the voltage rises, showing

similar delay effect for different values of the capacitor. However, because each point on the polarisation curve is obtained in steady state, the delay due to the capacitor does not affect the polarization curve of the PEM fuel cell. The analysis represented is centred in the step-up current at an instant time of 27s.

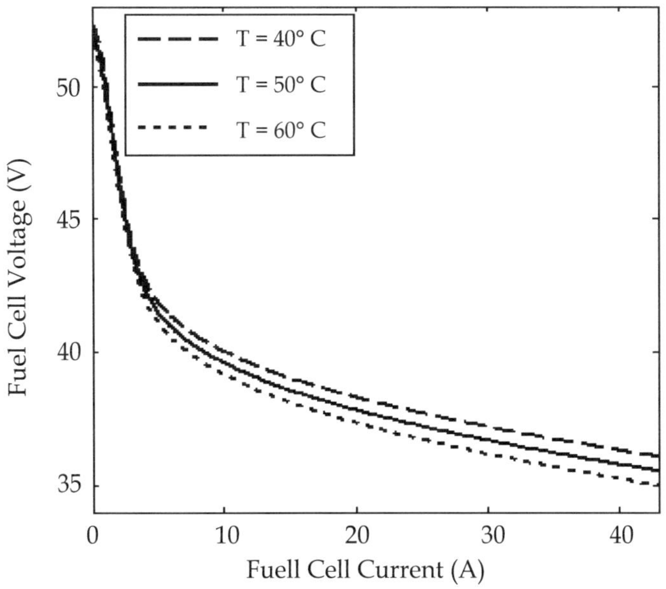

Fig. 33. Effect of the temperature in the dynamic response of the PEM

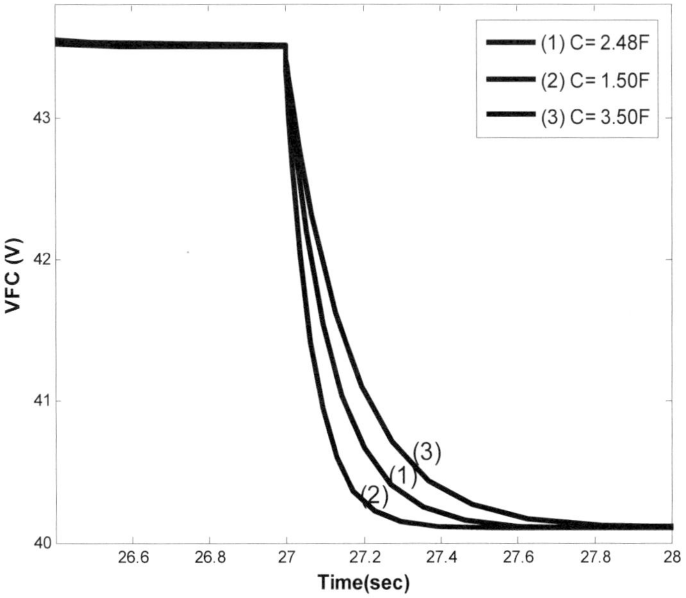

Fig. 34. Effect of the capacitor value on fuel cell voltage

3.4.3 Analysis of the converter behaviour in open loop

Fig. 35 shows how in open loop mode, the operation of the power converter is affected through small variations in the reference signal VCO. It appears as an output voltage variation of the converter. This is because if the value of VCO is changed, the frequency of operation of the resonant DC-DC converter is changed. In absence of control of the converter (in open loop), the higher the frequency of operation (that is to say, the VCO) the faster the response of the system and the output voltage value is at its highest, as can be seen by the three plots of the figure.

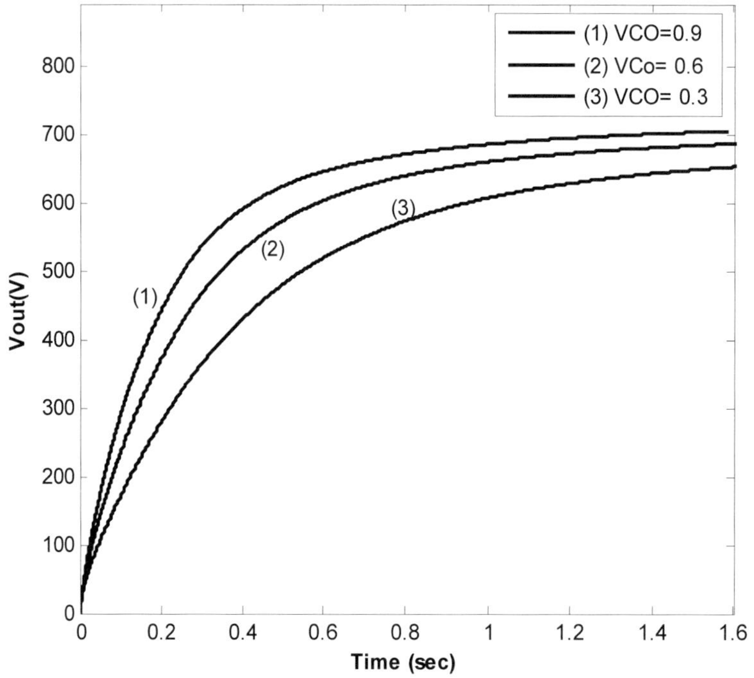

Fig. 35. Open loop response of the converter

3.4.4 Analysis of the converter behaviour in closed loop

Figs. 36, 37 and 38 below correspond to time responses of the main variables of the converter system in closed loop. The plot response of PEM fuel cell for a change in the load at time 0.04s is represented in Fig. 36. As can be seen, in closed loop, the response of PEM to a step load requested (IFC) results in a reduction in the output voltage (VFC). The PEM response is affected by the PI controller implemented which aims to put the PEM operating in accordance with the request load and maintaining a constant voltage of 400V at the converter output, as can be seen in the plot of Fig. 38, which corresponds to a change in the load at instant time 0.04s.

In Fig. 37 the LC series resonant tank waveforms are sinusoidal. The L and C components are placed on the primary side of the transformer and established for a resonant frequency of 50kHz. Obviously, other output powers demand lower converter frequency, operating around resonant pulses at the middle of the semi-period of the converter frequency.

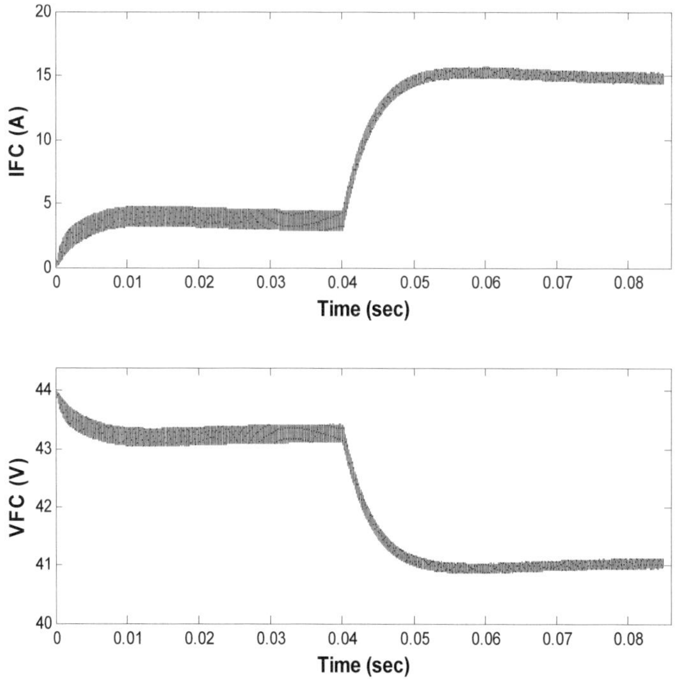

Fig. 36. Closed loop response of PEM fuel cell for a change in the load at time 0.04s

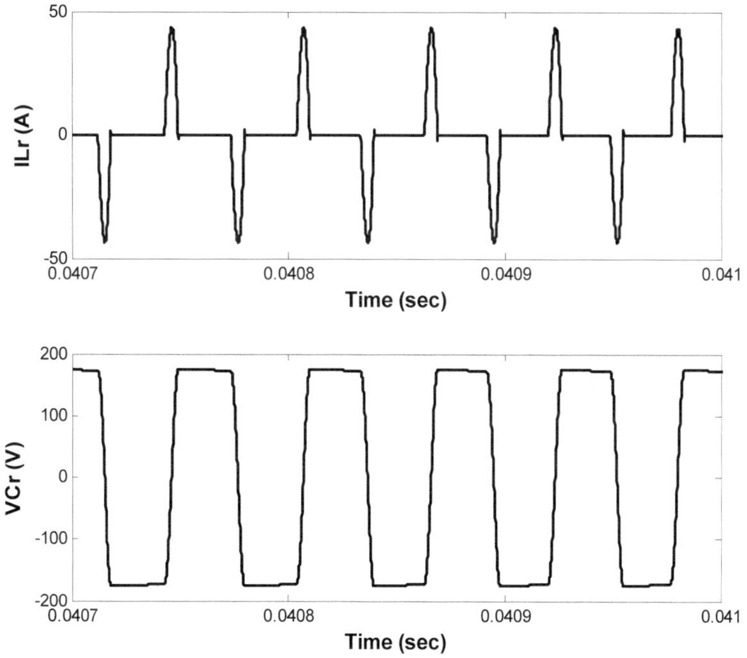

Fig. 37. Resonant waveforms ILr and VCr

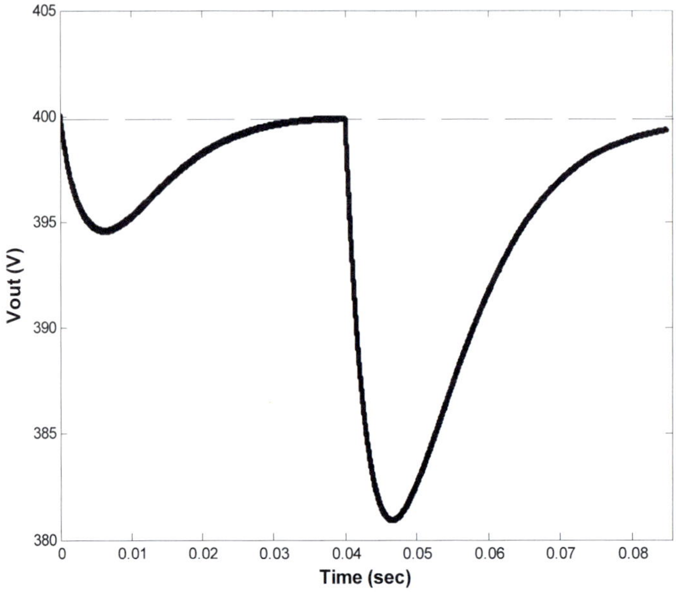

Fig. 38. Output voltage waveform for a change in the load at time 0.04s

3.5 Experimental results

Figs. 39 and 40 show some experimental results obtained in the digital oscilloscope Tektronix TDS2024. A Tektronix A622 is used for DC current measurement, while for the AC current measurement a CWT miniature Rogowski coil range from Powertek is used.

The fuel cell voltage in Fig. 39 is 20.6V and the current of the fuel cell is in this case 11.3A. Considering two points of the experimental PEM polarization represented in Fig. 26, (10A, 20.88V) and (12A, 20.68V9 it can be seen that the measured values in the output of the PEM, during the operation of the resonant converter, are in accordance with the respective curve for a given request load. Fig. 40 shows the series resonant converter waveforms, namely the resonant voltage VCr and resonant current ILr, which are both sinusoidal as expected. The operation frequency of the converter is in this case 33.38Khz.

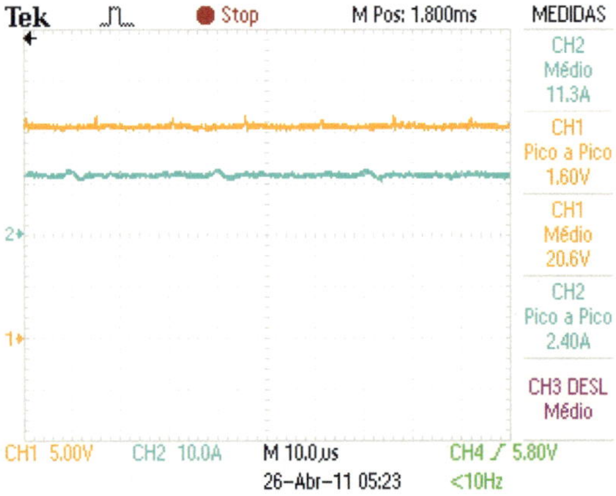

Fig. 39. Plots showing the fuel cell voltage (CH1) and current (CH2) for the load requested

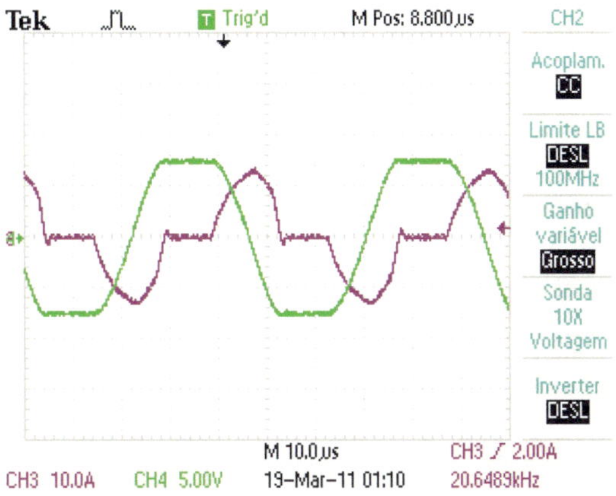

Fig. 40. Plots showing the series resonant converter waveforms - VCr (CH1) and ILr (CH3)

3.6 Conclusions

Similarly to the first case study presented, it was demonstrated in this second case that the MatLab tools could meet all the requirements of designing a power electronic converter for fuel cell (FC) based energy generation systems.

The modeling of the converter and the PEM in MatLab/Simulink allows a better understanding of the behaviour of the system and provides results that are an excellent tool in the project of the dynamics of the controller.

The case presentation is divided in two parts: in the first part the authors discuss the methodology for an accurate model for the fuel cell stack including its static and dynamical behaviour which is an essential aspect in the design of electrical power generation based on fuel cells. The design tool adopted is MatLab/Simulink, which proves to be a very common and easy tool for the design of electrical control systems.

However, due to the lack of manufacturer data-sheets about the exact values of the parameters needed for modelling, it is necessary to adopt a methodology in order to determine the optimum set of these parameters. The method adopted by the authors is the simulated annealing (SA) optimization algorithm, which proves to be well adapted to satisfy the goal of a fast convergence to establish the right values for the cell parameters. The good agreement between the simulation and the experimental results shows that the proposed model provides an accurate representation of the static and dynamic behaviour for the PEM fuel cell.

In the second part of the paper the authors give an overview of the possible topologies to be adopted for the DC/DC converter which are appropriate to take control and optimization of operation point of the fuel cell. In that sense, the soft switching proves to be particularly attractive and, in particular, the series resonant topology converters because they allow for reducing the switching losses and consequently increasing the efficiency. The simulation results are compared with real data obtained from a commercial system. Finally, the combination of a good power converter with a well-defined controller, together with the well-optimized fuel stack model, makes the electrical generation systems by FC very attractive indeed.

4. Conclusions

This chapter discusses the authors' approach to designing electrical generation systems based on MatLab/Simulink. It is shown, through explanation of development in MatLab using two examples, that MatLab is an appropriate tool for computational analysis of electrical systems in order to design physically controlled systems. In the first case in the chapter, it analyzed the implementation and control of a SER system, a conventional system based on power electronics and electrical drives.

For the second case, the design process of a completely different system is chosen, also demanding experimental validation of results.

The designing begins with the implementation of an appropriate model for PEM fuel cell behaviour based on analytical formulation of chemical processes behind fuel cell operation and the design of an equivalent and analogue electrical circuit describing the fuel cell operation. This case requires attention on the selection and implementation of an appropriated static power converter capable of either controlling and adapting the unregulated DC power generated by the fuel cell to a regulated electrical power source, or optimizing the efficiency of the fuel cell through appropriate input impedance. The power converter is a necessary sub-system for these kinds of systems, as it allows them to operate as controlled voltage sources for any operating point of the fuel cell.

The quality of the approach is demonstrated through implementation of the fuel cell and converter models, and other conventional sub-systems in a MatLab/Simulink model of the generation system.

The authors' approach allows for optimizing the design of electrical generation systems, both in economical terms and in performance quality, by making available accurate models that describe the electrical and chemical operations involved by simple methods when using the available toolboxes of the MatLab/Simulink.

The results illustrate in both cases that the MatLab/Simulink, being a cheap design environment tool software, can be generically adopted as an appropriate and accurate design tool.

5. Acknowledgment

The authors thank the following institutions which provided them with the conditions and financial support needed to conduct this research: Cimpor-Cements of Portugal, Institute of Telecommunications of Department of Electrical and Computer Engineering, University of Coimbra, Institute of Systems and Robotics, University of Porto and Foundation for Science and Technology.

6. References

Franz, M.B., "A new generation of standardised variable speed cascade systems", ABB Industries AG, Ch-5300 Turgi, Switzerland.

Mayer A., "La cascade de convertisseur statique hypossincrone, compte tenu des réctions sur le réseau et des couples oscillatoires"., Rev. Brown Boveri. pp. 133-141, April./May 1982.

Brown, J.E., "Analysis of the periodic transient state of a static Kramer drive", IEE Proceeding, vol. 133, pp. 21-29, Jan. 1986.

Akpinar, E, "Modelling and performance of slip energy recovery induction motor drives", IEEE Trans. Energy Conversion, vol. 5, No.1, pp. 203-210, Mar. 1990.

Marques, G.D., "Numerical simulation method for the slip power recovery system", IEE Proceedings of Electronic Power Applications, 1999, p. 17 a 24

Marques, G.D. and Verdelho, P. "A simple slip-power recovery system with a DC voltage intermediate circuit and reduced harmonics on the mains", IEEE Trans. on Industrial Electronics, vol. 47, pp 123-132, February 2000.

Hoshi, N., et al., "A compact type slip-power recovery system with sinusoidal rotor current for large pump/fan drives", IEEE Trans. Power Electronics, vol. 16, pp. 410-417, May 2001

Eskander, M.N., et al., "Comparison between two inverter topologies for application in industrial drives", ISIE 2001, Pusan, Korea

Hanna, R., "Harmonics and technical barriers in adjustable speed drives", IEEE Trans. Industry Application, 25 (5) (1989) 894-900

Baghzouz, Y., "Harmonic analysis of slip-power recovery drives", IEEE Trans. Industry Application, 28 (1) (1992) 50 -56

Refoufi, L. and Pillay, P., "Harmonic analysis of energy recovery induction motor drives", IEEE Trans. Energy Conversion, 9 (4) (1994) 665-672

Zakaria, W., Alwash, S. and Shaltout, A., "A novel double-circuit-rotor balanced induction motor for improved slip-energy recovery drive performance, Part II - Experimental verification and harmonic analysis", IEEE Trans. Energy Conversion, 11 (3) (1996) 563-569

Dell'Aquila, A., Lassandro, A. and Zanchetta, P., "Modeling of line side harmonic currents produced by variable speed induction motor drives", IEEE Trans. Energy Conversion, 13 (3) (1998) 263-269

Marques, G.D. and Verdelho, P., "A simple slip-power recovery system with a DC voltage intermediate circuit and reduced harmonics on the mains", IEEE Trans. Industrial Electronics, 47 (1) (2000) 123-132

Faiz, J., Batari, H. and Akpinar, E., "Harmonic analysis and performance improvement of slip energy recovery induction motor drives", IEEE Trans. Power Electronics, 16 (3) (2001) 410-417

Hoshi, N., et al., "A compact type slip-power recovery system with sinusoidal rotor current for large pump/fan drives", IEEE Trans. Power Electronics, 139 (2) (2002) 52-60

Chatelein, J., Machines Électriques, Tome I, Dunod, 1983

Amphlett, J.C., et al., "A model predicting transient responses of proton exchange membrane fuel cells", Journal of Power Sources, 1996, 61: p. 183-188

Corrêa, J.M., Farret, F.A. and Canha, L.N., "An analysis of the dynamic performance of proton exchange membrane fuel cells using an electrochemical model" in 27th Annual Conference on the IEEE Industrial Electronics Society 2001

Hatti, M., M. Tioursi, and W. Nouibat, "Static Modelling by Neural Networks of a PEM Fuel Cell", IEEE Proceedings, 2006: p. 2121-2126

Shaoduan, O. and E.K. Luke, "A hybrid neural network model for PEM fuel cells", Journal of Power Sources, 2005, 140: p. 319-330

Saengrung, A., Abtahi, A. and Zilouchian, A., "Neural network model for a commercial PEM fuel cell system", Journal of Power Sources, 2007, 172: p. 749-759

Jemei, S., et al., "On-board fuel cell power supply modelling on the basis of neural network methodology", Journal of Power Sources, 2003, 124: p. 479-486

Zuyev, S., Fuel Cell Power System Efficiency Calculation, 2004, Central Washington University, Mechanical Engineering Technology: Washington, USA. p. 16

Wang, C. and M. Nehrir, "Dynamic models and model validation for PEM fuel cells using electrical circuits", IEEE Transactions on Energy Conversion, 2005, 2(20): p. 442-451

Al-Baghdadi, M. and H. Al-Janabi, "Optimization study of proton exchange membrane fuel cell performance", Turkish Journal Eng. Env. Science, 2005, 29: p. 235-240

Bina, M.T. and D.C. Hamill, "Optimizing a discrete switching pattern using two simulated annealing algorithms", The 7th Workshop on Computers in Power Electronics 2000: p. 129-133

Fouskakis, D. and D. Draper, "Stochastic optimization: a review", International Statistical Review, 2002, N° 3(70): p. 315-349

Pham, D.T. and D. Karaboga, Intelligent optimisation techniques: genetic algorithms, tabu search, simulated annealing and neural networks, 2000, New York: Springer

Zolfaghari, S. and M. Liang, "Comparative study of simulated annealing, genetic algorithms and tabu search for solving binary and comprehensive machine-grouping problems", International Journal of Production Research, 2002, 9(40): p. 2141-2158

Romero, D., J. Rincón, and N. Almao, "Optimization of the thermal behaviour of tropical buildings", in 7th International IBPSA Conference, 2001: Rio de Janeiro, Brazil. p. 1079-1084

Zhi-Jun, M., et al., "Parameter optimization for a PEMFC model with a hybrid genetic algorithm", International Journal of Energy Research 2006, 30: p. 585-597

Anagnostopoulos, A., et al., "A simulated annealing approach to the traveling tournament problem", Journal of Scheduling, 2006 9(2): p. 177-193

Meireles M., A.P.M., Simões M. G., "A Comprehensive Review for Industrial Applicability of Artificial Neural Networks", IEEE Transactions on Industrial Electronics, 2003, 50(3): p. 585-601

Won-Yong Lee , G.-G.P., Tae-Hyun Yang , Young-Gi Yoon and Chang-Soo Kim "Empirical modeling of polymer electrolyte membrane fuel cell performance using artificial neural networks", International Journal of Hydrogen Energy, 2004, 29(8): p. 961-966

Ou, S., Modeling and optimization of PEM fuel cells, in Institute of Technology, 2006, University of Connecticut: Beijing. p. 129

Haque, M.T.a.K.A.M., "Application of Neural Networks in Power Systems: A Review", World Academy of Science, Engineering and Technology, 2005, 6: p. 53-57

Kalogirou, S.A., "Artificial neural networks in renewable energy systems applications: a review", Renewable and Sustainable Energy Reviews, 2001, 5: p. 373-401

Rivera E.I.O. , R.L.A., "The Z-source converter as an introduction to power electronics and undergraduate research", IEEE 37th annual Frontiers in Education conference, FIE '07, 2007: p. T2C-5-T2C-10

Xu L., L., J., "Comparison study of DC- DC-AC combined converters for integrated starter generator applications", 4th International Power Electronics and Motion Control Conference, IPEMC'04 2004, 3: p. 1130- 1135

Yoon-Ho Kim, H.-W.M., Soo-Hong Kim, Eun-Jin Cheong , Chung-Yeon Won, "A fuel cell system with Z-source inverters and ultracapacitors", 4th International Power Electronics and Motion Control Conference, IPEMC'04, 2004

Shiju, W., Design and hardware implementation of a soft-switched converter for fuel cell applications., in Faculty of the Graduate School. 2006, The University of Texas: Arlington. p. 109

Abu-Qahouq, J.B., I., "Generalized analysis of soft-switching DC-DC converters", in IEEE Proceedings of Circuits and Systems, ISCAS 2000, Geneva

Acik Adnan, A.I.s.k.C., "Active Clamped ZVS Forward Converter With Soft-Switched Synchronous Rectifier", Turk Journal of Electrical Engineering, 2002, 10(3)

Cancelliere, P., et al., "Modeling and Control of a Zero-Current-Switching DC/AC Current-Source Inverter", IEEE Transactions on Industrial Electronics 2007, 54(4): p. 2106-2119

Converter, I.Z.S.-C.B.-d. "Inverting ZCS Switched-Capacitor Bi-directional Converter", in IEEE Power Electronics Specialists Conference, PESC'06, 2006

Ivensky, G., et al., "Reducing IGBT Losses in ZCS Series Resonant Converters", IEEE Transactions on Industrial Electronics, 1999, 46(1): p. 67-74

5

Mixed-Signal Circuits Modelling and Simulations Using Matlab

Drago Strle
University of Ljubljana, Faculty for electrical engineering, Tržaška 25, Ljubljana, Slovenia

1. Introduction

Continuous advances in IC (integrated circuits) processing technologies offer the possibility to produce integrated circuits with increased complexity and capability at a reduced cost. In addition, integrated circuits are composed more and more of heterogeneous embedded systems with various kinds of digital, analogue, and mixed-signal circuits and sensors that are integrated on the same IC. In the future, the number of different embedded systems integrated on the same IC, as well as the number of all modules and the complexity of all modules, will increase. In addition, more and more heterogeneous modules (including analogue and mixed-signal circuits, sensors and actuators, micro-electro-mechanical-systems) will be integrated on the same IC.

Currently, well-established circuit design tools exist for the circuit level design of analogue circuits; even better design tools exist for the systematic and hierarchical design of large digital circuits, including an important aspect of any reliable digital circuit, that is, testability, which is also well covered by existing digital EDA tools (EDA stands for Electronic Design Automation tools). There are no such tools available at the moment for analogue and mixed-signal circuits except maybe Saber. Saber can help to model, design, and simulate a complete mixed signal system in a short amount of time. It may also be used in several analogue and mixed signal blocks and different kinds of integrated sensors. With Saber (Synopsis, 2004) it is possible to model such circuits; however, Matlab/Simulink is much more convenient because of many different toolboxes and libraries available. Matlab, together with Simulink, offers a hierarchical environment and computation engines that make it possible to model, simulate and design complex circuits in a very efficient way on a high hierarchical level. In addition, modules may be described, modelled, simulated, and designed at different abstraction levels and at different levels of detail. For example, analogue circuits could be modelled in a very simple way, that is, taking into consideration only system level aspects like transfer functions; conversely, more details about the implementation, such as offset voltage, gain bandwidth product, slew rate, thermal and 1/f noise, and parameters such as nonlinearity, could be added, when necessary. For digital circuits, it might be necessary to produce a bit-true model early in the design to take all aspects of the design into consideration. Appropriate decisions early in the design can improve the efficiency of the design process. Since large modern IC's usually contain many mixed-signal functions, it is necessary to model and simulate the analogue and the digital

part of the mixed-signal circuits, and possibly also the sensors, with most important non-ideal effects included.
Good examples of complex mixed-signal circuits are high-resolution Σ-Δ AD and/or DA converters. These mixed-signal circuits trade time with accuracy. To get some samples of digital results, many clock samples of analogue circuits must be processed. Using circuit simulator for the verification of such a module would require enormous amount of time. For example, to be able to simulate and calculate the performance of a fifth order modulator using normal EDA tools, more than 1000 hours on a 3GHz computer would be required; this amounts only to some simulations, which of course is not acceptable. The simulation of a high-level model of the same circuit, with most of the important non-ideal effects included, takes only a couple of minutes if the circuit is modelled on a high hierarchical level using the Matlab. In addition, because of the speed of simulation, depending on the specifications, such a methodology could be used to optimize certain parameters and determine the minimum requirements for the building blocks.
This chapter will explain how to model, design, and simulate mixed-signal circuits efficiently by using Matlab and Simulink. The design, modelling and simulation of a fifth order Σ-Δ A/D converter will be used as an example for high-resolution mixed-signal circuit. Generally, analogue and digital parts, and possibly even the sensors, are modelled according to needs. At the beginning of the design process, only high-level models are used; non-ideal effects are not yet implemented and only basic functionality is checked. For example, a transfer function for linear circuits can be used to verify the concept and later on, non-ideal effects are added to the model to verify parameters of analogue circuit implementation. For the digital part, only a discrete time model with double precision of variables are used at the beginning, while later on, a bit-true model is used. In this way, it is possible to verify the correctness of the design at an early stage of the design process. Since a complete mixed-signal circuit is verified on a high hierarchical level, it is possible to simulate all parts of the circuit at the same time and in a very short time. In this way, the efficiency of the design process is highly improved and the design time is shortened. The main objective of this chapter is to explain how we can model and simulate mixed-signal circuits in an efficient way, using a fifth order Σ-Δ A/D converter as an example.
For digital design, one of the trends is to integrate Matlab/Simulink tools into EDA CAD tools (CAD stands for computer aided design) for IC design (Perelroyzen, 2007) in order to facilitate and speed up the design of the digital integrated circuits and more specifically, to simplify and speed-up the design of the digital signal processing modules. For digital DSP (digital signal processing) designs, the Matlab/Simulink environment provides the opportunity to design and use DSP IP blocks and their models, to simulate those models on a functional level. Some companies (Xilinx, Altera, Synplicity) use Simulink for the implementation of IP-based design flow. The design starts with Matlab with the design of the signal processing algorithm; when the algorithm is developed, the corresponding IP blocks are selected from the library and then the RTL (register transfer logic) description of the system is synthesized (Moris, 2004). RTL description is then used in the synthesis of FPGA (field programmable gate array) content. For VLSI (very large scale integrated circuits) design, the net-list is synthesized from the RTL or HDL (hardware description language) code.
The methodology and tools for analogue and mixed-signal circuits that are currently used are based on a Spice-like simulation environment; that is good for simple analogue circuits. As soon as many modules are involved, or, as in modern heterogeneous designs, many

different modules are integrated, no tool exists that can handle the complex nature of such circuits and no tool is currently available for the design of such heterogeneous and complex systems. For such designs, many different specialists must work together. Because of that, there is a real need for heterogeneous design environment and simulation tool that can be used on a high hierarchical level and that integrates the design solutions of many different specialists. We believe that the Matlab/Simulink environment provides the appropriate tools where representations at the high hierarchical level enables the efficient design of digital, analogue, and mixed-signal circuits/systems.

In this chapter, we will present a methodology for the efficient design, modelling, and simulation of mixed-signal integrated circuits using the Matlab/Simulink environment; specifically and as our example, we shall design and model a fifth order Σ-Δ analogue to digital converter module. In Section 2, a short description of a top-down approach for design of a mixed-signal circuit is given, together with a short description of what is needed to design such circuits/systems successfully. It is assumed that the readers know all the basic tips and tricks of the Matlab/Simulink environment. In section 3, the definition of a mixed-signal circuit is given, together with the list of some of the libraries and elements used for modelling such circuits. In section 4, a system level design procedure is given for the Σ-Δ modulator that is used as our example together with the description of the Simulink blocks that are used to model such nonlinear system. In section 5, the basic behaviour, the mathematical model, and the Simulink model of the discrete-time integrator is presented, together with the mathematical and Simulink models of the most important non-ideal effects. Two-simulation results will be presented in this section: the Spectrum of a BS (bit-stream) including non-ideal effects and a "scatter" plot of the SnR that results from the Monte Carlo analysis. Section 6 presents the decimator bit-true modelling and design, and a complete mixed-signal circuit/system simulation result.

2. Top down design approach

To verify a functional property of a complex system early in the design phase, the design starts from a simplified description at a high hierarchical level. This then proceeds to the modelling of each constituent building block in a more detailed way. Eventually, such a modelling is applied to the transistor level. Later on, the description and modelling of each constituent module is improved by adding lower level detailed information that comes either from experience or from the detailed design process that use other design tools and simulation results. For example, for analogue interface circuits, the following might be important parameters: thermal noise, 1/f noise, open loop gain, gain bandwidth, slew rate, nonlinearities, sampling, kT/C noise; for the DSP, on the other hand, a bit-true model might be important to be able to see the influences. For example, one circuit level simulation of a simple 2nd order Δ-Σ modulator using Spectre simulator requires more than 160 hours of the processor time; such simulation makes sense when the design is finished, that is, the simulation acts as a final check to see the effect of parasitic capacitances, for example. If such simulation tools are used throughout the entire design process, the simulation should be repeated several times, so the time needed for the complete design cycle would be prohibitively long. When such a modulator is modelled on a high hierarchical level that includes the important non-ideal effects, the simulation needs only a couple of minutes. This means that such a tool could really be used very efficiently: once the model fulfils the specifications, including the specifications of the most important non-ideal effects, the model could be taken as a specification limit for the detailed circuit design. Once the detailed circuit and layout design is finished, the results of the "Spice" simulations of each module are taken and added into the Matlab model, and the whole simulation cycle could be repeated again on a high hierarchical level. This methodology is very efficient; it shortens the design time for mixed-signal circuits considerably.

3. Mixed-signal integrated circuits

Mixed-signal integrated circuits contain analogue and digital modules that are integrated on a single semiconductor chip; these circuits are closely interconnected and interrelated. It is difficult or not appropriate to design, model, and simulate analogue and digital modules separately. A very simple example from a complexity point of view are the Δ-Σ A/D or D/A converters that include low noise analogue signal processing blocks as well as digital blocks that are used for dynamic element matching, decimation, clock-form generation, and others. Furthermore, in modern heterogeneous systems, different kinds of sensors are integrated and their operation quality is closely related to the operation of analogue and digital interface circuits for data acquisition, for controlling of the properties and for driving the sensors. Digital signal processing is included as the integral part to extract useful information and/or to prepare/correct the driving signals; an example of such a complex system is the integrated inertial measurement system, which, besides the analogue and the digital signal processing modules, also includes the MEMS accelerometers and Gyro sensors (Strle & Kempe, 2007).

For a mixed-signal heterogeneous system, there are no synthesis algorithms available and most of the work must be done "by-hand" by specialists, that is, by a system designer, a mixed-signal and/or analogue designer together with a digital designer. Therefore, it is very important for the whole design team to use a common design environment where everybody could participate efficiently in the design procedure. In addition to the design of a mixed signal circuit on a high hierarchical level, the design of functional tests for a mixed-signal system can be performed and verified on a high hierarchical level by using Matlab/Simulink. This makes the design procedure even more efficient. Last but not least, during the design of a mixed signal circuit, a Monte Carlo simulation might be needed to verify efficiently whether the specifications are fulfilled for the whole spread of certain process parameters.

3.1 Basic building blocks of mixed-signal circuits

Analogue circuits are composed of a variety of modules built of CT (continuous time) and/or DT (discrete time) circuits. The operation of CT circuits (linear or nonlinear) is best described by a system of linear or nonlinear algebraic and/or differential equations, while the discrete time systems are best described by a system of linear and/or nonlinear difference equations. Linear systems of both kinds can be described by corresponding S-domain (for CT circuits) or Z-domain (for DT circuits) transfer functions. Usually the System on Chip (SoC) contains a mixture of some or all of the mentioned modules that are implemented either in an analogue and/or in a digital way. Some of the most popular high-level building blocks that are used in mixed-signal systems are the following:

- Analogue signal processing blocks
  - Amplifiers, comparators, switches, trans-conductors,
  - CT filters, S-C filters, S-I filters

  - Mixers
  - Signal generators
  - A/D and D/A converters
  - And many others
- Digital signal processing blocks
  - Adders, multipliers, CPU
  - Filters, mixers
  - Memory, Ram, counters, shifters
  - I/O

Many other blocks not mentioned above might be needed for a complete description of a SoC (System on Chip).

3.2 Simulink blocks that can be used for mixed-signal modules

Matlab/Simulink offers many different libraries. In this chapter we will use only the most common libraries and the most common elements that are available in many versions of Matlab/Simulink. Some of the libraries and some of the library elements are listed below. The meanings and the settings of the important parameters of each individual block will be explained when we will use a particular block in our Σ-Δ modulator design example. The libraries (bold face list) and the most useful blocks within a library for modelling mixed signal circuits are the following:

- **Commonly used blocks**
  - Constant
  - Gain
  - In, Out, Terminator
  - Sum, Product
  - Scope
  - Data Type Conversion
  - Subsystem definition
  - Saturation
  - Etcetera
- **Continuous time blocks**
  - Derivative
  - Integrator, Transfer function, Zero-Pole
  - State-Space
  - Variable Time Delay
- **Discontinuous**
  - Saturation, Relay
  - Dead Zone
  - Quantizer
- **Discrete time blocks**
  - Zero-Order Hold
  - Integer Delay, Unit delay
  - Discrete time Transfer function
  - Discrete time Zero-Pole
  - Discrete State-Space

  - Discrete time Integrator
- **Logic and Bit Operations**
- **Math operations**
  - Gain, Product, Slider Gain, Bias
  - Sum, Sum of Elements, Product, Divide, Dot Product
  - Sign, MinMax
  - Math Function
- **Ports and Subsystems**
  - In, Out
  - Subsystem
- **Signal attributes**
  - Data Type Conversion
  - Signal Conversion
- **Sinks**
  - Out, Terminator
  - Display, Scope
  - To File, To workspace
- **Sources**
  - Constant, In
  - From File
  - Sine Wave, Pulse generator, Repeating sequence
  - Signal generator, Step
  - Band-Limited White Noise, Uniform Random Number
- **User defined functions**
  - Fcn, MATLAB Fcn

Of course, for different systems, it might be necessary to use some additional libraries such as:

- Communication library
- Signal processing library
- Control system library

4. System level design

The design, modelling, and simulations of a complex mixed-signal module using Matlab/Simulink will be presented, using a fifth order Σ-Δ A/D converter as a design example. Σ-Δ converters are currently very popular because of the possibility to achieve high-resolution A/D conversion with great efficiency using the elements from VLSI process with characteristics that are not very good and stable. Σ-Δ converter is composed mostly of analogue modules and small digital circuit for generating clock signals, executing dynamic element matching algorithm and in addition, a digital decimation filter that is a fixed-point digital circuit. Many books and articles have been written about the subject; two of them are (Schrier & Temes, 2005) and (De la Rosa, 2011). Most of them deal with basic synthesis algorithms and properties. However, practical design recommendations of how to bring such designs into life in the shortest time possible are not presented in those books. Predicting final characteristics early on in the design, taking into considerations the most important non-ideal effects based on real circuit behaviour (kT/C noise, thermal and 1/f noise, offset voltages, finite gain-bandwidth product (GBW), finite open loop gain (A0), slew rate (SR), spread of parameters due to technology spread, stability issues, latency issues, meta-stability issues, etcetera), are usually not taken into considerations. In this chapter, we will try to model the additional characteristics that are essential for a successful design and use this information as a kind of specifications for the circuit design process.

4.1 The basics of a Σ-Δ A/D converter design

The design of an A/D converter usually starts with specifications. The simple specifications may be the following:

- Nyquist rate after decimation (BW=425kHz),
- Required signal to noise ratio (SnR>80dB),
- Required Harmonic distortions (THD≤80dB),
- Maximum signal level and its spectral contents,
- Reference level,
- Supply voltage and supply current, and others.

The data in brackets are the specifications of our sample A/D converter. Usually, the designer selects the architecture according to her/his experience. We will select a Σ-Δ A/D converter architecture with as small oversampling ratio as possible and as small order as possible in order to have as small power consumption as possible. Since the required HD is very demanding, we do not want to use any of the available linearization and/or dynamic-element-matching techniques. The natural choice in that case is to use a single bit internal quantizer and single bit internal D/A converter. It is difficult to design such an A/D converter correctly. The design presents many design challenges from the system level to the modelling and the circuit level because it needs a deep understanding of the system level design as well as the circuit level design issues. In addition, for a one bit internal quantizer, the circuit is highly nonlinear, which means that it is not possible to complete the design using simple AC design principles, transformations, and methods that are valid for the design of "linear" circuits. Despite the fact that linear models offer a simplified insight into the operation of the Σ-Δ modulator, the design is not complete without extensive simulations where influences of nonlinearity and other circuit parameters to the SnR (signal to noise ratio), BW (bandwidth), HD (harmonic distortions), noise, and stability may be checked. Modelling on a high hierarchical level makes it possible to explore the design space very efficiently and the results of high-level simulations could be used as inputs to the circuit design.

4.2 Synthesis of a discrete time noise transfer function

The NTF (noise-transfer-function) can be synthesized according to the definition given in subsection 4.1. The selected implementation might be an S-C (switched capacitor) loop transfer function implementation and therefore a discrete time model is selected. The simplest way to synthesize the noise transfer function is to use the appropriate tool; one such tool that is using Matlab is described in (Schrier & Temes, 2005). The link to download a latest version of toolbox called "delsig" is given in (Schreier, 2009). With the help of this toolbox, it is possible to synthesize the required NTF(z) in an efficient way; z-domain equation for the specifications given in subsection 4.1 is given in equation (1). Fig. 1 shows the plot of the |NTF(z)| and the pass-band detail.

$$NTF(z) = \frac{(z-1)(z^2-1.998\cdot z+1)(z^2-1.994\cdot z+1)}{(z-0.8116)(z^2-1.676\cdot z+0.7128)(z^2-1.837\cdot z+0.8782)} \quad (1)$$

It is possible to implement such transfer function in many different ways. Based on additional requirements such as small power supply consumption and stability under different signal conditions, we selected feed-forward architecture with only one feedback, presented in Fig. 2. It has a one-bit internal quantizer, a one bit internal D/A converter, and a feed-forward structure with one feedback coefficient b_{ref1}.

Coefficients α_0, δ_0, $\beta_{1,2}$, $\gamma_{1,2}$, $\eta_{1,2}$ and $\lambda_{1,2}$ from (2) are related in a complex way to the feedback and feed-forward coefficients represented by vectors **a, g, b, c** of the circuit shown on Fig.2. They can be calculated using function: **[a,g,b,c]** = realizeNTF(NTF, FORM, STF) from package "delsig" (Schreier, 2009), where **[a,g,b,c]** are vectors of coefficients from Fig. 2. The NTF (noise transfer function) is given by (1); STF (signal transfer function) STF=1 and FORM refers to the form of the architecture and are selected as the feed-forward structure.

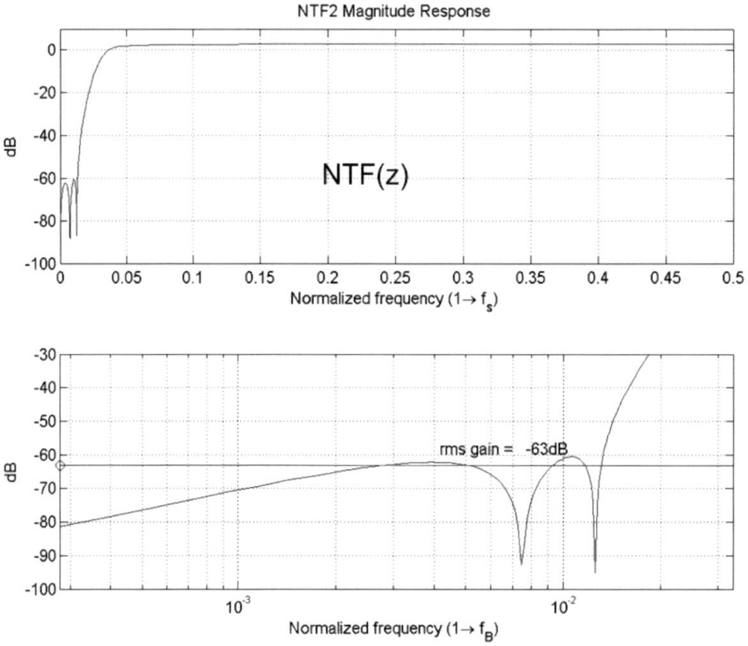

Fig. 1. Noise transfer function plot of (1). Upper plot: |NTF(z)| from 0 to 0.5*fs. Lower plot: |NTF(z)| pass-band detail

Input signal is added to the first integrator through coefficient b_{in1} and to the quantizer input through coefficient b6. The state variables $x_1(z)$ through $x_5(z)$ are the outputs of discrete time integrators. The coefficients g_1 and g_2 determine the positions of complex conjugate poles, while weighted state variables with weights a_1 through a_5 that are added together, with weighted input signal (b_6), contribute to the signal at the input of one bit internal quantizer. In this way, a complex conjugate zeros of (1) are formed. A linear model is formed if the internal quantizer is replaced by an adder that adds signal $x_6(z)$ with quantization noise $Q(z)$ and use gain $k=1$. One can determine the poles and the zeroes of noise transfer function $NTF_x(z)$ of the block diagram on Fig. 2. using symbolic and optimization toolbox of the Matlab and some "hand" written state space equations. The result is given in (2).

$$NTF_C(z) = \frac{V(z)}{Q(z)} = \frac{(z-\alpha_0)(z^2-\beta_1 z+\gamma_1)(z^2-\beta_2 z+\gamma_2)}{(z-\delta_0)(z^2-\eta_1 z+\lambda_1)(z^2-\eta_2 z+\lambda_2)} \tag{2}$$

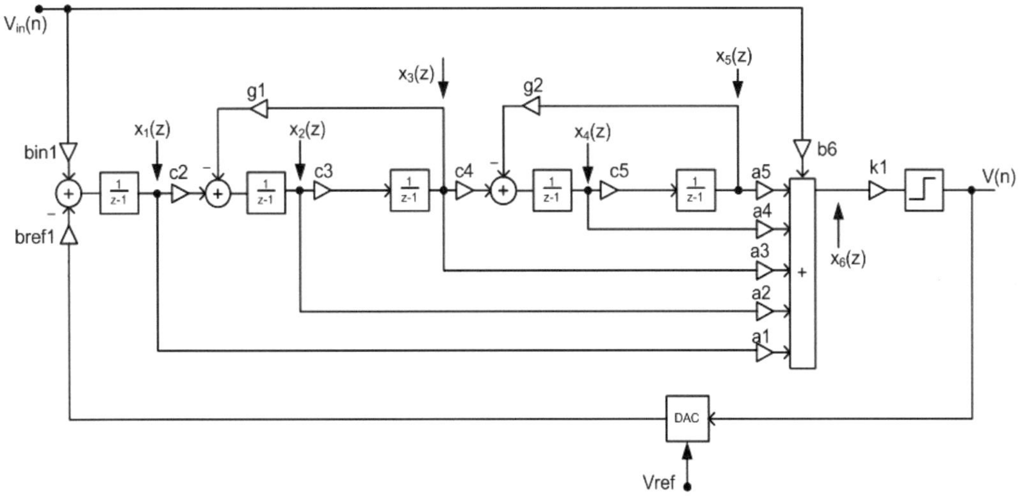

Fig. 2. Block diagram of a fifth order Σ-Δ modulator with feed-forward architecture. State variables $x_i(z)$ are outputs of the integrators

All coefficients are calculated by assuming the linear model of the Σ-Δ modulator. Of course, coefficients obtained in this way do not produce appropriately scaled state variables of the modulators' loop transfer function and further scaling steps will be needed; these are explained in the following subsections. For NTF(z) from (1), STF(z)=1, and for the selected feed-forward architecture the coefficients are (3):

$$\begin{aligned} \mathbf{a}^T &= [1.43\ 1.35\ 0.98\ 0.53\ 0.067] \\ \mathbf{g}^T &= [0.0090\ \ 0.0633] \\ \mathbf{b}^T &= [0.23\ 0\ 0\ 0\ 0\ 0.5] \\ \mathbf{c}^T &= [0.23\ 0.33\ 0.25\ 0.18\ 0.099] \end{aligned} \tag{3}$$

To check the validity of the synthesis algorithm, we can calculate the spectrum of the linear model of the modulators' bit-stream *V(n)*. The state space description of the linear model of the circuit from Fig. 2 is defined in (4).

$$\begin{aligned} y(n) &= \mathbf{a}^T\mathbf{x}(n) + b_6 v_{in}(n) \\ v(n) &= k_1 y(n) + q(n) \\ x(n) &= \mathbf{A}\mathbf{x}(n) + \mathbf{b}_{in} v_{in}(n) + b_{ref} v(n) v_{ref} \end{aligned} \tag{4}$$

The elements of the (4) are defined in (5) and (6). The meanings of the symbols are the following: $\mathbf{x}(n)$ is a vector of state variables, $v_{in}(n)$ is input voltage, $y(n)$ is the output of the loop-filter, $q(n)$ is quantization noise, and $v(n)$ is a bit-stream output. The spectrum obtained by the FFT function from Matlab is given in Fig. 3.

$$\mathbf{A} = \begin{bmatrix} 1 & 0 & 0 & 0 & 0 \\ c_2 & 1 & -g_1 & 0 & 0 \\ 0 & c_3 & 1 & 0 & 0 \\ 0 & 0 & c_4 & 1 & -g_2 \\ 0 & 0 & 0 & c_5 & 1 \end{bmatrix} \tag{5}$$

$$\mathbf{b}_{in}^T = \mathbf{b}(1:5); \quad b_6 = \mathbf{b}(6); \quad b_{ref} = \mathbf{c}(1) \tag{6}$$

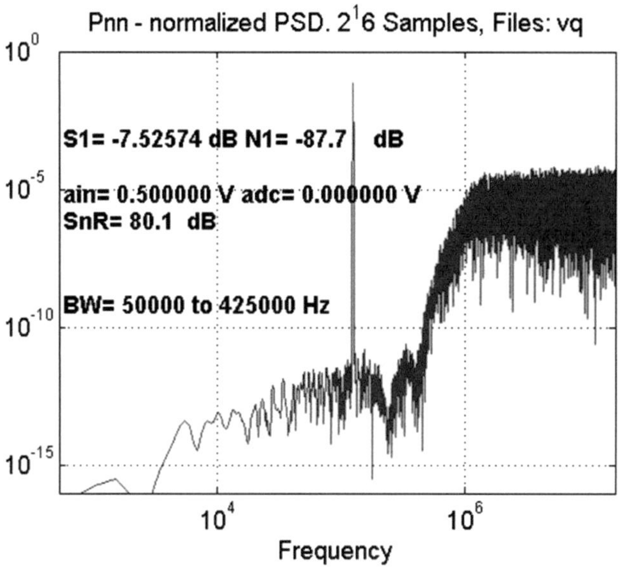

Fig. 3. Power spectral density of the bit-stream of ideal linear model of Sigma-Delta modulator. The output signal v(n) is a consequence of input signal v_{in} (a sine-wave) with frequency 125kHz, amplitude 0.5V_{rms} and sampling frequency f_s=32 MHz

Further checks require a nonlinear model of a one bit quantizer. For the first tests, a "signum" function instead of linear model of a quantizer can be used. In that case, the description is similar to (4) except that v*(n)* is modelled by a *sign()* function. The Matlab simulation result using nonlinear state-space description (7), with sine-wave input at a frequency of 125 kHz and an amplitude of 0.5 V_{rms} , is presented in Fig. 4.

$$\begin{aligned} y(n) &= \mathbf{a}^T\mathbf{x}(n) + b_6 v_{in}(n) \\ v(n) &= sign\left[k_1 y(n)\right] \\ x(n) &= \mathbf{A}\mathbf{x}(n) + \mathbf{b}_{in} v_{in}(n) + b_{ref} v(n) v_{ref} \end{aligned} \tag{7}$$

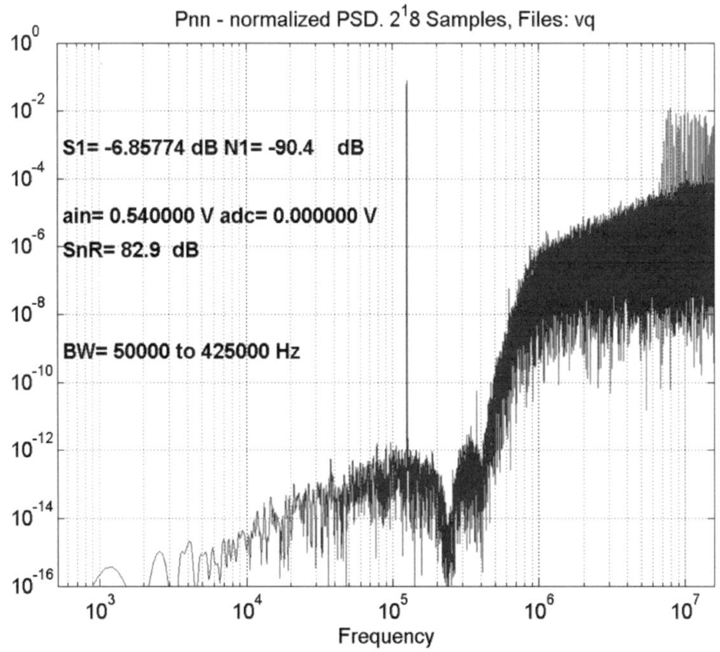

Fig. 4. Power spectral density of the bit-stream of a nonlinear model (7) at the output of a Sigma-Delta modulator v(n) with input signal v_{in} that is a sine-wave with a frequency 125kHz, an amplitude of $0.5V_{rms}$; sampling frequency is f_s=32 MHz

Simulation results in Fig. 3 and Fig. 4 show almost identical spectrums. The main spectral component at 125 kHz is due to the input signal and the noise spectrum is a consequence of noise shaping of quantization noise of 1 bit internal quantizer. The biggest difference between linear and nonlinear model appears at high frequency; the quantization noise spectrum of the nonlinear model is shaped differently for frequencies above 1MHz. In addition, for the nonlinear model, the "tones" can be observed close to fovs/2 as sharp peaks of the spectrum. "Tones" can be removed by adding the appropriate dither signal to the quantizer input. The procedure for detecting tones and a methodology for their removal is presented in subsection 4.4.

4.3 Simulink model

The Simulink model of ideal Σ-Δ modulator is equivalent to the block diagram presented in Fig. 2. All coefficients are available in the work-space and are set in a Matlab m-file according to the values given in (3). The Simulink symbols used and the settings of some of their parameters are the following:

- **Gain:** All coefficients are implemented with the symbol, "Gain" (Fig. 5). The main parameter is the gain factor that multiplies the input signal to get the output signal. The coefficients are defined in the m-file. After running the m-file, the coefficients are available in the Matlab workspace. In pane "Main", the gain factor and the "Sample time" are defined. In the "Signal attributes" pane the min-max values for the output and the data type of the output are set. They are set to their default values. In pane "Parameter Attributes", the parameter attributes are set as follows: min-max values and output data types are set to "Inherit: Same as input", so their data types are double. The rounding in this case is of no importance since the variables and constants are represented in a double floating-point format.

- **Zero-Order-Hold:** Each input connection of the modulator is assumed to have a continuous time signal; therefore, it is sampled and held by using the Zero-Order-Hold symbol, which closely follows the behaviour of the S-C circuits. Signals like In1 and Vref from the modulators block diagram are equipped with the Zero-Order-Hold element (Fig. 6). Sampling period of the block is set to T_s.

Fig. 5. Gain symbol

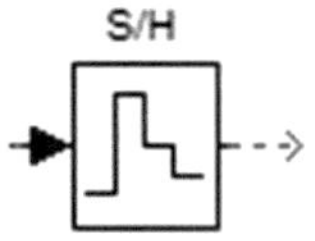

Fig. 6. Zero-Order-Hold symbol

- **Sum:** The block "Sum" (Fig. 7) adds input signals to get the output. The number of input signals is dependent on the number of + or - symbols that appear in the "list of signs". In our example, several differently shaped "sum" symbols are used: ++, +−, and +++++++. Number of + or − symbols signify how many and what kind of inputs are used (these are present in the "List of signs"). In addition, the shape of the symbol can be selected (round or rectangle). For example, for feed-forward architecture, the sum of weighted state variables appears at the input of the quantizer. In the same pane, the sampling time is set as "-1", which means that it is "Inherited". In pane "Signal attributes", the "Accumulator data type" is selected as either "Inherit" or "double"; the output min-max values are not limited and the output data type is selected as "Inherit". Since input signal data type is double, all other signals are also double.

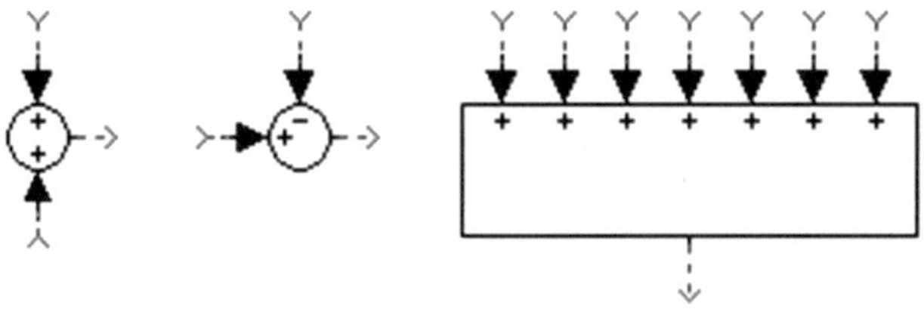

Fig. 7. The Sum symbols

- **Product:** The block which multiplies v(n) (bit-stream BS) with reference voltage is a "Product" shown in Fig. 8. It is possible to define the "Number of inputs" and the "type of multiplication". In our case two inputs need simple element-wise multiplication. In addition, Sample time is set to "-1=Inherited". In the pane "Signal Attributes", the output minimum and output maximum can be defined. The default value is "unlimited", while the output data type is set to "Inherited", and therefore the data type is double.

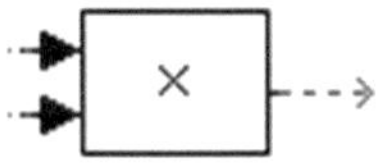

Fig. 8. The Product symbol

- **Relay:** The comparator can be in the simplest way modelled as a relay. The parameters that must be set are the following: Switch on point (VH), Switch off point (VL), Output when on (1), Output when off (-1), Enabled zero crossing, and sample time (-1=Inherited). The switching levels are defined in the main Matlab m-file. In our case, a small hysteresis is built-in and taken into consideration as follows: VH=1mV and VL=-1mV. The output levels (BS) are set to ±1.

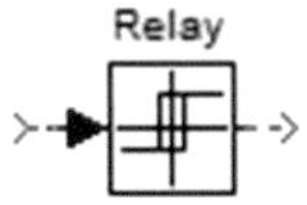

Fig. 9. The Relay symbol

- **DT integrator:** The last element used in the simplified model of our example modulator is a discrete time integrator shown in Fig. 10. In the ideal and simplest case, it can be modelled by a discrete transfer function with pole at z=1, followed by a Zero-Order-Hold block. The transfer function coefficients are defined in the "Main" pane of the parameter settings, with Numerator coefficients set to [1] and Denominator coefficients set to [1 -1]. In addition, the Sample time is set to T_s, and is defined in the main Matlab routine before running the Simulink simulation. The State attributes in this case are unimportant and default settings can be accepted. All five integrators are equivalent for the ideal Simulink model.

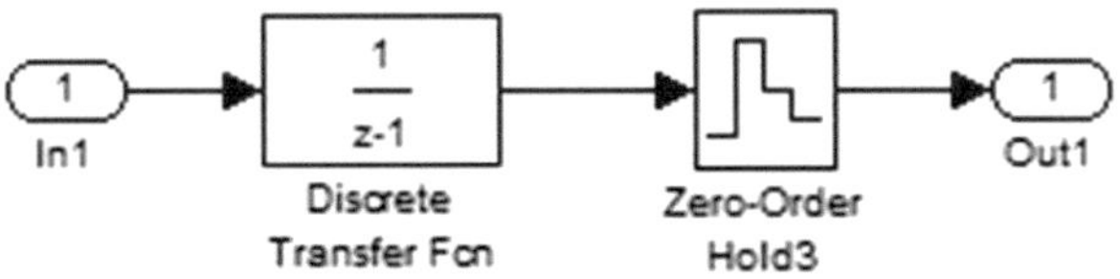

Fig. 10. Discrete time integrator model used in example modulator

- **Top level**: To run the simulation and to store some results, a top-level scheme is needed that consists of system to be simulated (Modulator_5th_order on Fig. 11), signal generators, and some elements that help store the selected results to the workspace or to the disk. The scope (osciloskope) is useful for observing some internal signals in time domain.The top-level Simulink scheme for our example modulator is presented in Fig. 11. It consists of a sine-wave generator, a constant for the reference input, the circuit to be modelled and simulated (in our case, a fifth order modulator), the scope, and two sinks with names bs_mod5.mat and Comp_in.mat that store the results to the disk.

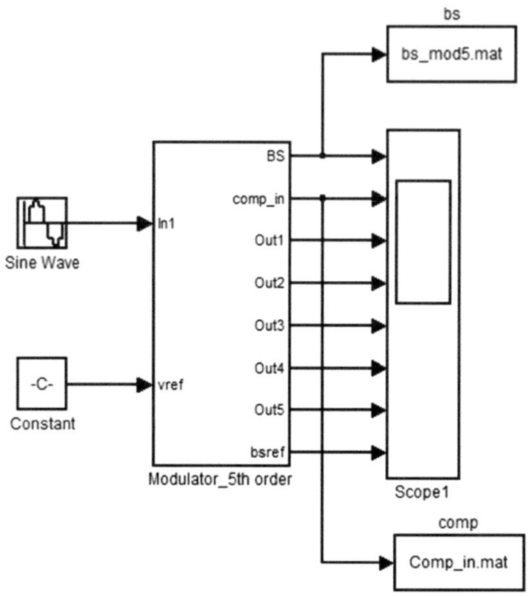

Fig. 11. Top level Simulink symbol with generators, constants, and sinks

- **Sine-Wave**: The definition of sine-wave signals needs many parameters with the following settings: "Sine Type" is Time based, "Amplitude = ain_real", "Bias = adc", "Frequency = 2*pi*fin", "Phase = 0", and "Sample Time= Ts". Variables ain_real, adc, fin and Ts are defined in the main Matlab routine and are available in the Matlab workspace.
- **Constant:** This is used to define the reference voltage of the modulator. The parameters are "Constant value = Vref_real" and "Sample Time = Ts"; both are defined in a Matlab workspace.
- **To file:** The data or variables are written to the disc. Two such blocks are available in Fig. 11: bs and comp. The data are stored to the files bs_mod5.mat and Comp_in.mat. The Parameters are the following: "Filename" that is set to, for example, bs_mod5.mat; "Variable name" is set to bs; "Decimation" is set to 1 (all samples are stored); and "Sample time" is set to Ts that is defined in the Matlab work-space. The stored data can be used for further analysis and plots.
- **Scope:** It is possible to observe the time-domain responses of the different connected signals. Fig. 12 shows time-domain signals of simulated modulator for: BS, Comp_in, and Out1 to Out5 that are state variables x(1) to x(5) and bsref that is a feedback signal BS multiplied by Vref.

The time-domain simulation results that use the ideal Simulink model, which is composed of the symbols defined above are presented in Fig. 12. The simulation parameters are specified in the Fig. 12 caption text. The signals observed are marked on the left hand side of the picture; BS stands for bit-stream, Comp_in for comparator input signal, X1 through X5 for state variables (outputs of the integrators), and BS_ref for the BS multiplied by the reference signal. The spectrum of a bit-stream signal for the same simulation is presented in Fig. 13; it is almost equal to the spectrum obtained by simulation of an ideal nonlinear Matlab model defined with (7) and presented on Fig. 4.

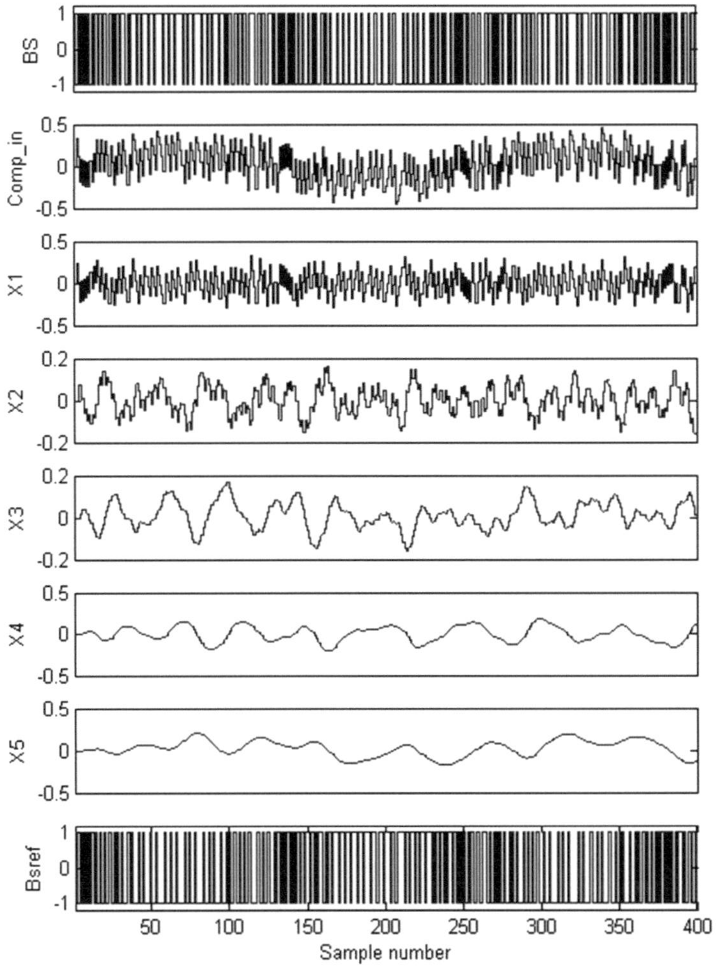

Fig. 12. Simulation results for 5th order modulator with vref_real=1, ain_real=0.54, fin=125kHz, fs=32MHz

4.4 Limit cycles analysis

Σ-Δ modulators are nonlinear devices/systems and therefore some characteristic problems related to such systems can happen. An important and difficult problem is related to "Limit-Cycles" (Mann, 1999) and (Strle, 2006). It is possible that under certain conditions, the spectral components appear in the base-band ("tones") that are not present in the input signal. This problem is severe in low order modulators but also not negligible in the high order modulators, where it is not so pronounced compared to low order modulators because of higher order noise shaping. Because of the non-linearity of the loop, it is very difficult to analyze the problem theoretically and no analytic result exists for high order modulators. A possible way to analyze the problem is to use a High level Simulink model and to perform many systematically prepared simulations at different conditions to locate eventual limit-cycles. The Matlab/Simulink environment is efficient because simulations run on a high hierarchical level. The results of a set of such simulations are presented in Fig.

14 as a 3D plot of spectrums, where the x-axis represents the frequency, y-axis represents DC input voltage, and the z-axis represents the PSD (power spectrum density) of a bit-stream. For our experiment a small AC signal with an amplitude of V_{inac}=68 uV and a frequency of 250 kHz is connected to the input of the modulator at different DC input voltages (V_{inDC}=-5mV to +5mV). On the left part of Fig. 14, the peaks ("tones") can be observed at a certain DC input voltages even in the base-band. A spectrum is presented for the original fifth order modulator from Fig. 2.

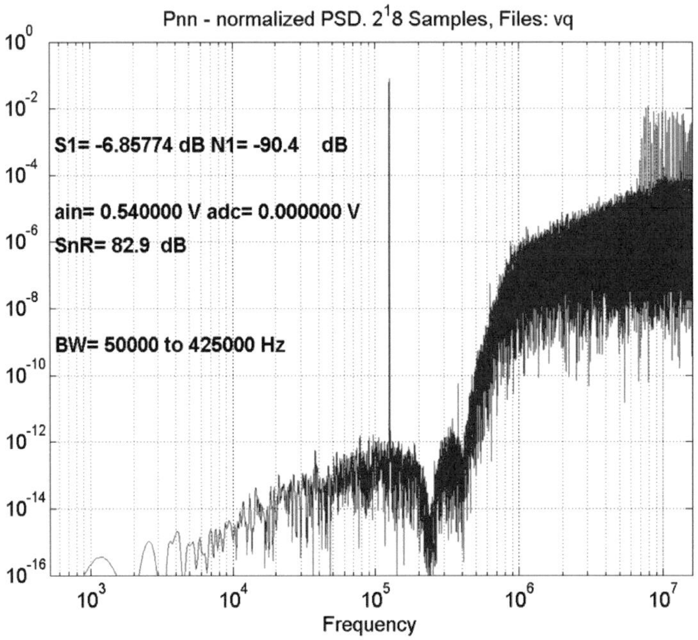

Fig. 13. Spectrum of a BS (bit-stream) for ideal Simulink model of a fifth order modulator

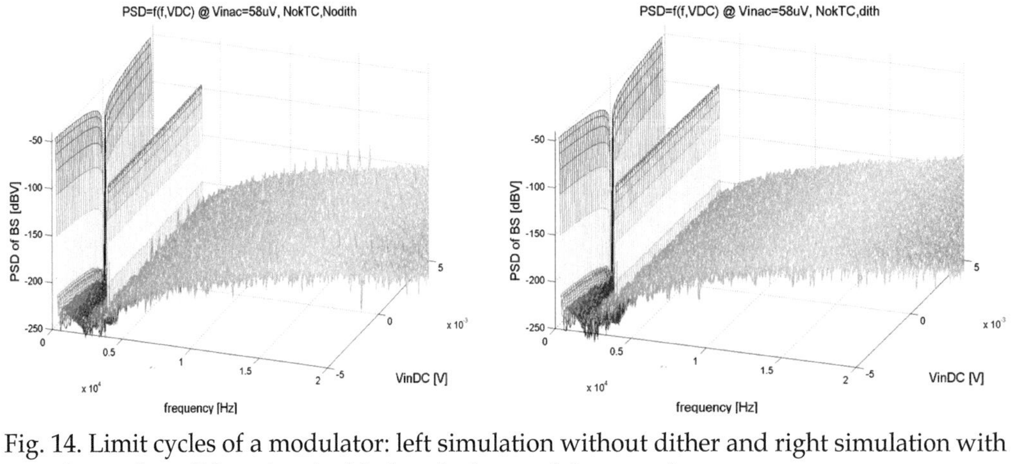

Fig. 14. Limit cycles of a modulator: left simulation without dither and right simulation with pseudo-random dither signal added to the input of the quantizer

The right side of Fig. 14 shows the spectrum after adding a dither signal to the quantizer input. A dither signal is a one bit pseudo-random signal connected to the input of the internal quantizer, according to the Simulink scheme on Fig. 15. The weight of the dither signal is 0.3*Vref. A pseudo-random-noise signal (PRS) (Zepernick, 2005) that is used as a "dither" is for the simulation purposes generated off-line and stored into the file. A dither signal de-correlates "tones" and spreads their energy over the entire band, which is then shaped by the noise transfer function of the modulator. A 3D plot of a bit-stream's PSD after adding the dither signal is presented on the right side of Fig. 14. The tones have disappeared but there is some small noise penalty in the base-band; the SnR is reduced by approximately 1.5 dB.

4.5 Scaling

The initial implementation of a discrete-time loop filter with feed-forward structure does not take into consideration the real voltage levels of state-variables at maximum input voltage signal, as well as the real reference voltage. At the beginning of the design process, the state variables are almost arbitrary; their relationship is such that poles and zeroes are implemented, while the state variable levels are not defined. The scaling is a semi-automatic procedure where maximum levels of the state-variables are adjusted to the required values. Scaling is needed to optimize signal levels in comparison to the noise levels and to adjust maximum voltage levels of the integrator outputs. In this way the performance parameters like SnR (signal to noise ratio), HD (harmonic distortions), SR (slew-rate) requirements are optimized. In the first step the real reference voltage (vref_real=0.6V for our example modulator) and the maximum input signal voltage (vin_real=0.54V) are connected to the modulator. A long simulation is then performed to get the distribution of state-variables. Long simulations are needed because Σ-Δ modulator is a chaotic device and it is difficult to predict voltage levels of the state variables in a short simulation; the spectrum may contain some very low frequency components. The min/max values are obtained from the simulation results in the second step (see $|x_{i\_\max}|$ on the left side of Fig. 16). In the third step, the desired limit $L(i)$ of each state variable is compared to the $|x_{i\_\max}|$ and the vector of scaling coefficients **s** is calculated using (8).

$$s(i) = \frac{L(i)}{|xi\_\max|} \quad i = 1,2,.... \tag{8}$$

In the fourth step, the level of each integrator output is adjusted by multiplying all input coefficients that are connected to the integrator. For example, coefficients b_{in} and b_{ref} are multiplied by $s(1)$ to adjust the maximum level of $x(1)$; at the same time, the coefficient c_2 is divided by $s(1)$ to keep the positions of the poles unchanged. This scaling procedure is repeated for all state variables and for all coefficients using Matlab. After scaling, maximum state-variable voltage levels are adjusted to the desired level, as shown on the right side of Fig. 16. In a real circuit, the required voltage range of state variables is dependent on the architecture, technology, and design of the modules. Histogram plots for all state variables before and after the scaling procedure are, for our example modulator, shown in Fig. 16.

The maximum levels of the state variables for our example modulator are optimized to the following levels: $|x(1)|_{\max} = 0.4\,V$ down to $|x(5)|_{\max} = 0.2\,V$. All other state variables are scaled in such a way that the levels are linearly distributed between 0.4 V to 0.2 V. Such

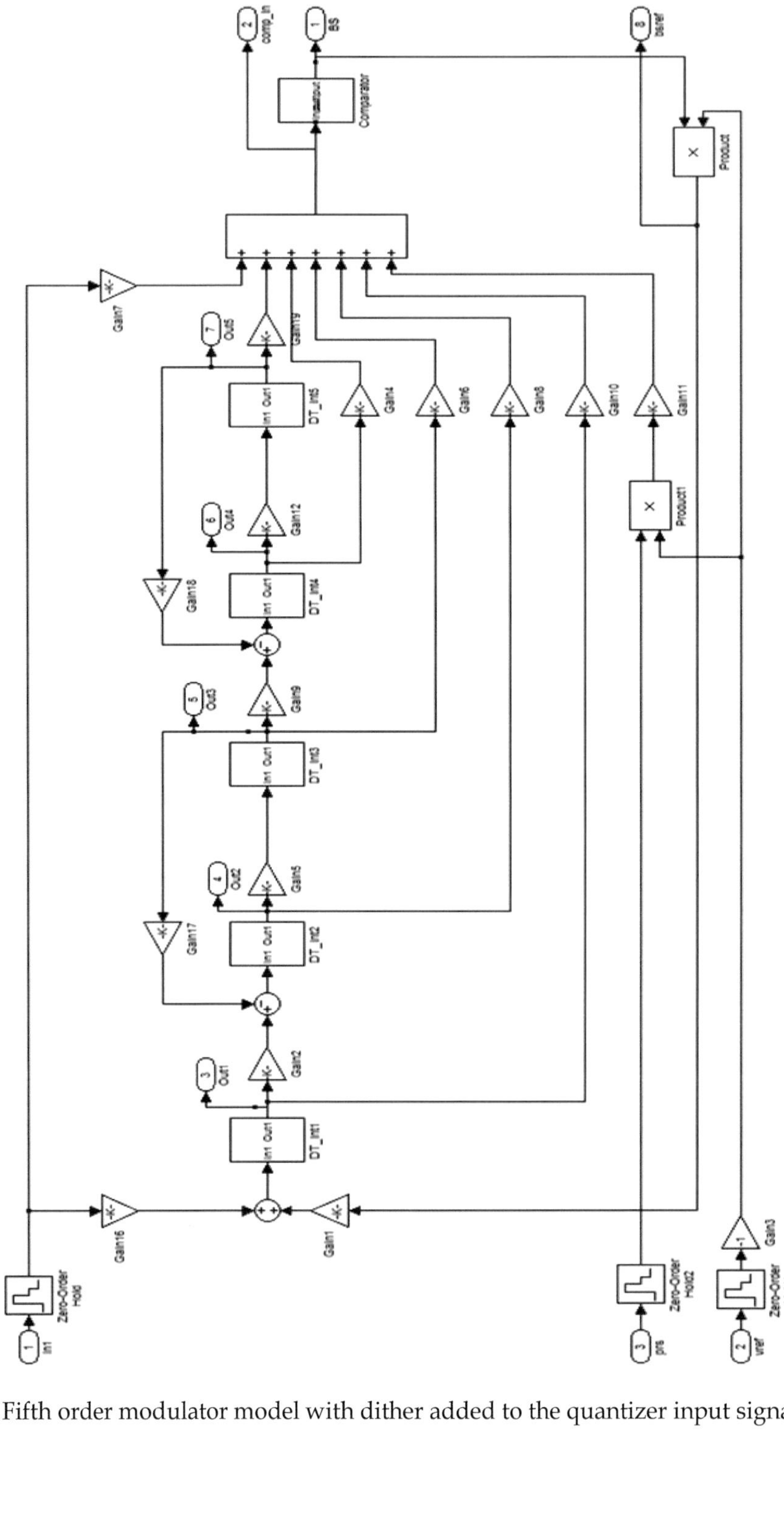

Fig. 15. Fifth order modulator model with dither added to the quantizer input signal

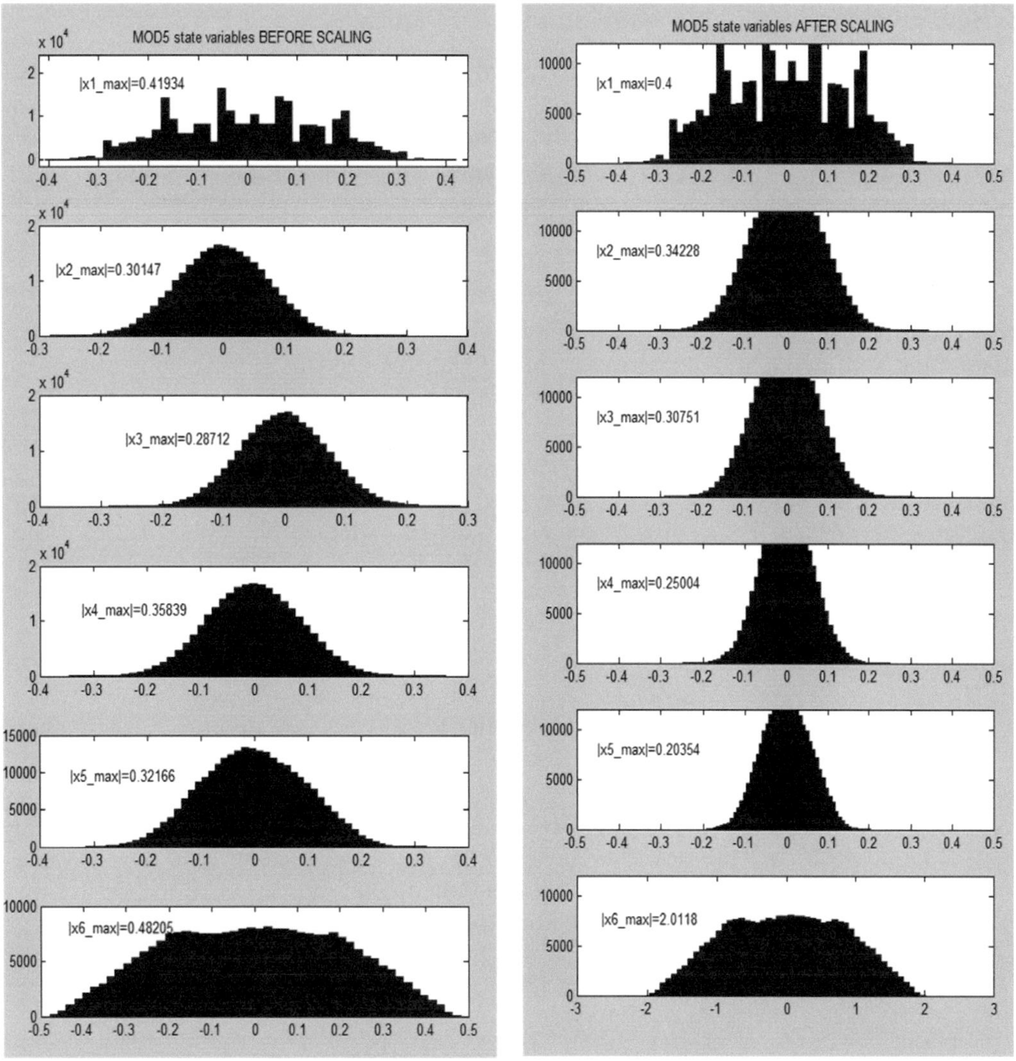

Fig. 16. Histograms of state variables for Vin=0.54 V and Vref=0.6V. Left figure: before scaling. Right histogram: after scaling

limits are selected because of the following stability considerations. With a large input voltage, the modulator could become unstable because of the high order loop filter and because the feedback cannot follow the input voltage. Therefore, for input voltage larger than the selected limit, the first state variable enters the saturation of the first integrator and reduces the loop filter order, and hence, the conditions for stability are improved. For slightly higher input voltage, the second integrating stage enters the saturation, and so on. Maximum voltage at the quantizer input ($|x_{6\_max}|$) is not important for the stability reasons but for the proper operation of the quantizer; a big input voltage is allowed (2 V in our example modulator) since we know that a passive adder before the quantizer will contain some parasitic capacitances that will reduce the level. The only requirement for the input signal of a one bit quantizer is that it is big enough to reliably drive the internal quantizer.

5. High level modelling of the mixed-signal circuits

Up to now, a discrete time loop-filter was implemented using ideal discrete time integrator transfer functions (see Fig. 2). The model is good enough if we are not interested in real implementation and circuit parameter influences. In real designs, it is beneficial if we can predict the influence of circuit parameters at a high hierarchical level; it is even better if we can determine the required circuit parameters from a system level model and simulation results.

The first step in including circuit non-ideal effects is to select the possible implementation of the discrete time integrators. In our case, we selected a Switched-Capacitor (S-C) implementation of the loop transfer function, which is composed of switched capacitor integrators, and therefore, it is necessary to develop the models of their behaviour. The procedure is defined in the following subsections.

5.1 Modelling Switched-Capacitor (S-C) circuits

Switched capacitor circuits are used in analogue and mixed signal circuits for a very long time. One of the first books that treated the subject systematically was *"Analog MOS Integrated Circuits for signal processing"* written by R. Gregorian and G.C. Temes (Gregorian, 1986); many other books about the subject were published until today. The most important block used extensively in most of the switched-capacitor circuits is the parasitic-capacitance insensitive discrete-time S-C integrator with a simplified electrical scheme presented in Fig. 17. The circuit is composed of switches, capacitors, and operational amplifier. The difference between left and right S-C integrator is the connection of phase *Φ1* and *Φ2* and how they drive the switches. For the circuit to function properly, the phases should be non-overlapping signals.

Assuming that input and output signals are discrete-time signals that change their states at the end of signal *Φ2*, we can describe the operation of the S-C integrator on the left (non-inverting integrator) by writing the difference equation that relate the output signal of the integrator and the input signal at discrete times according to (9). The C_1 and C_{int} are input and integrating capacitors respectively, while $V_1(n)$ and $V_{out}(n)$ are input and output voltages at time slot n, (see left part of Fig. 17).

$$-C_{\text{int}}\left[V_{out}(n)-V_{out}(n-1)\right]=-C_1V_1(n-1) \tag{9}$$

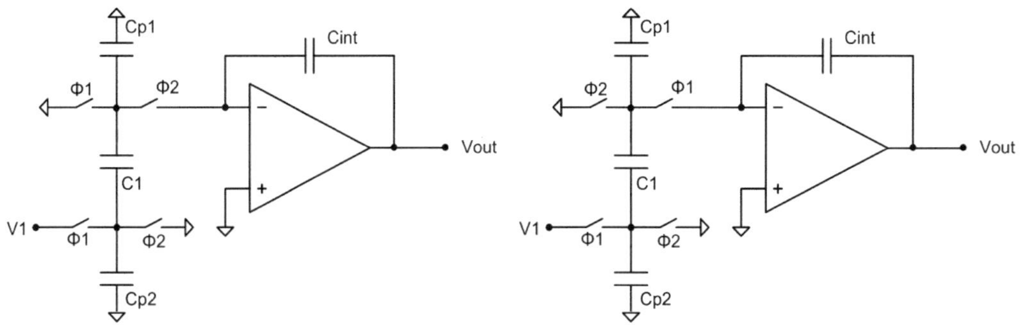

Fig. 17. Simplified circuit diagrams of S-C integrators. Left: non-inverting S-C integrator, Right: inverting S-C integrator

The output voltage for this simple integrator is, in time domain equal to (10).

$$V_{out}(n) = V_{out}(n-1) + \frac{C_1}{C_{int}} V_1(n-1) \tag{10}$$

Capacitor ratio determines the constant of the integrator. In z domain, the description becomes (11), so the transfer function of ideal **non-inverting S-C integrator** is (12).

$$V_{out}(z) = z^{-1} V_{out}(z) + \frac{C_1}{C_{int}} z^{-1} V_1(z) \tag{11}$$

$$H(z) = \frac{V_{out}(z)}{V_1(z)} = \frac{C_1}{C_{int}} \frac{z^{-1}}{1-z^{-1}} = \frac{C_1}{C_{int}} \frac{1}{z-1} \tag{12}$$

If switches are driven according to the right part of Fig. 17, the ideal z-domain transfer function is (13). Therefore, it implements an **inverting S-C integrator**.

$$H(z) = \frac{V_{out}(z)}{V_1(z)} = -\frac{C_1}{C_{int}} \frac{1}{1-z^{-1}} = -\frac{C_1}{C_{int}} \frac{z}{z-1} \tag{13}$$

Both integrators can be modelled by discrete time models where all voltages are described by double floating point numbers to be able to represent the continuum of analogue variables available in any analogue or mixed signal circuits. The models of discrete-time integrators are presented in Fig. 18. The left side shows the non-inverting S-C integrator and the right side shows inverting S-C integrator. Usually, this is the level of abstraction that is used in modelling mixed signal circuits. However, real circuit influences must be taken into consideration if one wants to see the contributions of these influences. The discrete time transfer function of the integrator $1/(z-1)$ is implemented with non-inverting S-C integrator, which is modelled on the left part of Fig. 18. A complete DT integrator that is used in the simplified model of our example modulator is presented in Fig. 19.

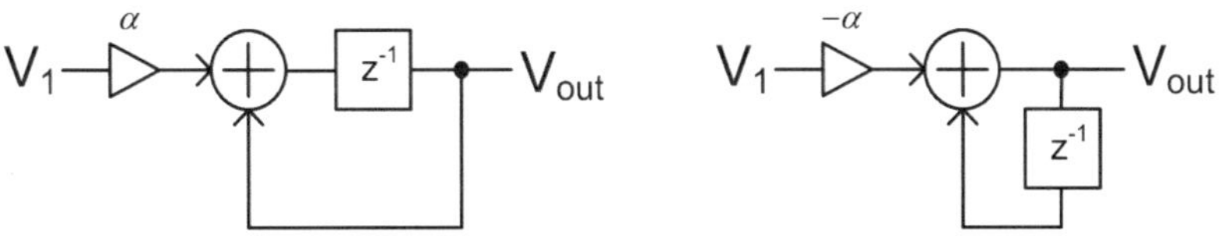

Fig. 18. Simulink model of ideal discrete-time (DT) integrator. Left: non-inverting; Right: inverting

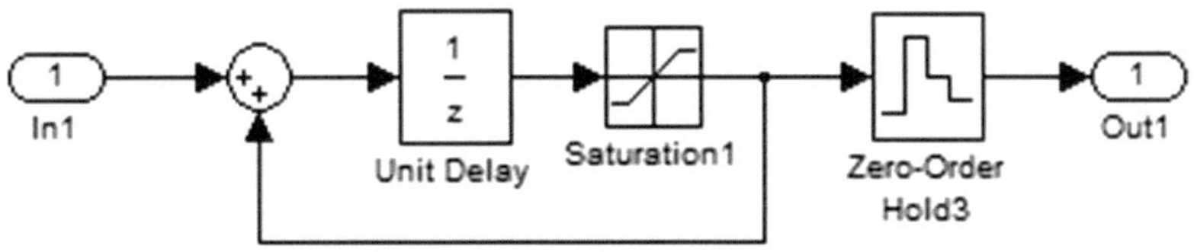

Fig. 19. DT non-inverting integrator Simulink model including Saturation and Zero-Order-Hold blocks

The architecture of the example modulator remains as it was defined in Fig. 15, except that all the blocks that implement the DT integrators are replaced with the model from Fig. 19; coefficients remain exactly the same and are shown in Fig. 15.
Only non-inverting integrators are used in our example circuit because of power consumption reasons. Two Simulink blocks in Fig. 19 were not described before: "Unit Delay" and "Saturation". "Unit delay" needs the settings of two Block Parameters: "Initial conditions" that are set to 0 and "Sampling time" that is set to Ts, as defined in a Matlab work-space. The block "saturation" is defined in the subsection 5.3.

5.2 Capacitor ratios

The coefficients are implemented with capacitor ratios as defined in (12). Each capacitor ratio defines one coefficient. For example, coefficient $b_{in}(1) = c_u(1)/C_I(1)$ is the ratio of input switched capacitor and the integrating capacitor of the first integrator. Assuming at the beginning that $b_{in}(1) \le b_{ref}(1)$ (see Fig. 2), then the input switched capacitor is selected as a unit $c_u(1) = 1$, while all other capacitors connected to the first integrator are bigger than $c_u(1)$. It is easy then to calculate the relative capacitance of, for example, $C_I(1)$. In this way, all coefficients can be replaced by corresponding capacitor ratios. For each integrator, the smallest coefficient determines the unit capacitor and all other capacitors in the same integrator stage are just multiples of the unit corresponding to that. How big the unit capacitance of each integrator stage must be is dependent on the required noise level allowed for each integrator stage i. and the architecture of the circuit. To reflect that, all coefficients implemented by the "Gain" blocks in Fig. 15 are changed; they now contain appropriate capacitor ratios expressed as the explicit quotient of two capacitors, where capacitance in the denominator is always corresponding to the integrating capacitor.

5.3 Adding circuit design parameters to the model

In a real S-C integrator, the charges are transferred from input capacitors to the integrating capacitors ideally without loss of charge, while the time of charge transfer is negligible. We can model that by difference equations (9) and the DT model in Fig. 18. In reality, this transfer is not complete and several additional non-ideal effects contribute to the results. It is beneficial if one is able to predict the influence of such effects on a high hierarchical level before the start of the circuit design. To be able to take into consideration the important circuit parameters of a mixed-signal circuit, the model of the S-C integrator must be improved by adding circuit design parameters such as: nonlinearity of the opamp characteristics, kT/C noise, thermal and 1/f noise, open loop gain of the amplifier (A0), offset voltage (V_{off}), unity gain bandwidth (GB), slew rate (SR), and others. In our improved model of the DT integrator, some discrete time processes will be influenced by the continuous time processes inside the sampling period. In addition, random signals will be added to model the kT/C noise and other circuit noise sources. The model parameters that give acceptable simulation results are the result of optimisation of power consumption, unit capacitor size, the architecture of the circuit and optimum selection of other parameters. Optimized parameters define the limits for the circuit design. The possible non-ideal effects that we modelled in our example modulator are the following:

- **Nonlinearities of the DT integrators** are modelled using the block "Saturation" on Fig. 19. Parameters that must be set in the block are the following: "Upper Limit" and "Lower limit"; they are set to +LIMIT and -LIMIT respectively and are defined in the

Matlab workspace. The element is treated as a gain when voltage is increasing and the "zero-crossing" detection is enabled. Sampling rate is "inherited", therefore Ts. The value of the LIMIT is obtained from the knowledge of the circuit behaviour of the opamp used in the S-C integrator. If the modulator is appropriately scaled as is presented on the right side of Fig. 16, we can be sure that under all normal conditions, the state variables will always remain within the linear region of the integrator. For our example design, the first integrator saturation level and limit is: $LIMIT(1) = |L(1)| = 0.4V$. Other limits can be obtained from the same figure.

- **kT/C noise:** Each switched-capacitor, in addition to the charge transfer, produces noise as a consequence of a thermal noise generated due to finite ON resistance of the switch (Gregorian & Temes, 1986). The noise power of the switched capacitor is independent of the switch ON resistance because the switch and the capacitor form a low-pass filter; with the increase of resistance comes the increase in noise power density and the decrease in bandwidth. Therefore, a smaller part of the noise gets under-sampled. Consequently, the noise power becomes independent of the resistance but inversely proportional to the capacitance. The noise-power of a switched-capacitor is distributed in the band from 0 to fs/2, which can be calculated according to (14), where $k = 1.38 \cdot 10^{-23} \left[J \cdot K^{-1} \right]$, T is absolute temperature in $°K$, c_i is relative capacitance of the switched capacitor, and $c_{unit}(i)$ is the absolute capacitance of the unit capacitor that corresponds to the integrator stage.

$$P_{n,i} = \frac{k\,T}{c_i \cdot c_{unit}(i)} [W] \tag{14}$$

Each coefficient implemented by the switched-capacitor generates a noise that is modelled in Simulink as a noise source by using a block "Random source" (see Fig. 20 for the 2nd integrator). The parameters are set as follows: "Source type" to Gaussian, "Mean" to 0, "Variance" to noise power according to (14), "Sample mode" to discrete, "Sample time" to Ts, "Samples per frame" to 1, "Output data type" to Double, and "Complexity" to Real.

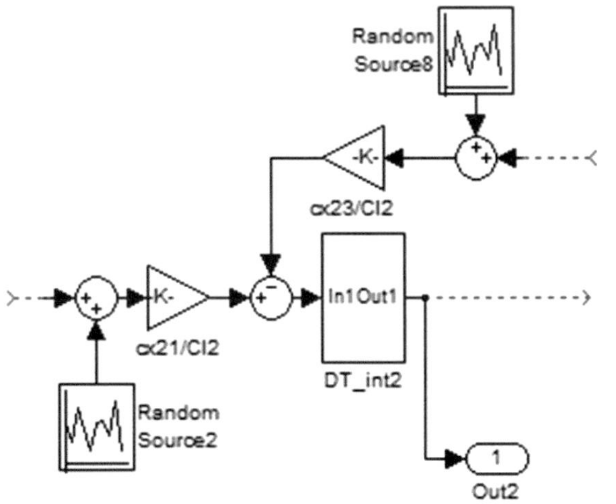

Fig. 20. kT/C noise modelling adding Random source to each S-C stage

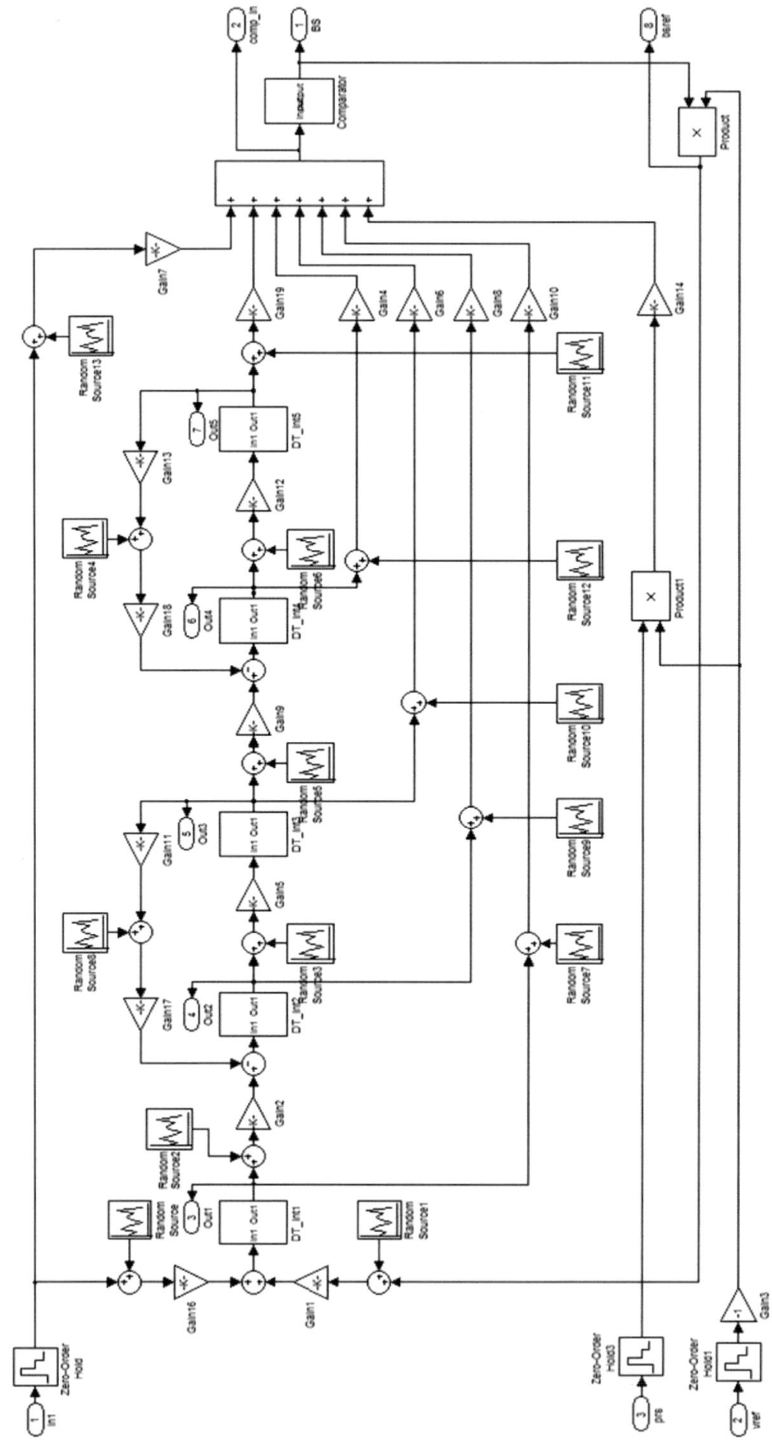

Fig. 21. Simulink model of the fifth order modulator, with kT/C noise sources included

Our fifth order modulator schematics is improved (Fig. 21) by adding appropriate noise sources, with noise power inversely proportional to the absolute value of the corresponding switched capacitance. The contribution of each noise source to the final noise level at the BS output is shaped by a particular noise transfer function. The biggest contributions (not attenuated) come from the input and reference switched capacitors. For high order circuits, the contribution of each k/TC noise source is hard to predict and optimize; hence, the Simulink model can be used to optimize all unit capacitor sizes, which may be different for each integrator in the loop. The power-consumption of each integrator is proportional to the absolute capacitance on one side, while kT/C noise of each S-C stage is inversely proportional to its capacitance, so the smallest power consumption could be achieved by optimizing the absolute value of the unit capacitor of each integrator stage.

- **Open loop gain A0:** Ideal charge transfer requires infinite open loop gain of the opamp that was used in the S-C integrator. In a real integrator, part of the charge that is supposed to be transferred to the integrating capacitor is lost. The consequences are that the pole is not anymore at z=1 and the coefficient is different than the ratio of input and integrating capacitance. The real transfer function of DT S-C integrator is given by (15). The model of DT integrator is changed to Fig. 22, where α can be calculated according to (16). The pole frequency is moved from an ideal location at $z_p = 1$ to $z_p = \alpha$, while the gain of the integrating stage is moved from k to $k \cdot \alpha$. In this expression, A_0 is low-frequency open loop gain of the amplifier, $\sum C_{x,i}$ is the sum of all switched capacitors connected to the integrator i and $C_{I,i}$ is the integrating capacitance of the integrator i .

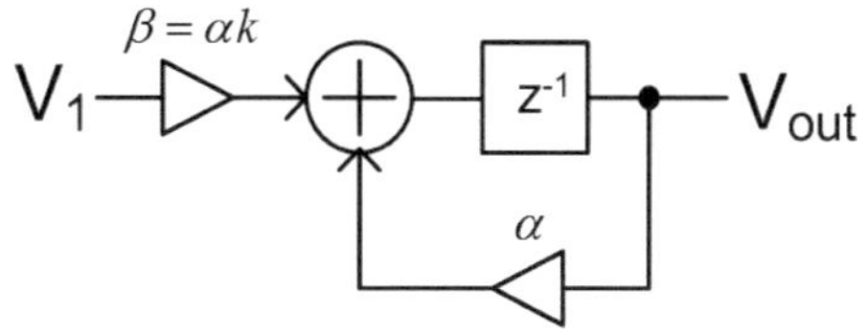

Fig. 22. DT integrator with a model of A0 influence

$$H(z) = \frac{k \cdot \alpha_i}{1 - \alpha_i z} \tag{15}$$

$$\alpha_i = \frac{\left[C_{I,i}(1 + A_0)\right]}{\left[C_{I,i}(1 + A_0)\right] + \sum C_{x,i}} \tag{16}$$

- **Dynamic properties of the integrator's opamp:** The response of each integrator during charge transfer depends on dynamic opamp characteristics: Slew-Rate (SR) and Gain Bandwidth Product (GB); in addition, it also depends on the finite open loop gain of the opamp (Maloberti, 2007). During charge transfer (phase Φ2 on the left part of Fig. 17), the opamp may enter 2 different modes of operation: SR limited mode at the first part of the transient, if the input charge is big enough, and the "linear" settling mode in the second part. The whole transient might follow a "linear" settling mode if input charge is small. For $G_{R0} \le SR$, where $G_{R0} = \left[dv_o(t)/dt\right]_{t=0}$ the time domain response of the output voltage can be modelled using (17), assuming the dominant pole model of the opamp with $1/\omega_p = \tau = 1/(2\pi \cdot GB)$; α is defined in (16), $k = C_{x,i}/C_{I,i}$ is the capacitor ratio, v_x is the voltage on the input capacitor slightly before the start of the charge transfer, and $v_{o1}(nT_s - T_s/2)$ is the output voltage of the integrator slightly before the start of the charge transfer. For $G_{R0} > SR$, the first part of the transient follows the SR limited behaviour according to (18), while the second part follows the "linear" settling behaviour according to (19). T_0 is the time where the slopes of the SR limited behaviour $v_{o1}(t)$ and settling limited behaviour $v_{o2}(t)$ are equal according to (20). The complete behaviour in that case is (21).

$$v_o(t) = v_o\left(nT_s - \frac{T_s}{2}\right) + \alpha k v_x\left(1 - e^{-\frac{t}{\tau}}\right) \text{ for } (nT_s - T_s/2) \le \text{t} < \text{n}T_s \tag{17}$$

$$v_{o1}(t) = v_o\left(nT_s - \frac{T_s}{2}\right) + SR * t \text{ for } t \le T_0 \tag{18}$$

$$v_{o2}(T_0) = (k \cdot \alpha \cdot v_x - SR * T_0)\left(1 - e^{-\frac{t-T_0}{\tau}}\right) \text{ for } t > T_0 \tag{19}$$

$$\left.\frac{dv_{o1}(t)}{dt}\right|_{t=T_0} = \left.\frac{dv_{o2}(t)}{dt}\right|_{t=T_0} \Rightarrow T_0 = \frac{\alpha k v_x}{SR} - \tau \tag{20}$$

$$v_o(t) = v_{o1}(T_0) + (\alpha \cdot k \cdot v_x - SR \cdot T_0)\left(1 - e^{-\frac{t-T_0}{\tau}}\right) \text{ for } T_0 < t \le nT_s \tag{21}$$

A complete Simulink model of the S-C integrator stage, excluding input coefficients (they are defined on the top level of the Simulink model shown in Fig. 21), is presented in Fig. 23. The model includes dynamic contributions due to SR and GB and the model of static error cause by A_0. The result of continuous time output voltage at the end of charge transfer that is at time nT_s is calculated by using an "Embedded" Matlab function, GBW_SR1, as shown on the left part of the S-C integrator Simulink model on Fig. 23. The constants for all integrators from Fig. 21 (constants for second integrator: Constant=tau(2), Constant1=alpha(2), Constant2=SR(2) and Constant3=Ts) are defined in the m-file and are available in the Matlab work-space. The code that evaluates (18) to (21) is presented in Fig. 24. Thermal noise generator (random Source8 on Fig. 23) is added at the output of the integrator and is thus multiplied by appropriate capacitor ratio. It models the contribution of the thermal noise generated in the opamp; input referred opamp noise power is multiplied by the appropriate coefficient $\sum(C_{x,i}/C_{I,i})$ so, that it can be added to the output of the integrator model.

5.4 Quantizer model

In a nonlinear model defined by state-space equations (7), it is assumed that the quantizer is described by a sign() function. This function has an infinitely steep response to the input signal. In reality, the gain of the quantizer alone is finite, which means that for very small

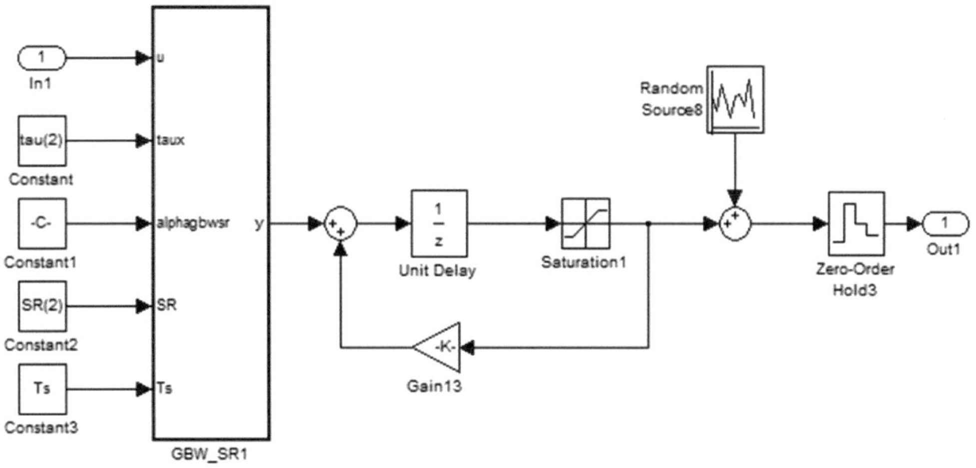

Fig. 23. Model of static and dynamic properties of non-inverting S-C integrator, including opamp thermal noise

```
function y     = gbwsr(u,taux,alpha,SR,Ts)

% this block calculates effects of GBW and Slew-Rate
% to the output voltage of an S-C integrator

Vs=u;
tau=taux;
if Vs<0
    SRx=-SR;
else
    SRx=SR;
end
GR0=alpha*Vs/tau;
if (abs(GR0)<=abs(SRx)) % gradient due to GBW smaller than SR
    y_Ts=alpha*Vs*(1-exp(-(Ts/(2*tau)))); % linear
else % GR0>SR % linear settling slower than SR
    T0=alpha*abs(Vs)/abs(SRx)-tau;
    if T0<Ts/2;
        y0=SRx*T0;
        y_Ts=y0+(alpha*Vs-SRx*T0)*(1-exp(-(Ts/2-T0)/tau));
    else
        y_Ts=SRx*Ts/2;
    end
end

y=y_Ts;
```

Fig. 24. Code that calculates output voltage of the S-C integrator, according to (18), (19), (20), and (21) signals, the decision may be wrong. For low resolution devices, this is of no consequence but for high resolution devices many wrong decisions could have consequences by increasing the noise in the base-band. It is very difficult to determine the gain of a one bit quantizer from a system point of view, that is, by just observing the reaction to the input signals. The output signal is always limited, whatever the input signal might be. The intuitive explanation is that the system gain of the quantizer is dependent on the amplitude of the input signal: it is large for small signals and small for large input signals. Therefore, it would be necessary to check the NTF and the stability of the loop as a function of the quantizer's gain. Some authors have proposed complicated statistical models of the one bit quantizer (Boche & Monich, 2010); however, we prefer to use simple intuitive understanding and as simple a model as possible. It is possible to check the NTF for the linear model as a function of the large signal gain (system gain) of the quantizer, taking into consideration the different values of k from Fig. 2. Further discussions about the problem are presented in the continuation of this subsection, where the influence of a small system gain on a more realistic model of the quantizer is presented, together with its influence to the operation of the modulator.

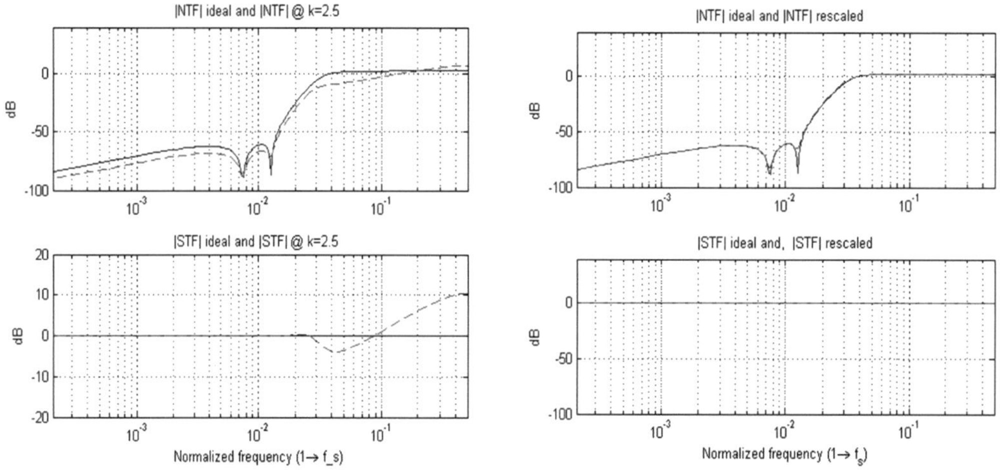

Fig. 25. |NTF| and |STF| plots for ideal quantizer and different system gain of the quantizer. Solid line: system gain of the quantizer k=1. Dashed line: system gain of the quantizer k=2.5. Upper plots: linear model of the |NTF|. Lower plots: |STF|. Left plots: un-scaled modulator; Right plots: rescaled modulator with system gain k=2.5 taken into considerations

Fig. 25 shows plots of the NTF and the STF for the ideal linear model of the fifth order modulator for different quantizers' gains. On both plots, the solid line presents the ideal linear model with system gain of the quantizer k=1, while the dashed lines represent plots of NTF and STF for system signal gain of a quantizer increased to k=2.5. The system gain of a linear model of a modulator (k=2.5) is deduced from extensive statistical simulations. Left plots are for an un-scaled modulator, while the right side of Fig. 25 plots the NTF and STF of rescaled linear model of the modulator. Rescaling is such that it compensates for the eventual change in the average system gain of the one bit quantizer in a linear model.

A simple nonlinear model of a one bit quantizer that includes the small signal gain of a differential stage, saturation block relay, offset voltage, input referred noise, and no latency is presented in Fig. 26. The model follows the implementation of the comparator, which is composed of the gain stage with gain G_comp, offset voltage Voff, and input referred noise power pncomp. The three blocks Fcn model the behaviour of the comparator in a good way: they calculate the decision under different conditions according to (22).

$$x = \begin{Bmatrix} 1 & u \geq V_{th\_H} \\ 0 & u < V_{th\_H} \end{Bmatrix} \quad y = \begin{Bmatrix} -1 & u \leq V_{th\_L} \\ 0 & u > V_{th\_L} \end{Bmatrix} \quad z = \begin{Bmatrix} 1 & V_{th\_L} \leq u \leq V_{th\_H} \\ 0 & \text{otherwise} \end{Bmatrix} \tag{22}$$

The decision is stable and correct if the difference between input voltage and the offset voltage of the comparator, multiplied by the gain of differential stage, is bigger than the threshold voltage high (x), or if the difference is smaller than the threshold voltage low (y). In those two cases, the decision is +1 or -1, respectively. However, for small input voltage, the decision is difficult and may be arbitrary because of comparator noise (z). Using this model, we can study the influence of some of the characteristics of the internal quantizer (comparator) as a function of its performance. In Fig. 27, the simulation results for different small signal comparator gains are presented. The spectrum on the left is for a small signal comparator gain Gcomp=1000, which gives a correct result, while the spectrum on the right side of Fig. 27 for Gcomp=100 is not acceptable because the SnR has been degraded considerably. The explanation for the increased base-band noise level is the following: because of very small signal gain of the comparator's differential stage, the decision was many times dictated by the random noise of the comparator instead of the signal, and this causes the increase of the baseband noise.

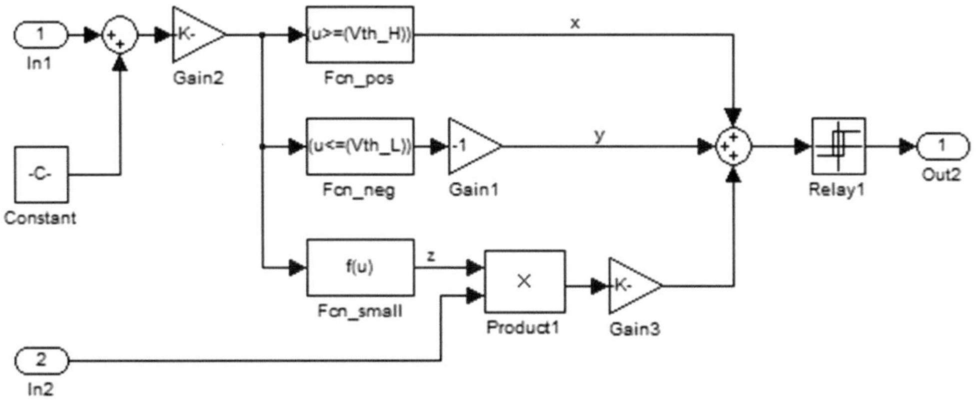

Fig. 26. Nonlinear model of the quantizer

5.5 Simulation and analysis

Using the models defined in the previous subsections, one can study the influence of many different effects due to non-ideal parameters. The complete model can also be used to optimize the main parameters of the circuit. Due to lack of space, only two simulation results will be presented for our fifth order modulator. In reality, many different simulations must be performed to verify the correctness of the design and to verify the influence of the non-ideal parameters on the behaviour of a mixed signal module.

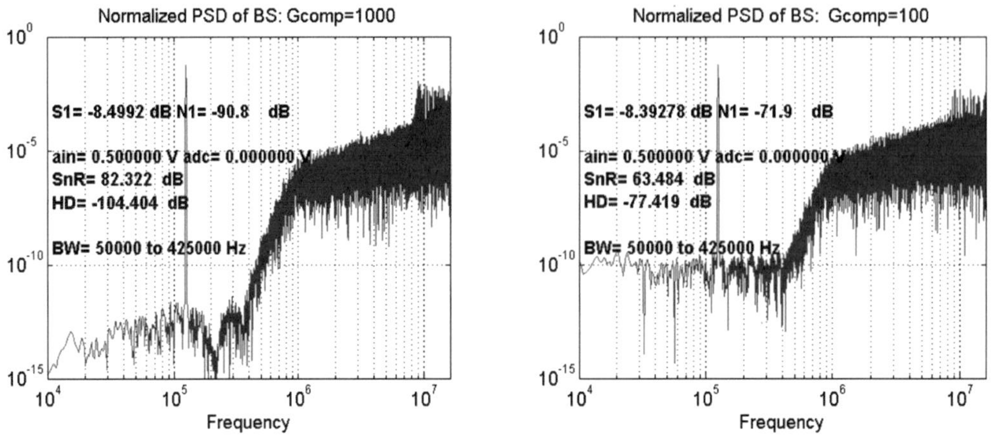

Fig. 27. BS spectrum of the example modulator for nonlinear Quantizer model. Left spectrum: Gcomp=1000, Right spectrum: Gcomp=100

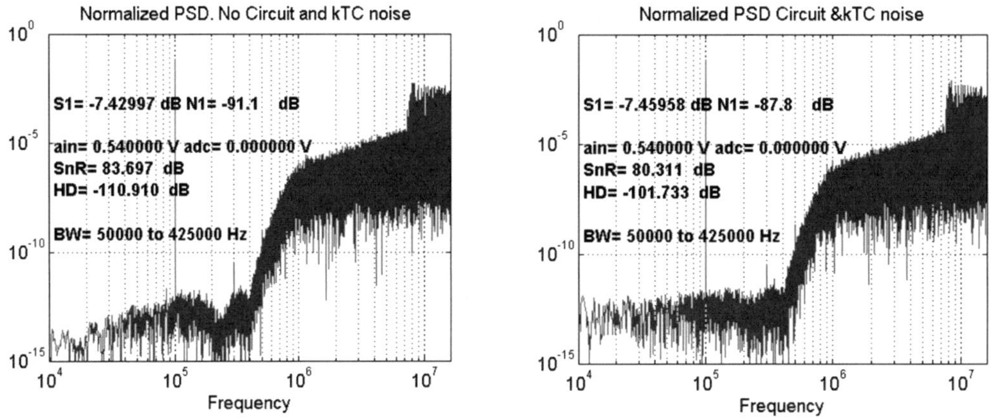

Fig. 28. Spectrum of the BS of the fifth order modulator, with non-ideal effects included. Left spectrum: No noise circuit included, Right spectrum: All noise sources and all other non-ideal effects included

Fig. 28 shows two simulation results. Both are calculated from the bit-stream of our fifth order example modulator. All non-ideal effects are included with parameters given in (23).

$$
\begin{aligned}
&A_{0,i} = 1000; \quad i = 1 \ldots 5 \\
&BW_i = 5 \cdot f_s \, [Hz]; \quad i = 1 \ldots 5 \\
&\mathbf{SR} = [70, 38, 14, 8, 8]\left[\frac{V}{\mu s}\right] \\
&\mathbf{V}_{ndop} = [15, 40, 80, 80, 80]\left[\frac{nV}{\sqrt{Hz}}\right] \\
&Temp = 150\ ^{\circ}C
\end{aligned}
\tag{23}
$$

The kT/C noise source effects have been excluded from the simulation for the left part of Fig. 28, while on the right side of Fig. 28, all noise sources have been included with optimized unit capacitor sizes. The evidence of circuit noise is clearly seen on the right part of the figure. The switched capacitors and integrator contributions have been optimized so that their influences are acceptable and power consumption is optimized.

The last simulation result shown in Fig. 29 presents a Monte Carlo analysis of our fifth order modulator, with all non-ideal effects included. The absolute values of the capacitances and the capacitor ratios were randomly changed around their nominal (mean) value, with standard deviations defined on the upper part of the scatter plot. This information is compliant with technology information. The capacitor ratios were spread according to the matching information from the process technology. The properties of the opamps and the comparator were kept constant, with values slightly different than the values defined in (23). It would be possible to include also the spread of this circuit parameter values obtained from the circuit simulation results. The x-axis of Fig. 29 represents rms "distance" of each experiment from its nominal value, while the y-axis shows the SnR in dB. Each circle represents one result.

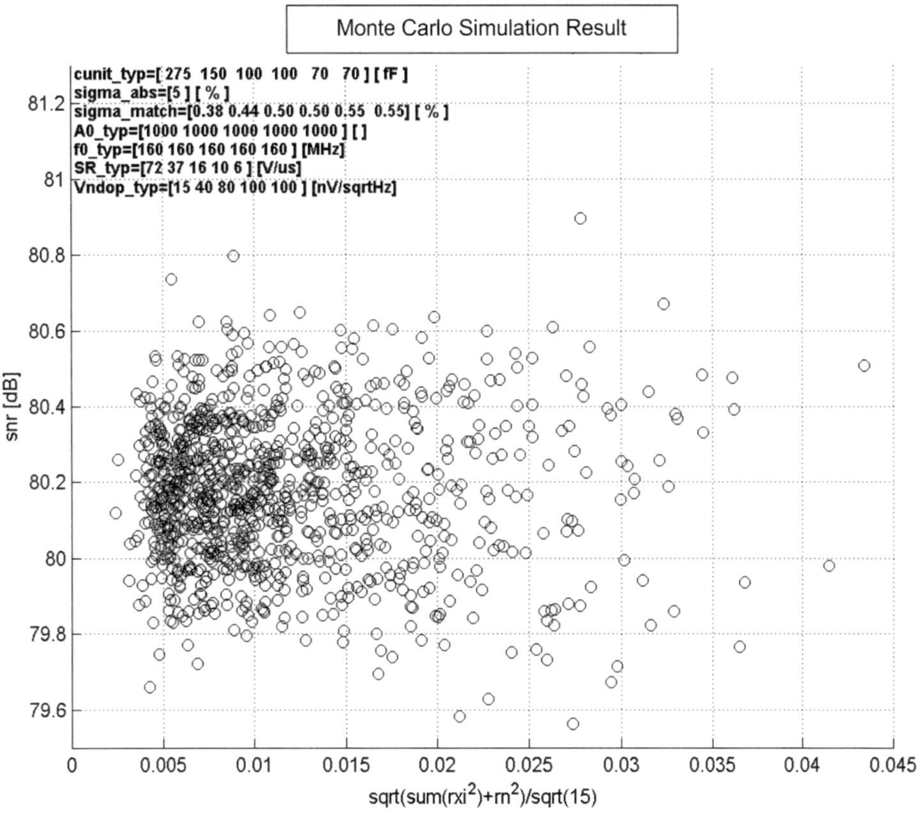

Fig. 29. Monte Carlo simulation result of the 5th order modulator. Each circle represent result (SnR) of one simulation at the conditions defined in upper left portion of the picture. The capacitors are spread by $|\sigma| = 5\%$. The x-axis is the rms distance of each capacitor set of the experiment from the nominal rms value

6. Decimator

Each Σ-Δ A/D converter is composed of a modulator and a decimation filter. This pair forms a simple mixed-signal system (circuit). Many different decimation filter architectures are possible (Schrier & Temes, 2005). In this chapter, we will not go into the details of a decimation filter design; rather, we will present the bit-true model of one example filter using simple Simulink element library and blocks. The model used is very simple. It leads to the efficient design of decimation filters.
The simplest decimation filter architecture is the so-called sinc filter defined in z-domain transfer function (24), where *ord* is the order of the filter and R_1 is the decimation factor. To implement that, a delay, registers, and adder Simulink blocks are needed; the structure is regular which leads to efficient VLSI design.

$$H(z) = \left[\frac{1 - z^{-R_1}}{1 - z^{-1}} \right]^{ord} \tag{24}$$

Usually, the order of the decimation filter must be bigger than the order of the modulator to suppress the out of band quantization noise sufficiently. For our example, a sixth order Sinc decimation filter is used. The block diagram of the filter is presented in Fig. 30. A complete filter is built with fixed word-length of WL=32 bits using so called wrap-around two's complement arithmetic. The digital integrator stages are running with f_s while differentiators are running with f_s/R_1 (R_1=32). The word length needed is calculated in such a way that no additional quantization noise is added into the process and that the wrap-around two's complement arithmetic works correctly. At the output of the filter, the word-length is reduced to 24 bits using block Gain6 with correct parameter settings.

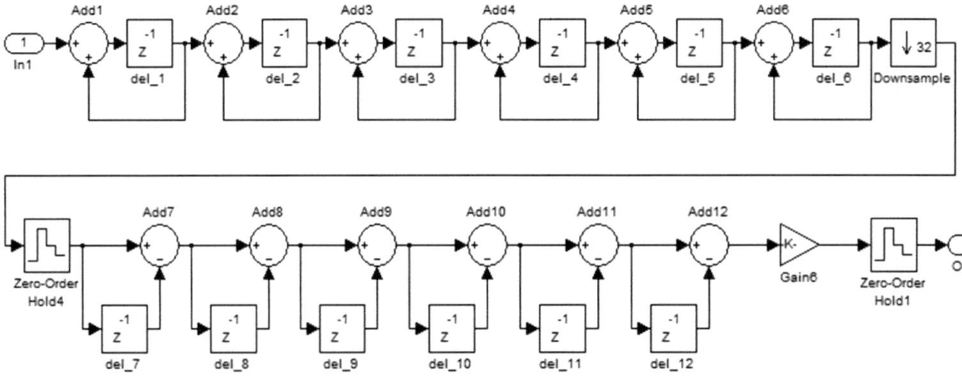

Fig. 30. 6th order sinc decimation filter structure

The number of bits used in integrator stages can be fixed by the appropriate number of bits of the input signal and appropriate settings of the adders. The input signal to the decimation filter is obtained from the bit-stream of the modulator; in our example, the modulator has a one bit internal quantizer with a data type double. For the fixed point arithmetic used in the decimation filter, the BS signal is first converted to an integer by using block Convert (SI) on Fig. 33. Fixed point arithmetic inside a decimation filter is defined by parameters inside the adders, as presented on the left part of Fig. 31, where accumulator data type is set to fixed point with WL1=32 bits. This number is calculated in Matlab m-file using formula $WL_1 = ceil(ord_1 * \log 2(R_1)) + WL_{in}$; the output data type of the adder block is also set to WL1. The adder must not saturate on integer overflow to accommodate wrap-around arithmetic.

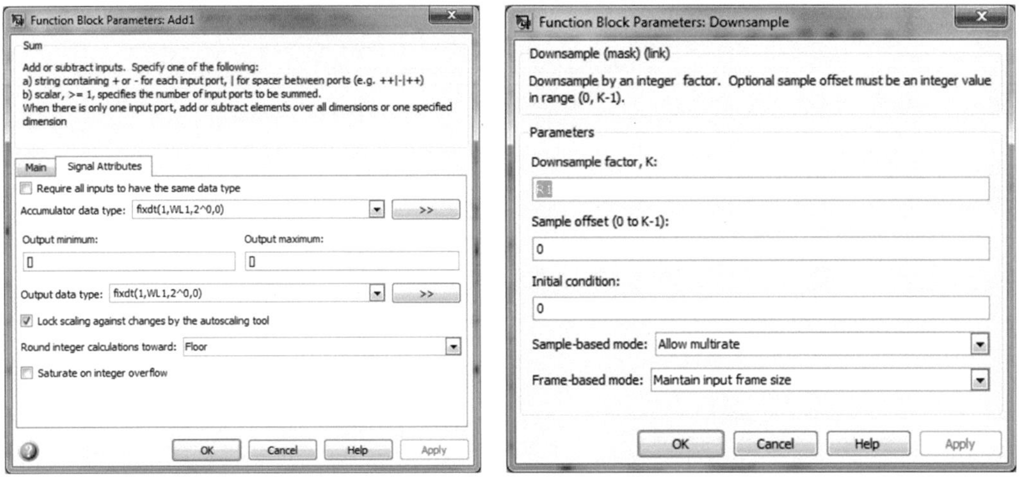

Fig. 31. Adder and Down-sampler parameters. Left: Adder. Right: Down-sampler

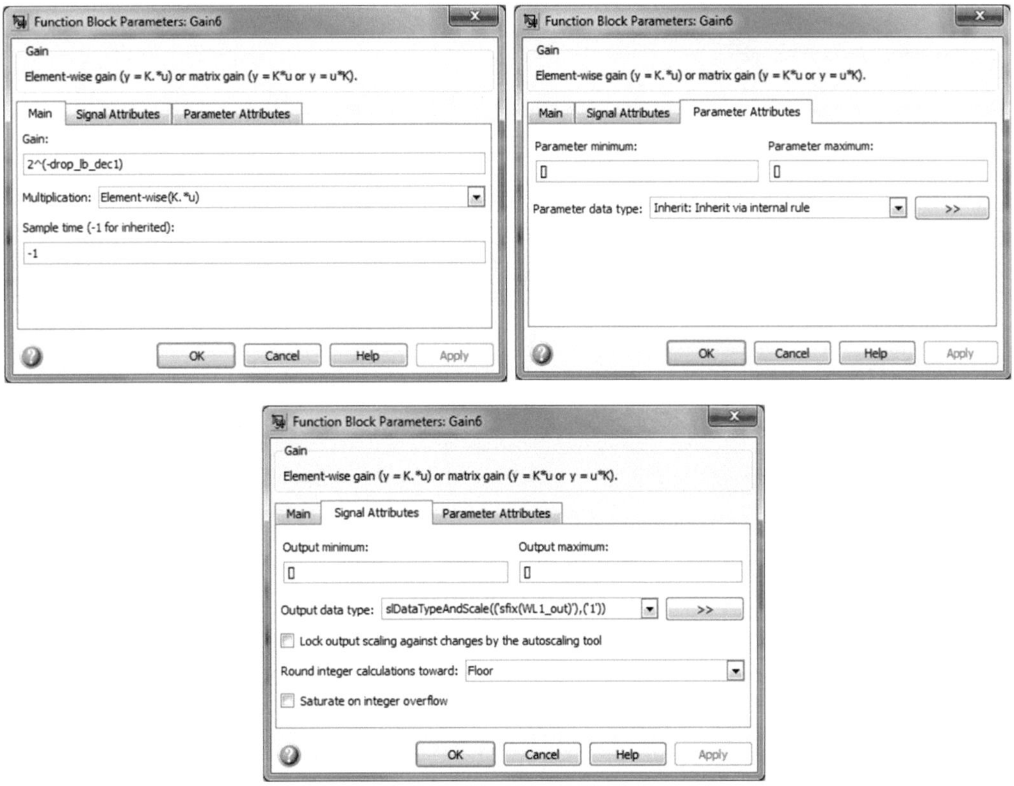

Fig. 32. Settings for block Gain6 that determines output word-length

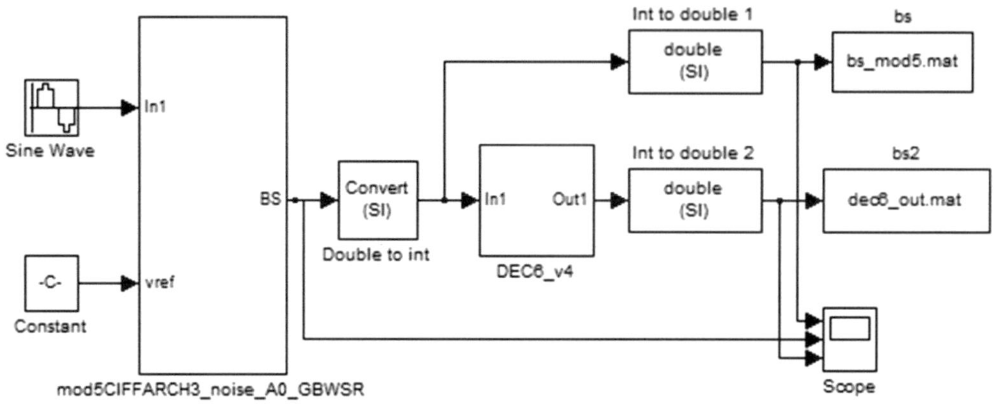

Fig. 33. Top-level Simulink block diagram for modulator-decimator simulation

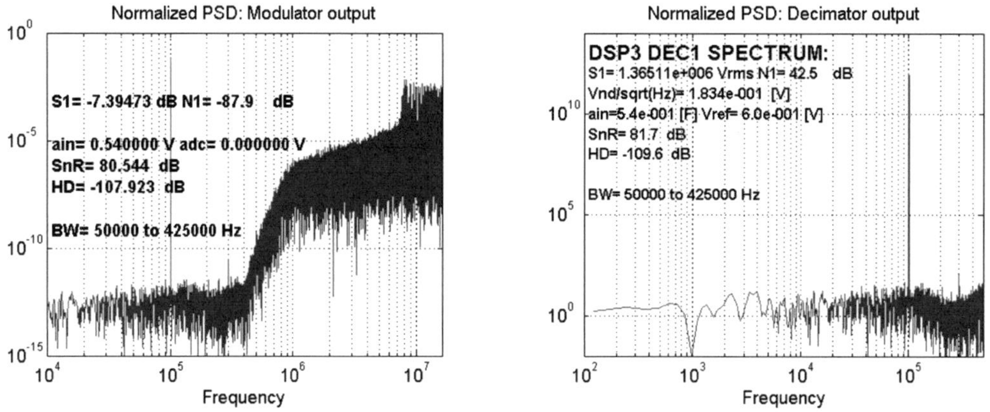

Fig. 34. Left spectrum: Spectrum of the modulator's BS including non-ideal effects. Spectrum on the right: The decimation filter output (the decimator is driven by the BS with spectrum on the left side

At the end of the sixth integrator stage, every R_1th sample is taken, which is implemented by a Down-sampler. The parameter settings are presented on the right side of Fig. 31. The whole decimator is running with the same number of bits WL1 because the structure in this case is more regular. Nevertheless, it is possible to use a smaller number of bits at the beginning of the chain and increase the word-length at the end of the structure, taking into consideration only the quantization noise penalty.

For our example decimator, the lower eight bits are removed by block Gain6 (from Fig. 30) at the output by setting appropriate parameters as shown in Fig. 32.

Fig. 33 shows a top-level Simulink block diagram that includes a modulator (mod5CIFFARCH3_noise_A0_GBWSR) with all previously defined non-ideal effects, and a model of a decimation filter (DEC6_v4) using previously defined settings for fixed-point arithmetic.

Fig. 34 shows the results of a Simulink simulations in two spectrums. The left plot shows the spectrum of the bit-stream of the 5th order modulator model that includes all non-ideal circuit effects defined before with nominal capacitor ratios, while the spectrum on the right side corresponds to the bit-true decimation filter output.

7. Conclusion

This chapter deals with modelling and simulation of a mixed-signal module (circuit) using high level Matlab/Simulink model on a high hierarchical level. More specifically, it presents an example design and the modelling details of a fifth order Σ-Δ A/D converter, which is built of a fifth order modulator and sixth order decimation filter. The modulator is modelled by using data types "double" and models of many non-ideal circuit effects, while the decimator is modelled by using different fixed-point data types. The most important non-ideal effects are included into the model of the "analogue part"; the decimation filter uses a bit-true, fixed-point arithmetic and hence we can say that it uses a bit-true model. Using the proposed modelling technique, one can speed up the design and simulations of complex mixed-signal circuits and systems considerably. For example, in the design shown in Fig. 34, less than one minute simulation time is needed to obtain 2^{18} samples and to get the presented final spectrums.

8. Acknowledgment

This work was partly supported by the NAMASTE Centre of Excellence.

9. References

Boche, H. &. Monich, U. J. (2010). Behavior of the Quantization Operator for Band-Limited, Nonoversampled Signals. *IEEE Trans. on Information Theory* , vol. 56, No. 5, pp. 2433-2440.

De la Rosa, J. M. (2011). Sigma_Delta Modulators: Tutorial Overview, Desing Guide, and State-of-Art Survey. *IEEE Trans. on Circuits and systems - I: Regular papers* ,vol. 58, no. 1, pp. 1-21.

Gregorian, R. T. & Temes, G.C. (1986). *Analog MOS Integrated Circuits for signal processing,* John Wiley & Sons, New York

Maloberti, F. (2007). *Data COnverters.* New York: Springer.

Moris, K. (2004). Destination DSP; Methodologies for signal processing success. *FPGA and Programmable Logic Journal (www.fpgajournal.com/articles/20041130_dsp.htm)* .

Perelroyzen, E. (2007). *Digital Integrated Circuits: Design-for-Test Using Simulink and Stateflow.* N.Y.: CRC Press.

S.Mann, D. (1999). Limit Cycle Behaviour in the Double Loop Band-pass Sigma-Delta A/D Converter. *IEEE Trans CAS.II, Analogue and digital Signal Processing* , vol .46, no. 8, pp. 1086 - 1089.

Schreier, R. (2009). *The Delta-Sigma Toolbox Version 7.3.* (http://www.mathworks.com/matlabcentral/fileexchange/delsig), Mathworks.

Schrier, R. T. & Temes, G.C. (2005). *Understanding Delta-Sigma Data Converters,* John Wiley & Sons, New York.

Strle, D. &. Kempe, V. (2007). MEMS-based inertial systems. *Inf. MIDEM*, pp. 199-209.

Strle, D. (2006). Limit Cycles in High Order Sigma Delta Modulators. *Inf. MIDEM,* vol. 36, No.1, pp. 11-18.

Synopsis. (2004). *Saber Users Guide.* Synopsis.

Zepernick, H. &. (2005). *Pseudo Random Signal Processing: Theory and applications,* John Wiley & Sons, New York.

6

Control Optimization Using MATLAB

Patic Paul Ciprian, Duta Luminita and Pascale Lucia
Automatics, Informatics and Electrical Engineering Department
Valahia University of Targoviste
Romania

1. Introduction

The automatic modelling system using MATLAB-Simulink software package applies the Cohen-Coon method for determining the closed loop PID parameters and plotting the system response clue. Implementing the same system in a closed loop PID adjustment using LabVIEW software package, requires, at first, an additional procedure, namely, the use of transfer functions in Z domain, which means the use of a sampling signal. The study in this paper intends to determine the parameters of a PID regulator using two software packages - MATLAB-Simulink and LabVIEW. As a mathematical pattern, a DC machine has been used. To exemplify regulators such as PID, LQR (Linear Quadratic Regulator) and PI-MIMO (PI - Multiple Input Multiple Output) were used. The application is easily implemented, the inverted pendulum being used to emphasize the results. The closed loop system and its evolution over time are easily implemented. This software package offers an easy user interface, which means it is convenient to introduce the programme functions (Nițu, C., et al., 1974).

MATLAB is a tool with high performance in technical estimations. It integrates the calculation, visualization and programming in an easy to use environment where problems and solutions are expressed in familiar mathematical notation. Using the MATLAB software package has the following main purposes: mathematical calculation, the development of algorithms, data acquisition, modelling, simulation and prototype development, visualization, exploration and data analysis, scientific graphics and engineering, and application development of a graphical user interface. MATLAB is an interactive system whereby the basic element to define data is the string that does not require sizing (Andrei, H., et al., 1999; Călin, S., 1970; Călin, S., et al., 1979, 2002; Dumitrache, I., 1971; Papadache, I., 1975).

With LabVIEW virtual instruments are built (VI), having the appearance of instruments or physical systems. Virtual instruments have an interactive user interface front panel - and with one part for the programmer - block diagram. For identification and use in other applications, each virtual instrument has an icon with specific entries and exits (Bishop, R., 2010).

Automatic systems modelling using the MATLAB-Simulink software package applied the Cohen-Coon method for determining the closed loop PID parameters and plotting the system response clue. The limit of the over adjustment was found to be 20%, the timing of the transitional regime - 3 seconds, and the maximum response time was 10 seconds. Also, one represented the chart of the evolution over time, in a closed loop system, to unit step input.

This software package offers an easy user interface, which means that it is convenient to introduce the programme functions. The application has implemented the conversion done from a field of definition of transfer functions to another (ex. obviously c2d function transforming the transfer function of s field in Z domain, using a sampling period by the user), and includes the Simulink tool that greatly facilitates the user's work as the user wants to consider in detail the operation of each block and many other features in the field of automation and theory systems.

MATLAB integrates the calculation, visualization and programming in an easy to use environment where problems and solutions are expressed in familiar mathematical notation.

Automatic systems modelling using the MATLAB-Simulink software package applied the Cohen-Coon method for determining the closed loop PID parameters and plotting the system response clue. This software package offers an easy user interface, which means that it is convenient to introduce the programme functions.

This paper intends to determine the parameters of a PID regulator using two software packages - MATLAB-Simulink and LabVIEW (Mahesh, L., et al., 1998).

To exemplify, PID, LQR (Linear Quadratic Regulator) and PI-MIMO (PI - Multiple Input Multiple Output) regulators types were used.

In the case of the LQR regulator, the Control System Toolbox was necessary since it is an extended version of the problem from the Simulink demo file.

Using LQG / LTR techniques, one can design a Kalman state estimator and a corresponding amplifier regulator for the linear system, by adding an integrator to ensure a zero steady error (Gibson, J., 1967; Ionescu, V., 1975).

An initial design regulator using the LQG / LTR methods is designed starting from a linear application.

The third problem of control design involves designing a centralized PI-MIMO regulator for a turbine engine of LVI00 fuel. The application is modelled as a system with two inputs, two outputs and a minimum of five phase states. Inputs are fuel flow and variable area turbine nozzle.

The work from this paper intended to determine the parameters of a PID controller using two software packages, namely MATLAB-Simulink and LabVIEW.

A comparative analysis of the features of the two programmes - MATLAB-Simulink and LabVIEW to determine the same automatic performances of the system – indicates that the MATLAB-Simulink software is more efficient. It has different features from its libraries already implemented, with coverage areas of automation and systems theory. LabVIEW is a software package dedicated to particular virtual instrumentation and graphical applications in time (Bishop, R., 2010).

Passing to study cases, first of all, one tries to present the classical case of the inverted pendulum and, also, the modelling of the robotic arm. We compared the results obtained using MATLAB-Simulink and LabVIEW software. The equations of the model are presented and the modelling results are given comparatively.

2. PID regulator

At first, the problem of control design is shaped by the transfer application as having a single input and a single output (Single Input Single Output, SISO) of third order, where a1 = 43 and a1=3 with an approximation of ± 0.7 and a non-linear saturation ± 1.5.

In addition, due to design tolerances, the current dynamics presents suggestive variations from the base model. Specifically, the denominator coefficient a2 varies between 40 and 50 and coefficient a1 between half and 1.5 times the nominal value of 3 (Franklin, G., et al., 1987; Potvin, A. F., 1991).

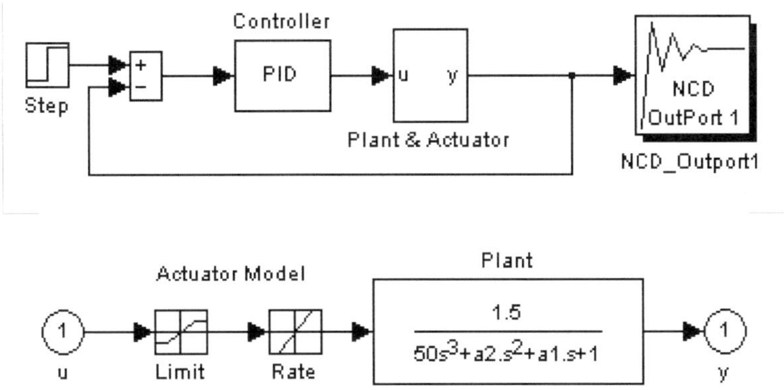

Fig. 1. NCD block attached to the result of the plant

$$G(s) = \frac{1.5}{50s^2 + a_2 s^2 + a_1 s + 1} \tag{1}$$

A PID regulator is designed so that closed-cycle system may meet the following specifications for tracking:

- Maximum oscillation 20%;
- Up to 10 seconds for the propagation;
- Maximum response time of 30 seconds (Franklin, G., et al., 1987; Potvin, A. F., 1991).

This results in the answer that the closed-cycle is resistant to uncertainty in the installation's dynamics.

The Simulink ncddemo1 system contains the application and the control structure. It is noted that non-linearity and saturation speed are included in the model plant. An input step drives the system. An NCD block is attached to the outlet installation (Figure 1) because it is the signal which will be restricted. On checking the System's Parameters dialog box one can notice that each simulation lasts 100 seconds.

Tuneable and uncertain variables are initialized. The uncertain variables a1 and a2 are initialized at nominal values of 40 and 3 respectively. Tuneable parameters Kp, Ki and Kd are initialized at 0.63, 0.05, 2.02 respectively. These values result from the use of the Ziegler-Nichols method for PID regulators.

The Ziegler-Nichols method for PID regulators can be summarized as follows:

- The entire amplification and derivative is established to zero. Than, all these are increased proportionally, until the system becomes unstable;
- This amplification is defined as Ku, the measure of the oscillation period is Pu;
- The coefficients are established one by one:

$$K_p = \frac{3 * K_u}{5}, \quad K_i = \frac{6 * K_u}{5 * P_u}, \quad si \quad K_i = \frac{3 * K_u * P_u}{50} \tag{2}$$

Then, the limitations of time are defined. Upper and lower restriction limits define oscillation, propagation time and response time (Franklin, G., et al., 1987; Potvin, A. F., 1991).
Note that the uncertainty in the parameters a1 and a2 is defined and that the restrictions are applied to the installation only nominally. After running optimization, the time, the cost function evolution and the final values for tunable parameters vary depending on computer's performance. Optimization should provide a regulator to satisfy any restrictions (National Instruments; MathWorks; MathWorks User's Guide, 2003).
The lower and superior limits are restricted and the optimizing process is started with uncertainty. One can consider that these restrictions cannot be satisfied, but the result shows a maximum violation of the restriction under the value of 0.01.
One can experiment by moving the limits of restriction to achieve better performances of the system. For example, one can reduce the time spread or decrease the restrictions of oscillation (Figure 2.)

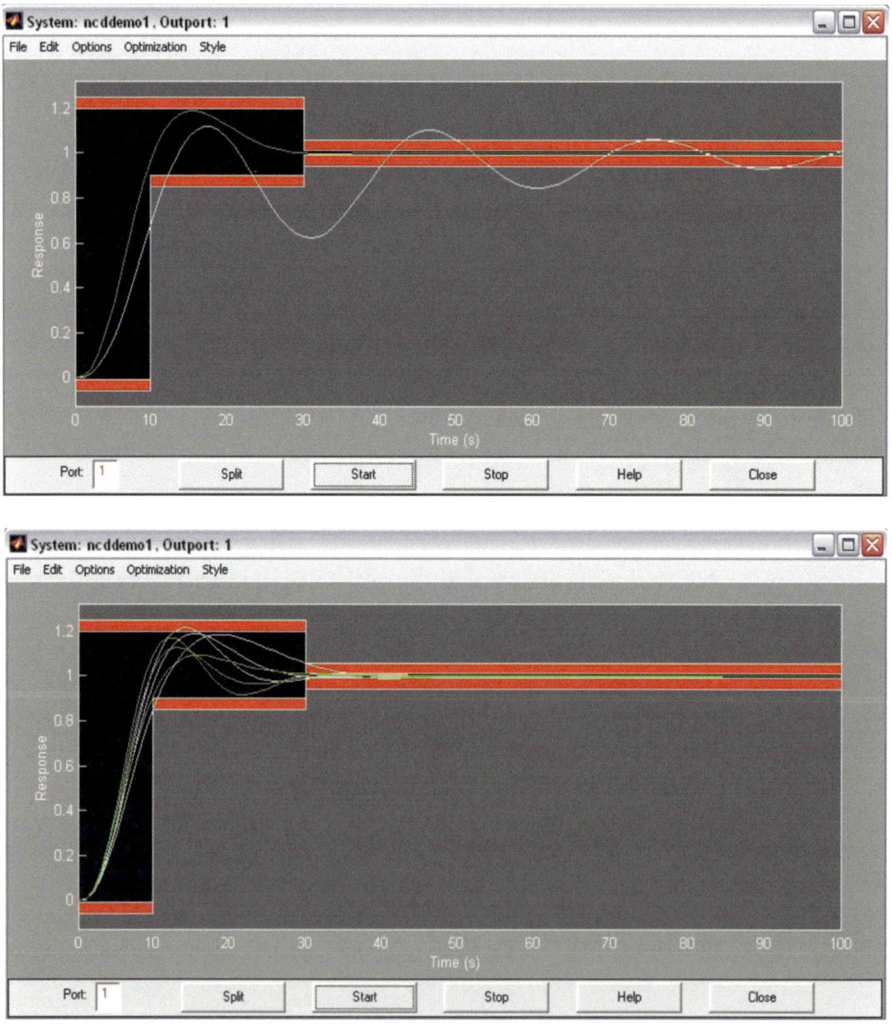

Fig. 2. Moving the limits of restriction to achieve better performance of the system

3. LQR regulator with feed-forward controller

The second problem requires a Control System Toolbox since it is an extended version of the problem from the Simulink demo *lqgdemos* file.
The SISO application can be modelled as a linear ranking 4 system with an enlarging saturation by ± 5 and a non-linear limit of error of ± 10.
The equations are (Franklin, G., et al., 1987; Potvin, A. F., 1991; National Instruments; MathWorks; MathWorks User's Guide, 2003):

$$\dot{x} = \begin{bmatrix} -1.0285 & 0.9853 & -0.9413 & 0.0927 \\ -1.2983 & -1.0957 & 2.8689 & 4.7950 \\ 0.1871 & -3.8184 & -2.0788 & -0.9781 \\ 0.4069 & -4.1636 & 2.5407 & -1.4236 \end{bmatrix} x + \begin{bmatrix} 0 \\ 6.6389 \\ 0 \\ 0 \end{bmatrix} u = Ax + Bu$$

$$y = \begin{bmatrix} -1.7786 & 1.1390 & 0 & -1.0294 \end{bmatrix} = Cx \qquad (3)$$

They define the nominal plant model. One allows the installation's matrix to vary between half to two times of its nominal value.
Using LQG / LTR techniques, one can design a Kalman state estimator and a k amplifier regulator for the linear system. Add an integrator to ensure a zero steady error.
To achieve an increased time response one adds a feed-forward amplifier (FF).
In the demo Simulink *Iqgopt* system, the control parameters k and FF are granted by 'the method presented above (National Instruments; MathWorks; MathWorks User's Guide, 2003).
These parameters can be accorded using the NCD Blockset.
In particular the control parameters k and FF are granted, so that the closed-cycle system may meet the following specifications:

- Maximum oscillation - 20%;
- Propagation time - one second;
- Response time - three seconds (Franklin, G., et al., 1987; Potvin, A. F., 1991; National Instruments; MathWorks; MathWorks User's Guide, 2003).

The Simulink system contains the application and the control structure below:
After starting the system, it is noted that the non-linearity error (± 10) and the saturation (± 5) are included in the model's installation.
Using the From Workspace block, one introduces a step that goes from zero to one in one second. An NCD block is attached to the result of the installation because there is a restricted signal. Checking the System's Parameters one observes that each simulation always lasts 10 seconds.
Tunable and uncertain variables are initialized. Domain restrictions for this demonstration are defined. Upper and lower restriction limits on the oscillation, propagation time and response time are defined. As described above, an initial design regulator using the LQG / LTR methods is designed starting from a linear application. For non-linear control optimization the feed-forward amplifier FF and regulatory matrix amplifier k are tunable (Franklin, G., et al., 1987; Potvin, A. F., 1991; National Instruments; MathWorks; MathWorks User's Guide, 2003).
Note how the installation (reaction) matrix A is defined and also that the optimization restrictions are applied only on nominal installation (reaction).

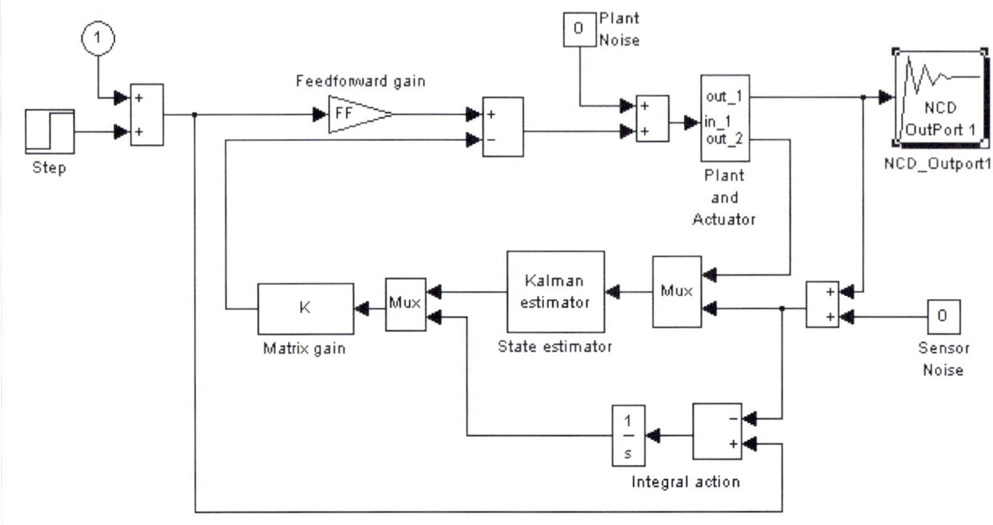

Fig. 3. NCD block attached to the result of the plant

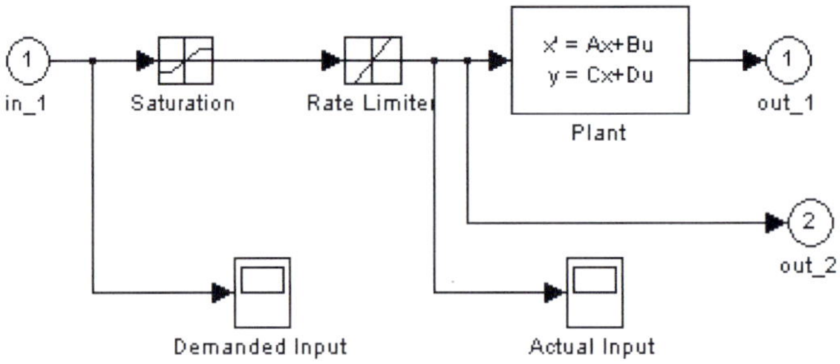

Fig. 4. Plant & Actuator

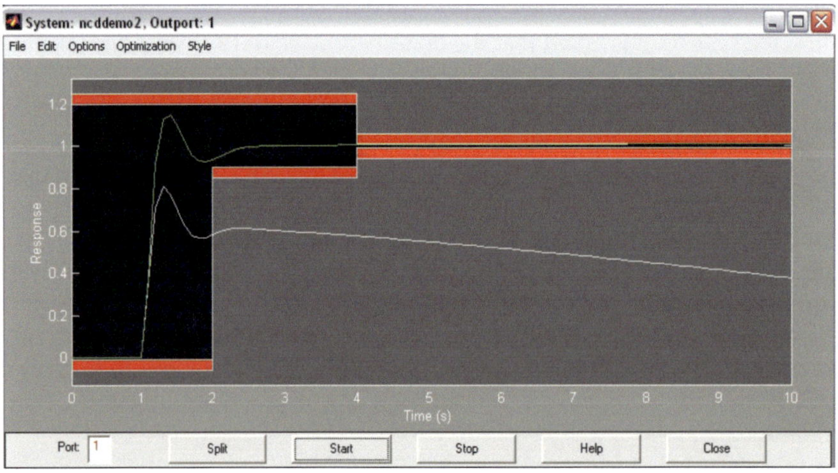

Fig. 5. Moving the limits of restriction to achieve better performance of the system

After the optimization starts, one monitors the response evolution in time. The optimization time, the cost function evolution and final values for tunable parameters vary depending on computer (Savant, C. J., 1967; Sprânceană, N., et al., 1978).
Optimization should produce a regulator which satisfies any restrictions.
One must always restrict the upper and lower limits and start the optimization with uncertainty. Considering that these restrictions can be satisfied, the result shows a maximum violation of the restriction under 0.01 (1%).
One can experiment by moving the limits of restriction to achieve better performances of the system; for example, reducing the propagation time or using restrictions on oscillation (Figure 5).

3.1 Results and simulation after using LQR

Simulation using the optimal LQR has been implemented. Figure 6 shows the unit step system response. As shown in the figure, the displacement reaches its final value in 3*10-6 sec., gives zero tracking error and the system has better stability. In comparison to the results obtained previously, it is quite clear that the use of LQR triggers a much better response (Jalili-Kharaajoo, M. and Dahastani, A., 2003; Roshan N., 2004).

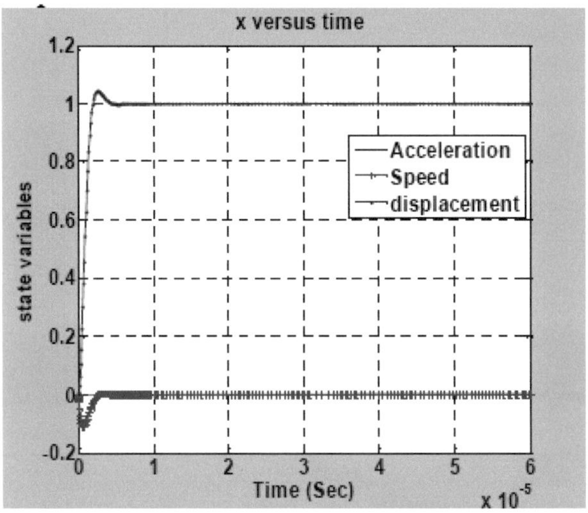

Fig. 6. State variables versus time for unit step input tracking

Figure 7 and Figure 8 show unit ramps and the unit acceleration system response. As shown from the figure the displacement reaches its final value in a few microseconds and gives zero tracking error, which means much better sensitivity and accuracy for the micro accelerometer compared to previous approaches.
The speed of reaching the final values depends on choosing the values of matrix Q, as choosing high values of Q means having faster response for any input signal and having better stability.
Finally, for all inputs, the mass speed when using the LQR is faster and almost has no oscillations, for example, for unit step input the average speed is 1.82*10-3 m/sec., compared to 1.71*10-4 m/sec. as described by some authors. That is, the mass reaches its final position faster with no oscillations.

Using LQR, has increased and improved the accelerometer bandwidth, stability, accuracy and response time (Ibrahim, H. E. A., 2010; Jalili-Kharaajoo, M and Dahastani, A., 2003).

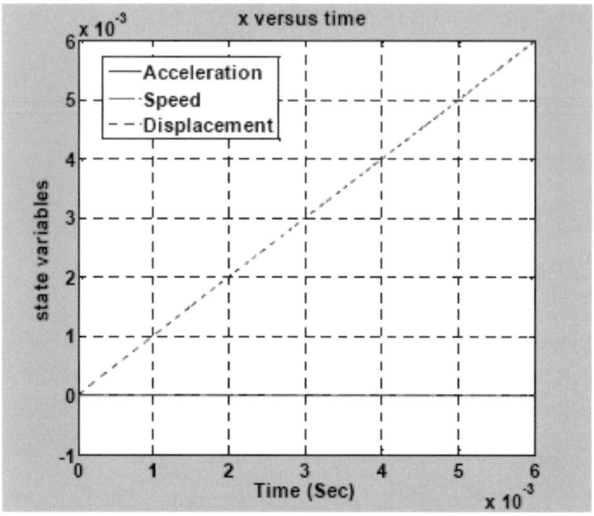

Fig. 7. State variables versus time for unit ramp input tracking

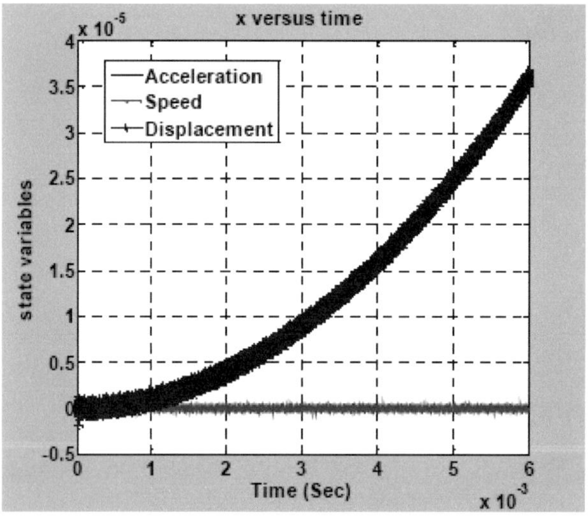

Fig. 8. State variables versus time for unit acceleration input tracking

4. PI-MIMO regulator

The third problem of control design involves designing a centralized PI-MIMO regulator for a turbine engine of LVI00 fuel. One models the application as a system with two inputs, two outputs and a minimum of five phase states. The inputs are fuel flow and variable area turbine nozzle. The outputs are speed coil generator fuel and temperature. The five stages are speed spool generator, the output power, temperature, the driving level of the fuel flow

and the driving level of the turbine nozzle (Franklin, G., et al., 1987; Potvin, A. F., 1991; National Instruments; MathWorks; MathWorks User's Guide, 2003).
Saturation non-linearities exist in the system as limited efforts and maximum temperatures. These non-linearities can be included in the problem formulation as in previous examples. Also, the demonstration plant will exaggerate uncertainty of installation.
More precisely, one permits a variation of a matrix A between half and twice its nominal value.
We want to design a centralized controller 2-by-2 PI for the application so that the system closed-cycle track meets the following specifications:

- Maximum propagation delay time of one second;
- 0 oscillation in the first channel and less than 10% in one second;
- Less than 5% across the channel coupling.

The Simulink system contains the software and control structure below (Figure 9).
To open the system this can be written in MATLAB prompt or double-click on the NCD block 3 demo Simulink system.
One model the PI regulator as a state-space system with the value 0 for matrix A and the identical matrix B.
The C and D matrix are variable tuneable K, and Kp, for a total of eight tuneable variables.

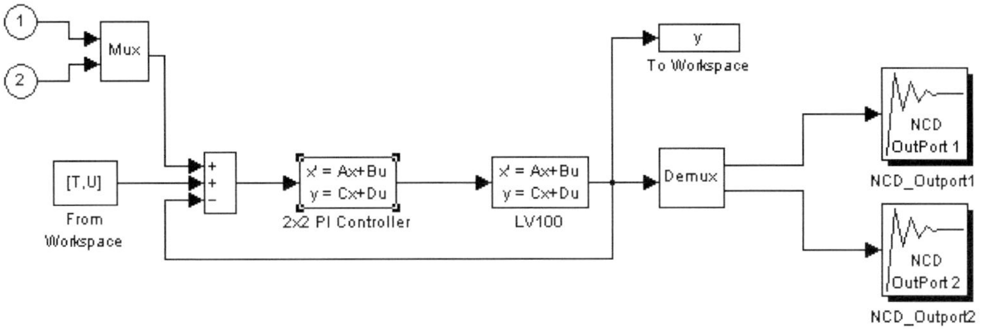

Fig. 9. Control structure of the system

One can note that there are two optimization of NCD blocks that can be displayed simultaneously (Mejhed, N. H., et al., 2005).
The approach suggested for MIMO regulator design requires the sequencing of input steps. When the first channel comes in, the first result should follow up the step and the other channels must reject the signal. When the second channel comes in, the second signal must follow up the step and the other channels must reject the signal etc. (Franklin, G., et al., 1987; Potvin, A. F., 1991; National Instruments; MathWorks; MathWorks User's Guide, 2003).
Note that we used the From Workspace block to enter the sequential steps inside the system. Double-click on the NCD blocks to open the restriction NCD images and to display all the other restrictions. It is noted that restrictions for the first result define the limits step response as shown above. Meanwhile, the output restrictions limits keep the signal near the $\pm$ 0.05 value.
Before starting the optimization, the Optimization Parameters dialog box opens by selecting Parameters from the Optimization menu and it should be noticed that 'how' is defined by

the Parameters Optimization. Also opened is the Uncertain Variables and one observes 'how' is defined by the A matrix installation and that optimization restrictions are only nominally applied on installation.

One can press Start or one can hold down the acceleration key and start the optimizing process. Then, follows the time response evolution, during the optimizing process. Optimization time, cost function evolution and final values for tuneable parameters vary depending on the computer. Optimization should produce a regulator that satisfies all restrictions (Franklin, G., et al., 1987; Potvin, A.F., 1991; National Instruments; MathWorks; MathWorks User's Guide, 2003).

Now, one returns to the Uncertainty Variables dialog box and one restricts the lower and upper limits. Press Start to begin optimizing with uncertainty. We can consider that these restrictions cannot be satisfied, since the result appears to show a maximum restraint violation of less than 0.01.

We can experiment by moving the restriction limits to achieve a higher system performance. For example, one reduces the propagation time or lessens the oscillation restrictions (Figure 10).

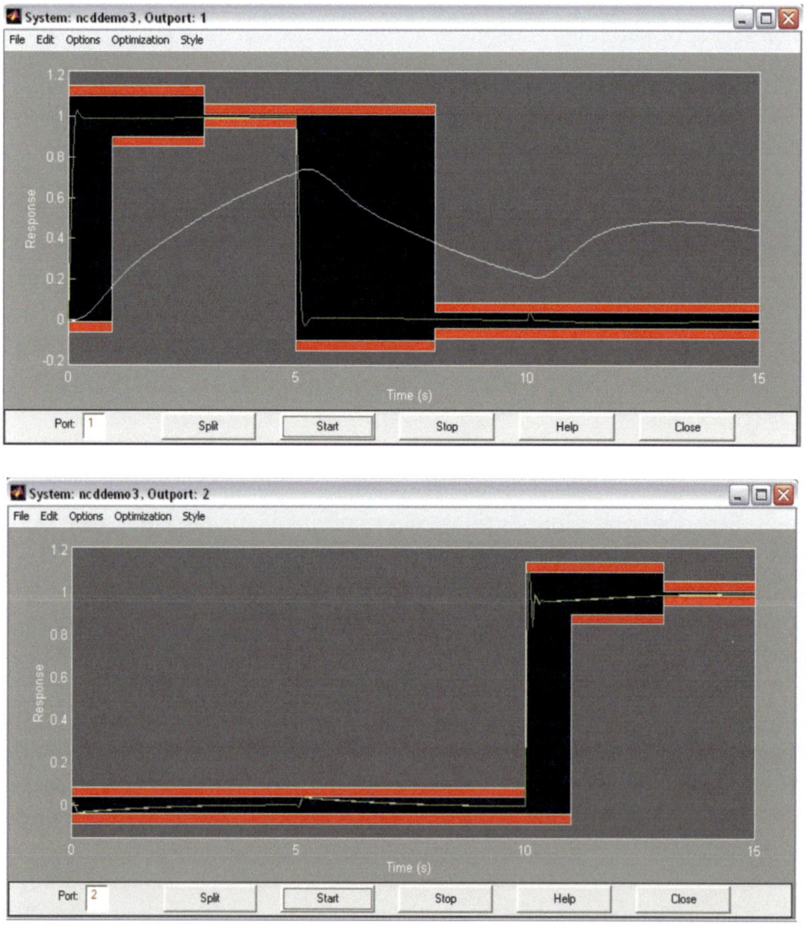

Fig. 10. Moving the limits of restriction to achieve better performance of the system

5. Case studies

We have chosen to present two case studies. The first is the inverted pendulum and the second is the modelling of a robotic arm.

5.1 Inverted pendulum

The inverted pendulum can be described as a cylindrical metal rod attached to a device controlled by an engine powered to revolve only around an axis. The device follows a linear track to create a stabilized problem (Figure 11).

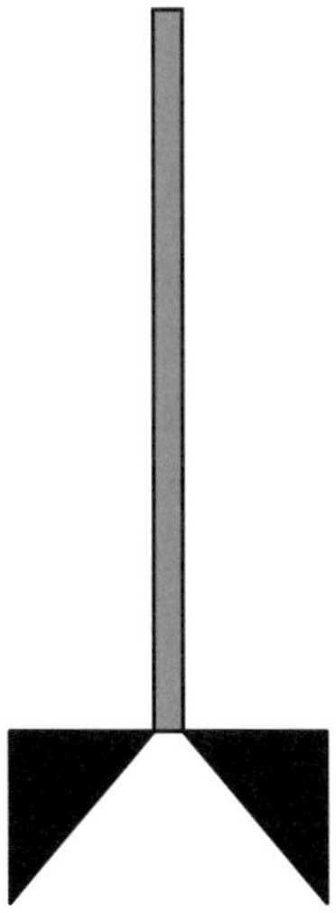

Fig. 11. Inverted pendulum

The inverted pendulum is a classic problem in dynamics and control theory, and is widely used as a benchmark for testing control algorithms (PID controllers, neural networks, fuzzy control, genetic algorithms, etc). Variations on this problem include multiple links, allowing the motion of the cart to be commanded while maintaining the pendulum and balancing the cart-pendulum system on a see-saw. The inverted pendulum is related to rocket or missile guidance, where thrust is actuated at the bottom of a tall vehicle. The understanding of a similar problem is built in the technology of Segway, a self-balancing transportation device. The largest implemented use of this is on huge lifting cranes in shipyards. When moving the shipping containers back and forth, the cranes move the box accordingly so that it never swings or sways. It always stays perfectly positioned under the operator, even when moving or stopping quickly.
Another way that an inverted pendulum may be stabilized, without any feedback or control mechanism, is by oscillating the support rapidly up and down. If the oscillation is sufficiently strong (in terms of its acceleration and amplitude) then the inverted pendulum can recover from perturbations in a strikingly counterintuitive manner. If the driving point moves in simple harmonic motion, the pendulum's motion is described by the Mathieu equation.
In practice, the inverted pendulum is frequently made of an aluminium strip, mounted on a ball-bearing pivot; the oscillatory force is conveniently applied with a jigsaw.

The equation of motion is similar to that for an un-inverted pendulum, except that the sign of the angular position is measured from the vertical unstable equilibrium position:

$$\ddot{\theta} - \frac{g}{l}\sin\theta = 0 \tag{4}$$

When added to both sides, it will have the same sign as the angular acceleration term:

$$\ddot{\theta} = \frac{g}{l}\sin\theta \tag{5}$$

Thus, the inverted pendulum will accelerate away from the vertical unstable equilibrium in the direction initially displaced and the acceleration is inversely proportional to the length. Tall pendulums fall more slowly than short ones.

The inverted pendulum with small parametric forcing is considered as an example of a wider class of parametrically forced Hamiltonian systems. The qualitative dynamics of the Poincare map corresponding to the central periodic solution is studied via an approximating integrable normal form. At bifurcation points we construct local universal models in the appropriate symmetry context, using the equi-variant singularity theory. In this context, structural stability can be proved under generic conditions (Van Noort, M., 2001).

The upper equilibrium of a pendulum can be stabilized by a vertical oscillation of the suspension point within a specific range of excitation frequencies and amplitudes. This follows from classical perturbation theory applied to the linearized equation of motion, e.g., according to van der Pol and Strutt, Stoker and Hale.

The corresponding bifurcation is determined by the non-linear dynamics. Our aim is to understand this dynamics in a qualitative way, with special interest in persistence.

Here, the symmetries of the system are first maintained. However, we consider a system that is slightly more general, but still in the 1 and ½ degree-of-freedom Hamiltonian setting (Van Noort, M., 2001).

We study the corresponding Poincare map, following the approach of Broer and Vegter.

Normal form theory yields a planar Hamiltonian vector field which gives an integrable approximation of this map, valid for every angular displacement and small velocity of the pendulum. The relation between the Poincare map and its approximation is briefly discussed in terms of perturbation theory (Sultan, K., 2003, 2007; Van Noort, M., 2001).

At each bifurcation point of the approximating vector field a model is constructed that is locally equivalent to this approximation, by performing small perturbations that respect the symmetries and conjugating these perturbations to the model by symmetry-preserving local morphisms (Van Noort, M., 2001).

The study of the inverted pendulum could be a collection of MATLAB functions and scripts, and SIMULINK models, useful for analyzing the inverted pendulum system and designing a control system for it.

The inverted pendulum is one of the most important classical problems of control engineering. 'Broom balancing' is a well known example of a non-linear, unstable control problem. This problem becomes further complicated when a flexible broom, in place of a rigid broom, is employed. The degree of complexity and difficulty in its control increases with its flexibility. This problem has been a research interest of control engineers. In this paper, however, we have analyzed the inverted pendulum only with a rigid broom (Sultan, K., 2003, 2007).

The aim of the study is to stabilize the inverted pendulum so that the position of the carriage on the track is controlled quickly and accurately so that the pendulum is always erected in its inverted position during such movements.
The inverted pendulum (IP) is among the most difficult systems to control in the field of control engineering. Due to its importance in the field of control engineering, it has been a task of choice to be assigned to control engineering students to analyze its model and propose a linear compensator according to the PID control law (Sultan, K., 2003, 2007).
For device, a stabilized runway requires the existence of the initial LQR stabilizer. The generation of this regulator rules is realized starting with writing the non-linear equations which define the inverted pendulum. Ignoring the dynamics of the engine, the non-linear equations of motion, for the inverted pendulum system, are (Franklin, G., et al., 1987; Potvin, A. F., 1991; National Instruments; MathWorks; MathWorks User's Guide, 2003):

$$\ddot{y} = \frac{\frac{f}{m} + l\theta \sin\theta - g\sin\theta\cos\theta}{\frac{M}{m} + \sin^2\theta} \tag{6}$$

$$\ddot{\theta} = \frac{-\frac{f}{m}\cos\theta + \frac{M+m}{m} g\sin\theta - l\theta^2 \sin\theta\cos\theta}{l\left(\frac{M}{m} + \sin^2\theta\right)} \tag{7}$$

Where:

- f is the force applied to the cart by the engine in Newton (N);
- m is the position of the cart in meters;
- y is the vertical angle of the pendulum in radians;
- θ is the mass of the cart (0.45 kg);
- M is the pendulum mass (0.21 kg);
- l is the distance from the mass centre of the pendulum (half of its length of 0.61 m);
- g is gravitational acceleration (m/s).

It is necessary that those equations to be linear in the operating point y=0 and (=0 to obtain the linear system:

$$\dot{x} = \begin{bmatrix} \dot{y} \\ \ddot{y} \\ \dot{\theta} \\ \ddot{\theta} \end{bmatrix} = \begin{bmatrix} 0 & 1 & 0 & 0 \\ 0 & 0 & -\frac{gm}{M} & 0 \\ 0 & 0 & 0 & 1 \\ 0 & 0 & \frac{g(M+m)}{lM} & 0 \end{bmatrix} \begin{bmatrix} 0 \\ \frac{11}{M} \\ 0 \\ -\frac{1}{lM} \end{bmatrix} f = Ax + bx \tag{8}$$

Using MATLAB command:

Klqr = lqr(A.b,diag([0.25 0 4 0],0.003)

one obtains the gained stability:

K1qr = (-28.86 -28.56 -145.00 14 -14.86)

Besides the obvious non-linearity of the system's equations, the voltage limit applied to the engine gives a restriction of the action saturation of 1 N (Franklin, G., et al., 1987; Potvin, A. F., 1991; National Instruments; MathWorks; MathWorks User's Guide, 2003).

The sensors measure the position and the angle of the pendulum device. In addition, according with the pendulum stability, one obtains a commanded reference signal for the presenting device. Specifically, one has to design a controller for the system to meet the following specifications of closed loop:

- up to 4 sec. for propagation time;
- up to 6 sec. for the response time;
- zero oscillation;
- less than 0.2 radians deviation from vertical.

It should be noted that the saturation non-linearity included in the process model and hidden pendulum block contain the motion system with non-linear equations.

One commands the input device position with a signal-type unit. NCD blocks are attached to the pendulum angle and device position signal (Figure 12). It is noted that each simulation lasts 15 sec.

The control structure contents have finite estimated status differences for the speed of the device and angular velocity of the pendulum.

As part of an internal control cycle, the estimations for the speed and angular velocity are multiplied by the amplification, collected and then introduced into the engine (Franklin, G., et al., 1987; Potvin, A. F., 1991; National Instruments; MathWorks; MathWorks User's Guide, 2003).

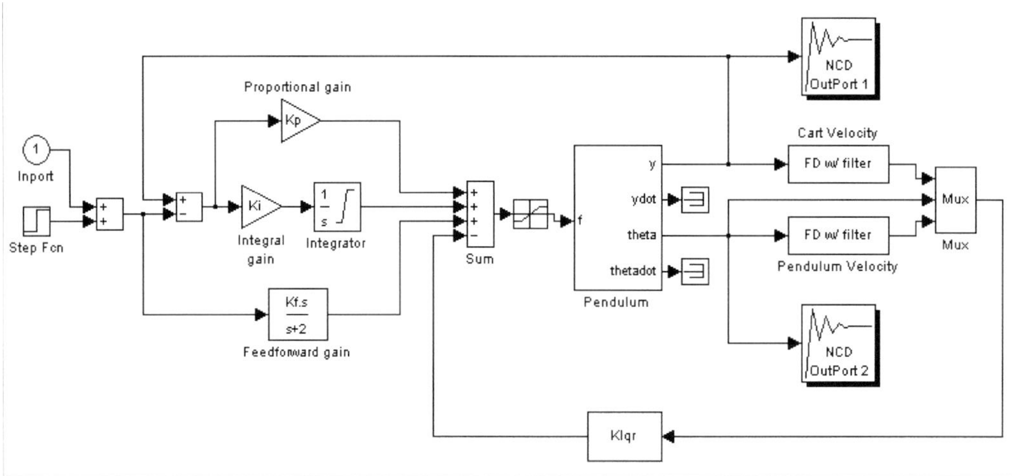

Fig. 12. NCD block attached to the result of the inverted pendulum

The gain is initialized from 1 at 3 with: Klqr = Clqr (2:4), where Clqr is the solution from 1 to 4 at LQR. In a series of external controls (used to allow the device to follow a commanded signal) a feed-forward amplifier Kf is initialized by Kf=C1qr(1) and an integral amplifier, Ki is initialized as zero. It is noted that, in the absence of a commanded signal, these baseline controllers reduce the control structure at LQR amplification described in the previous section (Andrei, H., et al., 1999; Călin, S. et al., 1979; Franklin, G., et al., 1987; Potvin, A. F., 1991).

Tunable variables are initialized and, in accordance, restrictions of time domain response are defined. The configuration of these restrictions should be known like a step response. Pendulum angle channel contains restrictions that define a disturbance rejection problem of

perturbations. In other words, while the device moves to the controlled position, the pendulum must remain in balance.
The optimization begins. The optimization time, the cost function evolution and final values for tunable parameters vary depending on computer. Optimization should produce a controller to meet any restrictions.
It is noted that this optimization runs slower than others. This is, due to the estimating finite-state involved, frequently updated during the simulation (Figure 13).

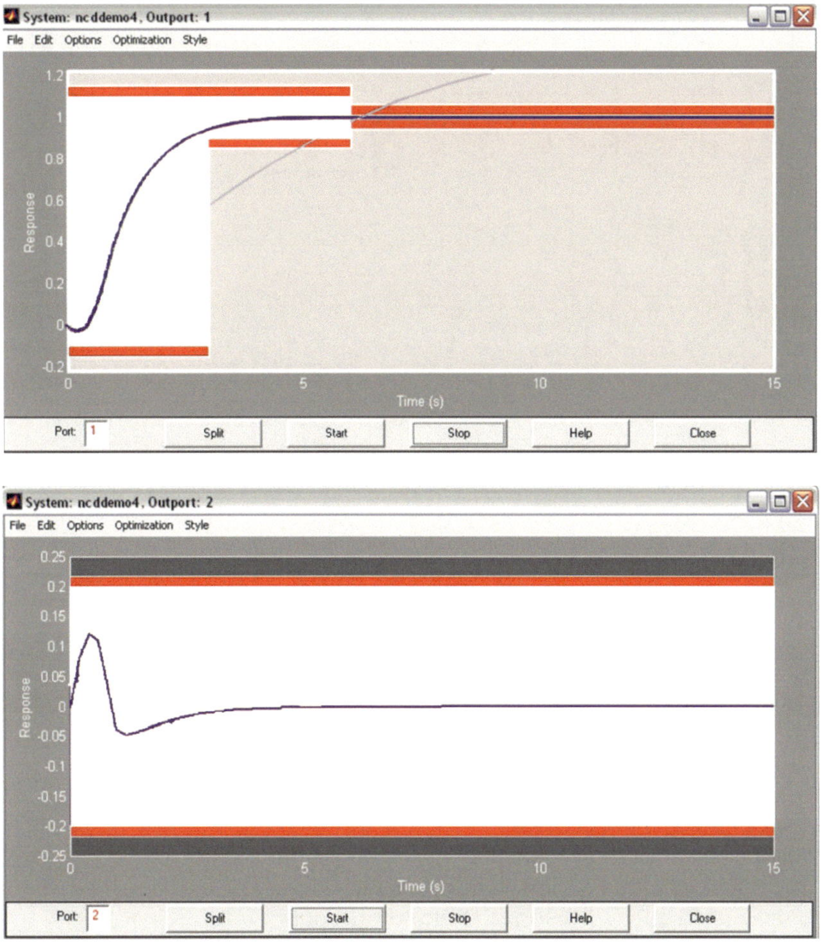

Fig. 13. Moving the limits of restriction to achieve better performance of the inverted pendulum

5.2 Modelling of a robotic arm

Modelling the manipulator's arm in a MATLAB-Simulink environment will be achieved by integrating the equations of state, twice. Note that the expressions depend, beside the mechanical parameters of the system, on the state variable and its first order derivative, which means considering them as integration reaction in the Simulink scheme of the two variables (Sciavicco, L., Siciliano, B., 2000; Stanciulescu F., 2003).

To obtain a general model that can be used regardless of the values of mechanical parameters of the system, the Simulink model will be developed with formal parameters. But, before starting the simulation, the numerical values of mechanical parameters (m1, m2, I2, b, g0) will be initialized in the MATLAB environment. The following scheme is done in Simulink (Patic, P. C., Gorghiu, G., 2009; Stanciulescu, F., 2003):

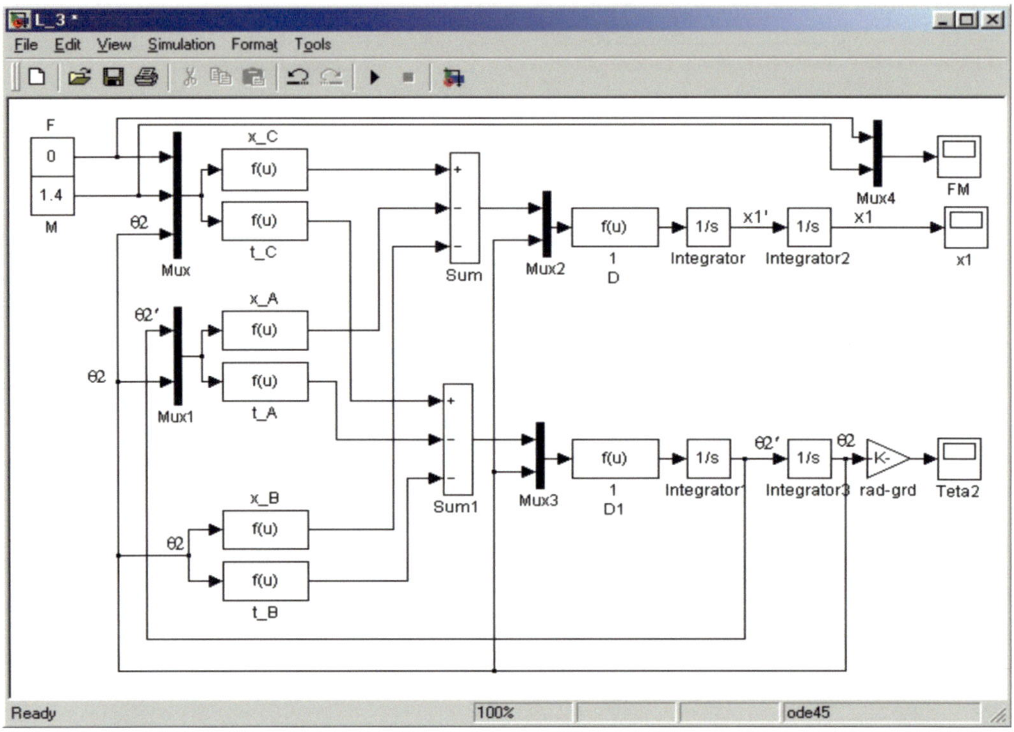

Fig. 14. Simulink scheme regarding the arm modelling

The localization of the blocks in Simulink sub-libraries is (Patic, P. C., Gorghiu, G., 2009; Stanciulescu, F., 2003):

x_A, x_B, x_C, 1/D, t_A, t_B, t_C, 1/D1 - blocks Fcn in Functions & Tables;
F, M - blocks Constant in Sources;
Sum, Sum1 - blocks Sum in Math;
Mux, Mux1 - blocks Mux in Signals&Systems;
Integrator, Integrator1, ... - blocks Integrator in Continuous;
Rad-grd - block Gain in Math;
FM, x1, Teta2 - blocks Scope in Sinks

The functions performed by each block are:

x_A: -(I2+m2*b^2*(sin(u[2]))^2)*m2*b*sin(u[2])*(u[1]^2);
x_B: -(m2*b)^2*sin(u[1])*cos(u[1])*g0;
x_C: (I2+m2*b^2*(sin(u[3]))^2)*u[1]-(m2*b*cos(u[3]))*u[2];
t_A: (m2*b)^2*sin(u[2])*cos(u[2])*(u[1]^2);
t_B: (m1+m2)*m2*b*sin(u[1])*g0;
t_C: -(m2*b*cos(u[3]))*u[1]+(m1+m2)*u[2];
1/D, 1/D1: u[1]/((m1+m2)*(I2+m2*b^2*(sin(u[2]))^2)-(m2*b*cos(u[2]))^2).

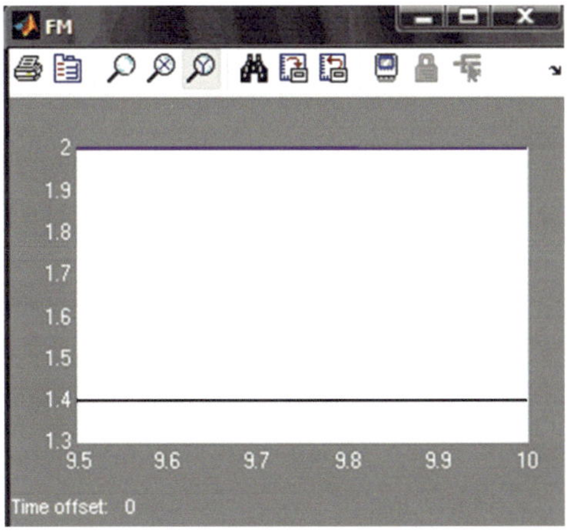

Fig. 15. The evolution of the system - changing external stimuli

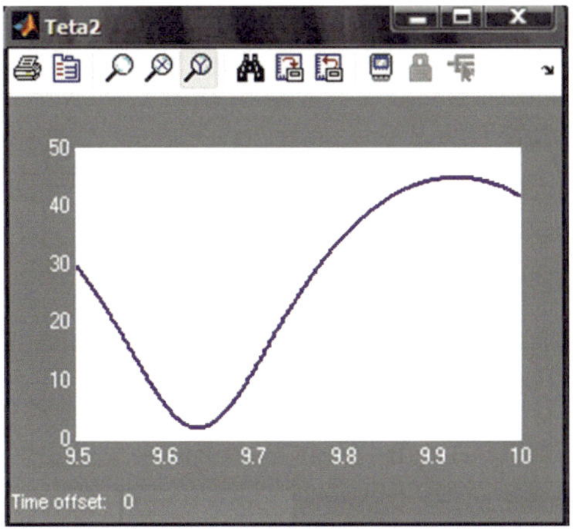

Fig. 16. The evolution of the system - changing external stimuli

Fig. 17. The evolution of the system - changing external stimuli

The block rad-grd being Gain type, with value 180/pi, transform the position θ2 from radians to degrees, just for viewing. As a method of integration, we will choose the method with variable step ode45, maximum integration step is imposed being 0.0001 [s], as well as the final time (stop time), which is 10 [s]. The maximum step 0.0001 was chosen to track the influence of changing values in the simulation stimuli on the evolution of the system (Stanciulescu, F., 2003; Stareţu, I., Ionescu, M., 2005).
After the model realization, a MATLAB file by "m" type is created in which are initialized the values of the mechanical parameters (Patic, P.C., Gorghiu, G., 2009):

```
m1=1;
m2=1;
I2=0.01;
b=0.2;
g0=9.81;
brat;
```

When typing in MATLAB window, the name of this file will be loaded in MATLAB space with the mechanic's parameter values, the last line of the file causing the opening model (Stanciulescu, F., 2003).
The simulation will aim to highlight the evolution of the system to changes in external stimuli.
The results exemplified correspond to a force application F = 2 [Nm] at time of t = 1 sec.

5.2.1 Simulation of the robotic arm using the 3rd degree polynomial interpolation

Continuing our study, for the proper representation of variations of positions, velocities and accelerations for these study couplers robots, we used two methods, utilized very often, to solve these problems of movements of a robot. The first method used was the 3rd degree polynomial interpolation. The other method is the connection of linear functions in parables (Pozna, C., 2000).
One can say that both methods transform the task space in joint coordinates. Polynomials can be used to approximate more complicated curves. A relevant application is the evaluation of the natural logarithm and trigonometric functions. This results in significantly faster computations. Polynomial interpolation also forms the basis for algorithms in numerical quadrate and numerical ordinary differential equations.
Polynomial interpolation is also essential to perform sub-quadratic multiplication and squaring, where an interpolation through points on a polynomial which defines the product, yields the product itself (Scritube Industrial Robots).
The interpolation polynomial of three degree is like below:

$$P(x) = a3x3 + a2x2 + a1x + a0 \quad (9)$$

The statement that P interpolates the data points means that:

$$P(xi) = yi, \text{ where } i \in \{0, 1, 2, 3\} \quad (10)$$

The second method is the connecting of the linear functions in parables. This method is generally used when the robot trajectory passes through several points, but can be used, also, to move from point to point. To join two different points, rectilinear trajectories are used and to respect the conditions of speed and acceleration (by crossing points) straight paths are connected in parables.

The trajectory of motion of the robot is studied from two points of the workspace (Patic, P. C., Gorghiu, G., 2009).
Below we represent only the polynomial interpolation of degree 3 method, with a view for further research to developing the other method - connecting linear functions in parables. So one can observe, graphically, the methods explained, theoretically, above.
First of all, we choose to determine a simulation of a robot arm translation (T) which moves from P1 (0, 0, 0) to P2 (150, 0, 200) (the shape of the trajectory is not required). In fact, in the next case:
the translation couple make a displacement by 150 mm:

di=0, df=150 mm.

the rotation couple make a rotation by 200 rad:

qi=0, qf=200 rad.

So, one tries to move the robotic arm from point P1(0, 0, 0) to P2(150, 0, 200), using two couples with two different degrees of freedom - Translation and Rotation.
After the graphic representation one obtains that both actions, the accelerations and breakings, are different from one couple to another, because the lengths of paths, which are moving, are different. The movement is performed simultaneously on all three directions (Pozna, C., 2000).
In figure 18 one represents the displacement versus time. The displacement from couple 1 is smaller than those from couple 2 (Patic, P. C., et al., 2010).
In figure 19 one determines the velocities versus time. Like above, the speed for couple 1, is smaller than for couple 2.
The graphical differences are more evident than above, when one uses the displacements.
In figure 20 one has the accelerations versus time. The acceleration has a decreasing trend, being noted that in five seconds the accelerations for those two couples is zero (Patic, P. C., et al., 2010).

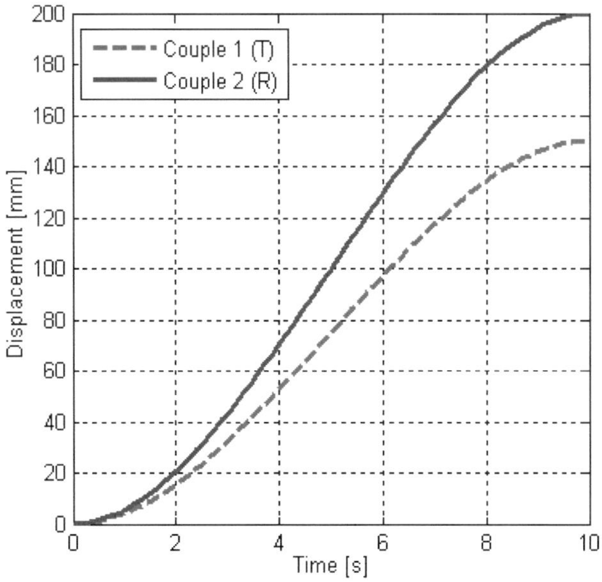

Fig. 18. The displacements of the robotic arm

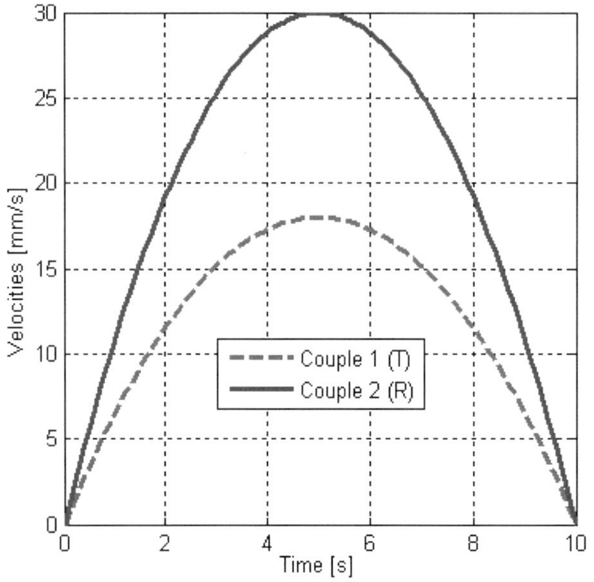

Fig. 19. The velocities of the robotic arm

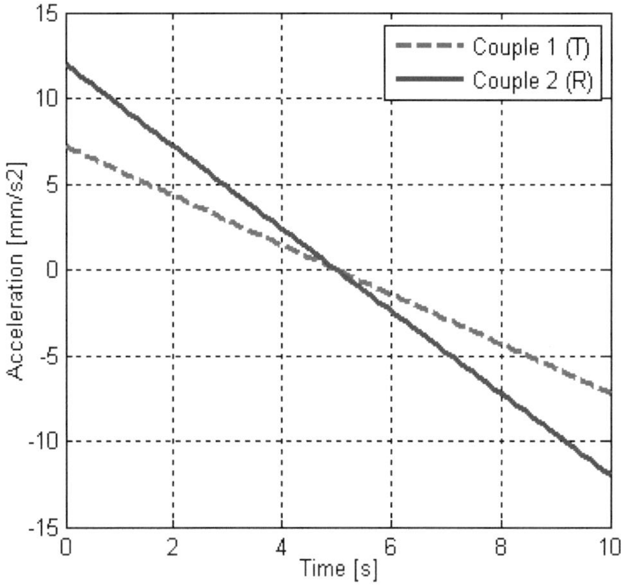

Fig. 20. The accelerations of the robotic arm

6. Conclusion

The work from this paper intended to determine the parameters of a PID controller using two software packages, namely MATLAB-Simulink and LabVIEW. As a mathematical model, a DC machine was used.

Automatic modelling systems using MATLAB-Simulink software packages applied the Cohen-Coon method for determining the closed loop PID parameters and plotted the system response clue. The limit of the over adjustment was found to be of 20%, the timing of the transitional regime - 3 seconds, and maximum response time was 10 seconds. Also, one represented the chart of the evolution over time, in a closed loop system, to unit step input. The use of these software packages offers an easy way of working, which means that it is convenient to utilize the programme functions.

Implementing the same system in a closed loop PID adjustment using the LabVIEW software package, one requires, at first, an additional procedure, namely, the use of the transfer functions in Z domain. For the displayed example the sampling period is 60 μs and so can be determined the transfer function graph, sampled to the entry with a unitary step.

By the use of the graphical features of the LabVIEW software package for the adjustment of the PID controller, one recorded the best performance, since they include zero stationary error due to the integrative component for minimum stabilization time, due to the anticipatory component derivative etc.

Using the LabVIEW package to study the reaction systems involved additional procedures.

A comparative analysis of the two programmes using MATLAB-Simulink and LabVIEW to determine the same automatic performances of the system indicates that MATLAB-Simulink software is more efficient, having different features of its libraries already implemented, with coverage areas of automation and systems theory. LabVIEW is a software package dedicated to particular virtual instrumentation and graphical applications in time.

For the robotic simulation one can say that a functional simulation, using a 3D model is very important for obtaining an optimum version of a robotic arm and for a robot. After the graphic representation, one obtains that both actions, the accelerations and breakings, are different from one couple to another, because the lengths of paths, which are moving, are different. The movement is performed simultaneously on all three directions. In conclusion, one recorded the maximum values of the couples that make big displacements, so the engines that lead such couples are very loaded.

7. References

Andrei, H., Brezeanu, I., Enciu, G., Enciu, M., *Elements of Adjustment Theory*, Ed. Macarie, Târgovişte, 1999

Călin, S., Tertişco, M., Dumitrache, I., Popeea, C., Popescu, D., *Optimisation in Industrial Automatisation*, Ed. Tehnică, Bucharest, 1979

Călin, S., Brezeanu, I., Popescu, M., Ispas, G., *Automatic Tuning System Theory. MATLAB Application*, Ed. Biblioteca, Târgovişte, 2002

Franklin, G. F., David Powell, J. and Emami-Naeini, A., *Feedback Control of Dynamic Systems*, Addison-Wesley Publishing Company, 1987

Dumitrache, I., *State-space Method for Linear Systems Automatic Analysis, Continuous and Discrete*", U.P.B. Litography, Bucharest, 1971

Gibson, J., *Linear Automatic System*, English translation, Ed. Tehnică, Bucharest, 1967

Ibrahim, H.E.A., *LQR Optimal Control for Micro-machined Tunnelling Accelerometer*, Proceedings of the 9th WSEAS International Conference on Signal Processing, Robotics and Automation, ISPRA '10, February 20-22, Cambridge, U.K., p.40-45, 2010.

Ionescu, V., *Introduction in Structural Theory of a Linear Systems*, Academy Edition., Bucharest, 1975

Jalili-Kharaajoo, M., Dehestani, A., Active Queue Management: Comparison of Sliding Mode Controller and Linear Quadratic Regulator, *WSEAS Transactions on Circuits and Systems,* Issue 3, Volume 2, July 2003, ISSN 1109-2734, p. 594-599

Sultan, K., Inverted Pendulum, MATLAB Central, 2003 and 2007, Available from http://www.mathworks.com/MATLABcentral/fileexchange/3790-inverted-pendulum

Chugani, M. L., Samant, A. R., Cerna, M., *LabVIEW Signal Processing,* Pearson, 1998

MathWorks, Using MATLAB-Simulink, n.d., Available from http://www.mathworks.com/access/helpdesk_r13/help/toolbox/ncd/case.html

Mejhed, N. H., Hmamed, A., Benzaouia, A., Continuous Time Regulator for Linear Systems with Constrained Control, *WSEAS Transactions on Systems,* Issue 5, Volume 4, May 2005, ISSN 1109-2777, p. 537-545.

National Instrument, NI Developer Zone, n.d., Available from http://zone.ni.com/devzone/conceptd.nsf/webmain/2F266590B802FEFD8625686500609588/AN039.pdf

Nițu, C., Jora, B., Popeea, C., Georgescu, E., *Automatic Regulators. Laboratory Guide,* UPB, Bucharest, 1974

Non-linear Control Design Blockset, for use with Simulink - User's Guide - The MathWorks, 2003

Papadache, I., *Choosing and According of the Regulators,* Ed. Tehnică, Bucharest, 1975

Patic, P. C., Pascale, L., Popa, F., Ardeleanu, M., *Modelling and Simulation of a Column Industrial Robot Type Used in Mounting Processes,* 10th Wseas International Conference on Signal Processing, Computational Geometry and Artificial Vision (ISCGAV '10), Taipei, Taiwan, August 20-22, 2010, ISBN 978-960-474-217-2, ISSN 1792-4618, pp. 122-127

Patic, P. C., Gorghiu G., *The Modelling and Simulation of a Robotic Arm, The Scientific Bulletin of Electrical Engineering Faculty,* ISSN 1843-6188, 2009, No. 2 (11), pp. 85 - 90

Potvin, A. F., *A Unified Solution to Constrained Configuration Control Law Design,* Master's Thesis, MIT EECS Dept., 1991

Pozna, C., *Command and Control of the Industrial Robots,* CIT Publishing House, Brasov 2000

Bishop, R., *LabVIEW 2009 Student Edition,* Prentice Hall, 2010

Roshan N., *Application of Linear Quadratic Regulator (LQR) in Displacement Control of an Active Mass Damper,* 4th WSEAS International Conference on Systems Theory And Scientific Computation *(ISTASC'04),* December, 17-19 2004, Tenerife, Spain.

Savant, C. J., *Automatic System Calculus,* Ed. Tehnică, Bucharest, 1967

Sciavicco, L., Siciliano, B., *Modelling and control of robot manipulators,* Springer, 2000

Scritube Industrial Robots, n.d., Available from http://www.scritube.com/tehnica-mecanica/Roboti-Industriali-Introducere45272.php

Călin, S.,, *Automatic Regulators,* Ed. Didactică şi Pedagogică, Bucharest, 1970

Sprânceană, N., Dobrescu, R., Borangiu Th., *Discrete Automation in Industry,* Ed. Tehnică, Bucharest, 1978

Stanciulescu, F., *The Complex System Modelling,* Ed. Tehnică, 2003

Starețu, I., Ionescu, M., Kinematics and Functional Simulation of a Robotic Arm from a Pyrotechnic Robot, 2005, Available from http://www.imsar.ro/SISOM_Papers_2005/1_R.pdf

Van Noort, M., Dissertaties - Rijksuniversiteit Groningen, 2001, Available from http://dissertations.ub.rug.nl/FILES/faculties/science/2001/m.van.noort/c2.pdf

7

MATLAB GUI Application for Teaching Electronics

Ali H. Assi, Maitha H. Al Shamisi and Hassan A. N. Hejase
United Arab Emirates University
United Arab Emirates

1. Introduction

The Electrical Engineering (EE) Department at the University Arab Emirates (UAE) University incorporates numerous software tools in teaching the diverse electrical engineering (EE) courses imparted at undergraduate and graduate level. The most common being the use of MATLAB, Simulink and LabView, in addition to standard circuits, electronics, and power systems software packages such as OrCAD, MultiSim and PSCAD. Instructors also make use of free available online JAVA applets that apply to specific advanced EE courses such as signals and systems, electromagnetics, antenna engineering, among others. The variety of tools used in each EE course makes it difficult for students to learn a new tool or program for each course. This suggests that MATLAB can be used as a common platform for all courses given its rich library and available tools. Student evaluations over the past years have reflected favourably on the use of MATLAB tools as a valuable support in graphical visualization, numerical evaluation and modelling tasks in the diverse EE course. Most books published nowadays in the various EE subjects include MATLAB exercises and applications in each chapter. The use of these software tools is intended to enhance student appreciation of theoretical concepts and as support tools for hands-on analysis and design experience. Most EE students use the limited MATLAB/Simulink Student Version which does not include many of the needed MATLAB toolboxes. As a result students have to work on campus in order to access the specialized toolboxes. Developing GUI-based applets offers the advantage of providing more independent MATLAB-based tools for use by students on their own Laptop anywhere.

Numerous educators have been developing software applets in different electrical engineering subjects. Such tools are indispensable in helping students better understand basic scientific and engineering concepts through a user-friendly interactive environment that also counts with an adequate help menu to guide students through the application. (Azemi & Stook, 1996) utilized MATLAB in undergraduate electric circuit courses. They focused on features of MATLAB that have not been adapted by other educators before. They worked on generating analytical solutions with the Symbolic Math toolbox, creating interactive simulations with user interface control, and the use of MATLAB Compiler and MATLAB C Library to produce stand-alone applications. They presented examples illustrating the above mentioned features and made the code available on their website.

They also discussed student response to use of the developed MATLAB software package in circuits analysis. (Andreatos & Michalareas, 2008) developed a MATLAB-based application for e-assessment in an introductory analog electronic design course. The application included separate MATLAB GUI interfaces for students and instructor. The applet was intended to help students design a transistor amplifier and in parallel provide an automated qualitative and quantitative assessment tool for instructors. The added assessment tool aimed at ensuring that students engage in actual circuit evaluation rather than making random guesses. (Andreatos & Zagorianos, 2009) also presented a MATLAB-based GUI tool for teaching Automatic Control Systems. The tool is demonstrated using a step-by-step exercise on a typical aircraft control system. (Attia, 1995, 1996) designed AC circuits and electronics teaching tools using MATLAB to teach circuit theory, filter design, random processes, control system and communication theory. The tools employ matrix functions for experimental data analysis as well as graphical features to display the frequency response of amplifiers and illustrate the principles and concepts of semiconductor physics. The circuits MATLAB exercises cover sinusoidal ac analysis, network characteristics and frequency response. The interactive programming and versatile graphics of MATLAB are especially effective in exploring some of the characteristics of devices and electronic circuits. (Rajashekar & Bovik, 2000) presented a suite of user-friendly interactive Digital Signal Processing (DSP) demonstration modules using MATLAB. Their focus was on providing visualization tools that emphasize the intuitive aspects of DSP algorithms. A MATLAB/GUI based educational tool was developed by (Koç & Aydoğmus, 2009) for power system fault calculations. This software provides a user-friendly interface to help the student understand the symmetrical components and fault calculations. The tool allows students to choose one of four fault options for which fault current and voltage calculations are performed. The GUI provides a graphical output representation of currents and voltages. For such application, the instructor expects students to check their answers with hand calculations.

The EE Department at UAE University offers two circuits courses, namely, Electric Circuits I (ELEC 320) and Electric Circuits II (ELEC 325). The Electric Circuits I course runs through both semesters of the academic year. It focuses on the analysis of basic DC and AC electric circuits. Among the topics covered in this introductory course are operational amplifier (OP-AMP) circuits. The average student population each year ranges from 25 to 30 students. At the beginning of the course, students have background knowledge of basic mathematics, physics, and MATLAB programming skills needed throughout the course. One of the most significant course design objectives is the development of a tool for achieving improved learning process. Today, during the teaching process of the fundamentals principles of Electronics, the emphasis is not given on tedious calculations, but rather on offering engineering education, by utilizing efficient software tools. Computer-aided applications are appropriate tools, because they improve the efficiency of learning. In this chapter, basic electronic and electric circuits are investigated using an interactive MATLAB GUI program applet (MATLAB, 2010). The developed comprehensive and user-friendly tool called Electronics Teaching Assistant (abbreviated herein as ETA) can perform typical operational amplifier (OP-AMP) gain calculations and displays analog graphs for input and output currents and voltages in a user friendly MATLAB environment.

Section 2 will address the operational amplifier and basic configurations used in teaching OP-AMP circuits. Section 3 briefly discusses the voltage and current divider circuits. Section 4 explains in detail the development of the GUI tool including code used and input and output windows. Conclusions are then presented in Section 5.

The authors intend to develop more GUI-based applets for numerous circuits and electronics subjects with the objective of making student learning of basic electrical topics fun and interactive. Proper assessment of student learning is followed each semester in line with the ABET outcome assessment process.

2. Operational amplifiers

Operational amplifiers (op amps) typically have 2 inputs, a positive (non-inverting) input and a negative (inverting) input. A signal fed into the positive (non-inverting) input will produce an output signal which is in phase with the input. If the signal is fed into the negative (inverting) input, the output will be 180 degrees out of phase when compared to the input.

The following sub-sections represent an attempt to give you the basic understanding of OP-AMP configurations. None of the power supply connections are shown. Most OP-AMP circuits used in audio applications use a ±15 volts power supply. They can also be used with a single ended supply (no negative voltage).

The diagram below (Fig. 1) shows the OP-AMP symbol.

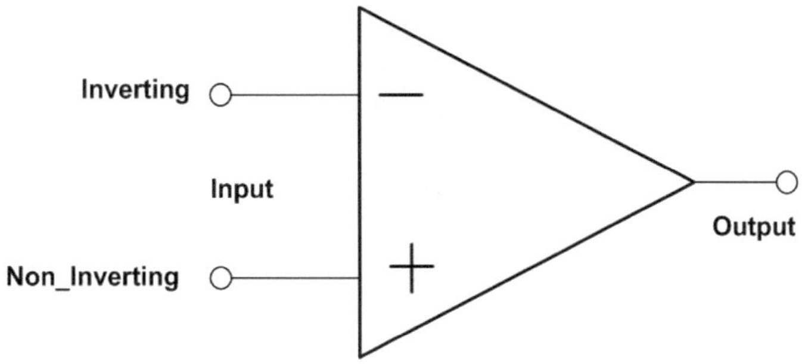

Fig. 1. The OP-AMP symbol

2.1 Inverting amplifier

This is a fundamental OP-AMP configuration whose schematic diagram depicted in Fig. 2 shows the basic circuit configuration.

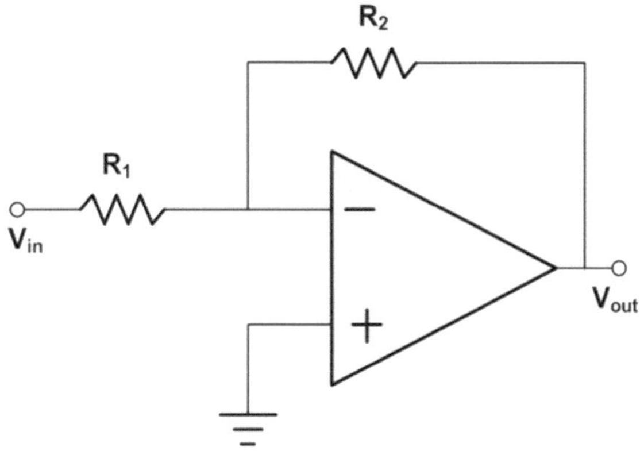

Fig. 2. The inverting configuration

An input voltage, V_{in} is applied to the input resistor, R_1. The OP-AMP amplifies the input voltage it receives and inverts its polarity, producing an output voltage, V_{out}. This same output voltage is also applied to a feedback resistor, R_2, which is connected to the amplifier input along with R_1.
The OP-AMP itself has a very high voltage gain. As a result, the junction of the two resistors, which is also the OP-AMP input, must be virtually at ground potential. A non-zero input voltage will be amplified so that the output voltage would try to exceed its electronic limits. At the same time, the OP-AMP requires an extremely small input current to operate. Therefore, the input current (Vin/R_1) must be the same as the feedback current (V_{out}/R_2). This implies that the effective gain of the circuit with feedback in place is simply the resistance ratio, R_2/R_1. With such configuration, we can obtain accurate results if we use precision resistors, and yielding a gain of:

$$Gain = \frac{V_{out}}{V_{in}} = \frac{R_2}{R_1} \tag{1}$$

2.2 Non-inverting amplifier

Fig. 3 shows a non-inverting OP-AMP circuit. In this circuit, the input signal is effectively used as the reference voltage at the "+" input, while the "-" input is indirectly referenced to ground. In order to keep the two input voltages the same, the OP-AMP must set V_{out} to whatever voltage is required to make the feedback voltage to the "-" input match the input voltage to the "+" input.

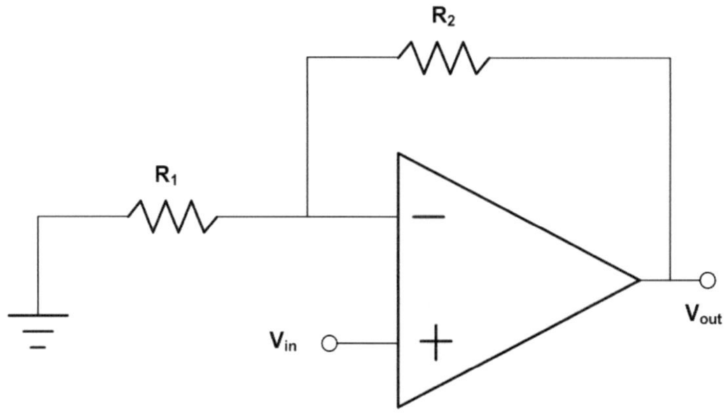

Fig. 3. The non-inverting configuration

Since R_2 and R_1 form a voltage divider, the feedback voltage will be:

$$V_{out} \times \frac{R_1}{R_2 + R_1} \tag{2}$$

The gain of this circuit becomes:

$$Gain = \frac{V_{out}}{V_{in}} = 1 + \frac{R_2}{R_1} \tag{3}$$

2.3 Voltage follower

This is a special case of the non-inverting amplifier with $R_1 = \infty$ and $R_2 = 0$. Fig. 4 shows the voltage follower circuit.

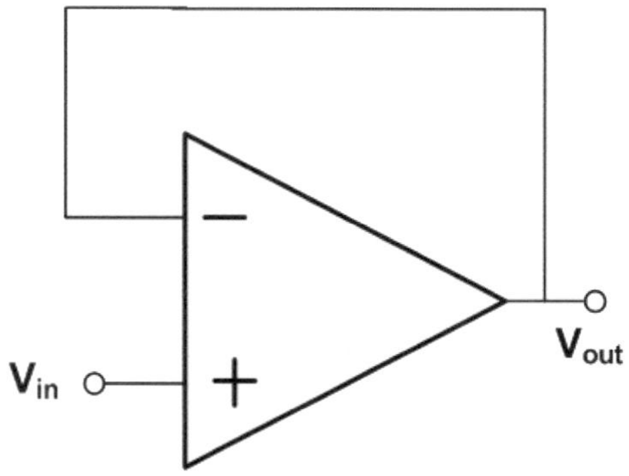

Fig. 4. The voltage follower

For the circuit shown in Fig. 4, and using equation (3), one can easily find:

$$V_{out} = V_{in} \tag{4}$$

This is a very useful circuit, because the input impedance of the OP-AMP is very high, giving effective isolation of the output from the signal source. The circuit draws very little power from the signal source, avoiding "loading" effects. This circuit in general is a useful first stage. The voltage follower is often used for the construction of buffers for logic circuits.

2.4 Summing amplifier

This is special case of the inverting configuration with more than one input as shown in Fig. 5.

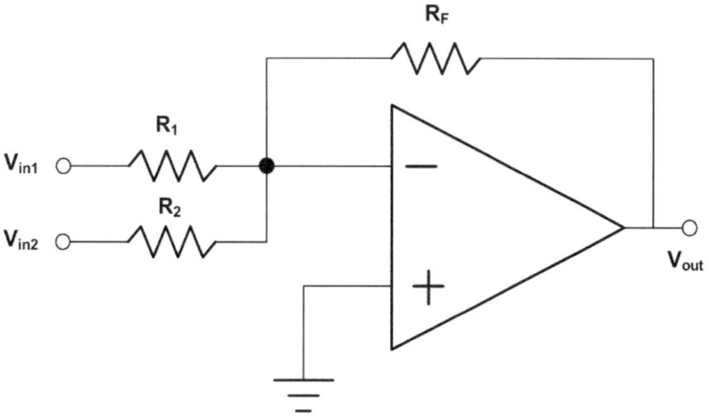

Fig. 5. The summing amplifier

This circuit will amplify each individual input voltage and produce an output voltage signal that is proportional to the algebraic "SUM" of the two individual input voltages V_{in1} and V_{in2}. We can also add more inputs if required. The point of using an OP-AMP to add multiple input signals is to avoid interaction between them, so that any change in one input voltage will not have any effect on the other input. This is because the input signals are effectively isolated from each other by the "virtual earth" node at the inverting input of the OP-AMP.

For the circuit shown in Fig. 5, the voltage at the output is given by:

$$V_{out} = -R_F\left(\frac{V_1}{R_1} + \frac{V_2}{R_2}\right) \tag{5}$$

A direct voltage addition can also be obtained when all the resistances are of equal value (i.e. $R_F = R_1 = R_2$):

$$V_{out} = -(V_1 + V_2) \tag{6}$$

2.5 Differential amplifier

The circuit of a differential amplifier is shown in Fig. 6. Apply the superposition principle to obtain the gain expression:

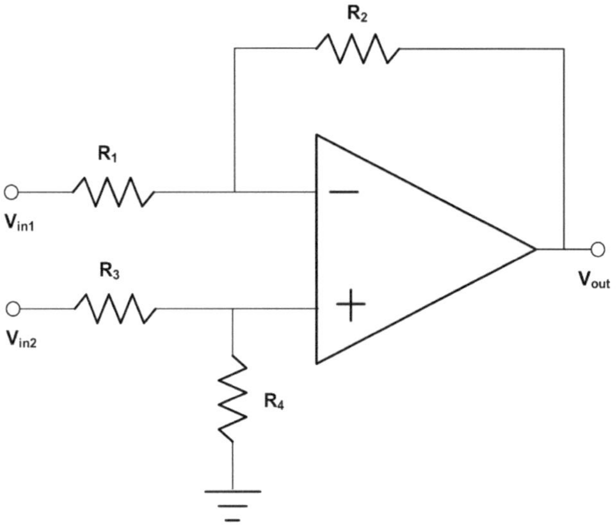

Fig. 6. The differential amplifier

$$V_{out} = -\frac{R_2}{R_1}V_{in1} + \frac{R_4}{R_3 + R_4}\left(1 + \frac{R_2}{R_1}\right)V_{in2} \tag{7}$$

For $R_2 = R_4$, the output will be:

$$V_{out} = -\frac{R_2}{R_1(V_{in2} - V_{in1})} \tag{8}$$

Finally, for $R_2 = R_1$ one can obtain the exact difference of V_{in2} and V_{in1}:

$$V_{out} = V_{in2} - V_{in1} \tag{9}$$

3. Basic electric circuits

This section explains briefly two basic circuit configurations of general use in electronic circuit analysis.

3.1 Voltage divider

The two resistor voltage divider, shown in Fig. 7, is used often to supply a voltage different from that of an available battery or power supply. In practice, the output voltage depends upon the resistance of the load it drives. Note here that R_2 includes also the load resistance.

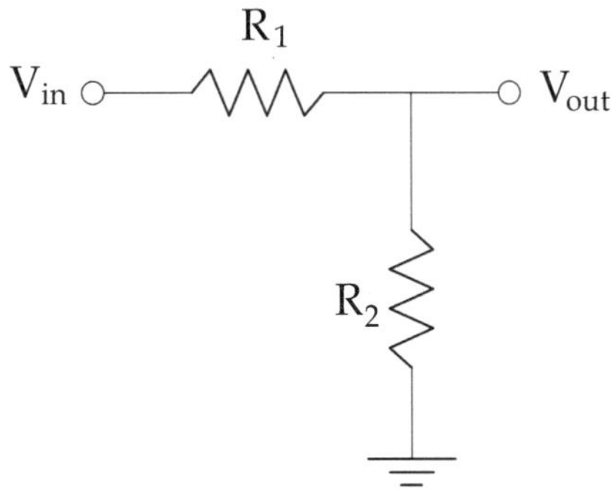

Fig. 7. The voltage divider

$$V_{out} = V_{in} \times \frac{R_2}{R_2 + R_1} \tag{10}$$

3.1 Current divider

For the circuit shown in Fig. 8, one can easily derive the following relation:

$$I_1 = I_3 \times \frac{R_2}{R_2 + R_1} \tag{11}$$

and

$$I_2 = I_3 \times \frac{R_1}{R_2 + R_1} \tag{12}$$

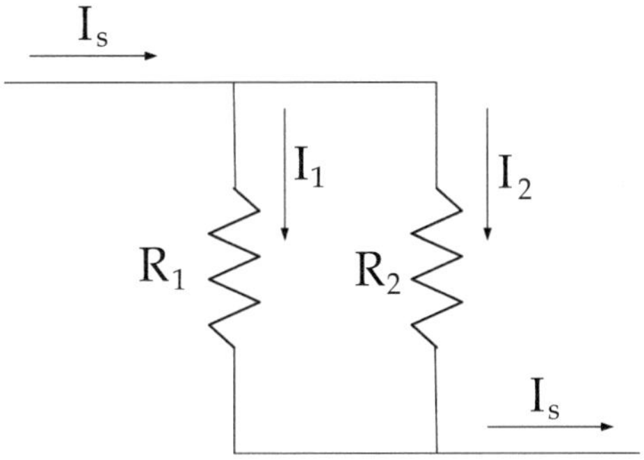

Fig. 8. The current divider

4. Graphical MATLAB-based tool

A graphical user interface tool was designed using the Matlab **GUIDE** environment which greatly simplifies the process of building and developing GUIs. **GUIDE Layout Editor** allows the user to populate a GUI by clicking and dragging GUI components namely, axes, panels, buttons, text fields, sliders into the layout area. Moreover, from the Layout Editor, the user can size the GUI, modify component look and feel, align components, set tab order, view a hierarchical list of the component objects, and set GUI options.
GUIDE automatically generates a program file containing MATLAB functions that controls how the GUI operates. This code file helps initialize the GUI and contains a framework for the GUI callbacks; the routines that execute when a user interacts with a GUI component. The MATLAB Editor should be used to add code to callbacks in order to perform the required actions [MATLAB Creating Graphical User Interfaces, 2004].

4.1 GUI layout and programming

The main window (Electronics Teaching Assistant) is designed to allow the user choose between Operational Amplifier circuits and Electric Circuits and exit the tool as shown in Fig. 9. It consists of two Axes, text and three push buttons namely, **OP AMP Circuits**, **Electric Circuits** and **Close**. The two axes are used for presenting images: one for logo and the other for background. The text displays the tool's name. OP AMP Circuits button will allow the user to analyze different types of OP AMP Circuits. Electric Circuits button will let the user analyze different types of electric circuits (voltage and current dividers). Close button will simply close the whole program.
The following code blocks show how the three buttons are programmed. The set function **set(handle, 'PropertyName', value)** is used to set a property value of buttons.

```
% --- Programming theOP_AMP_Circuits_Button.
functionOP_AMP_Circuits_Button_Callback(hObject, eventdata, handles)
% hObject=handle to OP_AMP_Circuits_Button (see GCBO)
% eventdata= reserved to be defined in a future version of MATLAB
% handles = structure with handles and user data (see GUIDATA)
%---- To open Electric Circuits window ---------%
set(ETA_OP_AMP_Circuits,'Visible','on')
 %---- To Close Electronics_Teaching_Assistant window ------%
set(Electronics_Teaching_Assistant,'Visible','off')
functionElectronic_Circuit_Button_Callback(hObject, eventdata, handles)
%---- To open Electric Circuits window ---------%
set(ETA_Electric_Circuits,'Visible','on')
%---- To close main window window ------------%
set(Electronics_Teaching_Assistant,'Visible','off')
functionClose_Button_Callback(hObject, eventdata, handles)
%---- To terminate the program ---------%
delete(get(0,'Children'));
```

In order to show the logo and background images and their axes, the code is written under **Opening Function**. **Axes function** is used to determine which axes the image should display followed by **imshowfunction**.

```
functionElectronics_Teaching_Assistant_OpeningFcn(hObject, eventdata, handles, varargin)
% This function has no output arguments. See OutputFcn.
% hObject= handle to figure
% eventdata reserved = to be defined in a future version of MATLAB
% handles = structure with handles and user data (see GUIDATA)
% varargin= command line arguments to Electronics_Teaching_Assistant (see VARARGIN)
% Choose default command line output for Electronics_Teaching_Assistant
handles.output = hObject;
%------------- Add logo---------------------------%
axes(handles.Axes_UAEU_Logo);
imshow('uaeu_logo.png');
%------------- Add Background --------------------%
axes(handles.Axes_Background)
imshow('Electronic_Circuit.jpg');
% Update handles structure
guidata(hObject, handles);
```

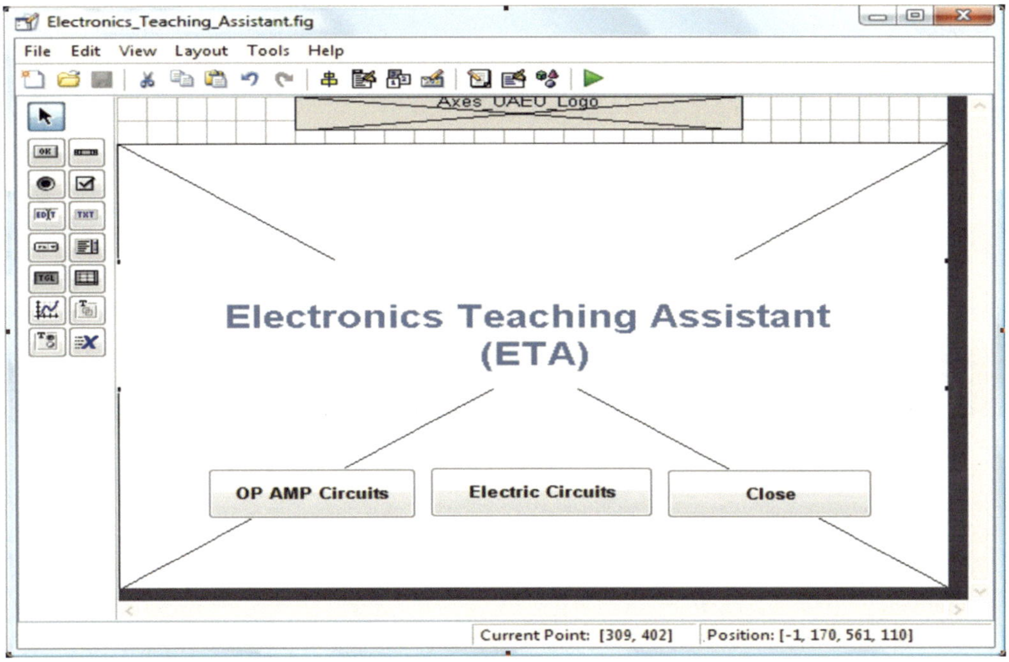

Fig. 9. Electronics Teaching Assistant

The ETA_Op_AMP_Circuits window shown in Fig. 10 is designed to allow the user choose between different types of circuits through a pop-up menu. The user can also visualize the circuit diagram when updated according to the user choices. This diagram is presented on Circuit Axes which is located on the top right hand. Input and output parameters vary according to circuit types. All circuit components are first laid out then their values are defined. For example, the R_1 and R_3 text located in the background of R_1 has its visibility property set to off. Once the user selects the differential amplifier circuit, the text becomes visible and R_1 text will become invisible.The relationship between input and output voltage (i.e. the gain) is plotted on Vin_Vout_Axes which is located underneath Circuit Axes. Three push buttons are presented namely; **Calculate**, **Reset** and **Main**. The calculate button computes gain(s) and plots input and output voltages. The Reset button clears the contents of input and output texts and axes. The Main button opens the main window and closes current window.

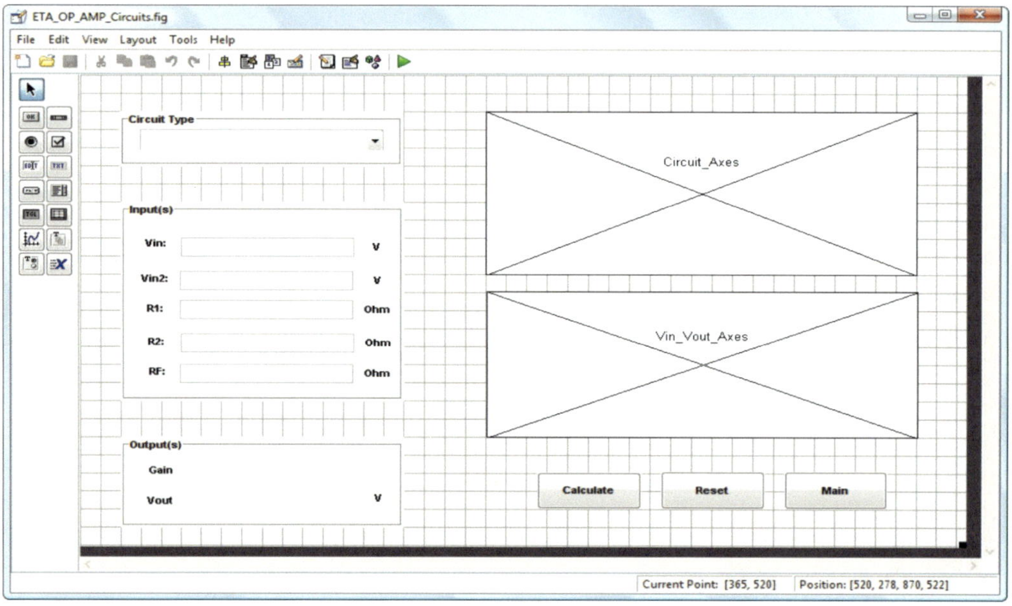

Fig. 10. ETA_OP_AMP_Circuits GUI Layout

The program code of pop-upmenu and Calculate_Buttoncall functions for case 4 (Summing Amplifier) are listed below.

```
functionCircuit_Type_Popupmenu_Callback(hObject, eventdata, handles)
% hObject handle theCircuit_Type_Popupmenu (see GCBO)
% eventdata reserved - to be defined in a future version of MATLAB
% handles structure with handles and user data (see GUIDATA)
% Hints:
% contents = get(hObject,'String') returns Circuit_Type_Popupmenu contents as cell array
% contents{get(hObject,'Value')} returns selected item from Circuit_Type_Popupmenu
switch get(handles.Circuit_Type_Popupmenu,'Value')
        %------------------ Summing Amplifier-------------------%
case 4
axes(handles.Circuit_Axes);
imshow('Summation.png');
set(handles.Gain_Text,'Visible','off');
set(handles.Gain_Out_Text,'Visible','off');
        %------------------ IF follower was chosen---------------%
        %----------------- Extra inputs -------------------------%
```

```
set(handles.Vin_2_Text,'Visible','on'); %Vin 2 label invisible
set(handles.R1_Edit,'Visible','on');
set(handles.R2_Edit,'Visible','on');
%************** R1 & R2 *****************%
set(handles.R1_Text,'Visible','on');
set(handles.R1_Edit,'Visible','on');
set(handles.R1_Unit_Text,'Visible','on');
set(handles.R2_Text,'Visible','on');
set(handles.R2_Edit,'Visible','on');
set(handles.R2_Unit_Text,'Visible','on');
        %---------------- Extra inputs ------------------------%
set(handles.Vin_2_Text,'Visible','on'); %Vin 2 label visiable
set(handles.Vin_2_Edit,'Visible','on'); %Vin 2 Edit text visiable
set(handles.V_Text,'Visible','on');  %Measure Unit of Vin2 visiable
set(handles.RF_Text,'Visible','on');  % Rf text visible
set(handles.R_FEdit,'Visible','on');  % Rf Edit visible
set(handles.RF_Unit_Text,'Visible','on');  % Rf unit text visible
set(handles.R1_R3_Text,'Visible','off');
set(handles.R2_R4_Text,'Visible','off');
        %----------------- Clear All the Edit Text ------------------------%
set(handles.Vin_Edit,'string', ' ')
set(handles.Vin_2_Edit,'string', ' ')
set(handles.R1_Edit,'string', ' ')
set(handles.R2_Edit,'string', ' ')
set(handles.R_FEdit,'string', ' ')
set(handles.Gain_Out_Text,'string', ' ')
set(handles.Vout_Out_Text,'string', ' ')
        %------------ Clear Vin-Vout axes before plotting, clear previous plot ---------------%
axes(handles.Vin_Vout_Axes)
cla
   functionCalculate_Button_Callback(hObject, eventdata, handles)
   % hObject  handle theCalculate_Button (see GCBO)
   % eventdata reserved - to be defined in a future version of MATLAB
   % handles  structure with handles and user data (see GUIDATA)
   %------------ Clear Vin-Vout axes before plotting, clear previous plot ---------------%
   axes(handles.Vin_Vout_Axes)
   cla %
   %-------------------- Basic inputs------------------------------%
   Vin   = str2double(get(handles.Vin_Edit, 'string'))% Input voltage
   R1   = str2double(get(handles.R1_Edit, 'String'));  % input Resistor1
   R2   = str2double(get(handles.R2_Edit, 'String'));  % input Resistor2
   %-------------------------------------------------------------------%
   %Menu List :
   % 1 :Default setting
   % 2 : Inverting Amplifier
   % 3 : Non- Inverting Amplifier
   % 4 : Voltage Follower
```

```
% 5 : Summing Amplifier
% 6 : Differential Amplifier
%--------------------------------------------------------------------%
switch get(handles.Circuit_Type_Popupmenu,'Value')
%--------------------------- Summing Amplifier---------------------------%
case 4
    Vin2  = str2double(get(handles.Vin_2_Edit, 'string'))  % Input voltage 2
    Rf  = str2double(get(handles.R_FEdit, 'string'));  % input Resistor 3
    %-------------Summing Equation -------------%
Gain_Result  = -Rf/R1  % Gain 1
Gain_Result_2 = -Rf/R2  % Gain 2
    %-------output voltage---------%
    Vout_1 = Gain_Result * Vin
    Vout_2 = Gain_Result_2 * Vin2
Vout = Vout_1+ Vout_2;
set(handles.Vout_Out_Text,'String',num2str(Vout))
    n = 1; % one cycle
t = 0 :pi/8 : 2*n*pi        % time domain
Vin_Plot  = Vin * sin(t)
Vout_Plot = Vout * sin(t)
if (abs (Vout) <= abs(Power_Supply)) % Check if clipping problem is occurred
plot(t, Vin_Plot,'RED' ,'linewidth',2)
grid on
axis([ 0 max(t) -20  20])
hold on
plot(t,  Vout_Plot,'GREEN' ,'linewidth',2)
grid on
xlabel('Time (t)','fontweight','bold')
ylabel('Input - Output Voltage (V)','fontweight','bold')
legend('Vin', 'Vout');
else
axes(handles.Vin_Vout_Axes)
Vin_Plot  = Vin * sin(t)
Vout_Plot = Vout * sin(t)
for i = 1 : length(Vout_Plot)
if (Vout_Plot(i)>Power_Supply)
Vout_Plot(i)= Power_Supply
elseif (Vout_Plot(i) < -Power_Supply)
Vout_Plot(i)= -Power_Supply
end
end
plot(t, Vin_Plot,'RED' ,'linewidth',2)
grid on
axis([ 0 max(t) -20  20])
hold on
plot(t,  Vout_Plot,'GREEN' ,'linewidth',2)
grid on
```

```
xlabel('Time (t)','fontweight','bold')
ylabel('Input - Output Voltage (V)','fontweight','bold')
legend('Vin', 'Vout');
end
    %------------------------ Display warning message (Clipping)-------------%
if abs(Vout) > 15
msgboxText{1} = 'Clipping!';
msgbox(msgboxText,'Clipping Phenomena', 'warn');
end
% --- ExecuteReset_Button.
functionReset_Button_Callback(hObject, eventdata, handles)
% hObject    handle to Reset_Button (see GCBO)
% eventdata  reserved - to be defined in a future version of MATLAB
% handles    structure with handles and user data (see GUIDATA)
%---------- Clear the contents----------------%
set(handles.Vin_Edit,'string', ' ')
set(handles.Vin_2_Edit,'string', ' ')
set(handles.R1_Edit,'string', ' ')
set(handles.R2_Edit,'string', ' ')
set(handles.R_FEdit,'string', ' ')
set(handles.Gain_Out_Text,'string', ' ')
set(handles.Vout_Out_Text,'string', ' ')
set(handles.Circuit_Type_Popupmenu, 'value', 1)%popup menu go to default
axes(handles.Circuit_Axes);
imshow('White_Background.jpg');
axes(handles.Vin_Vout_Axes)
cla % Clear current axis
% --- Execute Main_Button.
functionMain_Button_Callback(hObject, eventdata, handles)
% hObject    handle theMain_Button (see GCBO)
% eventdata  reserved - to be defined in a future version of MATLAB
% handles    structure with handles and user data (see GUIDATA)
%---- To open Main Window window ------%
set(Electronics_Teaching_Assistant,'Visible','on')
%---- To close Main Window window ------%
set(ETA_OP_AMP_Circuits,'Visible','off')
```

The Electric Circuits window, shown in Fig. 11, is designed to allow users analyze voltage and current dividers. This window consists of a pop-up menu where the user can choose between voltage and current dividers. The Electric Circuit Axes is updated accordingly. The inputs and outputs are varied between the different circuit types, with all components laid out first then their values specified. Three buttons are used namely; Calculate, Reset and Main, to perform the following functions: compute voltage and current, clear input and output text, and navigate to education window, respectively.
The codes shown below define the pop-up menu of the callback function and calculated push button callback function for case 3 (Current Divider).

```
functionElectric_Circuit_Popupmenu_Callback(hObject, eventdata, handles)
```

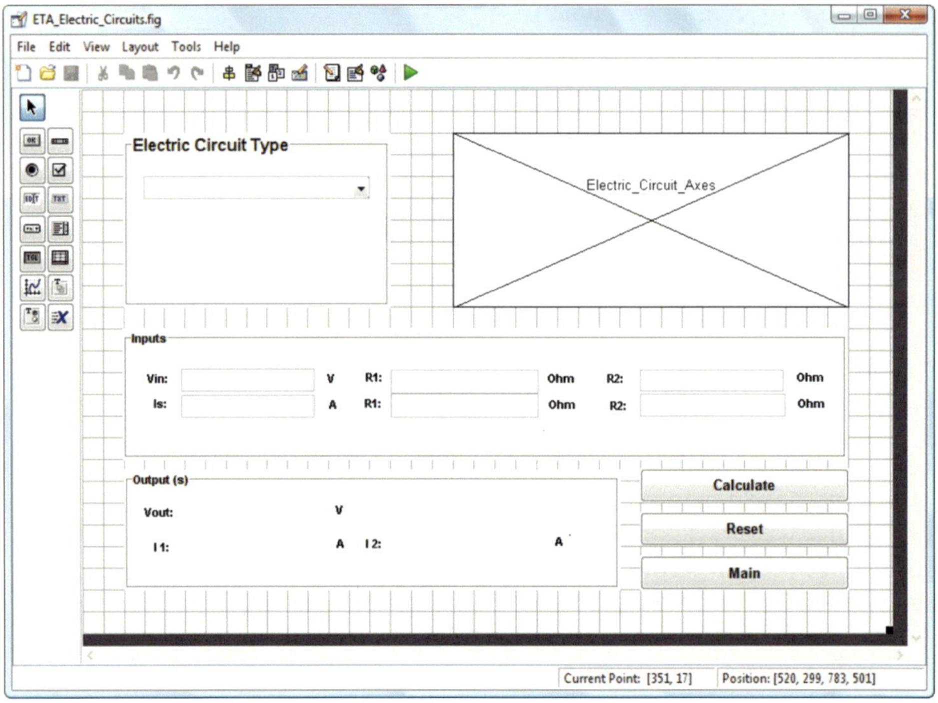

Fig. 11. ETA_Electric_Circuits GUI Layout

```
% hObject= handle theElectric_Circuit_Popupmenu (see GCBO)
% eventdata= reserved to be defined in a future version of MATLAB
% handles = structure with handles and user data (see GUIDATA)
switch get(handles.Electric_Circuit_Popupmenu,'Value')
%---------------- current divider ----------------------%
case 3
axes(handles.Electric_Circuit_Axes);
imshow('Current_Divider.png');
    %----------- Current divider inputs are visible------------%
set(handles.Is_Text,'Visible','on');
set(handles.Is_Edit,'Visible','on');
set(handles.Is_Unit_Text,'Visible','on');
set(handles.R1_Current_Edit,'Visible','on');
set(handles.R1_Current_text,'Visible','on');
set(handles.R1_Unit_Text,'Visible','on');
set(handles.IR2_Text,'Visible','on');
set(handles.R2_Current_Edit,'Visible','on');
set(handles.R2_Unit_Text,'Visible','on');
   %----------- Current divider outputs are visible------------%
set(handles.I1_Text,'Visible','on');
set(handles.I_1_Edit,'Visible','on');
set(handles.I1_Unit_Text,'Visible','on');
set(handles.I2_Text,'Visible','on');
```

```
set(handles.I_2_Edit,'Visible','on');
set(handles.I2_Unit_Text,'Visible','on');
    %----------- Voltage divider inputs are invisible------------%
set(handles.Vin_Text,'Visible','off');
set(handles.Vin_Edit,'Visible','off');
set(handles.Vin_Unit_Text,'Visible','off');
set(handles.R1_Text,'Visible','off');
set(handles.R1_Voltage_Edit,'Visible','off');
set(handles.Voltage_R1_Unit_Text,'Visible','off');
set(handles.Rb_Text,'Visible','off');
set(handles.R2_Voltage_Edit,'Visible','off');
set(handles.Rb_Unit_Text,'Visible','off');
    %----------- Voltage divider output is invisible------------%
set(handles.Vout_Text,'Visible','off');
set(handles.Vout_Edit,'Visible','off');
set(handles.Vout_Unit_Text,'Visible','off');
end
functionCalculate_Button_Callback(hObject, eventdata, handles)
% hObject= handle theCalculate_Button (see GCBO)
% eventdata=reserved to be defined in a future version of MATLAB
% handles =  structure with handles and user data (see GUIDATA)
switch get(handles.Electric_Circuit_Popupmenu,'Value')
case 3
    Is = str2double(get(handles.Is_Edit, 'string'))% Input current
    R1 = str2double(get(handles.R1_Current_Edit, 'String')); % input Resistor
    R2 = str2double(get(handles.R2_Current_Edit, 'String')); % current drain
    I1 = (R2/(R1+R2)) * Is
    I2 = (R1/(R1+R2)) * Is
set(handles.I_1_Edit,'Visible','on');
set(handles.I_2_Edit,'Visible','on');
set(handles.I_1_Edit,'String',num2str(I1))
set(handles.I_2_Edit,'String',num2str(I2))
end
```

4.2 Running the GUI

When the program is running, the main window appears as shown in Fig. 12. As mentioned earlier, this window allows the user to open the "OP AMP circuits" window by clicking the 'OP AMP Circuits' button. One can also open "Electric Circuits window" by clicking the 'Electric Circuits' button. Finally, the program can be closed by clicking the 'Close' button.
When the 'OP AMP Circuits' button is clicked, the OP_AMP_Circuits window opens while the main window (Education) disappears. The user can choose one of the following basic OP-AMP circuits types: Inverting Amplifier, Non Inverting Amplifier, Summing Amplifier, Voltage Follower and Differential Amplifier (Fig. 13). By selecting the circuit type from the menu; the schematic of the selected circuit will display on the upper axes and the inputs and outputs will change accordingly. The **Calculate**, **Reset**, and **Main** buttons perform functions as described earlier.

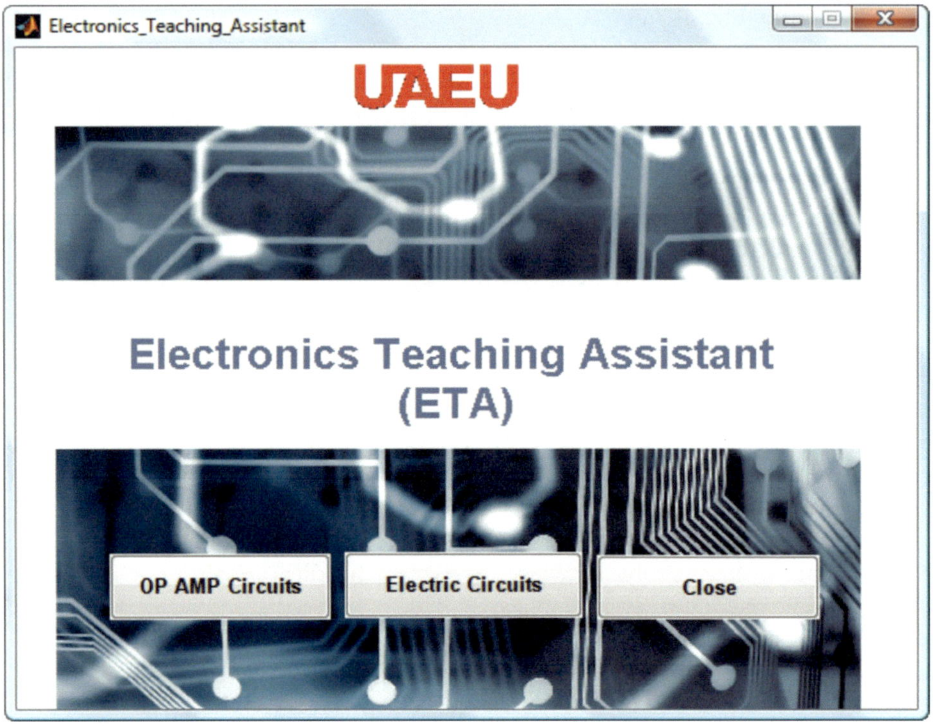

Fig. 12. Running Electronics Teaching Assistant GUI

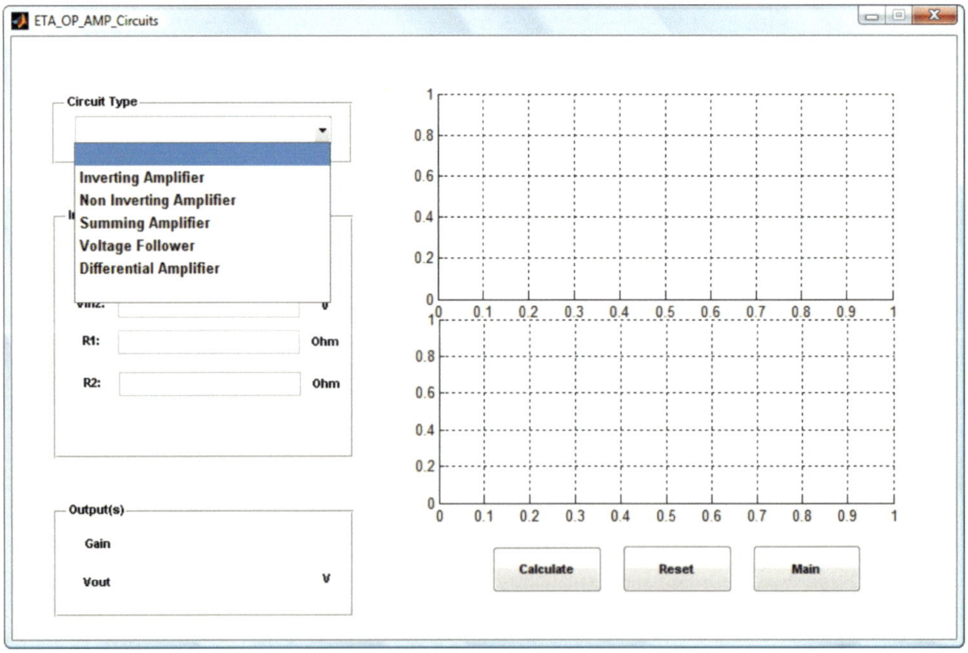

Fig. 13. Running the Operational Amplifier GUI

Figures 14 and 15 show the functions of the inverting and non- inverting amplifier circuits, respectively. The inputs for these circuits are named V_{in} (V), R_1 (Ohm) and R_2 (Ohm). The inputs and outputs are represented as sinusoidal waves and the relationship between them (i.e. gain) can be plotted. The red waveform represents the input of the amplifier while the green waveform represents the output. The value of the gain and V_{out} are displayed numerically.

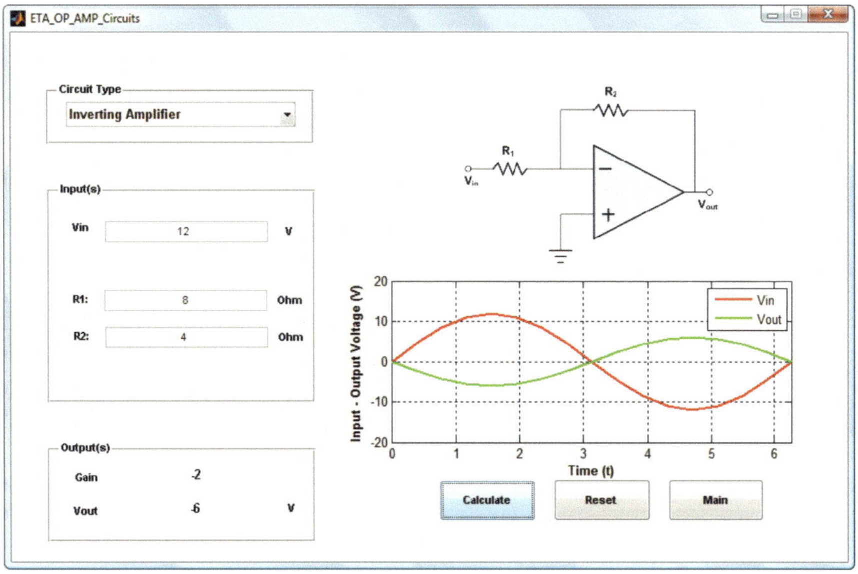

Fig. 14. Running the Inverting Amplifier GUI

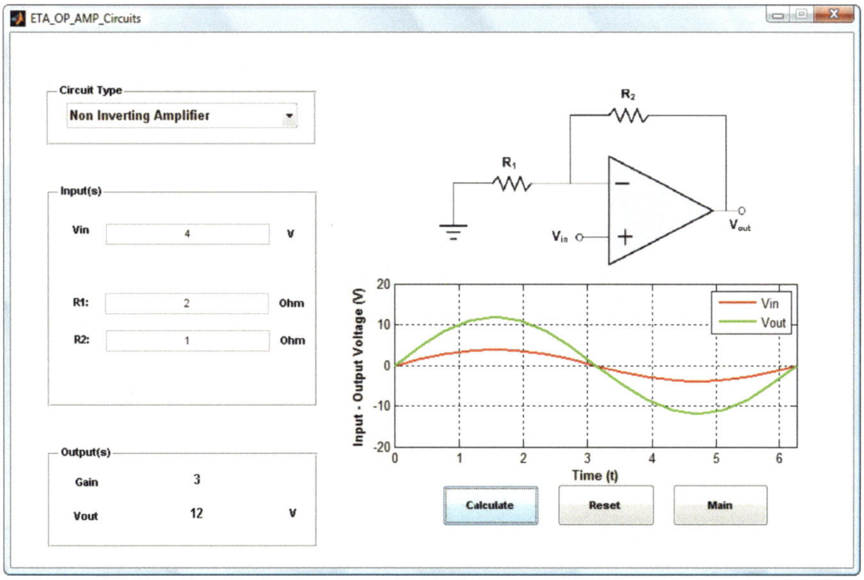

Fig. 15. Running the Non Inverting Amplifier GUI

The Summing Amplifier function is shown in Fig. 16. The inputs areV_{in1} (V), V_{in2} (V), R_1 (Ohm), R_2 (Ohm) and R_F (Ohm) while the output is V_{out} (V).

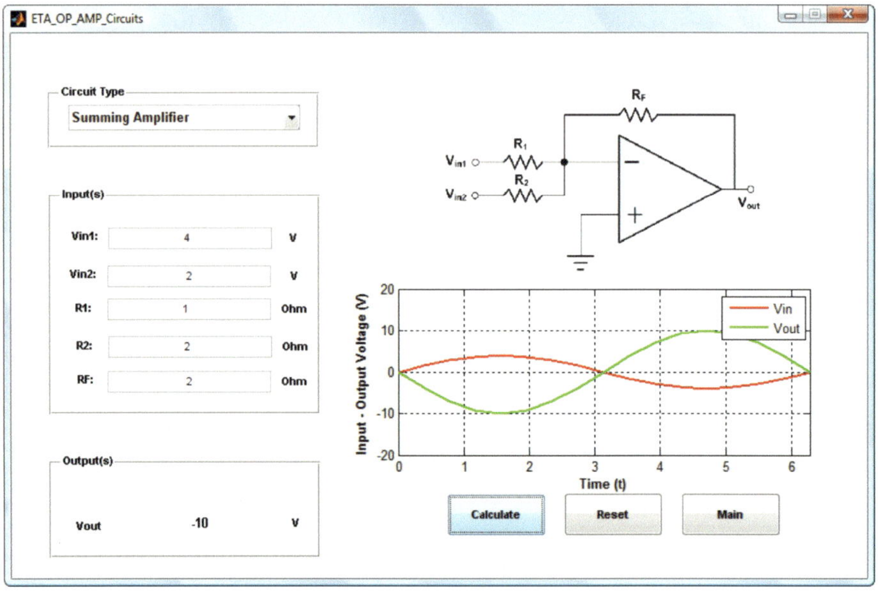

Fig. 16. Running the Summing Amplifier GUI

TheVoltage Follower function is shown in Fig. 17. This circuit has only one input V_{in} (V) with unity gain implying that the input and output values are equal. The V_{in} waveform does not appear because $V_{out} = V_{in}$.

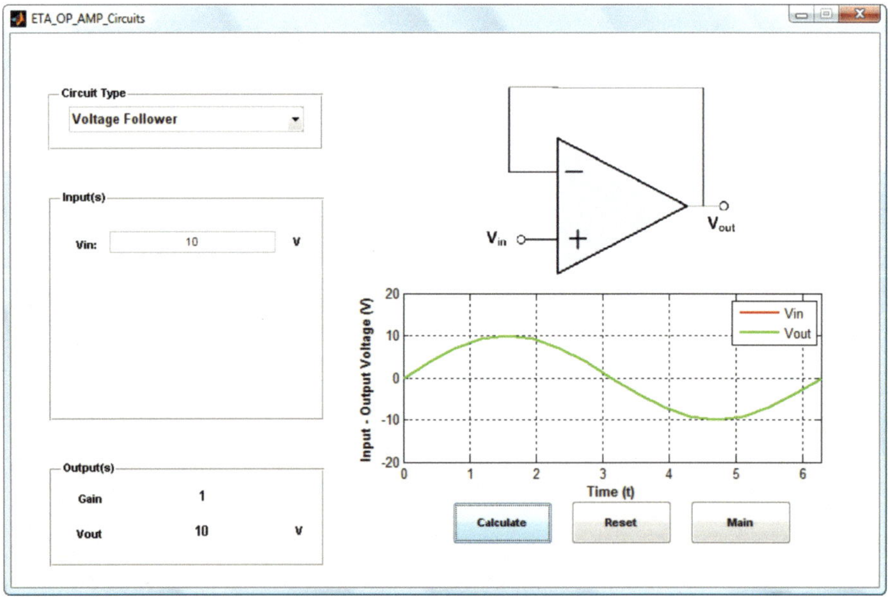

Fig. 17. Running the Voltage Follower GUI

The Differential Amplifier function is shown in Fig. 18. Parameters V_{in1}, V_{in2}, (R_1, R_3), and (R_2, R_4) are the inputs of the differential amplifier circuit, while V_{out} is the output.

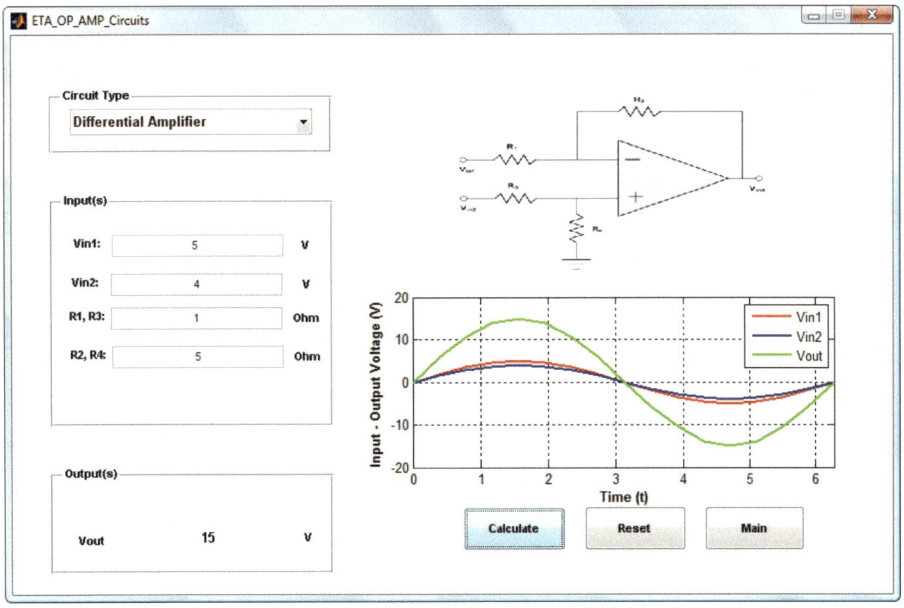

Fig. 18. Running the Differential Amplifier GUI

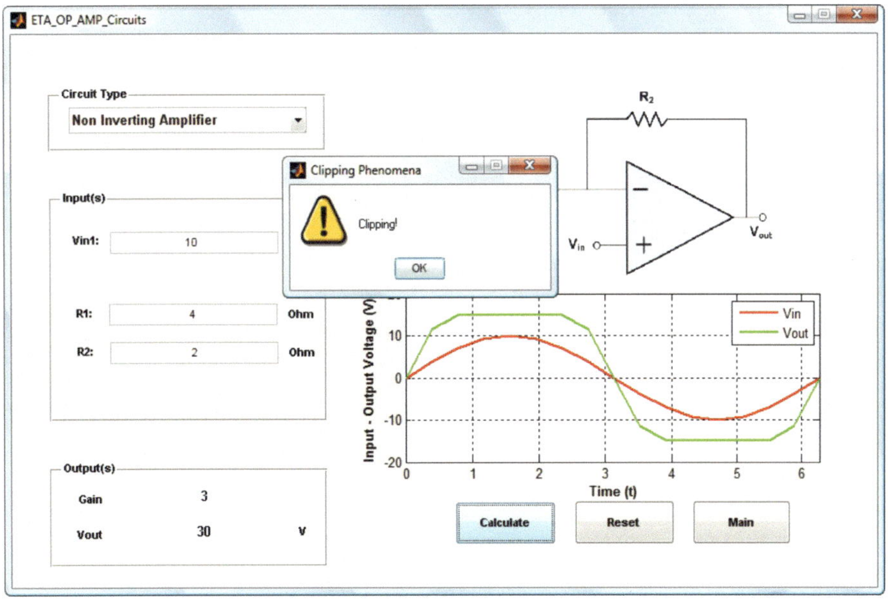

Fig. 19. Clipping Phenomena Warning Message

This ETA program has the ability to check if the clipping phenomena is occurring and notifies the user by displaying a warning message as illustrated in Fig. 19. Moreover, it checks user inputs; if the user unintentionally enters a non-numeric value, the error message will be shown as Fig. 20. The error message will be display if the user attempts to enter a voltage input that exceeds power supply voltage values (-15 V, 15V) as shown in Fig. 21. In case the user enters maximum input voltage, a warning message will be shown as shown in Fig. 22.

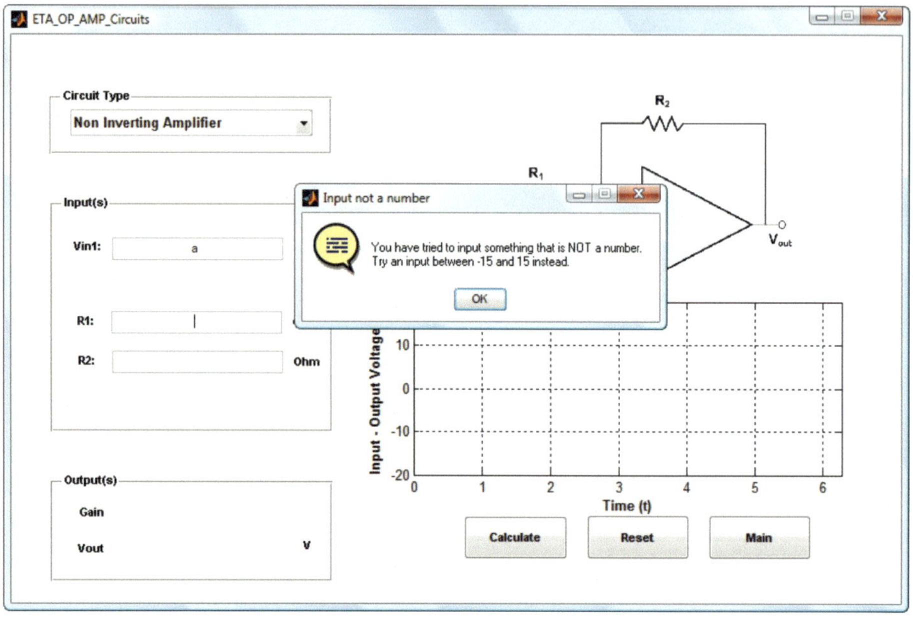

Fig. 20. The Input is not a Number Warning Message

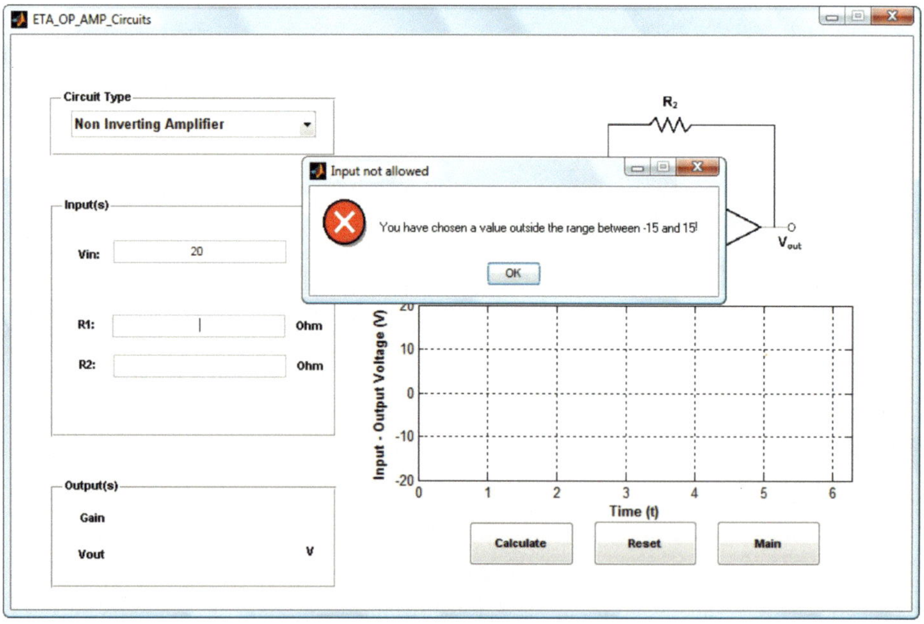

Fig. 21. The Input is out of the Range Error Message

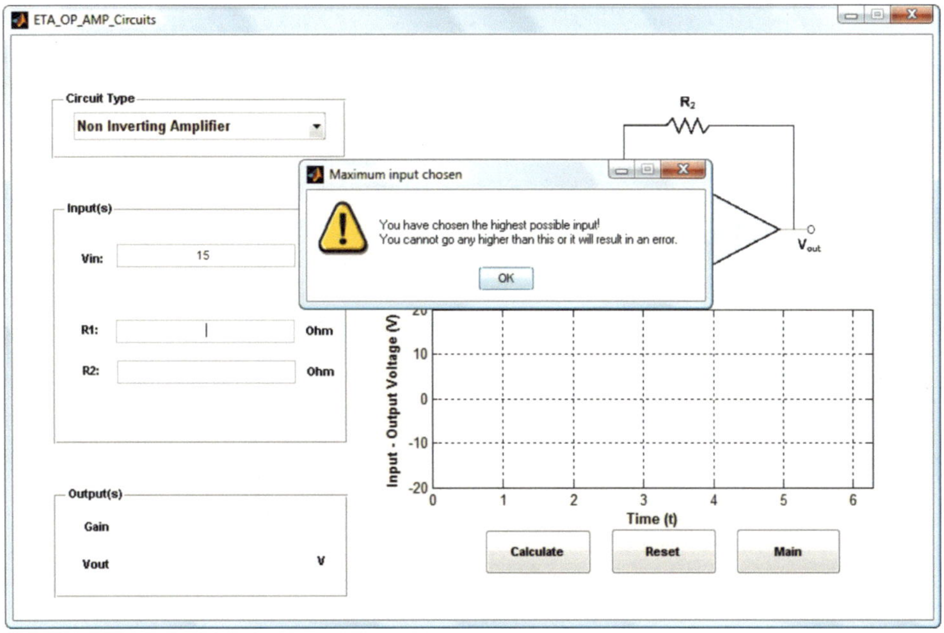

Fig. 22. The Maximum input chosen Warning Message

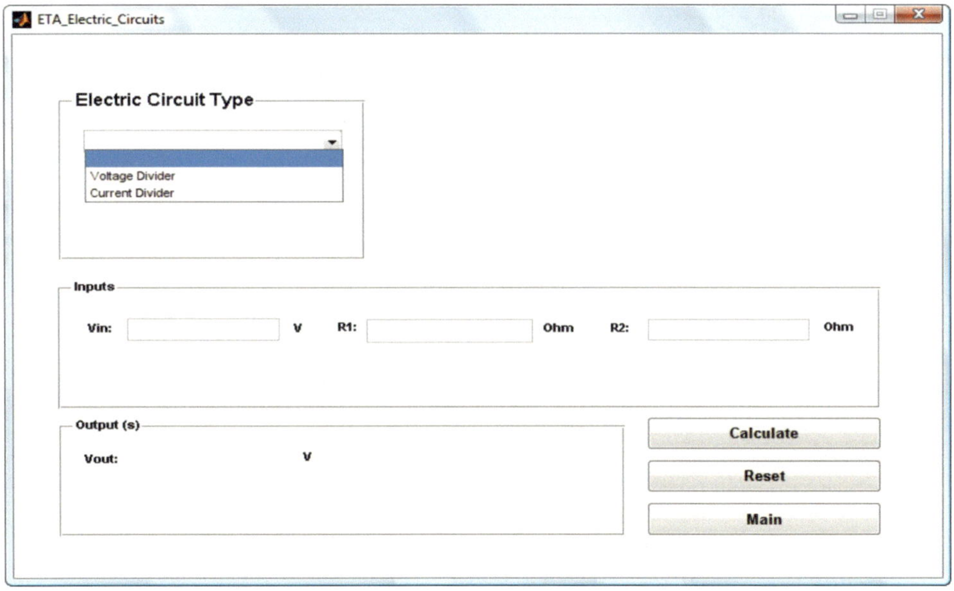

Fig. 23. Running the Electric Circuit GUI

When the user clicks the 'Electric Circuits' button, the ETA_Electric_Circuits window opens while the main window (Electronics Teaching Assistant) disappears. For this version of the ETA tool, the user can choose the electric circuit type (i.e. Voltage divider or Current divider) from the menu as shown in Fig. 23. By selecting the circuit from the menu; the schematic of the selected circuit will be shown on the upper axes and the inputs and outputs will change accordingly. The **Calculate**, **Reset**, and **Main** buttons perform functions as described earlier.

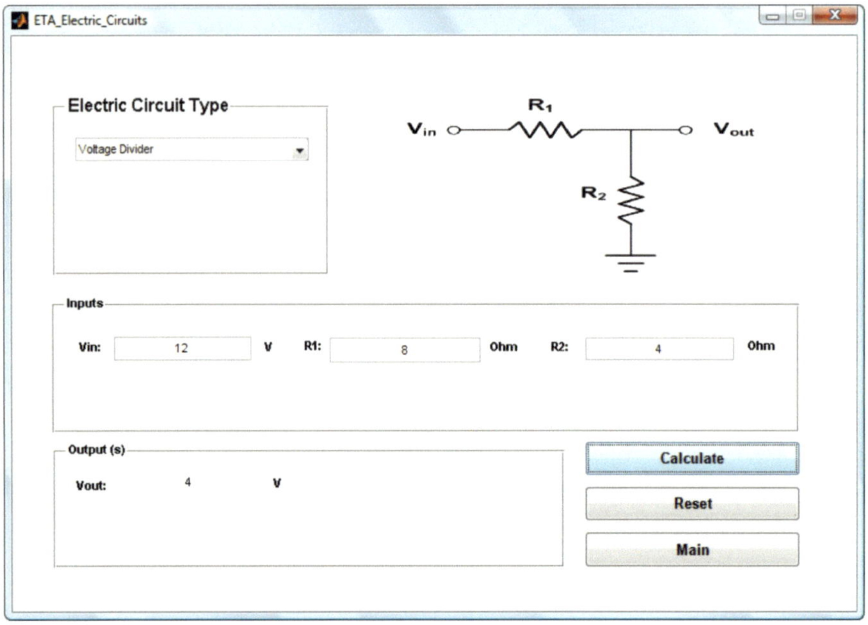

Fig. 24. Runningthe Voltage Divider GUI

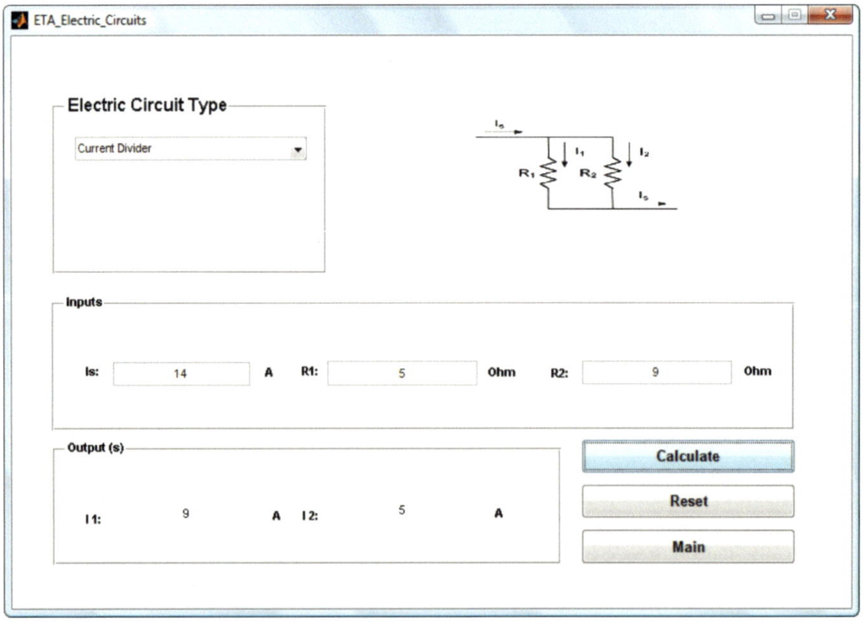

Fig. 25. Running the Voltage Divider GUI

Fig 24 shows the function of the basic voltage divider circuit. When the voltage divider circuit is selected from the menu, the circuit's schematic is displayed on axes. The inputs of this circuit are: Vin (V), R1 (Ohm) and R2 (Ohm).The Calculate, Reset, and Main buttons perform functions as described earlier.
Fig. 25 shows the function of the current divider circuit. When the current divider circuit is selected from the menu, the circuit's schematic is displayed on axes. The inputs of this circuit are: Is (A), R1 (Ohm) and R2 (Ohm). The values of I1 and I2 are displayed. The Calculate, Reset, and Main buttons perform functions as described earlier.

5. Conclusion

This chapter presented a user-friendly interactive MATLAB-based GUI tool for teaching basic electrical OP-AMP circuits. The programming code for the GUI tool development was also addressed in addition to explanation of input and output parameters needed for different types of OP-AMPs. In addition, MATLAB has a rich collection of mathematical functions and tools to compute and visualize data for different circuit applications. Students can use OrCAD PSpice to compare with the developed applet results. The interactive and friendly nature of MATLAB and its immediate graphing tools are indispensable for helping electrical engineering students achieve a better understanding of basic concepts and principles of semiconductor fundamentals and other electrical topics.

6. References

Andreatos A.S. & Michalareas G. (2008).Engineering education e-assessment with Matlab; Case study in electronic design, *Proceedings of the 5th WSEAS / IASME International Conference on ENGINEERING EDUCATION (EE'08)*, pp. 172-177, Heraklion, Greece, July 22-24, 2008.

Andreatos A.S. & Zagorianos A. (2009).Matlab GUI Application for Teaching Control Systems, *Proceedings of the 6th WSEAS International Conference on ENGINEERING EDUCATION*, pp. 208-211, Rodos (Rhodes) Island, Greece, July 22-24, 2009.

AttiaJ. O. (1995). Teaching AC circuit analysis with MATLAB.*Proceedings of the 25th Frontiers in EducationConference*, Vol. 1, pp.2c6.9-2c612, Atlanta, GA, USA, November 01- 04, 1995.

AttiaJ. O. (1996).Teaching Electronics with MATLAB. *Proceedings of the 26th Frontiers in Education Conference*, Vol. 2, pp. 609-611, Salt Lake City, UT, USA, November 06- 09, 1996.

Azemi A. & Stook C. (1996). Utilizing MATLAB in undergraduate electric circuits courses, *Proceedings of the 26th Annual Conference Frontiers in Education Conference (FIE '96)*, Vol. 2, pp. 599-602, Salt Lake City, Utah, USA, November 06-09, 1996.

Azemi A. & Yaz E. (1994). PSpice and MATLAB in Undergraduate and Graduate Electrical Engineering Courses. *Proceedings of the 24th Frontiers in Education Conference*, pp. 456-459, San Jose, CA, USA, November 02-06, 1994.

Koç S. & AydoğmusZ. (2009).A MATLAB/GUI Based Fault Simulation Tool for Power System Education, *Mathematical and Computational Applications*, Vol. 14, No. 3, pp. 207-217.

MATLAB (2010). MATLAB Creating Graphical User Interfaces, revision of March 2010 for MATLAB 7.10 (Release 2010a), The MathWorks Inc., Natick, MA, USA.

Rajashekar U. &Bovik A.C. (2000).Interactive DSP education using MATLAB demos, *IEEE SignalProcessing Education Workshop*, Hunt, Texas, USA, October 15-18, 2000.

8

MATLAB-Assisted Regression Modeling of Mean Daily Global Solar Radiation in Al-Ain, UAE

Hassan A. N. Hejase and Ali H. Assi
United Arab Emirates University
United Arab Emirates

1. Introduction

Many researchers have modeled weather data using classical regression, time-series regression and Artificial Neural Networks (ANN) techniques. MATLAB is used in handling data and writing task specific codes for models as well as in performing statistical analysis and curve fitting works. This is due to the dynamic nature of MATLAB and its rich toolboxes that cover almost every aspect of mathematical and statistical engineering applications.

Numerous authors (Abdalla & Feregh, 1988; Assi & Jama, 2010; Akinoglu & Ecevit, 1990; Al Mahdi et al., 1992; Ampratwum & Drovlo, 1999; Elagib & Mansell, 2000; Khalil & Alnajjar, 1995; Menges et al., 2006; Newland, 1988; Podesta' et al., 2004; Sahin, 2007; Samuel, 1991; Ulgen & Hepbasli, 2002) to count few developed empirical regression models to predict the monthly average daily global solar radiation (GSR) in their region using various parameters. The mean daily sunshine duration was the most commonly used and available parameter. The most popular model was the linear model by Angström-Prescott (Podesta' et al., 2004; Assi & Jama, 2010) which establishes a linear relationship between GSR and sunshine duration with knowledge of extra-terrestrial solar radiation and the theoretical maximum daily solar hours. Many studies with empirical regression models were done for diverse regions around the world. (Menges et al. 2006) reviewed 50 GSR empirical models available in literature for computing the monthly average daily GSR on a horizontal surface. They tested the models on data recorded in Konya, Turkey for comparison of model accuracy. The number of weather parameters varied between models. The diverse regression models used include linear, logarithmic, quadratic, third order polynomial, logarithmic-linear and exponential and power models relating the normalized GSR to normalized sunshine hours. Other models included in Menges work used direct regression models involving various weather parameters such as precipitation, cloud cover, etc., in addition to geographical data (altitude, latitude). (Şahin, 2007) presented a novel method for estimating the solar irradiation and sunshine duration by incorporating the atmospheric effects due to extra-terrestrial solar irradiation and length of day. The author compares his model with Angström's equation with favourable advantages as his method does not use Least Square Method in addition to having no procedural restrictions or assumptions. (Ulgen & Hepbasli, 2002) developed two empirical correlations to estimate the monthly average daily GSR on a horizontal surface for Izmir, Turkey. Their models resemble Angström type equations. They compared their models with 25 models previously reported in literature on the basis of statistical error tests (MBE (mean bias error), RMSE (root mean square error), MPE (mean percentage error), and R^2 (coefficient of determination)) with favourable results.

Other authors worked on prediction models based on artificial neural network techniques and most specifically Multi-Layer Perceptron (MLP) and Radial-Basis Function (RBF) methods (Al-Alawi & Al-Hinai, 1998; Assi et al., 2010; Behrang et al., 2010; Benghanem et al., 2009; Boccol et al., 2010; Elminir et al., 2005; Krishnaiah et al., 2007; Mohandes et al., 1998; Mohandes et al., 2000; Rehman & Mohandes, 2008). The advantage of the ANN models is their ability to handle large amounts of data as well as the ability to handle random data without worry of incomplete, inaccurate or noise-contaminated data.

Another approach followed by many researchers is using time-series modeling techniques which employ regression for the deterministic component and Box-Jenkins Auto-Regressive Integrated Moving Average (ARIMA) modeling for the stochastic residual component (Box & Jenkins, 1994; Enders, 2010). (Sulaiman et al., 1997) and (Zaharim et al., 2009) use the ARMA Box-Jenkins method to model GSR data in Malaysia. They model the data using non-seasonal autoregressive models where the model adequacy is checked using the Ljung-Box statistic for diagnostic data. However, only short-term data was used for testing their model. (Reikard, 2009) employs a combination of logarithmic regression and ARIMA modeling to predict solar radiation at high resolution and compares his models with other forecast methods such as ANN and considered the 24-hour daily seasonality not taken into account in most modeling approaches. (Boland, 1995) and (Zeroual et al., 1995) use a combination of regression model with Fourier series for the deterministic part and ARMA modeling for the residual stochastic component.

The potential of solar energy harvesting in the UAE is significant, with an average annual sunshine hours of 3568 h (i.e. 9.7 h/day), which corresponds to an average annual solar radiation of approximately 2285 kWh/m^2, i.e. 6.3 kWh/m^2 per day (Assi & Abdi, 2010).The main limitation of using many weather parameters is the difficulty of obtaining this data due to the high expenses and availability of recording equipment. Some of the regression models are more accurate for monthly data than daily data and most published works only show monthly data comparison results as the daily mean data are less accurate.

The authors are doing extensive work on the analysis of weather data in three UAE cities, namely, Al-Ain, Abu Dhabi and Sharjah. The prediction techniques employed range from classical one-parameter based regression techniques (Sunshine data), Artificial Neural Networks (ANN) Multi-Layer Perceptron (MLP) and Radial-Basis Function (RBF) techniques, and lately using time-series regression techniques with Auto-Regressive Integrated Moving-Average (ARIMA) modeling. Most of the work done relies on the use of MATLAB as a common platform for preparing and processing data as well as for testing the suggested prediction models. MATLAB was also used in curve fitting the output data and finding the statistical error parameters that judge the accuracy and dependability of our prediction models. The used correlations included the linear Angstrom-Prescott model and its derivations, namely, the second and third order correlations, in addition to the single term exponential model, logarithmic model, linear logarithmic model and power model.

This chapter uses examples with classical empirical regression techniques and time-series techniques to predict the monthly average daily GSR data in Al-Ain, UAE. In time-series regression technique, the deterministic component was modeled by decomposing it into a multiple linear regression component as a function of the available weather variables plus a seasonal component accounting for the annual periodicity and a linear trend. The residual error is studied using Box-Jenkins ARIMA modeling techniques for the sake of further enhancing the predicted solar radiation data. The resultant noise residual error renders Auto-Correlation Function (ACF) and Partial Auto-Correlation Function (PACF) plots within the 95 % confidence interval bounds and a quasi-normal noise error with zero mean and constant variance. The stationary form of the resulting time-series and the white-noise type residual error provide extra confidence of the long-term prediction accuracy of the estimated model. The MATLAB codes written by authors and their group involve employing various data modeling techniques such as linear regression, curve fitting, de-trending, FFT algorithm, statistical data analysis as well as Box-Jenkins method to predict a time-series model for the residual error.

The current work on solar radiation data in Al-Ain City, UAE will be correlated with other ongoing studies by authors to come up with solar radiation prediction models for the UAE cities of Abu Dhabi and Sharjah. The final objective is to come up with a good national weather model capable of predicting the mean monthly GSR for the whole UAE within an acceptable prediction error.

2. Methodology

The weather database meteorological data provided by the National Center of Meteorology & Seismology (NCMS) in Abu Dhabi) for the periods between 1995 and 2007 was divided into two sets: A model data set with daily record of the variables: air temperature, wind speed, sunshine hours and relative humidity for the years 1995- 2004 (10 years), and a test data set for the years of 2005-2007. All regression modeling and simulation work is done using MATLAB tools and with the help of the statistical software packages Minitab (Minitab, 2010) and SPSS (IBM SPSS Statistics, 2010). The next section will explain the modeling procedure for both the classical empirical regression and time-series regression techniques. Validation of model accuracy is presented along with corresponding error statistics. Then, a comparison between both empirical approaches is made.

2.1 Procedure

In this section we discuss two methods used to generate the weather data models for Al-Ain, UAE for years 1995-2004. Selected models are validated with data from years 2005-2007. The two models discussed in this chapter are:

1. Classical regression methods (Empirical models)
2. Time-series regression model (Regression with Box-Jenkins ARIMA method)

The use of MATLAB in each approach will be fully discussed along with the details of commands used and computation results for the models under investigation.

2.1.1 Classical regression modelling approach (empirical models)

The empirical regression models are generated with help of MATLAB and verified using SPSS. The appropriate MATLAB commands used are addressed with each procedural step.

2.1.1.1 Data preparation for nonlinear regression models

The 10-year mean daily GSR data in Al-Ain, UAE is computed for both sunshine hours and mean daily GSR yielding a data set of size N=365 for each variable. In MATLAB, this is done as follows:

```
N= 365;  NY= 10;
% N= 365 days of the year and NY= # years of model data used (1995-2004)
for k=1:N,    % Day index of year
   GSR(k)= mean( GSR_10yr (k:N:(NY-1)*N+k));
end
```

where GSR_10yr is the data sheet containing the daily mean GSR data array of size 3650 days (1995-2004). Similarly, we generate the 10-year average daily SSH from the sunshine hours data.

2.1.1.2 Extra-terrestrial radiation parameters

Mean daily values of GSR data are calculated from the knowledge of the latitude and longitude in the city of Al-Ain (Latitude = $24^0 16'$ and Longitude = $55^0 36'$). The extraterrestrial solar radiation on horizontal surface in kWh/m^2 (G_0) and theoretical maximum daily sun hours (S_0) are calculated from the equations (Assi et al., 2010):

$$G_0 = \frac{24G_{SC}}{\pi}\left[1 + 0.033\cos\left(\frac{360n}{365}\right)\right]\left[\cos(\phi)\cos(\delta)\sin(\omega_s) + \omega_s\sin(\phi)\sin(\delta)\right] \tag{1}$$

$$S_0 = \frac{2}{15}\omega_s \tag{2}$$

where n is the day index, ω_s the mean sunrise hour angle for the month, ϕ the latitude, and δ the declination angle. G_{SC} is a constant representing the daily extraterrestrial solar radiation on horizontal and is given by 1.367 kWh/m^2. The declination angle (δ) is defined by the equation:

$$\delta = \sin^{-1}\left[\sin\left(\frac{23.45\pi}{180}\right)\sin\left(\frac{2\pi[n + 284]}{365}\right)\right] \tag{3}$$

The GSR and SSH data are next normalized to the extraterrestrial values G_0 and S_0 described in eq. (1)-(2), and the resulting normalized data arrays denoted by clearness index (RSSH=GSR/G_0) and Sunshine duration ratio (RSSH = SSH/S_0) are stored in excel file solardata.xlsx in the form:

```
>> gsrdata=[N, S0, G0, RSSH, RGSR];
>> s=xlswrite('solardata.xlsx',gsrdata,'Sheet1', 'A1:E365');
```

The RGSR-RSSH data is then fitted to different nonlinear regression models as per Table 1.

Model reference	Type	Equation
(Podesta, 2004)	Linear	$y= b_1+b_2* x$
(Akinoglu & Ecevit, 1990)	Quadratic	$y= b_1+b_2* x+b_3* x^2$
(Samuel, 1991)	Cubic	$y= b_1+b_2* x+b_3* x^2+b_4* x^3$
(Ampratwum & Dorvlo, 1999)	Logarithmic	$y= b_1+ b_2 *\log(x)$
(Newland, 1988)	Log-Linear	$y= b_1+ b_2* x+ b_3*\log(x)$
(Elagib & Monsell, 2000)	Exponential	$y= b_1* \exp(b_2*x)$

Table 1. Nonlinear empirical regression models used for Al-Ain, UAE weather data

2.1.1.3 MATLAB application in nonlinear regression

The nonlinear regression in MATLAB is performed using two tools:
1. Interactive nonlinear regression toolbox (nlintool)
2. Nonlinear mixed-effects estimation (nlmefit)

The procedure followed in each approach is discussed in the next sections including sample output results from the weather GSR modeling. Alternative approaches include specifically written MATLAB m-files or the use of commercial statistical software packages such as SPSS, Minitab or SAS. All our MATLAB results agree well with results obtained using SPSS and Minitab.

2.1.1.3.1 Use of the interactive nonlinear regression toolbox (nlintool)

The MATLAB procedure to use "nlintool" is explained through the application of the log-linear regression model, described in Table 1, to model the relation between the clearness index (RGSR) and sunshine duration ratio (RSSH) through the following steps:
1. Given RSSH and RGSR data (N points each). Read the input data to MATLAB workspace from an Excel data sheet "GSRdata.xlsx" as follows:

```
>> inputdata=xlsread ('GSRdata.xlsx', 'sheet1','A1:B365')
>> RSSH=inputdata(:,1);
>> RGSR=inputdata(:,2);
```

   The input data array contains two columns of length N=365, namely, RSSH (independent variable or predictor) and RGSR (dependent variable).
2. Next, generate an m-file script called "loglinear.m" containing the regression function as follows:

```
function yhat = loglinear(beta, x)
     b1 = beta(1);
     b2 = beta(2);
     b3 = beta(3);
yhat = b1 + b2*x + b3*log(x);
```

3. In command window type:

```
>> beta0=[ 0 0 0]; % define initial guess of constants beta(k), k=1,2,3
>> nlintool(RSSH, RGSR,@loglinear,beta0)  % Invoke the interactive
   nonlinear regression toolbox
```

The output is the log-linear regression curve with error bounds as shown in Fig. 1.

4. Data that can be downloaded to MATLAB workspace include the regression coefficients (beta) and root-mean square error (rmse). This is done as follows:

```
>> rmse   % root mean-square error
rmse =
  0.0262
>> beta   % regression model coefficients
beta=
  -0.1778  6.1287E-05   0.2251
```

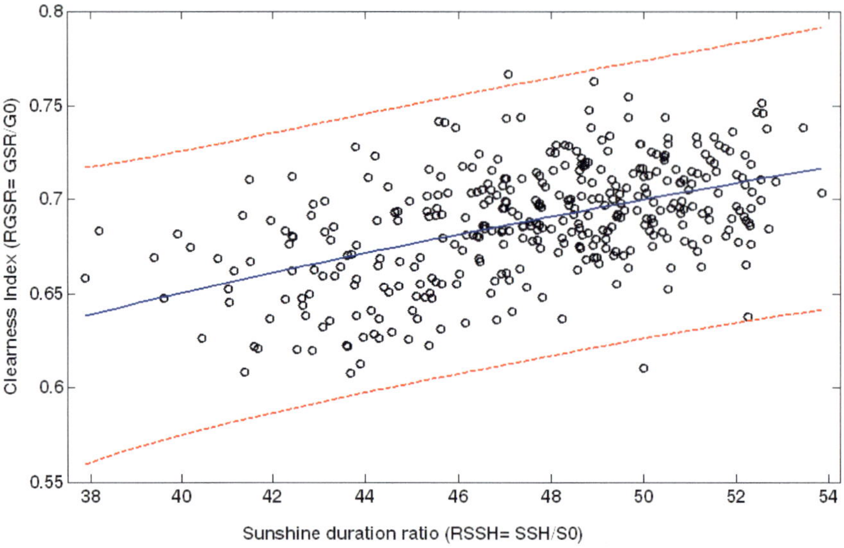

Fig. 1. Nonlinear regression curve with a log-linear function between Clearness index (RGSR) and sunshine duration ration (RSSH)

The command "whos" provides information on available workspace variables. Similarly, other nonlinear regression curve fits could be obtained by generating the corresponding m-file for each regression function and specifying the corresponding initial guess values for the unknown parameters.

Table 2 shows the coefficients obtained for each regression model shown in Table 1. The statistical error parameters resulting from each regression model can be computed using SPSS, Minitab or using MATLAB from the expressions displayed in section 2.3.

Type	Equation	b1	b2	b3	b4
Linear	y= b1+b2* x	0.4619	0.0047		
Quadratic	y= b1+b2* x+b3* x2	0.2980	0.0118	-7.400E-05	
Cubic	y= b1+b2* x+b3* x2+b4* x3	8.4297	-0.5183	0.0114	-8.2410E-05
Logarithmic	y= b1+b2*log(x)	-0.1697	0.2223		
Log-Linear	y= b1+ b2* x+ b3*log(x)	-0.1778	-6.133E-05	0.2252	
Exponential	y= b1* exp(b2*x)	0.4948	0.0069		

Table 2. Estimated coefficients for empirical regression models of weather data for years 1995-2004 in Al-Ain, UAE. Variables are y = RGSR = GSR/G0 and x = RSSH = SSH/S0

2.1.1.3.2 Use of the nonlinear mixed-effects estimation (nlmefit)

The nonlinear regression in MATLAB can also be performed using the nonlinear mixed-effects estimation (nlmefit). This tool fits the model by maximizing an approximation to the marginal likelihood with random effects integrated out, assuming that [See MATLAB help] random effects are multivariate normally distributed and independent between groups, and that observation errors are independent, identically normally distributed, and independent of the random effects. As an example, the format for the log-linear regression equation is as follows:

```
>> model = @(phi,t)(phi(:,1)+ phi(:,2).*t + phi(:,3).*log(t));
>> phi0 =[0 0 0];
>> group=[1:365];
>> [beta,psi,stats] = nlmefit(RSSH(:),RGSR(:),group,[],model,phi0)
```

The arguments of the MATLAB function 'nlmefit' used for our regression are:
RSSH: is an n-by-1 array of n observations on 1 predictor.
RGSR: is an n-by-1 vector of responses.
Group: is a grouping variable indicating m groups in the observations. Here, we enter size of rows of predictors, i.e. group=[1:365].
Model: is a function handle that accepts predictor values and model parameters and returns fitted values.
phi0: contains the initial values of the regression for equation parameters.
The program outputs are:
beta= contains the estimated regression model parameters
psi= an r-by-r estimated covariance matrix for the random effects. By default, r is equal to the number of model parameters p.
stats= returns a structure with the following parameters:

- logl – The maximized log-likelihood for the fitted model
- mse – The estimated error variance for the fitted model
- aic – The Akaike information criterion for the fitted model
- bic – The Bayesian information criterion for the fitted model
- sebeta – The standard errors for beta
- dfe – The error degrees of freedom for the model

The following is the MATLAB output to the log-linear regression model:

```
beta =
 -0.1778
 -6.1336E-05
  0.2252
psi =
 1.0e-003 *
  0.6821        0         0
     0       0.0000       0
     0          0       0.0000
stats =
logl: 8.1257e+002
mse: 3.7845e-028
rmse:1.9454e-014
aic: -1.6111e+003
bic: -1.5838e+003
sebeta: [1.3834 0.0104 0.4869]
dfe: 358
```

The regression model parameters obtained using the 'nlmefit' function match with the values computed using the "nlintool" function and listed in Table 2. The best regression model should yield the lowest value of AIC, BIC and RMSE in addition to the autocorrelation test requirements discussed later in the chapter. Fig.2 shows the ten-year mean daily GSR computed from the log-linear regression model with estimated coefficients listed in Table 2. Note the very good agreement between regression model and measured data. The error statistics yield a deterministic coefficient of R^2= 97.74 % in addition to low statistics RMSE = 0.2104, MBE = -0.0755, MABE = 0.1872, and MAPE= 3.11 %. A comparison of the remaining regression yields excellent agreement with measured data with R^2 values exceeding 96 %.

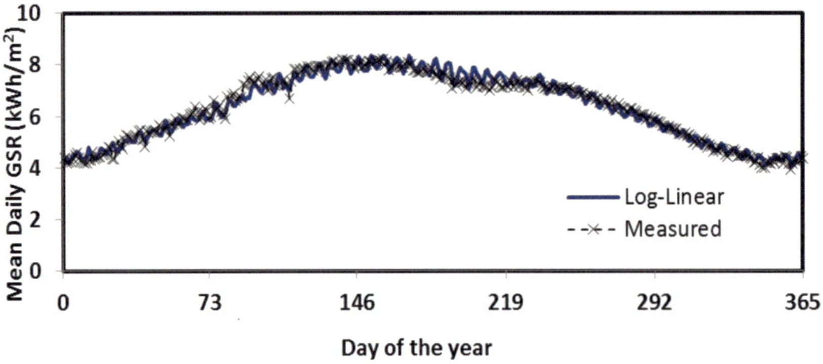

Fig. 2. Ten-year mean daily GSR data comparison between the empirical log-linear regression model and measured data in Al-Ain, UAE for years 1995-2004

2.1.1.4 Validation of empirical regression models

The six selected empirical regression models are validated by computing the predicted GSR data from these models using the test data set of years 2005-2007. The empirical models compare very well with measured data for the test data period as depicted in Fig. 3. All models yield deterministic coefficients values R^2 better than 98 %. The models also yield low values for RMSE, MBE, MABE and MAPE indicating their adequacy as weather prediction models for Al-Ain, UAE. The 3rd-order polynomial regression model (Cubic) outperforms the other five empirical models with lowest error statistics and highest deterministic coefficient.

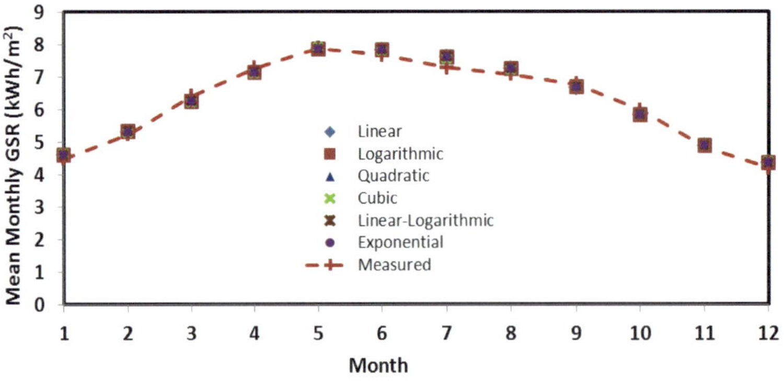

Fig. 3. Comparison of monthly mean regression model GSR with measured data for test period of 2005-2007

2.1.2 Time-series regression modelling with ARIMA approach

The time-series regression modelling approach makes use of the four weather parameters measured daily over a period of 10 years, i.e. 1995-2004 in Al-Ain, UAE. These parameters are:

1. Mean daily temperature (^0C) abbreviated as T
2. Mean daily wind speed (knots) abbreviated as W
3. Daily sunshine hours abbreviated as SSH
4. Mean daily relative humidity (%) abbreviated as RH
5. Mean daily global solar radiation (kWh/m2) abbreviated as GSR

The modeling procedure steps are as follows:

Step 1. Explore the form and characteristics of the dependent variable (GSR) and the predictors (T, W, SSH and RH) by looking at their time-series plots with the help of MATLAB. These plots will help in identifying the behavior of each variable and to check the trend and seasonality of GSR data.

Step 2. Compute the descriptive statistics of the four independent variables (T, W, SSH, and RH) and the dependent variable (mean daily GSR). The correlation between these variables is shown in Table 3. It shows that wind speed has the least effect on GSR performance. From the time-series plots of GSR, T and SSH data we can observe a cyclical behavior. Wind and humidity data on the other hand are more random. The best model is obtained when all four independent variables are considered in the GSR regression model.

	T	**W**	**SSH**	**RH**	**GSR**
T	1.0000	0.1907	0.4555	-0.7419	0.7958
W	0.1907	1.0000	-0.1099	-0.2170	0.1425
SSH	0.4555	-0.1099	1.0000	-0.4566	0.6972
RH	-0.7419	-0.2170	-0.4566	1.0000	-0.6761
GSR-kWh/m^2	0.7958	0.1425	0.6972	-0.6761	1.0000

Table 3. Correlation between the measured weather data parameters for the city of Al-Ain, UAE for years 1995-2004

The Pearson correlation values between the response (GSR) and the four predictor variables (T, W, SSH, RH) are found in MATLAB using the command:

```
>> corr(T, W, SSH, RH, GSR)
```

Table 3 shows that the temperature and sunshine hours have dominant effect on the GSR parameter followed closely by relative humidity and with less influence by wind speed.
The computation of the descriptive statistics can be done directly in SPSS or Minitab. In MATLAB we can either write a script m-file to compute all needed statistical parameters or we can use the already available functions in MATLAB and other functions that can be run under the **Statistics toolbox**. One MATLAB command that generates some statistical parameters is:

```
>> [xds,yds] = datastats (xdata, ydata)
```

which returns statistics for the column vectors xdata and ydata to the structures xdata and ydata, respectively. xdata and ydata must be of the same size. The returned statistics include: sample size, maximum value, minimum value, mean, median, range, and standard deviation. MATLAB also has standalone functions for statistical values such as: max, min, length (sample size), mean, median, mode, std (standard deviation), and var (variance). The coefficient of variation is found from the ratio of std(x)/mean(x). One can also use hist(x) to get a histogram of the sample data. Other statistical measures need to be programmed or can be determined using the MATLAB Statistics toolbox. Table 4 lists the commands that can be employed to obtain the central and dispersion measures for the data sets under study.

Central Measures		**Dispersion Measures**	
Command	**Description**	**Command**	**Description**
geomean	Geometric mean	iqr	Interquartile range
harmean	Harmonic Mean absolute deviation	mad	Mean absolute deviation
mean	Arithmetic mean	moment	Central moment of all orders
median	50 % Percentile	range	Range
trimmean	Trimmed mean	std	Standard deviation
mode	Most frequent value	var	Variance

Table 4. MATLAB commands for computing central and dispersion measures of a data set

The following commands can be used under the Statistics toolbox:

```
>> locate = [geomean(x) harmmean(x) mean(x) median(x), trimmean(x,25)]
>> stats = [iqr(x) mad(x) range(x) std(x)]
```

On the other hand, measures of shape are found using quantiles ($0 < p < 1$) or percentiles ($0 < p < 100$). The percentiles for a data sequence xdata are found in the Statistics toolbox using the command:

```
>> y = prctile(xdata,p);   % p= percentile needed
>> y = quantile(xdata,p);   % p= quantileneeded
```

The shape of a data distribution is also measured by the Statistics Toolbox functions skewness, kurtosis, and, more generally, moment.

Table 5 shows the descriptive statistics obtained for the mean daily global solar radiation data for Al-Ain, UAE for period 1994-2005.

Step 3. Fig. 4 shows the time-series plot of the mean daily GSR for years 1995-2004 with leap days excluded. The plot shows a clear periodicity of one year (365 days).

Step 4. The partial least square regression technique is used to model the relation between GSR data for ten years (1995-2004) and the four aforementioned dependent weather variables. The model equation obtained using MATLAB or using either software packages SPSS or Minitab is of the form:

$$GSR_{regression}(t) = a_1 + a_2 * T(t) + a_3 * W(t) + a_4 * SSH(t) + a_5 * RH(t) \quad (4)$$

where the regression coefficients are given in Table 6.

Statistical Parameters	T	W	SSH	RH	GSR
Mean (μ)	36.501	7.5305	9.9472	44.0450	6.3332
StdDev (σ)	7.7250	1.9896	1.5849	16.8160	1.3962
SE Mean($\sigma / \sqrt{N}$)	0.1280	0.0329	0.2620	0.2780	0.0231
Variance (σ^2)	59.6690	3.9585	2.5121	282.7660	1.9494
CoefVar (σ/μ) in %	21.1600	26.4200	15.9300	38.1800	22.0500
Min	16.2000	0.2084	0.8000	7.3750	1.1350
Median	37.6000	7.2506	10.2000	43.4170	6.5540
Max	49.1000	22.7936	12.8000	97.2300	8.8210
Skewness (σ_k)	-0.3000	1.6000	-1.5200	0.2000	-0.3600
Kurtosis (ku)	-1.2100	5.7300	3.7700	-0.7000	-0.9000

Table 5. Descriptive data statistics for the measured weather data parameters for the city of Al-Ain (Years 1995-2004) where N= 3650 data samples

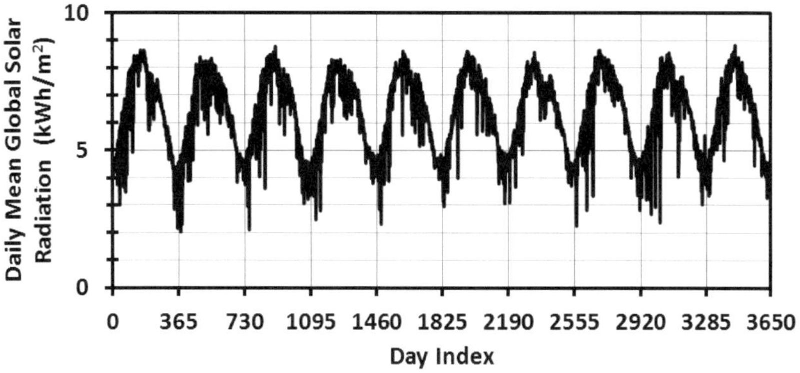

Fig. 4. Daily mean Global Solar Radiation (GSR) in Al-Ain, UAE for years 1995-2004

Coefficient	a_1	a_2	a_3	a_4	a_5
Value	-1.1973	0.0971	0.0513	0.3850	- 0.0052

Table 6. Regression coefficients of eq. (4)

The regression model of eq. (4) yields a deterministic coefficient $R^2 = 0.7824$ and MSE = 0.4247. In MATLAB, the regression between GSR and predictor variables (T, W, SSH, RH) is done using the Statistics Toolbox command

```
>> regcoef= robustfit(xdata, GSR )
```

Where '*xdata*' is an array matrix containing the four predictors, i.e. xdata=[T, WS, SSH, RH], and '*regcoef*' is a vector returning the regression coefficients between GSR and the four predictor weather variables resulting from the robust multi-linear regression process. The correlation between the regression component $GSR_{regression}$ and GSR can be found using

```
>> corr(GSR, GSRregression)
```

Step 5. Trend and Seasonality components of the residual regression error
The residual error from the multivariate linear regression model in eq. (4), denoted by $GSR_{residue1}$ (t) = GSR - $GSR_{regression}$(t), is shown in Fig. 5. The objective is to first examine it for trends and/or seasonality and decompose it to yield:

$$GSR_{residue1}(t) = GSR_{trend}(t) + GSR_{seasonal}(t) + GSR_{residue2}(t) \tag{5}$$

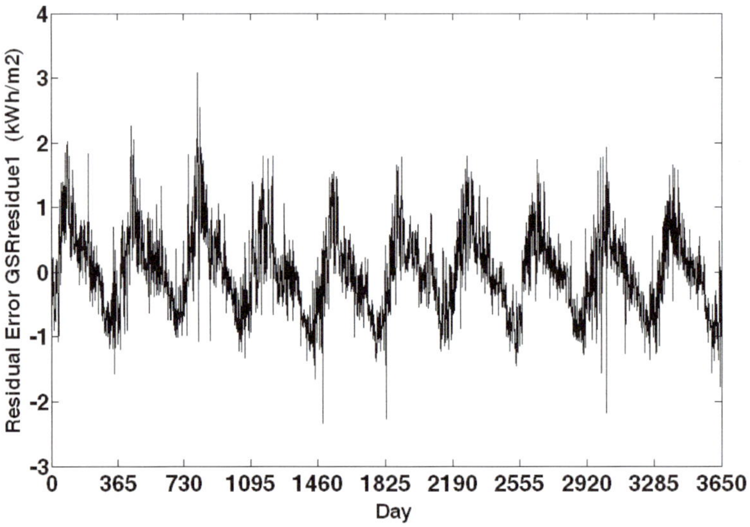

Fig. 5. Residual term of mean daily GSR after subtracting regression model of eq. (4)

The trend component is extracted in MATLAB using the statement

```
>> gsrdet=detrend(gsrresidue1`); % This gives GSRresidue1 with trend removed
>> gsrtrend=gsr-gsrdet;
```

The trend equation can be deduced using the *cftool* command in MATLAB that invokes the curve fitting GUI and then performs a linear polynomial fit to yield the linear trend equation:

$$GSR_{trend}(t) = 0.0771 - 4.2211E - 05 * t \tag{6}$$

The mathematical model for the seasonal component, i.e. $GSR_{seasonal}(t)$, is found from MATLAB using the FFT algorithm. The resulting model is:

$$GSR_{seasonal}(t) = \sum_{k=1}^{\frac{NP-1}{2}} \left[a_k \cos\left(\frac{2\pi}{NP}kt\right) + b_k \sin\left(\frac{2\pi}{NP}kt\right) \right] \tag{7}$$

The MATLAB statement to generate the Fourier Coefficients for a periodic sequence (period=NP=365) of data x[n], n=1, 2,.., N=3650 is done using:

```
>> N=3650;
>> y=fft(x,N);   % here x is an array representing the de-trendedGSR residual
```

The overall decomposition leads to the following regression model:

$$GSR(t) = GSR_{regression}(t) + GSR_{trend}(t) + GSR_{seasonal}(t) + \text{residual Error}(t) \quad (8)$$

where the multivariable linear regression, trend and seasonal components are described in eqs. (4), (6) and (7), respectively. The overall residual error of the time-series regression-based model is shown in Fig. 6.

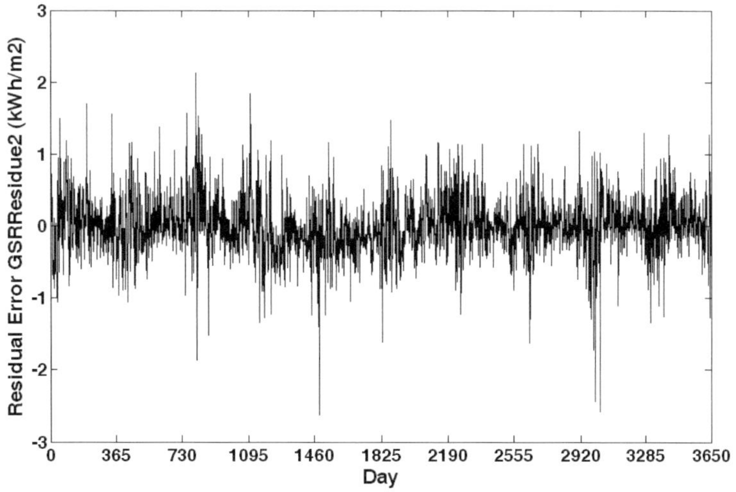

Fig. 6. Residual mean daily global solar radiation error for 1995-2004 data of Al-Ain, UAE

2.1.2.1 Time-series ARMA modelling for the residual term (stochastic component)

The Box-Jenkins models (Box & Jenkins, 1994) are only applicable to stationary time series. The identification of an appropriate box-Jenkins model for a particular time-series would first require a check for stationarity. If the residual term exhibits a normal distribution behavior with zero mean and constant variance then it resembles white noise error and there is no need for further ARIMA modeling.

The behavior of the ACF and PACF plots can help identify the ARMA model that best describes the resulting stationary time-series. Table 7 summarizes the ARMA model selection criteria (Enders 2010). In general, if the ACF of the time series value either cuts off or dies down fairly quick, then the time series values should be considered stationary. On the other hand, if the ACF dies down extremely slow, then the time series values may be considered non-stationary. If the model is adequate then these plots should show all spikes within the 95 % Confidence Interval (CI) bounds ($\pm 1.96/\sqrt{N}$) where N is the sample size. If the series results non-stationary, one could try to apply differencing or log- transformation and then check if these make the series stationary. A stationary time-series would have a quasi-normal distribution with zero mean and constant variance.

Fig. 7 shows the ACF and PACF plots for the residual component as obtained from Minitab. Note that the ACF decays in an oscillating form after few lags within CI bounds thus implying a fairly stationary time-series. Differencing the residual component made the ACF and PACF more unstable with further deterioration of their behavior thus implying that differencing is inappropriate for this data. The PACF plot cuts off quickly after 1 lag indicating that an AR(2) or higher could be adequate.

Model	ACF	PACF
AR (p)	Spikes decay towards zero. Coefficients may oscillate.	Spikes decay to zero after lag p
MA (q)	Spikes decay to zero after lag q	Spikes decay towards zero. Coefficients may oscillate.
ARMA (p,q)	Spikes decay (either direct or oscillatory) to zero beginning after lag q	Spikes decay (either direct or oscillatory) to zero beginning after lag p

Table 7. Behavior of ACF and PACF for each of the general non-seasonal models

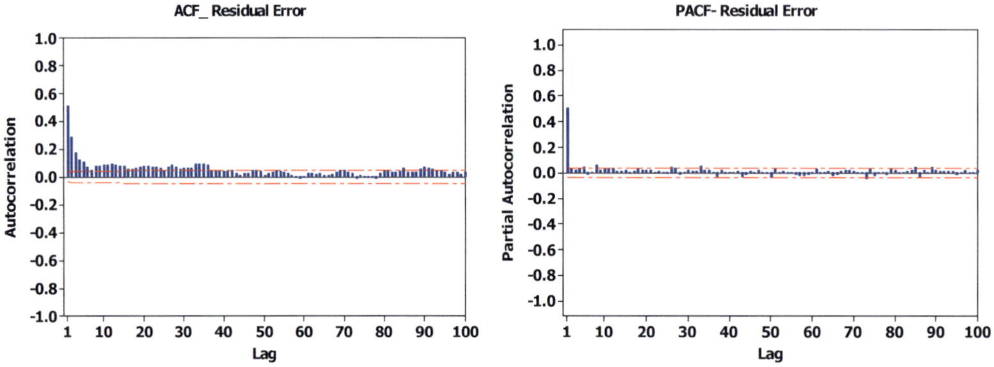

Fig. 7. Auto-Correlation Function (ACF) and Partial Auto-Correlation Function (PACF) for residual component of the mean daily GSR data

2.1.2.2 Description of ARMA modeling process

The time-series analysis of the residual stochastic component of the mean daily GSR data is conducted using SPSS and Minitab with help of MATLAB. The nature of the ARMA model used is first described followed by explanation of the model selection process with diagnostic measures used to validate the selected model.

The non-seasonal autoregressive-moving average of order (p, q), e.g. ARMA(p, q) is described by the equation (Enders, 2010):

$$y_t = \delta + \phi_1 y_{t-1} + \phi_2 y_{t-2} + \ldots + \phi_p y_{t-p} + \epsilon_t - \theta_1 \epsilon_{t-1} - \theta_2 \epsilon_{t-2} - \ldots - \theta_q \epsilon_{t-q} \, \epsilon \tag{9}$$

where δ is a random shock and $\phi_1, \phi_2, \ldots, \phi_p$ are unknown autoregressive model coefficients that are estimated from sample data. The constant parameter is proportional to the mean value μ which is zero in our case. $\theta_1, \theta_2, \ldots, \theta_q$ are unknown moving average model coefficients that depend on the sample data. Moreover, $\epsilon_t, \epsilon_{t-1}, \epsilon_{t-2}, \ldots, \epsilon_{t-q}$ are statistically independent random shocks assumed to be randomly selected from a normal distribution with zero mean and constant variance.

The ARMA(p, q) model parameters ($\phi_i, i = 1,2,\ldots,p$ *and* $\theta_j, j = 1,2,\ldots,q$) described in eq. (9) are estimated using Least Square methods with known values of y_t representing the residual component data. The estimated parameters of the selected ARMA(p, q) models should have t-values higher than 2.0 in order to be judged significantly different from zero at the 5 % level. Moreover, the coefficients should not be strongly correlated with each other in order to yield a parsimonious ARMA model, whilst passing the diagnostic checks. A parsimonious model is desirable because including irrelevant lags in the model increases the coefficient standard errors and therefore reduces the t-statistics. Models that incorporate large numbers of lags tend not to forecast well as they fit data specific features, explaining much of the noise or random features in the data. Therefore, model coefficients with p-values higher than 0.05 are insignificant and should be eliminated to avoid over-fitting as they have little effect on the prediction model (Enders, 2010). Different models can be obtained for various combinations of AR and MA individually and collectively. The best model is selected using the following diagnostics:

(a) Low Akaike Information Criteria (AIC)/ Schwarz-Bayesian Information Criteria (SBC, BIC)

These model parameters are dependent on the data sample size, model mean-square error (MSE), and the (p, q) values of the ARMA model. Their definition can be found in MATLAB help (MATLAB, 2010) or (Enders, 2010). SBC selects the more parsimonious model and is better than AIC for large samples. *The best model should have the lowest AIC/SBC value and the least MSE.*

(b) Plot of residual autocorrelation function (ACF)

The appropriate ARMA model, once fitted, should have a residual error whose ACF plot varies within the 95% CI bounds ($\pm 1.96 / \sqrt{N}$) where N is the number of observations upon which the model is based.

(c) Non-significance of auto correlations of residuals via Portmanteau tests (Q-tests based on Chi-square statistics) such as Box-Pierce or Ljung-Box tests(White noise tests)

Once the optimal ARMA(p,q) model for the residual GSR time-series is selected, there is a need to check the white noise test if the ACF/PACF correlograms show significant spikes at one or more lags that could be just by chance. These tests indicate whether there is any correlation in the time-series or whether the abnormal spikes encountered in the ACF and PACF of the residual error are just a set of random, identically distributed variables overall. The Ljung-Box Q-statistics can be used to check if the residuals from the ARMA(p, q) model behave as a white-noise process (Ljung & Box, 1978; Enders, 2010). Ljung & Box use the Q statistic:

$$Q = (n)(n+2)\sum_{k=1}^{K} \frac{r_k^2}{n-k} \tag{10}$$

which yields a more accurate variance of ACF [variance becomes $(n-K)/n^2$ instead of $1/n$] compared to the statistic defined earlier by(Box & Pierce, 1970). K is the degrees of freedom representing the maximum lags considered (normally 20). n = N-d with N being the number of data points and d the degree of differencing (no differencing is assumed in this work so d = 0), and r_k is the sample ACF at lag k.

Under the null-hypothesis that all values of autocorrelation $r_k = 0$, the Q Statistic is compared to critical values from chi-square distribution χ^2 distributed with K-degrees of freedom. If the model is correctly specified, the residuals should be uncorrelated and Q should be small and consequently the probability value should be large. A white noise process would ideally have $Q = 0$. Therefore, if $Q > \chi^2_{DF,\alpha}$ at the specified DF and significance level α, then the we can reject the null hypothesis.

Several ARMA models were analyzed based on the recommended criteria and two models surfaced out to be the best, namely, ARMA (2,1) and ARMA (4,3). Any further increase in the q-coefficients above 3 ($q > 3$) lead to over-fitting as witnessed by p-values exceeding 0.05. The best parsimonious model obtained based on the suggested diagnostics is the ARMA(2,1) model. Table 8 shows the ARMA (2, 1) model parameters obtained from SPSS. All the estimated model coefficients have p -value less than 0.05 (α= 5 %). This implies that all the coefficients of the selected Box-Jenkins model are significant since the null hypothesis H_0: ϕ= 0 (AR) or θ=0 (MA) can be rejected for the preset significance level α (can be chosen as 0.05 or 0.01). Table 9 shows the model fit statistics for the ARMA (2,1) model. The Ljung-Box statistic value **Q = 15.462** at lag 18 has a corresponding **p = 0.419** > 0.05. Hence, we cannot reject the adequacy of model by setting α = 0.05. The resulting ARMA (2,1) model will therefore yield a residual error that resembles white noise error. The ACF and PACF plots of the residual error of the ARMA(2, 1) model, shown in Fig. 8, vary within the 95% CI bounds. The spikes in the ACF and PACF at lag 7 are due to random events and thus cannot be explained. However, since it is a 95% confidence interval, one can expect this to happen once in every twenty lags and so we will not be concerned with this.

Parameter	Lag	Estimate	Standard Error	t-value	Sig. (p-value)
AR (1)	1	1.4504	0.0189	76.7886	0.000
AR (2)	2	-0.4568	0.0172	-26.5608	0.000
MA (1)	1	0.9699	0.0100	97.0868	0.000

Table 8. SPSS least square estimation of the model parameters for ARMA(2, 1) model of residual GSR component

Model Fit statistics								Ljung-Box Q(18)		
Stationary R2	R2	RMSE	MAPE	MAE	MaxAPE	MaxAE	Norm. BIC	Statistics	DF	Sig.
.265	.265	.337	458.224	.238	240313.424	2.491	-2.168	15.462	15	.419

Table 9. ARMA(2, 1) model statistics

Another method to ensure that the selected ARMA model yields a stationary residual error is by checking the **Unit-root rule** for stationarity. Assume that the lag operator in eq. (9) is B. Then $By_t = y_{t-1}$. Eq. (9) can then be written in the form (assume zero mean; δ= 0):

$$\left(1-\phi_1 B-\phi_2 B^2-\ldots-\phi_p B^p\right) y_t=\left(1-\theta_1 B-\theta_2 B^2-\ldots-\theta_q B^q\right) \epsilon_t \tag{11}$$

or

$$\phi(B) y_t=\theta(B) \epsilon_t \tag{12}$$

where

$$\phi(B)=1-\sum_{i=1}^{p} \phi_i B^i \; ; \quad \theta(B)=1-\sum_{i=1}^{q} \theta_i B^i \tag{13}$$

The stationarity of the time-series sequence y_t requires that all the roots of the AR(p) coefficients polynomial ϕ (B) should lie outside the unit circle (Enders, 2010).

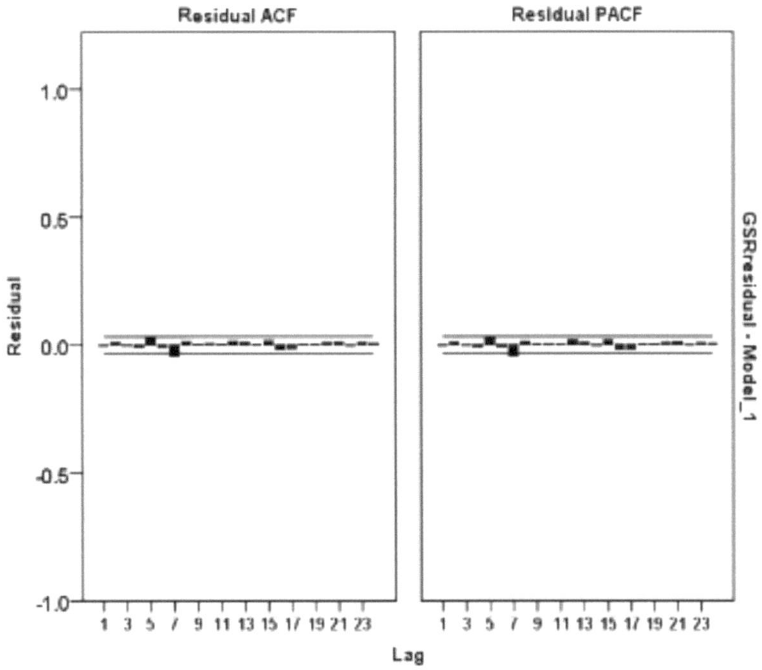

Fig. 8. ACF and PACF plots for the residual error of the ARMA(2, 1) model

The MATLAB function "**roots(c)**" computes the roots of the polynomial P(x) whose coefficients are the elements of the vector **c**. If **c** has (n+1) components, the polynomial is

$$P(x)=c(1)*x^{n}+ \ldots + c(n)*x + c(n+1).$$

Next, the ARMA(2,1) model parameters $\phi(B)$ obtained from SPSS are used in MATLAB to perform the stationarity unit-root test as follows :

```
>> phi=[1.4504   -0.4568];
>> phiB=[-phi(end:-1:1), 1]
     phiB=
     0.4568  -1.4504  1
>> roots(phiB)   % find roots of polynomial with coefficients phiB
     ans =
        2.1631
        1.0120
```

Note that all roots of $\phi(B)$ lie outside the unit circle thus implying a stationary ARMA(2, 1) model. Once the ARMA(p, q) model is selected and checked for stationary residual error, the GSR regression model involving the ARMA model becomes:

$$GSR(t) = GSR_{regression}(t) + GSR_{trend}(t) + GSR_{seasonal}(t) + GSR_{ARIMA}(t) + WN(t) \quad (14)$$

where WN(t) is the final residual error which resembles white noise with zero mean and constant variance.

2.1.2.3 Comparison of Time-series regression model with measured data

Use cftool MATLAB GUI toolbox to study the correlation between the regression model without (eq (8)) and with ARMA modeling (eq (14)) and the measured data set for years 1995-2004. This MATLAB tool sketches the data and finds the polynomial fit and descriptive statistics as depicted in Fig. 9 (a-b). The predicted time-series regression model with and without ARMA modeling yields deterministic coefficients of 94.4% and 92.4 %, respectively, as shown in Fig.9 (a)-(b).The ARMA-based model yields lower error statistics RMSE, MABE and MAPE and hence will do a better forecasting job.

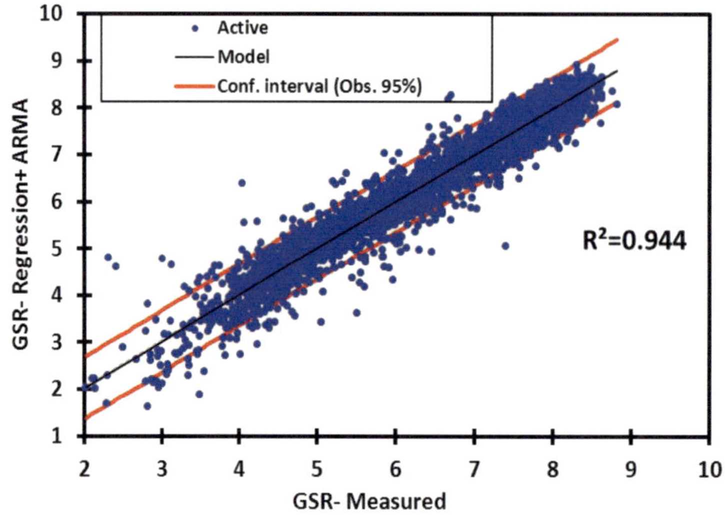

(a)

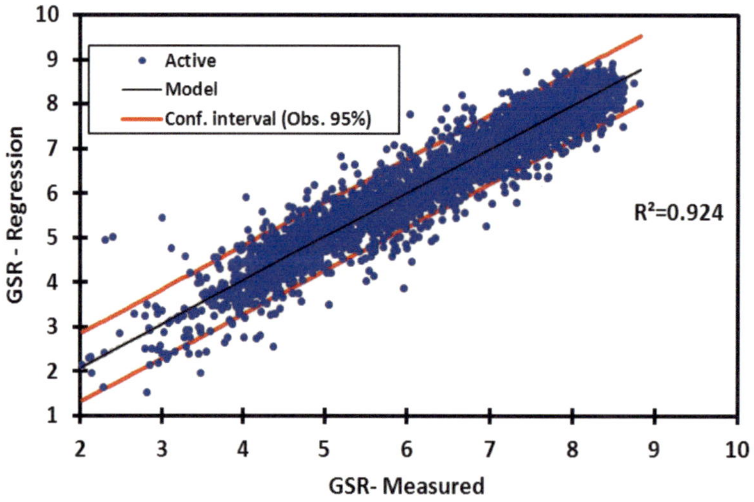

(b)

Fig. 9. MATLAB "cftool" GUI comparison between regression and measured data for years 1995-2004 (a) with, and (b) without ARMA model

The mean daily GSR data comparison between the measured and the regression model for years 1995-2004 in Al-Ain is shown in Fig. 10. The residual error term of GSR is written as:

$$GSR_{residual}(t) = GSR_{measured}(t) - GSR_{regression}(t) \tag{15}$$

This error is required to have normal distribution with zero mean and constant variance thus resembling a white noise error. The check of normality can be done in SPSS or Minitab or other statistical package. In MATLAB and after invoking the Statistics toolbox, we can use the command 'normplot(x)' where x is the time-series data array. We can also use the Quantile-Quantile Plots (Q-Q Plot) 'qqplot(x,xa)' where x and xa represent the measured and approximate data sequences. A linear relationship between x ad xa suggests that the two samples may come from the same distribution family and hence ensure a normally distributed residual error. Additional statistical studies may be done including ANOVA test and two-sample variance tests with the help of Minitab, SPSS or other statistical software packages. In MATLAB, we can use the Statistics toolbox functions ANOVA1 and ANOVA2.

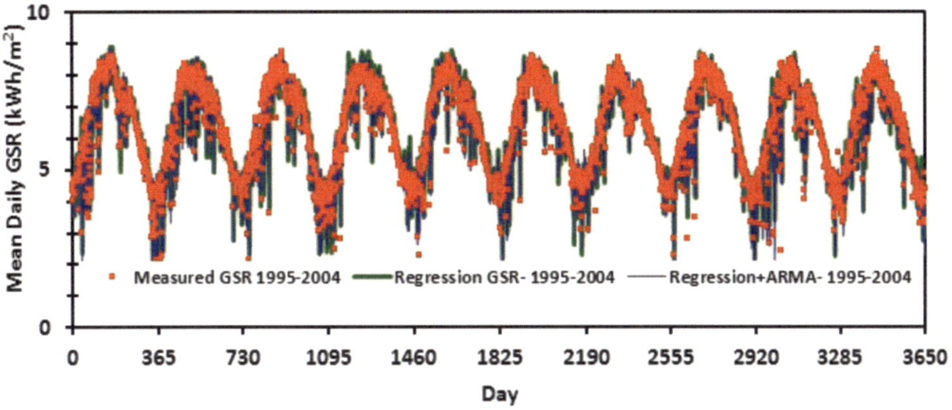

Fig. 10. Mean daily GSR data for years 1995-2004 in Al-Ain, UAE

The residual error of the GSR regression model was checked for normality in the previous section in order to ensure its stationarity for proper prediction of weather data. Minitab or SPSS are used to confirm the normality of the residual error. Fig. 11 shows the normality test results from Minitab showing a residual error with near zero mean (5.8380E-05) and a 0.3364 standard deviation. Note from Fig. 11 that the residual error moves along the normality line between 1 % and 95% percentiles. The computed Skewness (0.204) and Kurtosis (4.85) constants indicate a quasi-normal distribution behavior that is slightly shifted to the left of the mean and with more pointed bell shape than the normal distribution curve.

Table 10 shows the result of running Fisher's two-tailed F-test on the Regression and Measured data for years 1995-2004. This variance ratio test follows the Null hypothesis (H_0) that the ratio between variances is equal to 1 against the alternative (H_a) that the ratio between variances is different from 1. The computed p-value shown in Table 10 is greater than the significance level alpha=0.05 and thus we cannot reject the null hypothesis H_0. The risk to reject the null hypothesis H_0 while it is true is 22.04% and 18.23 % for Regression and Regression with ARMA cases, respectively.

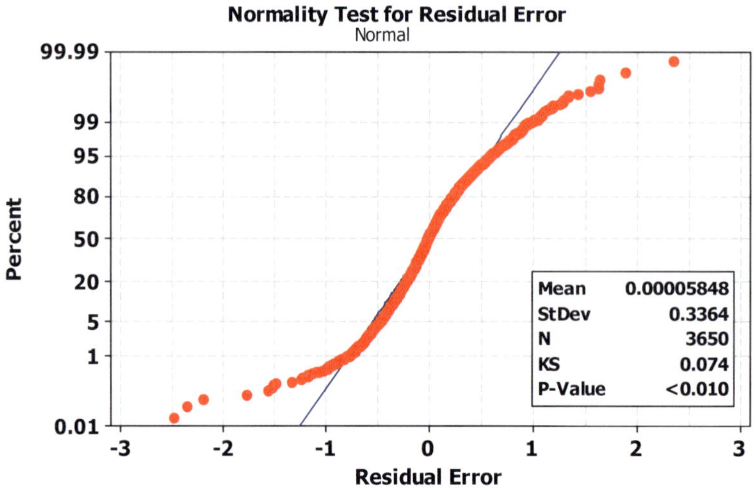

Fig. 11. Normality test for residual error with Minitab

Parameter	Regression vs. Measured	Regression with ARMA vs. Measured
95% CI on ratio of variances	] 0.976, 1.111 [	] 0.979, 1.115 [
Ratio of variances	1.041	1.045
F (Observed value)	1.041	1.045
F (Critical value)	1.067	1.067
DF1, DF2	3649, 3649	3649, 3649
p-value (Two-tailed)	0.2204	0.1823

Table 10. Fisher's two-tailed F-test for the model data of 10 years

Levene's equal variances test can also be applied as shown in Table 11. As the computed p-value in Tables 11 is greater than the significance level alpha=0.05, one cannot reject the null hypothesis H_0. The risk to reject the null hypothesis H_0 in Levene's test while it is true is 55.62% and 43.96% for Regression and Regression with ARMA cases, respectively. Levene's test is mostly used in samples with normal distribution.

Parameter	Regression Vs Measured	Regression with ARMA Vs Measured
F (Observed value)	0.346	0.597
F (Critical value)	3.843	3.843
DF1, DF2	1, 7298	1, 7298
p-value (one-tailed)	**0.5562**	**0.4396**

Table 11. Levene's two-tailed variance test

2.1.2.5 Validation of time-series regression model

In the following section, the time-series regression model is validated with measured test data set for years 2005-2007 in Al-Ain, UAE. A MATLAB code is written to implement the regression model for the input test data (1095 points). The generated regression model test data is then compared with the test data samples to check the correlation and to study the accuracy of the prediction model. An excellent agreement is noted between the mean daily regression and measured test data for years 2005-2007. The statistical error data computed with MATLAB yields deterministic coefficients R^2 = 92.6% and 90.77% with and without ARMA modeling, respectively, thus indicating good model prediction performance. MATLAB is again used to determine the monthly mean GSR data for the test data period (2005-2007). The resulting monthly mean GSR data comparison between test (measured) and regression model for years 2005-2007 is shown in Fig. 12. Note the excellent agreement between regression model and the test data. Fig. 12 also shows comparison results obtained using Multi-layer Perceptron (MLP) and Radial Basis Function (RBF) Artificial Neural Networks (ANN) obtained by the co-author (Al-Shamisi & Assi, 2011) using the same model and test data sets. Fig. 12 shows a better prediction performance for the regression models over the ANN-based models for Al-Ain test data. The low error parameters (RMSE, MBE, MABE, MBE, and MAPE) obtained for the regression models provide a clear indication of the potential of these techniques for long term GSR data prediction.

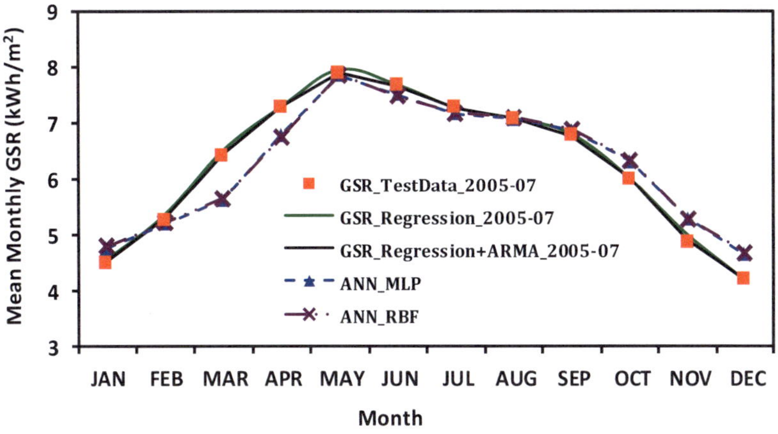

Fig. 12. Monthly mean GSR data comparison for test data 2005-2007 in Al-Ain city

2.2 Definition of the statistical error parameters

This section defines formulas used to compute the statistical error parameters in MATLAB. These parameters attest to the accuracy of the models used for predicting the mean daily global solar radiation (GSR). The error parameters were also computed using EXCEL and SPSS and values agree very well with MATLAB results. The formulas used are:

Mean Average Percentage Error: $$\text{MAPE} = 100 \times \frac{1}{N}\sum_{i=1}^{N}\left|\frac{GSR_m^i - GSR_p^i}{GSR_m^i}\right|$$

Mean Bias Error: $$\text{MBE} = \frac{1}{N}\sum_{i=1}^{N}\left(GSR_m^i - GSR_p^i\right)$$

Mean Absolute Bias Error: $$\text{MABE} = \frac{1}{N}\sum_{i=1}^{N}\left|GSR_m^i - GSR_p^i\right|$$

Root Mean-Square Error: $\text{RMSE} = \sqrt{\frac{1}{N}\sum_{i=1}^{N}\left(\text{GSR}_m^i - \text{GSR}_p^i\right)^2}$

Mean measured value: $\overline{\text{GSR}_m} = \frac{1}{N}\sum_{i=1}^{N}\text{GSR}_m^i$

Mean predicted value: $\overline{\text{GSR}_p} = \frac{1}{N}\sum_{i=1}^{N}\text{GSR}_p^i$

Deterministic coefficient: $R^2 = 1 - \frac{\text{SSE}}{\text{SST}} = 1 - \frac{\sum_{i=1}^{N}\left(\text{GSR}_m^i - \text{GSR}_p^i\right)^2}{\sum_{i=1}^{N}\left(\text{GSR}_m^i - \overline{\text{GSR}_m}\right)^2}$

where GSR_m^i is the ith measured value, GSR_p^i is the predicted value from the regression model, and N is the total number of data points.

3. Conclusion

This chapter addresses the MATLAB tools employed in finding appropriate prediction models for the mean daily and monthly global solar radiation in the city of Al-Ain, United Arab Emirates. A detailed description of tools used in obtaining the classical empirical regression models as well as time-series ARMA models is presented including computation of error statistics and use of diagnosis tests to validate the selected models. Excellent agreement is observed between the empirical regression and time-series prediction models and measured test data with high deterministic coefficients exceeding 90 % and low MBE, MABE, MAPE and RMSE error statistics that attest to the suitability of these models for long-term weather data prediction. The same MATLAB tools will be used to come up with prediction models for other UAE cities.

4. Acknowledgment

The authors would like to thank the National Center of Meteorology and Seismology (NCMS), Abu Dhabi for providing the weather data. Thanks are also due to Maitha Al-Shamisi for pre-processing the received data. This work is financially supported by UAE University Research Affairs under the contract #1542-07-01-10.

5. References

Abdalla Y.A.G. & Feregh G.M. (1988). Contribution to the Study of Solar Radiation in Abu Dhabi, *Energy Conver. Mgmt.*,Vol. 28, No. 1, pp. 63- 67.

Akinoglu B. G. & Ecevit A. (1990). A further comparison and discussion of sunshine based models to estimate global solar radiation, *Energy*, Vol. 15, pp. 865-872.

Al-Alawi S. & Al-Hinai H. (1998). An ANN-based Approach for Predicting Global Solar Radiation in Locations with no Measurements, *Renewable Energy*, Vol. 14, pp.199–204.

Al Mahdi N., Al Baharna N. S. & Zaki F. F. (1992). Assessment of Solar radiation models for Gulf Arabian Countries, *Renewable Energy*, Vol. 2, No. 1, pp. 65-71.

Ampratwum D. B. & Dorvlo A. S. S. (1999). Estimation of solar radiation from the number of sunshine hours, *Appl. Energy*, Vol. 63, pp. 161-167.

Al-Shamisi M. & Assi A. (January 2011). ANN Global Solar Radiation unpublished results for Al-Ain provided by personal communication.

Assi A. & Al-Shamisi M. (2010). "Prediction of Monthly Average Daily Global Solar Radiation in Al Ain City–UAE Using Artificial Neural Networks", *Proceedings of the 25th European Photovoltaic Solar Energy Conference*, pp. 508-512, Valencia, Spain, September 06-10, 2010.

Assi A., Al-Shamisi M. & Jama M. (2010). Prediction of Monthly Average Daily Global Solar Radiation in Al Ain City–UAE Using Artificial Neural Networks, *Proceedings of the 4th International Conference on Renewable Energy Sources (RES'10)*, pp. 109-113, Sousse, Tunisia ,May 03-06, 2010.

Assi A. & Jama M. (2010). Estimating Global Solar Radiation on Horizontal from Sunshine Hours in Abu Dhabi - UAE, *Proceedings of the 4th International Conference on Renewable Energy Sources (RES'10)*, pp. 101-108, Sousse, Tunisia, May 03-06, 2010.

Behrang M.A., Assareh E., Ghanbarzadeh A. & Noghrehabadi A. R. (2010). The potential of different artificial neural network (ANN) techniques in daily global solar radiation modeling based on meteorological data, *Solar Energy*, Vol. 84, pp. 1468-1480.

Benghanem M., Mellit A. & Alamri S. N. (2009). ANN-based modeling and estimation of daily global solar radiation data: A case study, *Energy Conversion and Management*, Vol. 50, pp. 1644-1655.

Boccol M., Willington E. & Arias M. (2010). Comparison of Regression and Neural Networks Models to estimate Solar Radiation, *Chilean Journal of Agricultural Research*, Vol. 70, No. 3, pp.428-435, July-Sept., 2010.

Boland J. (1995). Time series analysis of climate variables, *Solar Energy*, Vol. 55, pp. 377–388.

Box G. E. P., Jenkins G. M. & Reinsel G. C. (1994). *Time series analysis: Forecasting and control*, (3rd edition), Prentice-Hall International, Englewood Cliffs, N.J.

Box G. & Pierce D. (1970). Distribution of Autocorrelations in autoregressive Moving Average Time Series Models. *Journal of the American Statistical Association*, Vol. 65, pp. 1509- 1526.

Elagib N. & Mansell M. G. (2000). New approaches for estimating global solar radiation across Sudan, *Energy Conversion Management*, Vol. 41, pp. 419-434.

Elminir H., Areed F. & Elsayed T. (2005). Estimation of solar radiation components incident on Helwan site using neural networks, *Solar Energy*, Vol. 79, pp. 270-279.

Enders W. (2010). *Applied Econometric Time Series* (3rd edition), John Wiley & Sons, ISBN 978-0470-50539-7.

IBM SPSS Statistics for Windows, Version 19.0.0, 2010. SPSS Inc.

Khalil A. & Alnajjar A., (1995), Experimental and Theoretical Investigation of Global and Diffuse Solar Radiation in the United Arab Emirates, *Renewable Energy*, Vol. 6, No. 5-6, pp. 537-543.

Krishnaiah T., Srinivasa Rao S., Madhumurthy K. & Reddy K. S. (2007). A Neural Network Approach for Modelling Global Solar Radiation, *Applied Science Research*, Vol. 3, No. 10, pp.1105-1111.

Ljung G. & Box G. (1978). On a Measure of Lack of Fit in Time Series Models, *Biometrica*, Vol. 65, pp. 297-303.

MATLAB version 7.10.0.499 (R 2010 a), 2010.The MathWorks Inc.

Menges H. O., Ertekin C. & Sonmete M. H. (2006). Evaluation of solar radiation models for Konya, Turkey, *Energy Conversion and Management*, Vol. 47, pp. 3149-3173.

Minitab version 16.1.0, 2010. Minitab, Inc.

Mohandes M., Rehman S., & Halawani T. O. (1998). Estimation of Global Solar Radiation Using Artificial Neural Networks, *Renewable Energy*, Vol. 14, pp. 179-184.

Mohandes M., Balghonaim A., Kassas M., Rehman S. & Halawani T. O. (2000). Use of Radial Basis Functions for Estimating Monthly Mean Daily Solar Radiation, *Solar Energy*, Vol. 68, No. 2, pp. 161-168..

Newland F. J. (1988). A study of solar radiation models for the coastal region of south China, *Solar Energy*, Vol. 31, pp. 227-235.

Podestá G., Núñez G., Villanueva C. & Skanski M. (2004). Estimating daily solar radiation in the Argentine Pampas, *Agricultural and Forest Meteorology*, Vol. 123, pp. 41-53.

Rehman S. & Mohandes M. (2008). Artificial neural network estimation of global solar radiation using air temperature and relative humidity, *Energy Policy*, No. 36, pp. 571-576.

Reikard G. (2009). Predicting solar radiation at high resolutions: A comparison of time series forecasts, *Solar Energy*, Vol. 83, pp. 342–349.

Şahin A. D. (2007). A new formulation for solar irradiation and sunshine duration estimation, *International Journal of Energy Research*, Vol. 31, pp. 109-118.

Samuel T. (1991). Estimation of solar radiation for Sri Lanka, *Solar Energy*, Vol. 47, pp. 333–337.

Sulaiman M. Y., Hlaing O. W. M., Wahab M. A. & Sulaiman Z. A. (1997). Analysis of residuals in daily solar radiation time series, *Renewable Energy*, Vol. 11, No. 1, pp. 97-105.

Ulgen K. & Hepbasli A. (2002). Comparison of solar radiation correlations for Izmir, Turkey, *International Journal of Energy Research*, Vol. 26, pp. 413- 430.

Zaharim A., Razali A. M., Gim T. P. & Sopian K. (2009).Time Series Analysis of Solar Radiation data in the Tropics, *European Journal of Scientific Research*, Vol. 25, No. 4, pp. 672- 678.

Zeroual A., Ankrim M. & Wilkinson A. J. (1995). Stochastic modelling of daily global solar radiation measured in Marrakesh, Morocco, *Renewable Energy*, Vol. 6, No. 7, pp. 787-793.

9

Using MATLAB to Develop Artificial Neural Network Models for Predicting Global Solar Radiation in Al Ain City – UAE

Maitha H. Al Shamisi, Ali H. Assi and Hassan A. N. Hejase
United Arab Emirates University
United Arab Emirates

1. Introduction

Information about the availability of solar radiation on horizontal surface is essential for the optimum design and study of solar energy systems. For a country like UAE, the efficient application of solar energy seems inevitable because of abundant sunshine available throughout the year. The traditional way of knowing the amount of global solar radiation (GSR) in a particular region is to install pyranometers at as many locations as possible in this region thus requiring daily maintenance and data recording, and consequently increasing cost of GSR data collection. Therefore, it is rather more economical to develop methods to estimate the GSR using climatological parameters (Akhlaque et al., 2009; Kassem et al., 2009; Falayi et al., 2008; El-Sebaii & Trabea, 2005).

Many researchers estimated global solar radiation by using artificial neural networks. (Mohandes et al, 1998) applied ANN techniques to predict GSR using weather data from 41 stations in Saudi Arabia. Data from 31 stations was used in training the NN and the remaining data was used for testing. Input variables to the NN included 4 parameters: latitude, longitude, altitude and sunshine duration. Their sample data was not large enough to allow a credible comparison between the ANN models used and empirical regression models. (Lam et al., 2008) have used Artificial Neural networks ANNs to develop predication models for daily global solar radiation using measured sunshine duration for 40 cities covering 9 major thermal climatic zones and sub-zones in China. (Alam et al., 2009) used ANNs to estimate monthly mean hourly and daily diffuse solar radiation based on weather data from 10 Indian stations which have different climatic conditions. (Alawi & Hinai, 1998) applied ANNs to predict solar radiation in areas not covered by direct measurement instrumentation. The input data that was used for building the network were the location, month, mean pressure, mean temperature, mean vapor pressure, mean relative humidity, mean wind speed and mean duration of sunshine. (Tasadduq et al., 2002) have used neural networks for the prediction of hourly mean values of ambient temperature 24 hours in advance. Full year hourly values of ambient temperature are used to train a neural network model for a coastal location – Jeddah, Saudi Arabia. (Elminir et al., 2005) applied ANN modeling techniques to predict solar radiation data in different spectrum bands from data of meteorology for Helwan (Egypt) meteorology monitoring station. (Rehman & Mohandes, 2008) developed ANN-based estimation GSR for Abha city in Saudi Arabia; by using different combination of day of year, time day of year, air temperature and relative humidity. (Krishnaiah et al., 2007) considered the artificial neural network (ANN) approach for estimating hourly global solar radiation (HGSR) in India. The ANN models are presented and implemented on real meteorological data. The solar radiation data from 7 stations are used for training the ANN and data from two stations are used for testing the predicted values. (Mubiru, 2008) predicted a monthly average daily total solar irradiation on a horizontal surface for locations in Uganda by using artificial neural network technique, where both geographical and meteorological data are used to develop model.

For countries like UAE, where solar radiation has significant strength, the average annual solar hours is 3568 h (i.e. 9.7 h/day), which corresponds to an average annual solar radiation of approximately 2285 kWh/m^2 (i.e. 6.3 kWh/m^2 per day) (Assi & Jama, 2010).

This book chapter will show the potential of MATLAB tools in writing scripts that help in developing Artificial Neural Network (ANN) models for the prediction of global solar radiation in Al Ain city, UAE. The developed scripts use built-in commands and functions for customizing data processing, network architecture, training algorithms and testing performance of the ANN models.

2. Background

2.1 Neural network

A neural network is a massively parallel distributed processor made up of simple processing units that have a natural tendency for storing experiential knowledge and making it available for us. Artificial neural network (ANN) is a type of Artificial Intelligence technique that mimics the behavior of the human brain (Haykin, 2009).

ANNs have the ability to model linear and non-linear systems without the need to make assumptions implicitly as in most traditional statistical approaches. They have been applied in various aspects of science and engineering (Rivard & Zmeureanu, 2005; Chantasut et al., 2005).

ANNs can be grouped into two major categories: feed-forward and feedback (recurrent) networks. In the former network, no loops are formed by the network connections, while one or more loops may exist in the latter. The most commonly used family of feed-forward networks is a layered network in which neurons are organized into layers with connections strictly in one direction from one layer to another (Jain et al., 1996).

2.2 Multilayer preceptor (MLP)

MLPs are the most common type of feed-forward networks. Fig. 1 shows an MLP which has three types of layers: an input layer, an output layer and a hidden layer.

Neurons in input layer only act as buffers for distributing the input signals x_i (i=1, 2 ...n) to neurons in the hidden layer. Each neuron j (Fig. 2) in the hidden layer sums up its input signals x_i after weighting them with the strengths of the respective connections w_{ji} from the input layer and computes its output y_j as a function f of the sum.

$$y_j = f\left(\sum_{i=1}^{n} w_{ji}\, x_i\right) \tag{1}$$

f can be a simple threshold function or a sigmoidal, hyperbolic tangent or radial basis function.

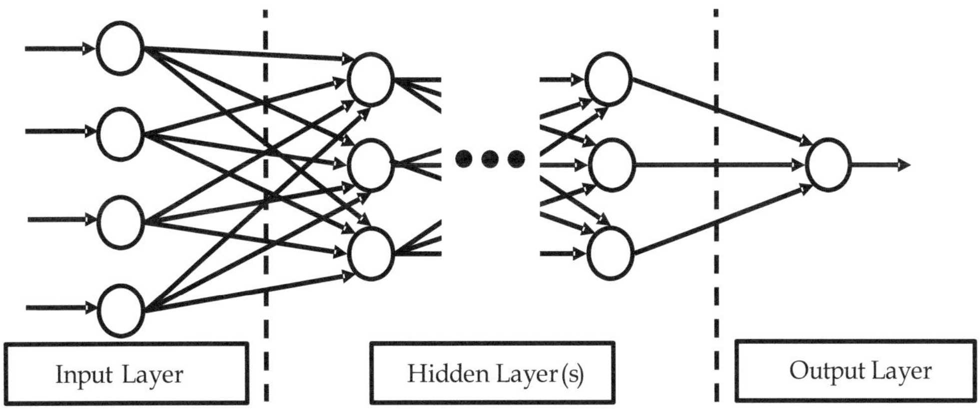

Fig. 1. A Multi-layered perceptron (MLP) network

The output of neurons in the output layer is computed similarly. The backpropagation algorithm, a gradient descent algorithm, is the most commonly adopted MLP training algorithm. It gives the change Δw_{ji} the weight of a connection between neurons iand j as follows:

$$\Delta w_{ij} = \eta\ \delta_j x_i \quad (2)$$

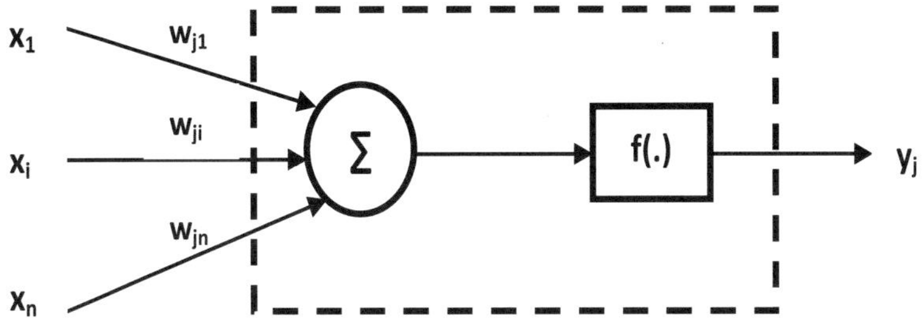

Fig. 2. Detail of the perceptron process

where η is a parameter called the learning rate and δ_j is a factor depending on whether neuron j is an input neuron or a hidden neuron. For output neurons,

$$\delta_j = (\partial f/\partial net_j)(y_j^{(t)} - y_j) \quad (3)$$

and for hidden neurons

$$\delta_j = (\partial f/\partial net_j)(\textstyle\sum_q w_{jq}\delta_q) \quad (4)$$

In Eq. (3), net_j is the total weighted sum of input signals to neurons j and $y_j^{(t)}$ is the target output for neuron j.

As there are no target outputs for hidden neurons, in Eq. (4), the difference between the target and actual output of a hidden neurons j is replaced by the weighted sum of the δ_q terms already obtained for neurons q connected to the output of j.

The process begins with the output layer, the δ term is computed for neurons in all layers and weight updates determined for all connections, iteratively. The weight updating process can happen after the presentation of each training pattern (pattern-based training) or after

the presentation of the whole set of training patterns (batch training). Training epoch is completed when all training patterns have been presented once to the MLP.
A commonly adopted method to speed up the training is to add a "momentum" term to Eq. (5) which effectively lets the previous weight change influence the new weight change:

$$\Delta w_{ij}(I+1) = \eta\, \delta_j x_i + \mu\, \Delta w_{ij}(I) \quad (5)$$

where $\Delta w_{ij}(I+1)$ and $\Delta w_{ij}(I)$ are weight changes in epochs $(I+1)$ and (I), respectively, and μ is "momentum" coefficient (Jayawardena & Fernando, 1998).

2.3 Radial Basis Function (RBF)

Radial basis function network consists of three layers Fig 3. The input layer has neurons with a linear function that simply feed the input signals to the hidden layer. Moreover, the connections between the input and hidden layer are not weighted. The hidden neurons are processing units that perform the radial basis function. Each unit is mathematically defined as

$$\varphi_j(x) = \varphi(\| x - x_j \|),\ j = 1, 2, \ldots, n \quad (6)$$

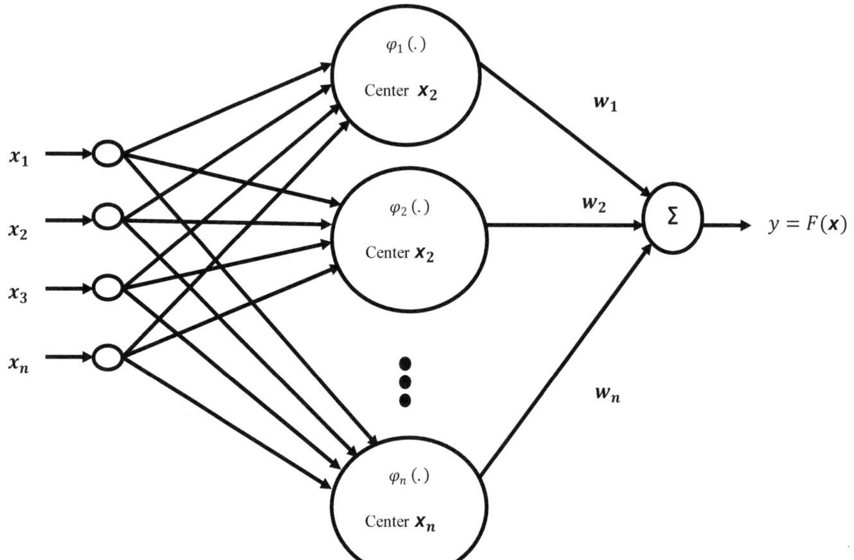

Fig. 3. Radial basis function network

The jth input data point x_j denotes the center of the radial basis function, and the vector x is the pattern applied to input layer. Selecting the basis function is not crucial to the performance of the network the most common being the Gaussian basis function which is used in this study. It is defined as

$$\varphi_j(x) = \exp(-1/2\sigma_j^2 (\| x - x_j \|^2)),\ j = 1, 2, \ldots, n \quad (7)$$

The output neuron is a summing unit to produce the output as a weighted sum of the hidden layer outputs as shown by

$$F(x) = \sum_{j=1}^{n} w_j \, \phi_j(x) \tag{8}$$

(Haykin, 2009; Jayawardena & Fernando, 1998)

3. Problem definition

Building reliable solar energy systems regardless whether the system is a photovoltaic or thermal solar energy system requires information on the GSR in the region where the system is to be built. Many countries developed models for the GSR to predict the solar radiation and help in building solar energy systems. In UAE we still lack such models for GSR, and this work is the first attempt to generate a weather model for Al Ain city (see Fig.4 for its geographical location in the UAE) and which will later be extended to other UAE cities.

In this work, the maximum temperature (°C), mean wind speed(knot), sunshine(hours), mean relative humidity(%) and solar radiation (kWh/m^2) for Al Ain city are provided by Abu Dhabi's National Center of Meteorology and Seismology (NCMS), for the period between 1995 and 2007. The data between 1995 and 2004 is used for training the MLP and RBF- based ANN techniques while the data between 2005 and 2007 is used for testing the models.

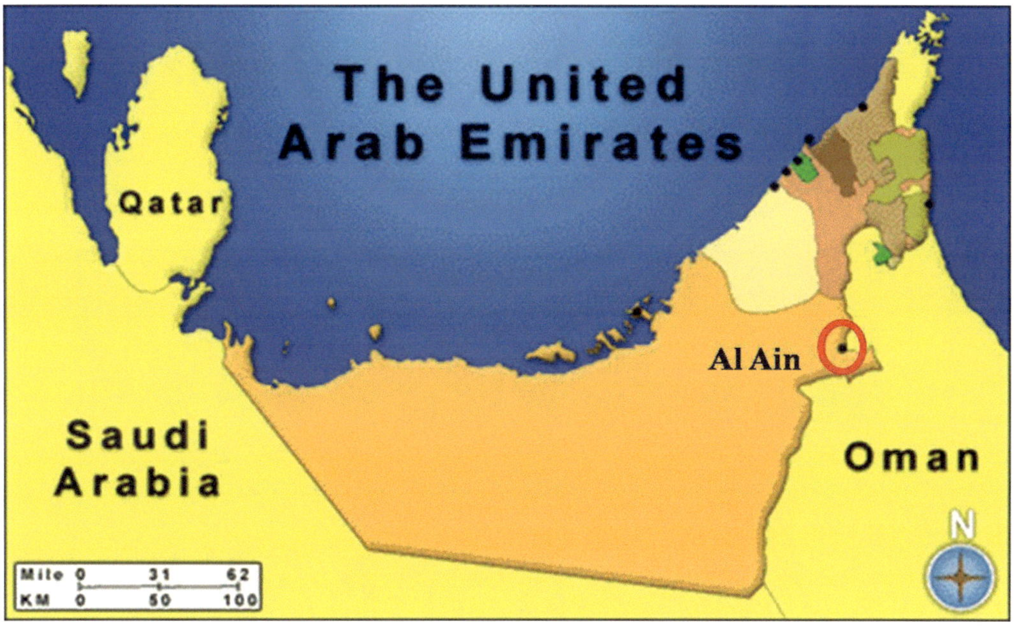

Fig. 4. Geographical location of Al Ain city in the UAE (southwest of UAE at Latitude: 24° 16′ N and Longitude: 55° 36′ E)

Fig. 5 shows the time-series plot of the four measured weather predictors namely, maximum temperature (T), mean wind speed (W), sunshine (SH), relative humidity (RH), as well as the mean daily global solar radiation (GSR, dependent model variable) for Al-Ain city between 1995 and 2007. All the plots show a clear seasonal component of period equals to

365 days. These plots can help examine the correlation between the output variable (GSR) and the four weather predictors.

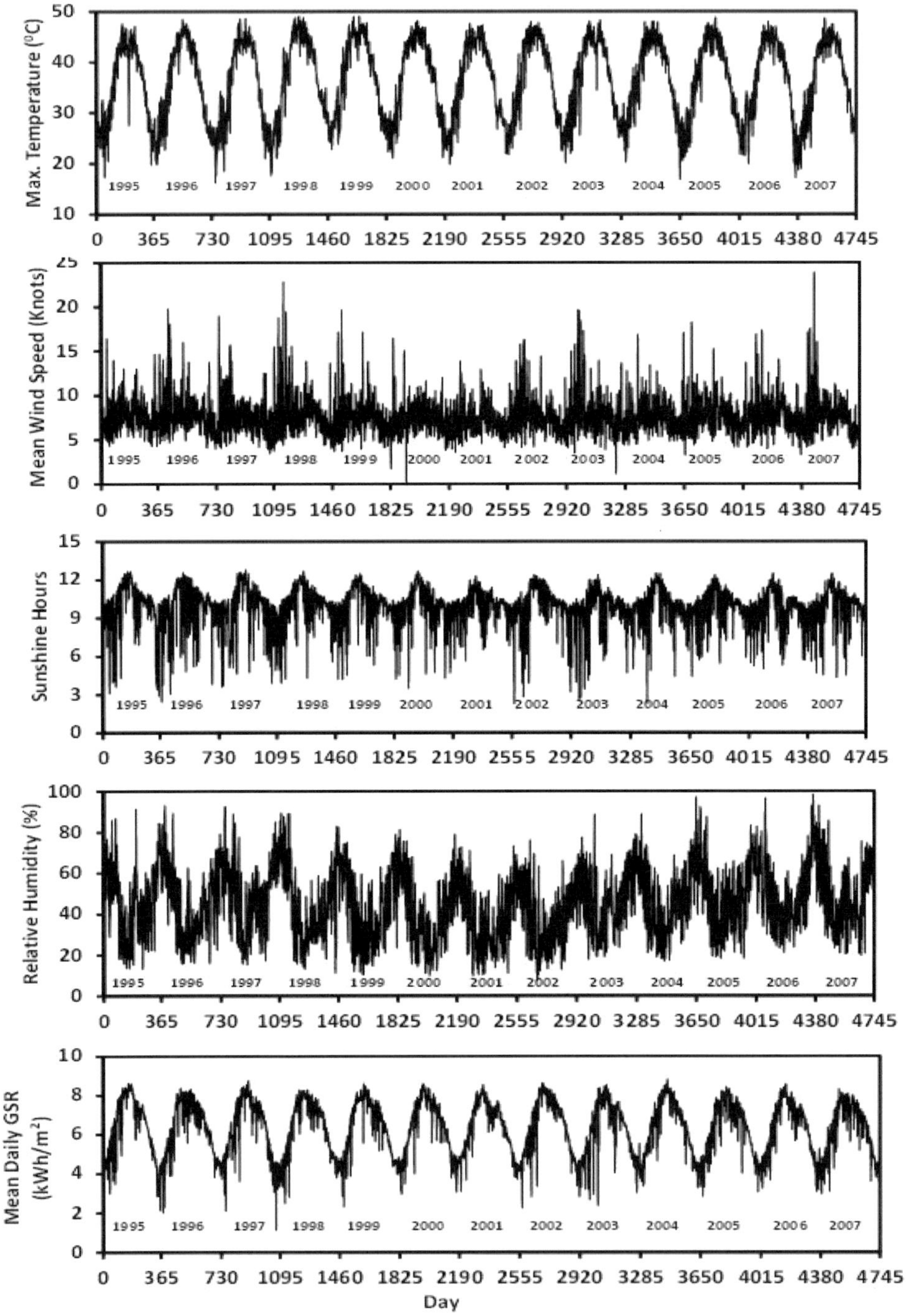

Fig. 5. Measured weather data for Al Ain City, UAE between 1995 and 2007

Eleven combinations of weather predictor variables were considered, as shown in Table 1, in order to investigate their effect on GSR. Both the MLP and RBF neural network methods are applied for predicting the GSR in Al-Ain city based on the combinations shown in Table 1.

Model No.	Input parameters	Model No.	Input parameters
1	T, W, SH & RH	7	T& SH
2	T, W & SH	8	T& RH
3	T, W & RH	9	W & SH
4	T, SH & RH	10	W& RH
5	W, SH & RH	11	SH & RH
6	T & W		

Table 1. Models based on different combinations of input parameters

Various network architectures were investigated in order to determine the optimal MLP architecture (i.e. the highest coefficient of determination, the lowest root mean square error and the lowest mean bias error) for each combination of input variables. Different training algorithms were used with changes in the number of neurons and hidden layers. In addition, different transfer functions including the tangent sigmoid, log sigmoid and linear functions in the hidden layer were also investigated.

Fourteen back-propagation training algorithms were tested in order to obtain the most appropriate algorithm for the training process. The algorithms include: Levenberg-Marquardt, Bayesian regularization, BFGS quasi-Newton, Powell -Beale conjugate gradient, Gradient descent, Gradient descent with momentum, Gradient descent with adaptive learning rate, Gradient descent with momentum & adaptive learning rate , One step secant, Fletcher-Powell conjugate gradient, Random order incremental training with learning, Resilient, Polak-Ribiere conjugate gradient, and Batch training with weight and bias learning rules.

The radius value (known as spread) of the function and the number of neurons are varied for best performance of the RBF network. Basically, the larger the value of spread, the smoother the function approximation will be. However, if the spread value is too large, many neurons may be required to fit the rapidly-changing function. On the other hand, very small spread values will require many neurons in order to fit the smooth function and networks cannot be generalized well (Beale et al, 2010). In this paper, the spread will be varied between 1 and 60 whereas the number of neurons is changed between 5 and 600 in order to come up with the most suitable ANN prediction models.

4. Designing and programming ANN models

4.1 Designing ANN models

Designing ANN models follows a number of systemic procedures. In general, there are five basics steps: (1) collecting data, (2) preprocessing data, (3) building the network, (4) train, and (5) test performance of model as shown in Fig 6.

4.1.1 Data collection

Collecting and preparing sample data is the first step in designing ANN models. As it is outlined in section 3, measurement data of maximum temperature (°C), mean wind speed(knot), sunshine (hours), mean relative humidity(%) and solar radiation (kWh/m^2) for Al Ain city for 13-year period from 1995 to 2007 was collected through the NCMS.

4.1.2 Data pre-processing

After data collection, three data preprocessing procedures are conducted to train the ANNs more efficiently. These procedures are: (1) solve the problem of missing data, (2) normalize data and (3) randomize data. The missing data are replaced by the average of neighboring values during the same week. Normalization procedure before presenting the input data to the network is generally a good practice, since mixing variables with large magnitudes and small magnitudes will confuse the learning algorithm on the importance of each variable and may force it to finally reject the variable with the smaller magnitude (Tymvios et al., 2008).

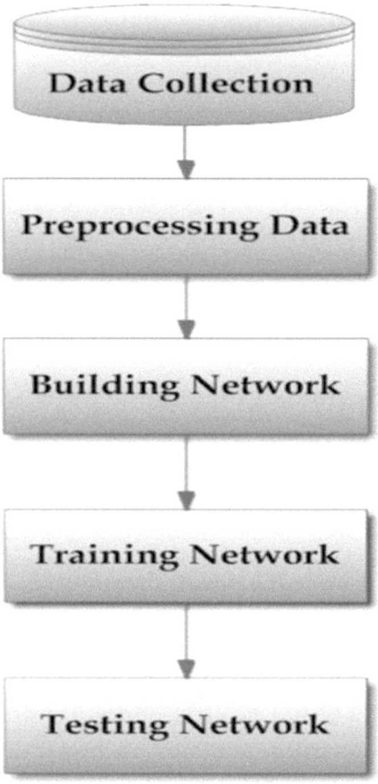

Fig. 6. Basic flow for designing artificial neural network model

4.1.3 Building the network

At this stage, the designer specifies the number of hidden layers, neurons in each layer, transfer function in each layer, training function, weight/bias learning function, and performance function. In this work, multilayer perceptron (MLP) and radial basis function (RBF) networks are used.

4.1.4 Training the network

During the training process, the weights are adjusted in order to make the actual outputs (predicated) close to the target (measured) outputs of the network. In this study, 10-year data period from 1995 to 2004 are used for training. As it is outlined in section 3, fourteen different types of training algorithms are investigated for developing the MLP network. MATLAB provides built-in transfer functions which are used in this study; linear (purelin),

Hyperbolic Tangent Sigmoid (logsig) and Logistic Sigmoid (tansig). The graphical illustration and mathematical form of such functions are shown in Table 2.

<table>
<tr><th>Function Name</th><th>Graphical Illustration</th><th>Mathematical form</th></tr>
<tr><td>Linear</td><td>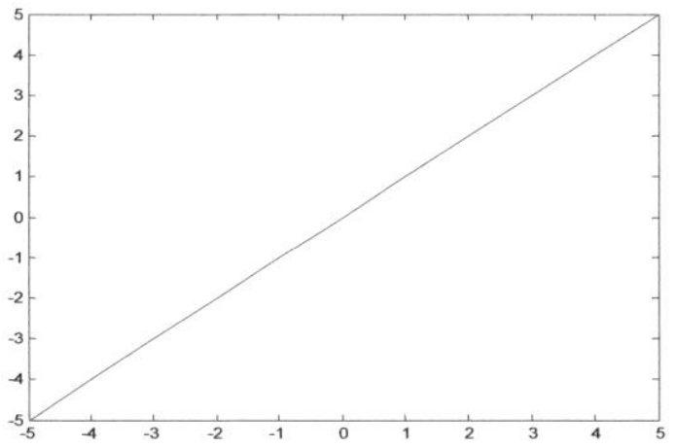
</td><td>$f(x) = x$</td></tr>
<tr><td>Hyperbolic Tangent Sigmoid</td><td>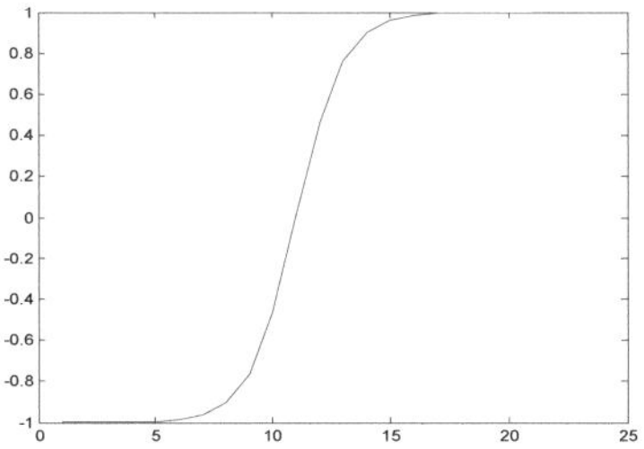
</td><td>$f(x) = \frac{e^x - e^{-x}}{e^x + e^{-x}}$</td></tr>
<tr><td>Logistic Sigmoid</td><td>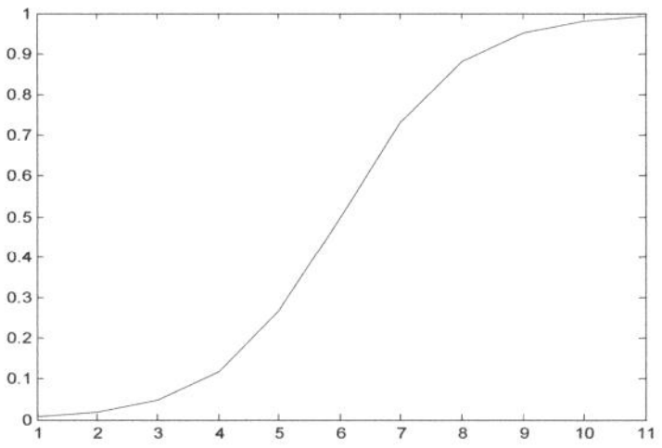
</td><td>$f(x) = \frac{1}{1 + e^{-x}}$</td></tr>
<tr><td>Gaussian RBF</td><td>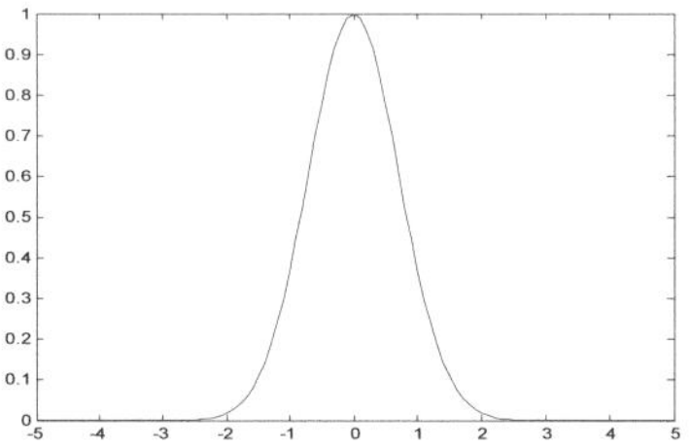
</td><td>$\varphi_j(x) = \exp\left(-\frac{1}{2\sigma_j^2}\left\|x - x_j\right\|^2\right)$</td></tr>
</table>

Table 2. MATLAB built-in transfer functions

4.1.5 Testing the network

The next step is to test the performance of the developed model. At this stage unseen data are exposed to the model. For the case study of Al-Ain city, weather data between 2005 and 2007 have been used for testing the ANN models.

In order to evaluate the performance of the developed ANN models quantitatively and verify whether there is any underlying trend in performance of ANN models, statistical analysis involving the coefficient of determination (R^2), the root mean square error (RMSE), and the mean bias error (MBE) were conducted. RMSE provides information on the short term performance which is a measure of the variation of predicated values around the measured data. The lower the RMSE, the more accurate is the estimation. MBE is an indication of the average deviation of the predicted values from the corresponding measured data and can provide information on long term performance of the models; the lower MBE the better is the long term model prediction. A positive MBE value indicates the amount of overestimation in the predicated GSR and vice versa. The expressions for the aforementioned statistical parameters are:

$$MBE = \frac{1}{n}\sum_{i=1}^{n}\left(I_{p,i} - I_i\right) \tag{9}$$

$$RMSE = \sqrt{\frac{1}{n}\sum_{i=1}^{n}\left(I_{p,i} - I_i\right)^2} \tag{10}$$

where $I_{p,I}$ denotes the predicted GSR on horizontal surface in kWh/m^2, I_i denotes the measured GSR on horizontal surface in kWh/m^2, and n denotes the number of observations.

4.2 Programming the neural network model

MATLAB is a numerical computing environment and also a programming language. It allows easy matrix manipulation, plotting of functions and data, implementation of algorithms, creating user interfaces and interfacing with programs in other languages. The Neural Network Toolbox contains the MATLAB tools for designing, implementing, visualizing and simulating neural networks. It also provides comprehensive support for many proven network paradigms, as well as graphical user interfaces (GUIs) that enable the user to design and manage neural networks in a very simple way(http://www.mathworks.com/products/neuralnet).

In this paper MATLAB (R2010a) is used to write script files for developing MLP and RBF ANN models and performance functions for calculating the model performance error statistics such as R^2, RMSE and MBE. Fig. 7 shows the procedural steps to develop the ANN models. The MLP program starts by reading data from an Excel file (Training.xlsx and Testing.xlsx). "xlsread" function is used to read the data specified in the Excel file.

```
Data_Inputs = xlsread('AlAin_TrainingSet_1995-2004_Model_1.xlsx');
Testing_Data = xlsread('AlAin_TestingSet_2005-2007_Model1.xlsx');
```

Training data samples are randomized by using the function "randperm". This function returns a random permutation of the 3650 integers (training samples) while the order of columns is kept unchanged (T, W, SH, RH & GSR).

```
Shuffling_Inputs = Data_Inputs(randperm(3650),1:5);
```

Next, the input variables (maximum temperature, mean wind speed, sunshine and mean relative humidity) and output variable (global solar radiation) are specified for training and testing. The first four columns present the inputs while the last column denotes the output data (target). The total number of training samples is 3650 (10 years from 1995 to 2004 excluding leap days) while the testing samples are 1095 (3 years from 2005 to 2007).

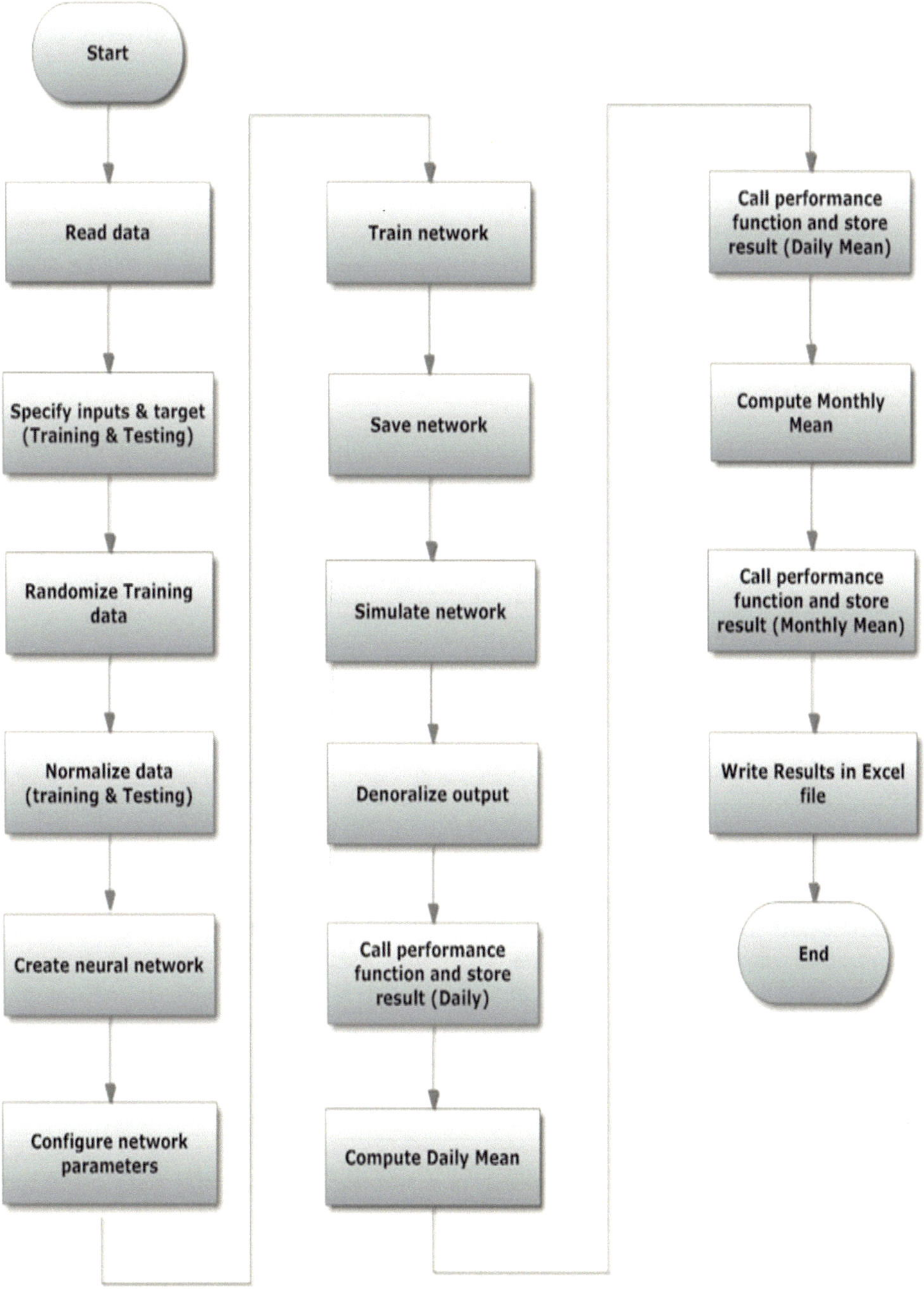

Fig. 7. Flow Chart for developing MLP and RBF networks using MATLAB

```
Training_Set = Shuffling_Inputs(1:3650,1:4)% specify training set [1995 - 2004]
Target_Set  = Shuffling_Inputs(1:3650,5)  % specify target set [1995 - 2004]
Testing_Set = Testing_Data(1:1095,1:4) % specify Testing set [2005- 2007]
Testing_Target_Set = Testing_Data(1:1095, 5)  % specify Testing set, Target [2005- 2007]
```

A normalization process is applied for training and testing the data. Function "mapstd" is used to normalize the inputs and target in order to yield zero mean and unity standard deviation. The output is converted back into the same unit that is used for the original target. Training and testing data are converted to rows (MATLAB requires that all data must be presented as row vectors).

```
[pn, ps] = mapstd(Training_Set');
[tn, ts] = mapstd(Target_Set');
```

The settings structures pn and tn contain normalized values of inputs and output, respectively, while ps and ts contain the means and standard deviations of the original inputs and targets.

MATLAB helps devise the MLP model by using the built-in function "newff" which creates a feed-forward back-propagation network. The designer can specify the number of hidden layers, the neurons in each layer, the transfer function in each layer, the training function, the weight/bias learning function, and the performance function. Moreover, this command will automatically initialize the weights and biases. The function is called as follows:

```
MyNetwork = newff(pn,tn, [i] , {tf});
```

where the arguments pn and tn are the normalized input and output, respectively. [i] implies that the network structure consists of one hidden layer and "i" neurons. For "j" hidden layers we use [i, j]. The argument {tf} denotes the transfer function of the ith layer.

The network is next configured as follows

```
MyNetwork.trainFcn = LM;
MyNetwork.trainparam.min_grad = 0.00000001;
MyNetwork.trainParam.epochs = 1000;
MyNetwork.trainParam.lr = 0.4;
MyNetwork.trainParam.max_fail =20;
```

where

"trainFcn": defines the function used to train the network. It can be set to the name of any training function (LM ='trainlm'; %Levenberg-Marquardt back-propagation)

"trainparam.min_grad": denotes the minimum performance gradient

"trainParam.epochs": denotes the maximum number of epochs to train

"trainParam.lr": denotes the learning rate

"trainParam.max_fail": denotes the maximum validation failures

The function "newrb" is used for iteratively creating an RBF network by including one neuron at a time. Neurons are added to the network until the sum squared error is found to be very small or the maximum numbers of neurons are reached. The call for this function is:

```
MyNetwork= newrb(pn,tn,goal,spread, mn, df);
```

where pn and tn are the input and target, respectively. The argument "goal" denotes the mean squared error goal, set here to be 0.01, and "spread" represents the spread of radial basis functions, changed between 1 and 60 and denoted here as "i". The argument "mn" is the maximum number of neurons, changed between 5 and 600 and denoted here "j', while "df" represents the number of neurons to add between displays and is set to 50.

The MLP network is trained using the "trainFcn" and "trainParam" train functions. The trained network is then saved in MATLAB by calling the functions

```
MyNetwork = train(MyNetwork,pn,tn);
save(NetworkName,'MyNetwork');
```

"NetworkName" is a variable name which can be changed according to the network train function and configuration in order to yield a meaningful name.

When the training is complete, the network performance should be checked. Therefore, unseen data (testing) will be exposed to the network. The testing simulation process is called with the statement:

```
y = sim(MyNetwork, testn); % simulate network
```

Fig. 8 and Fig. 9 show, respectively, screen captions of the MLP and RBF ANN training windows obtained using the "nntraintool" GUI toolbox in MATLAB.

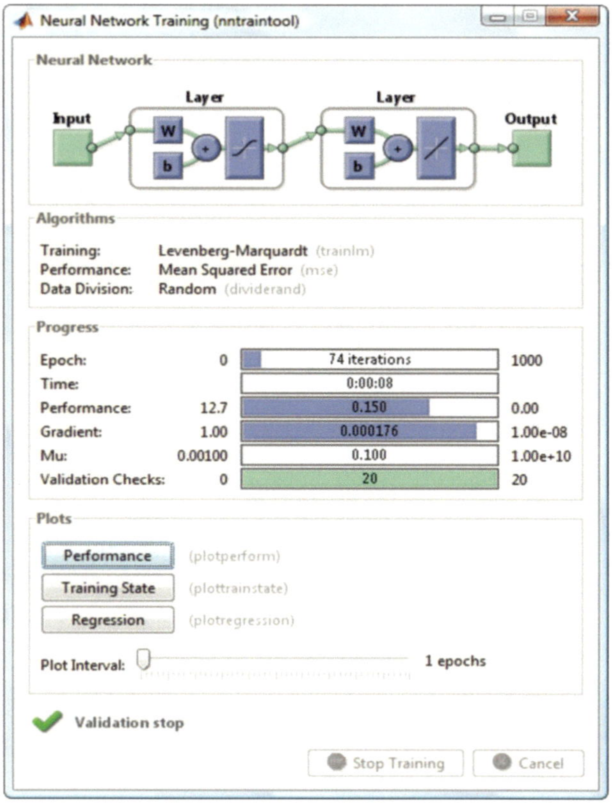

Fig. 8. MLP network Training Window

The output from the network (daily GSR) is denormalized in order to compare it with the measured data. After the network has been trained, one should use these settings to transform any future inputs that are applied to the network.

```
y_again = mapstd('reverse',y, targets) % denormlized
```

The performance function is then called to calculate and store the performance error statistics as follows

```
Daily_Result = performance(y,t,'all', 'v') % calculate statstics
```

Daily measured and predicted data are processed to compute and store the daily mean values along with corresponding error statistics. Afterwards, the daily mean of measured and predicted data are processed to produce monthly mean of measured as well as predicted data. This process is followed by using a MATLAB script to calculate the statistical results. The last step concludes with writing the mean daily and monthly test results along with corresponding statistical data to an Excel sheet.

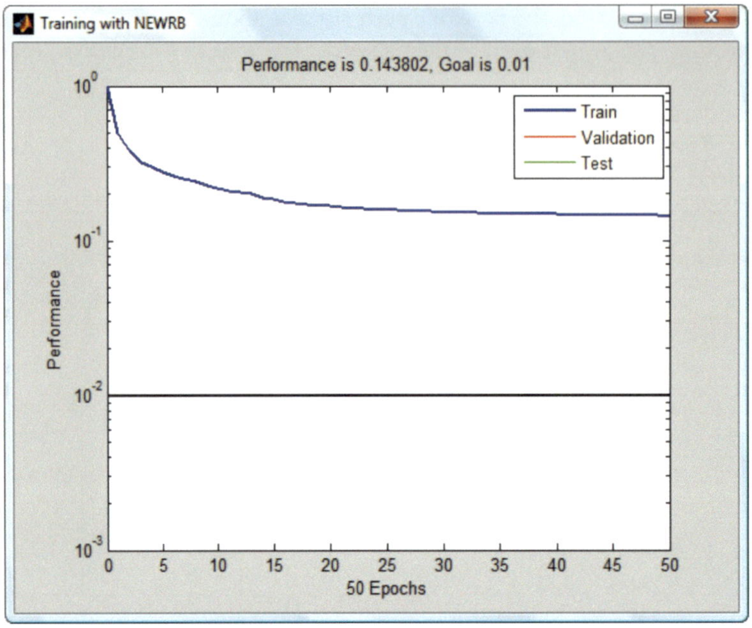

Fig. 9. RBF network Training Window

These steps are performed repeatedly where in MLP the control loop is a number of hidden layers and a number of neurons, while in RBF, the loop is controlled by spread and number of neurons. The stored results are checked and compared for all tested models in order to find the optimal network structure which has highest R^2 and lowest RMSE and MBE.

5. Results and discussion

This section presents the best achieved results for both the MLP and RBF ANN models. Tables 3 and 4 show the computed values of R^2, RMSE and MBE for the developed ANN models (MLP and RBF) considering different network structures. For the network structure identification used in the second column of Tables 3-4, the first number indicates number of neurons in the input layer, the last number represents neurons in the output layer, and the numbers in between represent neurons in the hidden layers.

From Table 3 we note that model one is the best among all the investigated MLP models for long performance prediction as it yields the lowest values of MBE, RMSE and a 92 % coefficient of determination. The input parameters used in the selected model are the maximum temperature, daily sunshine hours, and the mean relative humidity. Table 4 on the other hand, shows that model four is the best among all the investigated RBF models; the input parameters for this model are again the maximum temperature, sunshine hours, and mean relative humidity.

In the seventh, eighth and eleventh models, the MLP technique has better accuracy for predicting the average monthly GSR compared to RBF. For these models, the computed MBE values of 0.00376, 0.06900 and 0.00193, respectively, are promising and provide good accuracy for long term prediction. On the other hand, some RBF models perform better in terms of low MBE values.

Model	Network Structure	R^2	RMSE	MBE
1	4 -100- 1	0.92	0.349	-0.00571
2	3 - 30 -1	0.91	0.370	-0.00754
3	3 - 35 -1	0.84	0.495	-0.01611
4	3 - 20 - 30 - 25 -1	0.92	0.356	-0.02271
5	3- 125 - 1	0.95	0.351	-0.07429
6	3 - 190 -1	0.83	0.518	-0.05402
7	2 - 80 - 1	0.91	0.384	0.00376
8	2 - 195 - 1	0.89	0.485	0.06900
9	2 - 110 - 1	0.91	0.519	-0.03544
10	2- 85 - 1	0.91	0.576	-0.02722
11	2 - 155 - 1	0.93	0.435	0.00193

Table 3. Statistical error parameters of developed MLP models for different network structures

Model	Network Structure	R^2	RMSE	MBE
1	4- 50 -1	0.91	0.445	0.00069
2	3- 35 -1	0.86	0.459	-0.00055
3	3-75 -1	0.84	0.503	0.00073
4	3- 140 -1	0.92	0.356	-0.00307
5	3- 50 -1	0.93	0.446	0.01989
6	2- 50 - 1	0.80	0.556	-0.0208
7	2- 55- 1	0.90	0.401	-0.01835
8	2- 65 -1	0.85	0.483	0.48336
9	2- 15 -1	0.91	0.564	-0.03223
10	2 - 65 - 1	0.91	0.616	0.00611
11	2 - 385 - 1	0.92	0.466	-0.02073

Table 4. Statistical error parameters of developed RBF models for different network structures

Fig. 10 shows the comparison between predicted ANN models and the measured GSR data for all the eleven MLP and RBF-based networks models. This validation is done using measured GSR data for years 2005-2007. The predicted ANN models provide a very good prediction of monthly GSR behavior in Al-Ain, city.

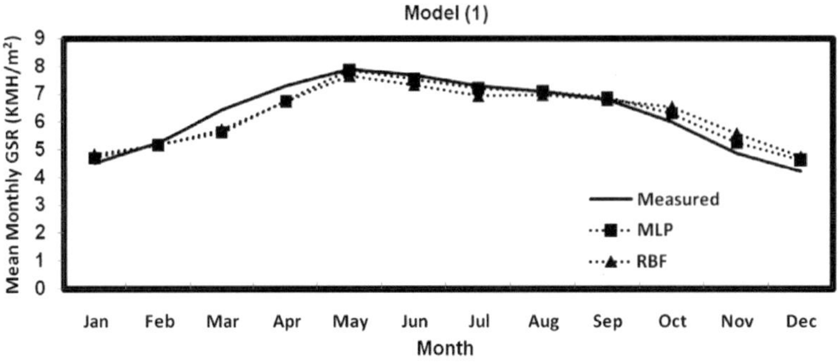
Model (1)
Mean Monthly GSR (KMH/m²)
0 1 2 3 4 5 6 7 8 9
Measured
MLP
RBF
Jan Feb Mar Apr May Jun Jul Aug Sep Oct Nov Dec
Month

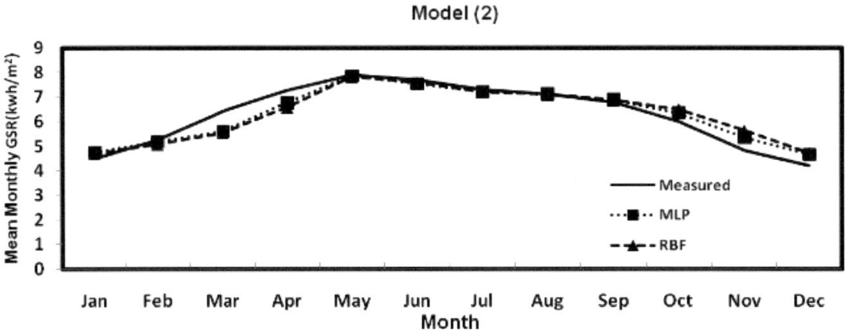
Model (2)
Mean Monthly GSR(kwh/m²)
0 1 2 3 4 5 6 7 8 9
Measured
MLP
RBF
Jan Feb Mar Apr May Jun Jul Aug Sep Oct Nov Dec
Month

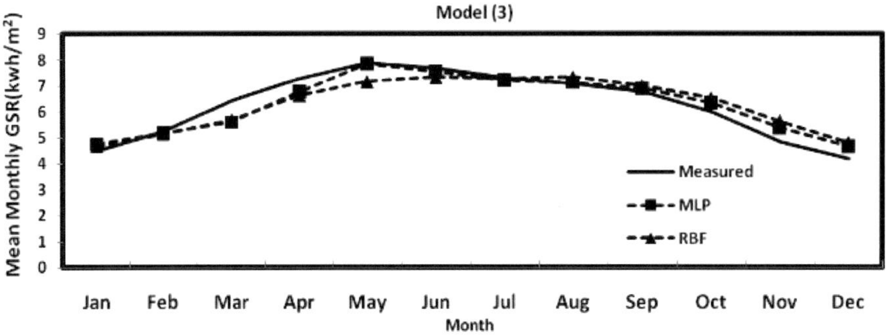
Model (3)
Mean Monthly GSR(kwh/m²)
0 1 2 3 4 5 6 7 8 9
Measured
MLP
RBF
Jan Feb Mar Apr May Jun Jul Aug Sep Oct Nov Dec
Month

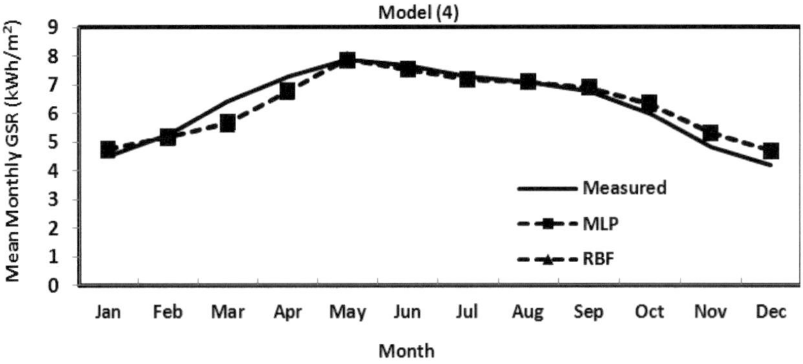
Model (4)
Mean Monthly GSR (kWh/m²)
0 1 2 3 4 5 6 7 8 9
Measured
MLP
RBF
Jan Feb Mar Apr May Jun Jul Aug Sep Oct Nov Dec
Month

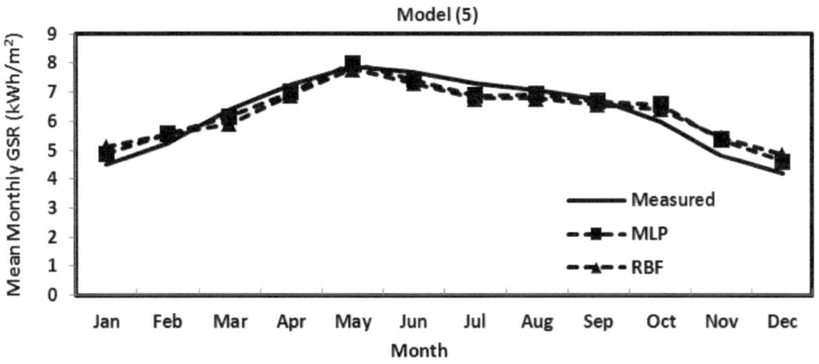
Model (5)
Mean Monthly GSR (kWh/m²)
Measured
MLP
RBF
Jan Feb Mar Apr May Jun Jul Aug Sep Oct Nov Dec
Month

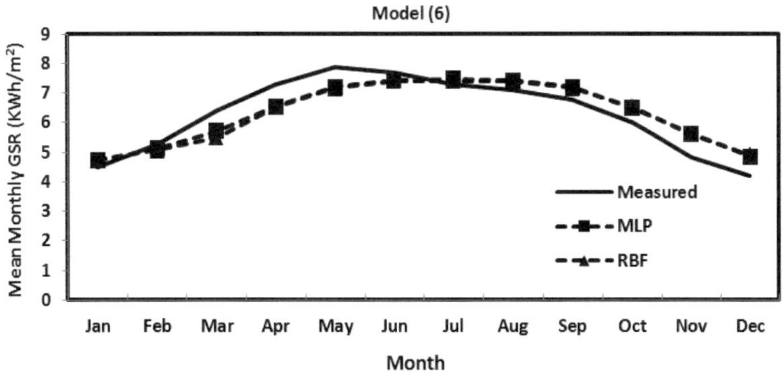
Model (6)
Mean Monthly GSR (KWh/m²)
Measured
MLP
RBF
Jan Feb Mar Apr May Jun Jul Aug Sep Oct Nov Dec
Month

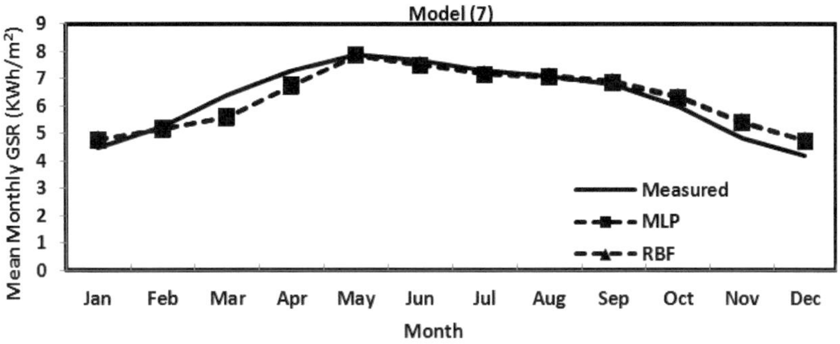
Model (7)
Mean Monthly GSR (KWh/m²)
Measured
MLP
RBF
Jan Feb Mar Apr May Jun Jul Aug Sep Oct Nov Dec
Month

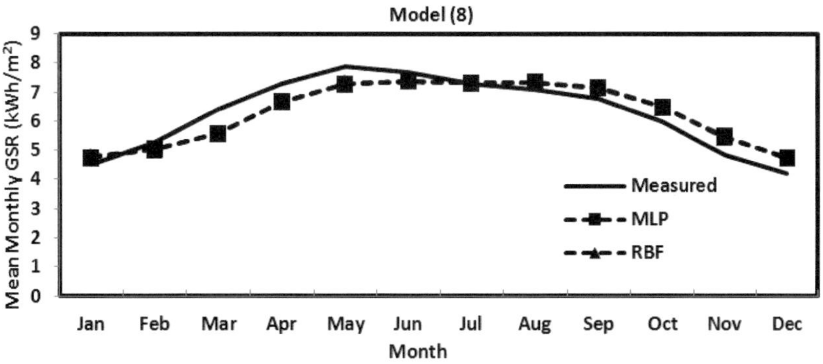
Model (8)
Mean Monthly GSR (kWh/m²)
Measured
MLP
RBF
Jan Feb Mar Apr May Jun Jul Aug Sep Oct Nov Dec
Month

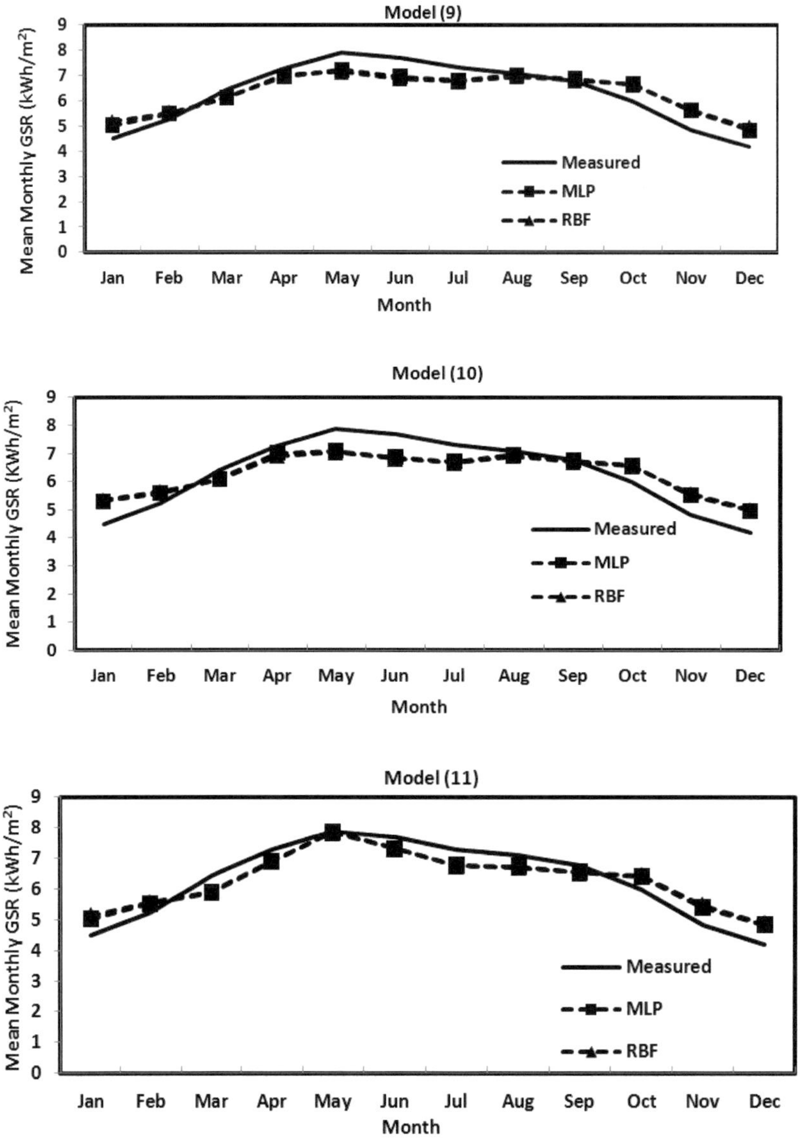

Fig. 10. Comparison between measured data and predicted ANN (MLP and RBF) models (1- 11)

6. Conclusion

In this work, MATLAB tools are used to predict monthly average global solar radiation in Al Ain city - UAE. Weather data between 1995 and 2004 are used for training the neural network, while data between 2005 and 2007 are used for testing. Eleven models with different input combinations are modeled with MLP and RBF ANN techniques. The obtained results confirm the superiority of the RBF technique over the MLP technique in most of the cases, namely, models 2- 6 and 9- 10, with deterministic coefficients near 90 %

and low MBE, MAPE and RMSE values. Moreover, ANN models have in general good performance even if one or more input parameters are unavailable. Currently, our focus is on modeling the GSR for other UAE cities and comparing the optimal ANN models with classical empirical regression and time-series regression models being investigated by this chapter's co-authors.

7. Acknowledgment

The authors would like to thank the National Center of Meteorology and Seismology (NCMS), Abu Dhabi for providing the weather data. This work is financially supported by UAE University Research Affairs under the contract #1542-07-01-10.

8. References

Ahmed, M., Ahmad, F. & Wasim Akhtar, M. (2009). Estimation of global and diffuse solar radiation for Hyderabad, Sindh, Pakistan, *Journal of Basic and Applied Sciences*, Vol. 5, No. 2, pp. 73-77.

Alam, S., Kaushik, S. & Garg, N. (2009).Assessment of Diffuse Solar Energy under General Sky Condition using Artificial Neural Network, *Applied Energy*, Vol. 86, pp. 554-564.

Al-Alawi, S. & Al-Hinai, A. (1998). An ANN-based Approach for Predicting Global Solar Radiation in Locations with no Measurements, *Renewable Energy*, Vol. 14, No, 1–4, pp. 199-204.

Assi, A. & Jama, M. (2010). Estimating Global Solar Radiation on Horizontal from Sunshine Hours in Abu Dhabi -UAE, *Advances in Energy Planning, Environmental Education and Renewable Energy Sources, 4th WSEAS international Conference on Renewable Energy Sources*, pp. 101 - 108, ISBN 978-960-474-187-8, Kantaoui, Sousse, Tunisia, May 3-6, 2010.

Beale, M., Hagan, M. & Demut, H. (2010). Neural Network Toolbox User's Guide, 14.03.2011, Available from http://www.mathworks.com/ help/pdf_doc/nnet/nnet.pdf

Behrang, M., Assareh, E., Ghanbarzadeh, A. & Noghrehabadi, A.(2010). The potential of different artificial neural network (ANN) techniques in daily global solar radiation modeling based on meteorological data, *Solar Energy*, Vol. 84, pp. 1468–1480.

Chantasut, N., Charoenjit, C. & Tanprasert, C. (2004). Predictive Mining of Rainfall Predictions Using Artificial Neural Networks for Chao Phraya River, *4th International Conference of The Asian Federation of Information Technology in Agriculture and The 2nd World Congress on Computers in Agriculture and Natural Resources*, August 9-12.

Elminir, H., Areed,F. & Elsayed, T.(2005). Estimation of solar radiation components incident on Helwan site using neural networks, *Solar Energy*, Vol. 79, pp. 270-279.

El-Sebaii, A & Trabea, A.(2005). Estimation of Global Solar Radiation on Horizontal Surfaces Over Egypt, Egypt. *J. Solids*, Vol. 28, No. 1, pp. 163-175.

Falayi,E., Adepitan, J. & Rabiu, A. (2008). Empirical models for the correlation of global solar radiation with meteorological data for Iseyin, Nigeria, *Physical Sciences*, Vol. 3, No. 9, pp. 210-216.

Haykin, S. (2009). Neural Networks and Learning Machines. 3rd edition, PearsonEducation, Inc.,New Jersey.

Jain, A., Mao, J. & Mohiuddin, K.(March 1996). Artificial Neural Networks: A Tutorial, *IEEE Computer*, Vol. 29, No.3, pp.31-44.

Jayawardena, A., Achela, D. & Fernando, K. (1998). Use of Radial Basis Function Type Artificial Neural Networks for Runoff Simulation, Computer-Aided Civil and Infrastructure Engineering, Vol. 13, pp. 91–99.

Kassem, A., Aboukarima, A. & El Ashmawy, N. (2009).Development of Neural Network Model to Estimate Hourly Total and Diffuse Solar Radiation on Horizontal Surface at Alexandria City (Egypt), *Journal of Applied Sciences Research*, Vol. 5, No. 11, pp. 2006-2015.

Krishnaiah, T., SrinivasaRao, S., Madhumurthy, K. & Reddy, K. (2007). A Neural Network Approach for Modelling Global Solar Radiation, *Applied Science Research*, Vol. 3, No. 10, pp. 1105-1111.

Lam, J., Wan, K. & Liu, Y. (2008), Solar Radiation Modeling Using ANNs for Different Climates in China, *Energy Conversion and Management*, Vol. 49, pp. 1080-1090.

Mohandes, M.; Rehman, S. &Halawani.T.(1998). Estimation of Global Solar Radiation Using Artificial Neural Networks, Renewable Energy, Vol. 14, pp. 179-184.

Mubiru J. (2008), Predicting total solar irradiation values using artificial neural networks, Renewable Energy, Vol. 33, No. 10, pp. 2329-2332.

Rehman, S. & Mohandes, M. (2008). Artificial neural network estimation of global solar radiation using air temperature and relative humidity, *Energy Policy*, (36), pp. 571-576.

Tasadduq,I., Rehman, S.& K. Bubshait. (2002). Application of neural networks for the prediction of hourly mean surface temperature in Saudi Arabia, *Renewable Energy*, Vol. 25, pp. 545-554.

The MathWorks (2011). MATLAB. URL: http://www.mathworks.com/products/neuralnet

Tymvios, F., Michaelides, S. & Skouteli, C.(2008). Estimation of Surface solar radiation with Artificial neural networks, In: *Modeling Solar Radiation at the Earth Surface,*Viorel Badescu, pp.(221-256),Springer, ISBN 978-3-540-77454-9, Germany.

Yang, J., Rivard, H. & Zmeureanu, R. (2005). Building Energy Predication with Adaptive Artificial Neural Networks, *Ninth International IBPSA Conference Montréal*, August 15-18.

10

Fractional Derivatives, Fractional Integrals, and Fractional Differential Equations in Matlab

Ivo Petráš
Technical University of Košice
Slovak Republic

1. Introduction

The term fractional calculus is more than 300 years old. It is a generalization of the ordinary differentiation and integration to non-integer (arbitrary) order. The subject is as old as the calculus of differentiation and goes back to times when Leibniz, Gauss, and Newton invented this kind of calculation. In a letter to L'Hospital in 1695 Leibniz raised the following question (Miller and Ross, 1993): "Can the meaning of derivatives with integer order be generalized to derivatives with non-integer orders?" The story goes that L'Hospital was somewhat curious about that question and replied by another question to Leibniz. "What if the order will be 1/2?" Leibniz in a letter dated September 30, 1695 replied: "It will lead to a paradox, from which one day useful consequences will be drawn." The question raised by Leibniz for a fractional derivative was an ongoing topic in the last 300 years. Several mathematicians contributed to this subject over the years. People like Liouville, Riemann, and Weyl made major contributions to the theory of fractional calculus. The story of the fractional calculus continued with contributions from Fourier, Abel, Leibniz, Grünwald, and Letnikov.
Nowadays, the fractional calculus attracts many scientists and engineers. There are several applications of this mathematical phenomenon in mechanics, physics, chemistry, control theory and so on (Caponetto et al., 2010; Magin, 2006; Monje et al., 2010; Oldham and Spanier, 1974; Oustaloup, 1995; Podlubny, 1999). It is natural that many authors tried to solve the fractional derivatives, fractional integrals and fractional differential equations in Matlab. A few very good and interesting Matlab functions were already submitted to the MathWorks, Inc. Matlab Central File Exchange, where they are freely downloadable for sharing among the users. In this chapter we will use some of them. It is worth mentioning some addition to Matlab toolboxes, which are appropriate for the solution of fractional calculus problems. One of them is a toolbox created by CRONE team (CRONE, 2010) and another one is the Fractional State–Space Toolkit developed by Dominik Sierociuk (Sierociuk, 2005). Last but not least we should also mention a Matlab toolbox created by Dingyü Xue (Xue, 2010), which is based on Matlab object for fractional-order transfer function and some manipulation with this class of the transfer function. Despite that the mentioned toolboxes are mainly for control systems, they can be "abused" for solutions of general problems related to fractional calculus as well.

2. Fractional calculus fundamentals

2.1 Special functions

Here we should mention the most important function used in fractional calculus - Euler's *gamma* function, which is defined as

$$\Gamma(n) = \int_0^\infty t^{n-1} e^{-t} \, dt. \tag{1}$$

This function is a generalization of the factorial in the following form:

$$\Gamma(n) = (n-1)! \tag{2}$$

This gamma function is directly implemented in the Matlab with syntax `[]=gamma()`.
Another function, which plays a very important role in the fractional calculus, was in fact introduced in 1953. It is a two-parameter function of the *Mittag-Leffler* type defined as (Podlubny, 1999):

$$E_{\alpha,\beta}(z) = \sum_{k=0}^{\infty} \frac{z^k}{\Gamma(\alpha k + \beta)}, \qquad (\alpha > 0, \quad \beta > 0). \tag{3}$$

The Mittag-Leffler function (3) can be expressed in the integral representation as

$$E_{\alpha,\beta}(z) = \frac{1}{2\pi i} \int_C \frac{t^{\alpha-\beta} e^t}{t^\alpha - z} dt, \tag{4}$$

the contour C starts and ends at $-\infty$ and circles around the singularities and branch points of the integrand.
There are some relationships (given e.g. in (Djrbashian, 1993; Podlubny, 1999)):

$$E_{1,1}(z) = e^z, \qquad E_{1/2,1}(\sqrt{z}) = \frac{2}{\sqrt{\pi}} e^{-z} \operatorname{erfc}(-\sqrt{z}),$$

$$E_{2,1}(z) = \cosh(\sqrt{z}), \qquad E_{2,1}(-z^2) = \cos(z), \qquad E_{1,2}(z) = \frac{e^z - 1}{z}.$$

For $\beta = 1$ we obtain the Mittag-Leffler function in one parameter (Podlubny, 1999):

$$E_{\alpha,1}(z) = \sum_{k=0}^{\infty} \frac{z^k}{\Gamma(\alpha k + 1)} \equiv E_\alpha(z). \tag{5}$$

For the numerical evaluation of the Mittag-Leffler function (3) with the default accuracy set to 10^{-6} the Matlab routine `[e]=mlf(alf,bet,c,fi)`, written by Podlubny and Kacenak (2005) can be used. Another Matlab function `f=gml_fun(a,b,c,x,eps0)` for a generalized Mittag-Leffler function was created by YangQuan Chen (Chen, 2008).
In Fig. 1(a) and Fig. 1(b) are plotted the well-known functions (e^z and $\cos(z)$) computed via the Matlab routine `[]=mlf()` created for the evaluation of the Mittag-Leffler function.
Another important function $\mathcal{E}_k(t, \lambda; \mu, \nu)$ of the Mittag-Leffler type was introduced by (Podlubny, 1999). The function is defined by

$$\mathcal{E}_k(t, \lambda; \mu, \nu) = t^{\mu k + \nu - 1} E_{\mu,\nu}^{(k)}(\lambda t^\mu), \quad (k = 0, 1, 2, \ldots), \tag{6}$$

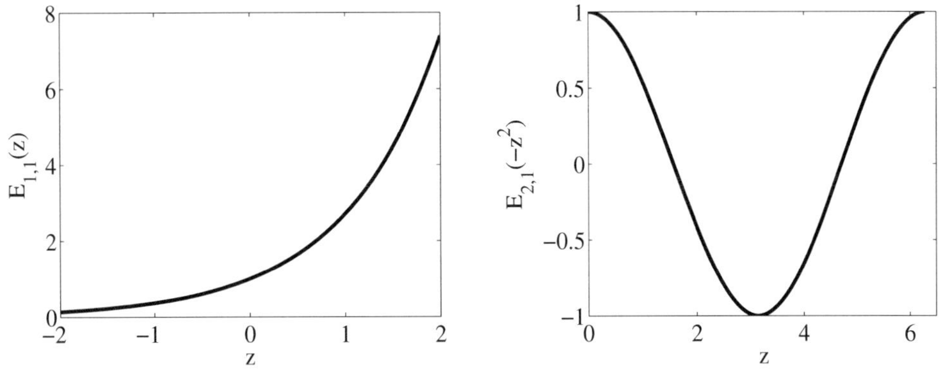

(a) $E_{1,1}(z)$, where $-2 < z < 2$ (b) $E_{2,1}(-z^2)$, where $0 < z < 2\pi$

Fig. 1. Mittag-Leffler function (3) for various parameters

where $E^{(k)}_{\mu,\nu}(z)$ is k-th derivative of the Mittag-Leffler function of two parameters given by

$$E^{(k)}_{\mu,\nu}(z) = \sum_{i=0}^{\infty} \frac{(i+k)!\; z^i}{i!\; \Gamma(\mu i + \mu k + \nu)}, \qquad (k = 0, 1, 2, \ldots). \tag{7}$$

2.2 Fractional derivatives and integrals

Fractional calculus is a generalization of integration and differentiation to non-integer-order fundamental operator ${}_aD^{\alpha}_t$, where a and t are the bounds of the operation and $\alpha \in$ R. The continuous integrodifferential operator is defined as

$${}_aD^{\alpha}_t = \begin{cases} \frac{d^{\alpha}}{dt^{\alpha}} & : \alpha > 0, \\ 1 & : \alpha = 0, \\ \int_a^t (d\tau)^{\alpha} & : \alpha < 0. \end{cases}$$

The three most frequently used definitions for the general fractional differintegral are: the Grünwald-Letnikov (GL) definition, the Riemann-Liouville (RL) and the Caputo definition (Miller and Ross, 1993; Oldham and Spanier, 1974; Podlubny, 1999). Other definitions are connected with well-known names as for instance Weyl, Fourier, Cauchy, Abel, etc.

The GL definition is given as

$${}_aD^{\alpha}_t f(t) = \lim_{h \to 0} h^{-\alpha} \sum_{j=0}^{\left[\frac{t-a}{h}\right]} (-1)^j \binom{\alpha}{j} f(t - jh), \tag{8}$$

where [.] means the integer part. The RL definition is given as

$${}_aD^{\alpha}_t f(t) = \frac{1}{\Gamma(n-\alpha)} \frac{d^n}{dt^n} \int_a^t \frac{f(\tau)}{(t-\tau)^{\alpha-n+1}} d\tau, \quad \text{for} \quad (n-1 < \alpha < n), \tag{9}$$

where $\Gamma(.)$ is the *gamma* function. The Caputo definition of fractional derivatives can be written as

$$ {}_aD_t^\alpha f(t) = \frac{1}{\Gamma(n-\alpha)} \int_a^t \frac{f^{(n)}(\tau)}{(t-\tau)^{\alpha-n+1}} d\tau, \quad \text{for} \quad (n-1 < \alpha < n). \tag{10} $$

In this chapter we will consider mainly the GL, the RL, and the Caputo definitions. This consideration is based on the fact that, for a wide class of functions, the three best known definitions - GL, RL, and Caputo - are equivalent under some conditions (Podlubny, 1999).

As it was already mentioned, under the homogeneous initial conditions the Riemann-Liouville and the Caputo derivative are equivalent. Let us denote the Riemann-Liouville fractional derivative as ${}_a^{RL}D_t^\alpha t(t)$ and the Caputo definition as ${}_a^{C}D_t^\alpha f(t)$, then the relationship between them is:

$$ {}_a^{RL}D_t^\alpha t(t) = {}_a^{C}D_t^\alpha f(t) + \sum_{k=0}^{n-1} \frac{(t-a)^{k-\alpha}}{\Gamma(k-\alpha+1)} f^{(k)}(a), $$

for $f^{(k)}(a) = 0 \ (k = 0, 1, \ldots, n-1)$.

The initial conditions for the fractional-order differential equations with the Caputo derivatives are in the same form as for the integer-order differential equations. It is an advantage because applied problems require definitions of fractional derivatives, where there are clear interpretations of initial conditions, which contain $f(a), f^{'}(a), f^{''}(a)$, etc.

In addition, for approximation purpose we consider the Laplace transform method of the fractional differintegral ${}_aD_t^\alpha$. The Laplace transform of the join operator of order α for the GL, RL and Caputo definitions, under the zero initial conditions is:

$$ \mathcal{L}\{{}_0D_t^\alpha f(t); s\} = s^\alpha F(s). \tag{11} $$

Laplace transform technique is considered as an efficient way in solving differential equations with integer order and fractional order as well. For differential equations with fractional order, the Laplace transform technique works effectively only for relatively simple equations, because of the difficulties of calculating inversion of Laplace transforms. This problem was solved by applying a numerical inverse Laplace transform algorithms in fractional calculus (Sheng et al., 2011). Three numerical inverse Laplace transform algorithms in Matlab, named `invlap()`, `gavsteh()`, and `nilt()`, were described there and tested.

The Laplace transforms for several known Mittag-Leffler type functions are summarized as follows (Magin, 2006; Podlubny, 1999):

$$ \begin{aligned} \mathcal{L}\{E_\alpha(-\lambda t^\alpha)\} &= \frac{s^{\alpha-1}}{s^\alpha+\lambda}, \quad \mathcal{L}\{t^{\alpha-1}E_{\alpha,\alpha}(-\lambda t^\alpha)\} = \frac{1}{s^\alpha+\lambda}, \\ \mathcal{L}\{t^{\beta-1}E_{\alpha,\beta}(-\lambda t^\alpha)\} &= \frac{s^{\alpha-\beta}}{s^\alpha+\lambda}, \quad \mathcal{L}\{\mathcal{E}_k(t,\pm\lambda;\alpha,\beta)\} = \frac{k!s^{\alpha-\beta}}{(s^\alpha\mp\lambda)^{k+1}}. \end{aligned} \tag{12} $$

2.3 Numerical methods for fractional calculus

There are many numerical methods appropriate for the fractional calculus computation. They were described in several works and a good survey can be found in (Vinagre et al., 2000; 2003). In the above-mentioned papers are described the time domain and frequency methods in the form of IIR and FIR approximations together with illustrative examples. Some of the mentioned frequency methods in both forms of approximation have been realized as the Matlab routines in Duarte Valerio's toolbox called *ninteger* (see detail review in (Valério, 2005)). Also created in this toolbox was a Simulink block *nid* for fractional derivative and integral, where the order of derivative/integral and method of its approximation can be selected.

2.3.1 Grünwald-Letnikov method

For numerical calculation of fractional-order derivatives we can use the relation (13) derived from the GL definition (8). This approach is based on the fact that for a wide class of functions the three definitions - GL (8), RL (9), and Caputo's (10) - are equivalent if $f(a) = 0$. The relation for the explicit numerical approximation of q-th derivative at the points kh, $(k = 1, 2, \ldots)$ has the following form (Dorčák, 1994; Podlubny, 1999):

$$ {}_{(k-L_m/h)}D^{q}_{t_k} f(t) \approx h^{-q} \sum_{j=0}^{k} (-1)^j \binom{q}{j} f(t_{k-j}) = h^{-q} \sum_{j=0}^{k} c_j^{(q)} f(t_{k-j}), \tag{13} $$

where L_m is the "memory length", $t_k = kh$, h is the time step of calculation and $c_j^{(q)}$ $(j = 0, 1, \ldots, k)$ are binomial coefficients. For their calculation we can use for instance the following expression (Dorčák, 1994):

$$ c_0^{(q)} = 1, \qquad c_j^{(q)} = \left(1 - \frac{1+q}{j}\right) c_{j-1}^{(q)}. \tag{14} $$

The binomial coefficients $c_j^{(q)}$ $(j = 0, 1, \ldots, k)$ can be also expressed by using a factorial. Writing the factorial as a *gamma* function (2), it allows the binomial coefficient to be generalized to non-integer arguments. We can write the relations:

$$ (-1)^j \binom{q}{j} = (-1)^j \frac{\Gamma(q+1)}{\Gamma(j+1)\Gamma(q-j+1)} = \frac{\Gamma(j-q)}{\Gamma(-q)\Gamma(j+1)}. \tag{15} $$

Obviously, for this simplification we pay a penalty in the form of some inaccuracy. If $f(t) \leq M$, we can easily establish the following estimate for determining the memory length L_m, providing the required accuracy ϵ:

$$ L_m \geq \left(\frac{M}{\epsilon |\Gamma(1-q)|} \right)^{1/q}. \tag{16} $$

The above-described numerical method is called Power Series Expansion (PSE) of a generating function. It is important to note that PSE leads to approximation in the form of polynomials, that is, the discretized fractional operator is in the form of FIR filter, which has only zeros (Chen and Moore, 2002; Vinagre et al., 2003).

The resulting discrete transfer function, approximating fractional-order operators, can be expressed in z-domain as follows:

$$ {}_0D^{\pm r}_{kT} G(z) = \frac{Y(z)}{F(z)} = \left(\frac{1}{T}\right)^{\pm r} \mathrm{PSE}\left\{ \left(1 - z^{-1}\right)^{\pm r} \right\}_n \approx T^{\mp r} R_n(z^{-1}), \tag{17} $$

where T is the sample period, PSE$\{u\}$ denotes the function resulting from applying the power series expansion to the function u, $Y(z)$ is the Z transform of the output sequence $y(kT)$, $F(z)$ is the Z transform of the input sequence $f(kT)$, n is the order of the approximation, and R is polynomial of degree n, respectively, in the variable z^{-1}, and $k = 1, 2, \ldots$. A Matlab routine `dfod2()` of this method (17) can be downloaded (see (Petráš, 2003b)).

EXAMPLE 2.1. Let us consider the fractional-order derivative $\alpha \in [0, 1]$ of the function *y=sin(t)* for $t \in [0, 2\pi]$. The following Matlab code using a function `fderiv()`, which was created by Bayat (2007) and is based on relation (13), can be used:

```
clear all; close all;
h=0.01; t=0:h:2*pi;
y=sin(t);
order=0:0.1:1;
for i=1:length(order)
     yd(i,:)=fderiv(order(i),y,h);
end
[X, Y]=meshgrid(t,order);
mesh(X,Y,yd)
xlabel('t'); ylabel('\alpha'); zlabel('y')
```

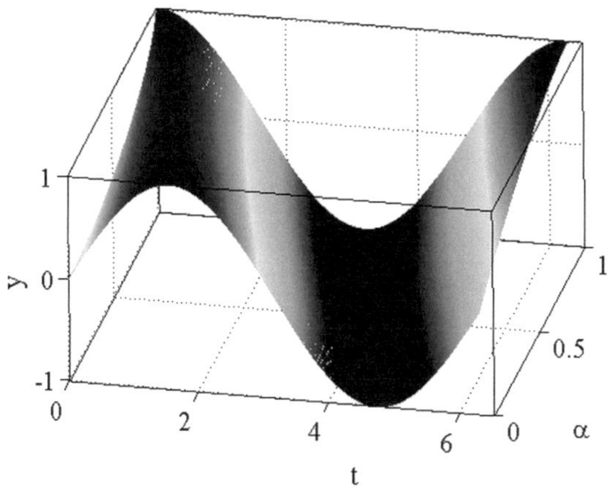

Fig. 2. Fractional derivatives of function *y=sin(t)*

In Fig. 2 is depicted the fractional derivative of the sine function for fractional order of derivative $0 < \alpha < 1$ and $0 < t < 2\pi$.

2.3.2 Continuous and discrete-time approximation techniques

Other approach can be realized by Continued Fraction Expansion (CFE) of the generating function and then the approximated fractional operator is in the form of IIR filter, which has poles and zeros.

Taking into account that our aim is to obtain equivalents to the fractional integrodifferential operators in the Laplace domain, $s^{\pm r}$, the result of such approximation for an irrational function, $G(s)$, can be expressed in the form (Vinagre et al., 2003):

$$G(s) \simeq a_0(s) + \cfrac{b_1(s)}{a_1(s) + \cfrac{b_2(s)}{a_2(s) + \cfrac{b_3(s)}{a_3(s)+\dots}}}$$

$$= a_0(s) + \frac{b_1(s)}{a_1(s)+} \frac{b_2(s)}{a_2(s)+} \frac{b_3(s)}{a_3(s)+} \dots \tag{18}$$

where a_is and b_is are rational functions of the variable s, or are constants. The application of the method yields a rational function, which is an approximation of the irrational function $G(s)$.

In other words, for evaluation purposes, the rational approximations obtained by CFE frequently converge much more rapidly than the PSE and have a wider domain of convergence in the complex plane. On the other hand, the approximation by PSE and the short memory principle is convenient for the dynamical properties consideration.

For interpolation purposes, rational functions are sometimes superior to polynomials. This is, roughly speaking, due to their ability to model functions with poles. These techniques are based on the approximations of an irrational function, $G(s)$, by a rational function defined by the quotient of two polynomials in the variable s in frequency s-domain:

$$G(s) \simeq R_{i(i+1)\dots(i+m)} = \frac{P_\mu(s)}{Q_\nu(s)} = \frac{p_0 + p_1 s + \dots + p_\mu s^\mu}{q_0 + q_1 s + \dots + q_\nu s^\nu}, \quad (m+1 = \mu + \nu + 1) \tag{19}$$

passing through the points $(s_i, G(s_i)), \dots, (s_{i+m}, G(s_{i+m}))$.

The resulting discrete transfer function, approximating fractional-order operators, can be expressed as (Vinagre et al., 2003):

$${}_0D_{kT}^{\pm r} G(z) = \frac{Y(z)}{F(z)} = \left(\frac{2}{T}\right)^{\pm r} \mathrm{CFE}\left\{\left(\frac{1-z^{-1}}{1+z^{-1}}\right)^{\pm r}\right\}_{p,n} \approx \left(\frac{2}{T}\right)^{\pm r} \frac{P_p(z^{-1})}{Q_n(z^{-1})}, \tag{20}$$

where T is the sample period, CFE$\{u\}$ denotes the function resulting from applying the continued fraction expansion to the function u, $Y(z)$ is the Z transform of the output sequence $y(kT)$, $F(z)$ is the Z transform of the input sequence $f(kT)$, p and n are the orders of the approximation, and P and Q are polynomials of degrees p and n, respectively, in the variable z^{-1}, and $k = 1, 2, \dots$.

In general, the discretization of fractional-order differentiator/integrator $s^{\pm r}$ $(r \in \mathrm{R})$ can be expressed by the *generating function* $s \approx \omega(z^{-1})$. This generating function and its expansion determine both the form of the approximation and the coefficients (Lubich, 1986).

In this section, for direct discretizing s^r, $(0 < r < 1)$, we will concentrate on the IIR form of discretization where as a generating function we will adopt an Al-Alaoui idea on mixed scheme of Euler and Tustin operators (Al-Alaoui, 1993; 1997), but we will use a different ratio between both operators. The mentioned new operator, raised to power $\pm r$, has the form (Petráš, 2003a):

$$(\omega(z^{-1}))^{\pm r} = \left(\frac{1+a}{T} \frac{1-z^{-1}}{1+az^{-1}}\right)^{\pm r}, \tag{21}$$

where a is the ratio term and r is the fractional order. The ratio term a is the amount of phase shift and this tuning knob is sufficient for most engineering problems being solved.

In expanding the above in rational functions, we will use the CFE. It should be pointed out that, for control applications, the obtained approximate discrete-time rational transfer function should be stable. Furthermore, for a better fit to the continuous frequency response, it would be of high interest to obtain discrete approximations with poles an zeros interlaced along the line $z \in (-1, 1)$ of the z plane. The direct discretization approximations proposed in this paper enjoy the desired properties.

The result of such approximation for an irrational function, $\widehat{G}(z^{-1})$, can be expressed by $G(z^{-1})$ in the CFE form (Vinagre et al., 2000):

$$G(z^{-1}) \simeq a_0(z^{-1}) + \cfrac{b_1(z^{-1})}{a_1(z^{-1}) + \cfrac{b_2(z^{-1})}{a_2(z^{-1}) + \cfrac{b_3(z^{-1})}{a_3(z^{-1}) + \ldots}}}$$

$$= a_0(z^{-1}) + \frac{b_1(z^{-1})}{a_1(z^{-1})+} \frac{b_2(z^{-1})}{a_2(z^{-1})+} \cdots \frac{b_3(z^{-1})}{a_3(z^{-1})+} \cdots$$

where a_i and b_i are either rational functions of the variable z^{-1} or constants. The application of the method yields a rational function, $G(z^{-1})$, which is an approximation of the irrational function $\widehat{G}(z^{-1})$.

The resulting discrete transfer function, approximating fractional-order operators, can be expressed as:

$$(\omega(z^{-1}))^{\pm r} \approx \left(\frac{1+a}{T}\right)^{\pm r} \mathrm{CFE}\left\{\left(\frac{1-z^{-1}}{1+az^{-1}}\right)^{\pm r}\right\}_{p,q}$$

$$= \left(\frac{1+a}{T}\right)^{\pm r} \frac{P_p(z^{-1})}{Q_q(z^{-1})}, = \left(\frac{1+a}{T}\right)^{\pm r} \frac{p_0 + p_1 z^{-1} + \cdots + p_m z^{-p}}{q_0 + q_1 z^{-1} + \cdots + q_n z^{-q}}, \quad (22)$$

where CFE$\{u\}$ denotes the continued fraction expansion of u; p and q are the orders of the approximation and P and Q are polynomials of degrees p and q. Normally, we can set $p = q = n$. A Matlab routine `dfod1()` for this described method (22) can be downloaded (see (Petráš, 2003a)).

EXAMPLE 2.2. Here we present some results for fractional order $r = \pm 0.5$ (half-order derivative/integral). The value of approximation order n is truncated to $n = 3$ and weighting factor a was chosen $a = 1/3$. Assume sampling period $T = 0.001$ sec.

For $r = 0.5$ we have the following approximation of the fractional half-order derivative:

$$G(z^{-1}) = \frac{985.9 - 1315z^{-1} + 328.6z^{-2} + 36.51z^{-3}}{27 - 18z^{-1} - 3z^{-2} + z^{-3}} \quad (23)$$

A Matlab sequence for the the fractional half-order derivative approximation (23) follows:

```
sys=dfod1(3, 0.001, 1/3, 0.5)
bode(sys)
step(sys)
```

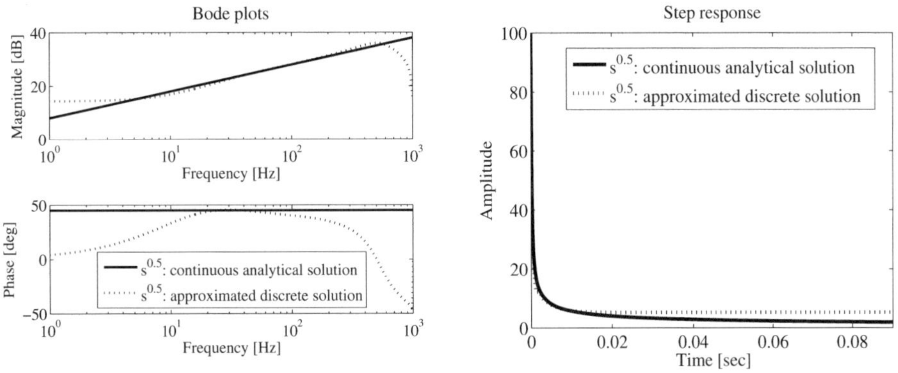

(a) Bode plots (b) Unit step responses

Fig. 3. Characteristics of approximated fractional-order differentiator (23) obtained from (22) for $r = 0.5$, $n = 3$, $a = 1/3$, and $T = 0.001$ sec

The Bode plots and unit step response of the digital fractional-order differentiator (23) and the analytical continuous solution of a fractional semi-derivative are depicted in Fig. 3. Poles and zeros of the transfer function (23) lie in a unit circle.

For $r = -0.5$ we have the following approximation of the fractional half-order integral:

$$G(z^{-1}) = \frac{0.739 - 0.493z^{-1} - 0.0822z^{-2} + 0.0274z^{-3}}{27 - 36z^{-1} + 9z^{-2} + z^{-3}} \tag{24}$$

A Matlab sequence for the the fractional half-order integral approximation (24) is the following:

```
sys=dfod1(3, 0.001, 1/3, -0.5)
bode(sys)
step(sys)
```

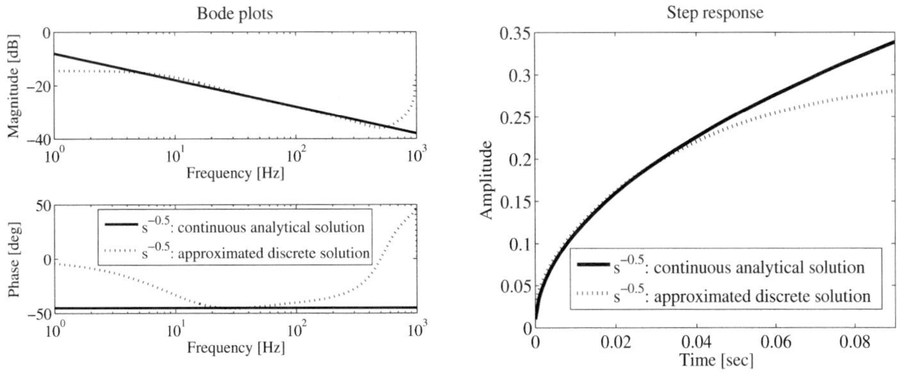

(a) Bode plots (b) Unit step responses

Fig. 4. Characteristics of approximated fractional-order integrator (24) obtained from (22) for $r = -0.5$, $n = 3$, $a = 1/3$, and $T = 0.001$ sec

The Bode plots and unit step response of the digital fractional-order integrator (24) and the analytical continuous solution of a fractional semi-derivative are depicted in Fig. 4. Poles and zeros of the transfer function (24) lie in a unit circle.
For simulation purpose, here we also present the Oustaloup's Recursive Approximation algorithm (Oustaloup et al., 2000). The method is based on the approximation of a function of the form:

$$H(s) = s^r, \qquad r \in R, \qquad r \in [-1;1] \tag{25}$$

for the frequency range selected as (ω_b, ω_h) by a rational function:

$$\widehat{H}(s) = C_o \prod_{k=-N}^{N} \frac{s + \omega'_k}{s + \omega_k} \tag{26}$$

using the following set of synthesis formulas for zeros, poles and the gain:

$$\omega'_k = \omega_b \left(\frac{\omega_h}{\omega_b}\right)^{\frac{k+N+0.5(1-r)}{2N+1}}, \quad \omega_k = \omega_b \left(\frac{\omega_h}{\omega_b}\right)^{\frac{k+N+0.5(1-r)}{2N+1}}, \quad C_o = \left(\frac{\omega_h}{\omega_b}\right)^{-\frac{r}{2}} \prod_{k=-N}^{N} \frac{\omega_k}{\omega'_k}, \tag{27}$$

where ω_h, ω_b are the high and low transitional frequencies. An implementation of this algorithm in Matlab as a function `ora_foc()` is given in (Chen, 2003).

EXAMPLE 2.3. Using the described Oustaloup's-Recursive-Approximation (ORA) method with:

$$\omega_b = 10^{-2}, \quad \omega_h = 10^2 \tag{28}$$

the obtained approximation for fractional function $H(s) = s^{-\frac{1}{2}}$ nad for $N = 3$ is as follows:

$$\widehat{H}(s) = \frac{0.03162s^7 + 22.42s^6 + 1940s^5 + 2.292 \times 10^4 s^4 + 3.755 \times 10^4 s^3 + 8523s^2 + 264.3s + 1}{s^7 + 264.3s^6 + 8523s^5 + 3.755 \times 10^4 s^4 + 2.292 \times 10^4 s^3 + 1940s^2 + 22.42s + 0.03162}. \tag{29}$$

A Matlab sequence for the the fractional half order derivative approximation (29) follows:

```
sys=ora_foc(-0.5,3,0.01,100)
bode(sys)
step(sys)
```

The Bode plots and the unit step response of the approximated half-order integrator (29) obtained for the frequency range (28) and $N = 3$ are depicted in Fig. 5.

2.3.3 Podlubny's matrix approach

This approach is based on the fact that operation of the fractional calculus can be expressed by matrix (Podlubny et al., 2009). It follows from Podlubny (2000), that the left-sided Riemann-Liouville or Caputo fractional derivative $v^{(\alpha)}(t) = {}_0D_t^{\alpha} v(t)$ can be approximated in all nodes of the equidistant discretization net $t = j\tau$ ($j = 0, 1, \ldots, n$) simultaneously with the help of the upper triangular strip matrix $B_n^{(\alpha)}$ as (Podlubny, 2000):

$$\left[v_n^{(\alpha)} \; v_{n-1}^{(\alpha)} \; \ldots \; v_1^{(\alpha)} \; v_0^{(\alpha)}\right]^T = B_n^{(\alpha)} \left[v_n \; v_{n-1} \; \ldots \; v_1 \; v_0\right]^T, \tag{30}$$

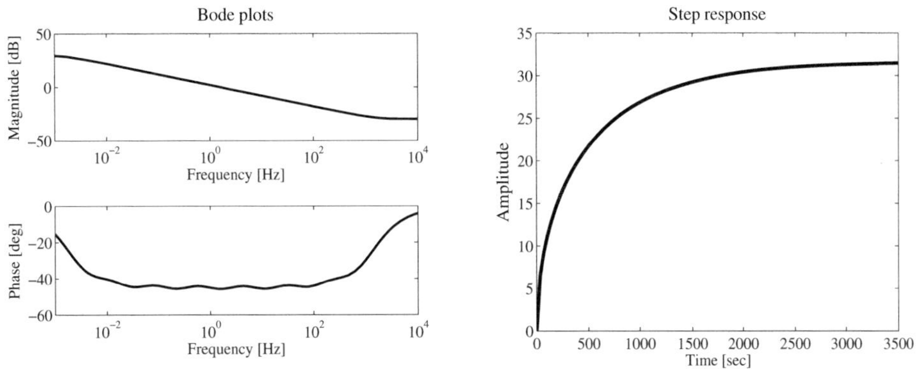

(a) Bode plots (b) Unit step response

Fig. 5. Characteristics of approximated fractional-order integrator (29) obtained from (27) for $r = -0.5$, frequency range (28) and $N = 3$

where

$$B_n^{(\alpha)} = \frac{1}{\tau^\alpha}\begin{bmatrix} \omega_0^{(\alpha)} & \omega_1^{(\alpha)} & \ddots & \ddots & \omega_{n-1}^{(\alpha)} & \omega_n^{(\alpha)} \\ 0 & \omega_0^{(\alpha)} & \omega_1^{(\alpha)} & \ddots & \ddots & \omega_{n-1}^{(\alpha)} \\ 0 & 0 & \omega_0^{(\alpha)} & \omega_1^{(\alpha)} & \ddots & \ddots \\ \dots & \dots & \dots & \ddots & \ddots & \ddots \\ 0 & \cdots & 0 & 0 & \omega_0^{(\alpha)} & \omega_1^{(\alpha)} \\ 0 & 0 & \cdots & 0 & 0 & \omega_0^{(\alpha)} \end{bmatrix}, \tag{31}$$

$$\omega_j^{(\alpha)} = (-1)^j \binom{\alpha}{j}, \qquad j = 0, 1, \dots, n. \tag{32}$$

Similarly, the right-sided Riemann-Liouville or Caputo fractional derivative $v^{(\alpha)}(t) = {}_tD_b^\alpha v(t)$ can be approximated in all nodes of the equidistant discretization net $t = j\tau$ $(j = 0, 1, \dots, n)$ simultaneously with the help of the lower triangular strip matrix $F_n^{(\alpha)}$ (Podlubny, 2000):

$$\begin{bmatrix} v_n^{(\alpha)} & v_{n-1}^{(\alpha)} & \dots & v_1^{(\alpha)} & v_0^{(\alpha)} \end{bmatrix}^T = F_n^{(\alpha)} \begin{bmatrix} v_n & v_{n-1} & \dots & v_1 & v_0 \end{bmatrix}^T, \tag{33}$$

$$F_n^{(\alpha)} = \frac{1}{\tau^\alpha}\begin{bmatrix} \omega_0^{(\alpha)} & 0 & 0 & 0 & \cdots & 0 \\ \omega_1^{(\alpha)} & \omega_0^{(\alpha)} & 0 & 0 & \cdots & 0 \\ \omega_2^{(\alpha)} & \omega_1^{(\alpha)} & \omega_0^{(\alpha)} & 0 & \cdots & 0 \\ \ddots & \ddots & \ddots & \ddots & \dots & \dots \\ \omega_{n-1}^{(\alpha)} & \ddots & \omega_2^{(\alpha)} & \omega_1^{(\alpha)} & \omega_0^{(\alpha)} & 0 \\ \omega_n^{(\alpha)} & \omega_{n-1}^{(\alpha)} & \ddots & \omega_2^{(\alpha)} & \omega_1^{(\alpha)} & \omega_0^{(\alpha)} \end{bmatrix}. \tag{34}$$

The symmetric Riesz derivative of order β can be approximated based on its definition as a combination of the approximations (30) and (33) for the left and right-sided Riemann-Liouville derivatives, or using the centered fractional differences approximation of the symmetric Riesz derivative suggested recently by Ortigueira (2006). The general formula is the same (Podlubny et al., 2009):

$$\left[v_m^{(\beta)}\ v_{m-1}^{(\beta)}\ \ldots\ v_1^{(\beta)}\ v_0^{(\beta)}\right]^T = R_m^{(\beta)} \left[v_m\ v_{m-1}\ \ldots\ v_1\ v_0\right]^T \tag{35}$$

In the first case, the approximation for the left-sided Caputo derivative is taken one step ahead, and the approximation for the right-sided Caputo derivative is taken one step back. This leads to the matrix

$$R_m^{(\beta)} = \frac{h^{-\alpha}}{2}\left[\ {}_{-1}U_m + {}_{+1}U_m\right] \tag{36}$$

In the second case (Ortigueira's definition) we have the following symmetric matrix:

$$R_m^{(\beta)} = h^{-\beta}\begin{bmatrix} \omega_0^{(\beta)} & \omega_1^{(\beta)} & \omega_2^{(\beta)} & \omega_3^{(\beta)} & \cdots & \omega_m^{(\beta)} \\ \omega_1^{(\beta)} & \omega_0^{(\beta)} & \omega_1^{(\beta)} & \omega_2^{(\beta)} & \cdots & \omega_{m-1}^{(\beta)} \\ \omega_2^{(\beta)} & \omega_1^{(\beta)} & \omega_0^{(\beta)} & \omega_1^{(\beta)} & \cdots & \omega_{m-2}^{(\beta)} \\ \ddots & \ddots & \ddots & \ddots & \cdots & \cdots \\ \omega_{m-1}^{(\beta)} & \ddots & \omega_2^{(\beta)} & \omega_1^{(\beta)} & \omega_0^{(\beta)} & \omega_1^{(\beta)} \\ \omega_m^{(\beta)} & \omega_{m-1}^{(\beta)} & \ddots & \omega_2^{(\beta)} & \omega_1^{(\beta)} & \omega_0^{(\beta)} \end{bmatrix} \tag{37}$$

$$\omega_k^{(\beta)} = \frac{(-1)^k\,\Gamma(\beta+1)\,\cos(\beta\pi/2)}{\Gamma(\beta/2-k+1)\,\Gamma(\beta/2+k+1)}, \qquad k = 0,1,\ldots,m. \tag{38}$$

Both these approximations of symmetric Riesz derivatives give practically the same numerical results and in the case of numerical solution of partial fractional differential equations lead to a well-posed matrix of the resulting algebraic system.

Similarly, if in addition to fractional-order time derivative we also consider symmetric fractional-order spatial derivatives, then we have to use all nodes at the considered time layer from the leftmost to the rightmost spatial discretization node.

Let us consider the nodes $(ih, j\tau)$, $j = 0,1,2,\ldots,n$, corresponding to all time layers at i-th spatial discretization node. It has been shown in Podlubny (2000) that all values of α-th order time derivative of $u(x,t)$ at these nodes are approximated using the discrete analogue of differentiation of arbitrary order (Podlubny et al., 2009):

$$\left[u_{i,n}^{(\alpha)}\ u_{i,n-1}^{(\alpha)}\ \ldots\ u_{i,2}^{(\alpha)}\ u_{i,1}^{(\alpha)}\ u_{i,0}^{(\alpha)}\right] = B_n^{(\alpha)}\left[u_{i,n}\ u_{i,n-1}\ \ldots\ u_{i,2}\ u_{i,1}\ u_{i,0}\right]^T. \tag{39}$$

In order to obtain a simultaneous approximation of α-th order time derivative of $u(x,t)$ in all nodes, we need to arrange all function values u_{ij} at the discretization nodes to the form of a column vector (Podlubny et al., 2009):

$$u_{nm} = \begin{bmatrix} u_{m,n}\ u_{m-1,n}\ \dots\ u_{1,n}\ u_{0,n} & & & & \\ & u_{m,n-1}\ u_{m-1,n-1}\ \dots\ u_{1,n-1}\ u_{0,n-1} & & & \\ & & \dots & & \\ & & & u_{m,1}\ u_{m-1,1}\ \dots\ u_{1,1}\ u_{0,1} & \\ & & & & u_{m,0}\ u_{m-1,0}\ \dots\ u_{1,0}\ u_{0,0} \end{bmatrix}^T$$

In visual terms, we first take the nodes of n-th time layer, then the nodes of $(n-1)$-th time layer, and so forth, and put them in this order in a vertical column stack.

The matrix that transforms the vector U_{nm} to the vector $U_t^{(\alpha)}$ of the partial fractional derivative of order α with respect to time variable can be obtained as a Kronecker product of the matrix $B_n^{(\alpha)}$, which corresponds to the fractional ordinary derivative of order α (recall that n is the number of time steps), and the unit matrix E_m (recall that m is the number of spatial discretization nodes):

$$T_{mn}^{(\alpha)} = B_n^{(\alpha)} \otimes E_m. \tag{40}$$

Similarly, the matrix that transforms the vector U to the vector $U_x^{(\beta)}$ of the partial fractional derivative of order β with respect to spatial variable can be obtained as a Kronecker product of the unit matrix E_n (recall that n is the number of spatial discretization nodes), and the matrix $R_m^{(\beta)}$, which corresponds to a symmetric Riesz ordinary derivative of order β (Ortigueira, 2006), (recall that m is the number of time steps):

$$S_{mn}^{(\alpha)} = E_n \otimes R_n^{(\beta)}. \tag{41}$$

Having these approximations for partial fractional derivatives with respect to both variables, we can immediately discretize the general form of the fractional diffusion equation by simply replacing the derivatives with their discrete analogs. Namely, the equation (Podlubny et al., 2009):

$${}_0^C D_t^{\alpha} u - \chi \frac{\partial^{\beta} u}{\partial |x|^{\beta}} = f(x,t) \tag{42}$$

is discretized as

$$\left\{ B_n^{(\alpha)} \otimes E_m - \chi\, E_n \otimes R_m^{(\beta)} \right\} u_{nm} = f_{nm}. \tag{43}$$

The initial and boundary conditions must be equal to zero. If it is not so, then an auxiliary unknown function must be introduced, which satisfies the zero initial and boundary conditions. In this way, the non-zero initial and boundary conditions moves to the right-hand side of the equation for the new unknown function.

3. Ordinary fractional differential equations

A general fractional-order system can be described by a fractional differential equation of the form

$$\begin{aligned} a_n D_t^{\alpha_n} y(t) + a_{n-1} D_t^{\alpha_{n-1}} y(t) + \ldots + a_0 D_t^{\alpha_0} y(t) = \\ = b_m D_t^{\beta_m} u(t) + b_{m-1} D_t^{\beta_{m-1}} u(t) + \ldots + b_0 D_t^{\beta_0} u(t), \end{aligned} \tag{44}$$

where $D_t^\gamma \equiv {}_0D_t^\gamma$ denotes the Grünwald-Letnikov, the Riemann-Liouville or Caputo fractional derivative (Podlubny, 1999). The corresponding transfer function of *incommensurate* real orders has the following form (Podlubny, 1999):

$$G(s) = \frac{b_m s^{\beta_m} + \ldots + b_1 s^{\beta_1} + b_0 s^{\beta_0}}{a_n s^{\alpha_n} + \ldots + a_1 s^{\alpha_1} + a_0 s^{\alpha_0}} = \frac{Q(s^{\beta_k})}{P(s^{\alpha_k})}, \tag{45}$$

where a_k $(k = 0, \ldots n)$, b_k $(k = 0, \ldots m)$ are constant, and α_k $(k = 0, \ldots n)$, β_k $(k = 0, \ldots m)$ are arbitrary real or rational numbers and without loss of generality they can be arranged as $\alpha_n > \alpha_{n-1} > \ldots > \alpha_0$, and $\beta_m > \beta_{m-1} > \ldots > \beta_0$.
In the particular case of *commensurate* order systems, it holds that, $\alpha_k = \alpha k, \beta_k = \alpha k, (0 < \alpha < 1), \forall k \in Z$, and the transfer function has the following form:

$$G(s) = K_0 \frac{\sum_{k=0}^{M} b_k (s^\alpha)^k}{\sum_{k=0}^{N} a_k (s^\alpha)^k} = K_0 \frac{Q(s^\alpha)}{P(s^\alpha)}. \tag{46}$$

With $N > M$, the function $G(s)$ becomes a proper rational function in the complex variable s^α which can be expanded in partial fractions of the following form:

$$G(s) = K_0 \left[\sum_{i=1}^{N} \frac{A_i}{s^\alpha + \lambda_i} \right], \tag{47}$$

where λ_i $(i = 1, 2, \ldots, N)$ are the roots of the pseudo-polynomial $P(s^\alpha)$ or the system poles which are assumed to be simple without loss of generality. The analytical solution of the system (47) can be expressed as

$$y(t) = \mathcal{L}^{-1} \left\{ K_0 \left[\sum_{i=1}^{N} \frac{A_i}{s^\alpha + \lambda_i} \right] \right\} = K_0 \sum_{i=1}^{N} A_i t^\alpha E_{\alpha,\alpha}(-\lambda_i t^\alpha), \tag{48}$$

where $E_{\mu,\nu}(z)$ is the Mittag-Leffler function defined as (3).
A fractional-order plant to be controlled can be described by a typical n-term linear homogeneous fractional-order differential equation (FODE) in the time domain

$$a_n \, D_t^{\alpha_n} y(t) + \cdots + a_1 \, D_t^{\alpha_1} y(t) + a_0 \, D_t^{\alpha_0} y(t) = 0 \tag{49}$$

where a_k $(k = 0, 1, \cdots, n)$ are constant coefficients of the FODE; α_k $(k = 0, 1, 2, \cdots, n)$ are real numbers. Without loss of generality, assume that $\alpha_n > \alpha_{n-1} > \ldots > \alpha_0 \geq 0$.
The analytical solution of the FODE (49) is given by general formula in the form (Podlubny, 1999):

$$y(t) = \frac{1}{a_n} \sum_{m=0}^{\infty} \frac{(-1)^m}{m!} \sum_{\substack{k_0 + k_1 + \ldots + k_{n-2} = m \\ k_0 \geq 0; \ldots, k_{n-2} \geq 0}} (m; k_0, k_1, \ldots, k_{n-2}) \tag{50}$$

$$\times \prod_{i=0}^{n-2} \left(\frac{a_i}{a_n} \right)^{k_i} \mathcal{E}_m(t, -\frac{a_{n-1}}{a_n}; \alpha_n - \alpha_{n-1}, \alpha_n + \sum_{j=0}^{n-2} (\alpha_{n-1} - \alpha_j) k_j + 1),$$

where $(m; k_0, k_1, \ldots, k_{n-2})$ are the multinomial coefficients.

Consider a control function which acts on the FODE system (49) as follows:

$$a_n D_t^{\alpha_n} y(t) + \cdots + a_1 D_t^{\alpha_1} y(t) + a_0 D_t^{\alpha_0} y(t) = u(t). \tag{51}$$

By the Laplace transform, we can get a fractional transfer function:

$$G(s) = \frac{Y(s)}{U(s)} = \frac{1}{a_n s^{\alpha_n} + \cdots + a_1 s^{\alpha_1} + a_0 s^{\alpha_0}}. \tag{52}$$

The fractional-order linear time-invariant (LTI) system can also be represented by the following state-space model:

$$\begin{aligned} {}_0D_t^{\mathbf{q}} x(t) &= \mathbf{A}x(t) + \mathbf{B}u(t) \\ y(t) &= \mathbf{C}x(t), \end{aligned} \tag{53}$$

where $x \in \mathrm{R}^n$, $u \in \mathrm{R}^r$ and $y \in \mathrm{R}^p$ are the state, input and output vectors of the system and $\mathbf{A} \in \mathrm{R}^{n\times n}$, $\mathbf{B} \in \mathrm{R}^{n\times r}$, $\mathbf{C} \in \mathrm{R}^{p\times n}$, and $\mathbf{q} = [q_1, q_2, \ldots, q_n]^T$ are the fractional orders. If $q_1 = q_2 = \ldots q_n \equiv \alpha$, system (53) is called a commensurate-order system, otherwise it is an incommensurate-order system.

EXAMPLE 3.1. Let us consider a simple two-term fractional differential equation with zero initial condition in general form:

$$aD_t^{\alpha} y(t) + by(t) = 1 \tag{54}$$

Solution can be obtained by using the Laplace transform method. In the Laplace domain we can express the solution as

$$Y(s) = \frac{1/a}{s(s^{\alpha} + b/a)} \tag{55}$$

and by using the useful relations (6) and (12), in the time domain we can write a general solution

$$y(t) = \frac{1}{a}\mathcal{E}_0(t, -\frac{b}{a}; \alpha, \alpha+1) \equiv \frac{1}{a} t^{\alpha} E_{\alpha,\alpha+1}\left(-\frac{b}{a}t^{\alpha}\right). \tag{56}$$

For obtaining the solution in Matlab we can use the following sequence of commands:

```
clear all; close all;
a=2;  b=1; alpha=1.5;
t=0:0.001:20; % for time step 0.001 and computational time 20 sec
y=(1/a)*t.^(alpha).*mlf(alpha,alpha+1,((-b/a)*t.^(alpha)));
plot(t,y);
xlabel('Time [sec]');
ylabel('y(t)');
```

EXAMPLE 3.2. Let us consider a three-term fractional differential equation in the form

$$a_2 D_t^{\alpha_2} y(t) + a_1 D_t^{\alpha_1} y(t) + a_0 y(t) = u(t). \tag{57}$$

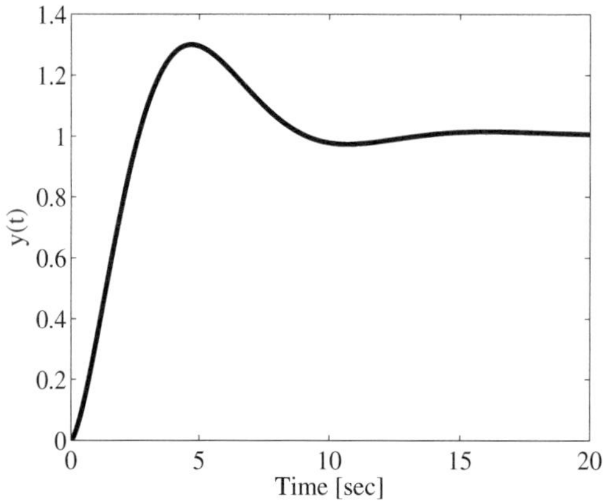

Fig. 6. Solution of the equation (55) for parameters: $\alpha = 1.5$, $a = 2$, and $b = 1$, under zero initial conditions, time step 0.001 and computation time 20 sec

Substituting (13) into the equation (57), one can write

$$\frac{a_2}{h^{\alpha_2}} \sum_{j=0}^{k} q_j^{(\alpha_2)} y(t_k - j) + \frac{a_1}{h^{\alpha_1}} \sum_{j=0}^{k} q_j^{(\alpha_1)} y(t_k - j) + a_0 y(t_k) = u(t_k), \tag{58}$$

where $t_k = kh$ $(k = 1, 2, \ldots, N)$ and $q_j^{(\alpha)}$ are binomial coefficients calculated according to (14). After some rearrangement of the terms in relation (58) we can obtain the numerical solution of the fractional differential equation (57) in the following form:

$$y(t_k) = \frac{u(t_k) - \frac{a_2}{h^{\alpha_2}} \sum_{j=1}^{k} q_j^{(\alpha_2)} y(t_k - j) - \frac{a_1}{h^{\alpha_1}} \sum_{j=1}^{k} q_j^{(\alpha_1)} y(t_k - j)}{\frac{a_2}{h^{\alpha_2}} + \frac{a_1}{h^{\alpha_1}} + a_0}, \tag{59}$$

where $k = 1, 2, \ldots, N$ for $N = T_{sim}/h$ and where T_{sim} is the total time of the calculation. The above approach is general and can be used for n-term fractional differential equation (44).

```
clear all; close all;
a2=0.8; a1=0.5; a0=1.0; alpha2=2.2; alpha1=0.9;
h=0.05; TSim=35;
n=round(TSim/h);
cp1=1; cp2=1; Y0=0; u=1.0;
for j=1:n
    c1(j)=(1-(1+alpha1)/j)*cp1;
    c2(j)=(1-(1+alpha2)/j)*cp2;
    cp1=c1(j);   cp2=c2(j);
end
Y(1)=Y0;
for i=2:n
  Y(i)=(u - (a2)*h^(-alpha2)*memo(Y,c2,i)- ...
  (a1)*h^(-alpha1)*memo(Y,c1,i))/(a2/(h^alpha2)+a1/(h^alpha1)+a0);
end
```

```
T=0:h:TSim;
plot(T,Y);
xlabel('Time [sec]'); ylabel('y(t)');

function [yo] = memo(r, c, k)
%
temp = 0;
for j=1:k-1
   temp = temp + c(j)*r(k-j);
end
yo = temp;
```

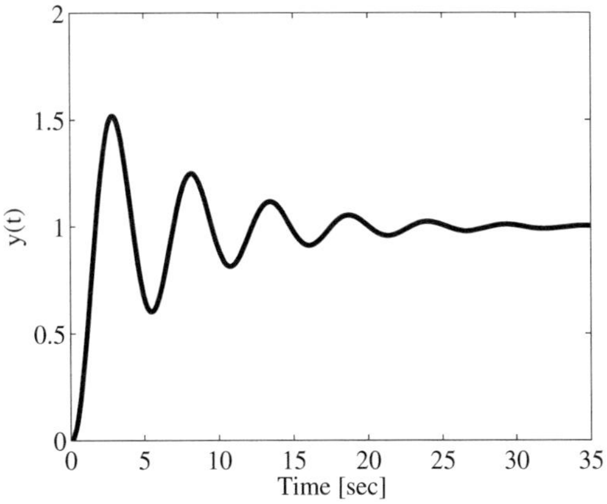

Fig. 7. Solution of the equation (57) for parameters: $a_2 = 0.8$, $a_1 = 0.5$, $a_0 = 1$, $\alpha_2 = 2.2$, $\alpha_1 = 0.9$ for $u(t) = 1$, under zero initial conditions, time step $h = 0.05$ and computation time $T_{sim} = 35$ sec

EXAMPLE 3.3. Let us consider the following three-term fractional differential equations, also called the Bagley-Torvik equation, in the form (Podlubny, 1999):

$$Ay''(t) + BD_t^{\alpha}y(t) + Cy(t) = F(t), \tag{60}$$

where $F(t) = 8$ for $0 \leq t \leq 1$ and $F(t) = 8$ for $t > 1$, and with zero initial conditions $y(0) = y'(0) = 0$.

In this case we will use a matrix approach and the following syntax of the Matlab functions (Podlubny et al., 2008):

```
clear all; close all;
alpha = 1.5; A = 1; B = 0.5; C = 1;
h=0.05;
TSim=40;
T=0:h:TSim;
N=TSim/h + 1;
M=zeros(N,N);
```

```
Dalpha = ban(alpha,N,h);
D2 = ban(2,N,h);
M=A*D2 + B*Dalpha + C*eye(size(Dalpha));
F=8*(T<=1)';
M = eliminator(N,[1 2])*M*eliminator(N, [1 2])';
F= eliminator(N,[1 2])*F;
Y=M\F;
Y0 = [0; 0; Y];
figure(1)
plot(T,Y0')
xlabel('Time [sec]');
ylabel('y(t)');
```

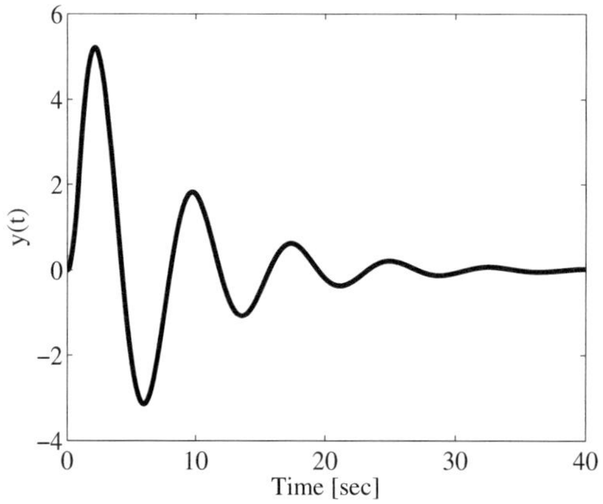

Fig. 8. Solution of the equation (60) for parameters: $A = 1$, $B = 0.5$, $C = 1$, and $\alpha = 1.5$ under zero initial conditions, time step $h = 0.05$ and computation time 40 sec

EXAMPLE 3.4. The transfer function of the closed feedback control loop with the DC motor (DCM) and the fractional-order controller designed for desired value of phase margin $\Phi_m = 45^o$ and gain margin equal to infinity, has the following form (Petráš, 2009):

$$G_c(s) = \frac{Y(s)}{W(s)} = \frac{G_o(s)}{1 + G_o(s)} = \frac{G_{DCM}(s)C(s)}{1 + G_{DCM}(s)C(s)} = \frac{0.05s + 1}{0.05s^{2.5} + s^{1.5} + 0.05s + 1}, \tag{61}$$

where $G_o(s)$ is the transfer function of the open control loop. Transfer function (61) corresponds to the fractional differential equation:

$$0.05D_t^{2.5}y(t) + D_t^{1.5}y(t) + 0.05y^{'}(t) + y(t) = 0.05w^{'}(t) + w(t) \tag{62}$$

The feedback control loop described above can be simulated in Matlab environment by using the approximation technique described in previous section, namely Oustaloup's recursive approximation function `ora_foc()` for desired frequency range $\omega_b = 10^{-2}$, $\omega_h = 10^2$, and $N = 6$.

```
close all; clear all;
Gs_DCM=tf([0.08],[0.05 1 0]);
Cs=(0.625*ora_foc(0.5,6,0.01,100))+(12.5*ora_foc(-0.5,6,0.01,100));
Gs_close=(Gs_DCM*Cs)/(1+(Gs_DCM*Cs));
step(Gs_close,15);
Gs_open=(Gs_DCM*Cs);
figure; bode(Gs_open);
[Gm,Pm] = margin(Gs_open);
```

The results obtained via described Matlab scripts are depicted in Fig. 9. The continuous model is shown with solid line. Phase margin is $\Phi_m \approx 44.9^o$ and gain margin is infinity.
The discrete version of the continuous fractional-order transfer function can be obtained by using the digital operator (21) and Matlab function for approximation of digital fractional-order derivative/integral `dfod1()` for sampling time $T = 1$ sec, ratio $a = 1/3$, and $n = 5$.

```
close all; clear all;
T=0.1; a=1/3;
z=tf('z',T,'variable','z^-1')
Hz=((1+a)/T)*((1-z^-1)/(1+a*z^-1));
Gz_DCM=0.08/(Hz*(0.05*Hz+1));
Cz=0.625*dfod1(5,T,a,0.5)+12.5*dfod1(5,T,a,-0.5);
Gz_close=(Gz_DCM*Cz)/(1+(Gz_DCM*Cz));
step(Gz_close,15);
Gz_open=(Gz_DCM*Cz);
figure; bode(Gz_open);
[Gm,Pm] = margin(Gz_open);
```

The results obtained via described Matlab scripts are depicted in Fig. 9. The discrete model is shown with dashed line. Phase margin is $\Phi_m \approx 45.1^o$ and gain margin is infinity.

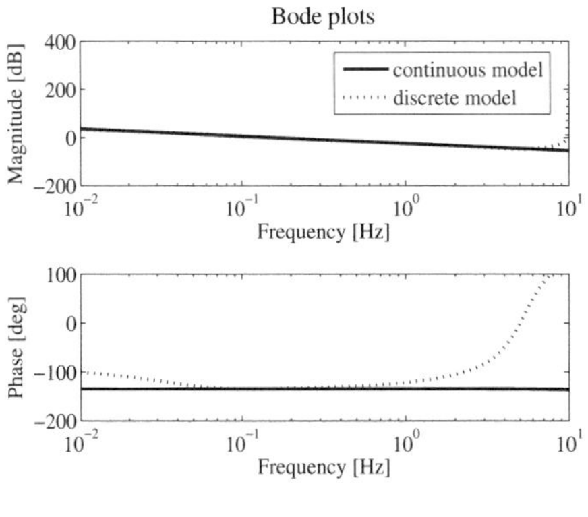

(a) Bode plots

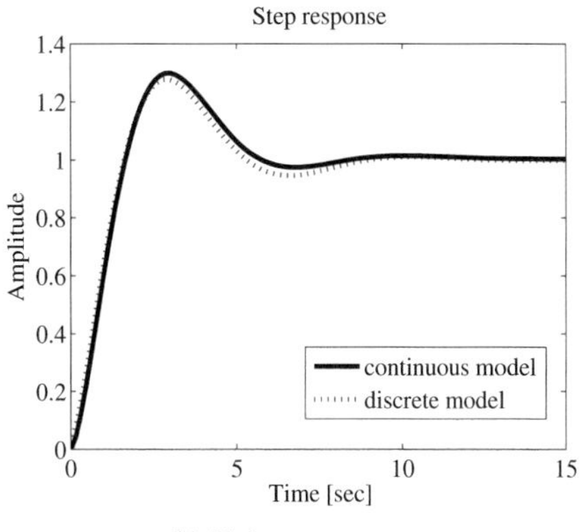

(b) Unit step responses

Fig. 9. Characteristics of fractional order transfer function (61)

4. Partial fractional differential equations

For the solution of partial differential equations with derivatives of any order (integer and non-integer), with time and space fractional derivatives, we can use a matrix approach.

EXAMPLE 4.1. Let us consider the following one-dimensional fractional diffusion equation with fractional derivatives with respect both to time and to the spatial variable:

$$ {}_0^C D_t^{\alpha} y(x,t) - a^2 \frac{\partial^{\beta} y(x,t)}{\partial |x|^{\beta}} = f(x,t) \tag{63} $$

with the initial condition $y(x,0) = h(x)$ and the boundary conditions $y(0,t) = y(L,t) = K$. Note that $\partial^{\beta} y(x,t)/\partial |x|^{\beta}$ is symmetric Riesz derivative. Let us consider the following parameters: $\alpha = 1.2$, $\beta = 2.1$, $a^2 = 1$, $f(x,t) = 5$, $L = 2$, $T_{sim} = 3$ sec and $K = 0$. The Matlab code is (for more details see also (Podlubny et al., 2008; 2009)):

```
clear all; close all;
% set the input parameters:
alpha =1.2; beta=2.1; a2=1; f_x=5; L=2; TSim=3; K=0;
% set the calculation parameters:
m = 21; n =148; h = L/(m-1); tau = TSim/n;
% alpha-th order derivative with respect to time:
B1 = ban(alpha,n-1,tau)';
% time derivative matrix:
TD = kron(B1, eye(m));
% beta-th order derivative with respect to x:
B2 = ransym(beta,m,h);
% spatial derivative matrix:
SD = kron(eye(n-1), B2);
% matrix corresponding to discretization in space and time:
SystemMatrix = TD - a2*SD;
S = eliminator (m, [1 m]);
SK = kron(eye(n-1), S);
SystemMatrix_without_columns_1_m = SystemMatrix * SK';

% remove rows with '1' and 'm' from SystemMatrix_without_columns_1_m
S = eliminator (m, [1 m]);
SK = kron(eye(n-1), S);
SystemMatrix_without_rows_columns_1_m = ...
SK * SystemMatrix_without_columns_1_m;

% initial conditions:
U0=zeros(1,m);

% right hand side:
F = f_x*ones(size(SystemMatrix_without_rows_columns_1_m,1),1);

% solution of the system:
```

```
Y = SystemMatrix_without_rows_columns_1_m\F;

% reshape solution array --
% values for k-th time step are in the k-th column of YS:
YS = reshape(Y,m-2,n-1);
YS = fliplr(YS);

% final solution (take into account the initial condition):
for k = 1:(n-1)
    U (:,k) = (YS(:,k)+U0(2:(m-1))');
end

% plot graph
[rows, columns] = size(U);
U = [ zeros(1, columns)+K; U;  zeros(1, columns)+K];
U = [U0' U];
[XX,YY]=meshgrid(tau*(0:n-1),h*(0:m-1));
mesh(XX,YY,U)
xlabel('t'); ylabel('x'); zlabel('y(x,t)');
title(['\alpha =', num2str(alpha), ',   \beta = ', num2str(beta)])
```

When we consider non-zero initial condition, e.g. in the form of auxiliary function $y(x,0) = h(x) = x(x-1)$ and non-zero boundary conditions in the form of the constant K, where $y(0,t) = y(L,t) = K$, we have to modify the following lines in above Matlab code:

```
K=2;
...
% initial conditions:
k = 1:m;
U0 = (k-1).*((m-1) - k + 1)*h^2 + K;
```

In Fig. 10(a) and Fig. 10(b) are depicted the solutions of the fractional partial differential equation (63) for zero and non-zero initial and boundary conditions, respectively.

5. Nonlinear fractional differential equations

A general numerical solution of the nonlinear fractional differential equation in the form

$$ {}_aD_t^q y(t) = f(y(t),t), $$

can be expressed by using the relations (13) and (14) as:

$$ y(t_k) = f\left(y(t_k), t_k\right) h^q - \sum_{j=v}^{k} c_j^{(q)} y(t_{k-j}). \tag{64} $$

For the *memory term* expressed by the sum, a "short memory" principle can be used. Then the lower index of the sums in relations (64) will be $v = 1$ for $k < (L_m/h)$ and $v = k - (L_m/h)$ for $k > (L_m/h)$, or without using the "short memory" principle, we put $v = 1$ for all k.

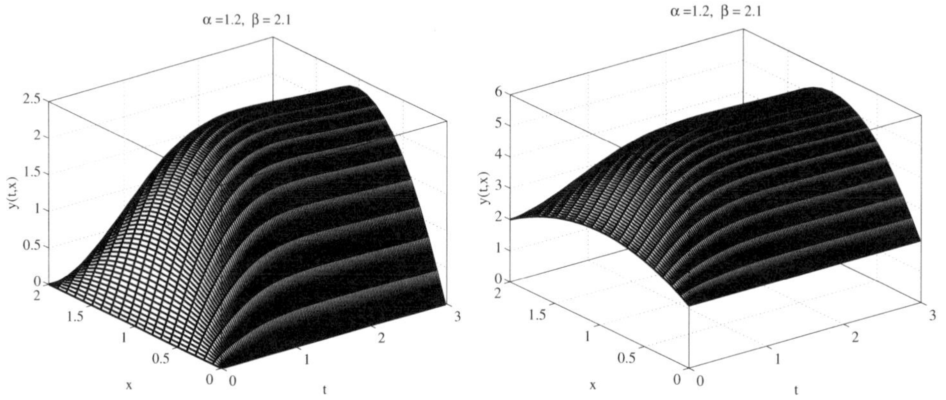

(a) For zero initial and boundary conditions: $y(x,0) = 0$ and $y(0,t) = y(L,t) = 0$

(b) For non-zero initial and boundary conditions: $y(x,0) = x(x-1)$ and $y(0,t) = y(L,t) = 2$

Fig. 10. Solution of the equation (63) for parameters: $\alpha = 1.2$, $\beta = 2.1$, $a = 1$, and $f(x,t)$=5 for $L = 2$ and $T_{sim} = 3$ sec

EXAMPLE 5.1. In this section, we will demonstrate the proposed numerical solution on the set of three nonlinear fractional differential equations, which are used for describing an economical system. The fractional-order financial system is described as follows (Chen, 2008):

$$\begin{aligned} {}_0D_t^{q_1}x(t) &= z(t) + (y(t) - a)x(t), \\ {}_0D_t^{q_2}y(t) &= 1 - by(t) - x(t)^2, \\ {}_0D_t^{q_3}z(t) &= -x(t) - cz(t), \end{aligned} \tag{65}$$

where the total order of the system is denoted by $\bar{q} = (q_1, q_2, q_3)$, a is the saving amount, b is the cost per investment, and c is the elasticity of demand of commercial market. The state variables are: $x(t)$ is the interest rate, $y(t)$ is the investment demand, and $z(t)$ is the price index.

The numerical solution of the fractional-order financial system (65) has the following form (Petráš, 2011):

$$\begin{aligned} x(t_k) &= (z(t_{k-1}) - (y(t_{k-1}) - a)x(t_{k-1}))\, h^{q_1} - \sum_{j=v}^{k} c_j^{(q_1)} x(t_{k-j}), \\ y(t_k) &= \left(1 - by(t_k) - x^2(t_k)\right) h^{q_2} - \sum_{j=v}^{k} c_j^{(q_2)} y(t_{k-j}), \\ z(t_k) &= (-x(t_k) - cz(t_{k-1}))\, h^{q_3} - \sum_{j=v}^{k} c_j^{(q_3)} z(t_{k-j}), \end{aligned} \tag{66}$$

where T_{sim} is the simulation time, $k = 1, 2, 3 \ldots, N$, for $N = [T_{sim}/h]$, and $(x(0), y(0), z(0))$ is the start point (initial conditions). The binomial coefficients $c_j^{(q_i)}$, $\forall i$, are calculated according to relation (14).

Let us consider the following parameters of the system (65): $a = 1.0$, $b = 0.1$, $c = 1.0$, orders $q_1 = 1.1$, $q_2 = 0.9$, $q_3 = 0.8$, computational time $T_{sim} = 200$ days, for time step $h = 0.04166$, and initial conditions $(x(0), y(0), z(0)) = (1, -1, 1)$. We will use $v = 1$ in (66) for all k.
The Matlab code for the solution of system (65) follows:

```
close all; clear all;
[t, y]=FOFinanc([1 0.1 1],[1.1 0.9 0.8],200, [1 -1 1]);
plot3(y(:,1), y(:,2), y(:,3),'k'); % in 3D state space
xlabel('x(t)'); ylabel('y(t)'); zlabel('z(t)'); grid;
figure; plot(y(:,1), y(:,2),'k'); % projection onto x-y plane
xlabel('x(t)'); ylabel('y(t)');  grid;
```

where routine `FOFinanc()` consists of the following code (Petráš, 2010):

```
function [T, Y]=FOFinanc(parameters, orders, TSim, Y0)
h=0.04166;
% number of calculated mesh points:
n=round(TSim/h);
%orders of derivatives, respectively:
q1=orders(1); q2=orders(2); q3=orders(3);
% constants of financial system:
a=parameters(1); b=parameters(2); c=parameters(3);
% binomial coefficients calculation:
cp1=1; cp2=1; cp3=1;
for j=1:n
    c1(j)=(1-(1+q1)/j)*cp1;
    c2(j)=(1-(1+q2)/j)*cp2;
    c3(j)=(1-(1+q3)/j)*cp3;
    cp1=c1(j); cp2=c2(j); cp3=c3(j);
end
% initial conditions setting:
x(1)=Y0(1); y(1)=Y0(2); z(1)=Y0(3);
% calculation of phase portraits /numerical solution/:
for i=2:n
    x(i)=(z(i-1)+(y(i-1)-a)*x(i-1))*h^q1 - memo(x, c1, i);
    y(i)=(1-b*y(i-1)-x(i)^2)*h^q2 - memo(y, c2, i);
    z(i)=(-x(i)-c*z(i-1))*h^q3 - memo(z, c3, i);
end
for j=1:n
    Y(j,1)=x(j);  Y(j,2)=y(j);  Y(j,3)=z(j);
end
T=0:h:TSim;
```

Supporting function `memo()` was already introduced in previous section of this chapter.
In Fig. 11 are depicted the simulation results of the financial system (65) for the following parameters: $a = 1$, $b = 0.1$, and $c = 1.0$, orders $q_1 = 1.1$, $q_2 = 0.9$, $q_3 = 0.8$, computational time 200 days, and for time step $h = 0.04166$ (i.e. approximately one hour sampling).

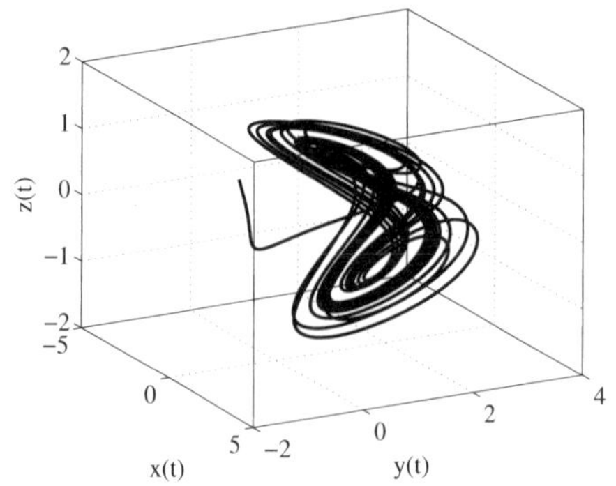

(a) State trajectory in 3D state space

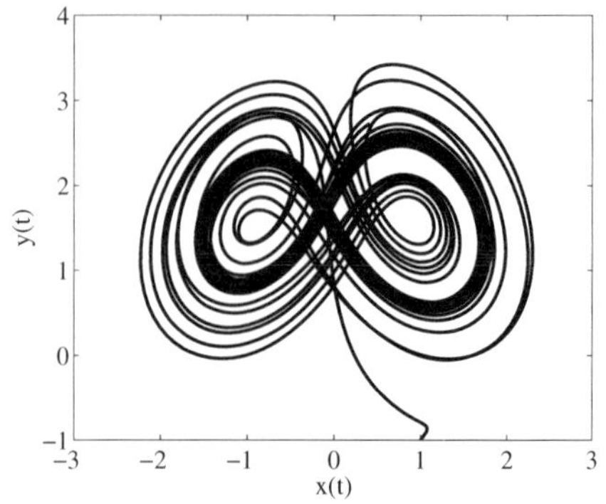

(b) State trajectory projected onto x-y plane

Fig. 11. Simulation result of the fractional-order financial system (65) in state space for the initial conditions $(x(0), y(0), z(0)) = (1, -1, 1)$

6. Conclusion

In this chapter are presented the methods for calculation of the fractional derivative and fractional integral together with methods for solution of the fractional differential equations in Matlab. Those methods are based on the numerical approximation of the fractional derivatives and integral in the continuos time, discrete time and frequency domains. For each mentioned methods are presented illustrative examples with a Matlab code. Moreover, all described problems can be solved also in Simulink environment but such approach was omitted in this chapter. Obviously the described problems could be solved via other methods and also by different Matlab functions but we shown the way how one can create its own *Fractional Calculus Toolbox* for Matlab from functions, which are freely downloadable from the MathWorks, Inc. Matlab Central File Exchange. It depends on the problem which should be solved in Matlab. Except above-mentioned open source routines, there are very useful and effective Matlab functions for solution and analysis of the fractional calculus problems, which are described in (Monje et al., 2010). Especially helpful is the linear fractional-order differential equations solver `fode_sol()` and also the set of functions already published in paper (Chen et al., 2009).

It is worth mentioning that there are many additional useful functions at the Matlab Central File Exchange web site, which are not used in this chapter. For instance variable-order, distributed-order, and random-order fractional equations, predictor corrector numerical method, impulse and step responses invariant discretization of fractional-order differentiators/integrators as well as various fractional-order digital filters.

7. References

Al-Alaoui, M. A. (1993). Novel digital integrator and differentiator, *Electron. Lett.*, Vol. 29, 376–378.

Al-Alaoui, M. A. (1997). Filling the gap between the bilinear and the backward difference transforms: An interactive design approach, *Int. J. Elect. Eng. Edu.*, Vol. 34, 331–337.

Bayat, F. M. (2007). Fractional Differentiator, MathWorks, Inc. Matlab Central File Exchange, URL: *www.mathworks.com/matlabcentral/fileexchange/13858*.

Caponetto, R.; Dongola, G.; Fortuna, L. and Petráš, I. (2010). *Fractional Order Systems: Modeling and Control Applications*, World Scientific, Singapore.

Chen, Y. Q. and Moore, K. L. (2002). Discretization Schemes for Fractional-Order Differentiators and Integrators, *IEEE Trans. On Circuits and Systems - I: Fundamental Theory and Applications*,Vol. 49, No. 3, 363–367.

Chen, Y. Q. (2003). Oustaloup–Recursive–Approximation for Fractional Order Differentiators, MathWorks, Inc. Matlab Central File Exchange, URL: *www.mathworks.com/matlabcentral/fileexchange/3802*.

Chen, Y. Q. (2008). Generalized Mittag-Leffler Function, MathWorks, Inc. Matlab Central File Exchange, URL: *www.mathworks.com/matlabcentral/fileexchange/20849*.

Chen, Y. Q.; Petráš, I. and Xue, D. (2009). Fractional order control - A tutorial, *Proc. of the American Control Conference*, pp. 1397–1411, June 10-12, 2009, St. Louis, USA.

Chen, W. Ch. (2008). Nonlinear dynamic and chaos in a fractional-order financial system, *Chaos, Solitons and Fractals*, Vol. 36, 1305–1314.

CRONE Research Group. (2010). CRONE Toolbox, URL: *www.ims-bordeaux.fr/CRONE/toolbox/*.

Dorčák, Ľ. (1994). Numerical Models for the Simulation of the Fractional-Order Control Systems, *UEF-04-94, The Academy of Sciences, Inst. of Experimental Physic*, Košice, Slovakia.

Djrbashian, M. M. (1993). *Harmonic Analysis and Boundary Value problems in the Complex Domain*, Birkhäuser Verlag, Basel.

Lubich, Ch. (1986). Discretized fractional calculus, *SIAM J. Math. Anal.*, Vol. 17, 704–719.

Magin, R. L. (2006). *Fractional Calculus in Bioengineering*, Begell House Publishers.

Miller, K. S. and Ross, B. (1993). *An Introduction to the Fractional Calculus and Fractional Differential Equations*, John Wiley and Sons. Inc., New York.

Monje, C. A.; Chen, Y. Q.; Vinagre, B. M.; Xue, D. and Feliu, V. (2010). *Fractional-order Systems and Controls*, Series: Advances in Industrial Control, Springer.

Oldham, K. B. and Spanier, J. (1974). *The Fractional Calculus*, Academic Press, New York.

Ortigueira, M. D. (2006). Riesz potential operators and inverses via fractional centered derivatives, *Int. J. Math. Math. Sci.*, Article ID 48391, 1–12.

Oustaloup, A. (1995). *La Derivation Non Entiere: Theorie, Synthese et Applications*, Hermes, Paris.

Oustaloup, A.; Levron, F.; Mathieu, B. and Nanot, F. M. (2000). Frequency-band complex noninteger differentiator: characterization and synthesis, *IEEE Trans. on Circuits and Systems I: Fundamental Theory and Applications I*, Vol. 47, 25–39.

Petráš, I. (2003a). Digital Fractional Order Differentiator/integrator – IIR type, MathWorks, Inc. Matlab Central File Exchange, URL: *www.mathworks.com/matlabcentral /fileexchange/3672*.

Petráš, I. (2003b). Digital Fractional Order Differentiator/integrator – FIR type, MathWorks, Inc. Matlab Central File Exchange, URL: *www.mathworks.com/matlabcentral /fileexchange/3673*.

Petráš, I. (2009). Fractional-Order Feedback Control of a DC Motor, *Journal of Electrical Engineering*, Vol. 60, No. 3, 117–128.

Petráš, I. (2010). Fractional Order Chaotic Systems, MathWorks, Inc. Matlab Central File Exchange, URL: *www.mathworks.com/matlabcentral/fileexchange/27336*.

Petráš, I. (2011). *Fractional-Order Nonlinear Systems: Modeling, Analysis and Simulation* Series: Nonlinear Physical Science, Springer, HEP.

Podlubny, I. (1999). *Fractional Differential Equations*, Academic Press, San Diego.

Podlubny, I. (2000). Matrix approach to discrete fractional calculus, *Fractional Calculus and Applied Analysis*, Vol. 3, 359–386.

Podlubny, I. and Kacenak, M. (2005). Mittag-Leffler Function, MathWorks, Inc. Matlab Central File Exchange, URL: *www.mathworks.com/matlabcentral/fileexchange/8738.*

Podlubny, I.; Skovranek, T. and Vinagre, B. M. (2008). Matrix Approach to Discretization of ODEs and PDEs of Arbitrary Real Order, MathWorks, Inc. Matlab Central File Exchange, URL: *www.mathworks.com/matlabcentral/fileexchange/22071.*

Podlubny, I.; Chechkin. A.; Skovranek, T.; Chen, Y. Q. and Vinagre, B. M. J. (2009). Matrix approach to discrete fractional calculus II: Partial fractional differential equations, *Journal of Computational Physics*, Vol. 228, 3137–3153.

Valério, D. (2005). Toolbox Ninteger for MatLab, v. 2.3, MathWorks, Inc. Matlab Central File Exchange, URL: *www.mathworks.com/matlabcentral/fileexchange/8312.*

Vinagre, B. M.; Podlubny, I.; Hernández, A. and Feliu, V. (2000). Some approximations of fractional order operators used in control theory and applications, *Fractional Calculus and Applied Analysis*, Vol. 3, 231–248.

Vinagre, B. M.; Chen, Y. Q. and Petráš, I. (2003). Two direct Tustin discretization methods for fractional-order differentiator/integrator, *J. Franklin Inst.*, Vol. 340, 349–362.

Sierociuk, D. (2005). Fractional Order Discrete State–Space System Simulink Toolkit User Guide, *www.ee.pw.edu.pl/d̃sieroci/fsst/fsst.htm.*

Sheng, H.; Li, Y. and Chen, Y. Q. (2011). Application of numerical inverse Laplace transform algorithms in fractional calculus, *J. Franklin Inst.*, Vol. 348, 315–330.

Xue, D. (2010). Computational Aspect of Fractional-Order Control Problems, Tutorial Workshop on Fractional Order Dynamic Systems and Controls, Proceedings of the WCICA'2010, Jinan, China. (URL: *mechatronics.ece.usu.edu/foc/cdc10tw /code-matlab-simulink /xdy_foccode.rar*).

11

Analysis of Dynamic Systems Using Bond Graph Method Through SIMULINK

José Antonio Calvo, Carolina Álvarez- Caldas and José Luis San Román
Universidad Carlos III de Madrid
Spain

1. Introduction

The dynamic systems analysis, very common in engineering studies, is relatively simple when the steady state behaviour is analyzed, or when the system has few degrees of freedom. However, for complex systems, the problem can be highly complicated and the classic way to establish the behaviour equations becomes inadequate.
In most of the cases, the main concern of engineering students is to establish the mathematical model that represents the dynamic behaviour of the system and how the different parameters influence the system behaviour, because the equations that represent the dynamic of the system are usually partial differential equations, whose solutions require deep mathematical knowledge that in most cases is not available for the students.
The *Bond Graph* technique (Blundell, 1982) is extraordinarily useful to overcome these difficulties. Bond Graph is a simple and effective method to set out the differential equations of any dynamic system independently of the physical field analyzed. *Bond Graph* provides a common model for a wide range of systems ranging from the usual Electric, Mechanics, Hydraulic, Thermals, etc., or combinations of them.
Depcik et al. (2004) compare different software and language options, which are available to build models of dynamic systems. They establish that *MATLAB*™ and *Simulink*™ might be the best choice if the teacher wishes to collaborate with students because engineering students are typically familiar with *MATLAB*.
Some commercial software allow working directly with *Bond Graph* concepts as CAMP-G, TUTSIM, BONDLAB, which allow drawing the flow lines of the Bond Graph method. However, in order to the students understand the physical and mathematical concepts involved on the dynamic system, the block diagram used in *Simulink* allows a better compression of physical behaviour of the system.
Simulink forms the core environment for Model-Based Design for creating accurate, mathematical models of physical system behaviour. The graphical block-diagram lets the user drag-and-drop predefined modelling elements, connect them together and create models of dynamic systems. These dynamic systems can be continuous-time, multi-rate, discrete-time, or virtually any combination of the three.
In this chapter, we present an application, developed in *Simulink* library, which allows the engineering students to learn easily and quickly about dynamic systems behaviour through *Bond Graph* method.

After a brief introduction to the *Bond Graph* method, it will be explained how *Simulink* can be applied to improve the method, transforming the *Bond Graph* graphical diagram to a *Simulink* block diagram. Next, some mechanical examples of the application will be presented, increasing complexity, to demonstrate the benefits of the method for building complex models from simpler ones. Finally, the results of the dynamic response to different excitations will be analyzed using the various tools provided by *Simulink*.

2. Bond Graph method

This paper does not aim to develop the *Bond Graph* method. There are many literatures about *Bond Graph* method and its applications to analyze dynamic systems, such as Vera et al. (1993), Thoma (1975), Margolis (1985) and Karnopp (1979) in which the method is explained adequately. However, we believe that it is appropriate to make a brief introduction for encourage uninitiated readers to extending the method.
In this paper, the fundamental bases of the *Bond Graph* theory will be presented, in order to understand how to implement a model in Simulink, but is not the focus of the present work to explain the *Bond Graph* method.

2.1 Bond Graph basis

Energy is a basic commodity in a system. It flows in from one or more sources, is temporarily stored in system components or partially dissipated in resistances as heat, and finally arrives at "*sinks*" or "*loads*" where it produces some desired effects. Power is the rate of flow energy and is a scalar with no direction.
Bond Graph represents this power flow between two systems. This flow is symbolized through an arrow (*Bond*) as figure 1 illustrated. Unfortunately, power is not easy to measure directly, and engineers prefer to work with two temporary variables called "*flow*" and "*effort*". Depending on the physical environment, these variables have different value. For example in electrical networks, flow represents the "current" and effort the "voltage", in mechanical linkages, flow represents the "velocity" and effort the "force". The product of both temporary variables is power as equation (1) shows in the case of a mechanical system:

$$Power = f(t) \cdot e(t) = v(t) \cdot F(t) \tag{1}$$

On each *Bond*, one of the variables must be the cause and the other the effect. This can be deduced by the relationship indicated by the arrow direction. Effort and flow causalities always act in opposite directions in a *Bond*.

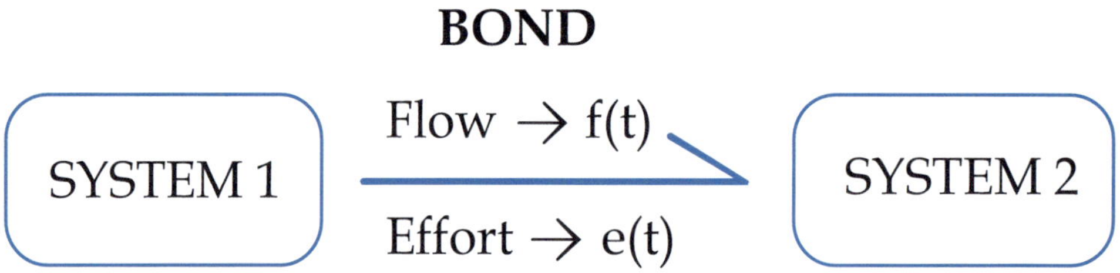

Fig. 1. Power flow in *Bond Graph*

Power bonds may join at one of two kinds of junctions: a *"0"* junction and a *"1"* junction. In a *"0"* junction, the flow and the efforts satisfy the expressions (2):

$$\begin{aligned} &\sum_n Flow_{input\_n} = \sum_m Flow_{output\_m} \\ &Effort_{input\_1} = Effort_{input\_2} = ... = Effort_{input\_n} = Effort_{output\_1} = ... = Effort_{output\_m} \end{aligned} \tag{2}$$

This corresponds to a node in an electrical circuit (where Kirchhoff's current law applies). In a *"1"* junction, the flow and the efforts satisfy the expressions (3):

$$\begin{aligned} &\sum_n Effort_{input\_n} = \sum_m Effort_{output\_m} \\ &Flow_{input\_1} = Flow_{input\_2} = ... = Flow_{input\_n} = Flow_{output\_1} = ... = Flow_{output\_m} \end{aligned} \tag{3}$$

This corresponds to force balance at a mass in a mechanical system. An example of a *"1"* junction is a resistor in series. In junction, the premise of energy conservation is assumed, no lost is allowed.
There are two additional variables, important in the description of dynamic systems. These variables, often called energy or dynamic variables are: *Momentum* [p(t)] and *displacement* [q(t)].
The variable "*Momentum*" is defined as the time integral of the effort as equation (4) shows.

$$p(t) = \int e(t)\,dt \;\Rightarrow\; \frac{dp}{dt} = e(t) \tag{4}$$

Likewise, the variable "displacement" is defined as the time integral of flow as equation (5) shows.

$$q(t) = \int f(t)\,dt \;\Rightarrow\; \frac{dq}{dt} = f(t) \tag{5}$$

In this way the energy of the system will be:

$$E = \int e(q)\,dq \tag{6}$$

The method makes possible the simulation of multiple physical domains, such as mechanical, electrical, thermal, hydraulic, etc., including combinations of these with each other, which can be treated as a unified set of elements. *Flows [f(t)]* and *efforts [e(t)]* should be identified with a particular variable for each specific physical domain which is working.
Table 1 shows the physical meanings of the variables considered in the general notation and their particular representation for different domains.
Once the system is represented in the form of *Bond-graph*, the state equations that govern its behaviour can be obtained directly as a first order differential equations in terms of generalized variables defined above, using simple and standardized procedures, regardless of the physical domain to which it belongs, even when interrelated across domains.
Bond Graph used a set of elements to model the real system such as:

- **Resistor**: This element represents situations where a lost of energy appears. (Electrical resistor, mechanical damper, Coulomb frictions, etc.). In these sorts of elements there is a relationship between flow and effort as the equation (7) shows. The value of "R" can be constant or function of any system parameter including time.

$$e(t) = R \cdot f(t) \tag{7}$$

- **Compliance:** This element represents the situations where a store of energy appears (electrical capacitors, mechanical springs, etc.). In these sorts of elements there is a relationship between effort and displacement variable as the equation (8) shows. The value of "K" can be constant or function of any system parameter including time.

$$e(t) = K \cdot q(t) \tag{8}$$

- **Inertia:** This element represents the relationship between the "flow" and Momentum (electrical coil, mass, moment of inertia, etc.) as the equation (9) shows. The value of "I" tends to be constant.

$$p(t) = I \cdot f(t) \tag{9}$$

- **Sources:** This element represents the energy sources. There are two kinds of sources: Flow source and Effort source.
- **Transformer:** A transformer adds no power but transforms it, such as an electrical transformer or a lever. Transformers represent those physical phenomena that are variation of the values of output flow and effort on the values of input flow and effort. If the transformation ratio is given by the "Tr" value, then the relationship between input and output is shown in Equation 10.

$$e_{output}(t) = T_r \cdot e_{input}(t) \qquad f_{output}(t) = \frac{1}{T_r} \cdot f_{input}(t) \tag{10}$$

Physical System	Effort Variable e(t)	Flow Variable f(t)	Momentum Variable p(t)	Displacement Variable q(t)
Mechanical Translation	Force F (N)	Speed V (m/s)	Momentum P (N s)	Displacement X (m)
Mechanical Rotation	Torque M (Nm)	Rotational speed w (Rad/s)	Angular Momentum H (N m s)	Angle q (Rad)
Electrical Systems	Voltage V (V)	Intensity I (A)	Current Flow F (V s)	Electrical Charge q (C)
Hydraulic Systems	Pressure P (N/m2)	Flow Q (m3/s)	Momentum R (N s/m2)	Volume V (m3)

Table 1. Generalized variables for different physical domains and units

Figure 2 shows the *Bond Graph* representation of the different basic elements available to model a system.

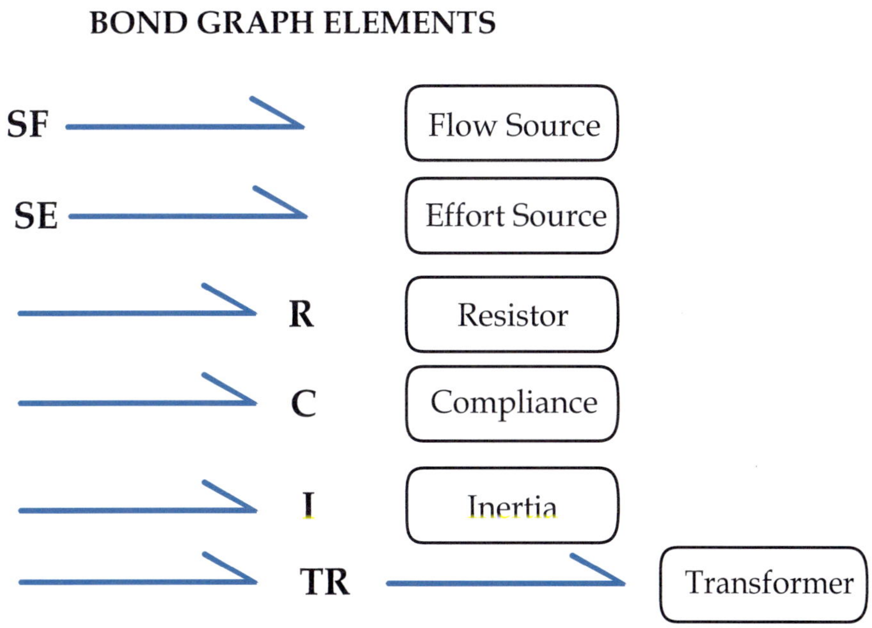

Fig. 2. *Bond Graph* basic elements

There are more elements in the *Bond Graph* method, but those showed above are enough for the following examples.

2.2 Mechanical example

In order to understand the *Bond Graph* method, a simple mechanical model will be used. Figure 3 illustrates a single degree of freedom (DOF) system composed by a rigid body that can only move up and down. This model is represented by a mass "m_1", a spring (K_1) and a damper (R_1). The source of energy is a known velocity of the ground $v_0(t)$. The output variable is the mass velocity $v_1(t)$.

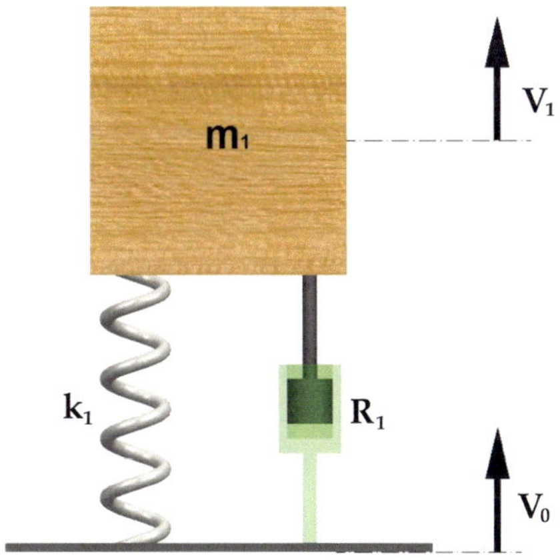

Fig. 3. One degree of Freedom System

Usually, the starting point to represent a real system as a *Bond Graph* diagram are the sources, in this case a flow source (ground velocity). The next step is to think about the power flows through the system components, power flows produced by the effort and flow variables. As figure 3 illustrates the spring and the damper are moved at a velocity that must be the difference between the mass velocity $v_1(t)$ and ground velocity $v_0(t)$. This means that a *"0"* junction must be used as figure 4 illustrates.
The spring is represented as a compliance bond and the damper as a resistance bond. Both components move at the same velocity, but each one needs different forces to move at this velocity. This means that a *"1"* junction must be used as figure 4 illustrates. Finally, the mass is represented as an inertia bond that moved at $v_1(t)$ velocity. Due to the fact that the system is under gravity of earth, an effort source must be used.
Bond Graph method calculates the flow and effort on each *Bond*, and uses as system variables the displacement associated to compliance (K_1) bond *[x(t)]* and momentum associated to inertia (m_1) b*ond [P(t)]*.

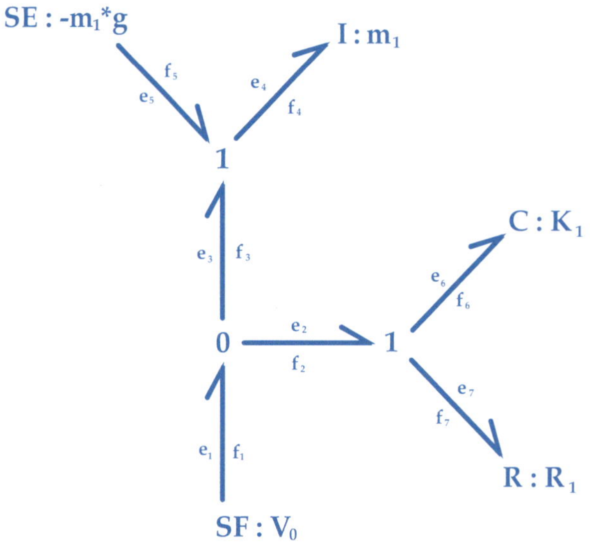

Fig. 4. *Bond Graph* of the one DOF system

According to the *Bond Graph* showed in figure 4, the flows in each bond are presented in the equations shown in (11):

$$
\begin{aligned}
f_1 &= V_0(t) \\
f_2 &= f_1 - f_3 = V_0(t) - \frac{P}{m_1} \\
f_3 &= f_4 = f_5 = \frac{P}{m_1} \\
f_6 &= f_7 = f_2 = V_0(t) - \frac{P}{m_1}
\end{aligned} \tag{11}
$$

The efforts in each bond are presented in the equations shown in (12).

$$\begin{aligned} &e_1 = e_2 = e_3 \\ &e_2 = e_6 + e_7 = K_1 \cdot X + R_1 \cdot \left(V_0(t) - \frac{P}{m_1} \right) \\ &e_7 = K_1 \cdot X \\ &e_6 = R_1 \cdot \left(V_0(t) - \frac{P}{m_1} \right) \\ &e_5 = -m_2 \cdot g \\ &e_4 = e_5 + e_3 = K_1 \cdot X + R_1 \cdot \left(V_0(t) - \frac{P}{m_1} \right) - m_1 \cdot g \end{aligned} \quad (12)$$

That system dynamic behaviour is represented by the following two equations shown in 13 and 14:

$$\frac{dX(t)}{dt} = f_7 = V_0(t) - \frac{P(t)}{m_1} \quad (13)$$

$$\frac{dP(t)}{dt} = e_4 = K_1 \cdot X(t) + \left(V_0(t) - \frac{P(t)}{m_1} \right) \cdot R_1 - m_1 \cdot g \quad (14)$$

These equations are achieved taking into account that the variation of the momentum is equal to the effort on the inertia bond, and the variation of the displacement is the flow in the compliance bond. These are two first order differential equations coupled as a function of the momentum [P(t)] associated to the inertia and displacement [X(t)] associated to the spring. These systems can be solved without major problems by using differential calculus.

3. Introduction to Simulink

Simulink is an environment for multidomain simulation and Model-Based Design for dynamic and embedded systems. It provides an interactive graphical environment and a customizable set of block libraries that allow to design, simulate, implement, and test a variety of time-varying systems, including communications, controls, signal processing, video processing, and image processing.

Simulink is integrated with *MATLAB*, providing immediate access to an extensive range of tools that make possible to develop algorithms, analyze and visualize simulations, create batch processing scripts, customize the modelling environment and define signal, parameters and test data.

With *Simulink*, a detailed block diagram of a system can be quickly created, modelled and maintained using a comprehensive set of predefined blocks. *Simulink* provides tools for hierarchical modelling, data management, and subsystem customization, making it easy to create concise, accurate representations, regardless of your system's complexity. *Simulink* software includes an extensive library of functions commonly used in modelling as:

- Continuous and discrete dynamics blocks, such as Integration and Unit Delay
- Algorithmic blocks, such as Sum, Product, and Lookup Table
- Structural blocks, such as Mux, Switch, and Bus Selector

Working directly in Simulink, these built-in blocks can be modified and new ones can be created and placed into customized libraries.
After building a model in *Simulink*, its dynamic behaviour can be simulated, and live results can be viewed. *Simulink* software provides several features and tools to ensure the speed and accuracy of the simulation, including fixed-step and variable-step solvers, a graphical debugger, and a model profiler.
All these features of the program allow generating a block model suitable to represent the *Bond Graph* model. The *Simulink* block model will solve the equations and allows the user to analyze the dynamic behaviour of the system.

4. Simulink application

After previous discussions about *Bond Graph* method and Simulink, this section explains how to use the benefits of *Simulink* to set up and solve the equations that manage system behaviour.
The procedure consist in convert the real model into a *Bond Graph* model and then translate it to the *Simulink* block diagrams, as can be seen in Figure 5.

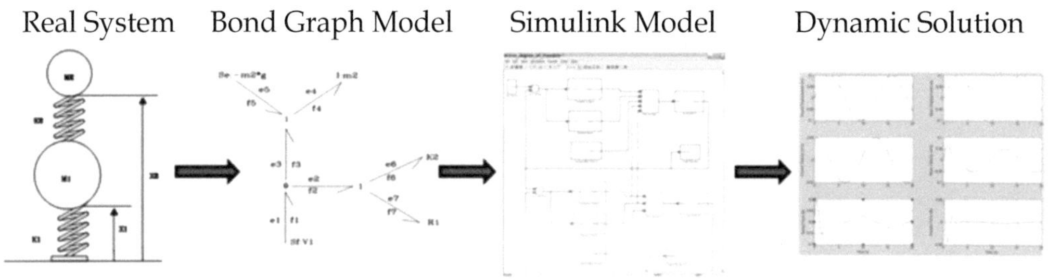

Fig. 5. Procedure to Analyze the Dynamic Behaviour of a System

Simulink provides a block-diagram that allows users to represent the equations involved on the *Bond Graph* model. These blocks of *Simulink* will be used to represent the action that occurs in each element of the *Bond Graph* model.
The different *Simulink* blocks that will be used to build the *Bond Graph* model are being described following.
It is assumed that readers know the basic operation of *MATLAB* and *Simulink*, so no details will be given regarding how to open the program, select Simulink blocks and build models from these *Simulink* blocks.
Figure 6 shows the main window of *Simulink* to build a new model, and the available blocks that have been selected. As it can be seen, very few blocks are needed to generate models.
From the working window of *MATLAB, Simulink* is accessed by clicking the icon at the top of the screen. Then, the user has to select open a new model and a new workspace appears.
From the *Simulink* library, the necessary blocks are selected and dragged to the working window. The blocks used for simple models are as follows:

- **Sources library:** *Time, Constant and Signal Generator*. These blocks provide an interface that allows the user to input energy into the system through a known flow or effort. *Simulink* provides different kinds of sources such as constant value, sinusoidal source, chirp signal, ramp, etc.

- **Continuous library:** *Derivate and Integrator*. These blocks provide an interface that allows to derive or integrate time-dependent variables of the dynamic system.
- **Math Operation library**: *Add, Divide, Product*. These blocks provide an interface that allows to add, subtract, multiply, divide, etc., time-dependent variables of the dynamic system.
- **Sinks library**: *XY Graph and To Workspace*. These blocks provide an interface that allows to display and store the variables of the dynamic system in order to analyze them.

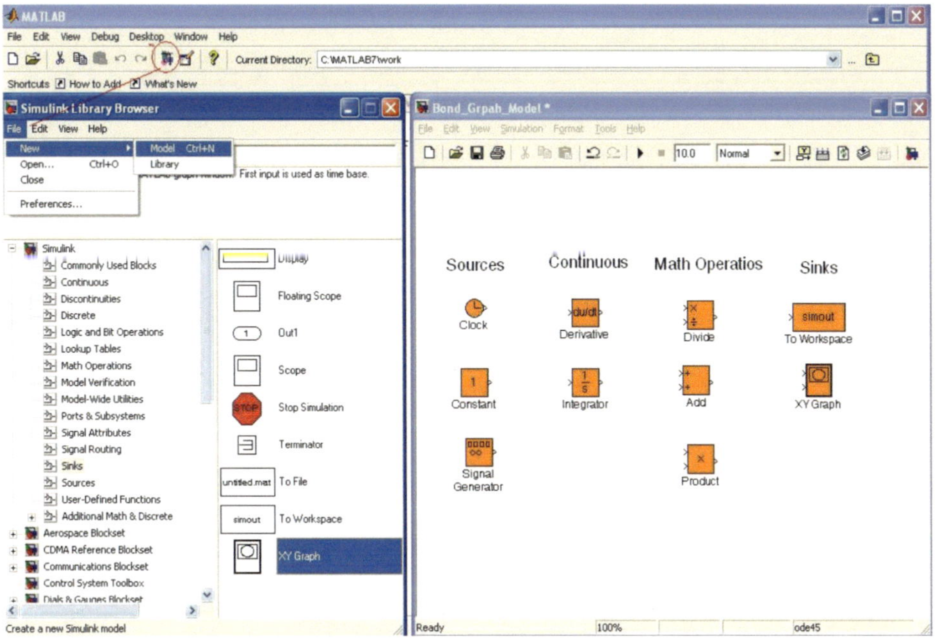

Fig. 6. Simulink working model window

Although there are many more blocks that the user can select and use to generate models, only those previously described are used in this work.

Taking into account the effect of each *Bond Graph* element on the flow and effort variables, the idea is to generate *Simulink* elements that perform the same actions.

Bond Graph and *Simulink* allows to work with discrete time dynamic systems, for instance, it is possible to simulate a variable damping shock absorber with two damping states (hard and soft). These two states could change as a function of other variable of the system.

On the other hand, as the equations and variables used for all physical systems are the same, it is possible to combine, in one model, mechanical and electrical systems or mechanical and hydraulic, etc. No changes are necessary in Simulink, just selecting the adequate block.

The first step is to select the necessary blocks to simulate the *Bond Graph* element behaviour. Then, it is possible to generate a new Simulink block through the "*sub-system create*" feature, that groups blocks to generate a user-defined one. Figure 7 illustrates how to create a subsystem: select the group of blocks to generate the subsystem and with the right button of the mouse, select the option "*create subsystem*". Then a new "S*ubsystem*" block appears.

In order to facilitate the user to enter parameter values, another *Simulink* feature called "*mask subsystem*" can be used.

The path to enter this feature is to click the right button of the mouse on the *Subsystem block* and select the option "*edit mask*". The window shown in Figure 8 will appear and the user has to select the tab "*parameters*". By clicking on the first icon on the left, a new line is added. This line allows entering the name of the variable and its abbreviation. It must be matched with what it was entered in the original block. It is necessary to define as many variables as defined in the *Subsystem* and variable names must be kept. Variable name must be introduced in the label called "Variable", and the label "Prompt" allows to introduce a variable description.

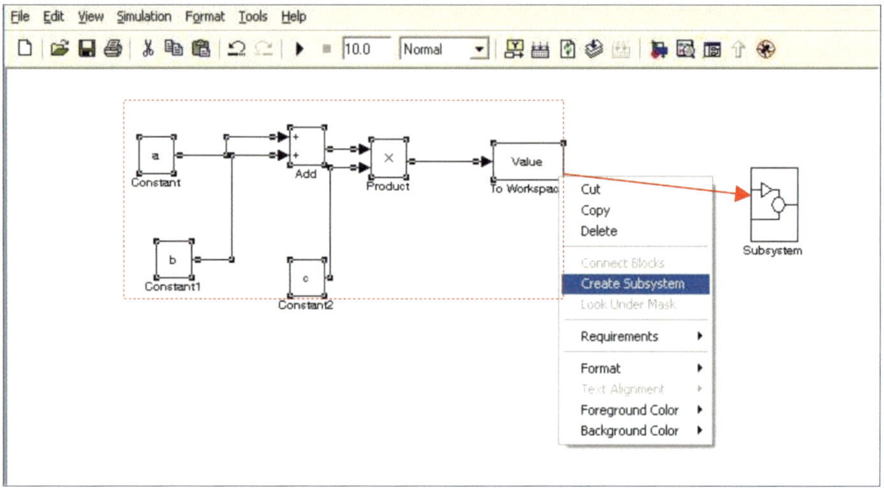

Fig. 7. Subsystem generation

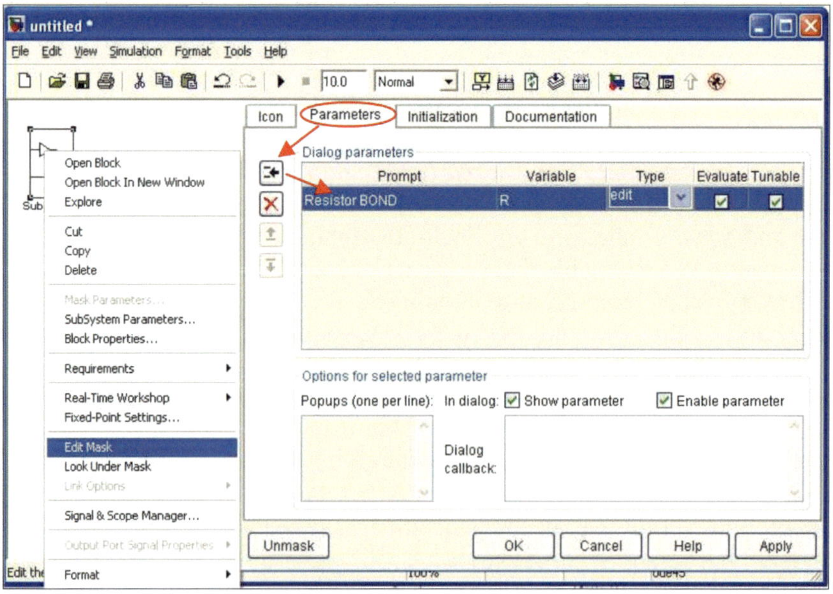

Fig. 8. Mask editor

Thus, when the user clicks on a *Subsystem block*, a new window appears to enter the parameter value as shown in Figure 9.

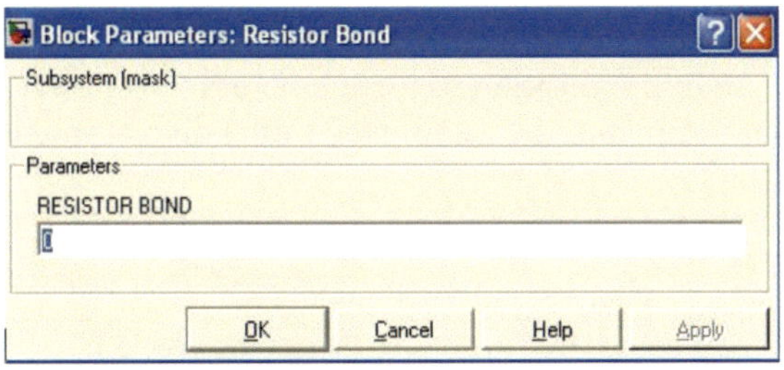

Fig. 9. Editor window for parameters

With exposed blocks, it is possible to generate the different elements to create a *Bond Graph* model following the next rules:

Source bond

This element, as has been already indicated, provides energy to the system, as a known flow or a known effort. So, the *Simulink* source blocks can be used directly.

Resistor bond

It provides an interface that allows the user to simulate a component that dissipates energy from the system. The input block is a known flow that is multiplied by the resistance value in order to obtain the output, which is a known effort as Figure 10 illustrates. The R value could be constant or variable. In each case, the necessary block is different (For instance a "*Lookup Table*").

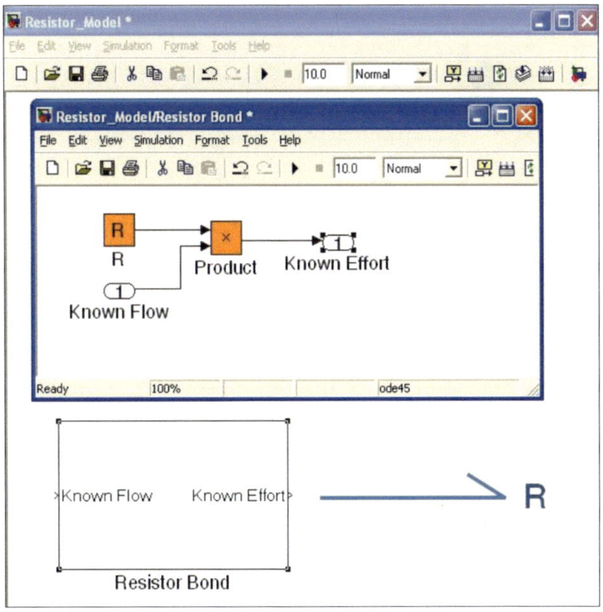

Fig. 10. Resistor bond

Compliance bond

It provides an interface that allows the user to simulate a component that stores energy from the system. The input block is a known flow that is integrated in order to obtain the displacement and multiplied by the compliance value to return a known effort as Figure 11 illustrates. To establish the initial position of the inertia at the beginning of the simulation, it is possible to preload the compliance by adding the initial displacement.

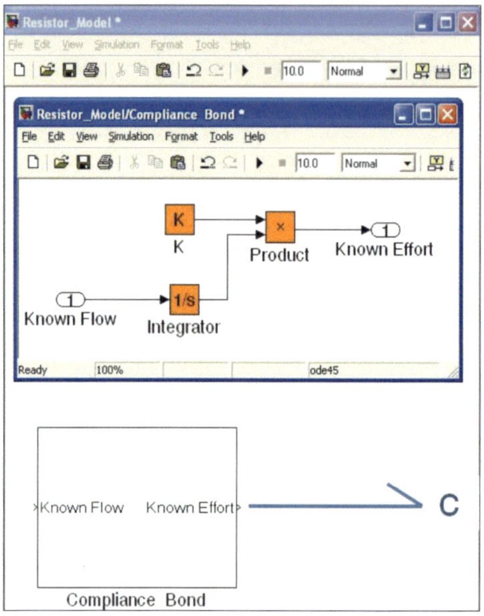

Fig. 11. Compliance bond

Inertia bond

It provides an interface that allows the user to simulate the system inertias. The input block is a known effort that is divided by the inertia value to obtain the flow derivate as equation (15) shows.

$$e(t) = I \cdot \frac{df(t)}{dt} \Rightarrow f(t) = \frac{1}{I} \cdot \int e(t)dt \tag{15}$$

Then, the value is integrated to return to a known flow as illustrated in Figure 12.

Junction "1" and "0"

They provide an interface that allows the user to simulate the junctions to sum flows or efforts. Both blocks are simple *Simulink's "add"* blocks. It is possible to add more input connections.

Transformer bond

It provides an interface that allows the user to simulate elements that modify the value of the flow and the effort. The input blocks are a known flow and effort, multiplied by the transformer ratio. Its inverse is calculated to obtain the flow and effort at the output. Figure 13 illustrates the block diagram.

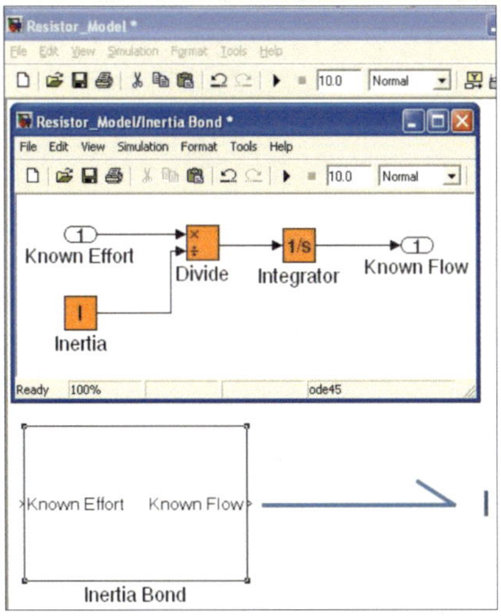

Fig. 12. Inertia bond

Display block

It provides a block that allows the user to store the system's variables in order to analyze and visualize results once the simulations are completed.

Finally, the working window with the blocks needed to create a model is presented in Figure 14. Three new blocks has been added, one of them (*XY Graph*) to display the variables of the model during the simulation at real time, the second one (*Simout*) to store the results in computer memory to be viewed later and the third one is a clock to manage the simulation time.

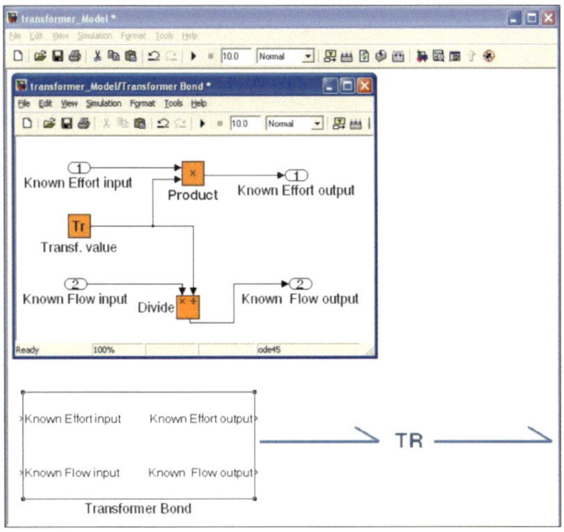

Fig. 13. Transformer bond

Finally, through *Simulink* interface, it is possible to select the method to integrate the equations, the simulation time and the integration step in order to adapt them to the user needs.

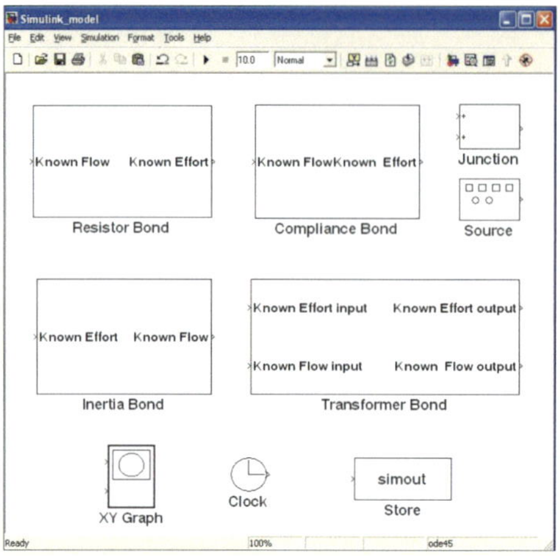

Fig. 14. Simulink Blocks built from Bond Graph Elements

5. Application example

This section illustrates how *Bond Graph* and *Simulink* were used by mechanical engineering students to analyze, in an easy way, the dynamic behaviour of some typical systems.
The analysis begins with the example of a one degree of freedom system, like the one used to introduce the *Bond Graph* method in the previous section (Figure 3). Table 2 shows the model parameters used as inputs.
Units are expressed in international unit system. It is assumed that the positive displacement of the mass is upward. Because of that, the weight force is negative.

Parameter	Value	Unit
Mass (m_1)	1	kg
Spring ratio (K_1)	9.8	N/m
Spring initial position (X_0)	1	m
Damper ratio (R_1)	1.88	N s/m
Weight (Se)	-9.8	N
Power Source System (Sf)	Variable	m/s

Table 2. Parameters for a One Degree of Freedom System

Figure 15 illustrates the *Simulink* block diagram of the one degree of freedom system based on *Bond Graph* method developed in Figure 4.
The *Flow* source (ground velocity) is connected to a sum block (*1 junction*) that calculates the difference of velocities between the ground (V_0) and the mass (V_1). This velocity is the input (known flow) for the spring (*Compliance Bond*) and the damper (*Resistor Bond*), that move at the same speed. They return to the system the spring force (F_k) and the damper force (F_r) that are connected to a sum block (*0 junction*) to calculate, by adding gravity force (*Effort Source*), the equilibrium force. This force will be the input to the *Inertia block* in order to calculate the velocity of the mass (V_1) that is used as an iterative loop to calculate the difference in velocity between the ground and the mass.

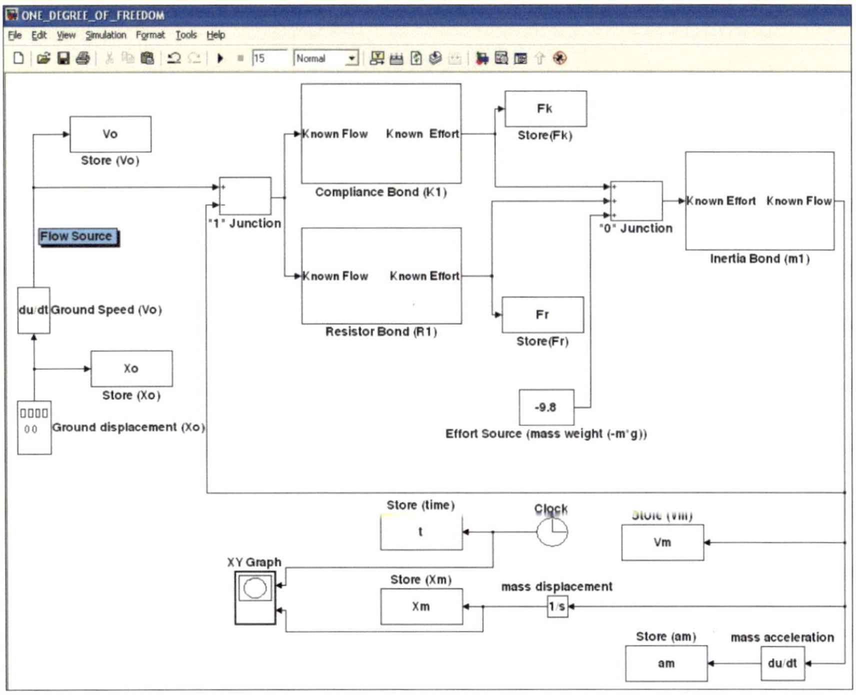

Fig. 15. One Degree of Freedom Model

The analysis parameters are the following:

- F_k Spring Force.
- F_r Damping Force
- X_m Mass Displacement
- V_m Mass Speed
- a_m Mass Acceleration
- X_0 Ground Displacement
- V_0 Ground Speed
- t Time

All of them have been stored in variables with their own names in order to analyze them and compare results by plotting graphs.

Due to the fact that the input to the system must be a flow (ground speed) it is necessary to derivate the ground displacement in order to obtain a flow source.

To decide the kind of solver that will be used to integrate the equations, it is necessary to select the *simulation* menu and then select the option *configuration parameters*. A new window will open as figure 16 shows. Simulation time, solver options and the sample time can be introduced in this window. For instance, the *Runge-kutta* integration method has been selected in this case, with a fixed step of 0.01 second. This method has been selected because it works with first-order differential equations and the convergence of this method is good without excessive computer time consumption, but any other method available in Simulink can be chosen since it will not influence the quality of the result. A step of 0.01 s allows to analyze the result with enough resolution to apply, for instance, a Fast Fourier Transform (FFT) without loss of information; but the user can try to adjust the best in each case.

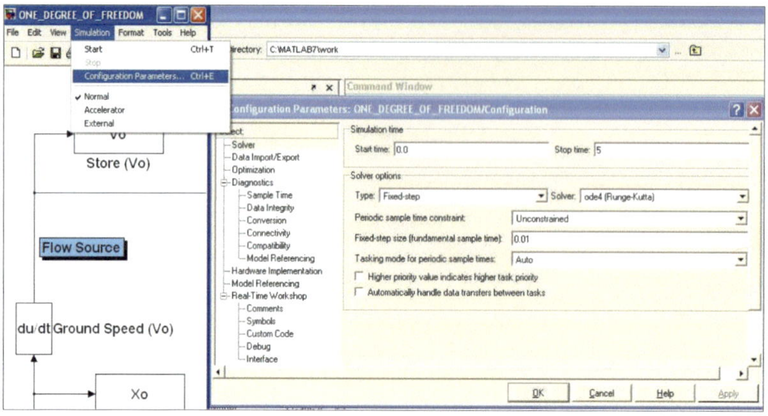

Fig. 16. Solver selection

Four different situations of the example model will be analyzed to show the advantages of using *Simulink* to generate, solve and analyze the results.

5.1 Free vibration

Firstly, the ground is stopped (v_o= 0 m/s) and the spring is not preloaded (*Xo* = 0 m), this means that the mass will fall on top of the spring and therefore the system moves (this is known as free vibration). Under the damper effect, the system will stop after a few cycles due to the lost of energy in each cycle.

The powerful tool of *MATLAB* to plot the results, the *MATLAB* Graphics Editor, will be used. Every variable has been stored in *MATLAB* workspace and is available to be represented. To access the graphics editor, the workspace flange must be selected in the *MATLAB* window, as figure 17 shows. Every available variable is showed in this window. The desired variable is selected with the button of the mouse. By clicking in the plot icon, a new window with the variable plotted will open. Then, it is possible to modify the chart by adding new variables, changing the scale or including legends.

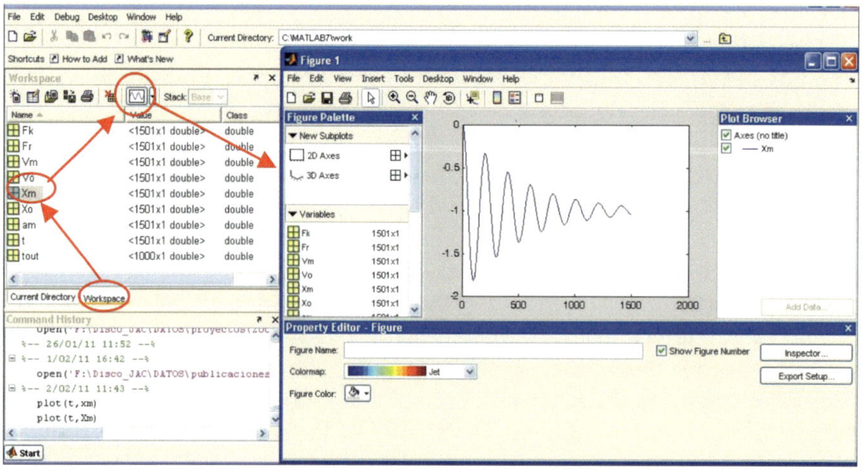

Fig. 17. *Matlab* graphics editor

Figure 18 illustrates the system behaviour. Different values have been analyzed, such as: ground displacement and velocity, mass displacement and acceleration and the force in the spring and the damper.

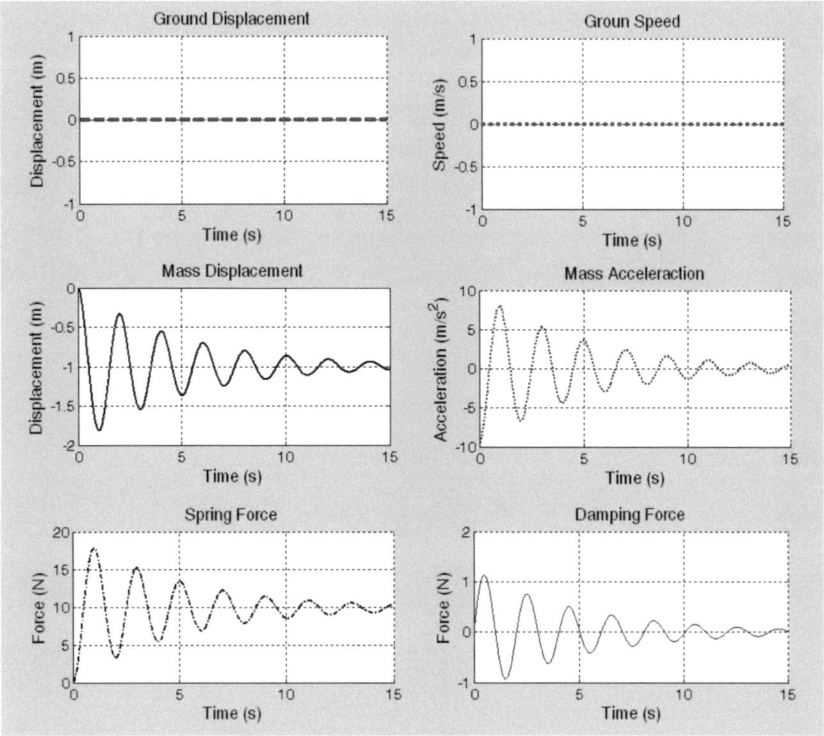

Fig. 18. Results for the One Degree of Freedom Model with no Ground Displacement

By looking the different graphs of the variables that have been plotted, it is possible to analyze what is happening to the model when the mass can move freely.
Initially, the mass falls and compresses the spring. Then, when the inertia and gravity forces achieve a value equal to the spring force, the mass returns to the steady state position. This movement is repeated but, as consequence of the damper, the system loses energy and finally stops after few cycles. When the system stops, the spring is loaded with a force equal to the mass weight (9.8 N) so the mass stabilizes at minus one meter from the initial position.

5.2 Forced vibration below natural frequency

In the second simulation, the system starts with the spring preloaded (Xo = 1m), and the ground has a sinusoidal movement with amplitude of 0.1 meter and a frequency of 0.1 Hz (This is known as forced vibrations) The natural frequency of the system, according to the equation 16, is under the frequency of the excitation

$$F(Hz) = \frac{1}{2\pi}\sqrt{\frac{K_1}{m_1}} = 0.498Hz \tag{16}$$

To change the model parameters, the user has to click on the block and put the new values. Taking into account that the system excitation is under the natural frequency, the mass movement will be similar to the ground movement as figure 19 illustrates.

As figure 19 shows, the system movement has a transitional state before stabilizing and oscillating around the initial position. Since the difference between the mass velocity and the ground velocity is very small, the energy dissipated by the damper is small too.

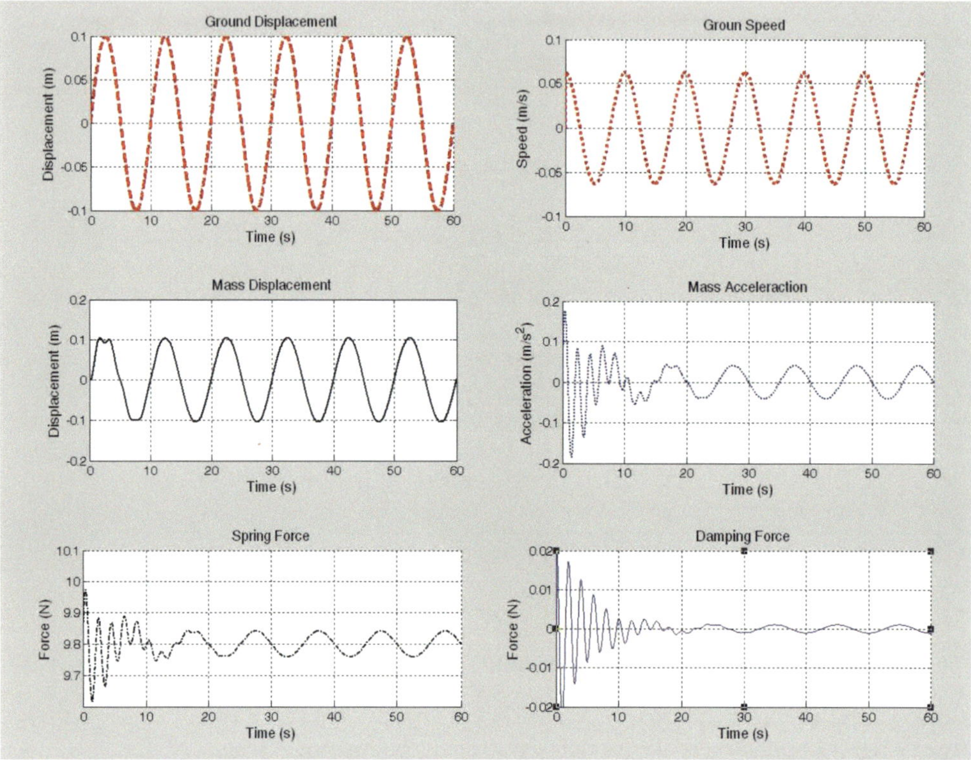

Fig. 19. Results for the One Degree of Freedom Model with Ground Displacement below the Natural Frequency

5.3 Forced vibration at natural frequency

In the third simulation, the sinusoidal movement of the ground is the natural frequency of the system. In this case, the movement of the mass is seven times higher than the ground movement due to the resonance phenomenon, as figure 20 illustrates. Again, after a little transitional period, the system achieves the steady state. Now, the energy dissipated on the damper is high as well as the force at the spring

5.4 Forced vibration up to natural frequency

In this simulation, the ground moves at a frequency (2 Hz) that is higher than the natural frequency of the system. Figure 21 illustrates the variable analysis.

In this case, the mass movement is lower than the ground movement, but as both of them are out of phase, the damper has to dissipate more energy than in the case analyzed in 5.2.

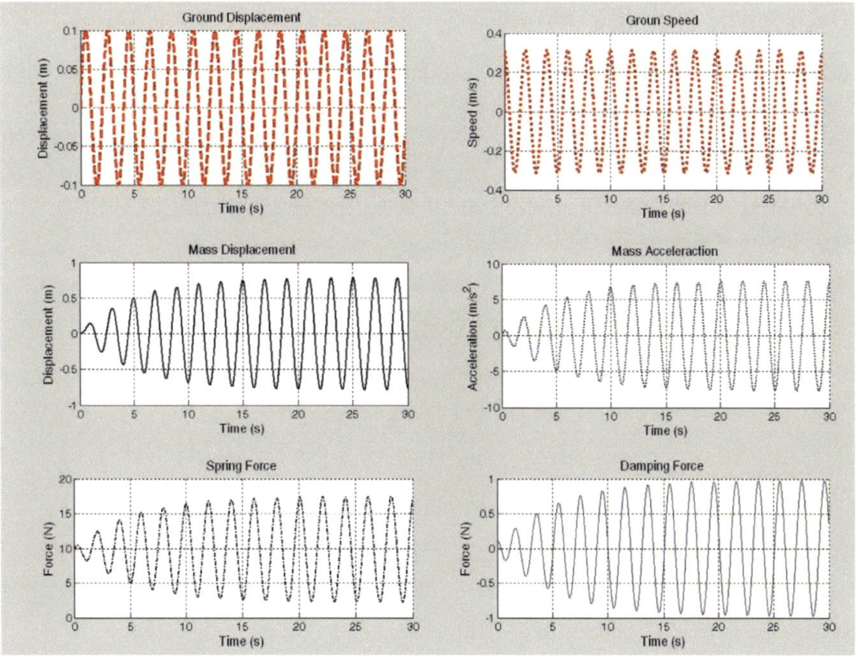

Fig. 20. Results for the One Degree of Freedom Model with Ground Displacement at Natural Frequency

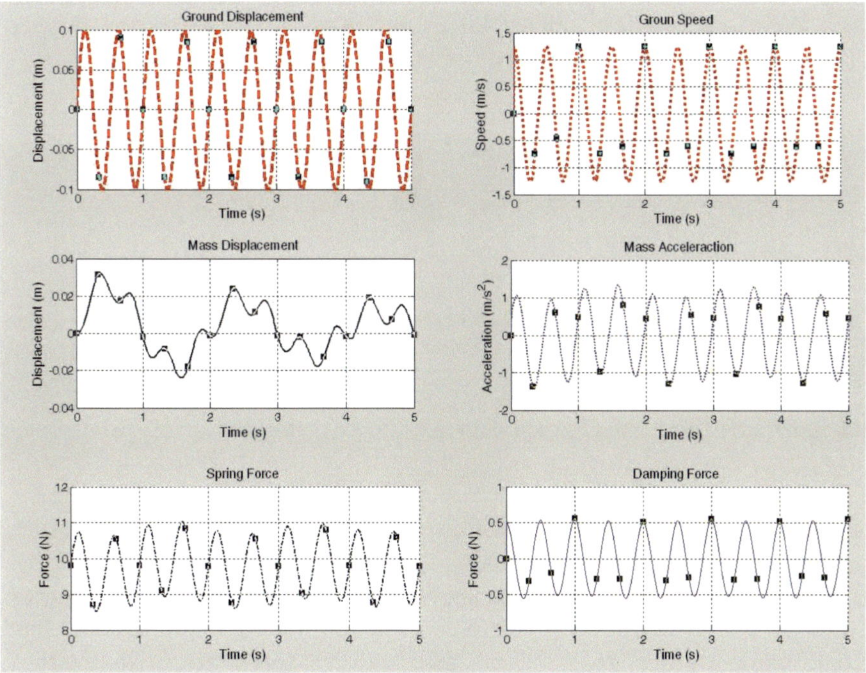

Fig. 21. Results for the One Degree of Freedom Model with Ground Displacement greater that the Natural Frequency

6. Two Degrees of Freedom Model

Finally, a more complex model will be simulated to demonstrate one of the advantages of the *Bond Graph* method and *Simulink* application. From the one degree of freedom model, the complexity of the system will be increased by adding an additional degree of freedom.
Figure 22 illustrates the physical model for a two degrees of freedom system created by adding two single degree of freedom systems.

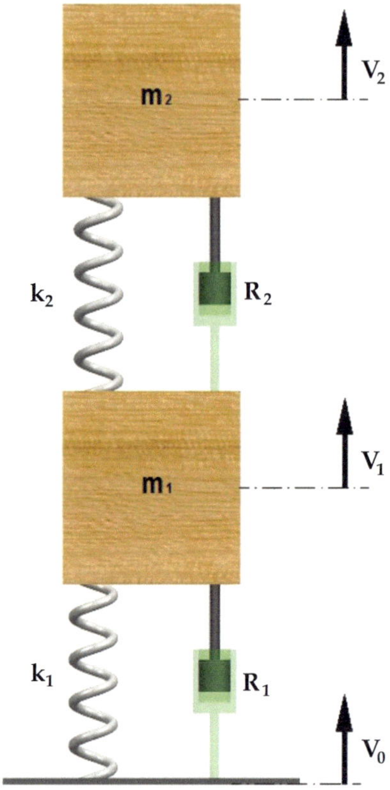

Fig. 22. Two Degrees of Freedom System

Figure 23 illustrates the *Bond Graph* model for the two degrees of freedom system. The system has been developed from the original one of one degree of freedom. The new part has been drawn in red:
As illustrated in figure 24, *Simulink* model it is relatively easy to built since the user only has to copy and paste the original model to obtain a system with two degrees of freedom.
The new part of the model is drawn in red. Only few lines, drawn in blue, are necessary to connect both parts of the model. The new blue lines transmit the effort from the spring (K_2) and the damper (R_2) to the *"zero junction"* that feed the inertia 1(m_1). The inertia 1 block returns a known flow to a *"one junction"* in order to calculate the velocity difference between the two masses that feed the spring K_2 and damper R_2.

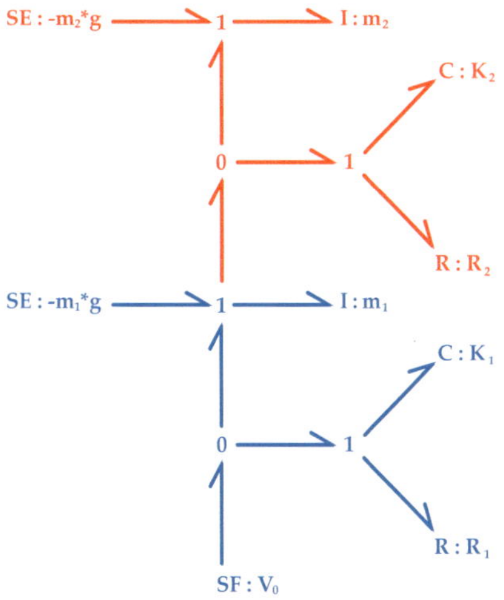

Fig. 23. Bond Graph chart of the Two Degree of Freedom System

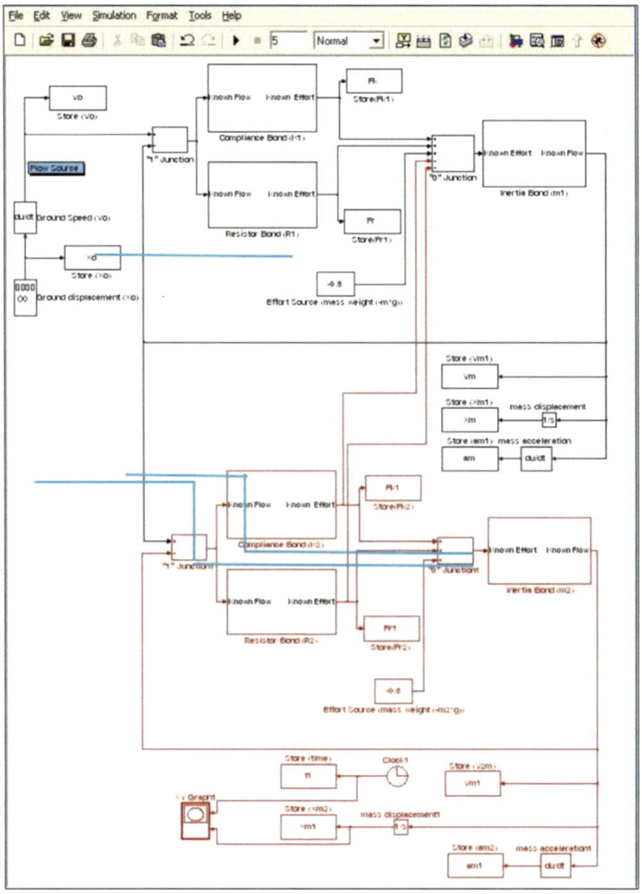

Fig. 24. Simulink blocks of a Two Degrees of Freedom System

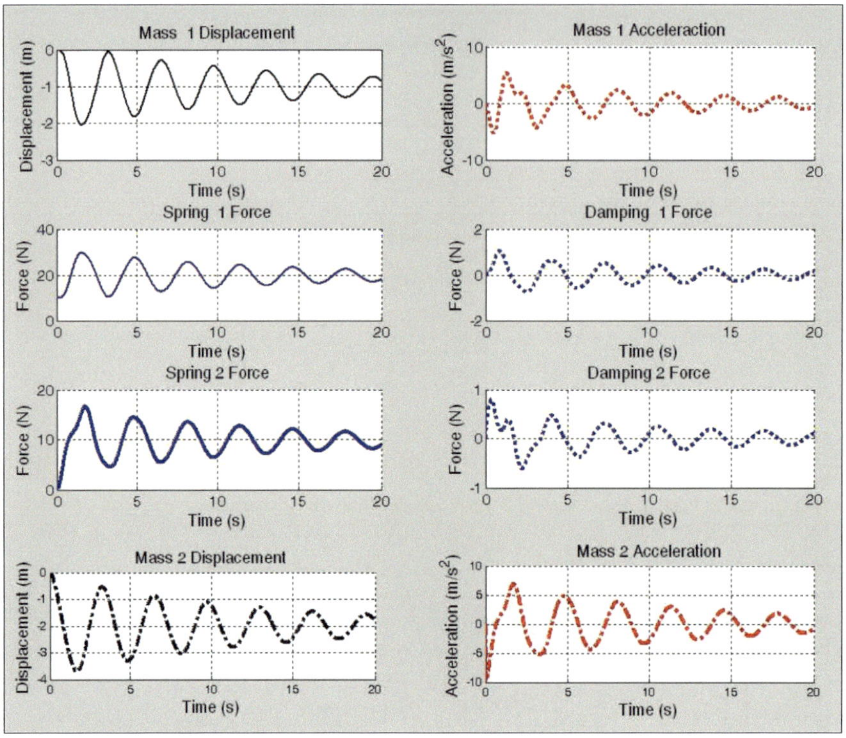

Fig. 25. Two Degrees of Freedom Results

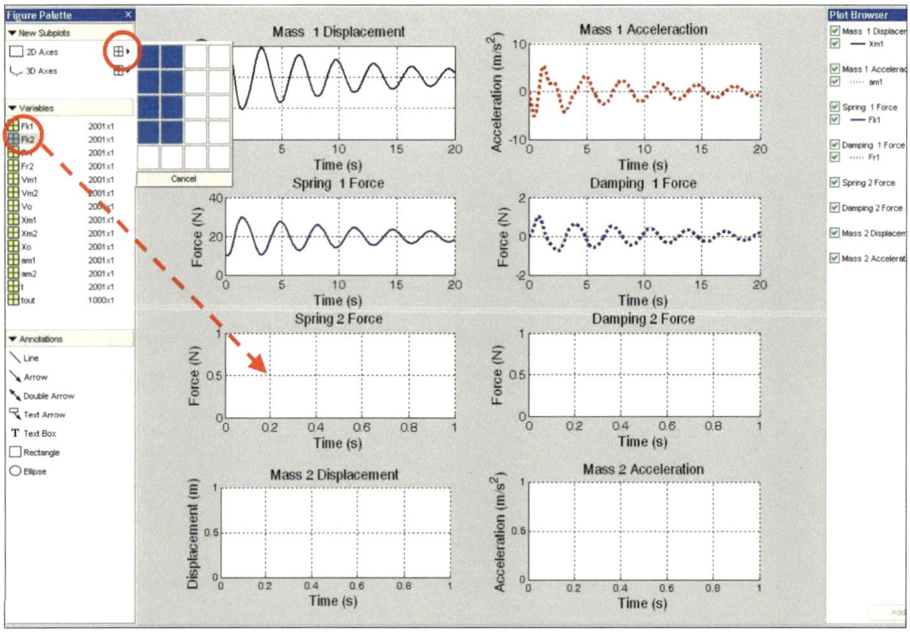

Fig. 26. How to add more plots

It will be necessary to rename the variables of the second part of the model. This requires accessing the *"mask editor"* by clicking with the right button of the mouse in each block, and changing the variable name (m_2, K_2, R_2 ...).
The model will be analyzed assuming that initially the ground is stopped, the spring 1 is preloaded, the spring 2 unloaded and mass m_2 falls over it. Figure 25 illustrates the results, analysing the mass displacement and the forces on the springs and the dampers.
In order to obtain the new graphics, the user has to open the plot window and add as many graphics as needed by clicking on the icon "*created titled subplots*" as figure 26 shows.
After that, the desired variable must be clicked and dragged to the blank plot window in which it is going to be represented.
Likewise, by changing model parameters, different inputs can be simulated and the results can be comfortably analyzed.
On the other hand, more complex models can be generated by adding more degrees of freedom following the procedure shown in this example.

7. Conclusion

This work presents a method to apply the *Bond Graph* technique to implement and solve the dynamic equations of a dynamic system by taking advantage of *MATLAB* and *Simulink.*
This method allows engineering students to quickly and easily gain experience and knowledge in systems dynamics and to learn which are the forces, accelerations, velocities and displacements of each component and each degree of freedom of the system.
It is very easy for the students to test the changes in the system and analyze how the results change.
The proposed method is designed with a user-friendly Windows interface in *MATLAB's Simulink.* The most important benefits of using the proposed method are the following:

- **MATLAB** toolboxes and functions can be used, allowing the program to simulate complex systems.
- It is easy to work with differential equations, matrixes and vectors.
- Students do not have to determine the dynamic equations, since the *Bond Graph* method allows to transfer from the graphics model to the block model the equations involved in the dynamic problem.
- *MATLAB* tools are easy to use when analyzing and comparing the model's results by numerical or graphics outputs.

It is noticeable the facility to generate complex models from simples ones and the facility to change the model parameters in order to obtain different results.
The user does not need to have a deep knowledge of differential equations to develop the expressions that represent the behaviour of the system and to solve them.
On the other hand, the *MATLAB* tools allow to generate models with complex behaviour, for instance, dampers with non-linear behaviour.

8. References

Blundell, A. (1982). *Bond Graph for modelling Engineering Systems*, Ellis Horword Publishers., UK

BONDLAB.PH (2007). Department Silicon Facility (DSF). http://ssd-rd.web.cern.ch/ssd-rd/bondlab/default.htm, (September 2007)

CAMP-G. (2007) *Computer Aided Modelling, Design and Simulation,* http://www.bondgraph.com, (September 2007)

Depcik, C. and Assanis, D.N., (2004). *Graphical user interfaces in an engineering educational environment,* Computer Applications in Engineering Education, Vol. 13, No. 1, pp. 48–59.

Karnopp, D., (1979). *On the Order of a Physical Model,* Trans. ASME Journal of Syst. Dyn. Meas. & Control. Vol 101, nº 3, pp. 102 - 118, ISSN: 0022-0434, New York, USA

Margolis, D. (1985). *Introduction into Bond Graph,* 3rd Seminar on Advanced Vehicle Dynamics. Amalfim Italy

The MathWorks Inc., (2009). *Creating Simulink Models,* http://www.mathworks.co.kr/matlabcentral/newsreader

Thoma, J.U., (1985). *Introduction to Bond Graph and their applications,* Pergamon Oxford. ISBN: 0080239366, New York, USA

TUTSIM (2007). *Technical University of Twente SIMulation,* University of Twente. http://www.20sim.com/tutsim.html, (September 2007)

Vera, C., Aparicio, F., Felez, J. (1993). *Simulación de sistemas dinámicos mediante la técnica del Bond Graph,* Sección de Publicaciones de la E.T.S.I.I. de Madrid, Universidad Politécnica de Madrid, ISBN: 84-7884-082-1, Spain

12

Solving Fluid Dynamics Problems with Matlab

Rui M. S. Pereira[1] and Jitesh S. B. Gajjar[2]
[1]*University of Minho*
[2]*University of Manchester*
[1]*Portugal*
[2]*United Kingdom*

1. Introduction

MATLAB (short for Matrix Laboratory) was created by Cleve Moler and Jack Little in the 1970's. It is a programming language for technical computing. Its environment is easy to work with, the syntax is very simple and intuitive, it has powerful toolboxes to treat many different problems in engineering, and it allows us to produce fantastic graphics as the programme runs. It also allows us to create a graphical interface (via graphical user interfaces - GUIs) that gives our programme a look that is very close to professional software.

Because of many of the mentioned features, a MATLAB code can be very compact, allowing anyone to have "the big picture" of any code without have to look at all its details. Another great advantage of Matlab is that, if the code is written in a vectorized form, the code can run much faster than if it was written in the traditional form (*'a la C/fortran'*). The fact that MATLAB allows us to use a powerful toolbox for sparse matrices, is also a great advantage since, many traditional linear algebra operations can be highly improved, allowing the codes to run much faster than it would run with the traditional linear algebra functions.

In our work we have made extensive use of MATLAB to do 'proof of concept' studies, especially when developing new algorithms and techniques for solving systems of coupled nonlinear partial differential equations, such as those which arise in fluid dynamics. This includes, for instance, codes for investigating instabilities in lid-driven cavities, Boppana and Gajjar (2010), instabilities in flow past circular cylinders, Boppana and Gajjar (2011), and transonic flow past aerofoils Pereira and Gajjar (2010). In some cases MATLAB is used in its own right for solving small problems, but the fact that MATLAB is an interpreted language means that for increasing problem sizes, the MATLAB version of the code can be much slower than equivalent versions in other languages especially when one is dealing with very large sparse matrices. On the other hand the beauty of MATLAB is that much of the hard work is buried in the simple syntax and hidden from the user. An example of this is the use of the backslash operator for solving linear systems. Whether the system is sparse or full, the manner in which the equations are solved is hidden from the user and this greatly facilitates code development. In the equivalent fortran versions of the code the replacement for the '\' operation requires considerable work and the code translation process is no longer a trivial exercise.

In this chapter we will discuss the use of hybrid spectral methods to solve two and three-dimensional problems using MATLAB. There is an excellent book by Trefethen (2000) which discusses the application of spectral methods using MATLAB to solve ordinary and partial differential equations, and which provides the foundation for the techniques described below.

To motivate the ideas we first consider the solution of a model elliptic equation of the form

$$a(x,y)\psi_{xx} + b(x,y)\psi_{yy} + c(x,y)\psi_x + e(x,y)\psi_y + f(x,y)\psi = g(x,y),$$

say with Dirichlet boundary conditions in a rectangular domain. To obtain a numerical solution to this problem the first step is to choose an appropriate method and discretization. In our work we have used a combination of spectral methods in one or two dimensions and high order finite difference methods in another dimension. The main reasons for this choice are that a hybrid approach combines the accuracy of spectral methods together with flexibility in comparison to using spectral methods on their own. One restriction with the use of spectral methods is that one needs to use somewhat simplified geometries. A hybrid approach gives more flexibility in this respect. Another important reason stems from consideration of the type of matrix patterns which arise. With finite differences in say the x direction and spectral collocation in the y direction, the coefficient matrix with the unknowns ordered in terms of increasing y values for a fixed x value, has a particular sparsity pattern dependent on the order of the finite-differencing used. Second order finite-differencing leads to a a block tridiagonal matrix whilst with fourth-order finite differences, the matrix is block-pentadiagonal of the form:

$$\mathbf{A}_q\mathbf{\Psi}_{q-2} + \mathbf{B}_q\mathbf{\Psi}_{q-1} + \mathbf{C}_q\mathbf{\Psi}_q + \mathbf{D}_q\mathbf{\Psi}_{q+1} + \mathbf{E}_q\mathbf{\Psi}_{q+2} = \mathbf{R}_q, \quad q = 0, 1, ..., M. \tag{1}$$

Here $\mathbf{\Psi}_q$ is the vector of unknowns at location $x = x_q$, $M+1$ is typically the number of points in the x direction and the block matrices are of size $N+1$ by $N+1$ where $N+1$ spectral points are used.

Using MATLAB it is not too difficult to generate a short code to solve the above discrete system and the book by Trefethen (2000) gives plenty of such examples. The problem becomes more challenging when N and M become large, as for example in some fluid flow applications where large N, M values are needed to resolve regions of the flow where the solution changes very rapidly. When using a large number of points the sparse matrix facilities of MATLAB come into their own. The whole coefficient matrix does not need to be stored and by declaring this as a sparse matrix, only the non-zero entries of the block matrices are calculated. This avoids having to store a very large and sparse matrix which can quickly lead to memory problems.

Increasing the order of the scheme leads to increased bandwidths. This sparsity pattern can be exploited for 2nd, 4th or even 6th finite-differencing with a *direct* solver. However, with spectral methods in two directions, unless the differential operator involved has a special form, it is not immediately possible to utilize the sparse nature of the matrix. Whilst this does not pose any intrinsic difficulties if one is coding in MATLAB, with increased number of points the solution phase can become very memory intensive and requires a lot of processor time. The use of the hybrid approach in our work is motivated in part by the observation that the sparse matrix structure can be exploited to write efficient solvers, which not only work well with MATLAB, but can be coded directly in other languages. MATLAB provides for an excellent environment in which one can test and develop solvers of this type.

The above techniques have been successfully applied to investigate a whole range of different flow problems governed by the Navier-Stokes and related equations. In the first example we consider the onset of instability in the lid-driven cavity flow. MATLAB was used to generate results on coarse grids and do preliminary eigenvalue computations. For very fine grids, the

computations were performed in Fortran 95. The problem is described in detail in Boppana and Gajjar (2010).
The second problem concerns the onset of instability in the flow past a row of circular cylinders. Again the same technqiues have been used but for a more complicated geometry. This problem is described in detail in Boppana and Gajjar (2011).
The third problem we discuss concerns the inviscid transonic flows past thin airfoils. Here the governing equations are nonlinear and of mixed type and the flow can contain shock wave discontinuities for certain parameter values. The full details are given in Pereira and Gajjar (2010). The same methods as described above are used except now type differencing needs to be incorporated to allow for the different flow behaviours in regions of subsonic and supersonic flow. The method is fast and very robust and we are able to compute steady flows with strong shocks. The code was written in MATLAB, using vectorization when possible, and, in order to produce a good interface with the user, we used GUIs (graphical user interfaces) from MATLAB. The result was a fast and accurate code, with the extra bonus of a very good interface with the user, without a lot of effort in terms of programming. The fact that graphical results can be shown immediately, saves us a lot of work, both on the analysis of the results and on its presentation.

2. Instabilities in lid-driven cavities

To motivate the techniques used in our work we first consider a model elliptic equation of the form

$$a(x,y)\psi_{xx} + b(x,y)\psi_{yy} + c(x,y)\psi_x + e(x,y)\psi_y + f(x,y)\psi = g(x,y) \tag{2}$$

with say Dirichlet boundary conditions in a square domain $0 \leq x, y \leq 1$. It is assumed that the functions a, b, c, e, f, g are smooth functions of x and y.
The discrete solution to the equations will be obtained at a set of grid points on an $(M+1) \times (N+1)$ grid say with the nodes, $x = x_j, \quad j = 0, \ldots, M$ with $x_1 = 0, x_M = 1$, and $y = y_k, \quad 0 \leq k \leq N$ with $y_0 = 0, y_N = 1$, and at these points we set $\psi_{j,k} = \psi(x_j, y_k)$.
We will assume that derivatives in the $x-$ and $y-$ directions may be approximated as

$$\frac{\partial \psi}{\partial x}(x_j, y_k) = \sum_{q=0}^{M} (\mathbf{D}_x)_{j,q}\psi_{q,k}, \qquad \frac{\partial^2 \psi}{\partial x^2}(x_j, y_k) = \sum_{q=0}^{M} (\mathbf{D}_{xx})_{j,q}\psi_{q,k},$$

$$\frac{\partial \psi}{\partial y}(x_j, y_k) = \sum_{q=0}^{M} (\mathbf{D}_y)_{k,q}\psi_{j,q}, \qquad \frac{\partial^2 \psi}{\partial y^2}(x_j, y_k) = \sum_{q=0}^{M} (\mathbf{D}_{yy})_{k,q}\psi_{j,q}. \tag{3}$$

Given the type and order of discretisation, the elements of the matrices $\mathbf{D}_x, \mathbf{D}_{xx}, \mathbf{D}_y, \mathbf{D}_{yy}$ are known. For example with second-order central finite differences, at an interior point of a uniform grid in x with $\Delta_x = x_j - x_{j-1}$, we have

$$(\mathbf{D}_x)_{j,j-1} = -\frac{1}{2\Delta_x}, \quad (\mathbf{D}_x)_{j,j+1} = \frac{1}{2\Delta_x},$$

$$(\mathbf{D}_{xx})_{j,j-1} = \frac{1}{\Delta_x^2}, \quad (\mathbf{D}_{xx})_{j,j+1} = \frac{1}{\Delta_x^2}, \quad (\mathbf{D}_{xx})_{j,j} = -\frac{2}{\Delta_x^2}, \quad 1 \leq j \leq M-1,$$

and zero otherwise. If we take Chebychev collocation in the $y-$direction, the $\mathbf{D}_y, \mathbf{D}_{yy}$ are the Chebychev differentiation matrices and are given in a number of places, see for example

Weideman and Reddy (2003) or Trefethen (2000), where MATLAB code to generate the matrices is given.
Discretization of the equation 2 leads to the set of equations

$$a_{j,k}\sum_{q=0}^{M}(\mathbf{D}_{xx})_{j,q}\psi_{q,k}+b_{j,k}\sum_{q=0}^{M}(\mathbf{D}_{yy})_{k,q}\psi_{j,q}+c_{j,k}\sum_{q=0}^{M}(\mathbf{D}_{x})_{j,q}\psi_{q,k}+e_{j,k}\sum_{q=0}^{M}(\mathbf{D}_{y})_{k,q}\psi_{j,q}+f_{j,k}\psi_{j,k}=g_{j,k}, \tag{4}$$

at the interior points $1 \leq j \leq M-1, \quad 1 \leq k \leq N-1$. At the boundaries we have $\psi = 0$.
The discrete set (4) can be combined into a compact form as

$$\begin{aligned}&[\mathrm{DIAG}(\mathbf{a})(\mathbf{I}_{N+1}\oplus\mathbf{D}_{xx})+\mathrm{DIAG}(\mathbf{c})(\mathbf{I}_{N+1}\oplus\mathbf{D}_{x})]\,\Psi+\\&\left[\mathrm{DIAG}(\mathbf{b})(\mathbf{D}_{yy}\oplus\mathbf{I}_{M+1})+\mathrm{DIAG}(\mathbf{e})(\mathbf{D}_{y}\oplus\mathbf{I}_{M+1})\right]\Psi+\mathrm{DIAG}(\mathbf{f})\Psi=\mathbf{g}\,,\end{aligned} \tag{5}$$

where Ψ denotes the vector of unknowns, $\mathbf{A} \oplus \mathbf{B}$ is the kronecker tensor product of two matrices $\mathbf{A}, \mathbf{B}$ (which in MATLAB is represented by the **kron(A,B)** operator), and DIAG($\mathbf{v}$) is as in MATLAB the diagonal matrix with entries given by the vector $\mathbf{v}$, and $\mathbf{I}_{M+1}$ is the identity matrix of order $M+1$. Certain rows of the matrix operator in (5) are also modified when the boundary conditions are incorporated.
The linear sytem may be represented as

$$\mathbf{S}\Psi = \mathbf{R}. \tag{6}$$

Once the coefficient matrix **S** and the right hand sides have been computed, the solution just involves the use of the \ operator with $\Psi = \mathbf{S}\backslash\mathbf{R}$. From the user perspective other than declaring that the matrices involved are sparse matrices, no additional special treatment is required to obtain the solution of the linear systems.
Given the discretization matrices, the above system is easy to code in MATLAB. For certain discretizations however, the linear systems outlined above can be huge and highly sparse. The bandwidth of the coefficient matrix increases with increasing order of differences used, and with spectral methods in two directions, the coefficient matrix has the sparsity pattern similar to that in figure 1(c), obtained using the **spy** function in MATLAB. On the other hand by taking second-order finite differences in the $x-$direction and spectral collocation in the $y-$direction, with a particular ordering of grid points, the matrices can be written in block tridiagonal form as shown in figure 1(a),1(b), or with fourth order finite-differencing in x the linear system is block pentadiagonal. With 2nd, 4th or even 6th finite-differencing the linear systems can be solved with a *direct* solver but with spectral methods in two directions, unless the differential operator involved has a special form, it is not immediately possible to utilize the sparse nature of the matrix. Whilst this does not pose any intrinsic difficulties if one is coding in MATLAB, with increased number of points the solution phase can become very memory intensive and requires a lot of processor time. The use of the hybrid approach in our work is motivated in part by the observation that the sparse matrix structure can be exploited to write efficient solvers, which not only work well with MATLAB, but can be coded directly in other languages. MATLAB provides for an excellent environment in which one can test and develop solvers of this type. In our work we have written our own direct block solvers as well as making direct use of the \ operator with a sparse matrix.
In the MATLAB codes when constructing the coefficient matrices, we use the functions **speye** or **spalloc** for initially creating the sparse matrices. After this only the non-zero elements of the matrices are assigned.

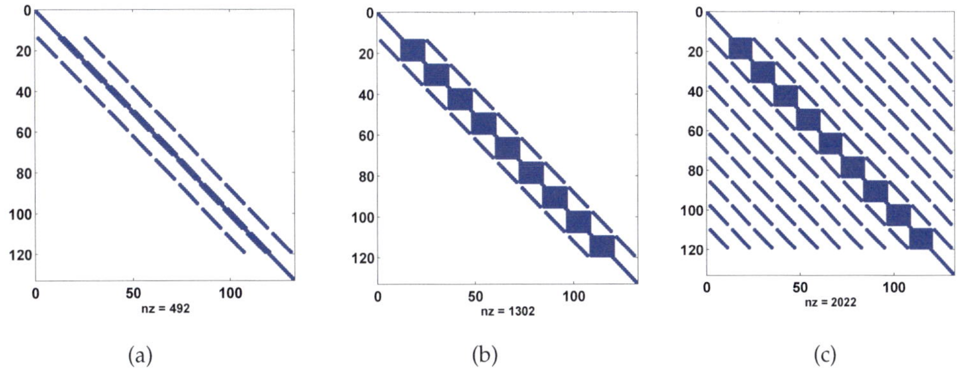

Fig. 1. Sparsity patterns for model problem with (a) second order finite-differences in both x and y with $N = 10, M = 11$, (b) second-order finite-difference in y and chebychev collocation in x with $N = 10, M = 11$, (b) chebychev collocation in both x and y with $N = 10, M = 11$.

2.1 Lid-driven cavity flow.

In this section we discuss the steps needed to go from the continuous model described by the set of coupled nonlinear partial differential equations, the Navier-Stokes equations, to solution using MATLAB. To focus attention we will consider the classic problem of flow in a lid-driven cavity which has been extensively studied in the literature. The governing equations for the problem are

$$\left.\begin{aligned} \nabla^2\psi &= \omega, \\ \text{and} \quad \psi_y\omega_x - \psi_x\omega_y &= \tfrac{1}{Re}\nabla^2\omega. \end{aligned}\right\} \tag{7}$$

Here Re is the Reynolds number defined as $\frac{Uw}{\nu}$, where U is the velocity of the lid, ν is the kinematic viscosity of the fluid, and w is the width of the cavity that are used to non-dimensionalize the velocity and length-scale variables respectively. The boundary conditions (see figure 2(a)) are given by

$$\left.\begin{array}{llll} \psi = 0 & \& \ \psi_x = 0 & \text{for} \ \ x = 0, & 0 \le y \le A, \\ \psi = 0 & \& \ \psi_x = 0 & \text{for} \ \ x = 1, & 0 \le y \le A, \\ \psi = 0 & \& \ \psi_y = 0 & \text{for} \ \ y = 0, & 0 \le x \le 1, \\ \psi = 0 & \& \ \psi_y = 1 & \text{for} \ \ y = A, & 0 \le x \le 1, \end{array}\right\} \tag{8}$$

where A is the aspect ratio of the cavity. The discrete solution to the equations will be obtained at a set of grid points on an $(M+1) \times (N+1)$ grid say with the nodes, $x = x_j, \quad j = 0, \ldots, M$ with $x_1 = 0, x_M = 1$, and $y = y_k, \quad 0 \le k \le N$ with $y_0 = 1, y_N = 1$, and at these points we set $\psi_{j,k} = \psi(x_j, y_k), \quad \omega_{j,k} = \omega(x_j, y_k)$.

We will assume that derivatives in the $x-$ and $y-$ directions may be approximated as in (3). The discretization leads to a set of nonlinear algebraic equations for the unknowns $\psi_{j,k}, \omega_{j,k}$, $0 \le j \le M, \quad 0 \le k \le N$. To solve these we use Newton linearization and this will lead to linear system of equations which are solved using MATLAB. Linearization of the nonlinear equations is performed by setting $\psi_{j,k} = \bar{\psi}_{j,k} + G_{j,k}, \quad \omega_{j,k} = \bar{\omega}_{j,k} + H_{j,k}$, the barred quantities representing a current iterate and $G_{j,k}, H_{j,k}$ begin small corrections, and substituting into the

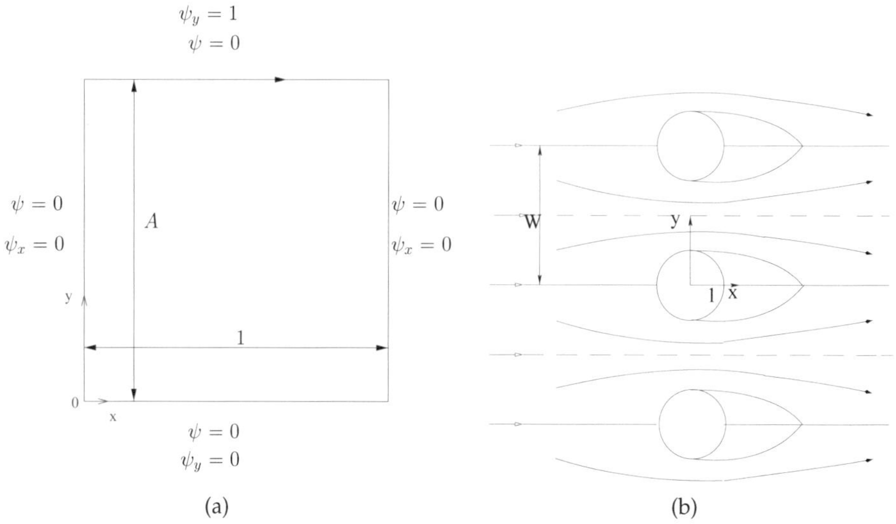

Fig. 2. Sketch of (a) the lid–driven cavity with boundary conditions, and (b) flow past a row of circular cylinders.

nonlinear equations and neglecting second order small terms. This leads to

$$(\mathbf{I}_{N+1} \oplus \mathbf{D}_{xx})\mathbf{G} + (\mathbf{D}_{yy} \oplus \mathbf{I}_{M+1})\mathbf{G} - \mathrm{DIAG}(\mathbf{H}) = \\ -(\mathbf{I}_{N+1} \oplus \mathbf{D}_{xx})\bar{\psi} - (\mathbf{D}_{yy} \oplus \mathbf{I}_{M+1})\bar{\psi} + \mathrm{DIAG}(\bar{\omega}),$$

$$\mathrm{DIAG}(\bar{\psi}_y)(\mathbf{I}_{N+1} \oplus \mathbf{D}_x)\mathbf{H} + \mathrm{DIAG}(\bar{\omega}_x)(\mathbf{D}_y \oplus \mathbf{I}_{M+1})\mathbf{G} \\ - \mathrm{DIAG}(\bar{\psi}_x)(\mathbf{D}_y \oplus \mathbf{I}_{M+1})\mathbf{H} - \mathrm{DIAG}(\bar{\omega}_y)(\mathbf{I}_{N+1} \oplus \mathbf{D}_x)\mathbf{G} \\ - \frac{1}{Re}\left[(\mathbf{I}_{N+1} \oplus \mathbf{D}_{xx})\mathbf{H} + (\mathbf{D}_{yy} \oplus \mathbf{I}_{M+1})\mathbf{H}\right] = -\mathrm{DIAG}(\bar{\psi}_y)(\mathbf{I}_{N+1} \oplus \mathbf{D}_x)\bar{\omega} \\ + \mathrm{DIAG}(\bar{\psi}_x)(\mathbf{D}_y \oplus \mathbf{I}_{M+1})\bar{\omega} + \frac{1}{Re}\left[(\mathbf{I}_{N+1} \oplus \mathbf{D}_{xx})\bar{\omega} + (\mathbf{D}_{yy} \oplus \mathbf{I}_{M+1})\bar{\omega})\right].$$

Here $\mathbf{G}, \mathbf{H}$ are the vector of unknown corrections.
Depending on the discretization, the above can be coded directly in MATLAB by constructing the coefficient matrix multiplying the vector of unknowns $(\boldsymbol{G}, \boldsymbol{H})^T$. Note that the size of the coefficient matrix is $2(N+1)(M+1) \times 2(N+1)(M+1)$ and even for modest N, M the above procedure leads to very large matrices and is not efficient. The approach we have adopted is to make use of the sparsity patterns for particular types of discretizations.

2.2 Use of Matlab for the solution of the discrete system

For the case when we use second order finite-differeces in the $x-$direction and chebychev collocation in the $y-$direction, the linear system may be written as

$$\mathbf{S}\boldsymbol{\Phi} = (\mathbf{S}_0, \mathbf{S}_1, \ldots, \mathbf{S}_M)^T = \mathbf{r},$$

where

$$\mathbf{S}_p = \mathbf{A}_p\boldsymbol{\Phi}_{p-1} + \mathbf{B}_p\boldsymbol{\Phi}_p + \mathbf{C}_p\boldsymbol{\Phi}_{p+1}, \quad 0 \le p \le M \tag{9}$$

$$\boldsymbol{\Phi}_p = (G_{p0}, G_{p1}, \dots, G_{pN}, H_{p0}, H_{p1}, \dots H_{pN})^T, \quad \boldsymbol{\Phi} = (\boldsymbol{\Phi}_0, \boldsymbol{\Phi}_1, \dots, \boldsymbol{\Phi}_M)^T,$$

with $\mathbf{A}_0 = \mathbf{C}_M = \mathbf{0}$. This represents a particular ordering of unknowns and gives rise to the block tridiagonal system in (9). With 4th order finite-differencing in x the linear system is block pentadiagonal.

The coefficient matrices $\mathbf{A}_p, \mathbf{B}_P, \mathbf{C}_p$ can be extracted from the discrete equations above and

$$\mathbf{A}_p = \begin{pmatrix} \frac{1}{\Delta_x^2}\mathbf{I}_{N+1} & \mathbf{O} \\ \frac{1}{2\Delta_x}\mathrm{DIAG}(\mathbf{D}_y \bar{\omega}_p) & -\frac{1}{2\Delta_x}\mathrm{DIAG}(\mathbf{U}_p) - \frac{1}{Re\Delta_x^2}\mathbf{I}_{N+1} \end{pmatrix},$$

$$\mathbf{B}_p = \begin{pmatrix} \mathbf{D}_{yy} - \frac{2}{\Delta_x^2}\mathbf{I}_{N+1} & -\mathbf{I}_{N+1} \\ \mathrm{DIAG}(\boldsymbol{\Omega}_{xp})\mathbf{D}_y & \mathrm{DIAG}(\mathbf{V}_p)\mathbf{D}_y + \frac{1}{Re}\left[\frac{2}{\Delta_x^2}\mathbf{I}_{N+1} - \mathbf{D}_{yy}\right] \end{pmatrix},$$

$$\mathbf{C}_p = \begin{pmatrix} \frac{1}{\Delta_x^2}\mathbf{I}_{N+1} & \mathbf{O} \\ \frac{1}{2\Delta_x}\mathrm{DIAG}(\mathbf{D}_y \bar{\omega}_p) & \frac{1}{2\Delta_x}\mathrm{DIAG}(\mathbf{U}_p) - \frac{1}{Re\Delta_x^2}\mathbf{I}_{N+1} \end{pmatrix},$$

with

$$\mathbf{U}_p = \mathbf{D}_y \bar{\boldsymbol{\psi}}_p, \quad \boldsymbol{\Omega}_{xp} = \frac{\bar{\omega}_{p+1} - \bar{\omega}_{p-1}}{2\Delta_x}, \quad \mathbf{V}_p = -\frac{\bar{\boldsymbol{\psi}}_{p+1} - \bar{\boldsymbol{\psi}}_{p-1}}{2\Delta_x}.$$

The above excludes the boundary conditions, but these just alter certain rows of the matrices. In MATLAB the individual entries of the block matrices are easily computed and the $\mathbf{S}$ matrix is updated via

$$\mathbf{S}(1+2p(N+1) : 2(p+1)(N+1), 1+2(p-1)(N+1) : 2p(N+1)) = \mathbf{A}_p,$$
$$\mathbf{S}(1+2p(N+1) : 2(p+1)(N+1), 1+2p(N+1) : 2(p+1)(N+1)) = \mathbf{B}_p,$$
$$\mathbf{S}(1+2p(N+1) : 2(p+1)(N+1), 1+2(p+1)(N+1) : 2(p+2)(N+1)) = \mathbf{C}_P,$$

for $1 \le p \le M-1$.

2.3 Results for lid-driven cavity

The method described above was used to compute the flow in a lid-driven cavity. The same techniques used were adapted to firstly compute the steady flow, and then to investigate the instability of the flow via simulations as well as solving the linear eigenvalue problem assuming normal mode disturbances proportional to $e^{\lambda t}$. Further details of the techniques may be found in Boppana and Gajjar (2010). MATLAB was also used in the eigenvalue analysis. In fact the eigenvalue problem required to be solved takes the form

$$S\boldsymbol{\Phi} = \lambda \mathbf{T},$$

which is a generalised eigenvalue problem. The matrix $\mathbf{S}$ is the same as the Jacobian matrix of the linear system after Newton linearization, and $\mathbf{T}$ is a singular diagonal matrix. The eigenvalue problem is solved in MATLAB using the **eig** function. In other related problems the routine **sptarn** available in the PDE toolbox was used for the solution of the generalised eigenvalue problem.

In figures 3, 4 we have shown the real and imaginary parts of eigenfunctions for the disturbance streamfunction ψ for aspect ratios of $A = 1$ and $A = 2$ at the onset of instability, obtained from a solution of the eigenvalue problem. The advantage of working with MATLAB is that such plots can be generated at the same time as the computation is in progress.

More extensive results and details are documented in Boppana and Gajjar (2010).

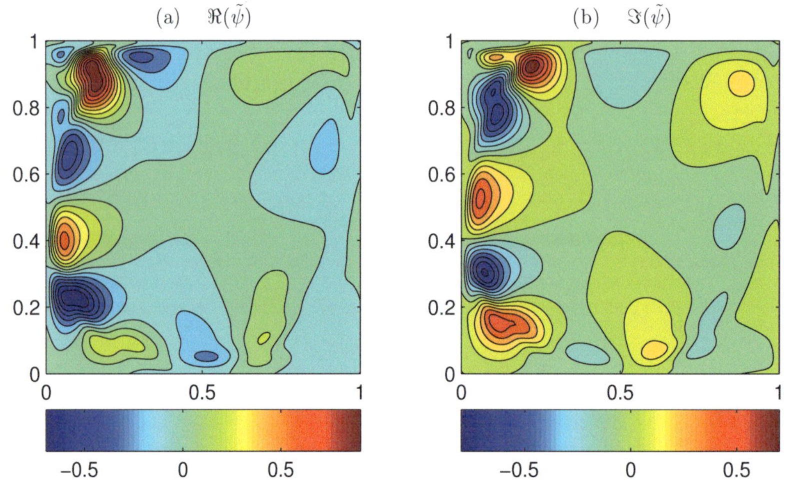

Fig. 3. Eigenfunctions of the streamfunction for lid-driven cavity at a critical Reynolds number of $Re = 8026.7$ and aspect ratio $A = 1$.

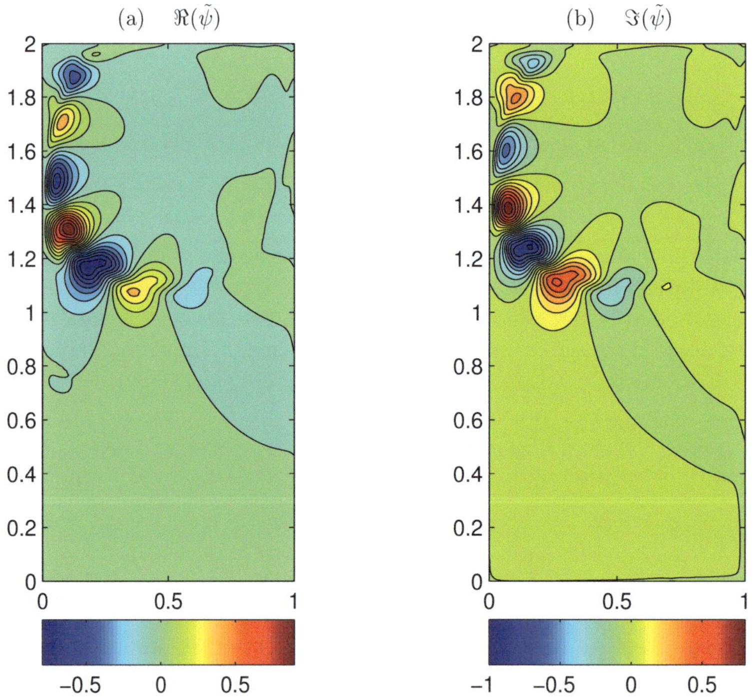

Fig. 4. Eigenfunctions of the streamfunction for lid-driven cavity at a critical Reynolds number of $Re = 5861$ and aspect ratio $A = 2$.

3. Flow past circular cylinders

The techniques described above have also been used to solve for the uniform flow past a row of circular cylinders, see figure 2(b). Here the Navier-Stokes equations are solved with boundary conditions of no slip on the cylinder surfaces and uniform flow far upstream. The two important parameters are the gap-width between the cylinder centres W (normalised with respect to cylinder radius) and the Reynolds number Re. Of particular interest is to ascertain when the flow first becomes unstable and the mode of instability. Experiments, see for example Mizushima & Ino (2008), for the flow past two such cylinders show a complicated dynamics as the parameters are varied. For large Reynolds numbers, and for large gap widths the flow is like that past an isolated cylinder and the observed shedding frequencies also similar. For $Re >> 1$ and intermediate gap widths (of 0.5 to 1 cylinder diameters), the flow can become deflected to one side and becomes asymmetric. For small gap widths, the flow is similar to that past a single bluff body. At low Reynolds numbers the flow dynamics is also complicated and with conflicting results.

In our work, MATLAB was used to first compute the base flows, and then for studies of the onset of instability, by solving the generalised eigenvalue problem. Full details of the numerical methods and results can be found in Boppana and Gajjar (2011). In figures 5, 6 we have shown the results for the streamfunction eigenfunctions. Modes which are symmetric and asymmetric with respect to the cylinder centreline, can be observed and it found that the critical Reynolds numbers for the onset of instabilties are very similar for both modes. However the symmetric modes as shown in figures 5(b), 6(b) for instance, have much lower critical Strohal frequencies as compared to asymmetric mode. The latter is the one which tends to that for the flow past an isolated cylinder as the gap width increases.

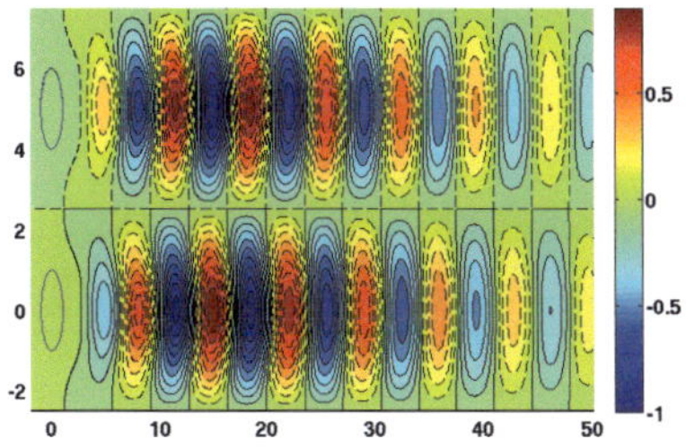

(a)

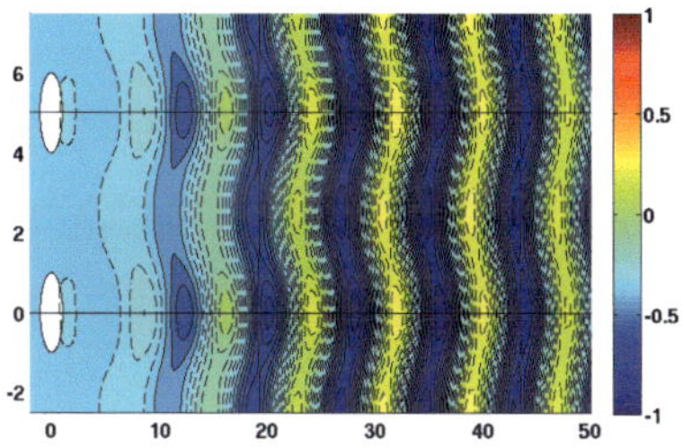

(b)

Fig. 5. Perturbation eigenfunctions the flow past a circular cylinder for a gap width $W = 5$ with (a) anti-phase oscillatory mode, (b) in phase oscillatory mode.

4. Transonic flows past airfoils

The study of transonic flows is motivated in part by the observation that many modern airplane carriers operate most efficiently when cruising at speeds which fall in the transonic range, that is close to the speed of sound. Mathematically the study of transonic flows is fascinating because the governing equations are nonlinear and of mixed type. The methods described above work have been applied to partial differential equations of mixed type containing shocks.

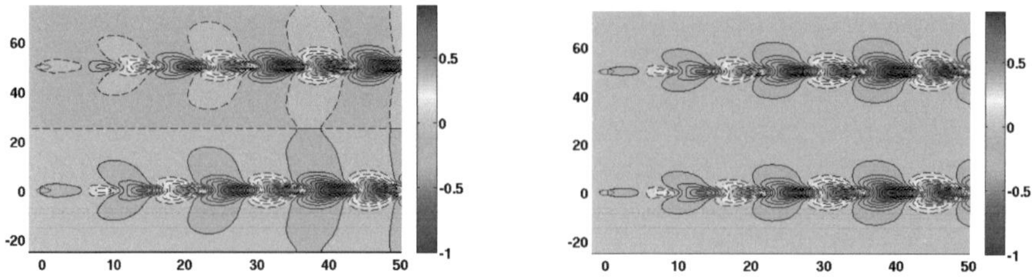

(a) (b)

Fig. 6. Perturbation eigenfunctions the flow past a circular cylinder for a gap width $W = 50$ with (a) anti-phase oscillatory mode, (b) in phase oscillatory mode.

4.1 The mathematical model

In this subsection we describe briefly a numerical method to deal with transonic flows past thin airfoils, based on the Kárman-Guderley equations. This method is discussed in detail in Pereira and Gajjar (2010). However the aim of this section in not to repeat once again the same work, but rather to focus on the use of the graphical interface which is extremely easy to program in MATLAB. First we will give an overview of how the mathematical model was built, and then we will explain how to use MATLAB graphics user interfaces (GUIs) in the context of our problem.

The governing equation may be obtained using asymptotic methods as described in Cole and Cook (1986). The starting point to our model was the full potential equation:

$$(a^2 - U^2)\Phi_{xx} - 2UV\Phi_{xy} + (a^2 - V^2)\Phi_{yy} = 0, \tag{10}$$

$$\frac{1}{2}(\Phi_x^2 + \Phi_y^2) + \frac{a^2}{\gamma - 1} = \frac{U_\infty}{2} + \frac{a_\infty^2}{\gamma - 1}, \tag{11}$$

where Φ represents the velocity potential, a is the local speed of sound, U_∞ is the velocity in the far field, a_∞ is the speed of sound in the far field, and $M_\infty = U_\infty / a_\infty$ is the free-stream Mach number. The velocity components (U, V) are defined as follows,

$$U = \Phi_x, \quad V = \Phi_y.$$

The density ρ and pressure p can be determined via the relationships,

$$\rho^{\gamma - 1} = M_\infty^2 a^2; \quad p = \frac{\rho^\gamma}{\gamma M_\infty^2},$$

where γ is the ratio of specific heats.

In order to define the boundary conditions we assume that the flow is uniform in the far field and that the flow is tangent to the airfoil on its surface. To construct this theory we also assume that we have a thin aerofoil with width ($\delta \to 0$) and that the air flow speed is close to sonic so $M_\infty^2 = 1 - k\mu(\delta)$, $\mu(\delta) \to 0$ where k is the transonic similarity parameter and μ is a function of the airfoil width (δ). The oncoming flow is assumed to be aligned with the x-direction.

In order to define the boundary conditions we assume that the flow is uniform in the far field and that the flow is tangent to the airfoil on its surface. To construct this theory we also assume that we have a thin aerofoil with width ($\delta \to 0$) and that the air flow speed is close to sonic so $M_\infty^2 = 1 - k\mu(\delta)$, $\mu(\delta) \to 0$ where k is the transonic similarity parameter and μ is a function of the airfoil width (δ). The oncoming flow is assumed to be aligned with the x-direction. The airfoil is defined by,

$$y = \delta F(x).$$

Introducing non dimensional variables,

$$U = uU_\infty, V = vU_\infty,$$

then the full potential equation becomes,

$$(\frac{a^2}{U_\infty^2} - u^2)\Phi_{xx} - 2uv\Phi_{xy} + (\frac{a^2}{U_\infty^2} - v^2)\Phi_{yy} = 0.$$

The expansion for Φ is described in Cole and Cook (1986) and is given by,

$$\Phi(x, y, M_\infty, \delta) = U_\infty(x + \epsilon(\delta)\phi(x, y, k) + ...).$$

It is well known that as $M_\infty \rightarrow 1$, the perturbations extend in the y direction significantly. Because of this, stretched coordinates were used and the governing equations and boundary conditions reduce to,

$$\phi_{xx}(k - \phi_x(\gamma + 1)) + \phi_{YY} = 0, \quad (12)$$

$$\phi_x = \phi_Y = 0, \quad x^2 + Y^2 \rightarrow \infty, \quad (13)$$

$$\phi_Y(Y = 0) = F'(x), \quad (14)$$

where (12) is the so called Kárman-Guderley equation. Equation (12) in conservative form is written as follows,

$$\frac{\partial}{\partial x}(k\phi_x - \frac{\gamma + 1}{2}\phi_x^2) + \phi_{YY} = 0, \quad (15)$$

and, if we denote,

$$\psi = kx - (\gamma + 1)\phi \quad (16)$$

then, we may rewrite (15) as,

$$(\frac{\psi_x^2}{2})_x + \psi_{YY} = 0. \quad (17)$$

The boundary conditions become,

$$\psi_x(x^2 + Y^2 \rightarrow \infty) = k, \quad \psi_Y(Y = 0) = -(\gamma + 1)F'(x). \quad (18)$$

When considering the non symmetric case, one has to introduce a new boundary condition - the Kutta condition. The Kutta condition is used at the trailing edge to ensure that the jump obtained in the integration of ψ_x along the lower and upper surfaces at the tail is zero.
Next we give a brief overview of the numerical method used to solve the above problem. Ee used finite differences for the derivatives in the x direction and a Chebyshev collocation method to describe the derivatives in the Y direction. As described in Cole and Cook (1986) each point of the domain may be either subsonic, sonic, supersonic or a shock point. Let,

$$P = (\frac{\psi_x^2}{2}),$$

then equation (17) becomes,

$$P_x + \psi_{YY} = 0. \tag{19}$$

Let $(\psi_x)_{i+1/2,j}$ represent the derivative with respect to x of ψ at the point $(x_{i+1/2}, Y_j)$, and let $h_i = x_i - x_{i-1}$. Using central differences for the x derivatives we may write (19) as,

$$\frac{(\psi_x)^2_{i+1/2,j} - (\psi_x)^2_{i-1/2,j}}{h_i + h_{i+1}} + (\psi_{YY})_{i,j} = 0,$$

or,

$$\frac{1}{h_i + h_{i+1}}((\psi_x)_{i+1/2,j} - (\psi_x)_{i-1/2,j})((\psi_x)_{i+1/2,j} + (\psi_x)_{i-1/2,j}) + (\psi_{YY})_{i,j} = 0. \tag{20}$$

As discussed in Cole and Cook (1986) if we have a subsonic point, the equation is elliptic and central differences should be used to calculate both $(\psi_x)_{i+1/2,j}$ and $(\psi_x)_{i-1/2,j}$. If we have a supersonic point, then equation (20) becomes hyperbolic and backwards differences should be used to calculate both $(\psi_x)_{i+1/2,j}$ and $(\psi_x)_{i-1/2,j}$. In the first case we can rewrite (20) as,

$$p_{i,j} + (\psi_{YY})_{i,j} = 0. \tag{21}$$

In the second case, we can rewrite (20) as,

$$p_{i-1,j} + (\psi_{YY})_{i,j} = 0. \tag{22}$$

where,

$$p_{i,j} = \frac{A_{i,j}}{h_i + h_{i+1}} \psi_x^c,$$

$$A_{i,j} = \frac{\psi_{i+1,j} - \psi_{i,j}}{h_{i+1}} - \frac{\psi_{i,j} - \psi_{i-1,j}}{h_i}. \tag{23}$$

and,

$$\psi_x^c = \frac{\psi_{i+1,j} - \psi_{i,j}}{h_{i+1}} + \frac{\psi_{i,j} - \psi_{i-1,j}}{h_i}. \tag{24}$$

Two other cases are considered, the case when the flow accelerates from subsonic to supersonic in which case we define a sonic point, and the opposite, when the flow decelerates form supersonic to subsonic in which case we call it a shock point. To deal with these cases we use artificial viscosity $(\mu_{i,j})$ Murman and Cole (1971), and equations (21) and (22) can be condensed as,

$$p_{i,j}(1 - \mu_{i,j}) + p_{i-1,j}\mu_{i-1,j} + \psi_{YY} = 0$$

where the values of $\mu_{i,j}$ and $\mu_{i-1,j}$ are taken from the following table:

TYPE OF POINT	$\psi_x^{central}$	ψ_x^{backWs}	$\mu_{i-1,j}$	$\mu_{i,j}$
ELLIPTIC	>0	>0	0	0
HYPERBOLIC	<0	<0	1	1
SONIC	<0	>0	0	1
SHOCK	>0	<0	1	0

Note that a shock point can be seen as an addition of both elliptic and hyperbolic x difference operators.
In the Y direction, the physical domain was first truncated to y_∞ and mapped into the Chebyshev space, as in Canuto et. all (1998),

$$Y \in [0, y_\infty] \to z \in [-1, 1]$$

where,

$$z_j = \cos(\frac{j\pi}{N}), j = 0, 1, ..., N$$

and,

$$Y_j = y_\infty(\frac{z_j + 1}{2}).$$

First and second derivatives in the Y directions were calculated as described earlier.
After applying the above discretizations we obtain a set of coupled nonlinear algebraic equations. These are linearized using Newton-Raphson linearization by setting

$$\psi_{i,j} = \overline{\psi_{i,j}} + G_{i,j},$$

where $\overline{\psi_{i,j}}$ represents the value of $\psi_{i,j}$ in a previous iteration and $G_{i,j}$ represents the update for $\psi_{i,j}$. This results in a linear system of equations for the $G_{i,j}$ of the form

$$A_{i,j}G_{i-2,j} + B_{i,j}G_{i-1,j} + C_{i,j}G_{i,j} + H_{i,j}G_{i+1,j} + E_{i,j}G_{i+2,j} = F_{i,j}. \tag{25}$$

Details on how to calculate the coefficients $A_{i,j}, B_{i,j}..., F_{i,j}$ can be found in Pereira and Gajjar (2010). The block pentadiagonal system of equations was solved directly using routines described in Korolev et all. (2002).

4.2 The use of GUIs

In this subsection we will focus on how to generate a good graphics interface using MATLAB GUIs in the context of the problem described in the previous subsection. In order to obtain a graphics interface to our programme, the first thing we have to do is to type **guide** in MATLAB's command window. The result is that MATLAB opens a window that has a graphics interface working environment(GIWE). The next thing to do, is to save it as **name.fig**. This action has as a result not only of saving the work done so far, but also to generate a file **name.m**, that has the MATLAB corresponding instructions.
Suppose next that we want to introduce a title on top of the graphics interface window. We select the *"Static text"* button in the GIWE. With the mouse one selects the location and the size of the text to input. Then after double clicking on it a new window appears, where one can choose options for the static text we want to introduce.

Another important feature on the design of an interface, is how to read data from this interface. To do so, one option is to select the *"Edit text"* button in the GIWE. With the mouse one selects the location and the size of the text to be read. Then, after a double click a new window appears where one can chose options for the text to be read from the keyboard. It is possible to choose a default text that can be attributed to a certain variable in the MATLAB code. If we fill in the field **"Tag"** with a name, that can be used to attribute the edited text to a variable. Suppose we fill the field "Tag" with **A1**. By doing this and saving it, one automatically obtains in the **.m file** two new functions **A1CreateFcn** and **A1Callback**. The first function executes during object creation, after setting all properties. The second function allows for the edited text to be attributed to a variable when the **enter key** is pressed. Say we want to attribute the edited text to the variable **"x"**, all you have to do is to write in the **A1Callback** function the following instruction:

```
x=str2double(get(handles.A1,'String'));
```

Here, the text read via the keyboard, once the **enter key** is pressed, is converted to double and attributed to a variable "x". This feature is very important for the user to be able to set the values of any variables to be used in the program.

In many codes, it is also very important to define a **push button**. This can be used to set up certain actions once it is pushed. An example is when one wants to read data from the keyboard, before starting a simulation. To implement this idea, we click the **push button** in the GIWE. Then one selects the size and place where to put it in the GIWE. Next, if one double clicks in it, a new window opens and the options for this **push button** are defined. Once this is done and it is saved, a new function is created in the **.m file** called **pushbuttonCallback**. All the actions that are to happen once the button is pushed are to appear in this function. For instance, one can attribute a set of values to a set of variables. This is done exactly in the same way as before. The difference is that this can be done to a set of many variables at once. The next instructions we put in this function are the ones that compose the **main code** of our programme.

Suppose that in the course of the simulation, we want to show a graphic object. This is done by choosing the **Axes button** in the GIWE. Then one selects the size and place where to put the graphic in the GIWE. Next, a double click on it and a new window opens and the options for this **Axes button** are defined. If we fill in the field **"Tag"** with a name, say **"graphics1"**, in order to plot a graphic $(x, f(x))$ in that window, we would write:

```
axes(handles.graphics1);
plot(x,f)
```

Using these features, we were able to define a useful graphics interface for the program to solve the transonic flow past an airfoil using the mathematical model presented in the previous section. The interface was built for the NACA0012 airfoil and is shown in figure 7.

The parameters considered were: Angle of attack (α), Mach number(M_∞), number of points in the x direction over the wing (nx), number of points in the Y direction (ny), maximum value for Y ($Ymax$), and relaxation factor (w).

In the figures 8, 9, we present the results obtained by our code for two classic examples extensively studied in the literature. The first example is for $M_\infty = 0.75$, $\alpha = 2.0$, $nx = 40$, $ny = 40$, $Ymax = 1.25$, $w = 0.5$.

The second example is for $M_\infty = 0.8$, $\alpha = 1.25$, $nx = 40$, $ny = 40$, $Ymax = 1.25$, $w = 0.6$.

The results of both examples agree with the literature, see for example Cole and Cook (1986) and Camilo (2003). As we can see, by using GUIs, we obtained a user friendly professional looking graphics interface, which allowed any other user to perform simulations and input their parameters for the run. The other users of the software did not need to be familiar with the underlying code and equations.

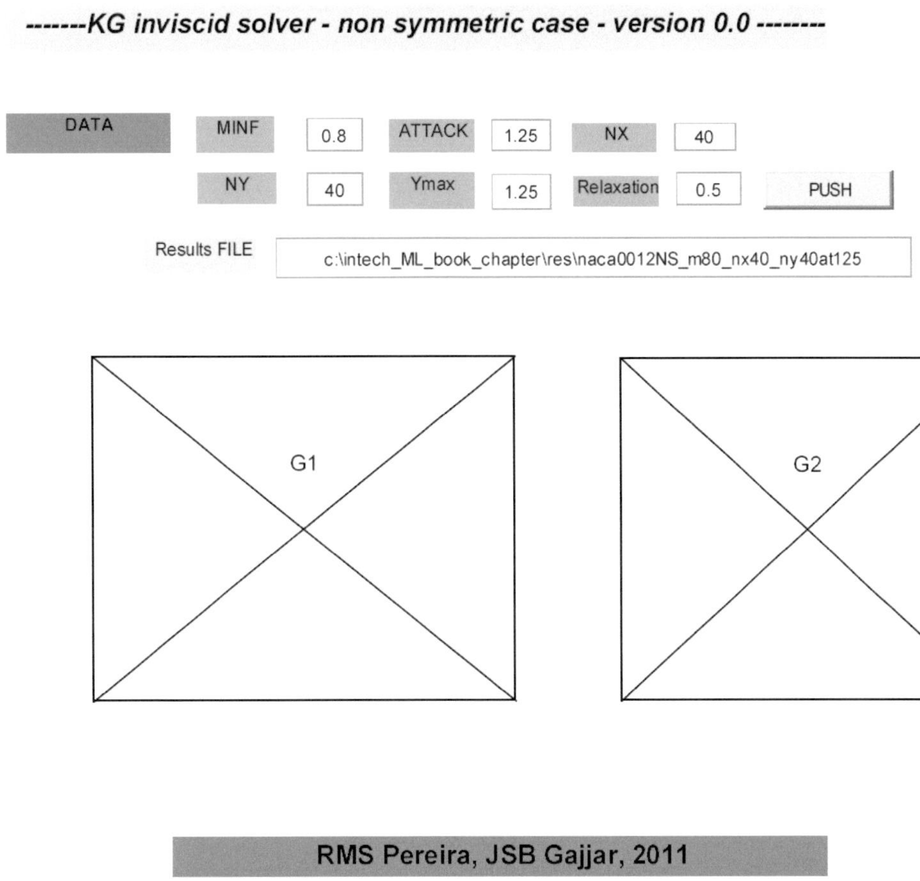

Fig. 7. The ".fig" file built for the example considered.

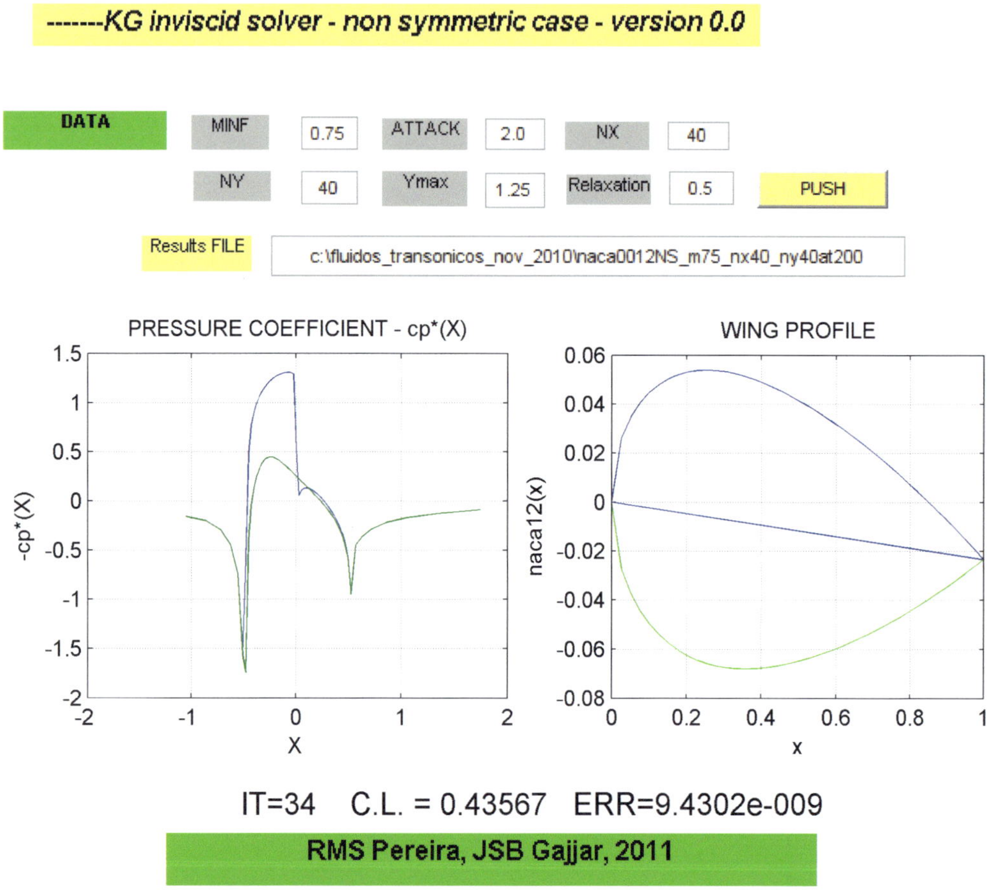

Fig. 8. Example of results for KG code for Transonic flows where $M_{inf} = 0.75; \alpha = 2.0; Nx = 40, Ny = 40, relaxation = 0.5$.

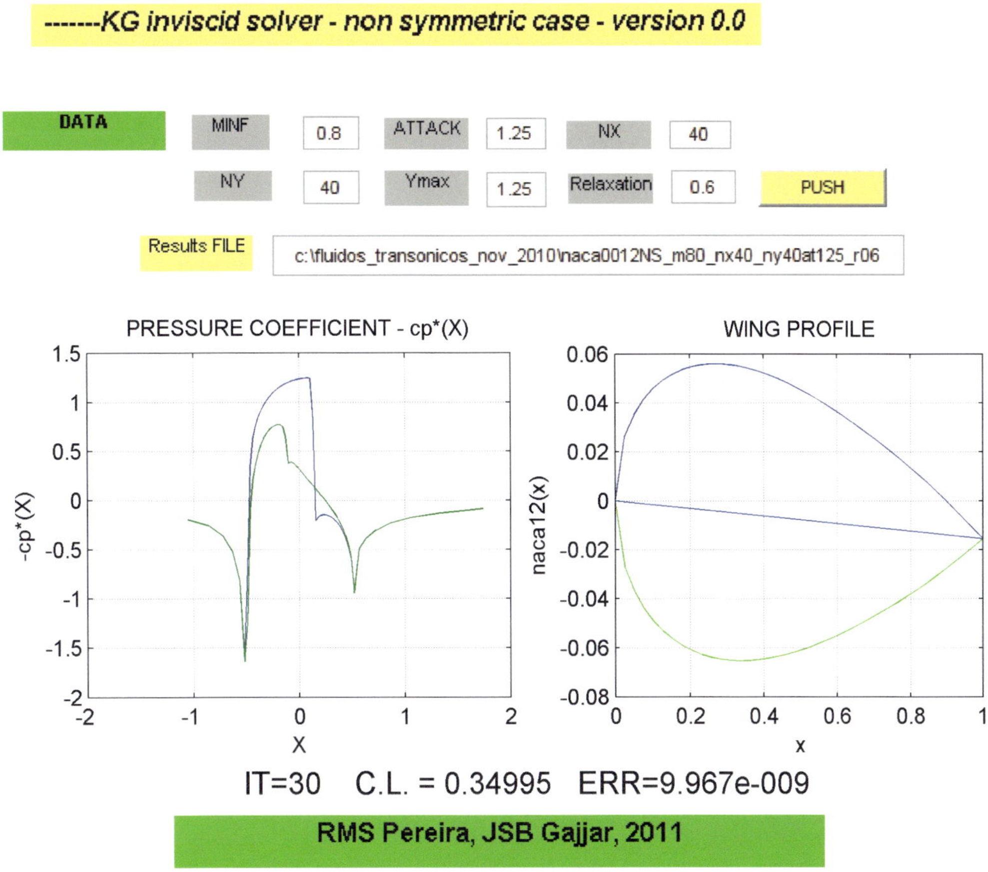

Fig. 9. Example of results for KG code for Transonic flows where $M_{inf} = 0.8; \alpha = 1.25; Nx = 40, Ny = 40, relaxation = 0.6$.

5. Conclusions

- The environment of MATLAB is easy to work, the syntax is very simple and intuitive, it has powerful toolboxes to treat many different problems in engineering, and it allows us to produce fantastic graphics as the program runs.
- A MATLAB code can be very compact, allowing anyone to have "the big picture" of any code without having to look at all its details.
- Another great advantage of Matlab is that, if the code is written in a vectorized form, the code can run much faster than if it was written in the traditional form (*'a la C/fortran'*).
- The fact that MATLAB allows us to use a powerful toolbox for sparse matrices, is also a great advantage since, many traditional linear algebra operations can be highly improved, allowing the codes to run much faster than it would run with the traditional linear algebra functions.
- The main drawback with the use of MATLAB is that when the number of points used in the discretization grows, which is necessary for finely resolved computations, the execution time and memory requirements can grow substantially. On multicore machines, the use of the *parallel toolbox* is recommended and this is supposed to provide superior performance making use of parallel linear algebra routines with minimal code changes. However we have not been able to test this with our codes.

6. References

Boppana, V.B.L. and Gajjar, J.S.B. (2010). *Global flow instability in a lid-driven cavity.* Int J. for Num Methods in Fluids, 62, 827-853.

Boppana, V.B.L. and Gajjar, J.S.B. (2011). *Onset of instability in the flow past a circular cylinder cascade.* J. Fluid Mech. 668, 303-334.

Camilo E. (2003). *Solução numérica das equações de Euler para representação do escoamento transónico de aerofólios.*M.Sc thesis, University of São Paulo, Brazil.

Canuto, C., Hussaini, M. Y., Quarteroni, A. and Zhang, T.A., (1998). *Spectral Methods in Fluid Mechanics.* Springer series in Comp. Phys., Springer Verlag.

Cole, J. D. and Cook, L. P., (1986). *Transonic Aerodynamics,* Elsevier Science Publishers B.V. .

Korolev G.L, Gajjar J.S.B., and Ruban A.I., (2002). *Once again on the supersonic flow separation near a corner.* J. Fluid Mech., 463, 173-199.

Mizushima, J. and Ino, Y., (2008). *Stability of flows past a pair of circular cylinders in a side-by-side arrangement.* J. Fluid Mech., 595, 491-507.

Murman, E. M. and Cole, J. D.,(1971). *Calculation of plane steady transonic flows.* Boeing Scientific Research Laboratories.

Pereira, R. M. S. and Gajjar, J. S. B. (2010). *Transonic Inviscid Flows Past Thin Airfoils: A New Numerical Method and Global Stability Analysis using MatLab.* International Journal of Mathematical Models and Methods in Applied Sciences, ISSN 1998-0140.

Trefethen L.N., (2000). *Spectral Methods in Matlab.* SIAM.

Weideman, J.A.C and Reddy, S.C (2003). *http://dip.sun.ac.za/~weideman/research/differ.html* .

13

The Use of Matlab in the Study of the Glass Transition and Vitrification in Polymers

John M. Hutchinson and Iria Fraga
Universitat Politècnica de Catalunya
Spain

1. Introduction

The glassy state of matter is common to all types of materials, be they metallic, inorganic or polymeric, for example. The transformation from an equilibrium liquid state to a non-equilibrium glassy state is usually achieved by cooling at a rate sufficiently rapid for crystallization to be inhibited. For metals, this generally requires cooling rates of the order of millions of degrees per second, whereas, for polymers that can crystallize, a glassy state can be achieved with cooling rates of only hundreds of degrees per second. Furthermore, for atactic polymers the irregularity of the chemical structure prevents crystallization and results naturally in an amorphous glassy state. Cooling is not the only way in which a glassy state can be achieved, though. The application of high pressure is another method, though it is rather rarely used for reasons of experimental difficulty and danger. On the other hand, an alternative method that is very commonly used is by means of a chemical reaction, and in particular the curing reaction of a thermosetting polymer. In the present paper we concentrate on the glass transformation process by these two commonly applied methods, namely cooling from the equilibrium liquid-like state and vitrification during the cross-linking reaction of a thermosetting polymer.

The glassy state is characterized by a lack of long range order, and is also referred to as an amorphous state. This does not, however, mean that there is no discernible structure of the glass; on the contrary, there is a structure to the glass, which can be quantified in respect of its short range order, and this structure is dependent on the way in which the glass was formed. A good example of this is the preparation of densified glasses by cooling from the melt state to the glassy state under high pressure and then releasing the pressure; the density, and other properties, of the glass formed under pressure in this way is greater than, and remains greater than, that of the glass formed from the same melt by cooling at atmospheric pressure. The fact that the structure of the glassy state depends on the way in which the glass was formed is important, because the properties of the glass are, in their turn, dependent on the structure.

A further important characteristic of the glassy state is that it is a non-equilibrium state. This was first recognized by Simon (Simon, 1931) the best part of a century ago, who proposed that, on cooling the equilibrium liquid at constant pressure, a transformation to a glass takes place at a temperature, known as the glass transition temperature, T_g, when the timescale for molecular rearrangements, which increases as the temperature decreases, becomes longer than that available corresponding to the imposed cooling rate. An immediate consequence of this is that the glass transition is a kinetic phenomenon, and that T_g depends on the cooling rate. Another consequence is that, if the temperature is held constant in the glassy state, the non-equilibrium glass will tend towards an equilibrium state at the same temperature. Thus, for example, the volume and the enthalpy of the glass will decrease as a function of time, in a process known as physical aging (Hutchinson, 1995), with consequent effects on other physical and mechanical properties. It is clearly of interest, therefore, not only from a fundamental scientific point of view but also with respect to the engineering applications of polymers, to be able to describe quantitatively the kinetic nature of the glass transition and the time dependence of the property changes that take place during physical aging.

The basic equations describing these kinetic aspects derive from the early experimental studies conducted by Tool in the 1930's and 1940's on silicate glasses (Tool, 1946, 1948; Tool & Eichlin, 1931), and later by Kovacs on polymer glasses (Kovacs, 1963), both making use of dilatometry. From these studies, two key features of structural relaxation of glasses were identified. First, Tool established that the relaxation time for structural relaxation of glass was dependent not only on the temperature but also on the instantaneous structure of the glass, and he proposed that the structure be characterized by the fictive temperature, T_f, to be defined below. Second, Kovacs showed that the relaxation process involved a distribution of relaxation times. Although nowadays such experiments are almost invariably made by Differential Scanning Calorimetry (DSC), the phenomenology is the same, and these two key features are necessary for any realistic description of the kinetics of structural relaxation. For reasons that will become clear later, they are now commonly referred to as non-linearity and non-exponentiality, respectively. In this paper, we apply a relatively simple theory for structural relaxation, in which these two aspects are intrinsic, to explore a number of different situations of practical importance involving the kinetic response of polymers in the glassy state, including the effect of cooling rate on the glass transformation process for polymers of different types, the relationship between cooling rate and frequency derived from Temperature Modulated DSC (TMDSC), and the identification of vitrification during the cure of thermosetting polymers. For all of these simulations we make use of Matlab and demonstrate the usefulness and ease of application of several of its basic attributes.

2. Theoretical aspects

The basic kinetic equation assumes that the rate of approach to equilibrium is proportional to the departure from equilibrium. For DSC, the departure from equilibrium is the difference between the instantaneous enthalpy, H, which is a function of both temperature T and time t, and the value of the enthalpy in equilibrium at the same temperature, H_∞, and is denoted as $\delta = H - H_\infty$, and hence:

$$\frac{d\delta}{dt} = -\frac{\delta}{\tau(T, T_f)} \tag{1}$$

In this equation τ is the relaxation time, which depends on both temperature and fictive temperature according to the original suggestion of Tool. The fictive temperature is defined as that temperature at which the glass would have an equilibrium value of enthalpy if it were immediately removed to that temperature. This is illustrated in the simulated cooling curve shown as an enthalpy-temperature diagram in Figure 1.

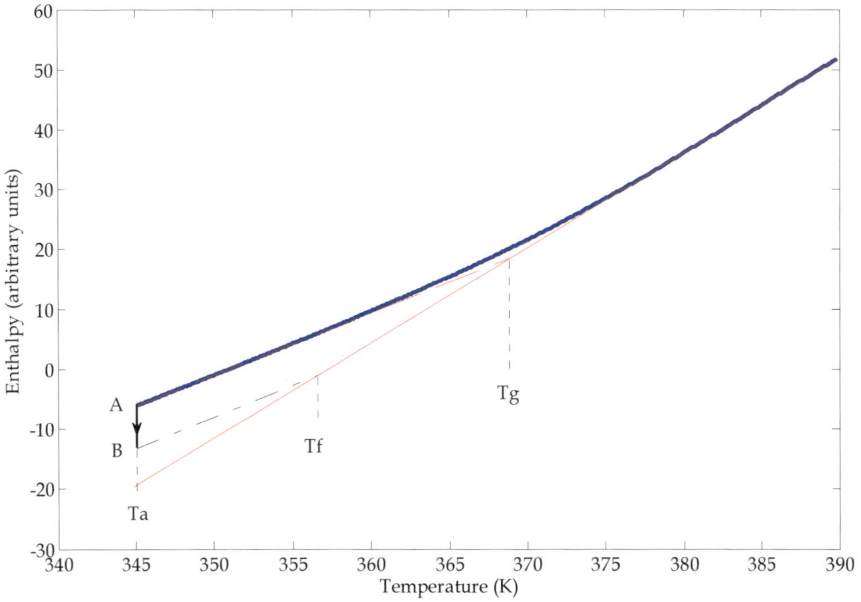

Fig. 1. Simulation of a DSC cooling curve, enthalpy versus temperature, showing the definitions of T_g and T_f. Parameter values: cooling rate –10 K/min, β=0.4, x=0.4, $\Delta h^*/R$=85 kK, τ=100 s at T_r=370 K. The full red line is the asymptote to the equilibrium liquid region; the dashed red line is the asymptote to the glassy region

In this simulation, the glass is formed by cooling at –10 K/min from 390 K to 345 K (state A), and from this cooling curve the glass transition temperature, T_g, is defined as the intersection of the equilibrium liquid and glassy asymptotes, as shown. If the cooling is arrested at A and the glass allowed to approach equilibrium isothermally by physical aging at the temperature T_a, a state B will be reached after some time. The state of the glass at B is defined conveniently by the fictive temperature, T_f, which is found as the intersection with the equilibrium asymptote of a line (dash-dotted) with the slope of the glassy asymptote and passing through state B. Various important aspects of the fictive temperature can be identified from this diagram: first, the fictive temperature of the glass in state A, immediately after cooling and forming the glass and without any physical aging, is identical to the glass transition temperature; second, as the glass is aged at the temperature T_a, below T_g, the fictive temperature decreases and in the limit is equal to the aging temperature; and third, T_f is related to δ by:

$$\delta = \Delta C_p \left(T_f - T_a \right) \tag{2}$$

where ΔC_p is the heat capacity difference between that of the liquid, C_{pl}, and that of the glass, C_{pg}.

Equation 1 introduces in a general way the dependence of the relaxation time on both the temperature and the fictive temperature of the glass, and is known as the single relaxation time model (Hutchinson & Kovacs, 1976). The specific dependence of τ on T and T_f is usually written in one of two ways. In the TNM equation (Moynihan et al, 1976; Narayanaswamy, 1971; Tool, 1946), the dependence is written in the form:

$$\tau(T,T_f) = \tau_g \exp\left[\frac{x\Delta h^*}{RT} + \frac{(1\text{-}x)\Delta h^*}{RT_f} - \frac{\Delta h^*}{RT_g}\right] \tag{3}$$

where τ_g is the average relaxation time in equilibrium at T_g, x ($0 \le x \le 1$) is the non-linearity parameter, Δh^* is the apparent activation energy at T_g, and R is the universal gas constant. An alternative expression derives from the concept of configurational entropy (Gibbs & DiMarzio, 1958) and is known as the Adam-Gibbs (AG) equation (Adam & Gibbs, 1965):

$$\tau = A \exp\left[\frac{N_A s_c^* \Delta\mu}{kTS_c}\right] \tag{4}$$

where N_A is Avogadro's number, s_c^* is the configurational entropy of the smallest cooperatively rearranging region that permits the transition of a molecular segment from one state to another, $\Delta\mu$ is the elementary activation energy per segment, k is Boltzmann's constant and S_c is the macroscopic configurational entropy of the sample.

To introduce a distribution of relaxation times, two approaches are possible: by means of a discrete distribution, as in the so-called KAHR model (Kovacs et al, 1979), or, much more commonly and mathematically more conveniently, by means of an empirical distribution function, namely the stretched exponential or Kohlrausch-Williams-Watts (KWW) function (Kohlrausch, 1866; Williams & Watts, 1970):

$$\varphi(t) = \exp\left[-\left(\frac{t}{\tau}\right)^{\beta}\right] \tag{5}$$

where the exponent β is inversely related to the width of the distribution of relaxation times. The set of equations 1, 2, 3 and 5 (or 1, 2, 4 and 5) is sufficient to simulate the response of a glass forming system to any prescribed thermal history. Matlab provides a very convenient environment in which to do this, and the results of such simulations in a variety of practical situations form the basis of this paper. In the first instance, the simple "three step cycles" thermal history is analysed, involving cooling at constant rate through the glass transition region to form the glass, isothermal annealing for various times to age the glass, and then reheating at constant rate through the transition region to simulate a typical DSC experiment, and in particular to examine the effects of the length of aging time at T_a on this reheating stage. Following this basic analysis of conventional DSC, the same procedure will be used to investigate the technique of TMDSC, in which a (usually) sinusoidally periodic modulation of the temperature is superimposed on the underlying cooling or heating rate (or isotherm).

3. Three step cycles

In this section, we outline first how the theoretical model can describe all the phenomenological aspects of the glass transition, and then show how the material parameters may be derived from experimental data by appropriate methods.

3.1 Phenomenology

A typical simulated cooling curve has been shown in Figure 1, together with an unspecified annealing period at temperature T_a. The three step thermal cycles consist of these two steps followed by heating at constant rate, which is the step that is obtained experimentally by

DSC in the study of the physical aging or enthalpy relaxation of polymer glasses (Hodge, 1994; Hutchinson, 1995). These cycles are therefore defined by several experimental variables: the cooling rate, q_1, the temperature T_a, the aging time, t_a, at T_a (or the enthalpy reduction during this time, $\bar{\delta}$), and the heating rate, q_2. In addition, there are several material parameters, the most important of which are: x, β, Δh^*, τ_g and ΔC_p. The heating step of these cycles is dependent on all of these variables, and the purpose of these simulations is, first, to describe and explain the experimentally observed behaviour, and subsequently to show how to obtain the material parameters from the experimental data. Figure 2 (full lines) shows two typical heating curves, for glasses aged for about one month (blue line) and four months (red line) at a temperature 20°C below T_g, in which large endothermic peaks appear. This is the most important characteristic of such experiments, and the magnitude and position of these peaks reflects the amount of aging that has taken place at T_a. To determine the amount of enthalpy lost during aging, it is necessary to do a second cycle, cooling at the same rate as for the first cycle, and then immediately reheating at the same rate as for the first cycle, without any aging time at T_a. This second heating stage is sometimes called the reference scan, and is shown in Figure 2 by the dashed line (green). Although hardly visible on the scale of this figure, there is in fact a small endothermic peak, referred to as an upper peak (Hutchinson & Ruddy, 1990) and here centred at about 65°C, even though there has been no aging; it can be shown that such a peak must always be present in these heating scans (Ramos et al., 1984) unless it is hidden under the main endothermic peak. The difference in areas under the first and reference scans is equal to the enthalpy lost during aging at T_a.

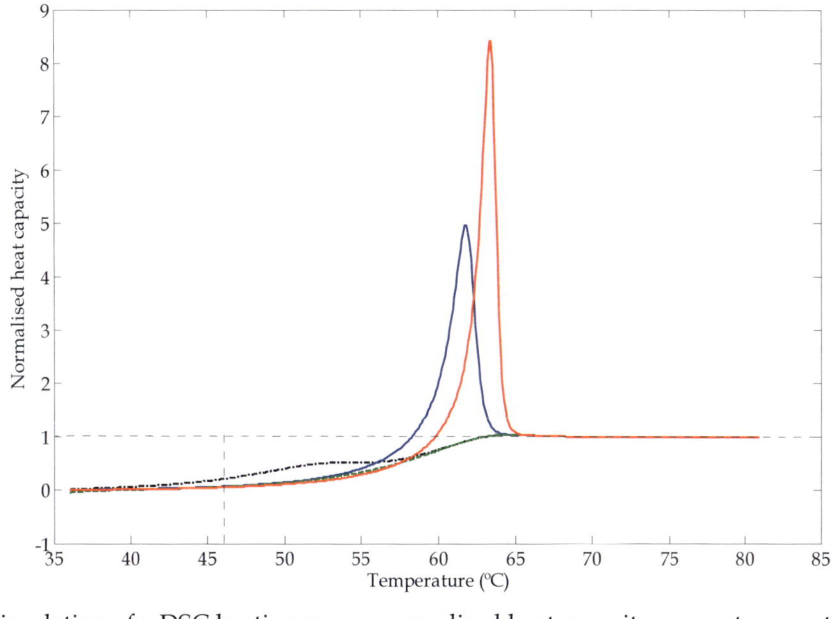

Fig. 2. Simulation of a DSC heating curve, normalised heat capacity versus temperature, for a glass formed by cooling at –40 K/min and then aged at T_a=36°C for 10^4 s (black dash-dotted line), 3×10^6 s (blue full line) or 10^7 s (red full line). Material parameter values: β=0.35, x=0.4, $\Delta h^*/R$=85 kK, τ=100 s at T_r=56°C. The horizontal dotted black line is the asymptote to the equilibrium liquid region, and the vertical dotted black line indicates the fictive temperature, T_f, after aging at T_a for 3×10^6 s

The fictive temperature of the glass in the aged state, for example in Figure 2 after about one month at T_a, can be found by the so-called equal areas method (Moynihan et al., 1976; Richardson & Savill, 1975). In this method, illustrated in Figure 2, the total area under the endothermic peak for the aged glass is equal to the area under the asymptote to the liquid-like region (dotted black line) and above the fictive temperature, T_f. Clearly, with increased aging, as the endothermic peak increases in magnitude, the fictive temperature moves to lower values, and in the limit will asymptotically approach the aging temperature, T_a.

The same Figure 2 also shows another characteristic feature of the heating scan of glasses which occurs under certain conditions. The dash-dotted black line is the heating scan following only about 3 hours aging at T_a, and shows the existence of what is often called a sub-T_g peak, here at about 52.5°C. When first observed by DSC, the appearance of double peaks in the glass transition region was considered something of a mystery (Illers, 1969; Neki & Geil, 1973; Retting, 1969), though they in fact arise quite naturally as a consequence of the distribution of relaxation times, and under certain quite well defined experimental conditions: a fast cooling rate in comparison with the subsequent heating rate, and little or no aging at the lower temperature of the cycle, the lower this temperature relative to the glass transition temperature the more likely being the appearance of a sub-T_g peak. In addition, although sub-T_g peaks are often observed for glasses with low values of β, in other words when the relaxation time distribution is broad (Ruddy & Hutchinson, 1988), such as is the case for poly(vinyl chloride) (Berens & Hodge, 1982), a broad distribution of relaxation times is not a pre-requisite for their appearance, as was demonstrated by the behaviour of some carefully prepared inorganic glasses (Pappin et al., 1994).

This phenomenology of the response of glasses to heating through the transition region, in which characteristic features such as the endothermic peak and its dependence on the aging time and heating rate are observed, the existence of the upper peak and its relative invariance with the experimental variables (Hutchinson & Ruddy, 1990), and the appearance of sub-T_g peaks and the conditions under which they are most likely to be observed, can be well described by the theoretical development outlined above. Simulations can be made very simply in the Matlab environment, and in particular, the ease of obtaining maximum values of a vector is of particular benefit. In the next section, these same simulations are used to show how the important material parameters may be derived from the experimental data.

3.2 The peak shift method

The theoretical development above includes one parameter in particular, the non-linearity parameter x, which, although defining the relative importance of temperature and structure (fictive temperature) to the relaxation time, does not have any obvious physical significance. Nevertheless, the excellent description of all the phenomenological aspects outline above suggests that there should be some physical significance, and considerable effort has been made by numerous workers to investigate this. The basic idea has been to evaluate x for different glass-forming systems in order to relate its value to the nature of the glass-former, and the review by Hodge (Hodge, 1994) gives an excellent summary. Fundamental to this approach is the need to have a reliable method for the evaluation of this parameter x. The majority of workers make use of what is termed the curve-fitting method, whereby a least-squares minimisation routine is used to fit the set of theoretical equations to the experimental DSC heating curve. While mathematically convenient, this approach suffers from some drawbacks: for example, it assumes a certain specific form for the distribution function, namely the stretched exponential. More importantly, though, it is often applied to fit heating curves for glasses aged only for short times, which consequently have little non-linearity; it is not appropriate to determine the non-linearity parameter by fitting curves which have no significant dependence on this parameter.

An alternative approach, which does not suffer from these drawbacks, was proposed some time ago. It is based upon the dependence of the endothermic peak temperature, T_p, on the experimental conditions defining the three step thermal cycles (Kovacs & Hutchinson, 1979; Ramos et al., 1984). This has become known as the peak shift method. From an extensive analysis of the response of glasses to such cycles, the dependence of T_p on each experimental variable (q_1, T_a, $\bar{\delta}$, q_2) while maintaining the others constant was found, in the limiting case of long aging times, to be linear. Thus one can define a set of shifts $\left[\hat{s}(q_1),\hat{s}(T_a),\hat{s}(\bar{\delta}),\hat{s}(q_2)\right]$, the most useful in respect of the experimental determination of x being:

$$\hat{s}(\bar{\delta}) = \Delta C_p \left(\frac{\partial T_p}{\partial \bar{\delta}}\right)_{q_1,T_1,q_2} \tag{6}$$

The interesting aspect of this approach is that these shifts are all inter-dependent, and are all functions of x:

$$F(x) = \hat{s}(\bar{\delta}) = -\hat{s}(q_1) = \hat{s}(q_2) - 1 \tag{7}$$

where the function $F(x)$, in limiting conditions, asymptotically approaches the simple hyperbolic function $F(x)=x^{-1}-1$, shown in Figure 3 and known as the master curve. Even more interestingly, this limiting function is essentially independent of the choice of distribution function used, be it a discrete distribution as in the multi-parameter KAHR model or the stretched exponential KWW function.

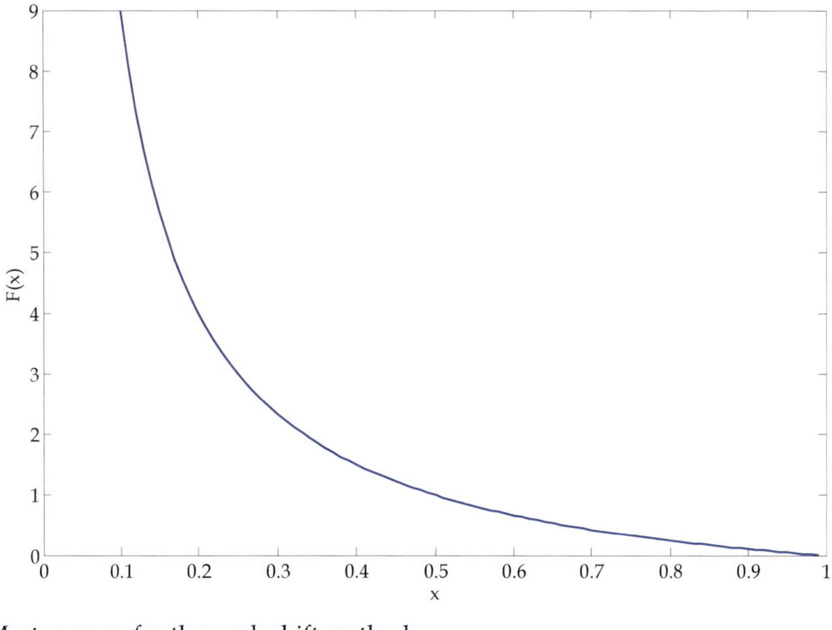

Fig. 3. Master curve for the peak shift method

The procedure (Hutchinson, 1987) is to determine, by a series of experiments, the peak endotherm temperatures, T_p, obtained on heating at constant rate, typically 10 K/min, for glasses which have been formed initially by cooling at the same rate, and then aged at a temperature, T_a, usually 10 to 20°C below T_g, for a range of times, which should extend ideally to periods as long as is convenient in order to approach the limiting conditions necessary. These lengths of time can be as much as several months, much longer than the timescales usually used in the curve-fitting method. For each endotherm, the associated enthalpy lost, $\bar{\delta}$, during the immediately previous aging can be determined from the area difference under this endothermic peak and under a reference scan made, for the same sample, under identical cycle conditions, but without any aging at T_a.

A plot of T_p as a function of $\bar{\delta}$ or as a function of the logarithm of the aging time, t_a, appears linear for values of $\bar{\delta}$ or t_a large enough for limiting conditions to be achieved, and from this linear region the slope is obtained which permits the evaluation of $\hat{s}(\bar{\delta})$ from Equation 6, and hence of $F(x)$ from Equation 7. The experimental value of x is then found from the master curve in Figure 3. The limiting dependence of T_p on $\bar{\delta}$ is essentially independent of all the other experimental variables (q_1, q_2, T_a) defining the thermal cycle, and of the distribution function for the relaxation times, and thus the peak shift method provides a rational means of evaluating experimentally the non-linearity parameter x (Hutchinson & Ruddy, 1988).

4. Temperature modulated DSC (TMDSC)

In the early 1990s, the idea of modulating the constant heating rate of conventional DSC was conceived by Reading and co-workers (Gill et al., 1993; Reading et al., 1993a). It was patented in the US in 1993 (Reading et al., 1993b), and commercialised by TA Instruments as Modulated DSC. Subsequently, other instrument manufacturers commercialised their own versions, including Alternating DSC (ADSC) from Mettler Toledo. Generically, such techniques are now referred to as Temperature Modulated DSC (TMDSC). The basic principle in all cases is to superimpose on the constant heating rate (or cooling rate, or isotherm) of conventional DSC a periodically (and in practice sinusoidally) varying modulation. The idea is that, in addition to the same information as is available from conventional DSC, TMDSC also provides, at any time during a scan, information about the instantaneous state of the sample.

The periodically modulated heating rate and heat flow signals can be analysed by Fourier Transformation, to give the amplitudes of the periodically varying heat flow and heating rate signals, and an average heat flow signal. The average signal is essentially the same signal as would be obtained by conventional DSC at the same rate as the underlying rate of TMDSC; the ratio of the amplitudes of the heat flow and heating rate is sometimes referred to as the "reversing" component; and the difference between the underlying signal and the reversing component is known as the "non-reversing" component. An alternative approach is to treat the reversing component as a complex heat capacity, C_p^*, and use the phase angle which results from the Fourier Transformation to separate C_p^* into its in-phase, C_p', and out-of-phase, C_p'', components (Schawe, 1995). With respect to the glass transition, the response of glasses in TMDSC during the heating stage of the three step thermal cycles shows some characteristic features: the average signal shows the usual endotherm associated with enthalpy relaxation which is seen by conventional DSC; the reversing component and C_p' show a sigmoidal change at an apparent glass transition temperature, T_g(dynamic), different from that found by conventional DSC, and without any endothermic peak; the non-reversing component and C_p'', as well as the phase angle, show a peak in the region of T_g(dynamic). Although this technique of TMDSC appeared from the outset to offer several advantages over conventional DSC, the initial interpretation of some of these features of the response in the glass transition region was rather confusing. For example, the observation that T_g(dynamic) is independent of the heating or cooling rate prompted the idea that this represented a rate independent T_g, in contradiction to the basic idea of the glass transition as a kinetic phenomenon, while the peak in the non-reversing heat flow was associated with enthalpy relaxation, since no peak appeared in the reversing component; this last, however, represents an interpretation difficult to reconcile with the fact that such a peak also appears in the non-reversing component during cooling, where enthalpy relaxation plays no part. There was clearly a need for a sound theoretical treatment of TMDSC in the glass transition region in order to interpret correctly the various signals. This could be based on the same formalism as had been adopted for the simulation of three step thermal cycles in conventional DSC, but now with a modulated temperature programme. These simulations were very conveniently made using Matlab, for which standard procedures exist for Fast Fourier Transformation (fft), for integrating the fundamental differential equation, Equation 1, for the kinetics of the relaxation process using the 4th-5th order Runge-Kutta routine (ode23), and for convolution integrals of the type required when the stretched exponential distribution is incorporated with the fictive temperature formulation (conv). Such simulations were able to describe quantitatively all the experimentally observed phenomena and thus permitted the interpretation of the signals in a logical way, as well as providing a means of investigating the effects of both the experimental and material parameters on the response. The most important aspects of these results are presented here.

The TMDSC experiment in the glass transition region is defined by a set of experimental parameters, which are: the underlying or average rate, either on cooling or heating (q_{av}), the period of the modulations (p), and the amplitude of the temperature modulations (A_T). The material parameters are the same as those for the simulation of conventional DSC. As an illustration of these simulations, Figure 4 shows the result for a modulated cooling curve, in the form of modulated heat flow (*HF*) as a function of time. It is clear that the amplitude of the modulations decreases markedly during cooling, corresponding to the sigmoidal change in the reversing or complex heat capacity. What is not so obvious is that the average value of the heat flow also decreases, though in a different way and over a different temperature (or time) range. In order to identify this effect, it is necessary to do a Fourier Transform (fft) of single cycles of these heat flow and heating rate modulations, using a window which is slid along the time scale to cover the whole cooling curve. From these Fourier Transformations, amplitudes and average values and the phase angle between heat flow and heating rate are obtained, from which the complex heat capacity and its in-phase and out-of-phase components, as well as the average heat capacity, are calculated:

$$C_P^* = \frac{A_{HF}}{A_\beta} \tag{8a}$$

$$C_P' = C_P^* \cos\varphi \tag{8b}$$

$$C_P'' = C_P^* \sin\varphi \tag{8c}$$

$$C_{\mathrm{P,ave}} = \frac{\langle HF \rangle}{\langle \beta \rangle} \tag{8d}$$

In these equations, A_{HF} is the amplitude of the heat flow modulations, A_β is the amplitude of the heating rate modulations, φ is the phase angle between the heating rate and heat flow modulations, and <*HF*> and <β> are the average values of the heat flow and heating rate, respectively. Because the phase angle is very small in the glass transition region, the in-phase heat capacity is approximately equal to the magnitude of the complex heat capacity. The variations of the in-phase and out-of-phase heat capacities and of the phase angle, obtained by Fourier Transformation of the modulations in Figure 4, are shown in Figure 5.

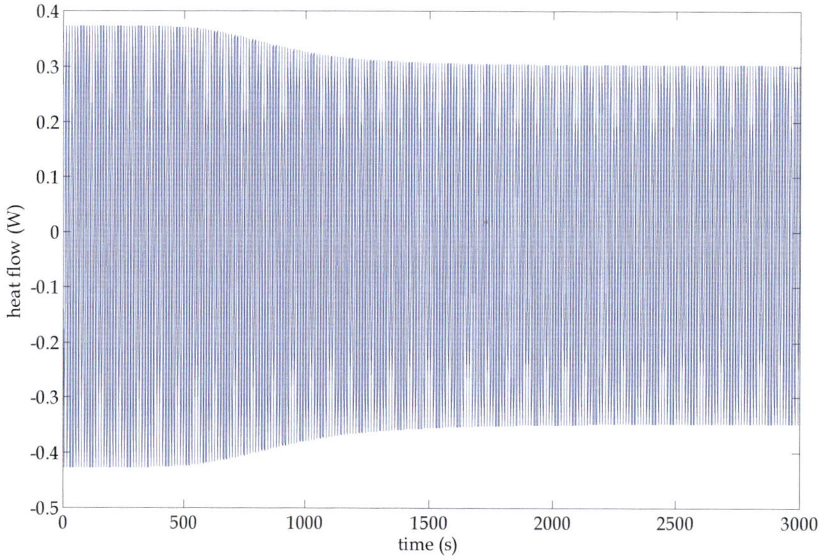

Fig. 4. Modulated cooling curve obtained by Matlab simulation with experimental and material parameters as follows: $q_{\mathrm{av}} = -1$ K/min, $p = 12$ s, $A_{\mathrm{T}} = 0.5$ K, $\beta = 0.4$, $x = 0.4$, $\Delta h^*/R = 85$ kK, $\Delta c_{\mathrm{P}} = 0.3$ J/gK, $c_{\mathrm{Pl}} = 1.6$ J/gK, $c_{\mathrm{Pg}} = 1.3$ J/gK

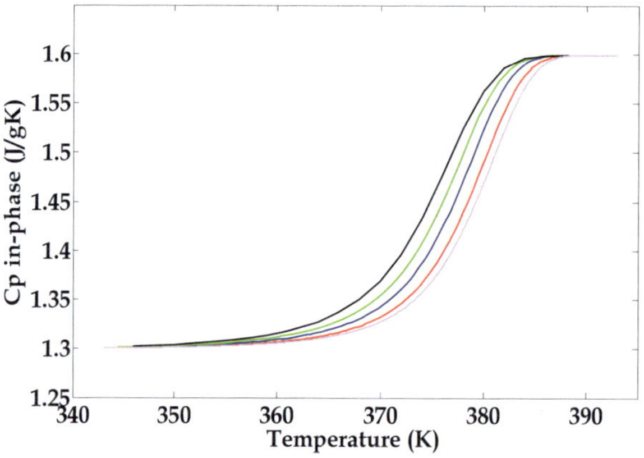

(a)

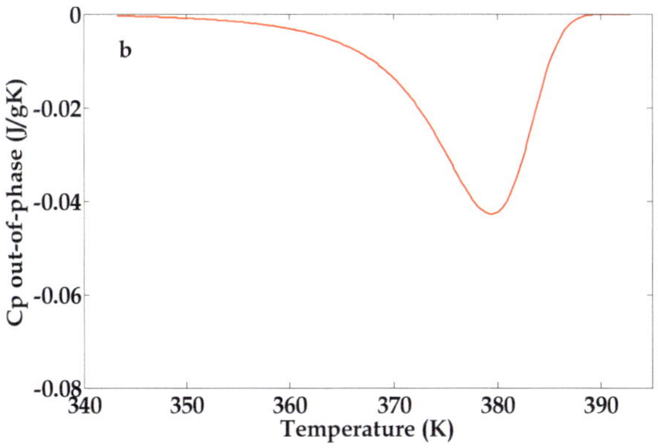

(b)

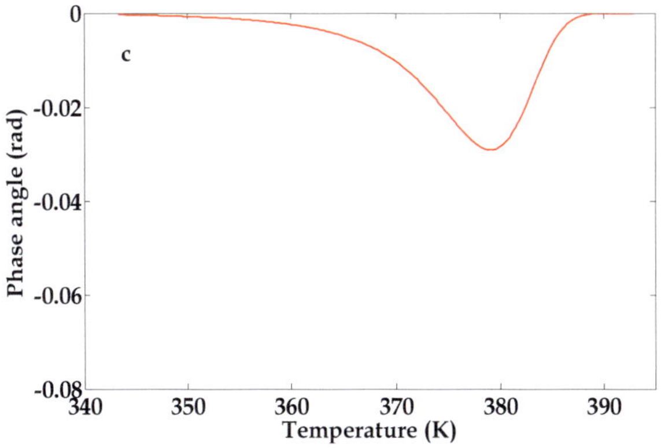

(c)

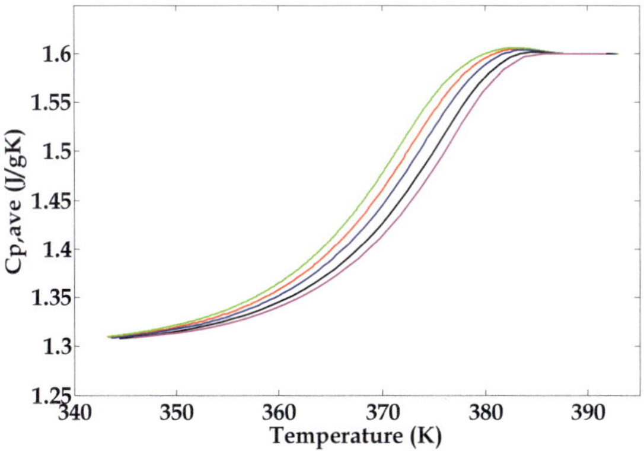

(d)

Fig. 5. Fourier transformed signals (red curves) for modulated cooling curve of Figure 4: (a) in-phase heat capacity; (b) out-of-phase heat capacity; (c) phase angle; (d) average heat capacity. In Figure 5a, modulation periods [s] are: 120 (black), 60 (green), 30 (blue), 12 (red), 6 (lilac). In Figure 5d, the cooling rates [K/min] are: –0.5 (green), –1 (red), –2 (blue), –5 (black), –10 (magenta)

The simulations of Figure 5 describe, both qualitatively and quantitatively, all the characteristic features of TMDSC experiments in the glass transition region. A number of comments may be made about these results in general, and also in respect of their dependence on both the experimental and material parameters. In the first place, it is evident that the dynamic glass transition (from c_P', Figure 5a) is quite different from the conventional glass transition (from $c_{P,ave}$, Figure 5d). Not only is the former considerably sharper, but also the glass transition temperature, obtained for example from the mid-point (in these simulations, for the red curves where c_P = 1.45 J/gK), is higher for the dynamic glass transition. These differences represent an important distinction between what are sometimes referred to as the thermal glass transition, from the average heat capacity of Figure 5d and equivalent to that obtained by conventional DSC, and the dynamic glass transition, from the complex or in-phase heat capacity of Figure 5a. In the former case, for the thermal glass transition, as the glass is cooled it departs from equilibrium (cf. Figure 1) at some temperature which depends on the cooling rate, and therefore the non-equilibrium state and the parameters describing non-equilibrium, in particular the non-linearity parameter x, play an important role in the kinetics of the transition. On the other hand, in the latter case, for the dynamic glass transition, the state is close to an equilibrium liquid in principle; the response of the sample is therefore glassy if the period of modulation is short, is liquid-like if the period is sufficiently long, and displays a transition region if the period is between these limits. The question of whether any given period is short or long has to be answered by comparing it with the instantaneous average relaxation time of the material. This average relaxation time increases as the temperature decreases, thus giving rise to the approximately Debye-type relaxation seen in Figure 5b for the out-of-phase component.

This situation is, however, complicated by the overlapping of the thermal and dynamic transitions, which can be demonstrated quite clearly by these Matlab simulations. It is a simple matter to run simulations for different values of period of modulation and of cooling rate to establish their separate effects, which are shown in Figures 5a and 5d, respectively. In Figure 5a, as the period of modulation increases, the dynamic glass transition temperature decreases, an effect which would, in principle, allow the determination of the apparent activation energy for the relaxation (Jiang et al, 1998). However, this determination of the activation energy supposes that the dynamic transition occurs entirely in equilibrium, analogous to the situation for dynamic mechanical analysis or dielectric analysis. However, it can be seen here from a comparison of Figures 5a and 5d that, even for the shortest modulation period of 6 seconds, the thermal transition begins before the dynamic transition has passed completely from a liquid to a glassy response.

There are two important conclusions that can be drawn from this observation. First, for the correct study of the dynamic glass transition, it is necessary to separate it from the thermal transition, which requires either a very slow cooling rate or a very short modulation period. The latter is limited by problems of heat transfer into the sample, and it is usually considered that the minimum period experimentally accessible is approximately 12 seconds. The former is limited only by available time, though it must be borne in mind that these experimental times can be very long; for example, the simulated experiment in Figure 5d for a cooling rate of –0.5 K/min takes almost 2 hours, and it would require a further reduction in the cooling rate by at least an order of magnitude for the complete separation of the dynamic and thermal transitions.

These considerations lead to the second important conclusion, which is that there must be some equivalence between the cooling rate and the frequency of modulation, and that this equivalence must be related to the material parameters, β and x. For example, it is almost always observed that, within what might be called typical ranges of values of the experimental variables (cooling rate and modulation frequency), these two types of transition overlap, with the dynamic glass transition usually being a few degrees higher than T_g (Donth et al, 1997; Hensel & Schick, 1998; Hutchinson, 1998; Montserrat, 2000; Weyer et al, 1997). A theoretical expression for the relationship between cooling rate and frequency can be derived from the fluctuation dissipation theorem for the glass transition (Donth et al, 1997), and can be written in the following form relating the angular frequency of modulation, ω (rad/s) in TMDSC and the cooling rate $|q|$ (K/s) in conventional DSC:

$$\omega = \frac{|q|}{a\,\delta T} \tag{9}$$

where a is a constant and δT is the mean temperature fluctuation of the cooperatively rearranging regions. By means of Matlab simulations in which the cooling rate in conventional DSC was determined such that it gave the same value of T_g as that for TMDSC with a period of 120 s (and an average cooling rate of –0.3 K/min), it has been shown (Hutchinson & Montserrat, 2001; Montserrat et al, 2005) that the magnitude of the temperature fluctuations increases the wider is the distribution of relaxation times (small β) and the greater is the non-linearity of the relaxation kinetics (small x), with interesting implications regarding the physical phenomena underlying the glass transition.

The effects of these material parameters, β and x, on the appearance of the TMDSC signals, such as those shown in Figure 5, are very different, as can be demonstrated rather simply by these Matlab simulations. In Figure 6 are shown the effects of changing x and β on the average heat capacity (Figures 6a and 6b, respectively) and on the complex heat capacity (Figures 6c and 6d, respectively).

With respect to the average heat capacity signals in Figures 6a and 6b, the effects of increasing x and of increasing β are very similar: in both cases the transition broadens as the parameter value decreases towards zero. In respect of x, this is explained by the response becoming more non-linear as x decreases, giving rise to a greater relative dependence on the fictive temperature (cf. Equation 3), which means that the relaxation time shortens and the transition occurs at ever lower temperatures, observed in Figure 6a as a shift, for example, of

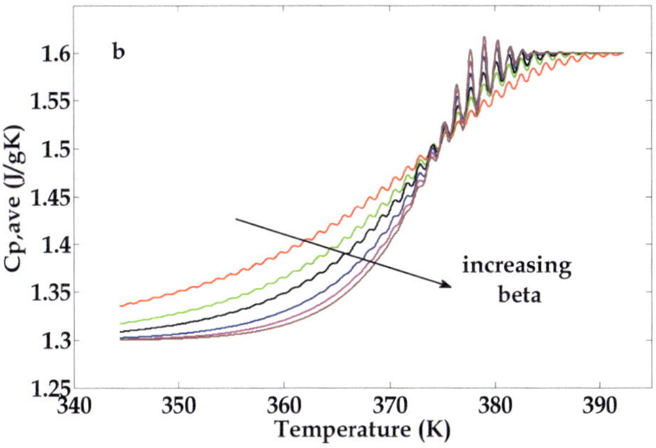

(a)

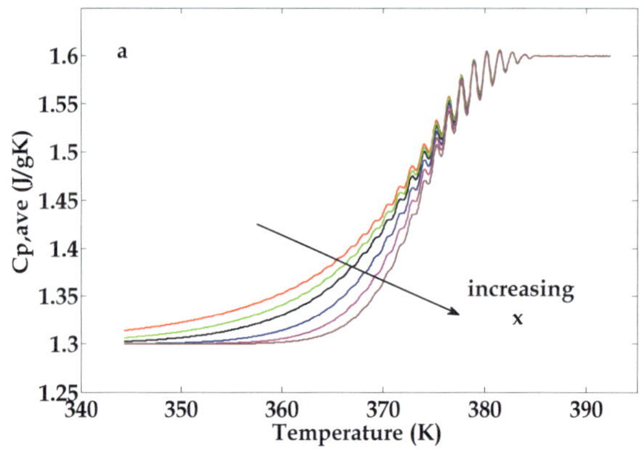

(b)

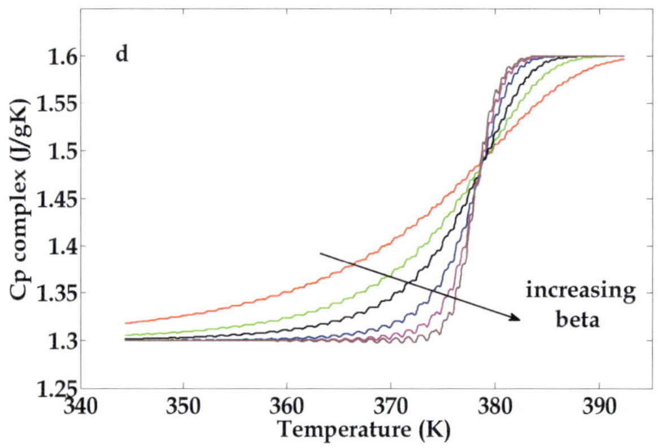

(c)

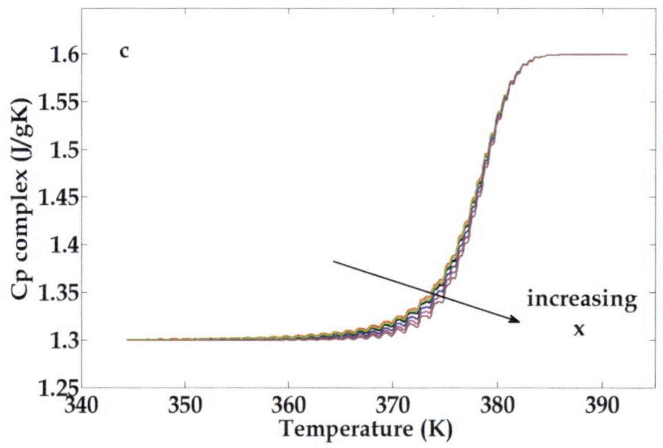

(d)

Fig. 6. Effects of x and β on the average and complex heat capacities in TMDSC on cooling through the glass transition region: (a) and (c) x=0.2, 0.3, 0.4, 0.6, 0.8, 1.0, with β=0.6; (b) and (d) β=0.2, 0.3, 0.4, 0.6, 0.8, 1.0, with x=0.4. Other parameters: q_{av}=–3 K/min, p=24 s, A_T=0.5 K, $\Delta h^*/R$=85 kK the mid-point temperature. In respect of β, reducing its value leads to a broadening of the distribution function (cf. Equation 5), with a consequent broadening of the response on cooling. In contrast, with respect to the complex heat capacity signals in Figures 6c and 6d, the effects of increasing x and of increasing β are very different: in one case (effect of x) the transition remains essentially unaffected, whereas in the other case (effect of β) the transition broadens as the parameter value decreases. In respect of x, this is explained by the fact that, in principle and as explained earlier, the dynamic transition occurs in equilibrium, where there is no effect of non-linearity since $T_f=T$ (cf. Equation 3). The small amount of deviation observed in Figure 6c from a unique curve for all values of x may be explained by the overlapping of the dynamic and thermal transitions, which results in the system's not remaining truly in equilibrium in the latter part of the relaxation. In respect of β, on the other hand, even in equilibrium the effect of the width of the distribution will be evident. Indeed, the breadth of the relaxation in the complex heat capacity is a function only of β, since it is essentially independent of x, which means that such curves can be used for the independent experimental determination of the parameter β (Montserrat & Hutchinson, 2002).

It is interesting also to note another characteristic feature of these curves, namely the appearance of ripples. These arise from the way in which the Fourier Transformation is made, in a window of a single cycle of the modulations, sliding this window along the time scale to cover the whole of the transition. In Figure 5, the window is slid by one whole cycle between Fourier Transformations, and hence the ripples do not appear. In Figure 6, the window is slid by the time step of the calculations, and hence the ripples do appear (Hutchinson & Montserrat, 1997). In the transition interval, the frequency of these ripples is twice the frequency of the heating rate modulations. In the experimental data these ripples should also appear, and indeed do so in the output signals from ADSC from Mettler Toledo, and their frequency is in agreement with the model predictions. These ripples do not appear in the output data from TMDSC equipment from other manufacturers, either because the data have been smoothed or because the Fourier Transformation window is slid along the time scale by integral cycles.

As a final comment on the use of TMDSC for the study of the glass transition in polymers, it is worth pointing out the relatively recent development of a multi-frequency technique, named TOPEM®, from Mettler Toledo. In this technique, instead of a periodic modulation of the temperature or of the heating rate as in TMDSC, the sample is subjected to a stochastic series of small temperature pulses, alternately positive and negative, with a user-defined range for the interval of time between these pulses, known as the switching time range. The combination of these two features, the stochastic nature and the use of pulses rather than modulations, allows an analysis of the frequency dependence to be made in a single scan, thus offering a significant advantage over TMDSC techniques which use only a single frequency in any one experiment. This advantage will become particularly apparent in the next section of this paper where the crosslinking reactions of thermosetting polymers are investigated. The method of analysis in TOPEM® is also different, using Laplace Transformation rather than Fourier Transformation, and is made in a Matlab environment using a Parameter Estimation Method (PEM). Amongst other output quantities, TOPEM® calculates what is called the quasi-static heat capacity, C_{p0}, which is the equivalent of the complex heat capacity of TMDSC, but for the limiting case of zero frequency. It is this quasi-static heat capacity which is first obtained from the experimental stochastic data, and is then separated into its frequency components. In a study of this technique applied to the glass transition of polymers (Fraga et al, 2007), the effects of a number of experimental parameters were investigated, including the range of frequencies over which the technique could usefully be applied.

5. Crosslinking reaction in thermosetting polymers

In the crosslinking (or cure) process for thermosetting polymers, a chemical reaction takes place between the resin and the crosslinking agent (hardener) such that the monomers of the un-reacted resin are incorporated into a three-dimensional rigid network structure. In this process, the viscous liquid resin, which has a very low T_g, usually sub-ambient, is transformed into a stiff and hard material, with a high T_g and with numerous industrial applications, from surface coatings to the matrix material for high performance fibre reinforced composites. Usually, a stoichiometric ratio of resin to hardener will be used, as this gives the optimum properties of the cured material, including a maximum value of the glass transition temperature. In addition, though, the conditions under which the cure reaction is conducted can also be important: for example, the cure may be isothermal, and the isothermal cure temperature may be selected within quite a wide range, or the cure may be non-isothermal, at a constant heating rate over a temperature range, with various possibilities for the heating rate. The selection of cure conditions can be important. For instance, in isothermal cure at low temperatures, the increase in T_g of the system that results from the crosslinking reaction can be such that it becomes higher than the isothermal cure temperature. Under these conditions, vitrification will occur, since the partially cured material will then be at a temperature below its T_g. Vitrification, followed by devitrification, can also occur under some circumstance during non-isothermal cure. When a crosslinking system vitrifies, the reaction rate changes dramatically, from a relatively rapid rate, controlled by the chemical rate constants of the reaction, to a much slower rate, which is controlled by the rate of diffusion of the reacting species. The ability to predict whether or not vitrification will occur under any given cure conditions is of some importance, and hence it is necessary to describe the kinetics of the reaction.

A particularly good illustration of the importance of understanding the cure kinetics is afforded by the cure reaction that takes place during the fabrication of epoxy-clay nanocomposites. These materials consist of a small proportion, typically less than 5 wt%, of organically modified clay in an epoxy resin matrix. The structure of the clay is laminar, and the fundamental idea is that the clay layers should separate completely (exfoliate) and be distributed uniformly throughout the epoxy matrix in the final cured nanocomposite: in this way, the nanoclay provides a very efficient reinforcement because of its large surface area, and thus can strengthen and stiffen the epoxy without significantly increasing its density, of particular importance for aeronautical applications, for example. However, to obtain an exfoliated structure is difficult, because it depends on the relative rates of cure of the resin in the intra-gallery and extra-gallery regions of the clay. Control of these rates, i.e. of the kinetics of the reaction, is therefore of crucial importance in obtaining an optimised nanostructure of these materials (Montserrat et al, 2008; Pustkova et al, 2009). The following sections discuss how the cure kinetics can be simulated using Matlab, to model both conventional and Temperature Modulated DSC experiments.

5.1 Theoretical aspects of cure kinetics

In the absence of vitrification, the cure reaction is chemically controlled and the time dependence of the degree of cure, which is denoted by α and which increases from 0 initially to 1 for the fully cured material, can be described by various different kinetic equations. One of the most widely used equations is that of Kamal (Kamal, 1974), which describes an autocatalytic reaction:

$$\left(\frac{d\alpha}{dt}\right)_{chem} = \left(k_1 + k_2\alpha^m\right)\left(1-\alpha\right)^n \tag{10}$$

where k_1 and k_2 are temperature dependent rate constants and the exponents m and n are the reaction orders. The rate constants depend on temperature according to the Arrhenius equation:

$$k_{c,1} = A_1 \exp\left(-\frac{E_{c,1}}{RT}\right) \tag{11a}$$

$$k_{c,2} = A_2 \exp\left(-\frac{E_{c,2}}{RT}\right) \tag{11b}$$

where A_1 and A_2 are pre-exponential constants, E is the activation energy, and R is the universal gas constant. In this equation, a subscript c has been added for k and E to indicate that that these are values for the chemically controlled reaction.

These Equations 10 and 11 are sufficient to describe the kinetics of the cure reaction when it is chemically controlled, in other words in the absence of vitrification (to be discussed in detail below), and the predictions of this model can be compared with experimental DSC data in the form of heat flow as a function of time (for isothermal cure) or as a function of temperature (for non-isothermal cure). The specific heat flow, HF [W/g] is given by:

$$HF = \Delta H_\infty \frac{d\alpha}{dt} \tag{12}$$

where ΔH_∞ is the total heat of reaction per unit mass [J/g] for a fully cured system. Typical results which emerge from this model are shown in Figures 7a and 7b for isothermal and non-isothermal cure, respectively, where the effects of some of the experimental parameters are included: in Figure 7a, four different isothermal cure temperatures (50°C, 60°C, 70°C and 80°C) are used, with the reaction occurring at shorter times as the cure temperature increases; in Figure 7b, four different heating rates are used (1, 2, 5 and 10 K/min), with the reaction shifting to higher temperatures with increasing heating rate.

By fitting these kinetic equations to the experimental data, it is possible to evaluate the various kinetic parameters, in particular the activation energies, the pre-exponential parameters, and the reaction exponents, m and n. In principle, the same parameter values will be obtained from both isothermal and non-isothermal experimental data. In practice, however, the kinetic equations are only an approximation to the real situation, which is generally much more complex, involving not just one reaction, for example the reaction of the primary amine of the cross-linking agent with the epoxy monomers, but also other reactions such as the reaction of secondary amines which result from the first reaction, and a homopolymerization reaction (etherification) which can be catalyzed by the tertiary amines resulting from the second reaction (Fernández-Francos et al, 2007; Kubisa & Penczek, 1999; Montserrat et al, 2008; Pascault et al, 2002; Tanaka & Bauer, 1988). The result of this added complexity is that a best fit to non-isothermal data does not always result in a best fit for the isothermal data. Nevertheless, in most instances a satisfactory fit can be obtained to all the experimental data, and the evaluation of the parameter values then provides useful information about the reaction kinetics.

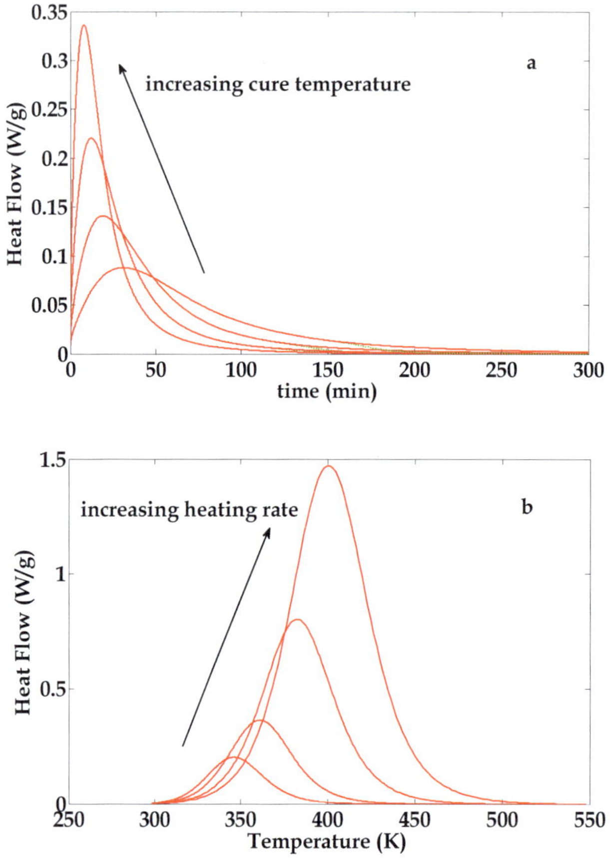

Fig. 7. Cure simulations under isothermal [(a): at 50°C, 60°C, 70°C and 80°C] and non-isothermal [(b): at 1, 2, 5 and 10 K/min] conditions. Parameters: m=0.5, n=1.5, $A_1=10^{3.6}$ s, $A_2=10^{3.4}$ s, $E_{c,1}$=51.8 kJ/mol, $E_{c,2}$=41.5 kJ/mol, ΔH_∞=520 J/g

The usual procedure for evaluating the parameter values from the experimental data is first to determine the total heat of reaction, per unit mass of sample, from the non-isothermal cure curves. This is calculated as the area under the cure curve of heat flow per unit mass of sample as a function of temperature, normalized by the heating rate. For a stoichiometric ratio of diglycidyl ether of bisphenol-A (DGEBA) epoxy resin and a diamine curing agent, for example, this is approximately 400 J/g. The reason for using the non-isothermal cure rather than the isothermal cure is that in isothermal cure it is possible that vitrification might occur. If this happens, then the cure does not proceed to completion, but the cure rate decreases to zero before the reaction is complete, and it is not possible to identify, by conventional DSC, whether or not this occurs. An analysis of the isothermal cure curve under these circumstances, using the kinetic Equations 10-12 above, would lead to erroneous results. In fact, it is also possible for vitrification to occur during non-isothermal cure, though the experimental circumstances for this (essentially, a very slow heating rate) are generally not those that are used in practice. The way in which the problem of vitrification during cure can be addressed by means of TMDSC is discussed in the following sections, first in a general way and then, separately, with respect to isothermal cure and non-isothermal cure. In these latter cases it will be shown how Matlab simulations of the cure under TMDSC conditions provide a rational way of interpreting the experimental results, and allow a comparison with other dynamic techniques operating over a quite different frequency range. The graphical representation aspects are particularly helpful.

5.2 Cure reaction with vitrification

Vitrification occurs, either in isothermal cure or in non-isothermal cure, when the glass transition temperature of the cross-linking system, which is continuously increasing as the degree of cross-linking increases, reaches and then exceeds the cure temperature. In isothermal cure, vitrification results in a rather rapid decrease in the rate of cure, as the rate of reaction changes from being controlled by the chemical rate constants, $k_{c,1}$ and $k_{c,2}$, to being controlled by the diffusion of the reacting species, with a much slower rate determined by a diffusion rate constant, k_d. As a consequence, the reaction effectively stops, and the system remains only partially cured. Likewise, in non-isothermal cure, it is possible for the glass transition of the curing system to increase beyond the instantaneous value of the (continually increasing) cure temperature, generally provided that the rate of heating is sufficiently slow. The system therefore vitrifies, but, in contrast to isothermal cure, the cure temperature continues to increase at the imposed rate, and so the system will eventually devitrify when the cure temperature again exceeds the glass transition temperature of the system. In the simulation of cure with vitrification, therefore, there are two important aspects to consider: first, the dependence of the glass transition temperature of the curing system on the degree of cure, and second, the expression for the diffusion rate constant, and its dependence on temperature.

The relationship between the degree of cure, α, and the glass transition temperature, T_g, of the curing system can be described by the DiBenedetto equation (DiBenedetto, 1987; Pascault & Williams, 1990):

$$\frac{T_g - T_{g0}}{T_{g\infty} - T_{g0}} = \frac{\lambda\alpha}{1-(1-\lambda)\alpha} \tag{13}$$

in which T_{g0} and $T_{g\infty}$ are the glass transition temperatures of the uncured (α=0) and of the fully cured (α=1) system, respectively, and λ is a fitting parameter related to the ratio of the heat capacities of the fully cured and of the uncured system.

There have been a number of different expressions proposed for the diffusion rate constant and its dependence on temperature, and a summary of these has been presented earlier (Fraga et al, 2008). The expression that is perhaps most widely used, and the one that is used here, assumes a WLF temperature dependence (Williams et al, 1955; Wise et al, 1997):

$$k_d = k_{dg} \exp\left[\frac{C_1(T-T_g)}{C_2+T-T_g)}\right] \tag{14}$$

where k_{dg} is the value of k_d when T_g is equal to the cure temperature, in other words at vitrification, and C_1 and C_2 are constants of the WLF equation, and are here taken to have their "universal" values of 40.2 and 51.6 K, respectively. As regards the value of k_{dg} for these simulations, there is a surprisingly large variation of values that are used in the literature; here we adopt the value of 0.0051 s^{-1} used in earlier work (Fraga et al, 2008).
The chemical rate constants, k_{c1} and k_{c2}, can be combined with the diffusion rate constant, k_d, to give overall rate constants, $k_{tot,1}$ and $k_{tot,2}$, for the reaction, according to the Rabinowitch equation (Rabinowitch, 1937):

$$\frac{1}{k_{\text{tot},1}} = \frac{1}{k_{\text{d}}} + \frac{1}{k_{\text{c},1}} \tag{15a}$$

$$\frac{1}{k_{\text{tot},2}} = \frac{1}{k_{\text{d}}} + \frac{1}{k_{\text{c},2}} \tag{15b}$$

These overall rate constants are used in place of the rate constants k_1 and k_2 of the Kamal equation, Equation 10, in order to describe the cure rate during either isothermal or non-isothermal cure, including that part in which vitrification occurs. This set of Equations 10-15 is solved using Matlab in order to simulate the cure of these reacting systems under isothermal and non-isothermal conditions, which are considered separately in the following sections. In particular, the vitrification time is determined as a function of the experimental conditions, being defined as the time at which the glass transition temperature of the reacting system becomes equal to the cure temperature.

5.2.1 Isothermal cure with vitrification

As mentioned above, it is not possible by conventional DSC to identify, directly from the cure curve, when vitrification occurs for a given isothermal cure temperature, T_c. To determine the vitrification time, it is necessary to repeat the isothermal cure for a series of different cure times, with a second (non-isothermal) scan after each isotherm in order to determine the glass transition temperature corresponding to each isothermal cure time. A plot of T_g as a function of cure time then allows the vitrification time, t_v, to be found as the cure time for which $T_g = T_c$. This procedure has been used in the past (Montserrat, 1992), but it is impractical on account of the length of time involved in making numerous repeated isothermal cure experiments. It is in this respect that TMDSC offers an important advantage: the reversing or complex heat capacity signal is responsive to the changes that take place when the system vitrifies, in just the same way as these signals respond to a glass transition on cooling, and hence at the time of vitrification in isothermal cure the complex heat capacity shows a sigmoidal change from a liquid-like to a glassy value. By TMDSC, therefore, it is possible to identify the vitrification time directly from the isothermal cure curve, and it is conventionally taken to be at the mid-point of the sigmoid.
This approach has been adopted successfully by a number of workers (Alig et al, 1999; Lange et al, 2000; Montserrat & Cima, 1999; Montserrat & Martin, 2002; Van Assche et al, 1998). Nevertheless, it raises the question of how this measurement of the vitrification time, which depends on the frequency of modulation, can be reconciled with that obtained by the lengthy conventional DSC procedure, which does not depend on the frequency. Clearly this leads again to the relationship between the frequency dependence and the rate dependence of T_g, which has been discussed above. In the present instance, the effect of frequency can be

demonstrated very clearly by means of Matlab simulations, and this approach transpires to be illuminating also about the study of vitrification by other techniques, such as Dielectric Analysis (DEA), which operate at much higher frequencies. The starting point for these simulations is that vitrification occurs when the glass transition temperature of the curing system, which increases with increasing frequency, reaches the cure temperature. However, rather than use this as the criterion for defining vitrification, we adopt here instead an alternative and simpler procedure, which is to assign a frequency dependence to the cure temperature, such that it *decreases* with increasing frequency according to the following equation (Fraga et al, 2008a):

$$\ln\left(\frac{f}{f_r}\right)=\frac{E_f}{R}\left(\frac{1}{T_c(f)}-\frac{1}{T_c}\right) \tag{16}$$

In this equation, E_f is the activation energy controlling the frequency dependence of T_c (equivalent to the activation energy for T_g), and f_r is a reference frequency for which the dynamic cure temperature, $T_c(f)$, is considered to be equal to the cure temperature, T_c. Since the vitrification time determined by conventional DSC makes use of a glass transition temperature determined on heating after cooling freely, the correspondence between cooling rate and frequency (Donth et al, 1997; Hensel & Schick, 1998; Hutchinson, 1998; Montserrat, 2000; Weyer et al, 1997) allows us to assign a value of 1/60 s^{-1} for the reference frequency. The results of such a simulation are shown in Figure 8, which shows the increase of T_g of the curing system as a function of isothermal cure time.

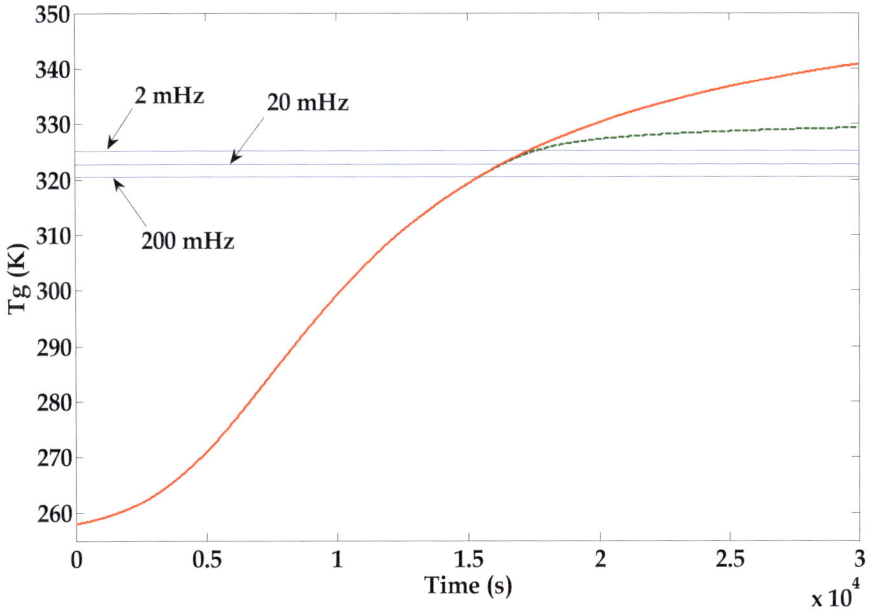

Fig. 8. Simulation of isothermal cure: chemical reaction without vitrification (full line, red curve); with vitrification (dashed line, green curve). Horizontal blue lines indicate frequency dependent isothermal cure temperature: 2 mHz (upper); 20 mHz (middle); 200 mHz (lower). Parameter values: m=1, n=2, λ=0.5, E_f/R=100 kK, T_{g0}=–15°C, $T_{g\infty}$=85°C, T_c=50°C

In the absence of vitrification, the T_g of the curing system increases from its value, T_{g0}, for the un-reacted resin monomer to a final value, $T_{g\infty}$, for the fully reacted system, as shown by the full line in Figure 8, though this final value is not reached within the time scale shown. On the other hand, if vitrification intervenes then the rate of cure will reduce dramatically and the system will not reach a full cure, as shown by the dashed line. The vitrification time, t_v, is determined as the time at which the T_g of the curing system becomes equal to the cure temperature, T_c. Since the cure temperature has been assigned a frequency dependence, this means that t_v will also depend on the frequency, and in a way this is clearly non-linear. It is a straightforward matter to evaluate t_v for a range of frequencies from such simulations, for a given isothermal cure temperature, and a typical result is shown in Figure 9.

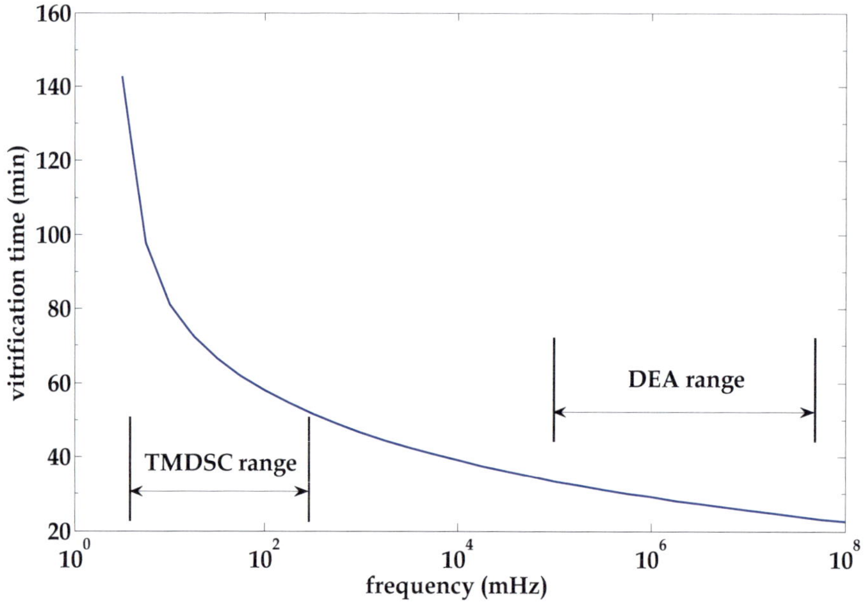

Fig. 9. Vitrification time as a function of frequency (on a logarithmic scale) for isothermal cure at 70°C with the following parameter values: m=0.23, n=1.43, λ=0.66, E_f/R=50 kK

As has been shown elsewhere (Fraga et al, 2008a), in a more extensive simulation covering a range of isothermal curing temperatures and examining the effects of various parameter values, such results are in excellent agreement with experimental data. In particular, the important feature of Figure 9 is that, at low frequencies, in the typical range available by TMDSC, there is a marked upward curvature, whereas at high frequencies, typical of those available in DEA, there is a good linear relationship between t_v and the logarithm of the frequency. The data obtained by TMDSC experiments are subject to a significant experimental error in view of the fact that this technique operates at only a single frequency; this means that a new sample must be prepared for each different frequency, which inevitably introduces some small variation in the resin to hardener ratio, which has a consequent effect on the cure kinetics. Nevertheless, it is possible to identify the upward curvature in the dependence of t_v on log(f) at low frequency from a close observation of some light-heating TMDSC experiments (Fraga et al, 2008a; Van Assche et al, 2001). In addition, the more recent technique of TOPEM®, a TMDSC technique which allows a range of frequencies to be studied in a single scan, shows this upward curvature even more clearly (Fraga et al, 2008b). On the other hand, at high frequencies the linear dependence of t_v on log(f) has been known for some time (Alig et al, 1999; Fournier et al, 1996; Mangion & Johari, 1990; Montserrat et al, 2003). Not only do these Matlab simulations describe very well the data at both low and high frequencies, but they also resolve the observation made by Montserrat et al (Montserrat et al, 2003) that the extrapolation of the t_v data from the high frequencies corresponding to DEA results did not coincide with the data at low frequencies corresponding to TMDSC data: it is clear from Figure 9 that this is simply because of the upward curvature in this representation. In fact, in DEA experiments it is not really the vitrification time, in the sense of a change from a chemical controlled to a diffusion controlled kinetics, that is being determined; rather it is the dynamic α-relaxation, for which the temperature of the relaxation peak is equal to the cure temperature at what might be called a dynamic vitrification time. This is clear from Figure 8, where at high frequencies the location of the dynamic vitrification time occurs well before the bifurcation which represents the change in kinetics of the reaction.

5.2.2 Non-isothermal cure with vitrification and devitrification

For the simulation of non-isothermal cure with vitrification (and devitrification), the same set of Equations 10 to 15 is solved using Matlab, and the same procedure is adopted of assigning a frequency dependence to the cure temperature according to Equation 16. If the heating rate is sufficiently slow, then the T_g of the reacting system can surpass the cure temperature, and vitrification will occur. This dramatically reduces the rate of reaction, and hence T_g increases only little while the cure temperature continuously increases according to the imposed rate of heating. Consequently, a point is reached where the cure temperature again exceeds the glass transition temperature, and the sample devitrifies and proceeds to a full cure. By conventional DSC these subtle changes in the rate of cure cannot be identified. On the other hand, by TMDSC the changes in the complex heat capacity allow both vitrification and devitrification to be identified, as a sigmoidal decrease and increase, respectively, in C_p^*, with their separation being greater the slower is the heating rate (Fraga et al, 2010a, 2010b). Generally, the heating rates need to be very slow in order to observe these phenomena: with an epoxy-amine system, for example, these rates are from 0.05 to 0.015 K/min. Furthermore, with TOPEM® the frequency dependence of vitrification and devitrification can be found experimentally, and Matlab simulations provide excellent agreement with the experimental observations.

Figure 10 shows an illustration of non-isothermal cure and the effect of a frequency dependent cure temperature. Here it can be seen that vitrification occurs at a temperature of about 310 K, depending on the frequency of modulation, and that shortly thereafter the cure rate decreases significantly. The rapidity with which the cure rate decreases and the extent to which the cure continues after the glass transition temperature reaches the cure temperature are dictated by the magnitude of the diffusion rate constant k_{dg} in Equation 14. As mentioned earlier, there is a surprisingly large variation in values assigned to this parameter in the literature, when one might have expected it to have approximately the same value for any vitrifying system, given that the glass transition is a universal phenomenon with a timescale that is conventionally taken to be around 100 seconds. Nevertheless, values for k_{dg} as different as 4×10^{-5} s^{-1} and 100 s^{-1} can be found in the literature (Fraga et al, 2008a). This remains an area for further investigation.

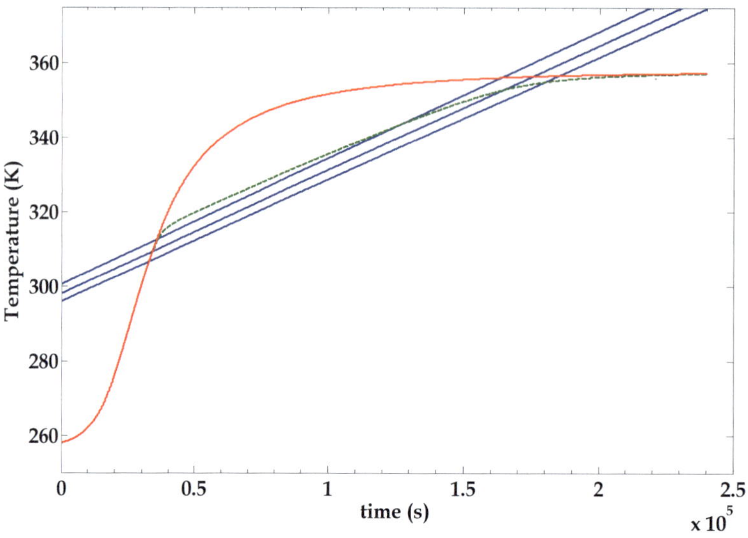

Fig. 10. Simulation of non-isothermal cure, showing variation of T_g during cure without vitrification (red full curve) and with vitrification and devitrification (green dashed curve). As there is now space available, following the format change, this caption could include the experimental conditions, which are: heating rate=0.02 K/min, m=1, n=2, λ=0.5, E_f/R=100 kK, T_{g0}=–15°C, $T_{g\infty}$=85°C

Following vitrification, the cure temperature continues to increase at the experimentally imposed rate, and consequently the system will devitrify when the cure temperature again exceeds the glass transition temperature. This generally occurs when the glass transition temperature is approaching its value for the fully cured system, $T_{g\infty}$. In Figure 10 this is seen as the crossing point of the cure curve and the heating rate curve, which is located in the region of the cure curve which is almost horizontal. The temperature at which devitrification occurs is therefore a good approximation to that of the fully cured system, and is almost independent of frequency (Fraga et al, 2010a; Fraga et al, 2010b). This is an important observation, as can be illustrated by a good example. The tri-functional epoxy resin, tri-glycidyl para-amino phenol (TGAP), when cured with diamino diphenyl sulphone (DDS), results in a very highly cross-linked network structure. In fact, the cross-link density is so high that the glass transition cannot be identified by DSC or TMDSC for this system, and it is common practice to determine the T_g instead by other techniques, for example by dynamic mechanical analysis (DMA) (Frigione & Calò, 2008). This is clearly not an ideal situation for studying the kinetics of cure and its effects on the structure and properties of the cured system: for instance, DMA does not measure the same T_g as for DSC or TMDSC, and operates at a higher frequency than does TMDSC (Hutchinson, 2010). However, by curing non-isothermally at a very slow rate, it is possible to identify both vitrification and devitrification in this system, with the temperature at which devitrification occurs being clearly defined, thus allowing the calorimetric determination of $T_{g\infty}$.

6. Conclusions

This paper summarises some aspects of the glass transition of polymers that have been investigated by means of simulations made in the Matlab environment. These aspects have included the following. First, the basic glass transformation process, involving cooling from an equilibrium melt to a non-equilibrium glass state, has been simulated by Matlab to show, in particular, the cooling rate dependence of the glass transition temperature and the endothermic peak that occurs in the heat flow, as measured by DSC, on reheating after annealing at a temperature within the glassy state. These simulations required the solution of a system of differential equations using the "ode" routines. The use of such simulations in which the effects of both experimental and material parameters were investigated led to a method (the peak shift method) for the determination of one of the material parameters, the non-linearity parameter, x.

Second, the technique of Temperature Modulated DSC was simulated by Matlab in order to better interpret the various new signals that this technique gives in addition to those available by conventional DSC. These simulations made use of "fft" routines in order to evaluate the average values and amplitudes of the periodically varying heating rate and heat flow signals. Again, these simulations were made so as to investigate the effects of both the experimental and the material parameters, and the results led to a clear interpretation of the complex heat capacity and its dependence on these parameters. Among other results, this approach allowed the clear distinction to be made between the thermal and dynamic glass transition temperatures, and led to an interpretation of the relationship between them in respect of the correspondence between cooling rate and frequency. Such simulations also led to a new method for the experimental determination of the other material parameter, the non-exponentiality parameter β.

Third, the processes of vitrification and devitrification that occur in thermosetting systems have been investigated by using Matlab to simulate the cure reaction in both isothermal and non-isothermal conditions. In particular, as regards isothermal cure, the effects of frequency have been simulated, and have allowed some hitherto apparently anomalous aspects of the frequency dependence of the vitrification time over a wide range of frequencies to be explained. With respect to non-isothermal cure, it has been shown that the devitrification process occurs at a temperature very close to the glass transition temperature of the fully cured system, and therefore provides a means of determining $T_{g\infty}$ calorimetrically for systems in which this is otherwise not possible. In the analysis and simulation of these processes, the graphical representation capabilities of Matlab were particularly useful.

7. Acknowledgement

This work was supported by a grant from the Spanish Ministry of Education and Science, Project MAT 2008-06284-C03-03.

8. References

Adam, G. & Gibbs, J.H. (1965). On Temperature Dependence of Cooperative Relaxation Properties in Glass-forming Liquids. *J. Chem. Phys.* Vol.43, Iss.1, pp. 139-146, ISSN 0021-9606

Alig, I.; Jenninger, W. & Schawe, J.E.K. (1999). Curing Kinetics of Phase Separating Thermosets Studied by DSC, TMDSC and Dielectric Relaxation Spectroscopy. *Thermochim. Acta*, Vol.330, Iss.1-2, pp. 167-174, ISSN 0040-6031

Berens, A.R. & Hodge, I.M. (1982). Effects of Annealing and Prior History on Enthalpy Relaxation in Glassy Polymers. I. Experimental Study on Poly(vinyl chloride). *Macromolecules*, Vol.15, Iss.3, pp. 756-761, ISSN 0024-9297

DiBenedetto, A.T. (1987). Prediction of the Glass-Transition Temperature of Polymers - a Model Based on the Principle of Corresponding States. *J. Polym. Sci. Part B. Polym. Phys.*, Vol.25, Iss.9, pp. 1949-1969, ISSN 0887-6266

Donth, E.; Korus, J.; Hempel, E. & Beiner, M. (1997). Comparison of DSC Heating Rate and HCS Frequency at the Glass Transition. *Thermochim. Acta*, Vol.305, Iss.Nov, pp. 239-249, ISSN 0040-6031

Fernández-Francos, X.; Salla, J.M.; Cadenato, A.; Morancho, J.M.; Mantecón, A.; Serra, A. & Ramis, X. (2007). Influence of the Initiating Mechanism on the Cationic Photopolymerization of a Cycloaliphatic Epoxy Resin with Arylsulfonium Salts. *J. Polym. Sci. Part A: Polym. Chem.*, Vol.45, Iss.1, pp. 16-25, ISSN 0887-624X

Fournier, J.; Williams, G.; Duch, C. & Aldridge, G.A. (1996). Changes in Molecular Dynamics during Bulk Polymerization of an Epoxide-Amine System as Studied by Dielectric Relaxation Spectroscopy. *Macromolecules*, Vol.29, Iss.22, pp.7097-7107, ISSN 0024-9297

Fraga, I.; Hutchinson, J.M. & Montserrat, S. (2010a). Vitrification and Devitrification during the Non-Isothermal Cure of a Thermoset. *J. Thermal Anal. Calorim.*, Vol.99, Iss.3, pp. 925-929, ISSN 1388-6150

Fraga, I.; Montserrat, S. & Hutchinson, J.M. (2007). TOPEM, a New Temperature Modulated DSC Technique - Application to the Glass Transition of Polymers. *J. Thermal Anal. Calorim.*, Vol.87, Iss.1, pp. 119-124, ISSN 1418-2874

Fraga, I.; Montserrat, S. & Hutchinson, J.M. (2008a). Vitrification during the Isothermal Cure of Thermosets: Comparison of Theoretical Simulations with Temperature-Modulated DSC and Dielectric Analysis. *Macromol. Chem. Phys.*, Vol.209, Iss.19, pp. 2003-2011, ISSN 1022-1352

Fraga, I.; Montserrat, S. & Hutchinson, J.M. (2008b). Vitrification during the Isothermal Cure of Thermosets. Part 1. An Investigation using TOPEM, a New Temperature Modulated Technique. *J. Thermal Anal. Calorim.*, Vol.91, Iss.3, pp. 687-695, ISSN 1388-6150

Fraga, I.; Montserrat, S. & Hutchinson, J.M. (2010b). Vitrification and Devitrification during the Non-Isothermal Cure of a Thermoset. Theoretical Model and Comparison with Calorimetric Experiments. *Macromol. Chem. Phys.*, Vol.211, Iss.1, pp. 57-65, ISSN 1022-1352

Frigione, M. & Calò, E. (2008). Influence of an Hyperbranched Aliphatic Polyester on the Cure Kinetic of a Trifunctional Epoxy Resin. *J. Appl. Polymer Sci.*, Vol.107, Iss.3, pp. 1744-1758, ISSN 0021-8995

Gibbs, J.H. & DiMarzio, E.A. (1958). Nature of the Glass Transition and the Glassy State. *J. Chem. Phys.* Vol.28, Iss.3, pp. 373-383, ISSN 0021-9606

Gill, P.S.; Sauerbrunn, S.R. & Reading M. (1993). Modulated Differential Scanning Calorimetry. *J. Thermal Anal.*, Vol.40, Iss.3, pp. 931-939, ISSN 0368-4466

Hensel, A. & Schick, C. (1998). Relation between Freezing-in due to Linear Cooling and the Dynamic Glass Transition Temperature by Temperature-modulated DSC. *J. Non-Cryst. Sol.*, Vol.235, Iss.Aug, pp. 510-516, ISSN 0022-3093

Hodge, I.M. (1994). Enthalpy Relaxation and Recovery in Amorphous Materials. *J. Non-Cryst. Sol.* Vol.169, Iss.3, pp. 211-266, ISSN 0022-3093

Hutchinson, J.M. (1987). Thermal Cycling of Glasses: a Theoretical and Experimental Approach, In: *Molecular Dynamics and Relaxation Phenomena in Glasses,* Th. Dorfmüller & G. Williams, (Eds.), pp. 172-187, Springer-Verlag, ISBN 3-540-17801-5, Berlin

Hutchinson, J.M. (1995). Physical Aging of Polymers. *Prog. Polym. Sci.,* Vol.20, Iss.4, pp. 703-760, ISSN 0079-6700

Hutchinson, J.M. (1998). Characterising the Glass Transition and Relaxation Kinetics by Conventional and Temperature-modulated Differential Scanning Calorimetry. *Thermochim. Acta,* Vol.324, Iss.1-2, pp. 165-174, ISSN 0040-6031

Hutchinson, J.M. (2010). Determination of the Glass Transition Temperature. *J. Thermal Anal. Calorim.,* Vol.98, Iss.3, pp. 579-589, ISSN 1388-6150

Hutchinson, J.M. & Montserrat, S. (1997). A Theoretical Model of Temperature-Modulated Differential Scanning Calorimetry in the Glass Transition Region. *Thermochim. Acta,* Vol.305, Iss.Nov, pp. 257-265, ISSN 0040-6031

Hutchinson, J.M. & Montserrat, S. (2001). The Application of Temperature-modulated DSC to the Glass Transition Region II. Effect of a Distribution of Relaxation Times. *Thermochim. Acta,* Vol.377, Iss.1-2, pp. 63-84, ISSN 0040-6031

Hutchinson, J.M. & Ruddy, M. (1988). Thermal Cycling of Glasses. II. Experimental Evaluation of the Structure (or Non-linearity) Parameter *x*. *J. Polym. Sci. Polym. Phys. Ed,* Vol.26, Iss.11, pp. 2341-2366, ISSN 0887-6266

Hutchinson, J.M. & Ruddy, M. (1990). Thermal Cycling of Glasses. III. Upper Peaks. *J. Polym. Sci. Polym. Phys. Ed,* Vol.28, Iss.11, pp. 2127-2163, ISSN 0887-6266

Hutchinson, J.M. & Kovacs, A.J. (1976). A Simple Phenomenological Approach to the Thermal Behavior of Glasses during Uniform Heating or Cooling. *J. Polym. Sci. Polym. Phys. Ed.* Vol.14, Iss.9, pp. 1575-1590, ISSN 0887-6266

Illers, K.H. (1969). Einfluss der Thermischen Vorgeschichte auf die Eigenschaften von Polyvinylchlorid. *Makromol. Chem.,* Vol.127, Iss.Sept , pp. 1-33, IDS E1355

Jiang, X.; Hutchinson, J.M. & Imrie, C.T. (1998). Temperature-Modulated Differential Scanning Calorimetry. Part II. Determination of Activation Energies. *Polymer Int.,* Vol.47, Iss.1, pp. 72-75, ISSN 0959-8103

Kamal, M.R. (1974). Thermoset Characterization for Moldability Analysis. *Polym. Eng. Sci.,* Vol.14, Iss.3, pp. 231-239, ISSN 0032-3888

Kohlrausch, F. (1866). Beitrage zur Kenntnifs der Elastischen Nachwirkung. *Annalen der Physik und Chemie* Vol.128, No.5, pp. 1-20.

Kovacs, A.J. (1963). Transition Vitreuse dans les Polymères Amorphes. Etude Phénoménologique. *Fortschr. Hochpolym. Forsch.,* Vol.3, pp. 394-507.

Kovacs, A.J.; Aklonis, J.J.; Hutchinson, J.M. & Ramos, A.R. (1979). Isobaric Volume and Enthalpy Recovery of Glasses. II. A Transparent Multiparameter Theory. *J. Polym. Sci. Polym. Phys. Ed.* Vol.17, Iss.7, pp. 1097-1162, ISSN 0887-6266

Kovacs, A.J. & Hutchinson, J.M. (1979). Isobaric Thermal Behavior of Glasses during Uniform Cooling and Heating: Dependence of the Characteristic Temperatures on the Relative Contributions of Temperature and Structure to the Rate of Recovery. II. A One-parameter Approach. *J. Polym. Sci. Polym. Phys. Ed.* Vol.17, Iss.12, pp. 2031-2058, ISSN 0887-6266

Kubisa, P. & Penczek, S. (1999). Cationic Activated Monomer Polymerization of Heterocyclic Monomers. *Prog. Polym. Sci.*, Vol.24, Iss.10, pp. 1409-1437, ISSN 0079-6700

Lange, J.; Altmann, N.; Kelly, C.T. & Halley, P.J. (2000). Understanding Vitrification during Cure of Epoxy Resins using Dynamic Scanning Calorimetry and Rheological Techniques. *Polymer*, Vol.41, Iss.15, pp. 5949-5955, ISSN 0032-3861

Mangion, M.B.M. & Johari, G.P. (1990). Relaxations of Thermosets. 4. A Dielectric Study of Cross-Linking of Diglycidyl Ether of Bisphenol-A by 2 Curing Agents. *J. Polym. Sci.: Polym. Phys.*, Vol.28, Iss.9, pp. 1621-1639, ISSN 0887-6266

Montserrat, S. (1992). Vitrification and Further Structural Relaxation in the Isothermal Curing of an Epoxy-Resin. *J. Appl. Polymer Sci.*, Vol.44, Iss.3, pp. 545-554, ISSN 0021-8995

Montserrat, S. (2000). Measuring the Glass Transition of Thermosets by Alternating Differential Scanning Calorimetry. *J. Thermal Anal. Calorim.*, Vol.59, Iss.1-2, pp. 289-303, ISSN 1418-2874

Montserrat, S.; Calventus, Y. & Hutchinson, J.M. (2005). Effect of Cooling Rate and Frequency on the Calorimetric Measurement of the Glass Transition. *Polymer*, Vol.46, Iss.26, pp. 12181-12189, ISSN 0032-3861

Montserrat, S & Cima, I. (1999). Isothermal Curing of an Epoxy Resin by Alternating Differential Scanning Calorimetry. *Thermochim. Acta*, Vol.330, Iss.1-2, pp. 189-200, ISSN 0040-6031

Montserrat, S. & Hutchinson, J.M. (2002). On the Measurement of the Width of the Distribution of Relaxation Times in Polymer Glasses. *Polymer*, Vol.43, Iss.2, pp. 351-355, ISSN 0032-3861

Montserrat, S. & Martin, J.G. (2002). The Isothermal Curing of a Diepoxide-Cycloaliphatic Diamine Resin by Temperature Modulated Differential Scanning Calorimetry. *J. Appl. Polymer Sci.*, Vol.85, Iss.6, pp. 1263-1276, ISSN 0021-8995

Montserrat, S.; Román, F. & Colomer, P. (2003). Vitrification and Dielectric Relaxation during the Isothermal Curing of an Epoxy-Amine Resin. *Polymer*, Vol.44, Iss.1, pp. 101-114, ISSN 0032-3861

Montserrat, S.; Román, F.; Hutchinson, J.M. & Campos, L. (2008). Analysis of the Cure of Epoxy Based Layered Silicate Nanocomposites: Reaction Kinetics and Nanostructure Development. *J. Appl. Polymer Sci.*, Vol.108, Iss.2, pp. 923-938, ISSN 0021-8995

Moynihan, C.T.; Easteal A.J.; DeBolt, M.A. & Tucker J. (1976). Dependence of Fictive Temperature of Glass on Cooling Rate. *J. Am. Ceram. Soc.* Vol.59, Iss.1-2, pp. 12-16, ISSN 0002-7820

Narayanaswamy, O.S. (1971). Model of Structural Relaxation in Glass. *J. Am. Ceram. Soc.* Vol.54, Iss.10, pp. 491-198, ISSN 0002-7820

Neki, N. & Geil P.H. (1973). Morphology-property Studies of Amorphous Polycarbonate. *J. Macromol. Sci. Phys.*, Vol.B8, Iss.1-2, pp. 295-341, ISSN 0022-2348

Pappin, A.J.; Hutchinson, J.M. & Ingram, M.D. (1994). The Appearance of Annealing Pre-peaks in Inorganic Glasses: New Experimental Results and Theoretical Interpretation. *J. Non-Cryst. Sol.*, Vol.172, Part.1, pp. 584-591, ISSN 0022-3093

Pascault, J.-P.; Sautereau, H.; Verdu, J. & Williams, R.J.J. (2002). *Thermosetting Polymers*, Marcel Dekker, ISBN 0-8247-0670-6, New York

Pascault, J.-P. & Williams, R.J.J. (1990). Glass-Transition Temperature Versus Conversion Relationships for Thermosetting Polymers. *J. Polym. Sci. Part B. Polym. Phys.*, Vol.28, Iss.1, pp. 85-95, ISSN 0887-6266

Pustkova, P.; Hutchinson, J.M.; Román, F. & Montserrat, S. (2009). Homopolymerization Effects in Polymer Layered Silicate Nanocomposites Based Upon Epoxy Resin: Implications for Exfoliation. *J. Appl. Polymer Sci.*, Vol.114, Iss.2, pp. 1040-1047, ISSN 0021-8995

Rabinowitch, E. (1937). Collision, Co-ordination, Diffusion and Reaction Velocity in Condensed Systems. *Trans. Faraday Soc.*, Vol.33, Iss.2, pp. 1225-1232, ISSN 0014-7672

Ramos, A.R.; Hutchinson, J.M. & Kovacs, A.J. (1984). Isobaric Thermal Behavior of Glasses during Uniform Cooling and Heating. III. Predictions from the Multiparameter KAHR Model. *J. Polym. Sci. Polym. Phys. Ed*, Vol.22, Iss.9, pp. 1655-1695, ISSN 0887-6266

Reading, M.; Elliott, D. & Hill, V.L. (1993a). A New Approach to the Calorimetric Investigation of Physical and Chemical Transitions. *J. Thermal Anal.*, Vol.40, Iss.3, pp. 949-955, ISSN 0368-4466

Reading, M.; Hahn, B.K. & Crowe, B.S. (1993b). Method and Apparatus for Modulated Differential Analysis. *United States Patent*, 5,224,775 (July 6, 1993)

Retting, W. (1969). Zur Abhängigkeit der Mechanischen Eigenschaften von Thermoplasten von ihrer Thermischen Vorgeschichte. *Angewandte Makromol. Chem.*, Vol.8, Iss. Sept, pp. 87-98, ISSN 0003-3146

Richardson, M.J. & Savill, N.G. Derivation of Accurate Glass-transition Temperatures by Differential Scanning Calorimetry. *Polymer*, Vol.16, Iss.10, pp. 753-757, ISSN 0032-3861

Ruddy, M. & Hutchinson J.M. (1988). Multiple Peaks in Differential Scanning Calorimetry of Polymer Glasses. *Polym. Comm.*, Vol.29, Iss.5, pp. 132-134, ISSN 0263-6476

Schawe, J.E.K. (1995). A Comparison of Different Evaluation Methods in Modulated Temperature DSC. *Thermochim. Acta*, Vol.260, Iss. Aug, pp. 1-16, ISSN 0040-6031

Simon, F. (1931). Über den Zustand der Unterkühlten Flüssigkeiten und Gläser. *Z. anorg. Allgem. Chem.*, Vol.203, Iss.1/2, (December 1931), pp. 219-227, ISSN 0044-2313

Tanaka, Y. & Bauer, R.S. (1988). Curing Reactions, In: *Epoxy Resins, Chemistry and Technology*, May, C.A. Ed., pp. 285-463, Marcel Dekker, ISBN 0-8247-7690-9, New York

Tool, A.Q. (1946). Relation between Inelastic Deformability and Thermal Expansion of Glass in its Annealing Range. *J. Am. Ceram. Soc.*, Vol.29, Iss.9, pp. 240-253, ISSN 0002-7820

Tool, A.Q. (1948). Effect of Heat-treatment on the Density and Constitution of High-silica Glasses of the Borosilicate Type. *J. Am. Ceram. Soc.*, Vol.31, Iss.7, pp. 177-186, ISSN 0002-7820

Tool, A.Q. & Eichlin, C.G. (1931). Variations in the Heating Curves of Glass by Heat Treatment. *J. Am. Ceram. Soc.*, Vol.14, Iss.4, (April 1931), pp. 276-308, ISSN 0002-7820

Van Assche, G.; Van Hemelrijck, A.; Rahier, H. & Van Mele, B. (1998). Modulated Temperature Differential Scanning Calorimetry: Cure, Vitrification, and Devitrification of Thermosetting Systems. *Thermochim. Acta*, Vol.305. Iss.Nov., pp. 317-334, ISSN 0040-6031

Van Assche, G.; Van Mele, B. & Saruyama, Y. (2001). Frequency Dependent Heat Capacity in the Cure of Epoxy Resins. *Thermochim. Acta*, Vol.377, Iss.1-2, pp. 125-130, ISSN 0040-6031

Weyer, S.; Hensel, A.; Korus, J.; Donth, E. & Schick, C. (1997). Broad Band Heat Capacity Spectroscopy in the Glass-transition Region of Polystyrene. *Thermochim. Acta*, Vol.305, Iss.Nov, pp. 251-255, ISSN 0040-6031

Williams, G. & Watts, D.C. (1970). Non-symmetrical Dielectric Relaxation Behaviour Arising from a Simple Empirical Decay Function. *Trans. Faraday Soc.* Vol.66, Iss.565P, pp. 80-85, IDS F3962

Williams, M.L.; Landel, R.F. & Ferry, J.D. (1955). Mechanical Properties of Substances of High Molecular Weight. 19. The Temperature Dependence of Relaxation Mechanisms in Amorphous Polymers and Other Glass-Forming Liquids. *J. Amer. Chem. Soc.*, Vol.77, Iss.14, pp. 3701-3707, ISSN 0002-7863

Wise, C.W.; Cook, W.D. & Goodwin, A.A. (1997). Chemico-Diffusion Kinetics of Model Epoxy-Amine Resins. *Polymer*, Vol.38, Iss.13, pp. 3251-3261, ISSN 0032-3861

14

Advanced User-Interaction with GUIs in MatLAB®

P. Franciosa, S. Gerbino and S. Patalano
University of Molise, School of Engineering; Termoli
Italy

1. Introduction

The advent of computer graphics and simulation software has strongly influenced the industrial design. Nowadays, when facing out the design of a new product or the re-design of an existing one, it is of interest evaluating different design scenarios, by comparing physical and functional behaviors and product performances. Engineers are aimed to explore many and many "what-if" design scenarios for design optimization.

MatLAB® scientific computing software offers powerful tools and mathematical utilities which can aid engineers in modeling and simulating their own applications, by using friendly graphical user interface (GUI) toolboxes.

Generally speaking, when developing software, toolbox or standalone applications, one may adopt specific programming languages, such as Visual C++®, Visual Basic®, or Java®. For a computer science or information technology engineer it is easy and natural to program in these environments but for other science and engineering researchers all this may be an obstacle since they are not so familiar with those languages and it is usually required a high programming expertise (Perutka, 2010).

In this contest, MatLAB® is a valid solution to develop powerful toolboxes and software by using its high programming language and its utilities (see linear algebra library collections and visualization toolkits, among others).

While most applications can work by just giving inputs and analyzing results in text or graphic format, the use of graphical interface offers many advantages for users who wish to solve complex problems interactively and obtain visual feedbacks.

There are several reasons for using MatLAB® as a GUI development tool (Holland & Marchand, 2002; Scott, 2006). First of all (I), MatLAB® offers a high-level scripting language. This allows researchers to focus on the problem they are trying to solve rather than spending time in developing a GUI architecture based on a low-level language. Second, (II) MatLAB®'s GUI applications can be fully integrated with the wide collection of computational routines. Moreover, (III) GUI applications are not dependent on OS architecture. Since MatLAB®'s code is not compiled, it may be run on any OS supported by MatLAB®. Finally, (IV) Graphic libraries allow to develop friendly GUI applications with powerful user interaction.

The high-level GUI development tool embedded in MatLAB® is called GUIDE (Graphical User Interface Development Environment) and it allows to automatically design the GUI layout and to handle control and object properties.

The scientific literature offers hundreds of valid GUI tools developed to easily solve practical engineering problems. For example, on the MathWorks website, under "file exchange" section, one can find several contributions covering data acquisition and monitoring, data analysis, image processing, mesh/surface visualization, 3D image rendering, FEM applications and so on.
This chapter focuses on two MatLAB®'s GUI applications, developed at University of Molise in collaboration with University of Naples (Italy): SVA-FEA (Statistical Variational Analysis & Finite Element Analysis) and PROMesh (PROcessing Mesh).
The aim is to show how to provide advanced user interaction in several common tasks such as importing data, editing data, controlling FEA runs, visualizing results, and exporting results.

SVA-FEA

SVA-FEA is a graphical tool able to statistically analyze variations occurring into assembly processes of compliant parts. Variations at part level propagate through the assembly due to both assembly sequence and process variability. One key issue to be faced-out when designing a new product is to reduce such a variation. Depending on the complexity of the process (number of assembly phases/stations) or on the physical laws governing the assembly process (see for example, plastic deformation or residual stresses occurring when joining two flanged-parts) manual approaches are often inadequate to give valuable results. In this contest, only a computer tool may help engineers in finding-out the best design setting. The implementation of SVA-FEA was motivated to quickly predict variation occurring into compliant assembly. Many efforts were done to develop a friendly GUI allowing to interactively define input data, assembly process and visualize final results. SVA-FEA is linked, in background mode, to MSC NASTRAN® solver, used to calculate elastic displacements and generalized forces. More details about the SVA-FEA methodology can be found in (Gerbino et *al.*, 2008).

PROMesh

The implementation of PROMesh was originally made within the PUODARSI (Product User-Oriented Development based on Augmented Reality and Interactive Simulation) Italian research project (http://www.kaemart.it/puodarsi), aiming to implement a tool to quickly perform stress-strain analyses and aerodynamic simulations, visualize results and keep them up-to-date while the shape of the object is modified interactively (Bordegoni et *al.*, 2010; Di Gironimo et *al.*, 2009). Starting from this general idea, we developed the PROMesh tool allowing to interactively modify any tessellated model by applying a morphing mesh procedure and to create a 3D closed domain starting from an open shell model. The so-edited geometry can be automatically converted into a suitable FE model, ready to be used for solving a steady fluid dynamic simulation. Comsol Multiphysics® is adopted as solver, working into background mode.
Both SVA-FEA and PROMesh were designed to be friendly as much as possible. Among other things, in order to provide high interaction tools, mouse events (mouse button- down, -up, -move) were programmed to allow fast selection tasks. In particular, mesh data information (see, for example, node coordinates) can be directly accessed just by mouse picking or dragging-dropping within the graphic area.
Some interesting features implemented in those MatLAB®-based applications are related to the possibility to select objects in a graphic window based on the current viewing

orientation. MatLAB®, which partially adopts an OpenGL® graphic engine, provides functionality, similar to that of a camera with zoom lens, which enables to control the viewing of the scene. By properly combining the camera orientation and the cursor-mouse position, mouse selection capabilities can be programmed.
This Chapter is arranged as follows: Section 2 provides an overview of SVA-FEA capabilities, highlighting its data structure and the main user-interaction features. PROMesh is discussed in Section 3. Finally, Section 4 draws final remarks and conclusions.

2. SVA-FEA overview

SVA-FEA provides functionalities to analyze variations occurring into assembly processes of compliant parts. Car body sheet-metal parts, aircraft structural components and plastic injected molded parts are typical elements with some compliance which makes no more applicable the assumption of rigid body when studying 3D tolerance stack-ups.

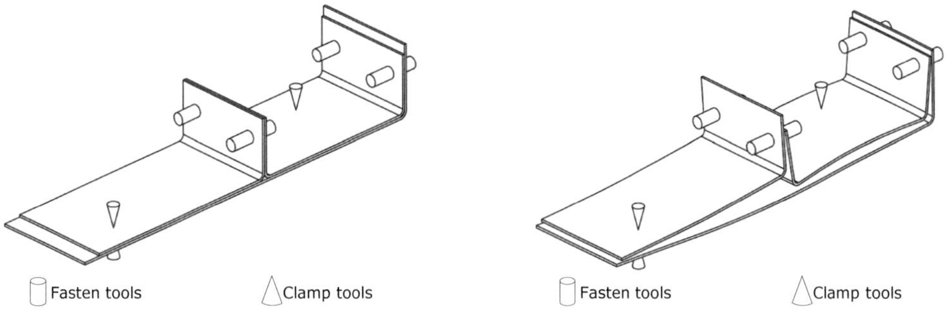

a. nominal geometry b. variational geometry

Fig. 1. Assembly of compliant parts

Following the classical PCFR cycle (Chang, 1996), with respect to the specific assembly station, parts are firstly positioned onto the fixture frame, then clamped and fastened and, finally, released, reaching the final sub-assembly configuration (Camelio et *al.*, 2004a). When analyzing variations of flexible assembly many factors should be accounted. First of all, the compliance of parts being assembled must be considered. Then, how parts interact each-other need to be investigated. Often, in real industrial applications, assembly processes are made of many sub-stations (Ceglarek et *al.*, 2009). When a part/sub-assembly moves from one station to another one, one should also consider that rigid location errors may add to elastic spring-back deviations. Looking at Fig. 1 one may observe that clamp and fasten tools may deform parts being assembled due to both part errors and clamp/fasten deviations. Understanding how deviations propagate through the assembly process it is of interest especially during the early design stages, when different design scenarios are aimed to be investigated and analyzed. In this contest, simulation environments are welcome as they allow to give valuable results into a reasonable time with no need to made very expensive and time-consuming real prototypes.
Mainly based on these needs, the implementation of SVA-FEA's GUI was motivated in order to analyze many different assembly configurations by varying few input parameters and to quickly view the simulation results.

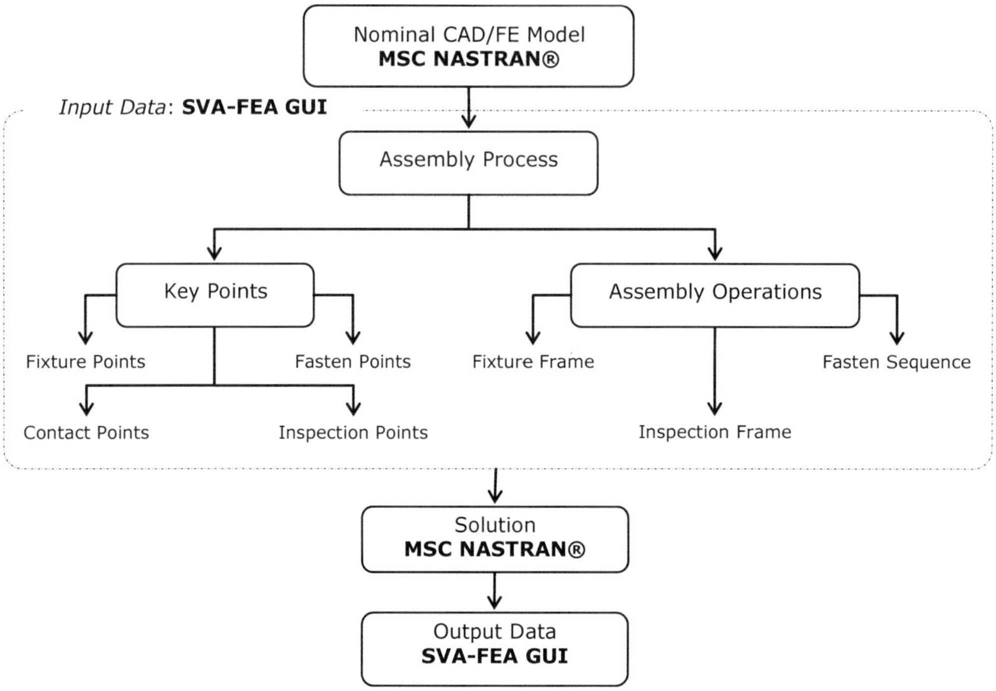

Fig. 2. SVA-FEA architecture (Franciosa, 2010a)

SVA-FEA allows to model both single- and, more in general, multi-station processes. Part deformation is calculated by adopting a FEM approach: forces and elastic displacements are calculated by solving a linear static FE model. The general SVA-FEA architecture (Franciosa, 2010a) is depicted in Fig. 2. Starting from the nominal assembly geometry, imported from a CAD system, the FE model is created and imported, accordingly, into MSC NASTRAN® format. For each sub-station, assembly operations have to be defined. In particular, four sets of Key Points (KPs) are identified: fixture points to model fixture tools; fasten points to model fasten operations; contact points to model the contact between parts to avoid part-to-part penetrations; and, inspection points related to points we want to check-out on the assembly at final stage. For each sub-station, these points must be assigned, accordingly. Moreover, statistical input data are provided in terms of mean and standard deviation. Once input data are correctly assigned, output data, in terms of statistical displacements, are given by solving two consecutive FEA runs.

The whole software architecture is based on MatLAB® environment which drives, in background mode, the MSC NASTRAN® solver. Fig. 3 depicts the SVA-FEA GUI and its main menus.

SVA-FEA's user interface was designed to easily allow: (I) importing mesh data; (II) selecting KPs; (III) defining assembly process; (IV) running FEA analysis; (V) and, viewing simulation results. The GUI layout was developed by using the GUIDE environment.

2.1 SVA-FEA data structure

This Section shows the general structure used to manage input data in SVA-FEA. Input data are managed by using *structure* arrays. The main data structure is depicted into Fig. 4.

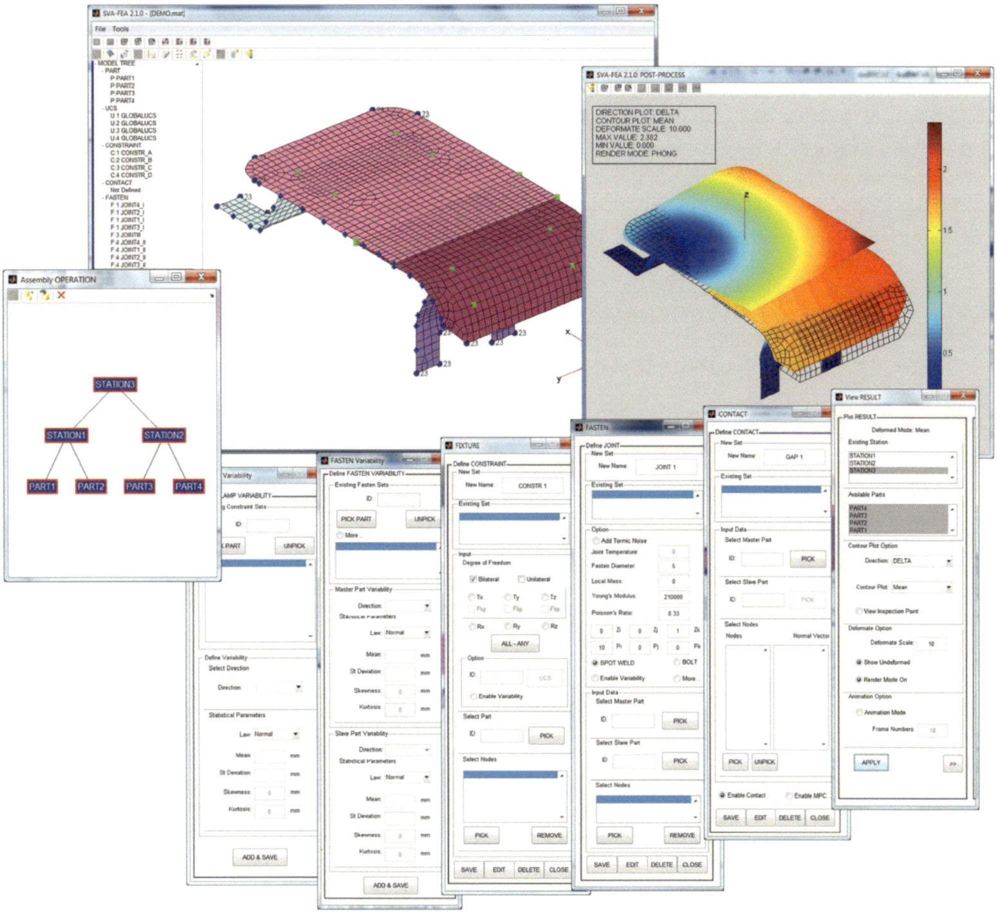

Fig. 3. SVA-FEA user interface

For each part ("part i"), six fields are available:

- MAT: material properties (Young's Modulus and Poisson's ratio) and shell thickness;
- NODE: coordinates of mesh nodes;
- ELEMENT: mesh elements; and,
- FIXTURE/FASTEN/CONTACT: input assignment for fixture, fasten and contact points.

With respect to the latter fields, the following sub-fields are available:

- DoF: list of constrained degrees of freedom (DoF);
- UCS: local coordinate frame definition;
- NodeIDf: node identification for fixture point assignment;
- NodeIDsrc / NodeIDdst: source and destination node identification;
- T: statistical input value in terms of mean and standard deviation.

2.2 SVA-FEA software: handling MSC NASTRAN® input files

The input information needed to do the numerical analysis in MSC NASTRAN® is contained into the ASCII .bdf (Bulk Data Format) file. This file is made of three sub-sections:

- *executive control statement*: includes solver options and diagnosis operations;
- *case control section*: includes sub-case entries and output queries; and,
- *bulk data section*: includes the FE model (nodes, elements and boundary conditions).

The general structure of a .bdf file (SVA-FEA supports the free field format, where data are separated by blanks) is listed below.

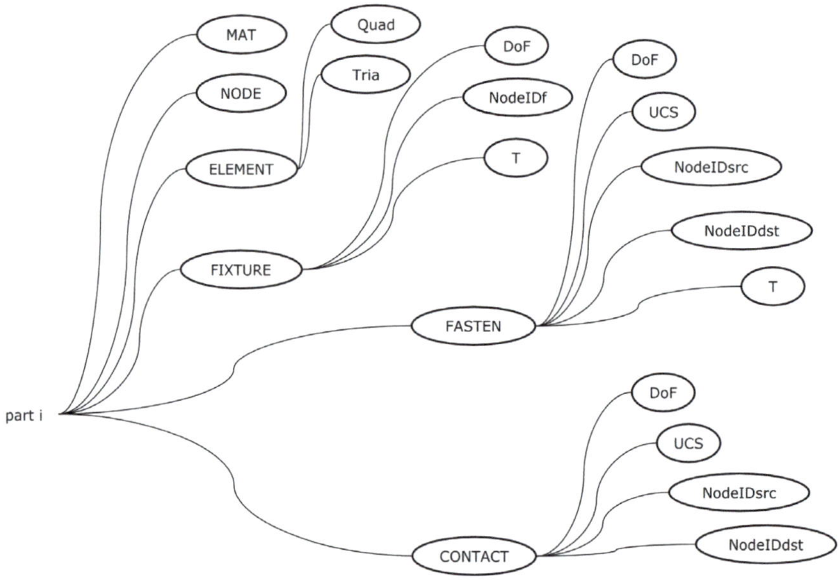

Fig. 4. SVA-FEA data structure (Franciosa, 2010a)

When the number of nodes or elements increases (in real industrial applications, meshes are made of many thousands of nodes) the .bdf file may become very huge and its reading, by using MatLAB® built-in functions, is often not efficient. To overcome this issue we implemented a MEX function (see Annex A.1 on how writing a MEX function) allowing to quickly read and import mesh elements (for example CQUAD4 and CTRIA3 elements by MSC NASTRAN®) and node coordinates. Material properties, geometry constants and node constraint settings will be defined through the SVA-FEA's GUI.

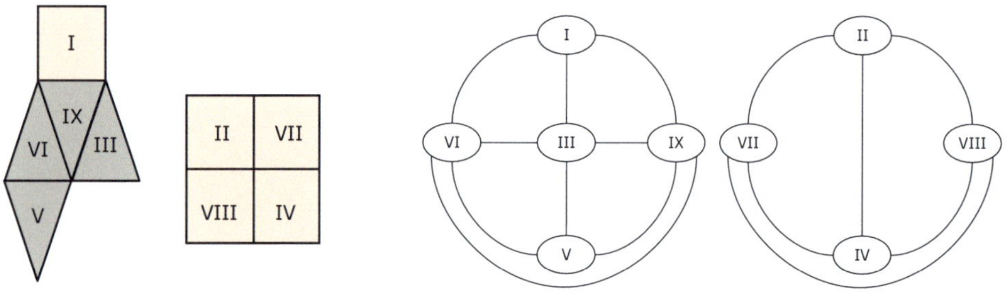

Fig. 5. Graph representation of mesh data (two domains)

```
$- executive control statement
SOL 101 $- solver type. "101" corresponds to the linear static solver
CEND

$- case control section
SUBCASE 1 $- sub-case entries

$- beginning bulk data section
BEGIN BULK
...
CQUAD4 104 1 122 123 134 133
$- element quad id=104, material id=1, connected nodes: 122,123,134,133
CTRIA3 105 1 150 151 152
$- element tria id=105, material id=1, connected nodes: 150,151,152
...
GRID 150  0.0 0.0 1.0 5
$- node id=150, coordinates [0.0, 0.0, 1.0], local UCS id=5
...
SPC 1 176 1 0.00
$- define single point constraint
...
PWELD 1 3 5.00
...
CWELD 1 1  ALIGN 125 9
$- cweld element to define fasten elements
....
FORCE 1 9 2 10.54 0.00 0.00 1.00
$- define load conditions
...
CORD2R 5  80.00 0.00 4.00 80.00 0.00 5.00 79.00 0.00 4.00
$- define local coordinate UCS
...
ENDDATA
$- ending bulk data file
```

When importing mesh data from .bdf formatted files, no geometric information is available about connected domains. We implemented an automatic procedure allowing to select and store connected domain. Every connected domain corresponds to a part, which can be introduced into the assembly process being simulated.

The general idea to extract connected domains is to consider the imported mesh as a graph in which mesh elements correspond to graph-vertices, while each edge represents an element-to-element connection (see Annex A.2 for a general overview on the main concepts of the Graph Theory used in the application). Looking at Fig. 5, 9 elements (five CQUAD4 and four CTRIA3) define two connected domains: (I, III, V, VI, IX) and (II, IV, VII, VIII). The graph representation depicted into Fig. 5b was obtained considering that two elements are connected if they share one edge or one node. For example, element I is connected to element IX, through one edge, and to elements III and VI, with one node.

Starting from the definition provided into equation (A.2), the adjacency matrix, "A", of the mesh-graph can be easily calculated. Knowing the adjacency matrix ($N_{quad}+N_{tria}$ x $N_{quad}+N_{tria}$ square matrix, where N_{quad} and N_{tria} are, respectively, the number of imported CQUAD4 and CTRIA3 elements), a growing procedure can be applied to detect all connected domains. Below the MatLAB®'s pseudo-code.

```
%- find-out connected domains
function domain=connectedDomain(A)

seed=1;
while true
    idConnect=[];
    visited(seed)=true; %- seed has been already visited

    for i=1:length(seed) %- loop over seed elements
        %- get connected elements by using "A" matrix
        [temp,visited]=getConnected(seed(i),A,visited);
        idConnect=[idConnect,temp];
    end

    %- "local domain"
    tempDomain=[tempDomain,idConnect];

    if ~isempty(idConnect)
        %- update seed counter
        seed=idConnect;
    else
        %- if no connected element is found then save "local domain"
        count=count+1;
        domain{count}=tempDomain; %- new domain counted

        %- look for a new seed (not yet visited)
        seed=getNotVisited(visited);
        tempDomain=seed;
    end

    %- break loop when there is no new seed (all elements were allocated)
    if isempty(seed)
        break
    end
end %- end loop
```

The procedure looks for those elements connected to the initial "seed element". Thus, iteratively, the seed counter is update with the so-connected elements ("idConnect"). When no other connected element is counted, then a connected domain has been selected and it is saved. These connected elements are classified as "visited". The iterative procedure stops when all elements have been marked as visited. Once connected domains are calculated, SVA-FEA updates its data structure: "ELEMENT.Quad", "ELEMENT.Tria" and "NODE" fields are filled, accordingly, with respect to the i-th connected domain (see Fig. 4). The "*patch*" MatLAB® built-in function is used to draw and visualize mesh data.

2.3 SVA-FEA software: selecting mesh nodes

Many efforts were done to make the SVA-FEA's GUI friendly as much as possible. In particular, when fixture or fasten points have to be assigned, the easiest way is just to select, by mouse picking, mesh node from the graphic area.

This task can be accomplished by using MatLAB® graphic tools. Fig. 6 reports the general scheme adopted in MatLAB® for defining a scene (MatLAB® supports both parallel and perspective projections; however, the actual implementation of SVA-FEA supports only the parallel projection).

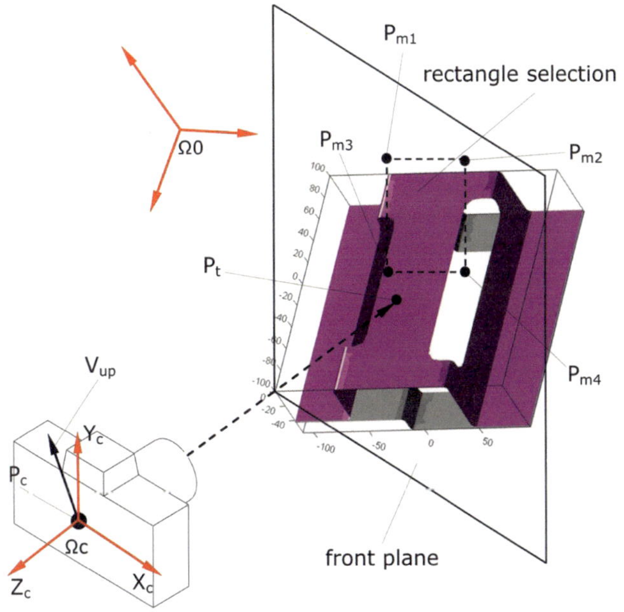

Fig. 6. Camera representation and mouse selection from graphic area

In Fig. 6 "P_t" is the position, in the coordinate frame (Ω_0), of the point the camera points to (*camera target*). "P_c" is the position of the camera frame (Ω_c) with respect to Ω_0 (*camera position*). "V_{up}" defines the rotation (*camera up-vector*) around the camera view axis, "Z_c". "P_{mi}" are the mouse picked points, defined with respect to Ω_0. "P_{mi}" correspond to the intersection between the camera view axis and the front plane (which is parallel to the camera plane X_c-Y_c). By using MatLAB® camera properties, "P_t", "P_c", "V_{up}" and "P_{mi}" can be obtained by:

```
Pc=get(gca,'CameraPosition'); %- camera position
Pt=get(gca,'CameraTarget');  %- camera target
Vup=get(gca,'CameraUpVector'); %- camera up-vector
Pmi=get(gca,'CurrentPoint'); %- picked point
```

The aim is to find-out the mesh node nearest to the picked point. To do this, the mesh node and the picked point have to be projected onto the front plane. After calculating the rotation matrix from the frame Ω_0 to Ω_c as into equation (1):

$$Z_c = \frac{P_c - P_t}{\|P_c - P_t\|}, X_c = \frac{V_{up} \wedge Z_c}{\|V_{up} \wedge Z_c\|}, Y_c = \frac{Z_c \wedge X_c}{\|Z_c \wedge X_c\|} \\ \downarrow \\ R = \begin{bmatrix} X_c \\ Y_c \\ Z_c \end{bmatrix} \tag{1}$$

one can obtain the index ("idSelected") of the nearest mesh node with respect to the picked point. Below the MatLAB® pseudo-code.

```
%- transform mesh-nodes, "Ncoord"
Ncoord=R*Ncoord';
Pmi=R*Pmi';

%- take just (x-y) components
Ncoord= Ncoord(1:2,:);
Pmi=Pmi(1:2);

%- calculate distances
diff=[Ncoord(1,:)-Pmi(1); Ncoord(2,:)-Pmi(2)];
dist=sqrt(sum(diff.^2,1));

%- finally, find-out the index related to the minimum distance
[~,idSelected]=min(dist); %- discard (~) first output
```

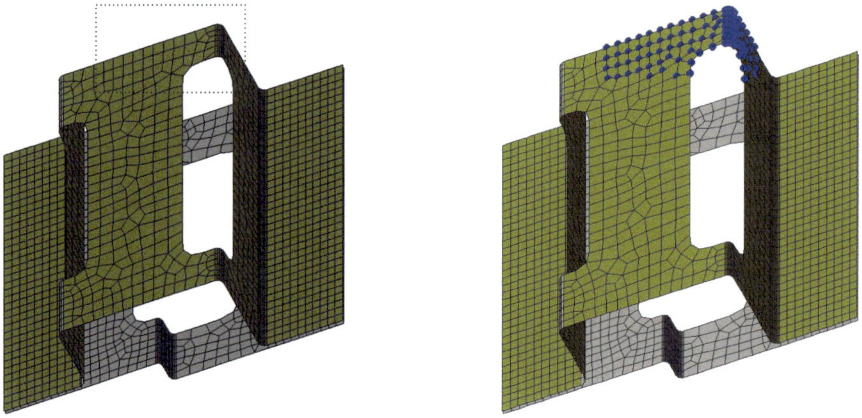

(a) drawing rectangle by mouse picking/moving (b) selecting mesh-nodes

Fig. 7. Application of the rectangle-area selection algorithm

The algorithm just described can be extended to allow rectangle-area selection from the graphic area by defining three sub-routines running when picking mouse buttons or moving mouse into the current MatLAB® figure. The procedure can be summarized as follows (see also Fig. 6):

- calculating "P_{m1}" point and "R" matrix when picking down the mouse button ("*WindowButtondownFcn*" callack);
- calculating "P_{m4}" point and draw rectangle-area selection when moving the mouse ("*WindowButtonMotionFcn*" callack); and,
- calculating mesh-nodes inside the rectangle-area selection ("*WindowButtonUpFcn*" callack).

"P_{m1}" is calculated once picking down the mouse button. "P_{m4}" corresponds to the actual position of the mouse cursor. The MatLAB® pseudo-code is reported below.

The "*patch*" and "*line*" MatLAB® built-in functions are used to draw, respectively, the rectangle-area selection and the selected mesh nodes. Furthermore, the "*inpolygon*" MatLAB®'s command is here adopted to check which nodes are inside the rectangle-area.

As example, in Fig. 7 a mouse selection is drawn into the upper side of figure (Fig. 7a). Then, the selected mesh nodes are marked as blue dots (Fig. 7b).

```
%- inizialize selection phase:
set(fig,'WindowButtondownFcn',{@sClick,Ncoord});

function sClick(Ncoord)

%- built frame
R=[Xc;Yc;Zc];

%- start selection
P1=get(gca,'CurrentPoint'); %- picked point

%- start mouse motion
set(gcf,'WindowButtonMotionFcn',{@moveMouse,P1,R,Ncoord})

function moveMouse(P1,R,Ncoord)

%- actual mouse position
P4 = get(gca,'CurrentPoint');

%- transform into the local frame
P1=R*P1';
P4=R*P4';

%- built rectangle selection
P2=[P1(1) P4(2) 0];
P3=[P4(1) P1(2) 0];

%- go-back into global frame
Vertext=R'*[P1;P2;P4;P3];';

%- draw rectangle
patch('Faces',[1 2 3 4],...
      'Vertices',Vertext');

%-call mouse button-up
set(fig,'WindowButtonUpFcn',{@endClick,R,Ncoord,Vertex});

function endClick(R,Ncoord,Vertex)

inPol=inpolygon(Ncoord(1,:),Ncoord(2,:),Vertex(:,1),Vertex(:,2));

Psel=Ncoord(inPol,:);

line('xdata',Psel(:,1),...
     'ydata',Psel(:,2),...
     'zdata',Psel(:,3))
```

In SVA-FEA, when defining fasten or contact points, mesh-nodes are directly selected from the graphic area (see Fig. 8) by using the rectangle-area selection tool. Once master and slave parts are picked, matched nodes are automatically assigned among parts. After selecting master node, the related matched node is calculated as the nearest one on the slave part. In Fig. 8, matched nodes are marked as circle dots.

2.4 SVA-FEA software: Tree view implementation

Imported connected domains and KPs can be edited and managed thought the MODEL TREE, serving as tree viewer (see Fig. 9). Specific programming languages, such as

Microsoft® Visual Basic or Visual C++, offer dedicated tools to develop tree viewers. In SVA-FEA we implemented the MODEL TREE based on a "*listbox*" control.

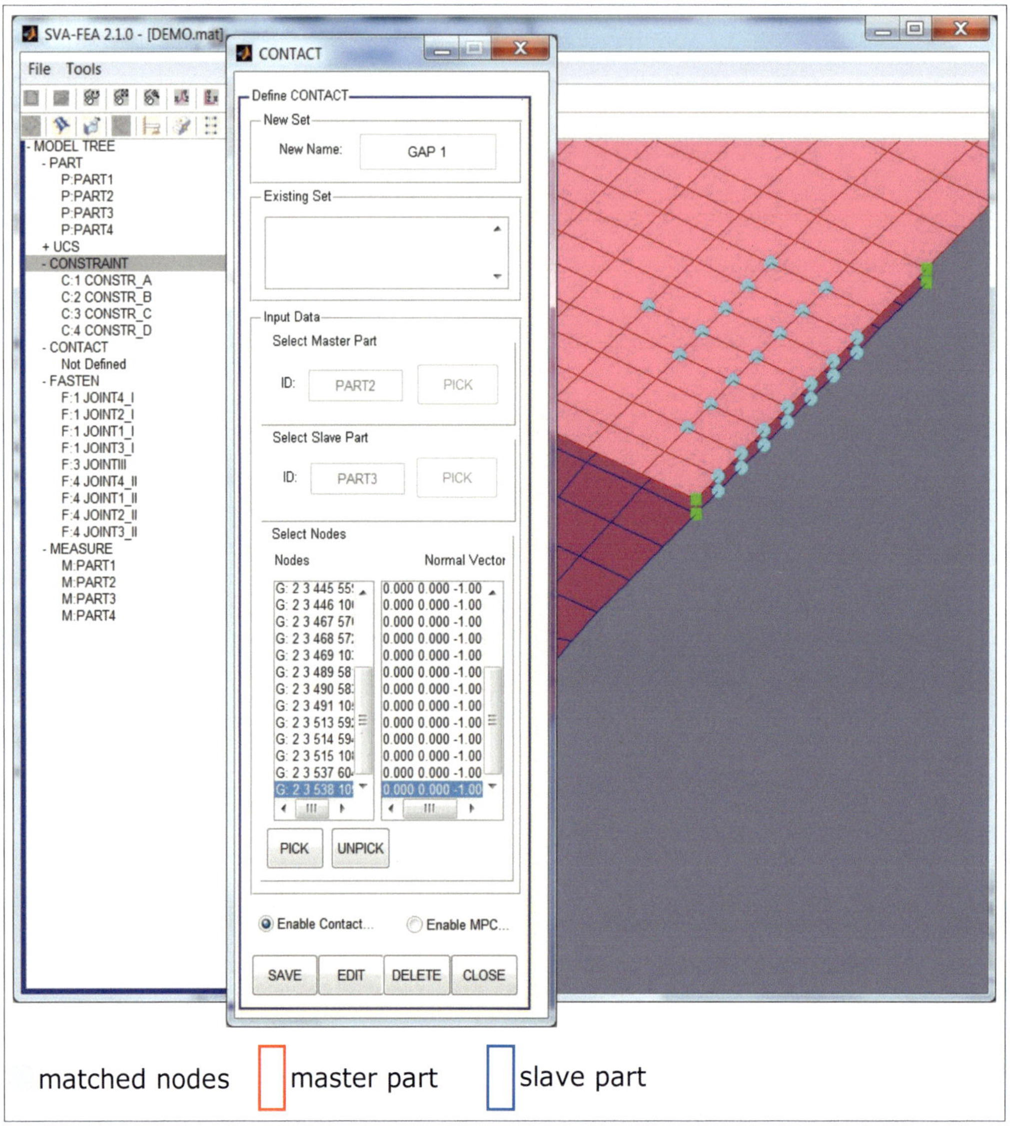

Fig. 8. Defining matched nodes among master and slave parts ("CONTACT" menu)

The "*listbox*" control differentiates its event call-backs depending on the "*SelectionType*" property. For example, if a single mouse click occurs, then the "*SelectionType*" property is automatically set to "*normal*". In presence of a double mouse click, "*SelectionType*" property becomes equal to "*open*".

The example below defines a new figure and a "*listbox*" control. The call-back function named "listCall" is associated to the "*listbox*". Every time clicking on that control, depending on the "*SelectionType*" property, "OPEN" or "NORMAL" strings are written.

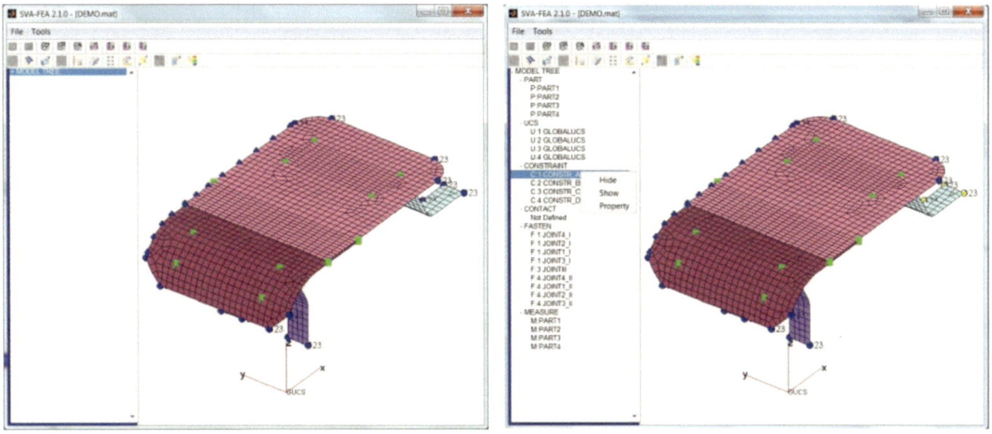

(a) collapsed MODEL TREE (b) expanded MODEL TREE

Fig. 9. MODEL TREE visualization

```
function testListbox

%- define a new figure
fig=figure('unit','characters','position',[20 5 160 45]);

%- define a listbox
hList=uicontrol('unit','characters','Style','listbox',...
                'position',[0 0 35 45],...
                'parent',fig,'enable','on');

%- set call-back function
set(hList,'callback',@listCall)

%- call-back function handling
function listCall(src,event)

%- differentiate depending on "SelectionType" property
if strcmp(get(gcf, 'SelectionType'), 'open') %- double-click
    set(src,'string','OPEN','value',1)
elseif strcmp(get(gcf, 'SelectionType'), 'normal') %- single-click
    set(src,'string','NORMAL','value',1)
end
```

Based on this key feature, the MODEL TREE was implemented in SVA-FEA to manage and visualize the modeling history. When importing new part or defining new KPs, the MODEL TREE is automatically updated. As example, Fig. 9 shows the MODEL TREE in which one can browse among part options (PART) and KPs (UCS, CONSTRAINT, CONTACT, FASTEN, MEASURE). Right-mouse-clicking was also programmed to allow a fast editing of the selected item.

2.5 SVA-FEA software: Assembly tree implementation

A crucial aspect to be achieved when performing the variation analysis of compliant parts is the assembly sequence, that is the sequence through which parts or sub-assemblies are put together. In (Ceglarek, 2009; Camelio et *al.*, 2004b) was reported that the assembly sequence may influence about 60% the final assembly variation. As stated before in this Chapter, for each assembly sub-station, a fixture frame and a fasten tool should be defined, simulating the classical PCFR cycle. As detailed in (Gerbino et *al.*, 2008; Franciosa, 2010a), SVA-FEA calculates the influence that previous sub-stations have on the actual assembly station. Such dependencies can be accounted considering the assembly process as an oriented graph, in which each vertex corresponds to a station, while every edge represents a station-to-station relationship.

Fig. 10 shows two assembly sequences and the related Laplace matrices (see Annex A.2). Knowing those matrices, dependencies among stations are univocally determined. For example, looking at the third column of the "L_b" matrix one can state that "Station 3" depends on "Station 1" and "Station 2". In SVA-FEA we developed the "Assembly OPERATION" tool able to interactively define parts to be assembled and the related station level. Moreover, for each assembly station the related fixture and fasten frame can be defined.

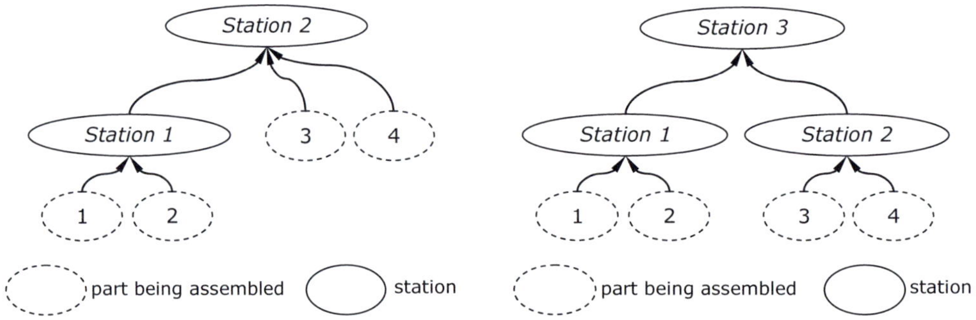

$$L_a = \begin{bmatrix} 0 & 1 \\ -1 & 0 \end{bmatrix} \qquad L_b = \begin{bmatrix} 0 & 0 & 1 \\ 0 & 0 & 1 \\ -1 & -1 & 0 \end{bmatrix}$$

Fig. 10. Two assembly sequences

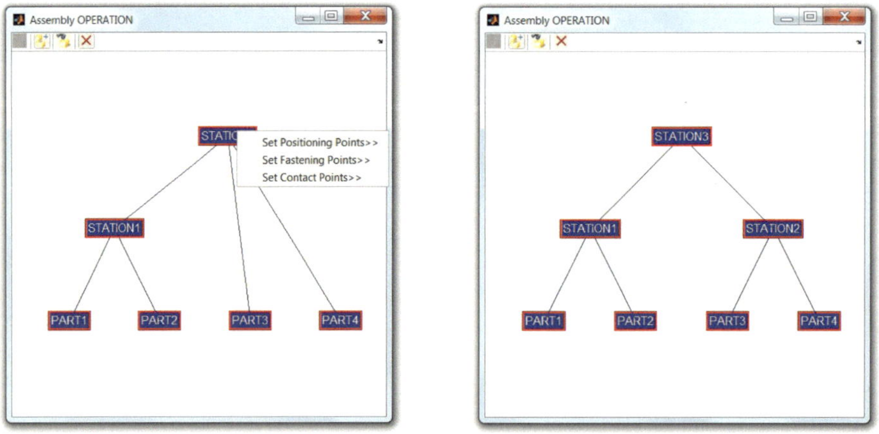

Fig. 11. Assembly OPERATION tool: two different assembly sequences

The "*text*" and "*line*" MatLAB® built-in functions were used to draw, respectively, part and station vertices and the edge links of the assembly graph. Fig. 11 reports the two assembly sequences as seen in SVA-FEA, related to ones depicted into Fig. 10.

2.6 SVA-FEA software: handling MSC NASTRAN output files

Once the assembly sequence is defined and the related KPs are set, accordingly, two consecutive FEA runs are solved, by running MSC NASTRAN®. Input files (in .bdf format) are automatically generated by SVA-FEA, and parsed to the MSC NASTRAN® solver. The following command lines are required to run MSC NASTRAN® from SVA-FEA:

```
%- MSC NASTRAN® path
pathsolve=sprintf('%s %s',cdNastran,filename);

%- run solver
dos(pathsolve);
```

where "cdNastran" is the MSC NASTRAN® installation path, whereas "filename" is the .bdf file to be solved.

FEA results coming from MSC NASTRAN® are stored in two main files: .op2 and .f06. The .op2 file contains post-processing data (see, for example, displacement fields), interpolated by using shape functions. However, the .op2 file has an owner format, not directly accessible or readable by users. On the contrary, the .f06 file is a text file containing node displacements and generalized forces. The general structure of the .f06 file is listed below. "Ti" and "Ri" are the translational and rotational degrees of freedom of the analyzed node, both related to displacements ("DISPLACEMENT VECTOR") and generalized forces ("FORCE OF SINGLE-POINT CONSTRAINT").

```
POINT-ID=241 // node id=241
                     DISPLACEMENT   VECTOR

SUBCASE    TYPE    T1          T2          T3          R1          R2          R3
1           G    -1.36E-05  4.81E-05 -1.38E-02  8.82E-03 -2.04E-03 -1.73E-06
2           G     1.36E-05 -4.81E-05  1.38E-02 -8.82E-03  2.04E-03  1.73E-06
// two sub-cases analyzed

POINT-ID=132
                     FORCE OF SINGLE-POINT CONSTRAINT

SUBCASE     TYPE    T1          T2         T3          R1         R2          R3
1           G      -3.96E-11 5.62E+00 8.94E+01  1.05E+03 -1.0E+02   -5.45E-03
// one sub-case analyzed
```

As described above for the MSC NASTRAN® input file, in order to speed-up the reading phase of the .f06 file, a compiled MEX functions was also here implemented.

2.7 SVA-FEA software: Post-processing simulation results

Simulation results can be easily analyzed and visualized from the POST-PROCESS main GUI (see Fig. 12): deformed or undeformed assembly (or sub-assembly) can be visualized; contour plots of mean or standard deviation values are available. Final results can be exported in Microsoft® EXCEL file, to quickly create graphs and diagrams. The interested reader is referred to (Franciosa et *al.*, 2009, 2010b) where more specific case studies are described and analyzed.

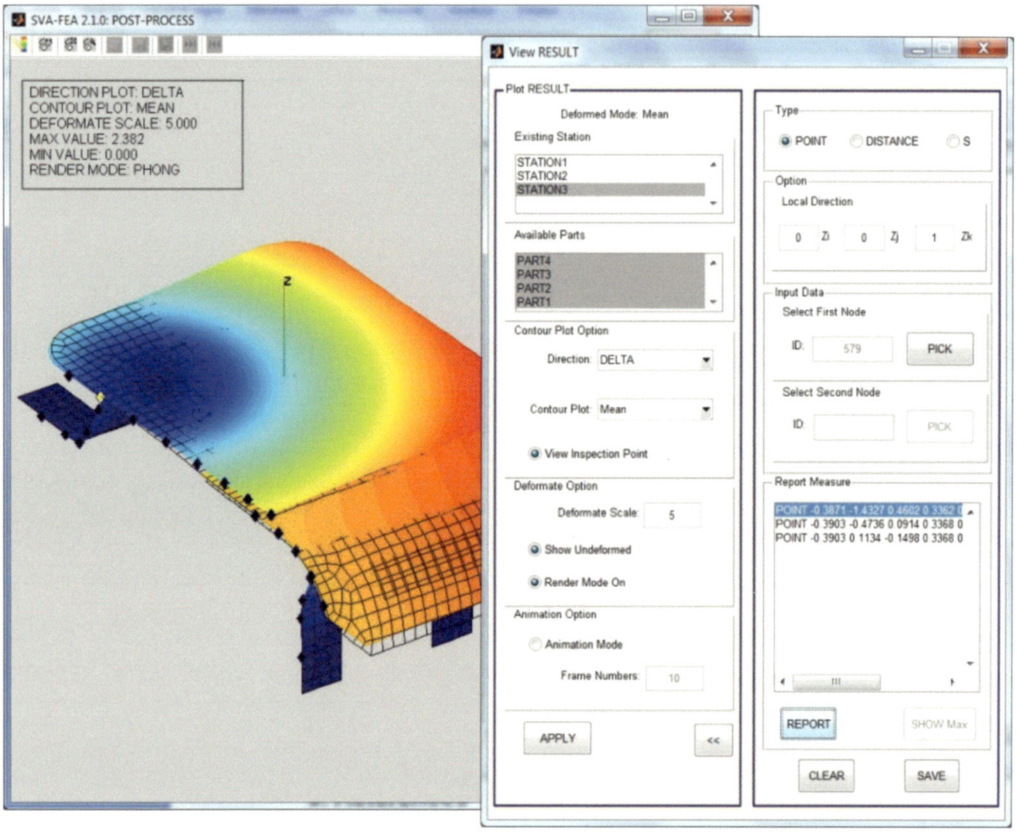

Fig. 12. POST-PROCESS tool

Contour plot utilities were implemented by using the MatLAB®'s "*patch*" function. This graphic object allows to visualize mesh data and to specify a color for each mesh-element or mesh-node. MatLAB® supports three shaders: flat, Gourand and Phong. The flat shader produces a uniform lighting across faces (that is, mesh-elements) of the object. Gourand and Phong algorithms, instead, calculate the mesh-node normals and interpolates linearly across the faces (Lengyel, 2003).

The code below can be adopted to generate a contour plot visualization (the related results are depicted into Fig. 13). "ELEMENT" contains the mesh-element connections (CQUAD4 and CTRIA3 elements imported from the input .bdf file). "cData" is a matrix containing contour data to be plotted (for example, the displacement field along the Z axis direction).

```
%- define a contour plot visualization (mesh edge shown)
patch('Faces',ELEMENT,'Vertices',Ncoord,... %- define mesh plotting
     'LineStyle','-','EdgeColor','k',... %- show "black" edge
     'FaceVertexCData',cData,'FaceColor','inter',... %- define contour data
     'FaceLighting','phong','EdgeLighting','phong') %- define shader

%- define a contour plot visualization (mesh edge hidden)
patch('Faces',ELEMENT,'Vertices',Ncoord,... %- define mesh plotting
     'LineStyle','none',... %- hide edge
     'FaceVertexCData',cData,'FaceColor','inter',... %- define contour
data
     'FaceLighting','phong','EdgeLighting','phong') %- define shader
```

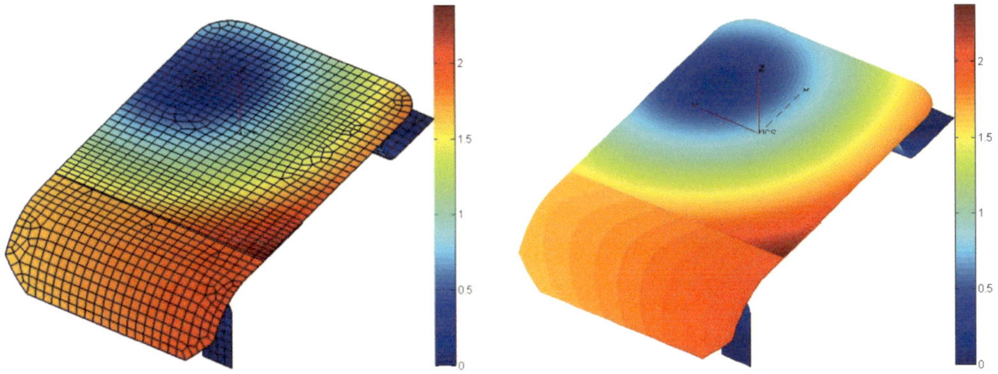

(a) mesh-edge shown (b) mesh-edge hidden

Fig. 13. Contour plot visualization

3. PROMesh overview

Re-designing real parts or, more generally, industrial products, involves different tasks. First of all, geometry shape must be digitalized in order to get a first geometrical model, which can be handled and edited. This model typically comes out as 3D tessellated model usually made of several thousands of nodes and triangles. Then, it needs to be processed in a CAE environment to simulate and understand its performances (in terms, for example, of structural or aerodynamic behavior). If the preliminary CAE results do not match design intents, the initial geometry has to be modified. The re-design loop is iterated until reaching a good balance among functional and esthetic requirements. Obviously, all this may become very time consuming and tedious when many geometry configurations need to be investigated. In this contest, interactive and automatic tools are welcome, since they may drive the designers to quickly test different design scenarios.

Within the PUODARSI Italian research project, PROMesh tool was implemented to quickly perform a fluid-dynamic simulation on any tessellated geometry object, after modifying it interactively (for example, by mouse drag-and-drop). PROMesh adopts Comsol Multiphysics® to solve Navier-Stokes equations, governing the fluid-dynamic phenomenon. Comsol Multiphysics® offers a powerful API interface allowing, among other things, to save and manipulate its data structure within the MatLAB® workspace and to extract and visualize simulation data.

Generally speaking, PROMesh allows: (I) loading any tessellated model, made of triangle or quadrilateral elements; (II) editing the imported geometry; (III) exporting that geometry to Comsol Multiphysics®; and solving a steady fluid dynamic simulation in automatic way. In particular, external flows around free shape objects are simulated. Further details about numerical algorithms can be found in (Di Gironimo et *al.*, 2009).
The PROMesh's software architecture borrowed several algorithms from SVA-FEA, for example, the mesh-node selection algorithm - Section 2.3. A new feature was implemented to allow user to interactively modify the geometry shape by the mouse control. To do this, a *Morphing Mesh Procedure* (MMP) was implemented.

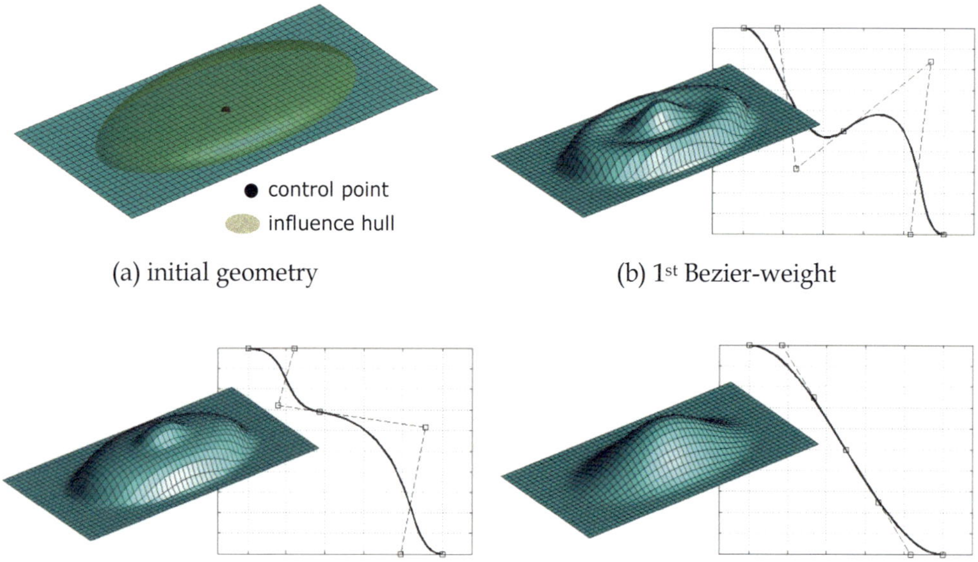

(a) initial geometry (b) 1st Bezier-weight

c. 2nd Bezier-weight d. 3rd Bezier-weight

Fig. 14. Generation of three different morphed geometries based on Bezier-weight functions

3.1 PROMesh software: MMP and user interaction

Morphing mesh is a well known technique used in computer graphic applications as a powerful tool for free-shape modeling and designing. The numerical procedure implemented in PROMesh may be summarized as follows (see (Franciosa & Gerbino, 2009) for more details). User defines a set of control points on the model, by picking them on the graphical interface. Then, the relative influence hull is assigned for each point. Control points directly influence final shape of the deformed object, and this shape can be fine-tuned by adjusting the influence hull's radius and/or the position of each control point. The influence hull defines the 3D region within which any mesh-node is influenced by the related control point. Based on this general idea, one can write:

$$\begin{aligned} &\Delta N_j = f\left(d_{i,j}\right)\cdot M \\ &\forall j = 1,\ldots,N_{node} \\ &\forall i = 1,\ldots,r \end{aligned} \tag{2}$$

where "ΔN_j" is the displacement of the j-th mesh-node, calculated once the morphing matrix, "M", and the weight function, "$f(d_j)$", are known. "r" is the number of control points. As demonstrated in (Franciosa & Gerbino, 2009), "M" matrix can be easily calculated from the control point coordinates. Moreover, the weight function is equal to 1 when the mesh-node "N_j" is coincident with the i-th control point and tends toward zero for points "N_j" whose distance from the i-th control point is greater than zero.

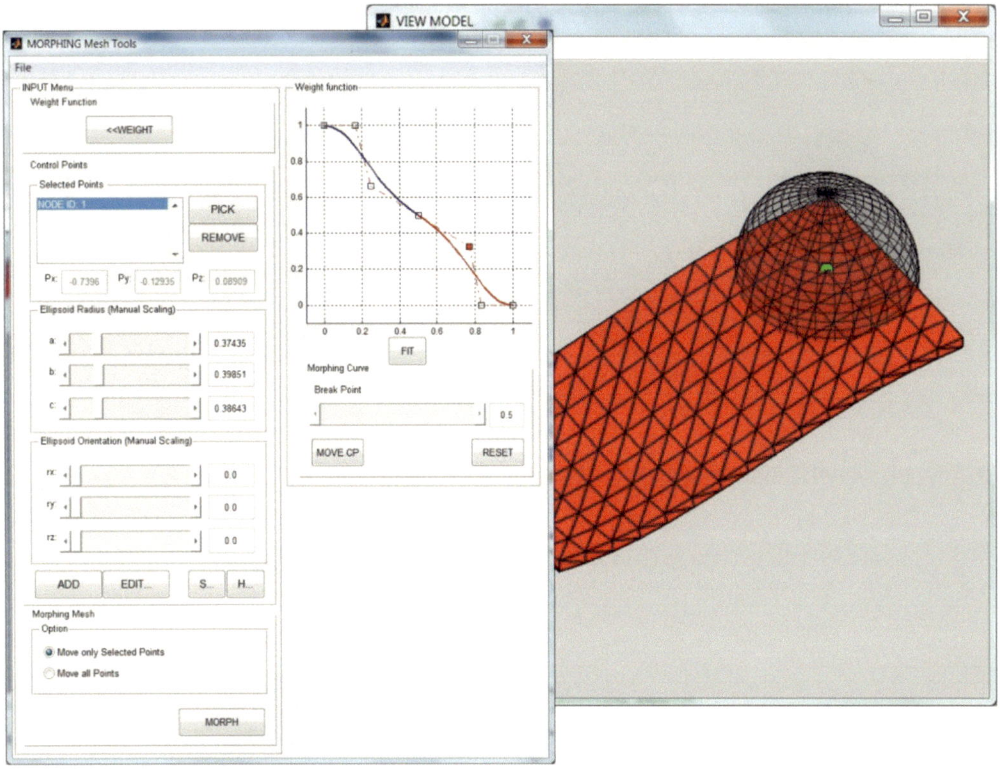

Fig. 15. PROMesh user interface: morphing mesh module

In PROMesh the weight functions was assumed as a piecewise Bezier curve, which can be modified by acting on its control polygon. As example, Fig. 14 shows the application of the MMP on an initial flat geometry. Once defined one control point and its influence hull (PROMesh supports only ellipsoid domains), three different geometries were generated, by varying the Bezier's shape. Since the morphing matrix depends on the control point coordinates, the geometry can be morphed with a mouse control in the graphical area. Partially based on the mouse selection algorithm (see Section 2.3), the interactive morphing procedure can be summarized as follows:

- calculate the selected control point "P_{ci}" and the camera rotation matrix, "R", when picking down the mouse button ("*WindowButtondownFcn*" callack);
- calculate the actual position of the control point "$P_{ci,act}$" point and apply the MMP, when moving the mouse ("*WindowButtonMotionFcn*" callack); and,
- end the procedure when releasing the mouse button ("*WindowButtonUpFcn*" callack).

Fig. 15 depicts the morphing mesh tool embedded in PROMesh. After picking some control points, the related influence hulls can be manually tuned by varying their sizes and their orientations ("*slider*" controls). Then, the weigh function can be edited by moving the control polygon of the Bezier curve, and the geometry changes in real time.
Figure 16 shows four morphed geometries obtained thought the high user-interaction offered by PROMesh.
Source files of PROMesh are available on:
http://www.mathworks.com/matlabcentral/fileexchange/authors/38957.

(a) 1st morphed geometry

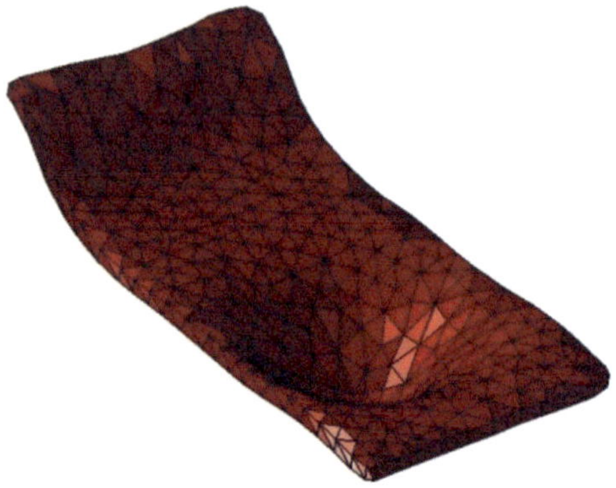

(b) 2nd morphed geometry

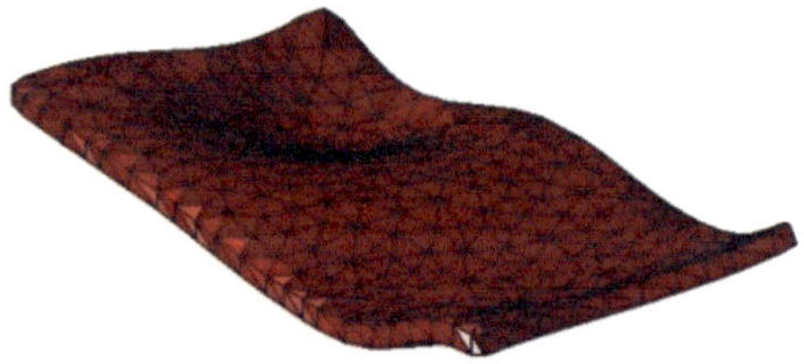

(c) 3rd morphed geometry

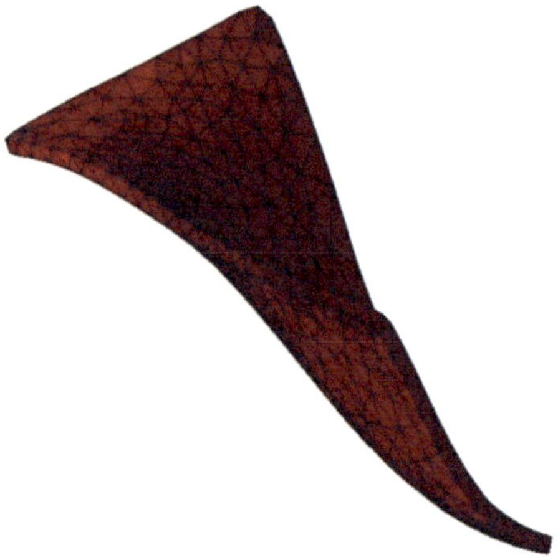

(d) 4th morphed geometry

Fig. 16. Application of the morphing mesh procedure

4. Conclusions and final remarks

The Chapter focused on two MatLAB®'s GUI applications: SVA-FEA® and PROMesh®. SVA-FEA® is a graphical tool developed to do statistical tolerance analysis of compliant assembly. It allows to manage imported mesh data, define assembly key points and specify

the assembly sequence. On the other side, PROMesh® offers dedicated algorithms to handle tessellated data geometry. The implementation of such tools was characterized by the inner needs to have friendly GUIs, allowing an advanced user-interaction. In particular, the following goals were achieved: (I) selection of mesh nodes through mouse clicking or mouse area-selection; (II) tree view and assembly tree implementations, based on graphs; (III) implementation of compiled MEX functions to speed-up huge calculations, involving the reading and writing tasks of formatted ASCII files. Furthermore, PROMesh® was oriented to allow user to interactively select mesh nodes and "morph" the mesh geometry.
The experiences made in developing these computer tools demonstrates that it is possible to provide advanced user-interaction without a specific skill in computer science.

Annex A: Methods and tools

A.1 Handling large data set in MatLAB®

When large data sets are allocated and accessed within loops, MatLAB® is not too much efficient. This is especially true when managing formatted text files rather than binary files. One manner to optimize and speed-up MatLAB® accessing data is by using compiled source codes, written in FORTRAN or C++ language (Kernighan & Dennis, 1978). This Annex describes how to write and compile a MEX function, written in C++ language, for MatLAB®.
Assume to create an array, A, whose entries are all integers from 1 to 10^8 (obviously, such as array may be easily defined as “A=1:1e8”; this example wants to show, instead, how loops are not so efficient into MatLAB®). From MatLAB® script one can write:

```
%- define array size
N=1e8;

%- initialize array
A=zeros(1,N);

%- start loop
for i=1:N
    A(i)=i; %-allocate "integer" value
end
```

On a Win 7 64bit, 8GB RAM, 2 i7 quad-core processors machine the run-time is 0.9441 s. The same array will be now generated by using a MEX compiled function.
The source code for a MEX file consists of two main distinct parts:

- *computational routine*: it contains the code performing the needed computations; and,
- *gateway routine*: it is the main function which links with MatLAB®.

The general form of a source MEX file is shown below:

```
// include mex header
#include "mex.h"

// COMPUTATIONAL ROUTINE SECTION
void userfnc#1(...)
{
```

```
    //… routine code…
}

double userfnc#2(…)
{
//… routine code…
}

// GATEWAY ROUTINE SECTION
void mexFunction(int nlhs, mxArray *plhs[], int nrhs,
                 const mxArray *prhs[])
// nlhs = number of output items
// nrhs = number of input items
// plhs = output pointers
// prhs = input pointers

{
// get pointer from MatLAB® input
A = mxGetPr(plhs[…]);

// create MatLAB® variable
  plhs[…] = mxCreateDoubleMatrix(…);

// allocate output variable
userfnc(…);
}
```

The name of the gateway function is always "mexFunction". This function parses all MatLAB® inputs into pointer variables ("mxGetPr") and create the output MatLAB® variables ("mxCreateDoubleMatrix"). Assuming "testmex.c" is the source code file, the following line should be written to compile it from MatLAB® (for 64bit MatLAB® distributions the Microsoft® Visual C++ compiler is suggested by MathWorks; how to install the Microsoft® Visual C++ for MatLAB® can be found in (Baker, 2009)).

```
%- link and compile mex source code
mex testmex.c
```

Therefore, one can now write a MEX file which creates the A array. The source C++ code of the "testmex.c" file is something like this:

```
#include "mex.h"

// computational routine
void allocateArray(double A[], int nr)
{
int i; // locale variable
for (i=0; i<nr; i++){
          A[i]=i+1; // "fill" array
                    }
}
// gateway routine
void mexFunction(int nlhs, mxArray *plhs[], int nrhs,
                 const mxArray *prhs[])
{
```

```
    double *A; // pointer to "int" type
    int nr; // define "int" variable

    // get "int" value from the input pointer
    nr = (int)*mxGetPr(prhs0]);

    // allocate MatLAB® double matrix
    plhs[0] = mxCreateDoubleMatrix(nr,1, mxREAL);

    // get the pointer to the output
    A = mxGetPr(plhs[0]);

   // allocate the output array by using the computational routine
    allocateArray(A,nr);
}
```

The compiled function may be easily called from MatLAB®, typing:

```
%- use compiled function
A=testmex(N);
```

The elapsed run-time is now 0.2893 s, that is, about 70% faster than the previous MatLAB® script. This way is particularly useful when managing large data sets, or nested loops are required.

A.2 Adjacency matrix and Laplace matrix

A graph "G" is usually defined by means of the vector list of vertices, "V", and the edge matrix, "E" (Berge, 2001; Deo, 2004).

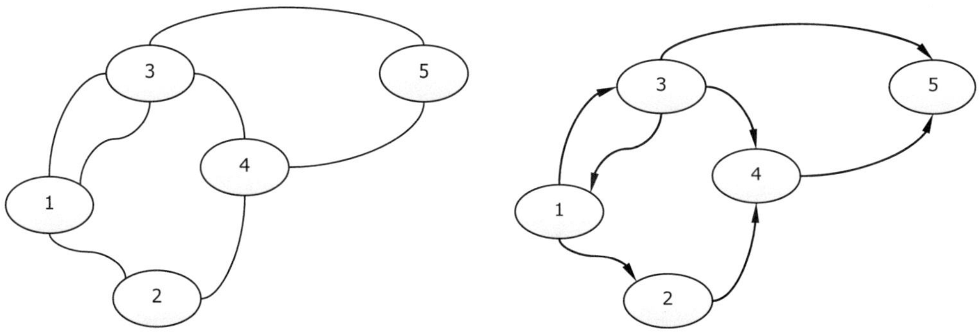

(a) not-oriented graph (b) oriented graph

Fig. A.1. Graph representation

"V" is a vector of integer ranging from 1 to N_v, where N_v is the total number of vertices. "E" is an N_ex2 matrix, in which the i-th row has the indices of vertices connected by that edge (N_e is the number of edges). Let (i, j) be the couple of entries on the i-th row. For not-oriented graphs (see Fig. A.1a) it is (i, j)=(j, i), whereas (i, j)≠(j, i) for oriented graphs (see Fig. A.1b). Moreover, the same couple of vertices may be connected with more than one edge (in Fig. A.1, vertices 1 and 3 are connected with 2 edges).

$$E_{NO}=\begin{bmatrix}1&2\\1&3\\3&1\\2&4\\3&4\\3&5\\4&5\end{bmatrix}\equiv\begin{bmatrix}2&1\\3&1\\1&3\\4&2\\4&3\\5&3\\5&4\end{bmatrix},\qquad E_O=\begin{bmatrix}1&2\\1&3\\3&1\\2&4\\3&4\\3&5\\4&5\end{bmatrix} \tag{A.1}$$

Looking at Fig. A.1, edge matrices, E_{NO} and E_O, for not-oriented and oriented graphs, respectively, are stated into equation (A.1). A useful representation of graphs, based on the edge matrix, may be achieved with the adjacency matrix, "A".

$$A(i,j)=\begin{cases}\sum_{k=1}^{Ne} edge_k, i\neq j\\ 0,\text{ otherwise}\end{cases}\qquad \forall i,j=1,2,\ldots,N_v \tag{A.2}$$

It is a symmetric square $N_v x N_v$ matrix and defined as in equation (A.2). The entry (i, j) in "A" counts all edges connecting the vertex V_i to V_j. For example, looking at Fig. A.1a, the adjacency matrix becomes as into equation (A.3).

$$A=\begin{bmatrix}0&1&2&0&0\\1&0&0&1&0\\2&0&0&1&1\\0&1&1&0&1\\0&0&1&1&0\end{bmatrix} \tag{A.3}$$

For oriented graph it may be useful to preserve the sign of the edge. For this purpose, the Laplace or Kirchoff matrix, "L" can be introduced. It is a square $N_v x N_v$ matrix and defined as in equation (A.4).

$$L(i,j)=\begin{cases}+\sum_{k=1}^{Ne} edge_k, i\neq j\text{ and }V_i\text{ directed to }V_j\\ -\sum_{k=1}^{Ne} edge_k, i\neq j\text{ and }V_j\text{ directed to }V_i\\ 0,\text{ otherwise}\end{cases}\qquad \forall i,j=1,2,\ldots,N_v \tag{A.4}$$

The entry (i, j) in "L" counts all edges directed from the vertex V_i to V_j. For example, looking at Fig. A.1b, it has:

$$L=\begin{bmatrix}0&1&1&0&0\\-1&0&0&1&0\\1&0&0&1&1\\0&-1&-1&0&1\\0&0&-1&-1&0\end{bmatrix} \tag{A.5}$$

5. References

Baker, L. (2009). *Microsoft 32/64-bit Visual C++ 2008 Express Support Files*, available online from http://www.mathworks.com/matlabcentral/fileexchange/22689-microsoft-3264-bit-visual-c-2008-express-support-files

Berge, C. (2001). *The Theory of Graph*, Dover Publications, ISBN-10: 9780486419756

Bordegoni M., Ferrise F., Ambrogio M., Caruso F., Bruno F. (2010). Data exchange and multi-layered architecture for a collaborative design process in virtual environments. *Journal on Interactive Design and Manufacturing*, Vol. 4, pp. 137-138.

Camelio, J. A., Hu, S. J., Ceglarek, D. (2004a). Modeling Variation Propagation in Multi-Station Assembly Systems with Compliant Parts, *ASME Journal of Mechanical Design*, Vol. 125, pp. 673-681

Camelio, J. A., Hu, S. J., Ceglarek, D. (2004b). Impact of Fixture Design on Sheet Metal Assembly Variation, *Journal of Manufacturing Systems*, Vol. 23, pp. 182-193

Ceglarek, D., Huang, W., Zhou, S., Ding, Y., Kumar, R., Zhou, Y. (2009). Time-Based Competition in Multistage Manufacturing: Stream-of-Variation Analysis (SOVA) Methodology - Review, *Journal of Flexible Manufacturing Systems*, Vol. 16, pp. 11-44

Chang, M., Gossard, D. C. (1996). Modeling the Assembly of Compliant, non-Ideal Parts, *Computer-Aided Design*, Vol. 29, pp. 701-708

Deo, N. (2004). *Graph Theory with Applications to Engineering and Computer Science*, Prentice-Hall of India, ISBN-10: 0133634736

Di Gironimo, G., Franciosa, P., Gerbino, S. (2009). An RE-CAE Methodology for Re-Designing Free Shape Objects Interactively, *Int. Journal on Interactive Design and Manufacturing*, DOI 10.1007/s12008-009-0082-8

Franciosa, P., Gerbino, S. (2009). Handling Tessellated Free Shape Objects with a Morphing Mesh Procedure in Comsol Multiphysics®, In: *Proc. of COMSOL Conference'09*, Milano (Italy), October 14-16, 2009

Franciosa, P., Gerbino, S., Patalano, S. (2009). Variation Analysis of Compliant Assemblies: A Comparative Study of a Single-Station Assembly, *Journal Anales de Ingenieria Grafica*, N. 20, pp. 57-64

Franciosa, P. (2010a). *Modeling and Simulation of Variational Rigid and Compliant Assembly for Tolerance Analysis*, PhD Dissertation, University of Naples, Federico II, School of Engineering-Italy, available online from http://www.fedoa.unina.it

Franciosa, P., Gerbino, S., Patalano, S. (2010b). Variation Analysis of Compliant Assemblies: A Comparative Study of a Multi-Station Assembly, *Journal Anales de Ingenieria Grafica*, N. 21, pp. 45-52

Gerbino, S., Patalano, S., Franciosa, P. (2008). Statistical Variation Analysis of Multi-Station Compliant Assemblies based on Sensitivity Matrix, *Int. Journal Computer Applications in Technology*, Vol. 33, 1, pp. 12-23

Holland, T. O., Marchand, P. (2002). *Graphics and GUIs with Matlab*, Chapman and Hall/CRC, 3rd edition, ISBN-10: 1584883200

Kernighan, B., Dennis, M. R. (1978). *The C Programming Language*, Englewood Cliffs, Prentice Hall, ISBN 0-13-110163-3

Lengyel, E. (2003). *Mathematics for 3D Game Programming and Computer Graphics*, Charles River Media, ISBN-10: 1584500379

Perutka, K. (2010). Tips and Tricks for Programming in Matlab, In: *Matlab - Modeling Programming and Simulation*, Edited by Emilson Pereira Leite, pp. 2-16, available online from http://www.intechopen.com/books

Scott, T. Smith (2006). *Matlab Advanced GUI Development*, Dog Ear Publishing, ISBN-10: 1598581813

15

Using MATLAB to Achieve Nanoscale Optical Sectioning in the Vicinity of Metamaterial Substrates by Simulating Emitter-Substrate Interactions

Kareem Elsayad[1]*, Marek Suplata[1] and Katrin Heinze[1,2]
[1]*Research Institute of Molecular Pathology (IMP) Dr. Bohr-Gasse 7, Vienna*
[2]*Rudolf Virchow Center,DFG Research Center for Experimental Biomedicine, University of Wuerzburg, Versbacher Str. 9, Wuerzburg*
[1]*Austria*
[2]*Germany*

1. Introduction

The imaging performance of a conventional far-field microscope is restricted by the so-called diffraction limit Born & Wolf (1997). For an imaging wavelength of λ this corresponds to a maximum attainable resolution of approximately $\lambda/4$ (laterally) and $\lambda/2$ (axially) when using a high numerical aperture objective lens. With recent advances in molecular biology some of the most interesting questions require a resolution beyond this. Higher resolution has been typically achieved using lower wavelength probing/scanning fields, or resorting to near-field scanning techniques (e.g. Scanning Near-field Optical Microscopy (SNOM) Betzig et al. (1991)). Unfortunately these come with their limitations and undesirable side effects, which prove to be limiting when it comes to studying molecular dynamics in their native environment. Furthermore, the use of fluorescent labels for studying specific processes and background suppression is desirable in many applications. Far-field optical microscopy still remains the only practical non-invasive technique suitable for imaging fast dynamics over extended periods and distances of interest with minimal perturbations to the system.

Fortunately, far-field optical microscopy capable of imaging beyond the conventional diffraction limit for life science applications has seen many advances over the last few decades. Our current arsenal of techniques include commercially well developed techniques such as confocal laser scanning microscopy Cremer & Cremer (1978) and Total Internal Reflection Fluorescence (TIRF) microscopy Axelrod (1981)[1]. The improved resolution with these techniques is in itself however only by a factor ~ 2 and often not sufficient in many cases. More powerful techniques such as Fluorescence PhotoActivatable Localization Microscopy (FPALM), Stimulated Emission Depletion (STED) Microscopy, Structured Illumination

[1] Although this is in itself not practically speaking a superresolution technique as it only achieves sub-diffraction limit axial localization over a single small axial region and can thus not be used to distinguish two emitters separated by distances smaller than $\sim \lambda/2$.

Microscopy (SIM), and variations thereof - see e.g. review Hell (2007) - have been developed which can offer lateral resolution improvements by factors of up to ≈ 20. Despite the great success of these techniques they struggle with achieving sufficient temporal resolution in many cases. They also struggle with achieving axial super-resolution, which when achievable usually requires elaborate modifications to the setup. Currently there exists to our knowledge no far-field optical microscopy technique that is capable of studying axial dynamics with < 20nm resolution in live cells without either significantly perturbing the sample or requiring an elaborate and/or costly microscopy setup.

Here we outline the computational aspects associated with a technique - Metamaterial Substrate Modified Fluorescence (MeSuMo) Microscopy - we have recently developed that allows for dynamic imaging with axial superresolution which is compatible with standard epifluorescence microscope setups. As with majority of optical imaging techniques currently used in the lifesciences, MeSuMo is essentially a fluorescence microscopy technique, requiring the objects of interest to be labelled with suitable fluorescent emitters. Compared to other techniques capable of achieving comparable resolution (e.g. Kanchanawong (2010)), MeSuMo microscopy is, once optimized, experimentally very simple to implement and suitable for fast dynamic studies on live cells. It relies on using microscope slides coated with an optimized metal-dielectric coatings (metamaterials) which modify the emission spectrum of fluorophores in a manner that is dependent on their separation from the surface of the substrate. A spectral analysis over a sampled area allows one to infer the average separation of the emitters in the studied region. In this chapter we will not aim to provide an exhaustive description of the underlying principles and details associated with the technique, but rather emphasis how the data analysis can be performed in a MATLAB environment. We note that there exists an extensive underlying theoretical body of work in the various areas of classical and quantum physics for modeling the near-field electromagnetic interaction with plasmonic structures and the photophysics of fluorophores, which the interested reader may learn more about through the referenced literature. To maintain the focus of the chapter we will thus in most cases only present qualitative interpretations of the effects when relevant and quote the essential results (equations and integrals) in a form that can be readily entered and computed using MATLAB.

The chapter is divided into five sections that include: (1) modeling the metamaterial coated substrates, (2) fitting the experimental data to the model, (3) modifying the model to obtain best fit results, and (4) an example of the technique being implemented. We conclude the chapter in section (5) with a discussion of future additions to the technique we are actively working on.

2. Modeling the metamaterial coated substrate

An optical metamaterial is an artificial material typically consisting of subwavelength scale metal and dielectric components. In the most general context its key feature is, in a nutshell, that it has a unique response to certain electromagnetic fields that can not be found in naturally occurring materials. This typically consists of negative refractive properties - namely that an incident field would refract in the opposite direction from the normal-axis as compared to a conventional naturally occurring material. Numerous interesting and potentially useful effects may result such as strong enhancements of the Purcell factor for nearby emitters Jacob et al. (2010), which allow for the realizations of devices such as SPASERs Bergman and Stockman (2003) and lasing SPASERs Zheludev et al. (2008). Here we focus on a relatively simple case of layered metallic-dielectric layers each having a thickness much smaller than or comparable to the wavelength. Depending on the precise thicknesses of the layers as well as their individual response properties such structures may exhibit Fabry-Perot resonances, resonant photon tunneling and other unusual transmission/reflection properties Belov and Hao (2006); Darmanyan and Zayats (2003); Elsayad and Heinze (2010); Ramakrishna et al. (2003). It turns out that many of these properties can quite intuitively be modeled analytically using MATLAB due to the matrix formalism often used to describe them.

In the context of the technique we will discuss there are two properties of interest to us. Firstly, there is the complex reflection coefficients of the structures. These determine the local field at the site of the emitter and hence also the excitation and decay rates. Secondly there is the dispersion relation of the supported modes of the structure which will give us physical insight into the type of excitations the emitters couple to at different distances and frequencies, and thereby allow us to tune our structures to obtain optimal results. Of particular relevance for the latter will be a so-called "cut-off energy" which exists in asymmetric structures at a given energy, where there is a transition from a bound to an unbound SPP mode Burke and Stegeman (1986).

For the case of the transmission/reflection coefficients one simple way to model the structures is to use transfer matrices which describe the propagation and attenuation in each layer Born & Wolf (1997). As mentioned such calculations are particularly well suited for MATLAB where, once the matrices are defined, the coefficients for arbitrary combinations of layers and structures can readily be determined and compared. The transfer matrices are generally defined in the Fourier domain parallel to the surface of the layers (k_x,k_y) and the real domain normal to the layers (z). This also allows for easy analysis of the contribution from different evanescent field components which are dominant in the near-field (distances smaller than about the wavelength). Once one has written matrices for the transmission through a given interface ($t_{i,j}$, where the superscripts i and j denote the regions on either side of the interface) and the attenuation through a certain thickness of a given material (p_i) in terms of the transverse wavevector(s) and - for the latter case - the thickness of the layer, one can obtain the total transmission function (or optical transfer function) of an n-layered structure t_n by

$$t_n = \Pi_i^{n-1} \; p_i \, t_{i,i+1} \, p_n. \tag{1}$$

Details on the implementation of transfer matrices can be found in most standard classical optics texts Born & Wolf (1997) and will not be elaborated on here. We only mention that the formalism will, for not too large transverse wavevectors, also be applicable for subwavelength laterally structured layers (e.g. layers containing split-ring, horse-shoe shaped, or fractal resonators). In such cases one would need to define suitable effective anisotropic permittivity and permeability matrices for them, e.g. in a 2D system one may have a permittivity `epsilon(a,b)` and permeability `mu(a,b)` where `a` and `b` are the x and z components required to describe the effective response properties of the structure. The cases of two polarizations (perpendicular magnetic and electric fields) can be treated separately by choosing the suitable Fresnel coefficients for the matrix elements of $t_{i,i+1}$. Alternatively one can also use a "brute force" approach for not too complicated structures and include the complete equations (e.g. as a function) into MATLAB. For example, for the case of a four layered structure (layers indexed by i, j, k, l) this would be:

$$r_{ijkl}^{P(S)} = \frac{r_{ij}^{P(S)} + r_{jkl}^{P(S)} \exp[2i(\varepsilon_j \mu_j (\varepsilon_i \mu_i)^{-1} - u^2)^{\frac{1}{2}} k_i d_j]}{1 + r_{ij}^{P(S)} r_{jkl}^{P(S)} \exp[2i(\varepsilon_j \mu_j (\varepsilon_i \mu_i)^{-1} - u^2)^{\frac{1}{2}} k_i d_j]} \tag{2}$$

with

$$r_{jkl}^{P(S)} = \frac{r_{jk}^{P(S)} + r_{kl}^{P(S)} \exp[2i(\varepsilon_k \mu_k (\varepsilon_i \mu_i)^{-1} - u^2)^{\frac{1}{2}} k_i d_k]}{1 + r_{jk}^{P(S)} r_{kl}^{P(S)} \exp[2i(\varepsilon_k \mu_k (\varepsilon_i \mu_i)^{-1} - u^2)^{\frac{1}{2}} k_i d_k]} \tag{3}$$

and

$$r_{ij}^{S} = \frac{\mu_j (1 - u^2)^{1/2} - \mu_i [\varepsilon_j \mu_j (\varepsilon_i \mu_i)^{-1} - u^2]^{1/2}}{\mu_j (1 - u^2)^{1/2} + \mu_i [\varepsilon_j \mu_j (\varepsilon_i \mu_i)^{-1} - u^2]^{1/2}} \tag{4}$$

$$r_{ij}^{P} = \frac{\varepsilon_j (1 - u^2)^{1/2} - \varepsilon_i [\varepsilon_j \mu_j (\varepsilon_i \mu_i)^{-1} - u^2]^{1/2}}{\varepsilon_j (1 - u^2)^{1/2} + \varepsilon_i [\varepsilon_j \mu_j (\varepsilon_i \mu_i)^{-1} - u^2]^{1/2}} \tag{5}$$

where ε_i, μ_i and d_i are the permittivity, permeability and thickness of the ith layer. The total wavevector in the ith layer is given by $k_i = \sqrt{\varepsilon_i \mu_i} \omega / c$ where ω is the frequency of the electromagnetic field and c is the speed of light in vacuum. Also a normalized in plane wavevector is defined as $u = k_x / k_1$, where k_x is the in plane wavevector component which is independent of the layer. The value of ε for the metal will in general be complex and frequency dependent, and is most easily obtained by fitting a high order polynomial to experimentally measured data (e.g. Drachev (2008) for silver). Alternatively for not to thin metal layers one may to a good approximation use a Drude-Sommerfeld model (e.g. Kittel (1995)) where the parameters can later be systematically varied to account for e.g. changes in temperature Elsayad and Heinze (2010b).

To determine the dispersion relation and the cut-off energy of a given structure one may also make use of the natural matrix calculation approaches of MATLAB. To do so one firstly writes a general expression for the parallel electric fields in each layer. For a layer-i extending from $z = z_{min}$ to $z = z_{max}$ this would be $A_i^{(1)} e^{k_{zi}(z + z_{min})} + A_i^{(2)} e^{-k_{zi}(z + z_{max})}$, where k_{zi} is the out of plane wavevector in the layer and $A_i^{(1)}$ & $A_i^{(2)}$ are at this point arbitrary complex coefficients. One may then write the corresponding magnetic induction fields for each layer using Maxwell's equations (i.e. by taking the normal derivative), so that for each layer one has two equations with two unknowns. This is done for each layer $i = 1, 2 \ldots N$. Finally one constructs a $2N \times 2N$ with the coefficients for each layer constituting the entries in each row. The determinant of this matrix will then give the dispersion relation $\omega(k_x)$ - see e.g. Dionne et al. (2008). Since k_x is complex one can not simply assign a solver such as `fzero` to the task. It is it turns out often necessary to evaluate this by brute force - i.e. letting MATLAB evaluate the determinant for a given complex transverse wavevector and checking how close it is to zero. In general it is important to provide a good starting guess of $\text{Re}(k_x)$ and $\text{Im}(k_x)$ for each frequency. For the cases of interest, where the frequencies of interest are close to the cut-off frequency, a good starting guess for the former is the light-line $\text{Re}(k_x) = n\omega / c$ of the medium with refractive index n in which the mode becomes unbound,

and then to progressively search further into the evanescent region, i.e. $\mathrm{Re}(k_x) = n\omega/c + \delta$ with $\delta \sim 0.01n\omega/c$. For the imaginary part $\mathrm{Im}(k_x)$ - which diverges at the cut-off - it is most efficient to employ an algorithm which calculates the gradient of the determinant between two nearby values of $\mathrm{Im}(k_x)$ [i.e. taking the difference in the determinant value and dividing by the difference in $\mathrm{Im}(k_x)$], and subsequently search for larger/smaller $\mathrm{Im}(k_x)$ values if the determinant is smaller/larger than zero. The stability of the solution should be checked to assure $\mathrm{Lim}_{\delta\to 0}\{\omega(k_x + \delta) - \omega(k_x - \delta) \to 0\}$. The above mentioned approach typically requires that $\mathrm{Im}(k_x)$ is well behaved and monotonous in the vicinity of the cut-off, which is fortunately often the case. Since the equation has to be satisfied for both $\mathrm{Re}(k_x)$ and $\mathrm{Im}(k_x)$ optimizations of both of these have to be performed simultaneously. For completeness an analysis can also be performed for transverse electric (TE) as well as transverse magnetic (TM) polarizations, although for the cases of the very thin non-magnetic plasmonic structures only the latter are usually relevant. For the case of highly asymmetric structures of few layers, coupling between the interfaces may be negligible and a single plasmonic mode at one interface can to a good approximation be assumed solely responsible for the dispersion of the cut-off mode Burke and Stegeman (1986). In this case the cut-off energy can for a non-magnetic structure be estimated by $E_c = \hbar c \varepsilon_j \varepsilon_k[\varepsilon_i(\varepsilon_j + \varepsilon_k)]^{-1}$, where ε_i is the permittivity of the medium where the cut-off occurs, and ε_j and ε_k are the permittivities on either side of the interface at which the mode is originally localized.
The principle of MeSuMo requires that the cut-off of the structure falls within the emission spectrum of the emitter. Since many common fluorophores and dyes have a fairly broad emission spectrum this criteria can usually be met quite easily and is generally quite robust. To calculate the change in intensity at a given frequency one firstly defines the change in the decay rate of a fluorophore as a function of distance and frequency. This may (at not too small distances) be modeled quite well in the dipole approximation using the classical Chance-Prock-Silbey (CPS) model Chance (Prock and Silbey). Under these conditions the decay rate in the $+\hat{z}$ and $-\hat{z}$ direction (away from and towards the substrate respectively) for perpendicular ($\perp$) and parallel ($||$) electric dipole like emitters can be obtained by:

$$\hat{\Gamma}_+^{\perp} = q - \frac{3q}{4}\mathrm{Im}\int_0^1 (\mathcal{I}_1 + \mathcal{I}_2)\,du$$

$$\hat{\Gamma}_-^{\perp} = \frac{3q}{4}\mathrm{Im}\left(\int_0^1 \mathcal{I}_1 du - \int_1^\infty \mathcal{I}_2 du\right) \tag{6}$$

$$\hat{\Gamma}_+^{||} = q - \frac{3q}{8}\mathrm{Im}\int_0^1 (\mathcal{I}_3 - \mathcal{I}_4)du$$

$$\hat{\Gamma}_-^{||} = \frac{3q}{8}\mathrm{Im}\left(\int_0^1 \mathcal{I}_3 du + \int_1^\infty \mathcal{I}_4 du\right) \tag{7}$$

in which the integrands are

$$\mathcal{I}_1 = 2u^3\frac{1-|r^P|^2}{(u^2-1)^{\frac{1}{2}}} \qquad \mathcal{I}_2 = u^3\frac{r^P}{(u^2-1)^{\frac{1}{2}}}\exp[2(u^2-1)^{\frac{1}{2}}k_1 z]$$

$$\mathcal{I}_3 = u\frac{(1-|r^S|^2)+(1-u^2)(1-|r^P|^2)}{(u^2-1)^{\frac{1}{2}}} \qquad \mathcal{I}_4 = 2u\frac{r^S+(1-u^2)r^P}{(u^2-1)^{\frac{1}{2}}}\exp[2(u^2-1)^{\frac{1}{2}}k_1 z] \tag{8}$$

where q is the quantum yield of the emitter, the superscripts $P(S)$ denote the transverse electric(magnetic) cases, and the z and ω dependence of $\hat{\Gamma}^{\perp(||)}_{+(-)}$ is implied. The integrals can in most cases quite easily be evaluated numerically (e.g. using quad). It may be the case that the structures have resonances (as can be determined by plotting the integrands as a function of u), in which case one may want to re-write the integrals to assure one integrates in a complex plane around them and account for the pole(s) in the conventional fashion. Integration can in almost all cases safely be cut-off at $u \sim 1000$, with the contribution beyond $u \approx 100$ becoming negligibly small for $z > 10$nm. In what follows we will sometimes make use of the notation $\Gamma_{ij} = \frac{1}{3}[(\Gamma^{\perp}_{+} + \Gamma^{\perp}_{-}) + 2(\Gamma^{||}_{+} + \Gamma^{||}_{-})]_{\omega_{ij}}$ to signify the isotropic average total decay rate from state i to j separated in energy by $\omega_{ij} = \omega_i - \omega_j$. The energy dependence of Γ_{ij} is understood to be contained in $r^{S,P} = r^{S,P}(\omega_{ij})$, $u = u(\omega_{ij})$ and $k_1 = k_1(\omega_{ij})$.
Besides the modification in the decay rate which has been described above, the measured emission intensity of an emitter will also depend on it's excitation rate. In particular the measurable emission intensity for the transition from the excited state a to a lower state b, which corresponds to a wavelength $\lambda_{ab} = 2\pi c/\omega_{ab}$ will be given by:

$$I(\omega_{ab}) \propto |\hat{\mu}_a \cdot \mathbf{E}_{ex}(\omega_{ab})|^2 f_{ab} \Gamma^R_{ab} \Gamma^{-1}_a \tag{9}$$

where $\mathbf{E}_{ex}(\omega_{ab})$ is the excitation field at the frequency ω_{ab}, and $\hat{\mu}_a$ is the dipole moment of the excited state a. Γ^R_{ab} and Γ_a are the radiative decay rate for the transition $a \to b$ and the total decay rate of the state a. f_{ab} is the Franck Condon coefficient between a and b, which is related to the rotational and vibrational configurations of the two energy states relative to each other, and can be thought of as the intrinsic favourability of the transition. For a realistic emitter there will in general be many other significant "down transitions" originating from the same excited state. For the decay of the state a to any other state x, one may thus write:

$$I(\omega_{ax}) = \frac{f_{ax}}{f_{ab}} \frac{\Gamma^R_{ax}}{\Gamma^R_{ab}} I(\omega_{ab}) \tag{10}$$

Subsequent decay of all states x (and state b) to a common ground state is assumed to proceed non-radiatively and at a rate several orders of magnitude larger than the radiative decay rate. For the case of spontaneous emission we consider it can for all intense and purposes be assumed to be instantaneous. If we neglect direct resonant energy transfer between emitters (i.e. assume sufficient dilution), then the total excitation field with a frequency ω_{ab} at the location of the fluorophore will be the sum of the external incident field $\mathbf{E}^0(\omega_{ab})$, the reflection of this field from the structure $re^{-2(1-u^2)^{1/2}k_1 z}\mathbf{E}^0(\omega_{ab})$ where r is the reflection coefficient, and the field generated from excitations in the material by all the fluorophores $\mathbf{E}_r(\omega_{ab}, z)$, i.e.

$$\mathbf{E}_{ex}(\omega_{ab}, u, z) = [1 + re^{-2(1-u^2)^{1/2}k_1 z}]\mathbf{E}^0(\omega_{ab}) + \mathbf{E}_r(\omega_{ab}, u, z) \tag{11}$$

The polarization for the reflected field can in most cases be taken as that of the incident excitation field. For the case of a single fluorophore $\mathbf{E}_r(\omega_{ab}, z)$ is given by the integrands of equations (6) and/or (7), which are identical to the reflected field for a given transverse wavevector component u, and will henceforth be written as $\mathbf{E}^0_r(\omega_{ab}, u, z)$. To calculate the reflected field from all of the fluorophores at various distances from the substrate one can proceed in several ways. It is of no practical relevance in our applications if one requires information on the position and orientation of each and every contributing fluorophore. We thus can proceed only via an effective medium approximation. We will assume a density ρ of fluorophores which may only vary in the axial (z) direction. In the case for $\rho(0 < z < z_{max}) = \rho$ and $\rho(z > z_{max}) = 0$ one obtains by integrating over $z = \{0, \infty\}$:

$$\mathbf{E}_r(\omega_{ab}, u, z) = (1 - e^{-(1-u^2)^{1/2}k_1 z_{max}}) \frac{\rho}{(1-u^2)^{1/2}k_1} \frac{\Gamma_{ab}(u,z)}{\Gamma_a(z)} \mathbf{E}_r^0(\omega_{ab}, u, z/2). \quad (12)$$

Alternatively one may represent the contribution from a collection of fluorophores by assigning a negative imaginary response function to the top layer (layer-1) in which they are immersed - i.e. set Im(ε_1)< 0 for non-magnetic structures. Whilst this may be computationally simpler for constant densities, for the case of a non-trivial z dependence the calculations become significantly more elaborate. We thus proceed with the former method.
For imaginary $(1-u^2)^{1/2}k_1$ the coupling fields are propagating and equation (12) can be reduced to the result for e.g. the field in a large semi-transparent 1D box filled with emitters. For real $(1-u^2)^{1/2}k_1$ the field will on the other hand decay rapidly with increasing z as one would expect. The contribution to $I(\omega_{ab})$ from equation (12) will in itself however only be small even for large ρ ($> 0.01\text{nm}^{-1}$).
There will be an additional second order contribution to the excitation field and hence the emission intensity at ω_{ab} from excited surface modes of energy ω_{ax} where $x \neq b$. This contribution is only significant because the SPP modes have very short decay times - typically $\Gamma \sim \mathcal{O}$(10-100fs), such that their uncertainty broadening is relatively large - $\mathcal{O}(1-10\text{eV})$. For $\omega_{ax} \sim \omega_{ab}$, or more specifically $|\omega_{ax} - \omega_{ab}| \sim \mathcal{O}$(meV), they will contribute significantly to $\mathbf{E}_R(\omega_{ab}, z)$. It follows that when the energy ω_{ab} corresponds to mainly real values of $(1-u^2)^{1/2}k_1$ (evanescent fields) whereas ω_{ax} to mainly imaginary values of $(1-u^2)^{1/2}k_1$ (propagating fields) this contribution becomes large near the surface as fluorophores far away from the substrate can effectively pump those nearby. To the lowest order the contribution can be written as:

$$\mathbf{E}_r^0(\omega_{ax}, u, z) = \int d\omega_\alpha \int d\omega_\beta f_{\alpha\beta} \frac{\Gamma_{a\beta}(u,z)}{\Gamma_{a\beta}} L_{a\beta} \mathbf{E}_r(\omega_{a\beta}, u, z) L_{\beta\alpha} \delta(\omega_\alpha - \omega_{ax}) \quad (13)$$

where

$$L_{a\beta} = \frac{1}{2\pi} \frac{\Gamma_{a\beta}(u,z)}{(\omega_a - \omega_\beta)^2 + [\Gamma_{a\beta}(u,z)/2]^2} \quad (14)$$

and $\Gamma_{ab}(u,z)$ and $\mathbf{E}_r(\omega, u, z)$ are the corresponding values of the total decay rate and reflected field as a function of transverse wavevector [i.e. the integrands of equations (2) and (2) &/or (3)]. We note that equation (13) accounts for the energy overlap between a state of energy ω_b and a continuum of states whose energy is given by the dummy variable ω_β. The ω_α integration is performed over a range of frequencies in the vicinity of the cut-off (typically corresponding to a wavelength range of 30-80nm), over which the energy range coincides with the emission spectrum of the fluorophore (i.e. are allowed transitions for the particular fluorophore). The weighting (Franck Condon) factors $f_{\alpha\beta}$ are empirically determined from the emission spectrum of an isolated fluorophore scaled so that the value at ω_{ab} it is unity. We note that it is usually practical or necessary to convert this integration into a discrete sum with an energy spacing of $\Delta\omega \sim 1$meV. Information particular to the type of fluorophore (e.g. energy level positions/separations and corresponding Franck Condon coefficients) may be implemented when constructing the summation.

Since we will not focus on single molecule studies we assume an isotropic average of dipole orientations for all cases. This can most easily be done by setting $\mathbf{E}_R^{iso} = (1/3)\mathbf{E}_R^{\perp} + (2/3)\mathbf{E}_R^{||}$ and/or $\Gamma^{iso} = (1/3)\Gamma^{\perp} + (2/3)\Gamma^{||}$ as appropriate. We also note to calculate the final measurable emission intensity the integral for Γ^R which appears in equations 9 & 10 (and is given by equations 6 & 7) should only be performed up to $\sqrt{\varepsilon_i}\cdot$NA, where NA is the numerical aperture of the measuring objective. It is possible to now predict the change in the measurable emission intensity for arbitrary z and fluorophores, near a metamaterial structure. In figure 1 we outline the basic backbone of a program that calculates the matrix `enhan(j,i)` which quantifies the measurable fluorescence enhancement at discrete distances (index `j`) and wavelengths (index `i`). The order of computations (top to bottom) is such that several independent calculations can depending on available resources be performed in parallel. The calculation is performed over all transverse wavevectors up to at least $|u| \sim 10z^{-1}$ and summed at the end (with the corresponding weighting factors to mimic integration).

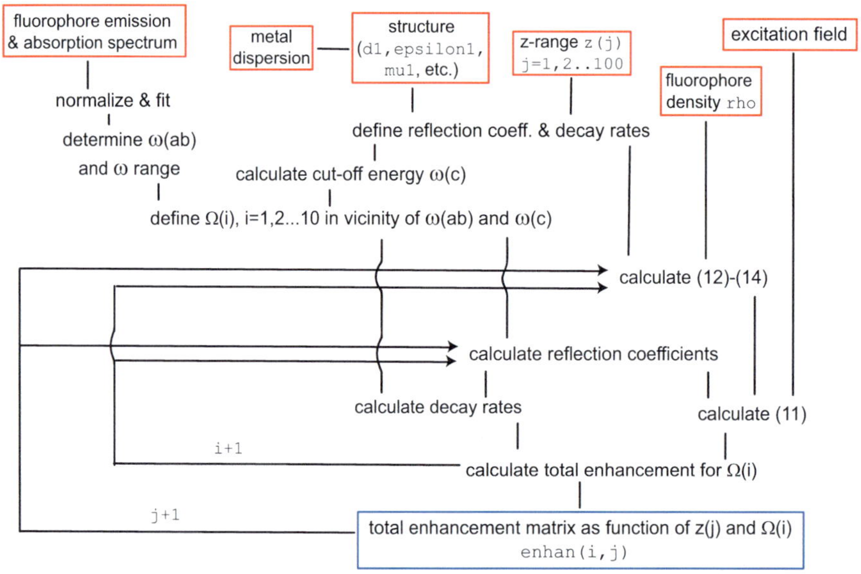

Fig. 1. Structure of program for calculating a matrix that predicts fluorescence enhancement

We now show how to implement equations 6 &7 (with the integrands defined by equation 9) in MATLAB, which are required for solving equation 10. To focus on the most relevant part of the code, we expect the reader to have some familiarity with basic MATLAB programming syntax (i.e. definition of functions and vector-based MATLAB notation). An example code for calculating the reflection coefficients [2 - 5] and subsequently performing the integration may look like:

Listing 1. Numerical integration

```
function main()
  % -- material permittivities
  sio2  = 2.13; glass = 2.46;
  water = 1.78; si3n4 = 4.15;
  % -- ranges for frequency & wavevectors
  w_vec = 0 : 0.01  : 4;
  kx  = 0 : 0.000001 : 0.02*pi;

  % -- permittivities & permeabilities &
  % -- thicknesses for each layer
  mu  = [1  1  1 1];
  d = [1e6 15 15 1e6];
  e = [ sio2 permitivity_silver(w,d(2)) si3n4 glass];

  % -- integrate Integrand_1
  lower = 0;  % limits for integrals
  upper = 1;
  b_up_a = quad(@(u) integrand_I1(u),lower,upper) );

  function [I1] = integrand_I1(u)
    [r_S,r_P] =  r_1234_vec = r_1234_PS(u,    );

     A = 1 - abs(r_P).^2;
     B = sqrt(u.^2 - 1);
    I1 = 2.*u.^3.*A./B;
  end

function r_1234 = r_1234_PS(u,polariz)
global d; global e; global k; global mu;

exp_term = exp(2i.*sqrt(e(2).*mu(2).*(e(1).*mu(1)).^(-1)-u.^2).*k(1).*d(2));
r_12_P  = r_ij_PS(u,1,2,"P");
r_12_S  = r_ij_PS(u,1,2,"S");
r_234_P = r_234_PS(u,"P");
r_234_S = r_234_PS(u,"S");

switch(polariz)
 case {"P"}
  num =    r_12_P  + r_234_P.*exp_term;
  den = 1 + r_12_P .* r_234_P.*exp_term;
  r_1234  = num ./ den;
 case {"S"}
num = r_12_S  + r_234_S.*exp_term;
  den = 1 + r_12_S .* r_234_S.*exp_term;
  r_1234 = num ./ den;
  end
end

function r_234 = r_234_PS(u,polariz)
global d; global e; global k; global mu;
```

```
exp_term = exp(2i.*k(1).*d(3).*sqrt(e(3).*mu(3).*(e(1).*mu(1)).^-1-u.^2));

  switch(polariz)
    case {"P"}
      r_23_P = r_ij_PS(u,2,3,"P");
      r_34_P = r_ij_PS(u,3,4,"P");
      num =     r_23_P +   r_34_P.*exp_term;
      den = 1 + r_23_P .* r_34_P.*exp_term;
      r_234 = num ./ den;
   case {"S"}
      r_23_S = r_ij_PS(u,2,3,"S");
      r_34_S = r_ij_PS(u,3,4,"S");
      num =     r_23_S +   r_34_S.*exp_term;
      den = 1 + r_23_S .* r_34_S.*exp_term;
      r_234 = num ./ den;
  end
end

function r_ij = r_ij_PS(u,i,j,polariz)
global e; global mu;

A = (1 - u.^2).^0.5;
B = ( e(j).*mu(j).* (e(i).*mu(i)).^-1 - u.^2).^0.5;

  switch(polariz)
    case {"S"}
      num    = mu(j).*A - mu(i).* B;
      den    = mu(j).*A + mu(i).* B;
      r_ij = num ./ den;
    case {"P"}
      num    = e(j).*A - e(i).* B;
      den    = e(j).*A + e(i).* B;
      r_ij = num ./ den;
  end
end
```

3. Fitting the experimental data to the model

Data can be acquired using a standard scanning epifluorescence microscope with a spectrometer and photomultiplier tubes. It is generally most practical to save images as `.lsm` files which can be directly read into MATLAB [In our setup each file contains a scanned image of the sample at ten different wavelengths (e.g. bins centered at $\lambda = 490$nm, 500nm, 510nm, etc.)]. For dynamic studies images at different time intervals can also be stored in a single `.lsm` file. Many spectrometers come with MATLAB drivers which allow for acquisition to also be controlled easily through MATLAB. Else for real time (video type) imaging it is necessary to save the data incrementally into a directory accessible to MATLAB. The spectral profile of the fluorophores of interest on an uncoated substrate immersed in a similar refractive index medium as the actual samples should also be available. The area under this spectrum should be normalized and extrapolated to a discrete matrix [e.g. fitted to a high order polynomial and evaluated at the discrete wavelengths indexed by `i`], and saved as a 1×10 matrix `Ilambda0(i)`.

Data analysis is performed on a pixel by pixel basis. For each pixel the spectrum area is normalized, fitted with a high order polynomial, evaluated at `i` discrete wavelengths, and written into a 1×10 matrix `data(i)`. The ratio `enhanobserved(i) = data(i)/Ilambda0(i)` is then calculated. A $1 \times j$ matrix `zn(j)` is defined which will represent the fraction of the emitters in the studied area at a distance corresponding to the index `j` from the interface. The task is now to solve `enhan*zn-enhanobserved=0`, which is in principle straight forward using a function such as e.g. `linsolve`. The result is best presented in a plot of `zn` as a function of `z` for each or a collection of pixels, which will show the distribution of fluorophore distances from the substrate at this particular lateral position. Depending on the sample studied and the information of interest this may be fitted with a suitable distribution function to obtain an average and spread in distances of emitters from the substrate within the analyzed region.

4. Optimizing the model and code

In many cases the initial fluorophore-concentration, metamaterial or coupling parameters may not be the best or correct parameters for the fit. This is usually evident when the results show an unexpected distribution for `zn`. Distances less than 10nm should be ignored as the approximations of the models (dipole approximation and local dielectric functions) are no longer valid at such small distances. The most significant source of uncertainty is the predefined and assumed constant value of the fluorophore concentration `rho`. To account for this one may redefine `rho` as being proportional to the integrated area of `zn` over `z`, and repeat the calculation of `zn`. Also to account for an axial variation in `rho` - as would be relevant for samples where the fluorophore density varies strongly with distance `z` - one may define `rho(j) = rho*(a + zn(j)/norm(zn))`, where `a` is normalization constant chosen so that on summation over the distances (i) one recovers the total intensity. In this case all subsequent calculations have to explicitly account for the additional distance dependence in *rho (j)*, which significantly increases the computational time. This may be efficiently achieved by defining `rho(j)` in a smaller parameter space indexed by `n` that corresponds to dividing `rho` into components where `rho(j)` is constant and non-zero only over a specified region. Once `zn` is calculated in this manner the optimization may be repeated for the new `rho` until the the calculation of the distribution of `zn` is stable and smooth or varies on the expected scale.

5. Example

Whilst elaborate custom substrates may be designed with effective parameters which yield the desired cut-off energy and dispersion relation, it is often possible to use combinations of no more than 3-4 layers with no lateral structuring to achieve satisfactory results. Here we give an example where we use a sample consisting of a thin silver film[2] (15nm) deposited on a thick quartz substrate ($\varepsilon = 2.13$), which is subsequently coated with a high permittivity dielectric film ($\varepsilon = 4.15$). The sample is immersed in a medium with a refractive index larger than that of

[2] Smoothness of the silver is guaranteed by using a Germanium wetting layer and is less than 0.4nm RMS as measured by Atomic Force Microscopy.

the quartz ($\varepsilon = 2.4$). The cut-off energy can be shown to occur within the emission spectrum of Alexa488 - a standard fluorescent marker with an emission spectrum peaking at a wavelength of around 528nm and extending all the way up to >550nm. To demonstrate the accuracy of the technique, fibroblast cells were grown on the laminin (thickness < 2nm, $\varepsilon \approx 2.15$) coated substrate and a particular protein found at adhesion sites close to the substrate called *Paxillin* Schaller (2001) was stained with Alexa488. The protein Paxillin has recently been shown to be separated from the substrate matrix by a distance of around 20-40nm using a 3D version of a technique based on Fluorescence Photoactivatable Localization Microscopy (FPALM) - known as interference-PALM or iPALM Kanchanawong (2010). In our study similar cells were used and the separation from the substrate surface can be expected to be comparable. In figure 2 we show a confocal fluorescence image of the cell we subsequently analyze (excitation wavelength = 488nm, emission filter ≈500-550nm). We focus on a region marked by the red box. A spectral analysis of the signal in this region shows an enhancement at longer wavelengths as expected. Using the procedure outlined in the previous sections we are able to calculate `zn` for the pixels in this box over the range `z = 1...130`. The fluorophore concentration (`rho`) was initially taken to be constant up to 2.4μm and the presented histogram in figure 2 is the result following four iterations of redefining `rho` according to the calculated `zn` in a `n=5` parameter space (see previous section). The size of the bin width for the spectral analysis was 9.7nm. As can be seen in figure 2 where the distance distribution (`zn` is plotted as a function of `z`), the fluorophores and hence the Paxillin are indeed localized at around the expected distance from the substrate (20-40nm). We note that compared to the iPALM setup used for these studies our technique is, once optimized, very simple and straight forward to implement. The analysis is sufficiently fast to allow for fast real-time studies (which is often impossible with e.g. iPALM) and also more versatile since there is no requirement for special photoactivatable fluorophorescent markers. We are currently using it to study the dynamics of other labeled proteins found in the vicinity of cell-substrate adhesion sites including the zinc-binding phosphoprotein *Zyxin* and the microfilament associated protein *VASP*.

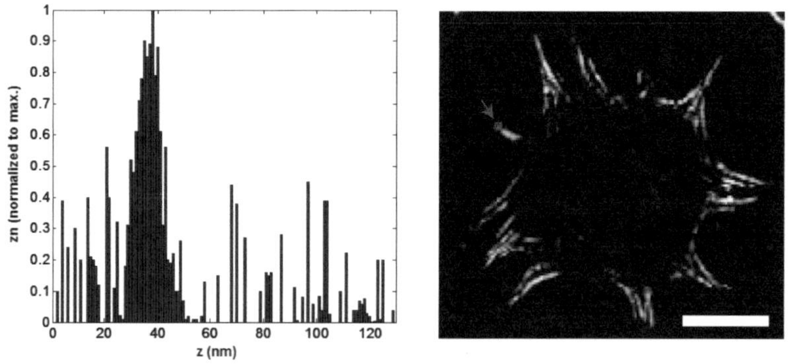

Fig. 2. Left: Axial distance profile of the protein *paxillin* (`zn` versus `z`) as inferred from $\Delta\lambda$ =9.7nm resolution spectrum (λ =480→800nm) of pixels at adhesion site. Right: image of cell. Red square shows pixels over which the spectrum was analyzed to obtain image on the left. [NIH 3T3 fibroblast with Alexa488 stained paxillin, scanning confocal microscope image at λ =519($\pm$9.7nm), with 1.4 NA objective and λ =465nm excitation. Scale-bar = 10μm].

6. Modifications & extensions

A natural extension to the presented nano-sectioning method would be to combine it with a different technique which allows for lateral (xy) superresolution. One such technique that is relatively straight forward to implement is FPALM which was already alluded to above. In FPALM photoactivatable fluorophores are stochastically turned on by a weak activations source so that individual molecules separated by distances larger than the diffraction limit can consecutively be localized provided one has knowledge of their point spread function and the instrument and detector response. Numerous algorithms exist for such 2D localization purposes most of which rely on fitting a normal 2D (Gaussian) intensity distribution to a region of interest surrounding each molecule. Several such routines have been made available in the form of MATLAB codes. For densely labelled samples it is often desirable to be able to fit multiple overlapping Gaussians so that the isolated single-molecule activation/excitation condition can be slightly relaxed. This is particularly useful where even a very weak activation signal is sufficient to activate a significant portion of fluorophores - which we have found to be the case for photoactivatable fluorophores near the metallic structures of interest. A MATLAB code capable of fitting "overlapping intensity distributions" may be written employing a Levenberg-Marquardt based multi Gaussian least squares optimization algorithm. The result of a multiple Gaussian fit is demonstrated in figure 3 for the distribution from two nearby molecules. We note that such algorithms are also conducive to parallel processing and thus in principle fast dynamic studies. Considering the fact that typical amount of data needed to be processed for each microscopy experiment is in the order of several hundreds of megabytes; the possibility to use acceleration power of modern GPUs to enable near real-time observation of reconstruction is welcomed. At this moment MATLAB allows us to develop our implementations for several image processing and optimization routines and possibly validate the results from our experimental parallel implementations. In following text we will focus on the use of Image processing and Optimization toolboxes to outline our framework for detection regions of interest around sparsely activated fluorophores. We expect that reader is familiar with basics of image processing and numerical optimization methods and so we only propose possible solution for stated problem. For further details about mathematical background regarding image analysis we suggest Sonka et al. (2001).
Current work is underway in our laboratory on combining this with the optical nanosectioning technique outlined above. A current obstacle appears to be the difficulty in rapidly photo-bleaching of the emitters - which is an essential feature of performing fast FPALM - near the substrates. This is a well known feature of fluorophores near metallic substrates and is understood to be due to the relative suppression of the triplet decay path, which is associated with the majority of the photobleaching. FPALM based nanosectioning as mentioned above is however still possible but at the price of lowered signal to noise ratio, and with properly designed image segmentation we are able extract regions aimed for further processing. The code shown below represents the necessary steps of the image processing required for detection of relevant fluorophores. This is based on dilation functions from the mathematical morphology toolset and subsequent segmentation with experimentally adjusted thresholding values.

Listing 2. Fluorophore segmentation based on thresholding and morphology

```
img         = lsm_read(fileName);
img_dbl     = im2double(img);
se          = strel("disk" , 5);
img_dil     = imdilate(img_dbl,se);
img_dil_bw = im2bw(img_dil,threshold);
```

Depending on the sample studied, one may observe an uneven background signal which systematically introduce errors into the model fitting which may prove detrimental. For these reasons we estimate the background intensity map based on uniform filtering over large region, e.g.:

Listing 3. Fluorophore segmentation with background correction

```
corrected_bg            = img_dbl - imfilter(img_dbl,fspecial("average",50));
img_corr_bg_closed_bw = im2bw(corrected_bg,0.60);
img_corr_bg_closed_bw_dil = imdilate(img_corr_bg_closed_bw,strel("disk",2));
```

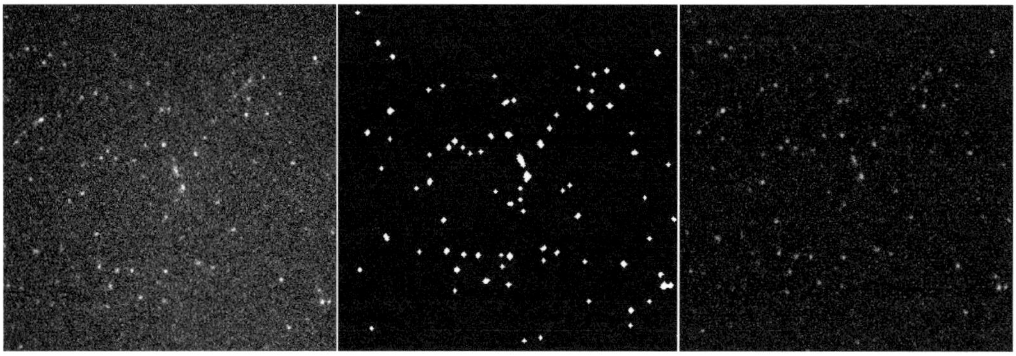

Fig. 3. a. sample of activated fluorophores with noisy background b. segmented fluorophores after background correction c. overlay of fluorophores positions and corrected background

The main algorithm framework for detection and precise position localization of activated fluorophores consists of two parts. Lines (1)-(9) set the size of the region of interest around the detected fluorophore candidates, *upscalefactor* determine up to a certain level precision for the fitting (with higher values at the expense of increased computational resources). The following lines are for loading of the acquired data-stack and the rescaling to the MATLAB native double format (images with scales from 0 to 1). The subsequent section is based on the code presented in listings 4 or 3 to detect local maxima and translate them to (x,y) coordinates. Here the for loop iterates over the range of all (x,y) fluorophore coordinates, and the code is built from 2 parts, extraction of the image region of interest around the position of the fluorophore and fitting to the image data model (a Gaussian function based on a nonlinear iterative least-squares fitting). For the main algorithm of Levenberg-Marquard, interested readers are referred to Marquardt (1963)

Listing 4. Fluorophore segmentation based on thresholding and morphology

```
win_W = 8; % -- moving window size
win_H = 8;
upscale_factor      = 5;
abs_dif_fit_values  = [];

stack = lsm_read("1.lsm");  % -- load LSM stack
img   = stack(1).data;
img   = im2double(img);   % -- change to 0-1 scale
[M,N] = size(img);

% -- find relevant positions of fluorophores
[pos] = find_local_maxima(img, 0.7);% -- detect fluorophore positions
[y,x] = find(pos == 1);          % -- get their coordinates
[x,y] = remove_bound(x,y,win_W,win_H,M,N);% -- remove spots near the boundary

% -- preallocated upscaled ROI
upscaled_window = zeros(M*upscale_factor,N*upscale_factor);

for k = 1 : 1 : length(x) % -- iterate over all fluorophore positions
  % -- get corners of the window from low-res image
  % -- where molecule was detected
  [win,corner_x,corner_y] = getROI(img,[y(k),x(k)],win_width,win_height);

  % -- rescale the window with nearest neighborhood interpolation
  %    & prepare the meshgrid of the same size for Gaussian 2d fitting
  [Mw,Nw] = size(win);
  ups_win =  imresize(win,[upscale_factor*Mw,upscale_factor*Nw],"nearest");
  [ny,nx] = size(ups_win);
  [px,py] = meshgrid(1:nx,1:ny);

  % -- prepare guess estimates for Gaussian fitting
  A = 10; z0  = 0;
  x0  = ny / 2;  y0 = nx / 2;
  sx  = 0.2 * upscale_factor;
  sy  = 0.2 * upscale_factor;
  param0 = [A, x0, sx, y0, sy, z0];

  % -- optimize parameters based on image data and gaussian model
  % params_fit = lsqnonlin(@(x) gaussian_fit_fun(x, px, py,window),param0);
  params_fit  =  lev_marq_gaussian2d(ups_win,px,py,[A,x0,sx,y0,sy 0]', ...
             1500,0.01,1e-6,0.01);
  % -- calculate goodness of fit for possible discarding of
  % -- incorrect values
  [F,Yfit, D] = gaussian_fit_fun(params_fit, px, py, ups_win);

  % -- calculate distance measure of model and image data
  abs_dif_fit_values  = [abs_dif_fit_values; sum(abs(D(:)))];
  fprintf("Absolute Difference of Fit : %.3f \n", sum(abs(D(:)) );
end
```

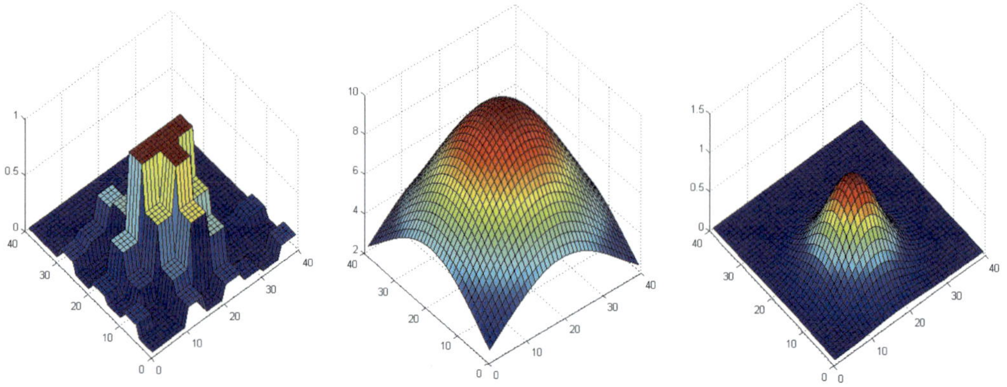

Fig. 4. a. Extracted ROI from raw microscopy data b. Initial shape of Gaussian model c. Fitted model

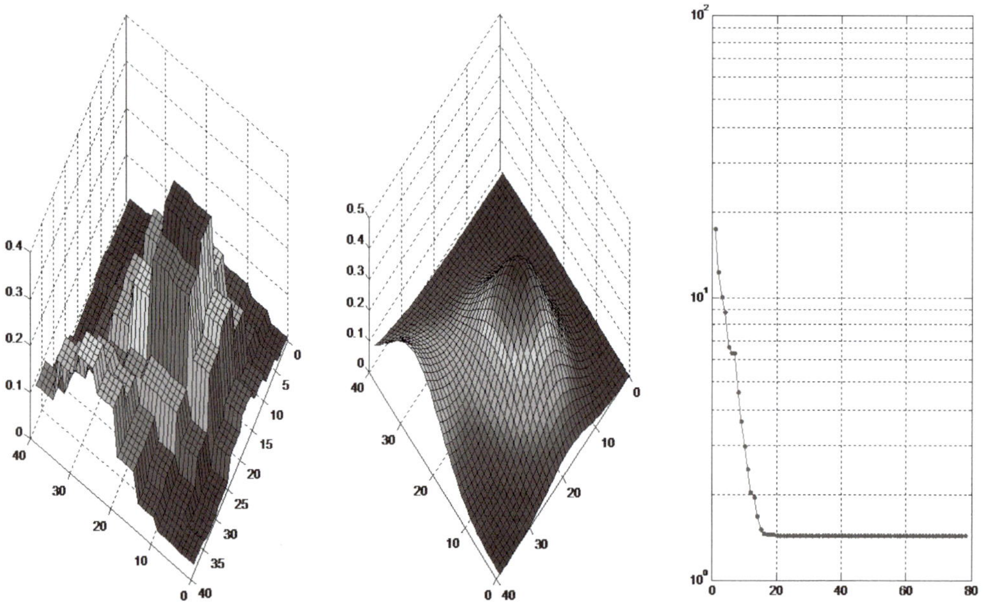

Fig. 5. Fitting two overlapping Gaussians to data using a Levenberg-Marquardt based routine. Left: raw data. Center: Gaussian Fits. Right: Wellness of fit as a function of number of iterations.

7. Concluding remarks

In summary we have outlined the data analysis protocol for a novel fluorescent imaging technique capable of performing sub-wavelength scale optical sectioning in the vicinity of metamaterial coated substrates - MeSuMo fluorescence microscopy. An outline of the approach one would take for analyzing the response properties of particular materials and how to go about fitting data to the model is explained from a perspective that may be readily implemented into MATLAB routines. Whilst the calculation can be performed by most software and self written codes, the intuitive matrix approach of MATLAB makes it well suited for the required tasks. Certain toolboxes may prove useful,[3] however no toolboxes are essential or required. The presented technique is likely to find a range of applications in the lifesciences related to studying membrane traffic or indeed any events that can be made to occur near a coated substrate and nanoscale axial dynamics are of interest. In practice a fundamental limitations of the technique is the rate and accuracy with which the spectral information over a give region can be acquired. Whilst the use of multiple photodetectors combined with fast scanning of the sample may be the most accurate and best suited for not so bright samples, one can in principle perform the spectral separation optically using dichroic mirrors & filters and an array of sensitive CCD cameras (or several with split chips). The latter would remove the need for scanning, with the imaging rate now limited primarily by photon statistics.

8. References

D. Axelrod (1981). Cell-substrate contacts illuminated by total internal reflection fluorescence. *Journ Cell Biol*, Vol.89, pp.141-145.

P.A. Belov and Y. Hao (2006). Subwavelength imaging at optical frequencies using a transmission device formed by a periodic layered metal-dielectric structure operating in the canalization regime. *Phys. Rev. B*, Vol.73, pp.113110-113113.

D.J. Bergman and M.I. Stockman (2003). Surface Plasmon Amplification by Stimulated Emission of Radiation: Quantum Generation of Coherent Surface Plasmons in Nanosystems. *Phys. Rev. Lett.*, Vol.90, pp.027402-027405.

Betzig, E. et al. (1991). Breaking the Diffraction Barrier: Optical Microscopy on a Nanometric Scale. *Science*, Vol.251, No.5000, pp.1468-1470.

M. Born and E. Wolf (1997). *Principles of Optics: Electromagnetic Theory of Propagation, Interference and Diffraction of Light*, Cambridge University Press, Cambridge, UK.

J.J. Burke and G.I. Stegeman (1986). Surface-polariton-like waves guided by thin, lossy metal films. *Phys. Rev. B*, Vol.33, pp.5186ï£¡5201.

R.R. Chance, A. Prock and R. Silbey (1978). Molecular fluorescence and energy transfer near interfaces. *Adv. Chem. Phys.*, Vol.37, pp.1ï£¡65.

C. Cremer and T. Cremer (1978). Considerations on a laser-scanning-microscope with high resolution and depth of field. *Microscopica Acta*, Vol.81, No.1, pp.31-44.

S.A. Darmanyan and A.V. Zayats (2003). Light tunneling via resonant surface plasmon polariton states and the enhanced transmission of periodically nanostructured metal films: An analytical study. *Phys. Rev. B*, Vol.67, pp.035424-035430.

J.A. Dionne et al. (2008). Are negative index materials achievable with surface plasmon waveguides? A case study of three plasmonic geometries. *Opt. Exp.*, Vol.16, No.23, pp.19001-19016.

V.P. Drachev (2008). The Ag dielectric function in plasmonic metamaterials. *Opt. Exp.*, Vol.16, No.2, pp.1186- 1195.

[3] In particular the *Symbolic Math* and *Curve-fitting* toolboxes for modeling the structures and fitting the spectrums, and the *Instrument Control* and *Image Acquisition* toolboxes for controlling optical components & shutters and data acquisition in MATLAB.

K. Elsayad and K.G. Heinze (2010). Temperature dependence of the near-field superlensing effect for single metal layers and stacked metal-dielectric films, *Proceedings of SPIE*, 77573L, San Diego, USA, Aug. 2010.
K. Elsayad and K.G. Heinze (2010). Multifrequency parallelized near-field optical imaging with anistropic metal-dielectric stacks. *Phys. Rev. A*, Vol.81, pp.053840-053845.
S.W. Hell (2007). Far-Field Optical Nanoscopy. *Science*, Vol.316, No.5828, pp.1153-1158.
Z. Jacob et al. (2010). Engineering photonic density of states using metamaterials. *App. Phys. B*, Vol.100, No.1, pp.215-218.
P. Kanchanawong et al. (2010). Nanoscale architecture of integrin-based cell adhesions. *Nat.*, Vol.468, pp.580-584.
C.Kittel (1995). *Introduction to Solid State Physics*, Wiley, ISBN 0471111813.
D. Marquardt (1963). An Algorithm for Least Squares Estimation on Nonlinear Parameters. SIAMJ. J. APPL. MATH.11, pp. 431-441.
S.A. Ramakrishna et al. (2003). Imaging the near field. *Journ. Mod. Opt.*, Vol.50, No.9, pp.1419-1430.
M.D. Schaller (2001). Paxillin: a focal adhesion-associated adaptor protein. *Oncogene*, Vol.20, No.44 pp.6459-6472.
M. Sonka et al. (2001). Image Processing: Analysis and Machine Vision, ISBN: 049508252X.
N.I. Zheludev et al. (2008). Lasing spaser. *Nat. Phot.*, Vol.2, pp.351-354.

16

A Methodology and Tool to Translate MATLAB®/Simulink® Models of Mixed-Signal Circuits to VHDL-AMS

Alexandre César Rodrigues da Silva[1] and Ian Andrew Grout[2]
[1]*Univ Estadual Paulista, UNESP;*
[2]*University of Limerick, UL;*
[1]*Brazil*
[2]*Ireland*

1. Introduction

Nowadays, due to the increasing complexity of circuits and systems incorporating mixed-signal components, many designers recognise the advantages of, and in some cases the necessity for, mixed-signal modelling and simulation of the circuits and systems as a whole prior to, during and post production of the circuit or system. This is particularly so within the microelectronics (semiconductor) arena. This, coupled with the emergence of a range of description languages that find use in the modelling and analysis via simulation of microelectronic circuit designs, means the ability now exists to design complex signal processing functions in both the digital and analogue domains. Modelling and simulation has increased the designer efficiency and ability to develop increasingly complex and useful electronic circuits, particularly at the integrated circuit (IC) level. Each type of circuit considered has its own particular requirements in terms of design performance (specifications), design methodologies required to realise a design, modelling and simulation toolsets utilised, designer experience and skills set.

This chapter will consider design aspects relating specifically to data converters, in particular the digital-to-analogue converter (DAC). In many electronic systems, the data converter (both the analogue-to-digital [A/D] and digital-to-analogue [D/A] converter) provides an important electronic function. The developed converter design will be provided to the end-user as either a discrete integrated circuit or as a macro cell within a larger design, see Fig. 1.

The data converter provides the primary interface block between the analogue 'real' world and the digital signal processing circuitry typically found in many control, instrumentation and, generically, 'mechatronic' systems. The converter design performance is continually increasing to meet the changing needs of the end-user applications, in particular: an increase in resolution (number of bits); an increase in speed of operation - driven primarily by the communications applications; the operation of the circuit on lower power supply voltages and with lower power consumption - driven primarily by the need for portable electronic circuit applications.

The focus area of this work was in the area of device modelling and simulation during the circuit design process, in particular, the conversion (translation) of model design descriptions between the different languages typically used by the design community, along with design synthesis requirements. The design and modelling of data converter algorithms was investigated using MATLAB®/Simulink® (The MathWorks Inc.) and then the conversion of the MATLAB®/Simulink® circuit model (of the data converter design) into a VHDL-AMS description was considered.

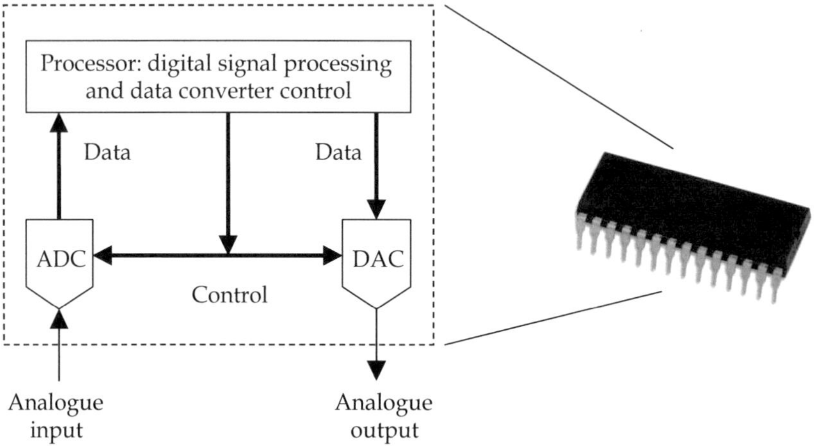

Fig. 1. Data converter designs embedded within a digital processor

A number of authors have already undertaken work in this area. In the next section, a summary of some of the prior work undertaken that have influenced the present work is presented.

1.1 Summary of related work

Electronic devices become more complex each day. To deal with this increasing complexity, design synthesis methodologies, assisted by suitable software tools, have been developed in order to allow designers to initially model their circuit or system at different design abstraction levels during the various design cycles and then ultimately synthesis of some or the whole design into an electronic circuit implementation within a particular design project.

In the work of Edenfeld (Edenfeld D. et al., 2004), the future trend of semiconductor technology is presented, with the advent of systems with mixing signals (mixed-signal). He noted that even in highly abstract projects, it is possible to discover potential problems in the initial stage of development, therefore reducing the project time and decreasing the cost.

In MacMillen's work (MacMillen D. et al., 2000), a complete overview of the technologies, algorithms and methodologies that are used in the EDA tools (electronic design automation) and the economic impact of these technologies is undertaken. They consider the different steps of the project: simulation, verification, synthesis and test. Also discussed are the types of necessary toolsets to support a project environment.

The necessity of behavioural modelling within mixed technology systems, that is systems with electronic, electric and non-electric (mechanical, pneumatic, etc.) parts operating together, is described in Wilson's work (Wilson P. R. et al., 1997). They present the interaction between the various domains and determine that the behavioural models in the different domains can be created using the VHDL-AMS (VHDL Analogue and Mixed-Signal) language.

In Christen's work (Christen E. & Bakalar L., 1999), a revision of the VHDL-AMS language for analogue applications and mixed-signal is provided. The main elements of the language are studied. Doboli's work (Doboli A. & Vermuri R., 2003) and that of Pêcheaus (Pêcheaus et al., 2005) also deal with the manner of modelling using VHDL-AMS.

Trofimov and Mosin (Travimov M. & Mosin S., 2004) note that one way of increasing the speed of undertaking project development is to use the top-down methodology. In analogue and mixed-signal circuit projects, the generation of analogue models is at a high level of abstraction. The use of models at high levels of abstraction permits a complete simulation of a mixed-signal device. However, an adequate tool must be used for modelling and simulation, and there must be a great interaction between the project tools.

Grout and Keane (Grout I. A. & Keane K., 2000) show a prototype of one tool (software toolbox) that analyses and processes a Simulink® block diagram model producing a VHDL representation of the model. The derived VHDL model will be a combination of behavioural, RTL (Register Transfer Logic) and structural definitions mapped directly from the Simulink® model. This approach was considered to enable a user to develop and simulate a digital control algorithm using MATLAB® and once the initial algorithm development was completed, to then convert this to synthesisable VHDL code.

In a study undertaken the following year, Grout (Grout I. A., 2001) show the application of the developed tool to transform a process modelled into Simulink® in a described model in VHDL. A closed-loop control system is used in this work.

Zorzi (Zorzi M. et al., 2004) describe a tool, called *I.M.A.Ge-AMS*, for writing new Spice models using the VHDL-AMS standard. The core of the *I.M.A.Ge-AMS* tool is a compiler derived from the VHDL-AMS compiler, developed for another EDA tool called *SANSA*.

In 2004, a paper by Grout and O'Shea (Grout I. A. & O´Shea T., 2004) discusses the need to provide suitable provision for, and flexibility in the use of, modelling and simulation languages suitable for supporting the range of mixed-signal microelectronic circuit design, test and test development activities that are encountered in today's complex microelectronic products. In this work, emphasis is placed on language support for test development activities. The target area considered is Delta-Sigma (Δ-Σ) modulation for on-chip signal generation in the support of mixed-signal built-in self-test (MS-BIST). In the same year, Zorzi's work (Zorzi M. et al., 2004) shows the tool to integrate the VHDL-AMS with Spice. The developed tool allows the user to write new models using VHDL-AMS and automatically generates the embedded codes to be used by Spice. This approach shows the advantage of using a behavioural language with a simulator that is the best known of all analogue simulators at the present time.

The following section will present the basic theory of digital-to-analogue converter operation and modelling with emphasis in the R-2R ladder networks. The mathematical model of R-2R ladder network is also presented.

2. Digital-to-analogue converter modelling

In this section, the concepts used in digital-to-analogue converter design modelling are reviewed. This type of circuit was selected because it is the most frequently encountered mixed-signal circuit. The data converter can be either an analogue-to-digital (A/D) (converting signals from the analogue to the digital domain) or a digital-to-analogue (D/A) converter (converting signals from the digital to the analogue domain).

With the increasing requirements on the design (and testing) of the data converter, the development of electronic design automation (EDA) tools for supporting design and testing of A/D and D/A converters are becoming more important. In addition, with the advances obtained in the development and use of hardware description languages (HDLs), new EDA tools which integrate different environments are being created. This has permitted the migration from development of structural representation (logic synthesis) to behavioural specifications (higher levels abstraction). The new behavioural specification has removed many of the traditional constraints to design and has given the designer freedom of choice as to the best solution to any particular problem.

One of the basic ideas developed was to create the model using mathematical blocks exercising a top-down design methodology for both continuous time and discrete time in nature. With the Simulink® toolbox, these models are represented using a graphical block diagram format, in a visual form that can aid in supporting the designer's understanding of the problem.

Digital-to-analogue conversion is the process in which data in discrete values are converted to a continuous variable form (current or voltage). A characteristic feature in digital-to-analogue conversion is the relative value of bits. In a binary code, each more significant bit has twice the value of the previous bit. That is, in the representation 2^n, where n = 0, 1, 2, 3, 4… etc., the n + 1th bit is in a more significant position than the bit in the nth position. An analogue voltage generated from a binary code will have components that are related by powers of 2.

In the present models for commercially available DACs, the output voltage of logic gates (output digital level) is used to activate electronic switches that apply zero voltage to the inputs of the digital-to-analogue converter for the logic 0 state and 5.0 V, or another reference voltage, for the logic 1 state. Fig. 2 shows the simplified circuit of the basic digital-to-analogue converter with 4 bits. It converts each bit of its inputs (digital data) that has a binary value of 1 to a current, and sums these currents into *Isum* at its analogue output. Each

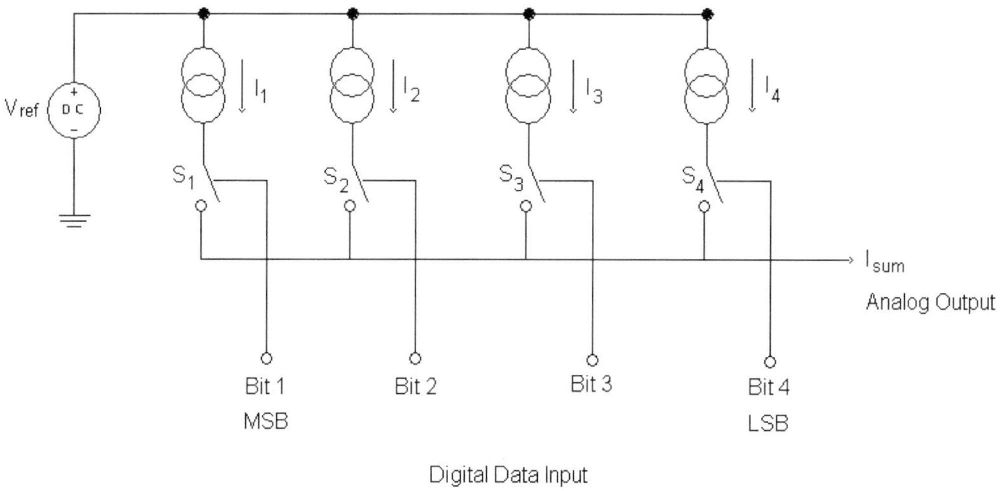

Fig. 2. Simplified circuit diagram of a basic digital-to-analogue converter with 4 bits

switch (*Sn*) controls a current source (*In*). When a switch is ON, its respective current source contributes its current to the output current (*Isum*), which becomes proportional to the parallel input presented as the digital input (*digital data input*).
A popular approach used within the digital-to-analogue converter available in IC form is the R-2R current ladder. Only two resistor values are required, regardless of the number of bits used, which simplifies resistor trimming during the IC fabrication process. The principle of the R-2R ladder is that at each node the ladder is divided in two. The current divides equally because the resistor values are 2R for each leg. All the models used in this work use the R-2R current ladder network. The R-2R ladder network is described in the next section.

2.1 The R-2R ladder network

The R-2R ladder network provides for a simple and inexpensive way in which to perform digital-to-analogue conversion. Its popularity is due to the networks' inherent accuracy superiority (when compared with other models) and ease of manufacture. Fig. 3 presents a diagram of the basic R-2R ladder network with *N* bits. Note that the network consists of only two resistors values. One resistor has *R* value and the other one has *2R* value (twice the value of *R*) no matter how many bits make up the ladder. The particular value of *R* is not critical to the function of the R-2R ladder.
The node labelled '*grd*' (at one end of the termination resistor) is connected to *ground*. The termination resistor assures that the Thevenin resistance of the network, as measured to ground looking toward the LSB (with all the bits grounded), is *R*. The Thevenin resistance of an R-2R ladder is always *R*, regardless of the number of bits in the ladder. From Fig. 3, it can be noted that the information is presented to the ladder as individual bits of a digital word switched between a reference voltage, labelled '*Vref*' and ground. The output voltage *Vout* is dependent on the number and location of the bits switched to *Vref* or ground. *Vout* will vary between 0 volts and *Vref* volts.

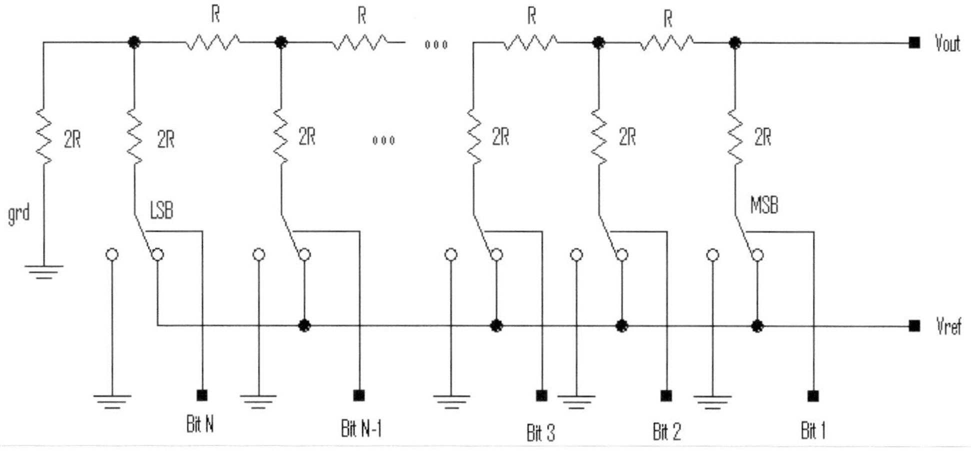

Fig. 3. The R-2R ladder network with N bits

If all inputs are connected to ground, 0 volts are produced at the output *Vout*. If all inputs are connected to *Vref*, the output voltage approaches *Vref*, and if some inputs are connected to ground and some to *Vref* then an output voltage between 0 volts and *Vref* appears at *Vout*. These inputs range from the most significant bit (MSB) to the least significant bit (LSB).

The MSB, when activated, causes the greatest change in the output voltage and the LSB, when activated, will cause the smallest change in the output voltage. The output voltage caused by connecting a particular bit to *Vref* with all other bits in grounded is *Vout= Vref / 2N*, where *N* is the bit number. Then for *N = 1, Vout = Vref / 2*, for *N = 2, Vout = Vref / 4*, etc. Table 1 shows the effect of individual bit locations to the Nth bit. Notice that since the bit *N =1* has the greatest effect on the output voltage, it is designated the MSB.

Bit number	Vout
1 (MSB)	Vr/2
2	Vr/4
3	Vr/8
4	Vr/16
5	Vr/32
6	Vr/64
7	Vr/128
8	Vr/256
9	Vr/512
10	Vr/1024
n (LSB)	$Vr/2^n$

Table 1. Effect of individual bits on *Vout*

The R-2R ladder is a linear circuit. Then, by the principle of superposition, the output can be calculated by taking the sum of the effect of all bits connected to *Vref*. For example, if bits *1* and *3* are connected to *Vref* with all other inputs grounded, the output voltage is calculated by *Vout = (Vref/2) + (Vref/8)* which reduces to *Vout = (5.Vref) /8.*

As the R-2R ladder is a binary circuit, the effect of each successive bit approaching the LSB (less significant bit) is half that of the previous bit. If this sequence is extended to a ladder of infinite bits, the effect of the LSB on *Vout* approaches 0. Conversely, the full-scale output of the network approaches *Vref.*

2.2 Mathematical model that represents the R-2R ladder

As shown in Table 1, each bit contributes one small part of the reference voltage in the generation of the output voltage. The sum of the contribution of each individual bit then represents the analogue signal output. For example, in a DAC with 8 bits, the most significant bit contributes 0.5 of the reference voltage. The least significant bit contributes only 0.00390625 of the reference voltage. Each bit then contributes one specific gain value to the output voltage. The sum of all gains multiplied by the reference voltage then generates the final output voltage.

A simple scheme for analogue signal generation using only the mathematical approach was created for this work. As shown in Fig. 4, the mathematical approach of R-2R ladder consists of an arrangement of *gain, sum* and *multiplier* blocks. Each of the *gain* blocks has a weighting factor that is added when its input is supplied with a logic 1 and multiplied by reference voltage, so generating the final output voltage.

In the example presented in Fig. 4, using *Vref = 1V* when *B3 = B0 = 1* and *B2 = B1 = 0*, the output value is *0.5625* which represents the addition of each input. The advantage of the approach is that the DAC using R-2R ladder can be easily simulated using the

MATLAB®/Simulink® or any other mathematical modelling environment. Note that this model is similar to R-2R ladder network presented in Fig. 3.

In this work, models of commercially available digital-to-analogue converters were developed. All converters considered had a resolution of 8 bits and used the R-2R ladder approach to implement the conversion circuitry. The IC designs used were the DAC08 (Analog Devices Inc. [a]), AD7524 (Analog Devices Inc. [b]) and AD5450 (Analog Devices Inc. [c]).

Today, the designer of digital circuits and systems typically uses hardware description languages (HDLs) such as VHDL or Verilog®-HDL in order model the circuit or system at a high level of design abstraction. Although these HDLs provide language constructs for behavioural simulation, their language subsets are far too restrictive for system level design. On the other hand, the MATLAB®/Simulink® modelling and simulation environment provides a powerful high level mathematical modelling environment for systems that can be widely used for high level algorithm development. It is a high-performance language for technical computing. It has a large collection of computational algorithms ranging from elementary functions, like summation and multiplication, through to complex arithmetic functions, such as fast Fourier transforms (FFTs).

A hardware description language, such as VHDL, can readily be used to describe a digital circuit or system. However, this language has a very limited capability when dealing with complex mathematical operations. The use of an interface, however, between MATLAB®/Simulink® and certain HDLs can fill the gap between an HDL and a high level mathematical modelling and simulation environment.

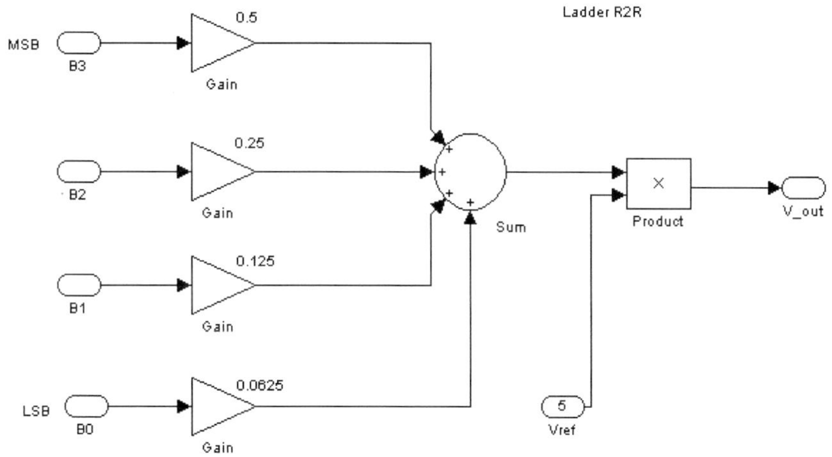

Fig. 4. Mathematical approach for modelling the R-2R ladder using Simulink®

In the next section, models developed in MATLAB®/Simulink® that implemented the digital-to-analogue converters selected for this work are presented.

3. Data converter models implemented in MATLAB®/Simulink®

A highly useful feature of Simulink® used in this work is the possibility of using it in the development of hybrid system models. In the DAC models developed, the use of *sum*, *multiplier*, *logic gates* and *shift register* components, along with components to generate input

signals and undertake results analysis was required. All these basic components are available in libraries provided with Simulink®. These components are found in different libraries named *toolboxes*. A list of professional *toolboxes* currently available can be obtained from The MathWorks Inc. This list is by no means static; more toolboxes are being created every year. For example, there are toolboxes for communication systems, control systems, frequency-domain design, fuzzy logic and digital signal processing. With the components available to the user, it is possible to create models of the DACs selected in order to undertake a suitable design modelling and simulation study. Components are available to implement the analogue and digital circuit parts of the data converter. In addition, there are components to generate the input signals and to perform results analysis.
Using the available *and*, *or* and *not* logic gates, all required digital parts were created; shift *register*, *counters*, *latches* and all the logic necessary to implement the ADC7524 and ADC5450 *control* using *subsystems*.
As the model increases in size and complexity, the model visualization can be kept manageable by grouping blocks into suitably defined *subsystems*. For example, an R-2R ladder network can be generated as a subsystem and used in all the models. Fig. 5 shows the R-2R ladder created as a *subsystem*. This *subsystem* may then be used in all the models.

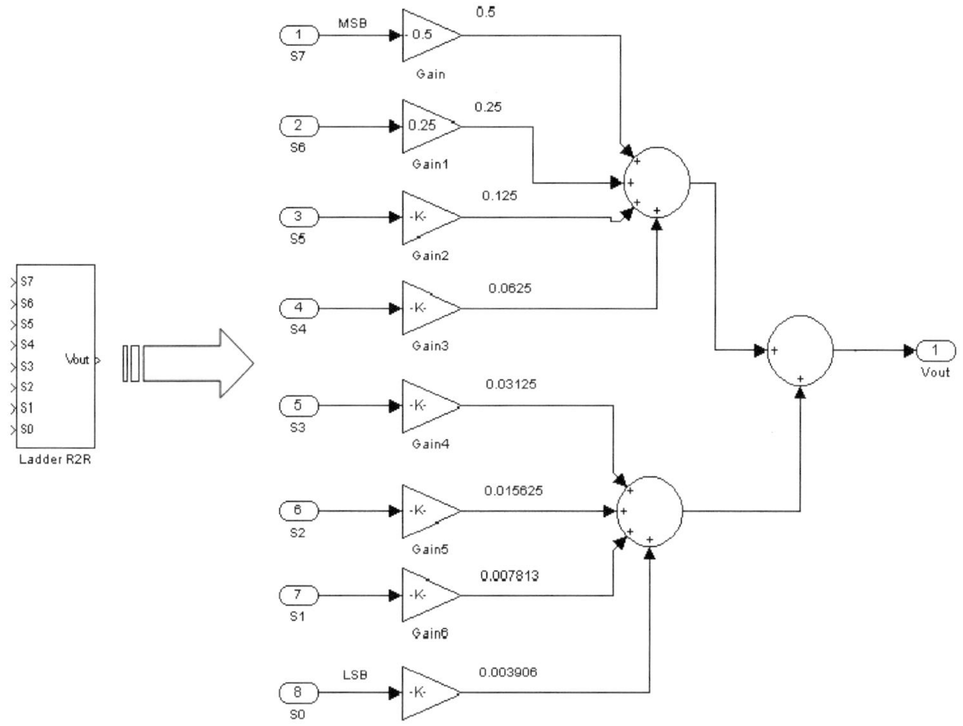

Fig. 5. R-2R ladder created as a *subsystem*

The *subsystem* named *R-2R* ladder is a block that has inputs labelled *S0* to *S7* (digital inputs) and an output *Vout* (analogue output). As shown in Fig. 5, the *subsystem* was created using the available *gain*, *sum*, *input* and *output* components, found in the Simulink® libraries.

3.1 DAC08 modelled in MATLAB®/Simulink®

The DAC08 is a multiplying D/A converter that uses the R-2R ladder in which an output current is the product of a digital number and an input reference current. Each digital input has a weight represented by the gain. These gains are added when their inputs have 1 logic and are multiplied by reference voltage, generating the output voltage. Table 2 shows the weight of each individual bit in the DAC08.

Bit position	Weight
S_7 (MSB)	0.5
S_6	0.25
S_5	0.125
S_4	0.0625
S_3	0.03125
S_2	0.015625
S_1	0.00781250
S_0 (LSB)	0.00390625

Table 2. Individual bit weighting in the DAC08 model

With this information it is possible to create the DAC08 converter model using the components available in the Simulink® libraries. Fig. 6 shows the DAC08 model implemented in Simulink®. It can be seen that the model is composed of the R-2R ladder network block, a product block and a subtraction block to generate the output currents (*Io* and *Iob*).
The multiplier block generates output voltage of the binary value in the digital input. The reference voltage will define the maximum output voltage. The commutation between the outputs, labelled *Io* and *Iob,* is performed by the subtraction block.

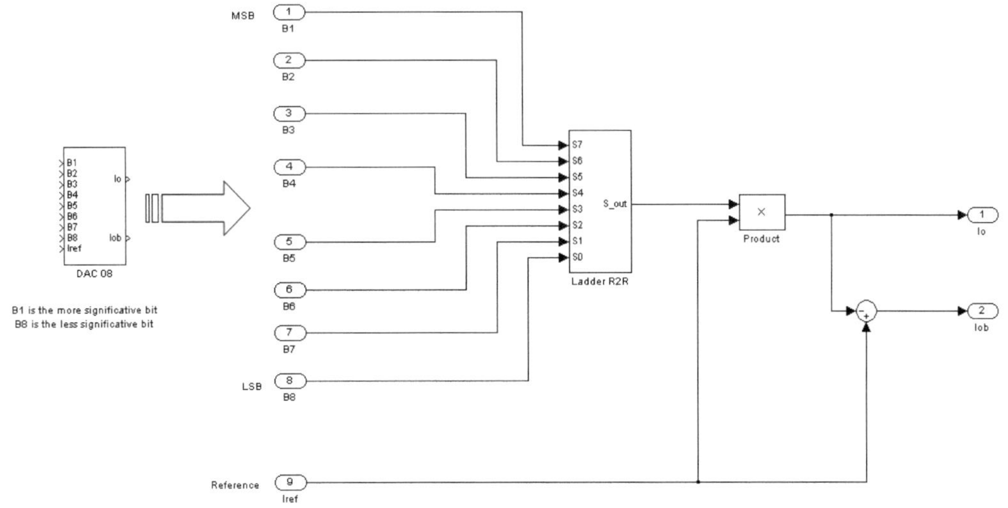

Fig. 6. DAC08 model implemented in Simulink®

As the R-2R ladder block is analogue in nature, there is a need to use the correct data type between the digital inputs and the analogue ladder network. In the R-2R ladder, the blocks labelled *Data type conversion* were used. These blocks implement the necessary conversion between different data types. Fig. 7 shows the used ladder R-2R network implemented as a subsystem. To test this model, an 8-bit sine waveform was generated as the converter signal input. To use the waveform as input of the model, the vectors *B1* (MSB) to *B8* (LSB) were generated from a MATLAB® M-file (with a file extension *.m*) and were used by Simulink® through the *From Workspace* block. The Simulink® model used to test the DAC08 is shown in Fig. 8 and the output signal, resulting from digital to analogue conversion, is shown in Fig. 9.

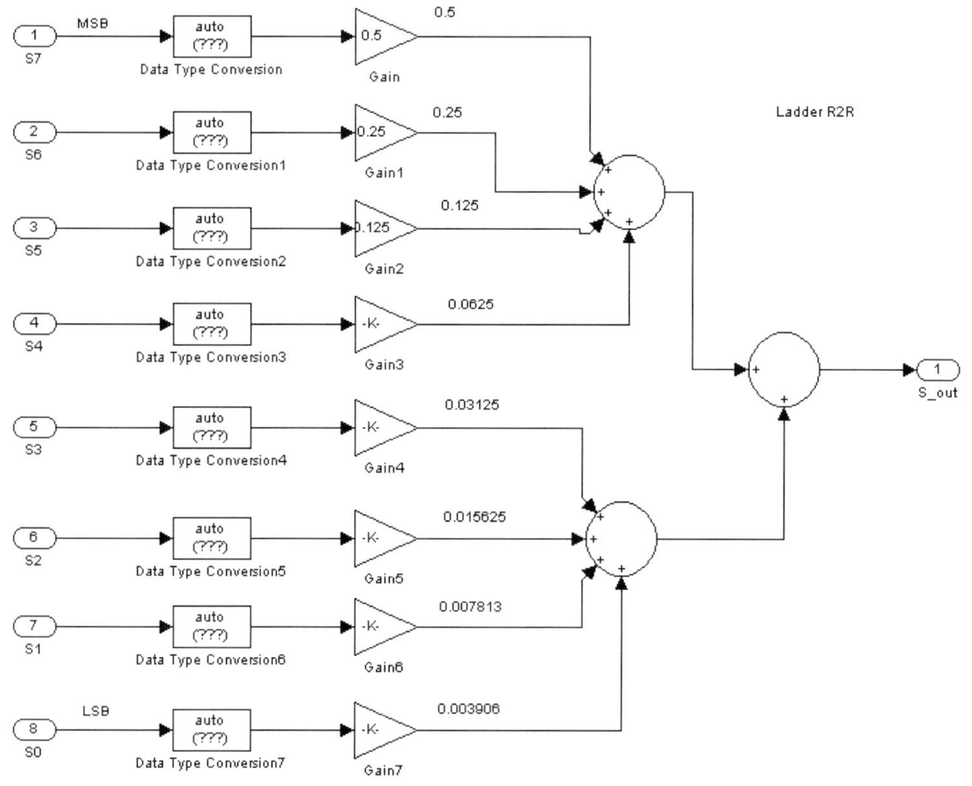

Fig. 7. R-2R ladder network implemented as *subsystem*

3.2 AD7524 modelled in MATLAB®/Simulink®

The AD7524 consists of an R-2R ladder and an input latch with 8 bits. The load cycle of the AD7524 is similar to the write cycle of a random access memory (RAM). In the *write mode*, when *CSb* (chip select - active low) and *WRb* (write - active low) are both LOW, the AD7524 is in the WRITE mode and the AD7524 analogue output responds to data activity at the *DB0-DB7* data bus inputs.

In all tests undertaken in the study, the *CSb* and *WRb* were set to a low level. In this mode, the AD7524 acts like a non-latched input D/A converter. Fig. 10 shows the AD7524 model implemented in Simulink®. We can see that the model is comprised of an R-2R ladder network block, a product block and a subtraction block to generate the outputs (*Out1* and *Out2*). This model also has *Data Latch* blocks with 8 bits of input. The R-2R ladder block is similar to the one used by the ADC08 converter presented in Fig. 5. In this model there is a

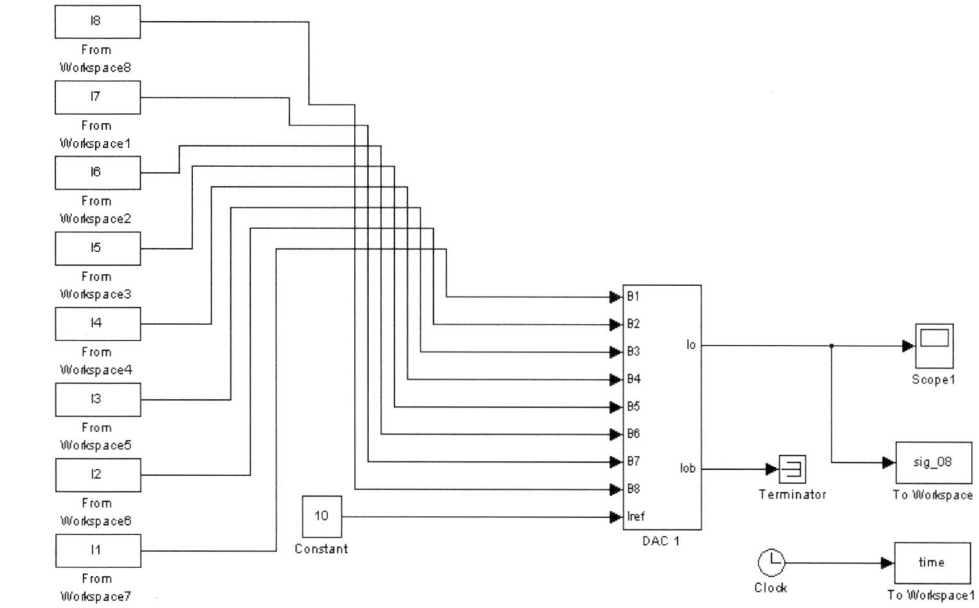

B1 IS THE MORE SIGNIFICANT BIT

Fig. 8. Simulink® model used to test the DAC08

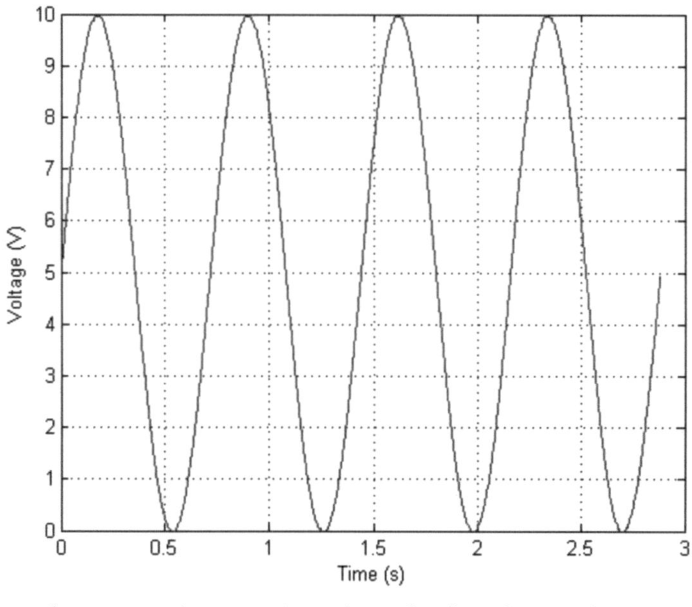

Fig. 9. Output analogue waveform resulting from the digital-to-analogue conversion

subsystem named *convertor* generated to implement the data type conversion that was used outside of the R-2R ladder block. The 8-bit input for the *Data Latch* block was constructed by two *latch* blocks with 4 input bits and by a single control circuit. This modularity is for easy construction of latch with 12, 16 and 20 bits. Fig. 11 shows the *Data Latch* block.

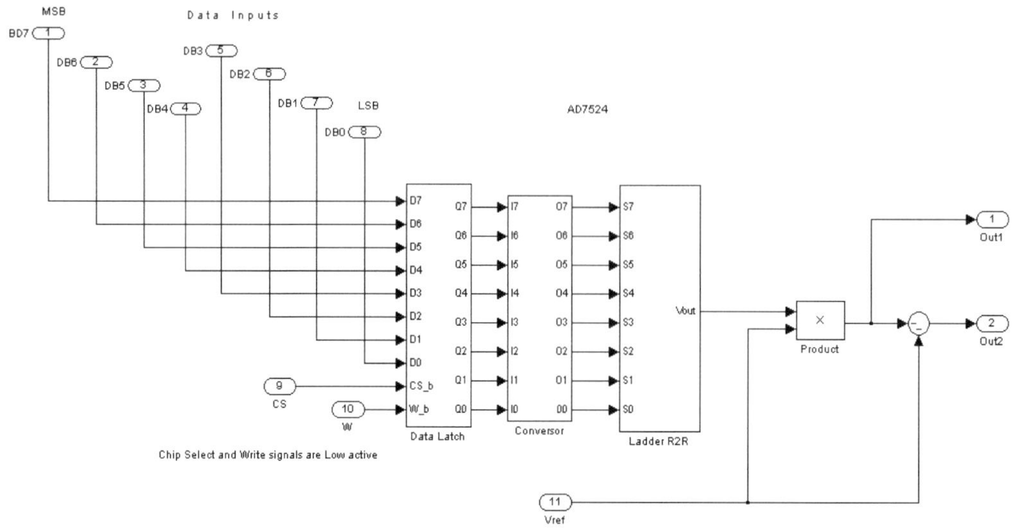

Fig. 10. AD7524 model implemented in Simulink®

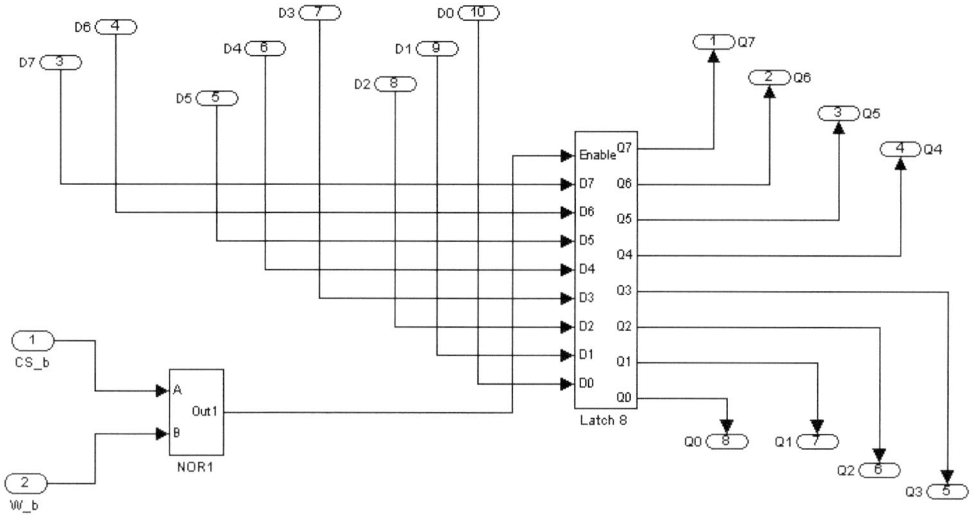

Fig. 11. 8-bit data latch block

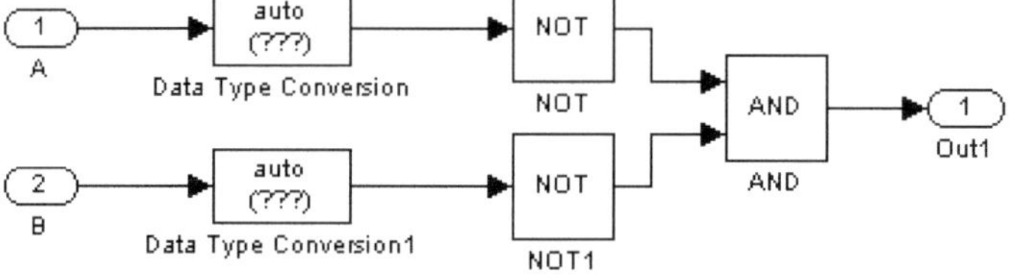

Fig. 12. Block for control of writing

The block for control of writing is a simple NOR gate. When the inputs labelled *CS_b* and *W_b* have low level logic applied, the output of the block is high level logic. In other words: *out = not (CS_b + W_b)*. This enables the latch to transfer the input to the output. Fig. 12 shows the control circuit to enable the transfer of data between the input and the output.
The block labelled *latch 8* was created using two *latch* blocks with 4 bits. The *latch* block with 4 bits is shown in Fig. 13.

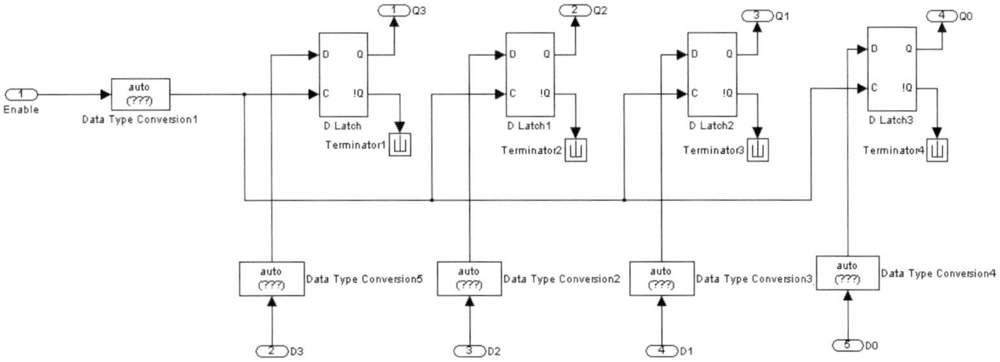

Fig. 13. Latch block with 4 bits

The same waveform was used for testing the Simulink® model as shown in Fig. 14.

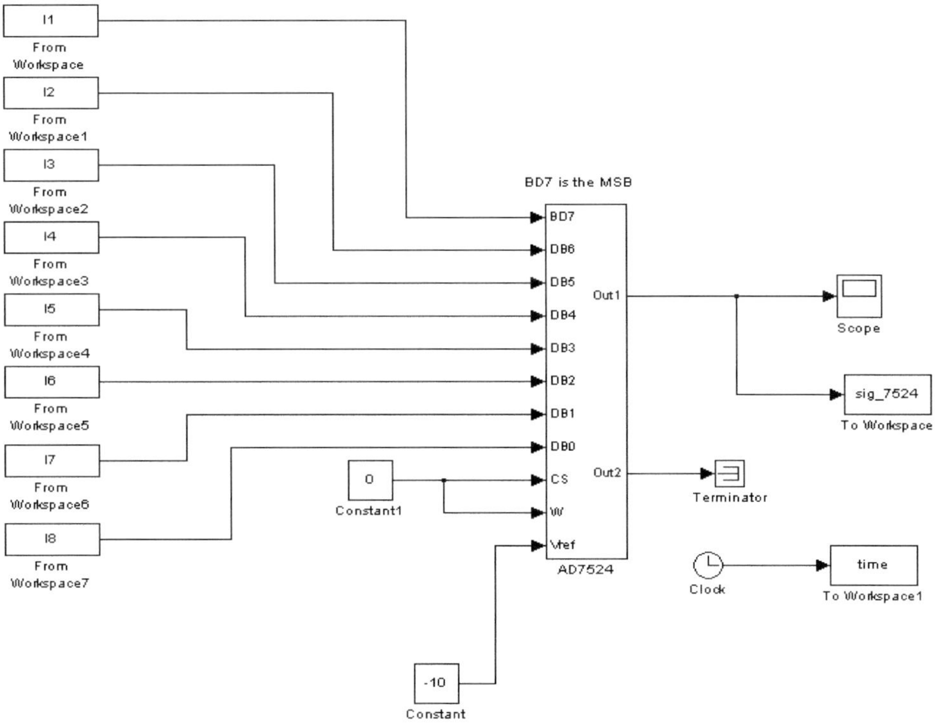

Fig. 14. Simulink® model to the ADC 7524 converter

3.3 AD5450 modelled in MATLAB®/Simulink®

The AD545n series (n = 0, 1, 2, 3) DAC has a 3-wire interface that is compatible with the majority of interface standards. Data is written to the device in 16-bit words. This word consists of two control bits and 14 data bits. The AD5450 uses 8 data bits and ignores the 6 LSBs. The controls bits *C1* and *C0* are used to load and update the code and change the active clock edge. Table 3 shows the control bits of the AD5450.

C1	C0	Function implemented
0	0	Load and update (power-on default)
0	1	Reserved
1	0	Reserved
1	1	Clock data to shift register upon rising edge

Table 3. AD5450 control bits

The SYNC function, low active, is an edge-triggered input that acts as a frame-synchronization signal and chip enable. Data can only be transferred to the device while SYNC is low. After the falling edge of the 16th SCLK pulse, bring SYNC high to transfer data from the input shift register to the DAC register. The AD5450 also uses the R-2R ladder network to do the conversion.

Fig. 15 shows the AD5450 model implemented in Simulink®. It can be seen that the model is composed of an R-2R ladder network block. The R-2R ladder block is similar in use to the ADC08 and AD7524 converters. In this model we also used the data type conversion outside of the R-2R ladder block. It can also been seen that there is a block named *DAC Data Latch* which implements the *control* blocks, the *latch* block and the *shift register* block.

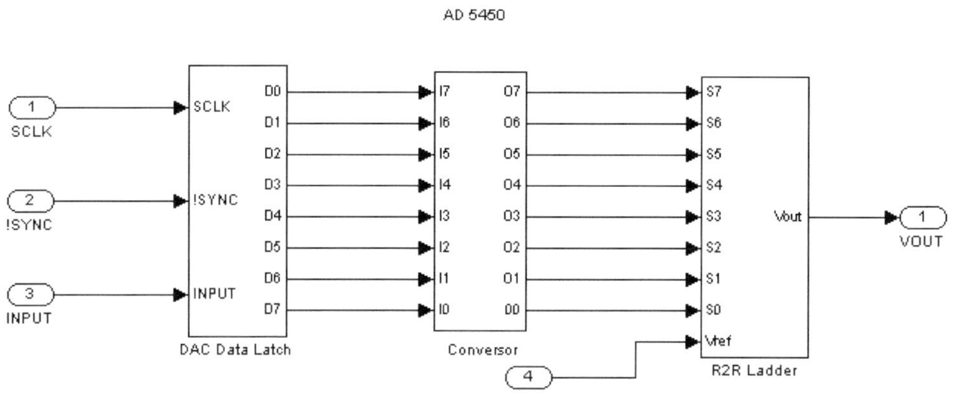

Fig. 15. Simulink® model to the AD5450 converter

Fig. 16 shows the *DAC Data Latch* block. This block has another 4 blocks called *Control Load, Control Latch, Data Latch* and *Shift Register.*

It can be seen that there are three *transport delay* blocks in this circuit required to enable the correct operation of the model. Without these timing delays, the model cannot have the correct functionality. When a *transport delay* block is used, there is also a need for a *Data Type Conversion* block. Fig. 17 shows the *Control Load* block. It has a circuit that counts the clock, called *Count Pulses,* and another circuit called *Set Trigger,* to set the trigger signal. The *Count*

Pulses block loads data into the latch to be converted after the count circuit receives 16 clock pulses.

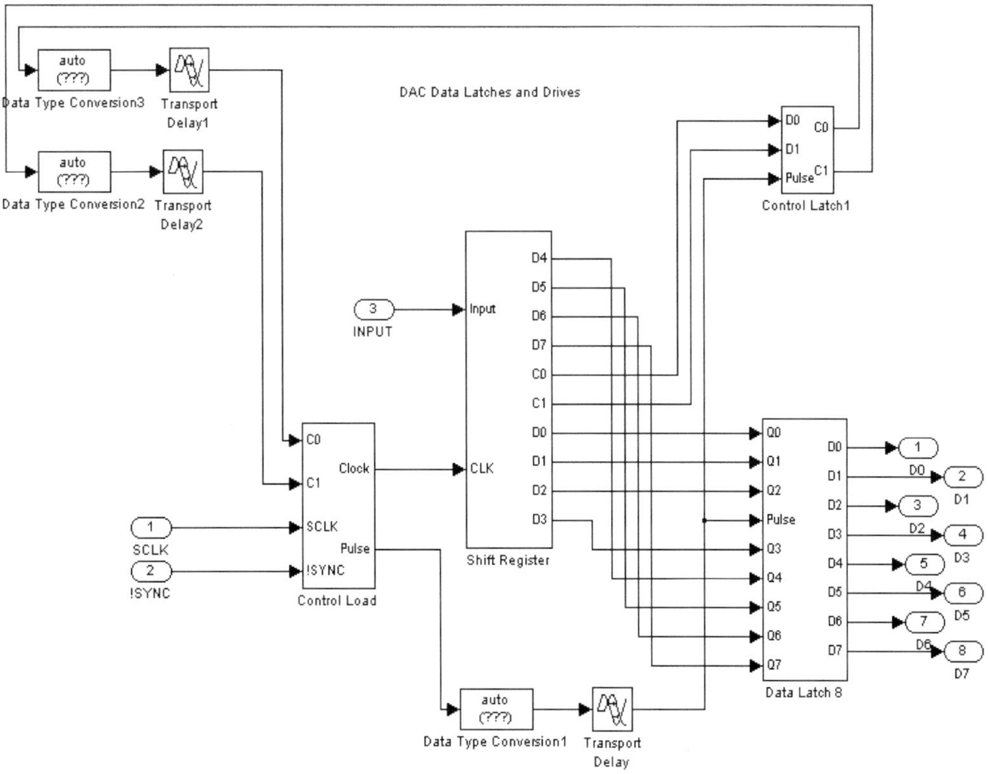

Fig. 16. AD5450 *data latch* block

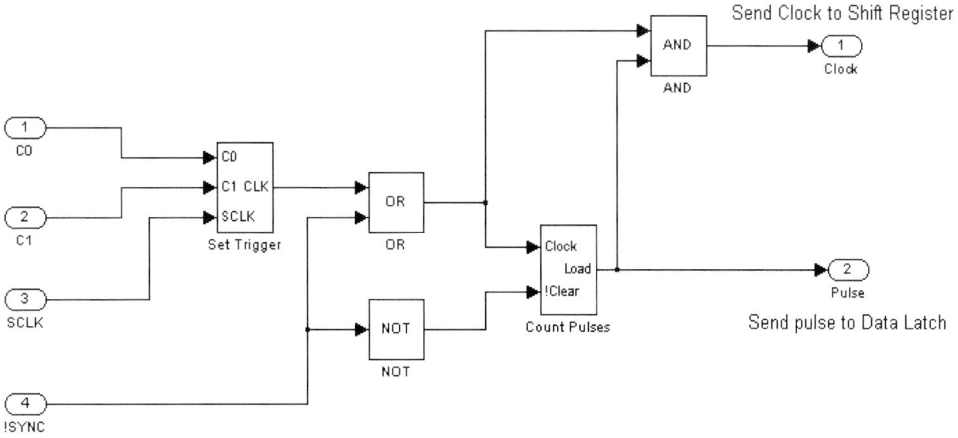

Fig. 17. The *Control Load* Block

Several other blocks created as subsystems are used to test the AD5450 model presented in Fig. 18.

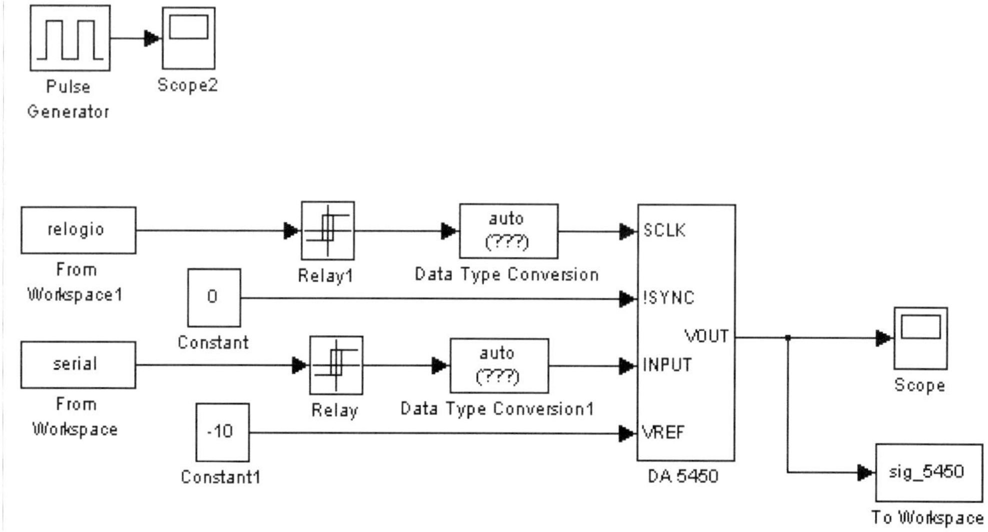

Fig. 18. Simulink® model used to test the AD5450 converter

In order to test this model, the same 8-bit sine waveform, as used previously, was used. This model uses the serial input. For each 8-bit vector generated, to represent the sine waveform, a bit stream (sequence of bits) was also generated. A MATLAB® M-file was created to generate the workspace bit stream.

The next section presents an approach developed to support mixed-signal circuit design and analysis. The methodology proposed is a novel approach to the problem of developing model descriptions of mixed-signal circuit topologies by the construction of a set of subsystems that support the automated mapping of MATLAB®/Simulink® models to structural VHDL-AMS descriptions. The tool developed, named *MS2SV* (MATLAB®/Simulink® to SystemVision™), reads a Simulink® model file and translates it to a structural VHDL-AMS code. It also creates the file structure required to simulate the translated model in the SystemVision™ environment from Mentor Graphics®. The *MS2SV* translator was developed using the C programming language and it has a number of predefined library components required for the translation process. The motivation for using Simulink® as a high level design model comes from the fact that it is the standard language used, for example, in areas of control. Simulink® is also a popular tool used in education and research. The choice of VHDL-AMS as the target language is motivated by the standard of hardware description language, available in the majority of synthesis environments. It is worth pointing out that Simulink® is purely a simulation language, therefore, the automatic translation of Simulink® to VHDL-AMS is highly desirable.

4. The MS^{2}SV model conversion toolbox

The *MS^{2}SV* conversion toolbox was developed using the C programming language. The developed program reads the file type *.mdl* (MATLAB®/Simulink® model) describing a model to be implemented and generates all the necessary structure for this model to be simulated in the SystemVision™ environment. The *.mdl* model is then described (translated) into VHDL-AMS code. In the process of translation, all the components presented in the Simulink® model are identified in the library of components previously developed for this specific use. An overview of methodology is shown in Fig. 19.

It can be seen that the steps involved are as below:

i. Initial specification of the model and model performance analysis through simulation using Simulink®.
ii. Conversion of the Simulink® model to a correspondent VHDL-AMS model.
iii. Simulation and analysis of the converted model using SystemVision™ environment.
iv. Comparison of simulation results from both model forms.
v. Continue the synthesis process (of the VHDL-AMS code parts) if the results comparison is acceptable, or return to a new specification if the results comparison is not acceptable.

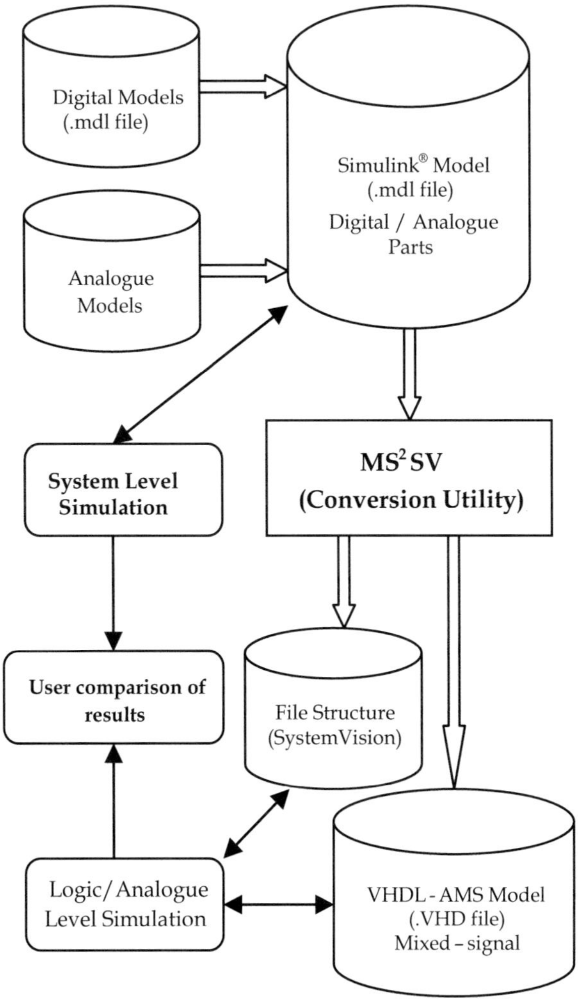

Fig. 19. Methodology used in the process of translation

In the initial phase of specification, the user can only use the components available in the library named *LIB_MS2SV*. This library has a set of combinational and sequential primitives, such as *or, and, not, latches, bistables* (flip-flops), counters and *shift registers*. In addition, it contains analogue primitives, such as *gain, product* and *sum*. Also available are a number of subsystems created for specific use, along with constant types and pulse sources. Fig. 20 shows some of the components available in the library *LIB_MS2SV*.

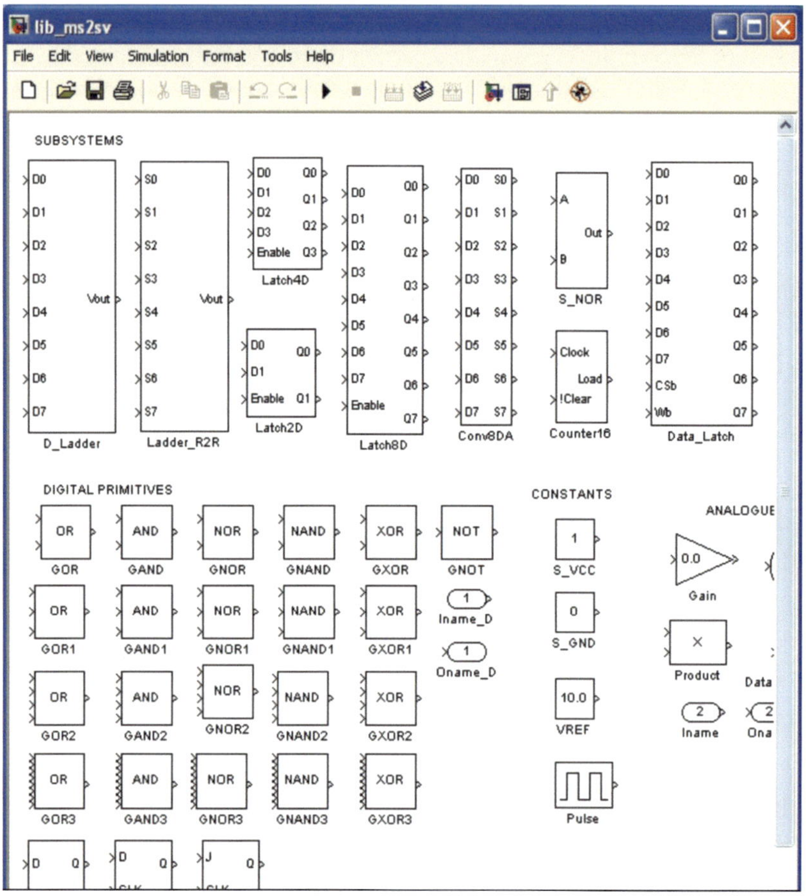

Fig. 20. LIB_MS2SV library of components

One important aspect of the design methodology is related to the names used to specify the input/output ports of the system. The name of all digital signals must finish with *_D* and cannot have names which are reserved words in VHDL-AMS. Note also that the names of components are different from the conventional names as in the conversion process, the conventional names are used as reserved words in the target models. They should also not have names that finish with a number, for example *CONVDA8*. This is because if there is a need to use two or more instantiations of the component *CONVDA8*, then Simulink® will automatically change the name of the second component to *CONVDA1*, *CONVDA2*, and so on. These new names will not then be recognized correctly. This naming rule is not however applied to logic gates. In this case the programme identifies only the name *GAND*, *GOR*, etc.

The number of the input is specified inside of the *.mdl* file. When the *MS²SV* programme is executed, the programme identifies all the important information inside the *.mdl* file and recognises this information in the library of components *LIB_MS2SV*. The translation of the structure of the original model into the corresponding VHDL-AMS code structure is then undertaken. Once the Simulink® model has been translated into VHDL-AMS code, a project set is created in the SystemVision™ project environment which allows for adequate simulation and analysis of the translated model.

4.1 Using the MS²SV toolbox

The *MS²SV* programme was developed using the C programming language and it is to be used with the computer command prompt. To call and run the program, the designer needs to use the following command:

```
C:> ms2sv_1 input_file output_file
```

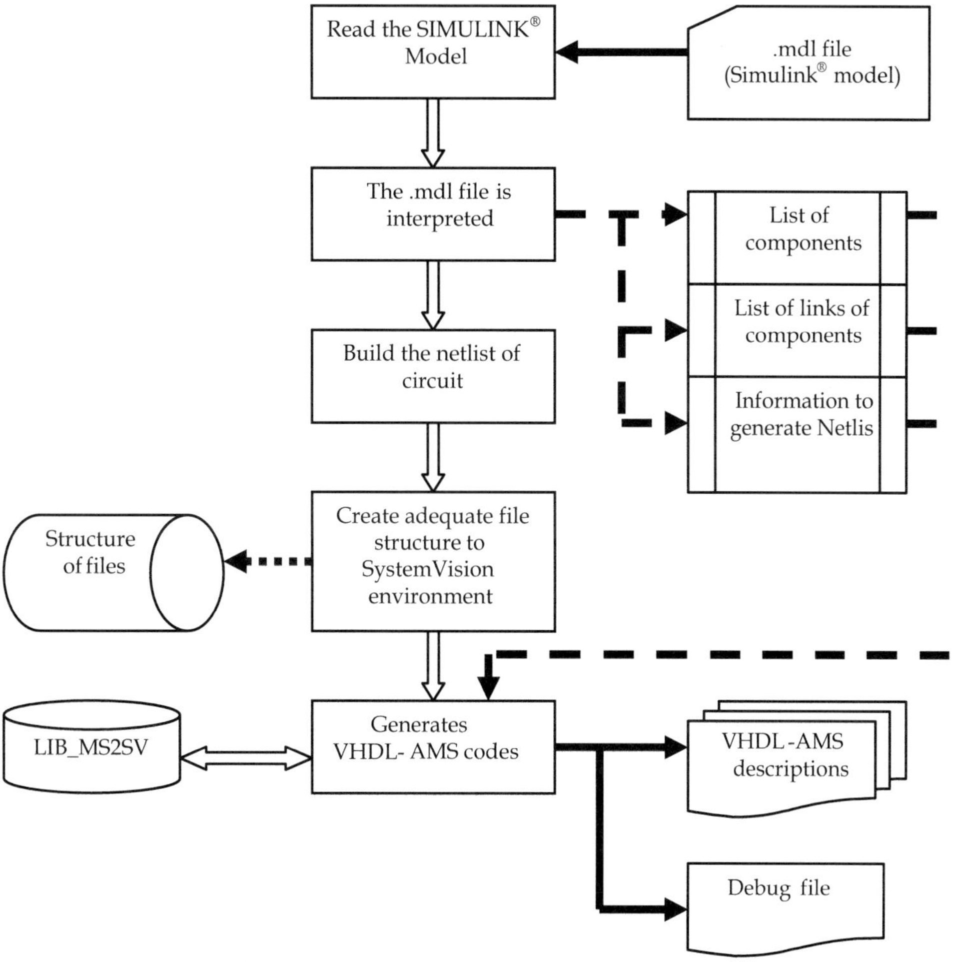

Fig. 21. Block diagram of *MS²SV* programme

The *ms2sv_1* is the name of executable file, the *input_file* is the name of model Simulink® (.mdl file) and the *output_file* is a text file (any name) used to save information of some steps of execution. This text file is very useful to find mistakes and debug. Fig. 21 shows the block diagram of the *MS²SV* programme.

It can be seen from Fig. 21 that the steps used by *MS²SV* to translate a Simulink® model to corresponding VHDL-AMS code are:

i. **Read the Simulink® model**: this model is a file type *.mdl* that was created by MATLAB®. The name of this file will be the name of the entity of the VHDL-AMS description translated.
ii. **Interpreter**: this step does the interpretation of the .mdl file. The .mdl file has a lot of different information that is not useful to be translated. As an example, the .mdl file has information about the position of the components in the screen, the orientation, the foreground colour, font name, font size and names other different information. It is the most difficult job of the programme. When finishing this step, the list of components, the list of links between components and the necessary information to build the circuits are generated.
iii. **Building the circuit**: all the information generated in the last step is arranged. Now the programme has the Simulink® model description in an adequate format to generate the corresponding VHDL-AMS code.
iv. **Create the file structure to SystemVision™**: all the necessary structure of the directory and file to a perfect compilation and simulation is created in this step. In the present version of the programme, all the structure is created under the SystemVision™ Project directory.
v. **Generate VHDL-AMS code**: all the identified components of the model have one corresponding code in VHDL-AMS. This code is at the library of components. This step identifies the corresponding code and generates all the VHDL-AMS description to the translated code. For all components not included at EDULIB, the library has one VHDL file. One VHDL-AMS file may need other VHDL-AMS files. This hierarchical structure is very important to be specified in the benchmark of SystemVision™. In this step the debug file is also generated.

4.2 MS²SV toolbox evaluation

To evaluate *MS²SV* toolbox, the models of digital-to-analogue converter designs implemented in MATLAB®/Simulink® (as presented in section 3) were developed again, however now using only the *LIB_MS2SV* library. These models were translated to VHDL-AMS code using the developed tool and the translated codes were compiled and simulated in the SystemVision™ environment. In this section, only the Simulink® model for the DAC08 data converter is presented and then translated to VHDL-AMS. The waveform used to simulate the operation of the circuit was the ramp function only, as the *LIB_MS2SV* library does not yet have any other sources to allow the generation of different waveforms. In the future, the intention is to generate additional types of sources for placement within the *MS²SV* library.

4.2.1 Project for the DAC08 data converter

The Simulink® model to DAC08 was translated by the *MS²SV* programme. The following VHDL-AMS code was generated:

Entity d08ramp - Top of hierarchy

```
  -- genhdl/d08ramp
-- Generatedby MS2SV toolversion 1.0
  LIBRARY ieee;
  USE ieee.std_logic_1164.all;
  USE ieee.electrical_systems.all;
  LIBRARY edulib;
  USE work.all;
  libraryfundamentals_vda;
  library spice2vhd;
  entity d08ramp is
  Port(
           terminal Vout :electrical);
  end entity d08ramp;
  architecture arch_d08ramp of d08ramp is
  terminal VREF :          electrical;
    terminal Sum2          : electrical;
    terminal Sum1          : electrical;
    terminal Sum           : electrical;
    signal Pulse7          : std_logic;
    signal Pulse6          : std_logic;
    signal Pulse5          : std_logic;
    signal Pulse4          : std_logic;
    signal Pulse3          : std_logic;
    signal Pulse2          : std_logic;
    signal Pulse1          : std_logic;
    signal Pulse           : std_logic;
    terminal Product       :electrical;
    terminal Gain7         :electrical;
    terminal Gain6         :electrical;
    terminal Gain5         :electrical;
    terminal Gain4         :electrical;
    terminal Gain3         :electrical;
    terminal Gain2         :electrical;
    terminal Gain1         :electrical;
    terminal Gain          :electrical;
    terminal Conversion7 :electrical;
    terminal Conversion6 :electrical;
    terminal Conversion5 :electrical;
    terminal Conversion4 :electrical;
    terminal Conversion3 :electrical;
    terminal Conversion2 :electrical;
    terminal Conversion1 :electrical;
    terminal Conversion  :electrical;
  begin
    V_VREF :entity EDULIB.V_CONSTANT(IDEAL)
  genericmap ( LEVEL => -10.0 )
  portmap ( POS => VREF,
            NEG => ELECTRICAL_REF );
    E_Pulse7 :entity EDULIB.CLOCK_FREQ(IDEAL)
  genericmap ( FREQ => 0.0078125 )
  portmap ( CLK_OUT => Pulse7 );
    D2A_Conversion7 :entity
EDULIB.D2A_BIT(IDEAL)
  genericmap( VHIGH => 1.0,
                       VLOW => 0.0 )
  portmap ( D => Pulse7,
                 A => Conversion7 );
    E_Gain7 :entity EDULIB.E_GAIN(BEHAVIORAL)
  genericmap ( K => 0.5 )
  portmap( INPUT => Conversion7,
                 OUTPUT => Gain7 );
    E_Pulse5 :entity
EDULIB.CLOCK_FREQ(IDEAL)
  genericmap ( FREQ => 0.03125 )
  portmap ( CLK_OUT => Pulse5 );
    D2A_Conversion5 :entity
EDULIB.D2A_BIT(IDEAL)
  genericmap( VHIGH => 1.0,
              VLOW => 0.0 )
  portmap ( D => Pulse5,
            A => Conversion5 );
    E_Gain5 :entity
EDULIB.E_GAIN(BEHAVIORAL)
  genericmap ( K => 0.125 )
  portmap( INPUT => Conversion5,
           OUTPUT => Gain5 );
    E_Pulse6 :entity
EDULIB.CLOCK_FREQ(IDEAL)
  genericmap ( FREQ => 0.015625 )
  portmap ( CLK_OUT => Pulse6 );
    D2A_Conversion6 :entity
EDULIB.D2A_BIT(IDEAL)
  genericmap( VHIGH => 1.0,
              VLOW => 0.0 )
  portmap ( D => Pulse6,
            A => Conversion6 );
    E_Gain6 :entity
EDULIB.E_GAIN(BEHAVIORAL)
  genericmap ( K => 0.25 )
  portmap( INPUT => Conversion6,
           OUTPUT => Gain6 );
    E_Pulse4 :entity
EDULIB.CLOCK_FREQ(IDEAL)
  genericmap ( FREQ => 0.0625 )
  portmap ( CLK_OUT => Pulse4 );
    D2A_Conversion4 :entity
EDULIB.D2A_BIT(IDEAL)
  genericmap( VHIGH => 1.0,
              VLOW => 0.0 )
  portmap ( D => Pulse4,
            A => Conversion4 );
    E_Gain4 :entity
EDULIB.E_GAIN(BEHAVIORAL)
  genericmap ( K => 0.0625 )
  portmap( INPUT => Conversion4,
           OUTPUT => Gain4 );
    E_Sum1 :entity
WORK.L_SUM4(ARCH_L_SUM4)
  portmap( IN1 => Gain7,
           IN2 => Gain5,
           IN3 => Gain6,
           IN4 => Gain4,
           OUTPUT => Sum1 );
  E_Pulse :entity
EDULIB.CLOCK_FREQ(IDEAL)
  genericmap ( FREQ => 1.0 )
  portmap ( CLK_OUT => Pulse );
    D2A_Conversion :entity
EDULIB.D2A_BIT(IDEAL)
  genericmap( VHIGH => 1.0,
              VLOW => 0.0 )
  portmap ( D => Pulse,
          A =>Conversion );
```

Fig. 22. (continues on next page) presents the simulation result in SystemVision™ using the translated VHDL-AMS codes

```
  E_Gain :entity EDULIB.E_GAIN(BEHAVIORAL)
  genericmap ( K => 0.003906 )
  portmap( INPUT =>Conversion,
           OUTPUT =>Gain );
    E_Pulse3 :entity EDULIB.CLOCK_FREQ(IDEAL)
  genericmap ( FREQ => 0.125 )
  portmap ( CLK_OUT => Pulse3 );
    D2A_Conversion3 :entity EDULIB.D2A_BIT(IDEAL)
  genericmap( VHIGH => 1.0,
              VLOW => 0.0 )
  portmap ( D => Pulse3,
            A => Conversion3 );
    E_Gain3 :entity EDULIB.E_GAIN(BEHAVIORAL)
  genericmap ( K => 0.03125 )
  portmap( INPUT => Conversion3,
           OUTPUT => Gain3 );
    E_Pulse2 :entity EDULIB.CLOCK_FREQ(IDEAL)
  genericmap ( FREQ => 0.25 )
  portmap ( CLK_OUT => Pulse2 );
    D2A_Conversion2 :entity EDULIB.D2A_BIT(IDEAL)
  genericmap( VHIGH => 1.0,
              VLOW => 0.0 )
  portmap ( D => Pulse2,
            A => Conversion2 );
    E_Gain2 :entity EDULIB.E_GAIN(BEHAVIORAL)
  genericmap ( K => 0.015625 )
  portmap( INPUT => Conversion2,
           OUTPUT => Gain2 );
    E_Pulse1 :entity EDULIB.CLOCK_FREQ(IDEAL)
  genericmap ( FREQ => 0.5 )
  portmap ( CLK_OUT => Pulse1 );
    D2A_Conversion1 :entity EDULIB.D2A_BIT(IDEAL)
  genericmap( VHIGH => 1.0,
              VLOW => 0.0 )
  portmap ( D => Pulse1,
           A => Conversion1 );
    E_Gain1 :entity EDULIB.E_GAIN(BEHAVIORAL)
  genericmap ( K => 0.007813 )
  portmap( INPUT => Conversion1,
           OUTPUT => Gain1 );
  E_Sum :entity WORK.L_SUM4(ARCH_L_SUM4)
  portmap( IN1 =>Gain,
           IN2 => Gain3,
           IN3 => Gain2,
           IN4 => Gain1,
           OUTPUT =>Sum );
    E_Sum2 :entity EDULIB.E_SUM(BEHAVIORAL)
  portmap( IN1 => Sum1,
           IN2 =>Sum,
           OUTPUT => Sum2 );
  E_Product :entity EDULIB.E_MULT(BEHAVIORAL)
  portmap( IN1 => VREF,
           IN2 => Sum2,
           OUTPUT =>Vout );
end architecture arch_d08ramp;
```

Fig. 22. (continues) presents the simulation result in SystemVision™ using the translated VHDL-AMS codes

5. Conclusions

In this chapter, work undertaken to investigate the modelling, simulation and synthesis of mixed-signal integrated circuit designs using a combination of hardware description languages (HDLs) and mathematical modelling tools was presented. Three different models of digital-to-analogue converter designs used in commercial applications were represented. These models were implemented in MATLAB®/Simulink® and then in SystemVision™ using the VHDL-AMS language. An approach to develop and support mixed-signal circuit design and analysis was shown. The methodology proposed shows a novel approach to the problem of developing model descriptions of a mixed-signal circuit topologies, by construction of a set of subsystems that support the automated mapping of MATLAB®/Simulink® models to structural VHDL-AMS description. The *toolbox* developed is named *MS²SV* (MATLAB®/Simulink® to SystemVision™) and this is used to read a Simulink® model file and then translate it to a structural VHDL-AMS code. It also creates the file structure required to simulate the translated model in the SystemVision™ environment from Mentor Graphics®. The results show the viability of this type of approach. It had a direct relation between the used elements by MATLAB®/Simulink® to implement the studied models and elements used by SystemVision™ to implement the same model functionality for a mixed-signal circuit design.

6. Acknowledgments

This work was supported by CNPq, Process N. 307255/2009-3 and CAPES Process N. 3359-05-0.

7. References

Analog Devices (a). 8-bit, High-Speed, Multiplying D/A Converter (Universal Digital Logic Interface), www.analog.com.

Analog Devices (b). CMOS 8-bits Buffered Multiplying DAC, www.analog.com.

Analog Devices (c). 8, 10, 12, 14-Bit High Band Width Multiplying DACs with Serial Interface, www.analog.com.

Christen E. & Bakalar K. (1999). VHDL-MAS - A Hardware Description Language for Analog and Mixed-Signal Applications, IEEE Trans. On Circuits and Systyems - II: Analog and Digital, Signal Processing, Vol. 46, No. 10, October, 1999, pp. 1263-1272.

Doboli A. & Vemuri R. (2003) . Behavioral Modeling for High-Level Synthesis of Analog and Mixed-Signal Systems From VHDL-AMS, IEEE Trans, on Computer-Aided Design of Integrated Circuits and Systems, Vol. 22, No. 11, November, 2003, pp. 1504-1520.

Edenfeld D. et al.,(2004). 2003 Technology Roadmap for Semiconductors, Computer, IEEE Computer Society, January 2004, pp. 47-56.

Grout I.A. & K. Keane,(2000). A Matlab to VHDL conversion toolbox for digital control, IFAC Symposium on Computer Aided Control Systems Design (CACSD 2000), Salford, UK, 11th - 13th September 2000.

Grout I. A. (2001). Modeling, simulation and synthesis: From Simulink to VHDL generated hardware, Proceedings of the 5th World Multi-Conference on Systemics, Cybernetics and Informatics (SCI 2001), July 22nd–25th 2001, Vol. 15, pp. 443-448.

Grout I. A. & O'Shea T. (2004). MATLAB/VHDL-AMS Modelling and Simulation Support for Microelectronic Circuit Design and Test, Proceedings of the 10th International Mixed-Signals Testing Workshop, 2004, pp. 178-183.

MacMillen D. et al., (2000). An Industrial View of Electronic Design Automation, IEEE Transactions on Computer Aided Design of Integrated Circuits and Systems, Vol. 19, No. 12, December 2000, pp. 1428-1448.
Pêcheus F., Lallement C. & Vachoux A. (2005). VHDL-AMS and Verilog-AMS as Alternative Hardware Description Languages for Efficient Modeling of Multidiscipline Systems, IEEE Trans. On Computer-Aided Design of Integrated Circuits and Systems, Vol. 24 No.2, February, 2005, pp. 204-225.
The MathWorks Inc. MatLab/Simulink, Version 4, USA.
Trofimov M. & Mosin S. (2004). The Realization of Algorithmic Description on VHDL-AMS, TCSET'2004, February 24-28, 2004, Lviv-Slavsko, Ukraine, pp. 350-352.
Wilson P. R., Ross J. N., Brown A. D. & Rushton A. (2004). Multiple Domain Behavioral Modeling Using VHDL-AMS, Proceedings of the 2004 International Symposium on Circuits and Systems, Vol. 5, 23-26 May 2004, pp. V644-647.
Zorzi M., Franzè F., Specialie N. & Masetti G.,(2004). A Tool for Integration of New VHDL-AMS Models in Spice, Proceedings of the 2004 International Symposium on Circuits and Systems, Vol. 4, 23-26 May 2004, pp. IV637-640.

17

Automated Model Generation Approach Using MATLAB

Likun Xia
Universiti Teknologi PETRONAS
Malaysia

1. Introduction

High level models comprise both faulty and fault-free models. High level fault-free modeling may simply indicate behavior of a fault-free circuit, but normally it is not able to cope with faulty conditions with strong nonlinearity. The only way to solve this is to replace the fault-free model with a faulty one. Furthermore, in fault-free simulation, the difference in term of simulation speed between transistor level and high level may not be obvious, but this can be shown under fault simulation. High level fault modeling (HLFM) techniques have shown the potential ability to deal with at least some degree of nonlinearity in large systems.

Unlike for linear systems, no technique currently guarantees for completely general nonlinear systems, even in principle, to produce a macromodel that conforms to any reasonable fidelity metric. The difficulty is due to the fact that nonlinear systems can be widely varied, with extremely complex dynamical behavior possible, which is very far from being exhaustively investigated or understood. Generally in view of the diversity and complexity of nonlinear systems, it is difficult to conceive of a single overarching theory or method that can be employed for effective modeling of an arbitrary nonlinear block.

Models can be obtained either manually or automatically. Automated model generation (AMG) approaches are becoming an increasingly important component of methodologies for effective system verification. Similar to manual creation, AMG can generate lower order macromodels via an automated computational procedure by receiving the information from transistor level models (Roychowdhury 2003; Roychowdhury 2004).

Unfortunately, there are not any approaches describing the use of AMG approaches for HLFM at a system level except for the publication in (Xia, Bell et al. 2010). For straightforward system simulation relatively simple models may be adequate, but they can prove inadequate during HLFM. The accuracy and speedup of existing models may be doubted when fault simulation is implemented because faulty behavior may force (nonfaulty) subsystems into highly nonlinear regions of operation, which may not be covered by their models. Multiple training data is required to cover the potentially wide range of operating conditions.

The chapter is organized as follows. Section 2 reviews various AMG approaches using MATLAB. A specific AMG approach using MATLAB is presented in sections 3. Section 4 demonstrates the results in simulated and real environments followed by conclusion for the chapter in section 5.

For clarity, an attempt has been made to adhere to a standard notational convention. Lower case **boldface** characters will generally refer to vectors. Upper case **BOLDFACE** characters will generally refer to matrices. Vector or matrix transposition will be denoted using $(.)^T$ and $(.)^*$ denotes conjugation for complex valued signals. $\Re^{K\times K}$ denotes the real vector space of $K\times K$ dimensions.

2. Review of automated model generation approaches using MATLAB

Automatic generation of circuit models for handling strong nonlinearity has received great interest over the last few years. It is essential for realistic exploration of the design space in current and future mixed-signal SoCs (system-on-chips) and SiPs (system-in-packages). Generally such techniques take a detailed description of a block such as SPICE level netlist and then generate a much smaller macromodel via an automated computational procedure. The advantage of this approach is its generality. As long as the equations of the original system are available numerically, knowledge of circuit structure, operating principles and so on are not very important (Roychowdhury 2003).

The model generated by AMG can be structured as either linear-time invariant (LTI), linear-time varying (LTV), nonlinear-time invariant or nonlinear-time varying. LTI no doubt form the most important class of dynamical systems. The basic structure of a LTI block for mixed mode circuits is illustrated in Fig. 1, where u(t) and y(t) represent inputs, and output to the system in the time domain, respectively. U(s) and Y(s) are forms in the Laplace domain. The definitive property of any LTI system is that the input and output are related by convolution with an impulse response h(t) in the time-domain, i.e., $y(t) = x(t) * h(t)$, their transforms are related to multiplication with a system transfer function H(s), i.e., $Y(s) = X(s) \cdot H(s)$. Their relationship can be expressed by partial differential equations (PDEs) or ordinary differential equations (ODEs). Such differential equations can be easily implemented using analogue hardware description language (AHDL).

A typical model structure for LTI is AutoRegressive with eXogenous (ARX) that is able to describe any single-input single-output (SISO) linear discrete-time dynamic system (Ljung 1999).

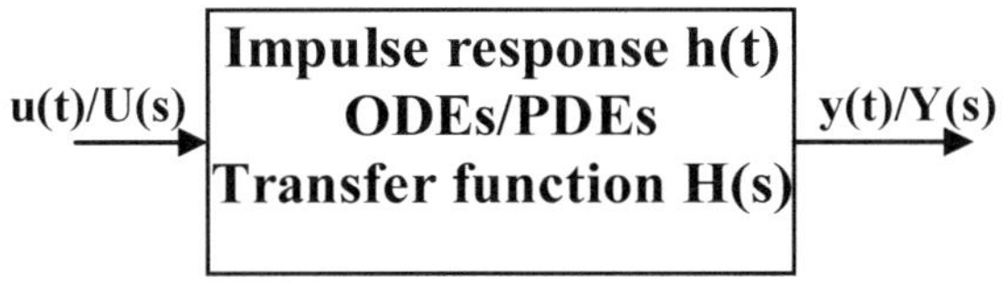

Fig. 1. Linear time-invariant block

LTV models are used in practice because most real-world systems are time-varying as a result of system parameters changing as function of time. They also permit linearization of nonlinear systems in the vicinity of a set of operating points of a trajectory. Similar to LTI systems, LTV can also be completely characterized by impulse responses or transfer functions. The main difference between them is that time-shift in the input of LTV does not necessarily result in the same time-shift of the output. A basic structure of LTV is depicted in Fig. 2, where u(t) and y(t) represent inputs, and output to the system in the time domain, respectively. U(s) and Y(s) are forms in the Laplace domain.

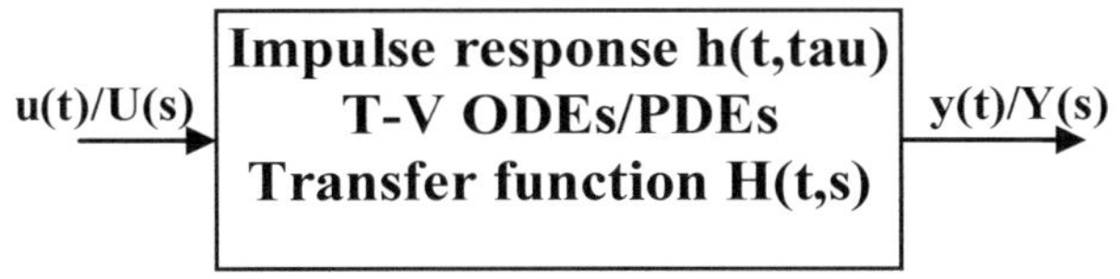

Fig. 2. Linear time-varying block

LTV are capable of handling time variation in state-space forms (Ljung 1999). Furthermore, nonlinear models such as the Wiener and Hammerstein model, and Situation-Dependent AutoRegressive with eXogenous (SDARX) give much richer possibilities to describe systems.

These models can be generated by using estimation algorithms, which comprise lookup tables (Yang and McGaughy 2004), radial basis functions (RBF) (Mutnury, Swaminathan et al. 2003), artificial neural networks (ANN) (Davalo and Naïm 1991; Zhang and Gupta 2000) and its derivations such as fuzzy logic (FL) (Verbruggen and Babuška 1999) and neural-fuzzy network (NF) (Uppal and Patton 2005), and regression (Simeu and Mir 2005). Model generators can also be categorized into the black, grey or white box approaches, depending on the level of existing knowledge of the system's structure and parameters. Dong et al (Dong and Roychowdhury 2005) indicates that white-box methods can produce more accurate macromodels than black-box methods. However, this work was only applied to a limited number of digital circuits.

Regression using MATLAB is an approach that is of interest in this chapter. It is a form of statistical modeling that attempts to evaluate the relationship between one variable (termed the dependent variable) and one or more other variables (termed the independent variables) (Ljung 1999). It can be divided into linear regression and nonlinear regression for generating linear or nonlinear models. (McConaghy, Eeckelaert et al. 2005; McConaghy and Gielen 2005) use the regression approach (Hong, Sharkey et al. 2003), via the predicted residual error sums of squares (PRESS) statistic (Breiman 1996), to test predictive robustness of linear models that are generated by an automatic symbolic model generator named CAFFEINE (Canonical Functional Form Expression in Evolution). CAFFEINE takes SPICE simulation data as inputs to generate open-loop symbolic models by using genetic programming (GP) via a grammar that is specially designed to constrain the search to a canonical functional form without cutting out good solutions. Results show that these models are interpretable, and handle nonlinearity with better prediction quality than posynomials (coefficients of a polynomial need not be positive, and the exponents of a posynomial can be real numbers, while for polynomials they must be non-negative integers). However, McConaghy et al did not address whether the generated model can be fitted into a large system and model nonlinearity well. Additionally, speed of model generation was not mentioned.

Unfortunately, AMG may produce high order models of excessive complexity for both continuous-time and discrete-time systems, so model order reduction (MOR) techniques are required. The purpose of MOR is to use the properties of dynamical systems in order to find approaches for reducing their complexity, while preserving (to the maximum possible extent) their input-output behavior. It comprises a branch of systems and control theory (Roychowdhury 2004). Combining MOR with the model structures produces new model structures dubbed LTI MOR (Pillage and Rohrer 1990), LTV MOR (Phillips 1998; Roychowdhury 1999) and weakly nonlinear methods including polynomial-based (Li and

Pileggi 2003; Li and Pileggi 2005), trajectory piecewise linear (TPWL) (Rewienski and White 2001), and piecewise polynomial (PWP) (Dong and Roychowdhury 2003).
Mathematically, a LTI model with a MOR method is expressed as a set of differential equations. In (1) u(t) represents the input waveforms to the block and y(t) are the outputs. The number of inputs and outputs is relatively small compared to the size of x(t), which is the state of the internal variables of the block. A, B, C, D and E are constant matrices, $E \,\&\, A \in R^{n\times n}, B \in R^{n\times p}, C \in R^{p\times p}, u(t) \in R^{p}$.

$$\begin{aligned} E\dot{x} &= Ax(t) + Bu(t) \\ y(t) &= C^{T}x(t) + Du(t) \end{aligned} \tag{1}$$

MOR methods for LTI systems fall into two major groups: Projection-based methods and Non-projection based methods. The former consists of such methods as Krylov-subspace (moment matching methods), Balanced-truncation method, proper orthogonal decomposition (POD) methods etc. Krylov-subspace based techniques such as Padé-via-Lanczos (PVL) techniques (Feldmann and Freund 1995), Krylov-subspace projection methods were an important milestone in LTI MOR macromodeling (Grimme 1997). Non-projection based methods comprise methods such as Hankel optimal model reduction, singular perturbation method, various optimization-based methods etc. Via Krylov-subspace operation, reduced models are obtained in (2), where $\tilde{E},\tilde{A},\tilde{B},\tilde{C}$ are reduced order matrices, $\tilde{E} \,\&\, \tilde{A} \in R^{q\times p}$, $\tilde{B} \in R^{q\times p}$, $\tilde{C} \in R^{p\times q}$, W and V are matrices for spanning the matrices.

$$\tilde{E} = W^{T}EV, \tilde{A} = W^{T}AV, \tilde{B} = W^{T}B, \tilde{C} = CV \tag{2}$$

However, the reduced models using Krylov methods retained the possibility of violating passivity, or even being unstable (Roychowdhury 2003).
LTI MOR may not be applicable for many functional blocks in mixed signal systems that are usually nonlinear. It is unable to model behaviors such as distortion and clipping in amplifiers. Therefore, LTV MOR is required. The detailed behavior of the system is described using time-varying differential equations as shown in (3):

$$\begin{aligned} E(t)\dot{x} &= A(t)x(t) + B(t)u(t) \\ y(t) &= C(t)^{T}x(t) + D(t)u(t) \end{aligned} \tag{3}$$

The dependence of A, B, C, D and E on t is able to capture time-variation in the system. This time-variation is periodic in some practical case such as in mixers, the local oscillator input is often a square waveform or a sine waveform, switched or clocked systems are driven by periodic clocks (Roychowdhury 2003).
Although LTV MOR may be used when modeling some weakly nonlinear systems, in most of cases nonlinear system techniques are required for such systems. A standard nonlinear system formation is based on a set of nonlinear differential-algebraic equations (DAEs) shown in (4), where, $x \in R^{n}$, n is the order of matrices, x(t) and y(t) indicate the vectors of circuit unknowns and outputs, u is the input, $q(\cdot)$ and $f(\cdot)$ are nonlinear vector functions, and b and c are input and output matrices, respectively.

$$\begin{aligned} \dot{q}(x(t)) &= f(x(t)) + bu(t) \\ y(t) &= c^{T}x(t) \end{aligned} \tag{4}$$

A polynomial approximation is simply extension of linearization, with f(x) and q(x) replaced by the first few terms of a Taylor series at the bias point x_0 as shown in (5), where q(x) = x (assumed for simplicity), $\otimes$ is the Kronecker tensor products operator, $A_i = \frac{1}{i!}\frac{\partial^i f}{\partial x^i}\Big|_{x=x_0} \in R^{n \times n^i}$. The utility of this system in (5) is that it becomes possible to leverage an existing body of knowledge on weakly polynomial differential equation systems.

$$\begin{aligned}&\frac{d}{dt}(x(t)) = f(x_0) + A_1(x - x_0) + A_2(x - x_0) \otimes (x - x_0) + \cdots A_i(x - x_0)^{(i)} + bu(t)\\&y(t) = c^T x(t)\end{aligned} \tag{5}$$

Volterra series theory (Schetzen 1980) and weakly nonlinear perturbation techniques (Nayfeh and Balachandran 1995) can then be used to justify a relaxation-like approach for this kind of systems. The former provides an elegant way to characterize weakly nonlinear systems in terms of nonlinear transfer functions (Volterra 2005). By using Volterra series, response x(t) in (5) can be expressed as a sum of responses at different orders, i.e., $x(t) = \sum_{n=1}^{\infty} x_n(t)$, x_n is the nth order response. The linearized first order through third order nonlinear responses in (5) need to be solved recursively using Volterra series as shown from (6) to (8), where $\overline{(x_1 \otimes x_2)} = \frac{1}{2}((x_1 \otimes x_2) + (x_2 \otimes x_1))$.

$$\frac{d}{dt}(x_1(t)) = A_1 x_1 + bu \tag{6}$$

$$\frac{d}{dt}(x_2(t)) = A_1 x_2 + A_2(x_1 \otimes x_1) - \frac{d}{dt}(x_1 \otimes x_1) \tag{7}$$

$$\frac{d}{dt}(x_3(t)) = A_1 x_3 + 2A_2\overline{(x_1 \otimes x_2)} + A_3(x_1 \otimes x_1 \otimes x_1) + \frac{d}{dt}(x_1 \otimes x_1 \otimes x_1) - 2\overline{(x_1 \otimes x_2)} \tag{8}$$

The nth-order response can be related to a Volterra kernel of order n, $h_n(\tau_1,...,\tau_n)$, which is an extension to the impulse response function of the LTI system exhibited in (9), to capture both nonlinearities and dynamics by convolution. Volterra kernels are the backbone of any Volterra series. They contain knowledge of a system's behavior, and predict the response of the system (Volterra 2005).

$$x_n(t) = \int_{\infty}^{\infty} \ldots \int_{\infty}^{\infty} h_n(\tau_1,\ldots,\tau_n) u(t-\tau_1)\ldots u(t-\tau_n) d\tau_1 \ldots d\tau_n \tag{9}$$

Alternatively, a variant that matches moments at multiple frequency points is shown in (10), where $h_n(\tau_1,...,\tau_n)$ is transformed into the frequency domain via Laplace transform.

$$H_n(s_1,\ldots,s_n) = \int_{-\infty}^{\infty} \ldots \int_{-\infty}^{\infty} h_n(\tau_1,\ldots,\tau_n) e^{-(s_1\tau_1 + \cdots + s_n\tau_n)} d\tau_1 \ldots d\tau_n \tag{10}$$

$H_n(s_1,\ldots,s_n)$ is referred to as the nonlinear transfer function of order n. The nth-order response, xn, can also be related to the input using $H_n(s_1,\ldots,s_n)$.
Unfortunately, the size of Volterra based nonlinear descriptions often increase dramatically with problem size. Li et al combines and extends Volterra and projection approaches using a method termed NORM (Nonlinear model Order Reduction Method) to reduce the model size (Li and Pileggi 2003).
Outside a relatively small range of validity, but polynomials are known to be extremely poor for global approximation (Roychowdhury 2004), so other methods such as piecewise approximation can be used to achieve better solutions. (Rewienski and White 2001) developed an approach termed trajectory piecewise-linear (TPWL) using a piecewise-linear (PWL) system. Initially Rewienski et al select a reasonable number of "centre points" along a simulation trajectory in the state space, which is generated by exciting the circuit with a representative training input. Around each centre point, system nonlinearities are approximated by implicitly defined linearization. A model is generated if the current state point x is 'close enough' to the last linearized point x_i, i.e., $\|x - x_i\| < \varepsilon$, which means that x lies within a circle of radius of ε and centred at x_i. Each of the linearized models takes the form shown in (11), with expansions around states $x_0, \ldots, x_{s-1}$: where x_0 is the initial state of the system and A_i are the Jacobians of f(.) evaluated at states x_i.

$$\frac{dx}{dt} = f(x_i) + A_i(x - x_i) + Bu \tag{11}$$

A Krylov subspace projection method is then used to reduce the complexity of the linear model within each piecewise region. Rewienski et al then combined all s linear models according to a weighting equation in (12), where $\tilde{w}_i(x)$ are weights depending on state x.

$$\frac{dx}{dt} = \sum_{i=0}^{s-1} \tilde{w}_i(x) f(x_i) + \sum_{i=0}^{s-1} \tilde{w}_i(x) A_i(x - x_i) + Bu \tag{12}$$

TPWL is more suitable for circuits with strong nonlinearities such as comparators, and has more advantages than PWL because as the dimension of the state-space in PWL grows one concern with these methods is a potential explosion in the number of regions which may severely limit simplicity of a small macromodel. However, Rewienski et al did not address the criterion of the training stimulus. Moreover, because PWL approximations do not capture higher-order derivative information, the ability of TPWL to reproduce small-signal distortion or intermodulation is limited. Therefore, Krylov-TBR TPWL was developed using TBR projection to obtain further order reduction (Vasilyev, Rewienski et al. 2003).
The piecewise polynomial (PWP) technique (Dong and Roychowdhury 2003), which is a combination of polynomial model reduction with the trajectory piecewise linear method, is able to improve TPWL by dividing the nonlinear state-space into different regions, each of which is fitted with a polynomial model around the centre expansion point. These points can be selected either from "training simulation" or from DC sweeps. The resulting macromodel is refined incrementally by new piecewise regions until a desired accuracy is reached. Firstly they expand a polynomial function into many points, each of them is then simplified by approximating the nonlinear function in each piecewise region to obtain much smaller size models. These models are then stitched together. Finally a scalar weight function is used to ensure fast and smooth switching from one region to another. A key advantage of PWP is that a macromodel generated can capture not only linear weakly

nonlinear (such as distortion and intermodulation) but also strongly nonlinear (such as clipping and slewing) system dynamics. Moreover, fidelity in large-swing and large-signal analysis can be retained. PWP is further implemented in (Dong and Roychowdhury 2004) for extracting broadly applicable general-purpose macromodels from SPICE netlists such that the generated model is able to capture different loading effects, simultaneous switching noise (SSN), crosstalk noise and so on. Furthermore, a speed up of eight times simulation speed is achieved (Dong and Roychowdhury 2005). However, multiple training data has to be used to cover different operating regions.

Xia et al (Xia, Bell et al. 2010) developed an algorithm to generate multiple macromodels automatically to perform HLFM and high level modeling (HLM). Moreover, the models generated contain low-orders (2nd), so MOR is not required. More details on the approach will be discussed in section 3.

3. The multiple model generation approach using MATLAB

3.1 Introduction to least square estimate

Linear models can be obtained using recursive least square (RLS) estimation. It is a mathematical procedure for finding the best-fitting curve to a given set of points by minimizing the sum of the squares of the offsets of the points from the curve (Ljung 1999). Its general process is shown in Fig. 3, where u(t) is the input stimulus, which is used to connect both a system and the estimator; y(t) is the output response from a system using the transistor level simulation (TLS); $y_E(t)$ is the output response using an estimation approach such as the RLS.

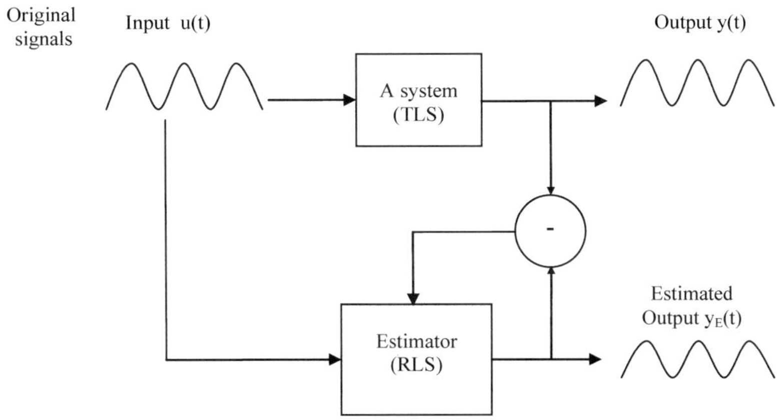

Fig. 3. General process of the estimation

Both the system and estimator use the input stimulus to produce individual output response, which are then compared, if the difference is significant, the parameters of the model need to be modified in order to reduce difference.

Wilkinson et al (Wilkinson, Roberts et al. 1991) combined RLS estimation with the delta operator (Middleton and Goodwin 1990) to obtain the transfer function of a real time controller for a servo motor system instead of using discrete-time transfer function because that model coefficients in discrete-time models strongly depend on the sampling rate, which result in aliasing and slow simulation time. By using the delta operator the coefficients produced relate to physical quantities, as in the continuous-time domain model, but are less susceptible to the choice of sampling interval (Wilkinson, Roberts et al. 1991). Initially a discrete-time system is given in (13):

$$y(t) = -a_1 y(t-1) - a_2 y(t-2) - \ldots a_{na} y(t-na) + b_1 u(t-1) + b_2 u(t-2) + \ldots b_{nb} u(t-nb) \quad (13)$$

A linear regression form of the system is shown in (14):

$$y(t) = \varphi^T(t)\theta \quad (14)$$

where θ is the parameter vector shown in (15), φ(t) is the regression vector displayed in (16).

$$\theta = \left[a_1\, a_2 \ldots a_{na}\, b_1\, b_2 \ldots b_{nb}\right]^T \quad (15)$$

$$\varphi^T(t) = [-y(t-1)\ldots - y(t-na) \quad u(t-1)\ldots u(t-nb)] \quad (16)$$

The least square estimate (LSE) of the parameter vector can be found from measurements of u(t) and y(t) using (17) (Ljung 1999):

$$\theta(t) = \left[\frac{1}{N}\sum_{t=1}^{N}\varphi(t)\varphi^T(t)\right]^{-1}\left[\frac{1}{N}\sum_{t=1}^{N}\varphi(t)y(t)\right] \quad (17)$$

Its recursive form is expressed in (18), where ε(t) is the prediction error, λ(t) represents forgetting factor (ff), P(t) indicates covariance matrix, and L(t) is the gain vector.

$$\begin{aligned}
\theta(t) &= \theta(t-1) + L(t)\varepsilon(t) \\
\varepsilon(t) &= y(t) - \varphi^T(t)\theta(t-1) \\
L(t) &= \frac{P(t-1)\varphi(t)}{\lambda(t) + \varphi^T(t)P(t-1)\varphi(t)} \\
P(t) &= \frac{1}{\lambda(t)}\left[P(t-1) - \frac{P(t-1)\varphi(t)\varphi^T(t)P(t-1)}{\lambda(t) + \varphi^T(t)P(t-1)\varphi(t)}\right]
\end{aligned} \quad (18)$$

The linear regression is then restructured using the delta operator as shown in (19) (Middleton and Goodwin 1990), where δ represents delta, q is the forward shift operator and Ts is the sampling interval. The relationship between δ and q is a simple linear function, so δ can offer the same flexibility in the modeling of discrete-time systems as q does.

$$\delta = \frac{q-1}{Ts} \quad (19)$$

This operator behaves as a form of the forward-difference formula, as shown in (20) (Burden and Faires 1985). This is used extensively in numerical analysis for computing the derivative of a function at a point.

$$f'(x) = \frac{f(x+h) - f(x)}{h} \quad (20)$$

The delta operator makes use of the discrete incremental difference (or delta) operator that whilst operating on discrete data samples, is similar to those of the continuous-time Laplace operator. A better correspondence can be obtained between continuous and discrete time if the shift operator is replaced by a difference operator that is more like a derivative (Middleton and Goodwin 1990).
A similar procedure is used to achieve regression based on the delta operator. This starts by considering a continuous time transfer function shown in (21).

$$G(s) = \frac{b_0 s^n + b_1 s^{n-1} + \dots b_n s^0}{s^m + a_1 s^{m-1} + \dots a_m s^0} \tag{21}$$

When Ts is sufficiently short, the continuous time transfer function G(s) is equal to the delta transfer function G(δ) (Middleton and Goodwin 1990) displayed in (22).

$$G(\delta) = \frac{y(t)}{u(t)} = \frac{b_0 \delta^n + b_1 \delta^{n-1} + \dots b_n \delta^0}{\delta^m + a_1 \delta^{m-1} + \dots a_m \delta^0} \tag{22}$$

After arranging this, equation (23) is obtained:

$$y(t)\delta^m = -(a_1 \delta^{m-1} + \dots + a_m) y(t) + (b_0 \delta^n + \dots + b_n) u(t) \tag{23}$$

This can be written as (24) (Middleton and Goodwin 1990), which is similar to (14):

$$\delta^m y(t) = \varphi^T(t)\theta \tag{24}$$

where

$$\theta = \left[a_1\, a_2 \dots a_m\, b_0\, b_1 \dots b_n\right]^T$$

$$\varphi^T(t) = [-\delta^{m-1} y(t) \dots - \delta^0 y(t) \quad \delta^n u(t) \dots \delta^0 u(t)]$$

Using a similar approach to LSE in the discrete-time transform, the parameter vector is obtained using the delta operator in (25):

$$\theta(t) = \left[\frac{1}{N}\sum_{t=1}^{N} \varphi(t)\varphi^T(t)\right]^{-1} \left[\frac{1}{N}\sum_{t=1}^{N} \varphi(t)\delta^m y(t)\right] \tag{25}$$

RLS is also obtained in (26), as shown that it is similar to equation (18), the difference is that the vectors including θ, ε, y have been deltarised.

$$\begin{aligned}
\theta(t) &= \theta(t-1) + L(t)\varepsilon(t) \\
\varepsilon(t) &= \delta^m y(t) - \varphi^T(t)\theta(t-1) \\
L(t) &= \frac{P(t-1)\varphi(t)}{\lambda(t) + \varphi^T(t)P(t-1)\varphi(t)} \\
P(t) &= \frac{1}{\lambda(t)}\left[P(t-1) - \frac{P(t-1)\varphi(t)\varphi^T(t)P(t-1)}{\lambda(t) + \varphi^T(t)P(t-1)\varphi(t)}\right]
\end{aligned} \tag{26}$$

However, the approach in (Wilkinson, Roberts et al. 1991) is only available to single-input single-output (SISO) systems.

3.2 System development using delta transfer function

In this section a novel AMG approach named multiple model gradation system using delta transfer operator (MMGSD) is developed. The concept of process is shown in Fig. 4. The MMGSD generates macromodels by observing the variation in output voltage error against input range. The advantage is that the estimated signal can be adjusted recursively in time to handle nonlinearity. It consists of two parts: the automated model estimator (AME) and automated model predictor (AMP). The AME implements the model generation algorithm, and the AMP uses these models from AME to predict signals in the simulation with different types of stimuli. The system is based on a set of models n. The location of each model is decided by the thresholds seen in u(t).

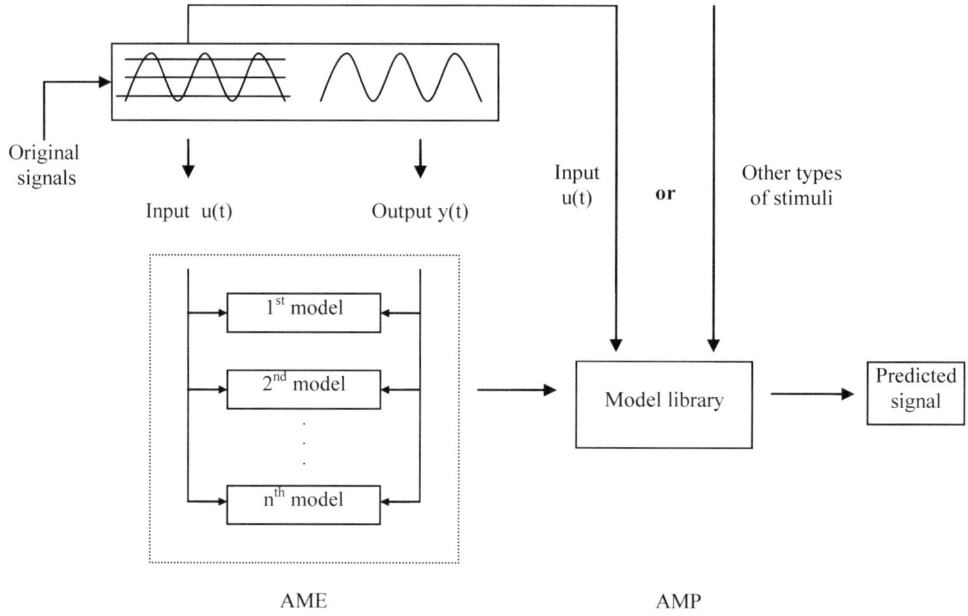

Fig. 4. Schematics for the procedure of MMGSD

The AME comprises three stages: the pre-analysis, estimator and post-analysis. The general structure is shown in Fig. 5.

Pre-analysis is mainly to set up conditions such as input range and the number of intervals for model creation and is only performed once; the estimator is used to determine the quality of output data; post-analysis is the critical step because procedures for creating models are implemented here. This process terminates when no new model is created.

Pre-analysis is mainly to set up conditions such as input range. In the whole algorithm, this stage is only run once. The Estimator process starts by running through all samples using the *for* loop in MATLAB. The indices for creating the threshold are found with a *find* statement. A statement *min* is used to guarantee that only the smallest index is selected, and then the new model pointed by this index is generated. Parameters (th) and the covariance matrix (p) in each model need to be created and updated. The innovation error (epsi) and residual error (epsilon) are all calculated. Moreover, the prefilter needs also to be updated. The estimation is not over until all samples finish (Ljung 1999).

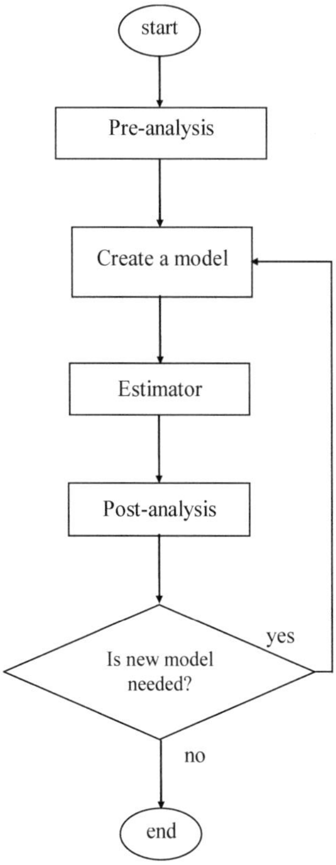

Fig. 5. The flowchart for the AME

Post-analysis is the critical step because procedures for creating models are run here. The workflow is described in Fig. 6. The decision to add a new model to an interval of input voltage is based on (27), where mediumRange is half of the difference between the maximum amplitude of the error (highInterval) and the minimum amplitude of the error (lowInterval) for the interval. criticalRange is the equivalent summation. criteria calculated for the interval results from the comparison of these measures and that of the central interval of the simulation (mediumRange(central)).

$$\begin{aligned} &mediumRange = (highInterval - lowInterval)/2 \\ &criticalRange = (highInterval + lowInterval)/2 \\ &criteria = [mediumRange - mediumRange(central)] - criticalRange \end{aligned} \tag{27}$$

If the difference between two mediumRange is greater than the criticalRange, one model is added within the jth interval (if there are j intervals), otherwise no action is taken. If j is greater than a central point, the threshold will be set at the lower range, otherwise it is set at the higher range in order to obtain the position close to the central point. In order to increase

simulation speed a shift mechanism is used to delete equivalent models. Finally the new threshold array is sorted into monotonic order. Only one model is created per iteration, because the error profile is recalculated whenever a model is added.
The AMP is used to verify the AME system. It loads models generated by the AME to predict output responses.

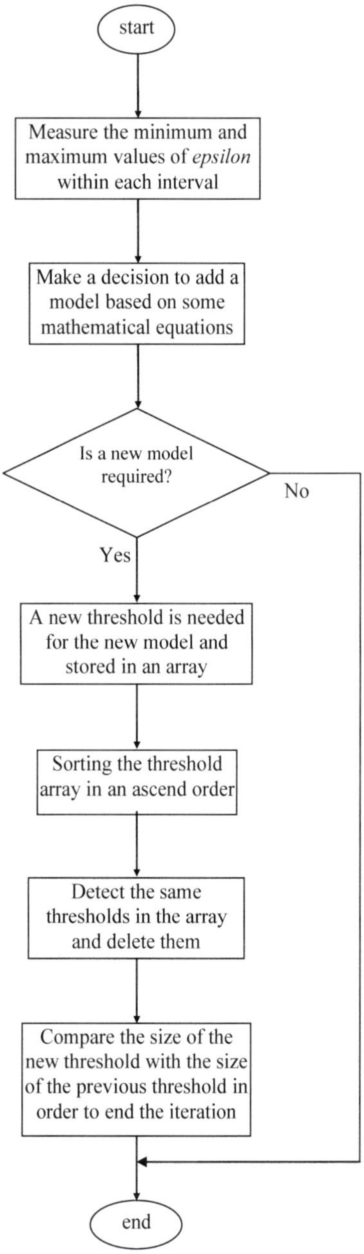

Fig. 6. The algorithm for post-analysis

The model structure is based on the RARMAX system (Ljung 1999) but with modification since RARMAX is under the discrete-time transform, whereas the MMGSD is based on delta transform. Therefore, during simulation (estimation) some quantities in the system need to be either deltarised or undeltarised, for example, the residual error epsilon in the AME and AMP is already deltarised, but during the vector update the undeltarised value is required. Therefore, we create two functions in the MMGSD: the Deltarise function and Undeltarise function. The former is to generate derivative vectors based on original vectors. The undeltarise function requires original data during the estimation. These two functions are used in different places in the MMGSD.

3.2.1 The deltarise function

The deltarise function is used to find the deltarised value using the delta operator given in (28), where delta (δ) is related to both the present and future values, Ts is the sampling rate, q is the forward shift operator used to describe discrete models, which is shown in (29).

$$\delta = \frac{q-1}{T_s} \cong \frac{d}{dt} \tag{28}$$

$$qx_k = x_{k+1} \tag{29}$$

The equivalent form of (29) is obtained in (30), the relationship between δ and q is a simple linear function, so δ can offer the same flexibility in the modeling of discrete-time systems as q does.

$$\delta x_k = \frac{x_{k+1} - x_k}{T_s} = \frac{x(kT_s + T_s) - x(kT_s)}{T_s} \cong \frac{dx}{dt} \tag{30}$$

The use of delta operator and its relationship is illustrated in the following example. It is a discrete-time model, but only output vectors are displayed in (31(a)). Initially each vector is subtracted from the one next to it, as seen in (31(b)), and is then divided by Ts, so deltarised value is obtained, as seen in (31(c)). However, the last one highlighted by the rectangle is not involved in the calculation.

$$y(t) \quad y(t-1) \quad y(t-2) \quad \boxed{y(t-3)} \tag{31(a)}$$

$$y(t-1) \quad y(t-2) \quad y(t-3) \tag{31(b)}$$

$$\delta y(t-1) \quad \delta y(t-2) \quad \boxed{\delta y(t-3)} \tag{31(c)}$$

$$\delta y(t-2) \quad \delta y(t-3) \tag{31(d)}$$

To achieve $\delta^2 y(t-3)$, equation (31(c)) is subtracted from (31(d)), and then divided by Ts. The procedure is used to obtain $\delta^3 y(t-3)$ seen in (31(g)).

$$\delta^2 y(t-2) \quad \boxed{\delta^2 y(t-3)} \tag{31(e)}$$

$$\delta^2 y(t-3) \tag{31(f)}$$

$$\delta^3 y(t-3) \tag{31(g)}$$

Thus, the deltarised version of (31(a)) is obtained shown in (32).

$$\delta^3 y(t-3)\ \ \delta^2 y(t-3)\ \ \delta^1 y(t-3)\ \ \delta^0 y(t-3) \tag{32}$$

The same procedure is also used for other vectors such as the inputs vectors u, e and the noise vector c. Delay is not included here. However, there is some difference such that in the input vector the current deltarised values (u(t), v(t)) are not required.

3.2.2 The undeltarise function

This function is based on (28) but with the modification, q = δTs+1, in order to model at the current time. An example is also used to demonstrate how this reverse algorithm works. It is a model in delta transform, but only the output vectors y are shown in (33(a)). Firstly each vector, except for the last one, highlighted by the rectangle because it is already undeltarised, is multiplied by Ts in (33(b)). We then add the output vectors as shown in (33(b)) and (33(c)), so undeltarised vectors are obtained in (33(d)), i.e., y(t-2) is obtained.

$$\delta^3 \mathrm{y}(\mathrm{t}-3)\ \ \delta^2 \mathrm{y}(\mathrm{t}-3)\ \ \delta^1 \mathrm{y}(\mathrm{t}-3)\ \ \boxed{\delta^0 \mathrm{y}(\mathrm{t}-3)} \tag{33(a)}$$

$$\mathrm{T_s}\delta^3 \mathrm{y}(\mathrm{t}-3)\ \ \mathrm{T_s}\delta^2 \mathrm{y}(\mathrm{t}-3)\ \ \mathrm{T_s}\delta^1 \mathrm{y}(\mathrm{t}-3) \tag{33(b)}$$

$$+\qquad\qquad +\qquad\qquad +$$

$$\delta^2 \mathrm{y}(\mathrm{t}-3)\qquad \delta^1 \mathrm{y}(\mathrm{t}-3)\qquad \delta^0 \mathrm{y}(\mathrm{t}-3) \tag{33(c)}$$

$$\|\qquad\qquad \|\qquad\qquad \|$$

$$\delta^2 \mathrm{y}(\mathrm{t}-2)\qquad \delta^1 \mathrm{y}(\mathrm{t}-2)\qquad \boxed{\mathrm{y}(\mathrm{t}-2)} \tag{33(d)}$$

To achieve y(t-1), equation (33(d)) is multiplied by Ts, and then we add the vectors shown in (33(e))- (33(g)).

$$\mathrm{T_s}\delta^2 \mathrm{y}(\mathrm{t}-2)\ \ \mathrm{T_s}\delta^1 \mathrm{y}(\mathrm{t}-2) \tag{33(e)}$$

$$+\qquad\qquad +$$

$$\delta^1 \mathrm{y}(t-2)\qquad \delta^0 \mathrm{y}(t-2) \tag{33(f)}$$

$$\|\qquad\qquad \|$$

$$\delta^1 \mathrm{y}(\mathrm{t}-1)\qquad \boxed{\mathrm{y}(\mathrm{t}-1)} \tag{33(g)}$$

Finally y(t) is obtained using the same procedure as above.

$$T_s\delta^1 \mathrm{y}(t-1) \tag{33(h)}$$

$$+$$

$$\mathrm{y}(t-1) \tag{33(i)}$$

$$\|$$

$$\boxed{\mathrm{y}(t)} \tag{33(j)}$$

Therefore, the undeltarised version of (33(a)) is achieved shown in (34).

$$y(t) \quad y(t-1) \quad y(t-2) \quad y(t-3) \tag{34}$$

The number of iterations depends on a variable called *numb*, the reason to use the variable is that during undeltarising, vectors such as output vector need to be undeltarised once to obtain the value at next time, but during the prefilter update, it needs to be fully undeltarsied. If a full undeltarisation is required, the variable is set to 0, otherwise an integer is selected. If the number is greater than the size of the vector array an error message is produced.

3.2.3 Two functions utility in MMGSD

It is known that the delta operator is a very high gain system because of the sampling interval T_s (10us in this case), so it is important not to put a vector or a variable in the wrong place during the manipulation, otherwise, the whole process may numerically explode very quickly.

In this subsection some key modifications in the MMGSD based on the functions defined above are described in the following subsections.

3.2.3.1 The AME

In order to obtain the deltarised output data dy at current time and the deltarised vector array dphi, the vector array phi (φ) and the original output data y at current time are needed. The deltarise function is employed in (35).

$$dphi4y = deltarise([\mathrm{y}\ phi(iiia)],\ Ts) \tag{35}$$

where iiia indexes the array for the output vector in phi. Ts is the sampling interval, dphi4y is the deltarised vector array for output, in which the first element is dy, and all other elements are assigned to dphi(iiia).

Similarly input vectors u and e, and the noise vector c are deltarised values for dphi. However, their deltarised values at the current time are not required.

Secondly in the prefilter ztil in RML, the relationship between psi (ψ) and phi (φ) in z transform is expressed as: phi(t) = c(z)*psi(t), or phi(t) = psi(t)+$c_1$psi(t-1)+…+c_{nc}psi(t-n_c), where c is the polynomial coefficients [1, c_1, …, c_{nc}] for noises to improve the property of psi so that the estimator converges more reliable. It is seen that phi(t) is related to psi at both current and previous time. The relationship between psi and phi in delta (δ) transform is expressed as in (36), where the c polynomial is a deltarised version of the coefficients,

$$phi(t) = c(\delta) \cdot psi(t) \tag{36}$$

or its full expression in (37).

$$\delta^{nc-1}phi(t-nc) = \delta^{nc-1}psi(t-nc) + c_1\delta^{nc-2}psi(t-nc) + \ldots + c_{nc}psi(t-nc) \tag{37}$$

To achieve deltarised psi at current time, this equation is manipulated as shown in (38). It is a two-dimensional array, the number of rows is equal to the size of vectors in phi and the number of columns is equal to the number of terms in the c polynomial.

$$\delta^{nc-1}psi(t-nc) = \delta^{nc-1}phi(t-nc) - c_1\delta^{nc-2}psi(t-nc) - \ldots - c_{nc}psi(t-nc) \tag{38}$$

When using the z transform, (Ljung 1999) makes use of the fact that past values of psi and phi are readily available in the estimator, so that psi(t) can be obtained easily from available data vectors in the estimator. This is because the nature of the data does not change with storage position in the data vector. However, when using the delta transform $\delta^{nc-1}psi(t-nc)$ cannot be obtained using the same procedure, because samples in the data vector are different orders of δ. All these data vectors have to be refilled at each sampling interval.
The vectors in $\delta^{nc-1}psi(t-nc)$ are shown in (39), if, for example, the coefficients array nn is [3 4 2 1 4].

$$-\delta^2 y(t-3)\ldots-\delta^0 y(t-3),\delta^3 u(t-4)\ldots\delta^0 u(t-4),\delta^1\overline{\varepsilon}(t-2)\ \delta^0\overline{\varepsilon}(t-2),1,\delta^3 v(t-4)\ldots\delta^0 v(t-4) \quad (39)$$

$-\delta^2 y(t-3)\ldots-\delta^0 y(t-3)$ are obtained by deltarising $-y(t-1)\ldots-y(t-3)$ using deltarise function. The undeltarise function in 0 is also required to firstly fully undeltarise each row of dpsi at previous time to achieve the current time psi(t), e.g., $-y(t-1)\ldots-y(t-3)$ is achieved by fully undeltarising $-\delta^2 y(t-3)\ldots-\delta^0 y(t-3)$. The undeltarise function is employed again but only for a single iteration (*numb* = 1) to obtain dpsi the next time, so this matrix is shifted forward once. The last term (δ^0psi) in the array is then thrown away, so δ^1psi becomes δ^0psi and so on in order to add the new array in front and keep the algorithm consistent.
Finally the vector array phi is updated with the new estimation including the noise vector that is updated by residual error epsilon. We must keep in mind that depsilon is the deltarised version of epsilon, in this case we only have depsilon at current time, thus the undeltarise function is needed for epsilon, as shown in (40).

$$epsilon = undeltarise([depsilon\ dphi(iiic)], Ts, 0) \quad (40)$$

where *dphi(iiic)* includes noise vectors at previous time, *iiic* is the index array for noise vectors in *dphi*, Ts is the sampling rate, 0 indicates the full undeltarisation as has been discussed above.

3.2.3.1 The AMP

Similar to the AME both the deltarise and undeltarise functions are required through the system. Unlike the AME, the predicted value y is used for updating the vector array phi, whereas in the AME inputs u, e and output y are obtained from the training data.
To obtain the output data *y*, *dy* is fully undeltarised by employing the undeltarise function shown in (41):

$$y = undeltarise([dy\ -dphi(iiia)], Ts, 0) \quad (41)$$

where *dphi(iiia)* includes the previous deltarised output vector, *iiia* is the array for the outputs in *dphi*, Ts is the sampling rate, 0 indicates the full undeltarisation is utilized.

4. Results and discussions

In this subsection the MMGSD is evaluated based on two experiments. The data obtained from a two-stage CMOS operational amplifier (op amp) as shown in Fig. 7. The op amp is used in an open-loop configuration.

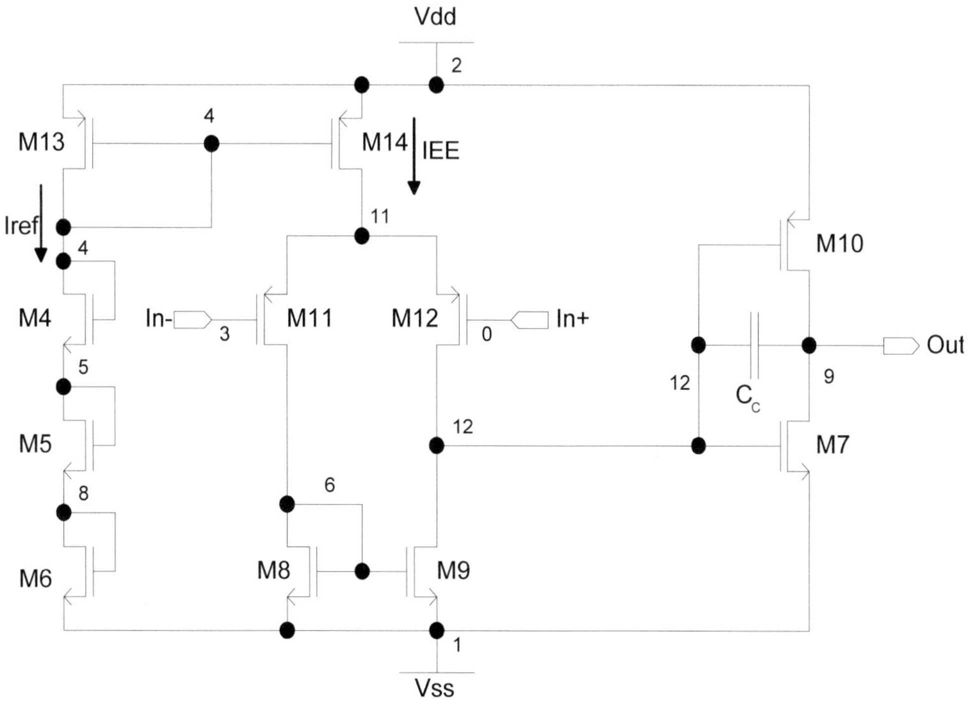

Fig. 7. Schematic of the two-stage CMOS operational amplifier

4.1 A single model detection

The aim of the experiment is to prove that it is able to hunt for known models and converges well. The process follows two steps:

1. The AMP system is applied to a known linear model. Both input data and output data are stored in a text file.
2. The AME generates the model based on these data.

The reason to work in the opposite way is that the AMP is less complicated than the AME and it is easier to find out whether or not the delta operator works well in the MMGSD. The system used in this example is a linear model given in (42).

$$V_o = \frac{-(20s+500)V_{in} + (10s+250)V_{ip} + 250V_{offset}}{s^2 + 20s + 500} \tag{42}$$

Two types of training data are generated from the PRBSG for the MISO AMP: one is a 0.6V, 50Hz square waveform with a 0.12V, 100kHz PRBS superimposed on it for the inverting input, a similar signal but with lower amplitude and frequency is applied to the noninverting input with 14,000 samples. Another training waveform is a 0.2V, 100Hz triangle waveform with a 0.05V, 100kHz PRBS superimposed on it for the inverting input, the second input is a similar signal but with lower amplitude and frequency for the noninverting input with 14,000 samples.

The AME is employed to generate the model seen in (43) with Ts of 10us. It is seen that two models can be matched referring to their coefficients.

$$V_o = \frac{-(20s+500)V_{in} + (10s+250)V_{ip} + 250.02V_{offset}}{s^2+20s+500} \tag{43}$$

4.2 High level fault modeling (HLFM)

In this subsection HLFM is performed to evaluate the models generated using AMG in MATLAB. The training stimulus is a 2.5V, 83.33Hz triangle waveform with a 0.5V, 100kHz PRBS superimposed on it and connects to the inverting input of the open-loop op amp. A similar signal but with lower amplitude and frequency is applied to the noninverting input. The MMGSD generated five models to cover both fault-free and faulty situations. The model thresholds were -2.5V, -1.5V -0.5V, 0.5, 1.5V and 2.5V and number of training samples used for these models were 2263, 2010, 2267, 2452 and 3048, respectively. The generated models are then used to perform a fault simulation of a circuit built from these op amps.

A standard quadratic low-pass filter, shown in Fig. 8, was used to investigate fault simulation with the generated model. The input signal was a 2.0V, 20Hz sinusoid. Transient analysis using SystemVision from Mentor Graphics results from 60ms to 200ms with a step of 0.1ms where used to compare output waveforms.

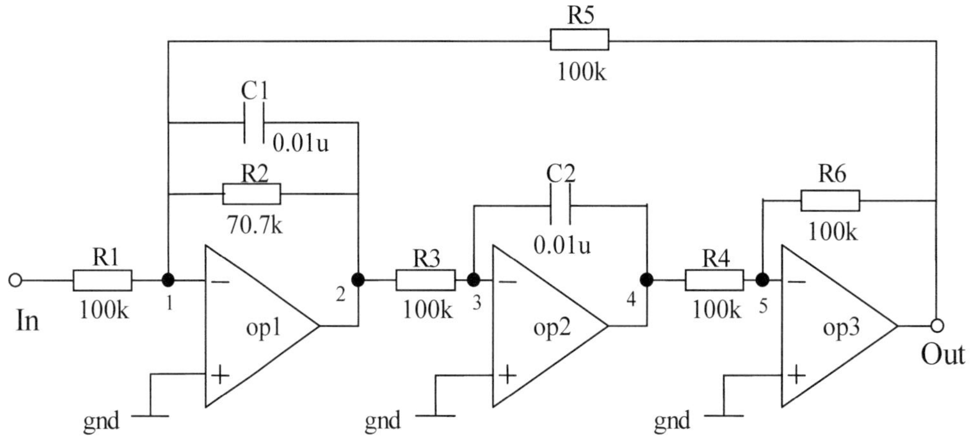

Fig. 8. The quadratic low-pass filter.

Simulation of fault M9_dss_1[1] is shown in Fig. 9. Again the signal becomes nonlinear compared with the fault free case and in this instance the TLFS and HLFS are well matched throughout. TLFS takes 1.297s to complete simulation, and HLFS requires 2.543s

5. Conclusion

In this chapter automated model generation (AMG) techniques using MATLAB were outlined. The models generated were able to generate either SISO or MISO models from transistor level SPICE simulations. They showed the advantage and ability to perform high level fault modeling (HLFM) with the reasonable accuracy compared with transistor level fault simulation (TLFS).

[1] short between drain and source on transistor 9 at op1

In section 1, various model structures were introduced, such as linear-time invariant (LTI) models, or nonlinear-time varying models.

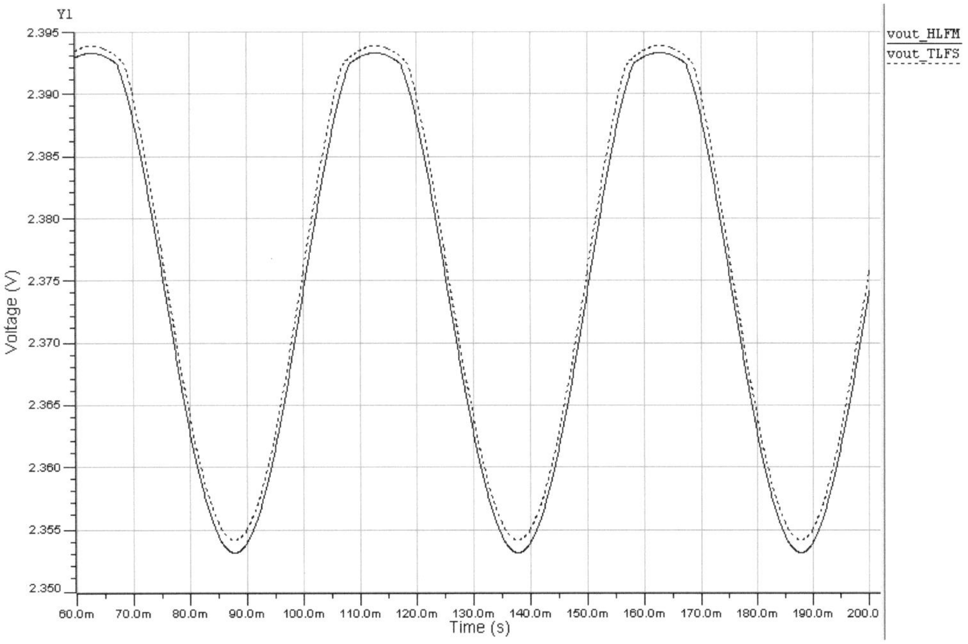

Fig. 9. The output signal from fault M9_dss_1

In section 2, various estimation methodologies were concluded, which consisted of regression, table lookup, neural networks and so on. Particularly regression approaches were focused in this case.

In section 3, an example of AMG termed multiple model generation system using delta operator (MMGSD) was introduced under MATLAB environment. We demonstrated how the delta operator was converted from the discrete-time operator, and how they could be used in the MMGSD.

In section 4, two experiments were implemented. The first one was to demonstrate that the MMGSD was capable of detecting an existing model accurately. The second experiment proved that it could handle the low-pass filter and model nonlinear behaviors accurately.

In summary, AMG approaches using MATLAB are efficient to support high level modeling and simulation, especially useful for high level fault modeling and simulation because of their accuracy.

6. Acknowledgment

The author would like to thank Universiti Teknologi PETRONAS for funding this project. The author wishes to give most special gratitude to his wonderful parents for their encouragement, tolerance and unconditional love during these years in China, United Kingdom and Malaysia. The author shows his appreciation to Miss Zahraa Osman for her contribution on the work. The authors also would like to thank Dr. Ian M. Bell and Dr.

Antony J. Wilkinson from Hull University, United Kingdom for their support and useful discussion throughout the work. And last but not least, the author wishes to thank his friends around of the world.

7. References

Breiman, L. (1996). "*Stacked Regressions.*" Machine Learning 24(1): 49-64.

Burden, R. and J. Faires (1985). *Numerical analysis*, Prindle, Weber & Schmidt.

Davalo, É. and P. Naïm (1991). *Neural networks*, Macmillan Education.

Dong, N. and J. Roychowdhury (2003). Piecewise polynomial nonlinear model reduction. *Design Automation Conference Proceedings:* 484-489.

Dong, N. and J. Roychowdhury (2004). Automated extraction of broadly applicable nonlinear analog macromodels from SPICE-level descriptions. *Proceedings of the IEEE Custom Integrated Circuits Conference (CICC2004)*: 117-120.

Dong, N. and J. Roychowdhury (2005). Automated nonlinear macromodeling of output buffers for high-speed digital applications. *Proceedings of the 42nd Design Automation Conference (DAC 2005)*: 51-56.

Feldmann, P. and R. W. Freund (1995). "Efficient linear circuit analysis by Pade approximation via the Lanczos process." *IEEE Transactions on Computer-Aided Design of Integrated Circuits and Systems* 14(5): 639-649.

Grimme, E. J. (1997). *Krylov Projection Methods for Model Reduction.* Electrical engineering department Urbana, Illinios, University Illinios. Doctor of philosophy

Hong, X., P. M. Sharkey, et al. (2003). "A robust nonlinear identification algorithm using PRESS statistic and forward regression." *IEEE Transactions on Neural Networks* 14(2): 454-458.

Li, P. and L. T. Pileggi (2003). NORM: compact model order reduction of weakly nonlinear systems. *Design Automation Conference Proceedings (DAC 2003):* 472-47.

Li, P. and L. T. Pileggi (2005). "Compact reduced-order modeling of weakly nonlinear analog and RF circuits." *IEEE Transactions on Computer-Aided Design of Integrated Circuits and Systems* 24(2): 184-203.

Ljung, L. (1999). *System identification: theory for the user*, Prentice Hall PTR.

McConaghy, T., T. Eeckelaert, et al. (2005). CAFFEINE: template-free symbolic model generation of analog circuits via canonical form functions and genetic programming. *Proceedings of Design, Automation and Test in Europe Conference* 2: 1082-1087.

McConaghy, T. and G. Gielen (2005). Analysis of simulation-driven numerical performance modeling techniques for application to analog circuit optimization. *IEEE International Symposium on Circuits and Systems (ISCAS 2005).* 2: 1298-1301

Middleton, R. H. and G. C. Goodwin (1990). Digital control and estimation: a unified approach, Prentice Hall.

Mutnury, B., M. Swaminathan, et al. (2003). Macro-modeling of non-linear I/O drivers using spline functions and finite time difference approximation. Electrical Performance of Electronic Packaging.

Nayfeh, A. H. and B. Balachandran (1995). *Applied nonlinear dynamics: analytical, computational, and experimental methods*, Wiley.

Phillips, J. R. (1998). Model reduction of time-varying linear systems using approximate multipoint Krylov-subspace projectors. *IEEE/ACM International Conference on Computer-Aided Design, ICCAD 98. Digest of Technical Papers.* Santa Clara, CA, USA: 96-102.

Pillage, L. T. and R. A. Rohrer (1990). "Asymptotic waveform evaluation for timing analysis." *IEEE Transactions on Computer-Aided Design of Integrated Circuits and Systems* 9(4): 352-366.

Rewienski, M. and J. White (2001). A trajectory piecewise-linear approach to model order reduction and fast simulation of nonlinear circuits and micromachined devices. *IEEE/ACM International Conference on Computer Aided Design (ICCAD 2001):* 252-257.

Roychowdhury, J. (1999). "Reduced-order modeling of time-varying systems." IEEE *Transactions on Circuits and Systems II: Analog and Digital Signal Processing* 46(10): 1273-1288.

Roychowdhury, J. (2003). Automated macromodel generation for electronic systems. *Proceedings of the 2003 International Workshop on Behavioral Modeling and Simulation (BMAS 2003)*: 11-16.

Roychowdhury, J. (2004). Algorithmic macromodeling methods for mixed-signal systems. *Proceedings of17th International Conference on VLSI Design (VLSID):* 141-147.

Schetzen, M. (1980). *The Volterra and Wiener theories of nonlinear systems*, Wiley.

Simeu, E. and S. Mir (2005). Parameter identification based diagnosis in linear and nonlinear mixed-signal systems. *11th International Mixed-Signals Testing Workshop*, France, TIMA laboratory

Uppal, F. J. and R. J. Patton (2005). "Neuro-fuzzy uncertainty de-coupling: a multiple-model paradigm for fault detection and isolation." *International Journal of Adaptive Control and Signal Processing* 19(4): 281-304.

Vasilyev, D., M. Rewienski, et al. (2003). A TBR-based trajectory piecewise-linear algorithm for generating accurate low-order models for nonlinear analog circuits and MEMS. *Proceedings of Design Automation Conference, (DAC 2003)*: 490-495.

Verbruggen, H. B. and R. Babuška (1999). *Fuzzy logic control: advances in applications,* World Scientific.

Volterra. (2005). "Volterra Series and Volterra Kernel." Retrieved 06/08, from http://ctas.east.asu.edu/chnam/ASE_Book/Volterra%20Theory.htm

Wilkinson, A. J., S. Roberts, et al. (1991). Real time plant monitoring using recursive identification. *Proceedings of COMADEM 91: The Third International Congress on Condition Monitoring and Diagnostic Engineering Management,* Southampton Institute, Adam Hilger.

Xia, L., I. M. Bell, et al. (2010). "Automated Model Generation Algorithm for High-Level Fault Modeling." *IEEE Transactions on Computer-Aided Design of Integrated Circuits and Systems (TCAD)* 29(7): 1140-1145.

Yang, B. and B. McGaughy (2004). An essentially non-oscillatory (ENO) high-order accurate adaptive table model for device modeling. *Proceedings of the 41st Design Automation Conference* (DAC 2003), San Diego, CA, USA 864-867
Zhang, Q. J. and K. C. Gupta (2000). *Neural networks for RF and microwave design*, Boston: Artech House.

18

A Matlab Genetic Programming Approach to Topographic Mesh Surface Generation

Katya Rodríguez V.[1] and Rosalva Mendoza R.[2]
[1]*National Autonomous University of México, Research in Applied Mathematics and Systems Institute;*
[2]*National Autonomous University of México, Engineering Institute;*
México

1. Introduction

The problem of surface approximation by means of soft mathematical functions is a relevant topic in Hydrology. The generation of these functions allows solving implicitly some of the most important calculation in order to predict the behavior of the hydrological basin. Thus, this work proposes the use of an Evolutionary Algorithm (EA) (Bäck, 1996) to generate 3-D mesh surface from a set of topographic data. In literature, there are only few existing works about the use of Evolutionary Algorithms (EAs) applied to the reconstruction of topographic surfaces, most of them are based on Genetic Algorithms (GAs) (Holland, 1975; Goldberg, 1989) as an approximation polynomial parameter estimator. Thus, this paper introduces a Genetic Programming (GP) approach whose aim is to obtain a mathematical function that allows a compact representation of the surface of the topographic information. This surface generation problem is then formulated as symbolic regression. The use of EAs, specifically GP (Koza, 1990; Banzhaf et al., 1998), constitute a promise alternative for the traditional interpolation techniques that employ approximation polynomials, due to GP integrates in a natural way the common non-linearities present in complex interpolation problems. This proposal is then applied to a set of topographic data corresponding to the Mezcalapa River zone, which is the local name of the Grijalva River located at the southeast of the Mexican Republic and it is one of the most important rivers due to its flow and generation of electric energy.

The GP algorithm is programmed in MATLAB® and the results produced by means of this GP approach give indication of a significant improvement in terms of the quality of the approximation in relation to the results obtained by means of approximation polynomials method applied to this region. In the following section a brief review of some works on mathematical modeling applied to Civil and Hydraulic Engineering are detailed. After that, description of genetic programming algorithm and its implementation in MATLAB are presented. The application of this evolutionary method to evolve mathematical models in order to construct topographic surface is presented. Finally results and conclusions are drawn.

2. Previous works

The literature related to the application of EAs to the problem of topographic surface generation is sparse. Some related papers, in terms of mathematical modeling, are the one by Fujiwara and Sawai (1999), where the use of EAs is proposed to optimize 3-D facial images. The problem is formulated as the selection of n points from a total set of N points that constitutes the original image; but, by selecting only n points ($n<N$), the image can be reconstructed with a good approximation to the original one.
Huang and Ho (2003) proposed a genetic algorithm again to select the n points where $n<N$ and N is the number of points of the original image in order to approximate a surface. In this work, a crossover operator named OAX (Orthogonal Arrays Crossover) was introduced. Kodoma et al (2005) proposed the use of hybrid algorithms by combining matrix-based representation genetic algorithm and a simulated annealing algorithm to reduce the computing time; however, performance presented by this hybrid algorithm and the original proposal based only on genetic algorithms are similar.
The work by Gálvez et al (2007) concerns to the problem of curve and surface fitting. They focus on the case of 3D point clouds fitted with Bézier curves and surfaces. Two Artificial Intelligence (AI) techniques are considered in this paper: the use of GAs and the functional networks scheme. Wagner et al (2007) present the ability of a state-of-the-art multi-objective EA to be successfully integrated in surface reconstruction software.
Goinski (2008) proposes a novel technique for surface reconstruction from a points cloud in 3D. The aim is to combine EAs with a recursive subdivision scheme. Paszkowicz (2009) reports recent use of GAs in various domains related to materials science, solid state physics and chemistry, crystallography, biology, and engineering. Shape and topology optimization is one of the applications reported in the field of engineering.
Periaux et al (2009) compare the performances of two different optimization techniques for solving inverse problems; the first one deals with the Hierarchical Asynchronous Parallel Evolutionary Algorithms software (HAPEA) and the second is implemented with a game strategy named Nash-EA.
In the context of GP, this has been used to solve symbolic regression problems. In Koza (1990), GP was used to generate a program to represent the colors of an image as a two dimensions array. Keller et al. (1999) proposed the use of GP to reconstruct surfaces of prototype pieces of industrial equipment. In this case, the objective is related to the works by Kodoma et al. (2005), Fujiwara and Sawai (1999) and Huang and Ho (2003).
The generation of mathematical function by means of symbolic regression has been widely studied in the GP field, as shown by the following papers by Keijzer (2003), Streeter and Becker (2001), Iba and Nikolaev (2001), Parasuraman et al (2007), Miller and Harding (2008), Baumes et al (2009), Barmpalexis et al (2011), among others. It seems that the representation of surface plays an important role in a variety of disciplines including aided-design, computer vision, graphic computation and geographical signal and image processing. Thus, evolutionary algorithms, in particular genetic programming, have been promising areas to these applications.
In the field of hydraulic engineering, the problem of approximating a soft mathematical function to a set of topographic data was considered (Mendoza et al., 1996). It required of getting an explicit mathematical expression and then the derivative of it in order to construct a model of coordinates curves adjusted to free surface. The problem was initially solved by representing the topographic elevation as a function of the dependent variables x-

y, which was approximated to a third order Taylor series (Arfken, 1980). Coefficients were adjusted by a Least Square Algorithm. Obtained results were, in general, acceptable. However, there were a significant number of points where the proposed method did not provide appropriate estimation (Mendoza et al., 1996). These points corresponded to regions of peaks and valleys surrounded by very different topographic points.

In order to improve the quality of the approximation, Mendoza (2002) proposed the use of algorithms belonging to the EAs field. As it is known, EAs are optimization techniques based on the concepts of natural selection and evolution. This work is then focused on the use of one of these evolutionary techniques, Genetic Programming (Banzhaf, et al., 1998).

In the present work, representing a topographic surface by means of a mathematical function is proposed and the problem is formulated as a symbolic regression using traditional genetic programming. A GP Toolbox for MATLAB is then developed and detailed in next sections.

3. Genetic programming

Nature has provided the inspiration for the design of computational algorithms in a variety of ways. These computational processes have taken two main natural systems as their basis that is the *brain* and the *genetic evolution theory*. EAs are one of these computational models and are proposed in this work for modelling topographic surface.

EAs, also known as Evolutionary Computation (EC), use computational models of evolutionary processes in the design and implementation of computer-based problem solving. A general definition and classification of these evolutionary techniques is given in Bäck (1996). He defines an EA as a search and optimisation algorithm, inspired by the process of natural evolution, which maintains a population of structures that evolve according to rules of selection and other operators such as recombination and mutation. Here, the structure of all evolution-based algorithms is shown in Figure 1.

The adaptive search algorithm called Genetic Programming (GP) was designed by Koza (1990). GP is an evolution-based search model that is a subclass of the popular GAs [Holland, 1975; Goldberg, 1989]. Koza introduced a more complex representation based on *computer programs*. Although finding algorithms or programs is more difficult than finding a single solution, it is more useful since generalised solutions work for an entire class of tasks.

```
PROGRAM Evolution-Based Algorithm
        t = 0
        Create Initial Population P(t)
        Evaluate Initial Population P(t)
        While (not termination_criterion) do
                t = t + 1
                Select Individuals for Reproduction P(t) from P(t-1)
                Alter P(t)
                Evaluate New Population P(t)
        end
```

Fig. 1. Evolution-based algorithm

To illustrate the hierarchical encoding used for GP, Figure 2 gives a simple example where the operations +, -, *, %, sin, cos, exp, sqrtp belong to the function set and the variables X and Y and the set of constants pi, 1, 2, 3, 4, and 5, constitute the terminal set. It is important to mention that division has been assigned the symbol "%"; this means protected division in order to avoid infinity results producing by operations like dividing by zero. It is also de case for square root operation where *sqrtp* function takes the absolute value of its argument. Note in Figure 2 that the parse tree is also equivalent to the prefix expression, as well as to the mathematical function and the MATLAB function.

Function_Set = [+, -, *, %, sin, cos, exp, sqrtp]
Arity_Set = [2, 2, 2, 2, 1, 1, 1, 1]
Terminal_Set = [X, Y, pi, 1, 2, 3, 4, 5]

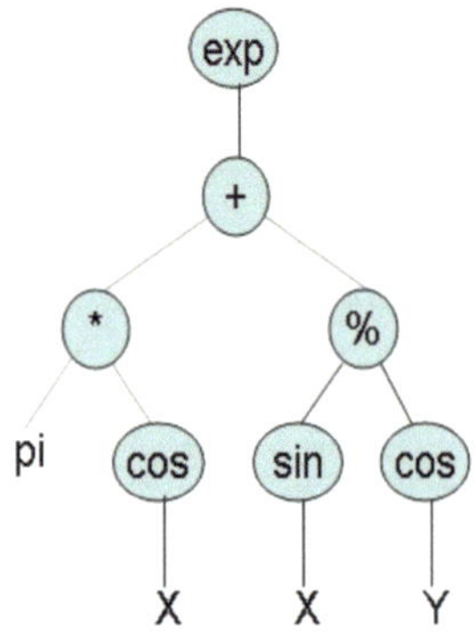

$$f = exp\left(\pi\, cos(X) + \frac{sin(X)}{cos(Y)}\right)$$

```
function  z = example(X,Y)

      z = exp(pi*cos(X)+(sin(x)/cos(y)));
```

(exp (+ (* pi (cos X)) (% (sin X) (cos Y))))

Fig. 2. A tree-based individual encoding and its equivalent representation in prefix notation, MATLAB program and mathematical function

3.1 Genetic programming operators

As for the conventional GA, reproduction and crossover are considered the main genetic operators, mutation being a secondary operator.

3.1.1 Reproduction

Reproduction in GP works in a similar way to that in a GA, being one of the foundations of the survival of the fittest. It is an asexual operator that selects an individual structure according to some selection method based on the fitness measures. The selected individual is then copied without any alteration to the new population.

3.1.2 Crossover

One of the main differences between GP and the traditional implementation of GA is the fact that GP crossover does not preserve any kind of context in the chromosome. This is due to the fact that the standard crossover defined by Koza (1990) exchanges subtrees which are chosen at random in both parents. Koza has pointed out that random subtree crossover maintains diversity in the population because crossing two identical structures, generally,

will create different offspring. This is because the crossover points are, in general, different in the two parents.
Crossover works by first selecting a pair of structures from the current population. Then, a node rooted from each parent is randomly selected. These nodes become the roots for the sub-structures lying below the crossover point. In the next step, the sub-structures are exchanged between the parents producing two new structures which are usually of different sizes to their parents. Figure 4 illustrates the crossover operation over a function set and terminal set defined as for Figure 2.
Note that for GP-crossover, the crossover point can be either a terminal or an internal point. If the crossover points in both parents are internal nodes, this means that function nodes are chosen as roots for the substructures to be exchanged. A second case of crossover occurs when a terminal node and an internal node, as the root of the substructure, are chosen in the first and second parents, respectively. When an internal node is selected, the number of arguments taken by the associated function must be considered in order to exchange a valid substructure.
A third case of crossover occurs when the crossover node is a terminal in both parents. In this case, the size and shape of the parents do not modify but the arguments of the two functions are swapped.

3.1.3 Mutation

Mutation is considered a secondary operator. It operates by randomly selecting a node, which can be either a terminal or internal point, and replacing the associated sub-structure with a randomly generated subtree up to a maximum size. A Maximum Mutation Size (MMS) parameter is introduced which is different from the maximum tree size parameter, MS.
In a conventional GA, the mutation operator introduces a certain degree of diversity into the population which is being beneficial. In contrast, the GP-crossover operation is the mechanism for diversification in the GP population. This fact is the justification given by Koza (1990) for using a 0% mutation probability. Hence, convergence of the population is unlikely in genetic programming.
Nevertheless, Angeline (1996) has described a set of mutation operators named: grow, shrink, cycle, switch and numerical terminal mutation. These mutation schemes are defined as follows:
Grow exchanges a randomly selected terminal point with a randomly generated subtree.
Shrink substitutes a selected subtree with a single terminal.
Cycle replaces a selected internal (a function) node by another function.
Switch selects two subtrees from the same parent and then switches their positions.
Numerical Terminal selects a single real-valued numerical (not a variable) terminal and adds to it Gaussian noise with a particular variance.

4. A GA toolbox for MATLAB

MATLAB is a high-level language and possesses a variety of already implemented functions, where problems can be easily coded in *m*-files. These facts make the programming of a GA in MATLAB an easy process.
The Genetic Algorithm Toolbox uses MATLAB matrix functions to build a set of routines for implementing a wide range of genetic algorithm methods (Chipperfield et al., 1994).

MATLAB essentially supports only one data type, a rectangular matrix of real or complex numeric elements. Thus, four data structures are defined for the implementation of the GA Toolbox developed by Chipperfield et al. (1994):

1. Chromosomes: It is a matrix of size *Nind*Lind*, where *Nind* is the population size and *Lind* is the length of the strings (rows of chromosomes) representing individuals.
2. Phenotypes: This data structure corresponds to the decision variables matrix and is obtained by applying a mapping process (decoding) from the chromosome representation into the decision variable space. Thus, this structure is a matrix of size *Nind*Nvar*, where *Nvar* is the number of variables that are encoding into chromosomes and each row corresponds to an individual's phenotype.
3. Objective Function: It is used to evaluate the performance of each individual (first chromosomes and after decoding phenotypes) of the population in the problem domain. This can be scalar (for mono-objective GA), or a matrix in the case of a multiobjective GA. Then, this data structure is a matrix of size *Nind*Nobj*, where *Nobj* is the number of objective (*Nobj*=1 for single objective problems).
4. Fitness Values: These are derived from the objective function by means of a fitness assignment function (scaling or ranking). Fitness values are defined in *Nind*1* matrix and are non-negative scalars.

5. GP structures in MATLAB

From Figure 2, it is seen that the parse-tree has an equivalent prefix notation (a LISP structure); thus, this codification is adopted in order to implement genetic programming in MATLAB. Then, a population is defined by a *Nind*Maxnodes* matrix whose content is initially zeros. By means of this encoding, the initial population matrix is:

$$pop = \begin{bmatrix} 0 & 0 & \cdots & 0 \\ 0 & 0 & \cdots & 0 \\ \vdots & \vdots & \ddots & \vdots \\ 0 & 0 & \cdots & 0 \end{bmatrix}$$

Then, random parse-trees are generated taking random values from the primitive sets. It is important to mention that the root node is always defined as a function node and the *arity* (number of input arguments of each function) is taking into account in order to generate syntactically valid structures. An example is presented as follows:

1. The root node has been randomly chosen from the function set. For this example, this function is *"exp"*.
2. This function takes one argument, thus another node is randomly selected from the function or terminal sets. Here, a function node was chosen ("+"); the *"exp"* function has its argument but the "+" function takes two arguments. Arguments for the "+" must be randomly selected.
3. This process continues until terminals are selected and the expression cannot increase its size and $(Nodes_{remain} < (Maxnodes - Nodes_{curr}))$, where $Nodes_{remain}$ means the nodes needed in the structure in order to produce a syntactically valid expression and $Nodes_{curr}$ is the number of nodes selected at the moment to conform an expression that is still incomplete. In the case where $(Nodes_{remain} = (Maxnodes - Nodes_{curr}))$, only terminal nodes are selected for a syntactically valid expression and the process concludes.

In Figure 3, it is then showed some parse-trees and their equivalent prefix notation into a population matrix.

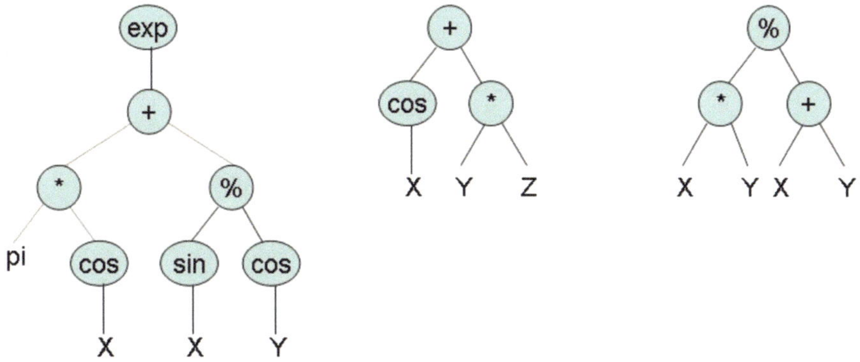

$$pop = \begin{bmatrix} exp & + & * & pi & \cos & X & \% & \sin & X & \cos & Y & 0 \\ + & \cos & X & * & Y & Z & 0 & 0 & 0 & 0 & 0 & 0 \\ \vdots & \vdots & \vdots & \vdots & \vdots & \vdots & \vdots & \vdots & \vdots & \vdots & & \vdots \\ \% & * & X & Y & + & X & Y & 0 & 0 & 0 & 0 & 0 \end{bmatrix}$$

Fig. 3. Initial GP population in MATLAB

But, in order to facilitate the use of MATLAB to manipulate matrix values of the same type, an identifier is considered for each primitive (function or terminal) as shown in Table 1.

Integer Indentifier	Primitive Value
1	+
2	-
3	*
4	%
5	exp
6	cos
7	sin
1000	random constant
1001	X
1002	Y
1003	Z
1004	pi

Table 1. ID for GP Primitive Sets

Then, matrix presented in Figure 3 is transformed to the following matrix:

$$pop = \begin{bmatrix} 5 & 1 & 3 & 1004 & 6 & 1001 & 4 & 7 & 1001 & 6 & 1002 & 0 \\ 1 & 6 & 1001 & 3 & 1002 & 1003 & 0 & 0 & 0 & 0 & 0 & 0 \\ \vdots & \vdots & \vdots & \vdots & \vdots & \vdots & \vdots & \vdots & \vdots & \vdots & & \vdots \\ 4 & 3 & 1001 & 1002 & 1 & 1001 & 1002 & 0 & 0 & 0 & 0 & 0 \end{bmatrix}$$

Genetic operators are applied on these prefix representations by selecting a random crossover node in the first parent in the interval [1, $MaxNodesPop_i$] and a random node in the second parent between [1, $MaxNodesPop_{i+1}$], where *MaxNodesPop* is a *Nind* column vector containing information related to the number of nodes of each individual into the population. This vector is updated each time crossover or mutation is performed. After that, associate expression to these selected nodes are taken and exchanged creating two new individuals.

In the case of mutation, again a node is randomly selected in the range [1, $MaxNodesPop_i$] and the syntactically valid associate sub-expression is eliminated and a new sub-expression is inserted. This is created from the primitive sets and using the routine of creating initial population.

If a new individual generated by means of crossover or mutation exceeds the allowed maximum size (maximum number of nodes), a new randomly selected node is taken in the range defined by the position of the previously selected node and $MaxNodePop_i$. This fact avoids that individuals grow rapidly causing bloat[1].

An example of crossover on the MATLAB GP representation is exemplified in Figure 4. Previous **pop** matrix is considered in this example. It is important to mention that the individual selection mechanism can be any method (roulette wheel, tournament, stochastic universal selection) and it is borrowed from the GA Toolbox, as well as the fitness assignment mechanism.

5.1 Function evaluation

In order to evaluate each individual into the population, a bottom-up parser must be constructed as a MATLAB function. Based on primitive set defined in Table 1 and the last individual of **pop** matrix from Figure 3, this program is evaluate as illustrated in Figure 5 considering that the variables X and Y take the following values $[-3, -2, -1, 0, 1, 2, 3]^T$ and $[0, 1, 2, 3, 4, 5, 6]^T$, respectively. The output of the evaluated individual (information at the root node) is a vector of size *Nx1*, where *N* is the number of data points, in this simple example *N* is equal 7. Thus, the objective function is defined as the minimization of the estimated mean quadratic error produced between the output of each program (individual) and the real values of the topographic elevation. This is expressed in the following equation:

$$f_i = \frac{1}{N} \sum_{j=1}^{N} \left| z_j - z'_{ij} \right|^2$$

where f_i is the objective value of the *i-th* individual, z is the vector of measured topographic elevations, z' is the vector of estimated topographic elevations for N recorded coordinates. The objective value is scalar and the fitness assignment mechanism described in Chipperfield et al. (1994) can be straightforward applied. Observe that for the GP Toolbox

---

[1] Bloat is the rapid growth of programs produced by genetic programming.

only three data structures must be defined: **pop**, a *Nind*MaxNodes* matrix; **objective value**, a *Nind* column vector; and a **fitness value**, a *Nind* column vector.

$$pop = \begin{bmatrix} 5 & 1 & 3 & 1004 & 6 & 1001 & 4 & 7 & 1001 & 6 & 1002 & 0 \\ 1 & 6 & 1001 & 3 & 1002 & 1003 & 0 & 0 & 0 & 0 & 0 & 0 \\ \vdots & \vdots & \vdots & \vdots & \vdots & \vdots & \vdots & \vdots & \vdots & \vdots & & \vdots \\ 4 & 3 & 1001 & 1002 & 1 & 1001 & 1002 & 0 & 0 & 0 & 0 & 0 \end{bmatrix}$$

$$pop = \begin{bmatrix} 5 & 1 & 1002 & 4 & 7 & 1001 & 6 & 1002 & 0 & 0 & 0 & 0 \\ 1 & 6 & 1001 & 3 & 1002 & 1003 & 0 & 0 & 0 & 0 & 0 & 0 \\ \vdots & \vdots & \vdots & \vdots & \vdots & \vdots & \vdots & \vdots & \vdots & \vdots & & \vdots \\ 4 & 3 & 1001 & 3 & 1004 & 6 & 1001 & 1 & 1002 & 1002 & 0 & 0 \end{bmatrix}$$

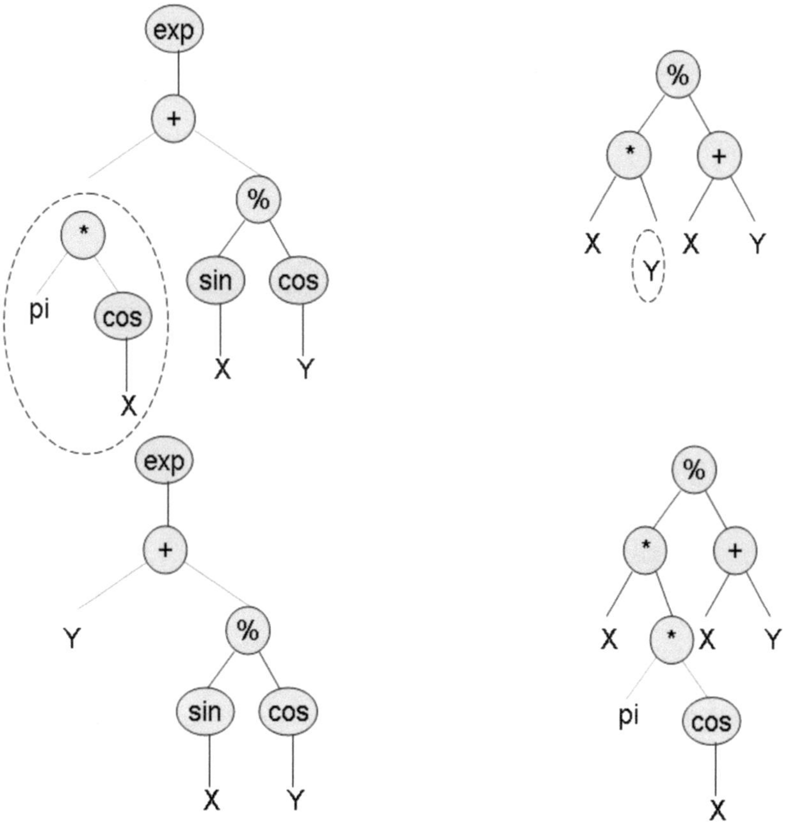

Fig. 4. GP toolbox crossover mechanism

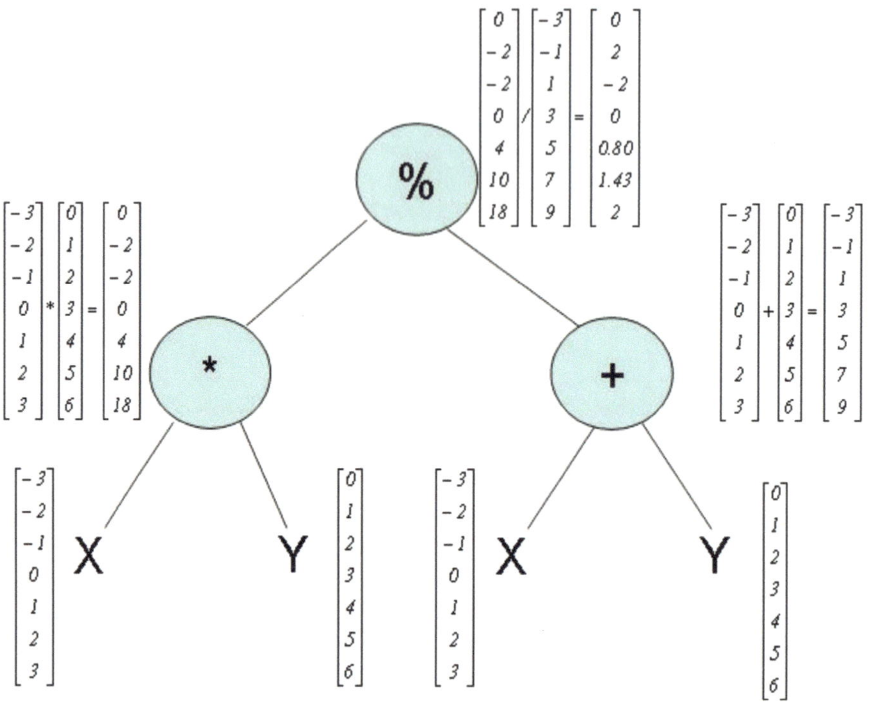

Fig. 5. A bottom-up parser to evaluate GP individuals

6. Estimation of topographic surface by means of GP toolbox in MATLAB

In this section, the MATLAB GP toolbox is applied to model and estimate the topographic elevation of the region shown in Figure 6. The number of available topographic data was 1600 points corresponding to the Mezcalapa river zone located at the southeast of the Mexican Republic. In order to apply the evolutionary methods, the following considerations were taken into account:

a. The function set was composed of the four basic arithmetic operators, trigonometric functions (sine and cosine) and the square root *sqrt* function. Thus, the arity set was defined as {2, 2, 2, 2, 1, 1, 1}, the arithmetic functions take two input arguments and the remaining functions take one input argument.
b. The terminal set consisted of the independent variables (coordinates) x and y, and the ephemeral random constants in the range [-1, 1].
c. The termination criterion was set as the maximum number of generations.
d. In order to evaluate the performance of each individual into the population, estimate mean squared error between the topographic elevation obtained by the individual and the known elevation z was used.
e. The selection mechanism used in these experiments was tournament selection with tournament of size 3.
f. The population was composed of 100 individuals of a maximum size of 256 nodes.
g. Probabilities of crossover and mutation were set to 0.95 and 0.05, respectively.
h. Finally, ten independent runs were carried out for each sub-region.

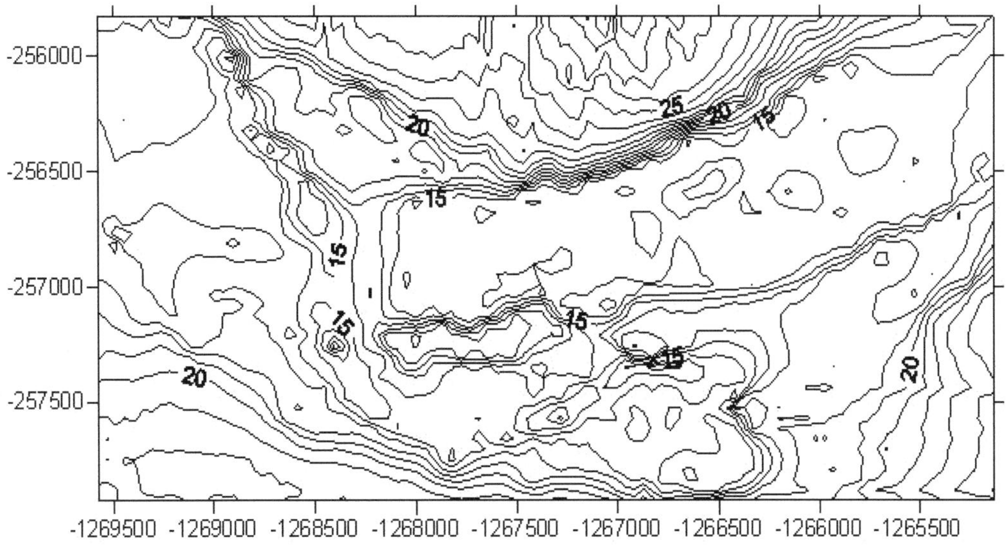

Fig. 6. Mezcalapa river zone, southeast of Mexican Republic

7. Results analysis

The strategy followed in order to reproduce the topography of The Mezcalapa fork River was to divide into ten regions the total area; each one of 160 triples of points with coordinates (x_i, y_i, z_i). In order to avoid numerical noise a constant value in x and y coordinates was added; then, the wireframe map of the total area is shown in Figure 7. Figure 8 shows a wireframe map of the same area reconstructed with the estimated values of the topographic level; comparing the results, they show that the map based on the estimated values is softer, reproduces well the peaks and the valleys but it does not reach the values they present.

The real topography is more rugged and steep; in general, the estimated values of the topographic height fall short in the values of the peaks and valleys, leading to smooth the values of these. Perhaps the most evidence of this softening is the upper right of the region, the real topography exhibits a series of peaks, which show vaguely in the topography generated with the estimated values. In general the border values are well reproduced, but the extreme internal values (peaks or valleys) are the ones with the information surrounding do not have a good estimate.

In general, when the estimate is good the calculated value is almost the same as the measured, however if the information does not help the estimation errors are large (over one meter) that future studies will try to improve.

The analysis of the results shows good estimations of the z values but there are some particular areas where it is necessary to refine the set of functions and terminals for better estimations of the value of the topographic level. The average error in the ten areas was 0.70 masl; the maximorum maximum value is in area 1 and is 4.4 masl; minimorum minimum value is in area 7 and it has a value of 0.0096 masl. Table 2 shows for each region, the average, the maximum and the minimum errors.

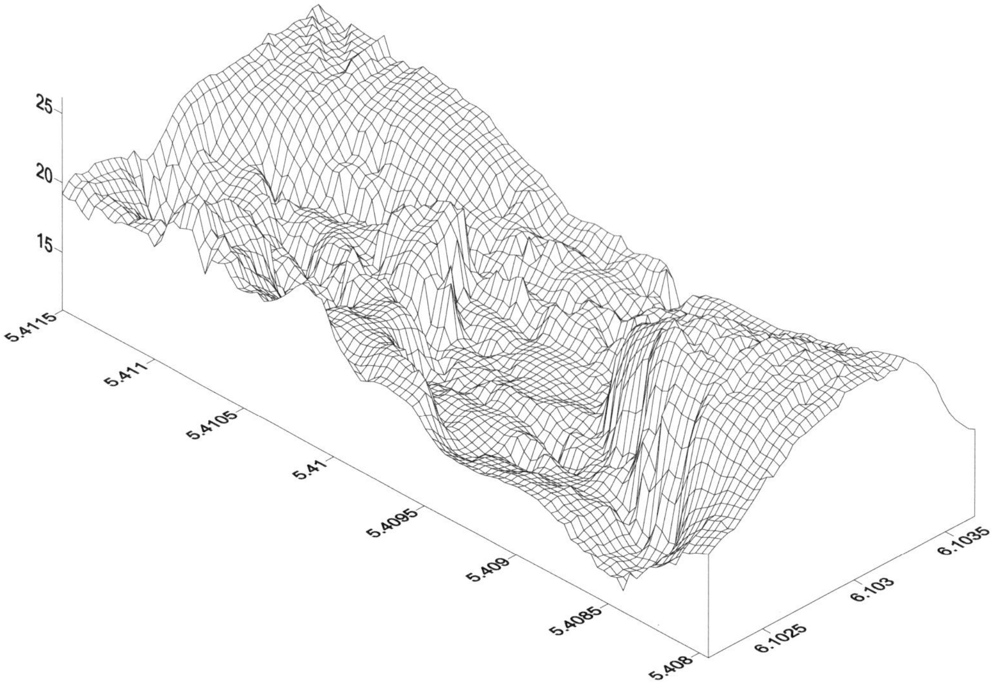

Fig. 7. Total region, real values of the topographic level

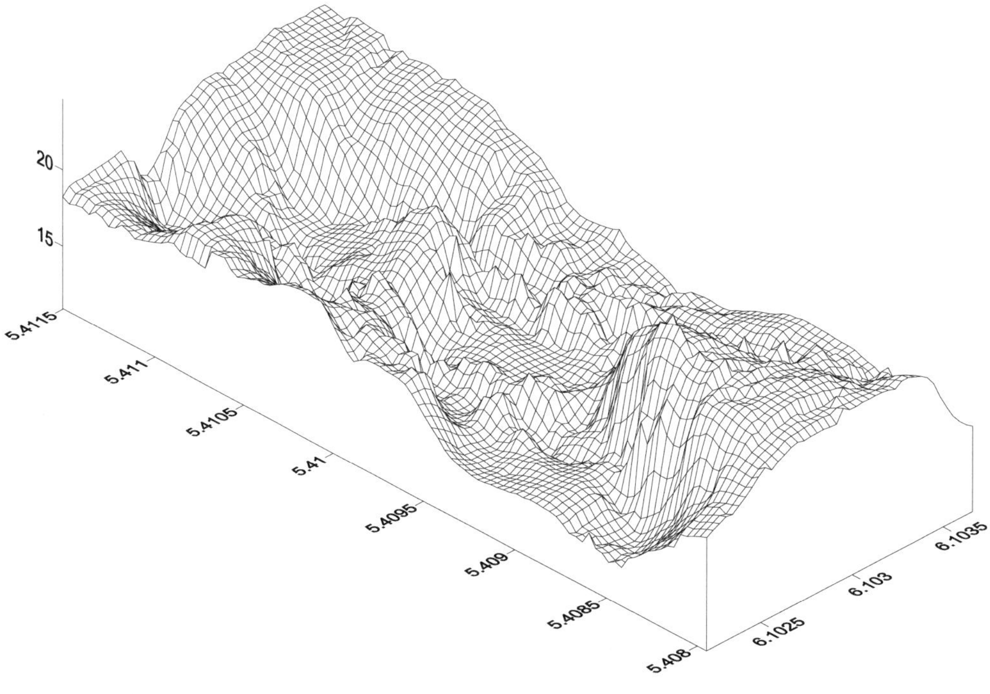

Fig. 8. Wireframe map, estimated values of the topographic level

Region	average error (masl)	max error (masl)	min error (masl)
1	0.64	4.39	0.0023
2	0.72	2.34	0.0014
3	0.68	2.92	0.012
4	0.74	3.26	0.033
5	0.83	2.87	0.0028
6	0.69	3.85	0.0042
7	0.71	3.68	0.00096
8	0.6	3.05	0.0013
9	0.69	2.83	0.0015
10	0.69	3.14	0.003

Table 2. Results for each region

Figure 9 shows the difference in absolute value between real *z* value and estimated *z* value. It can see that the vast majority of points are in the area where the error is less than 0.5 masl. However it is also showed that there are points where the estimation error exceeds the value of a meter, the latter leads to recommend a further study to refine the areas which have picks or valleys and normally these values are surrounded by information that does not provide much help for their estimation.

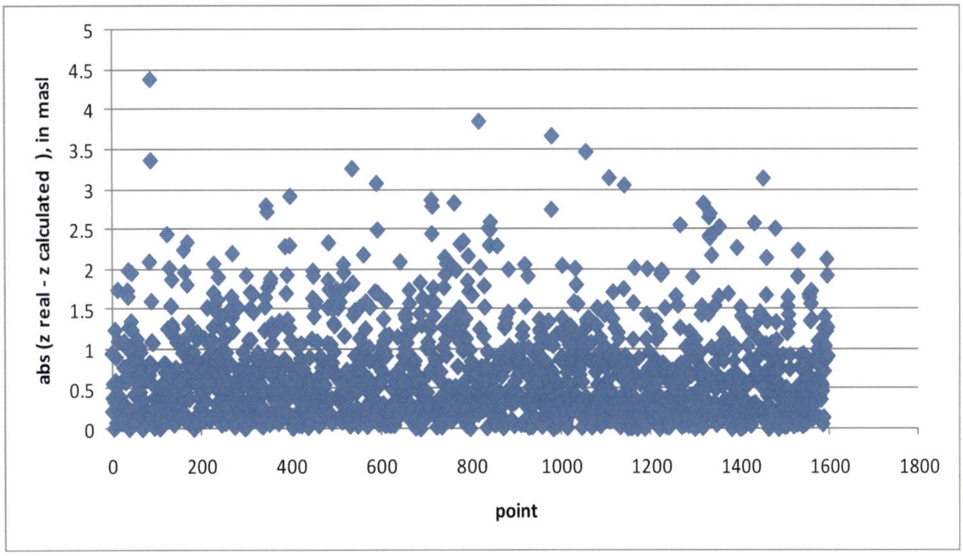

Fig. 9. Differences between real and estimated z values

8. Conclusions

In this work, a GP MATLAB Toolbox has been introduced exploiting the facilities that this interpreter offers. Individual trees are mapped into matrix where each row corresponds to an individual in prefix notation. This type of representation allows to exploit the MATLAB data type, rectangular matrix. Then, the GP Toolbox was applied to model topographic surfaces; the study region was, in this case the Mezcalapa fork river. Modeling problem was formulated as a symbolic regression and obtained results showed considerably good the reconstruction of the topographic surface. However, it is necessary to continue the study to refine the model's estimations in the areas in which the values of the peaks and valleys are not reached. In general, it reproduces well the topography but it can be improved by considering different function sets, genetic operators or more complex individuals in order to reduce the estimation errors since the standard GP was the one implemented in this work.

9. Aknowledgment

The authors wish to thank Dr. Abel A. Jiménez C, Researcher at the Engineering Institute, for providing the data set of Mezcalapa river for this study.

10. References

Angeline, P.J. (1996) An Investigation into the Sensitivity of Genetic Programming to the Frequency of Leaf Selection During Subtree Crossover. In *Proc. of the First Annual Conference on Genetic Programming*. MIT Press, pp. 21-29.

Arfken, G. (1980) *Métodos matemáticos para físicos*. Diana.

Bäck, T. (1996) Evolutionary Algorithms in Theory and Practice. Oxford University Press.

Banzhaf, W., P. Nordin, R.E. Keller and F.D. Francone (1998) Genetic Programming: An Introduction. Morgan Kaufmann Publishers.

Barmpalexis, K., K. Kachrimanis, A. Tsakonas and E. Georgarakis (2011) Symbolic Regression via Genetic Programming in the Optimization of a Controlled Release Pharmaceutical Formulation. *Chemometrics and Intelligent Laboratory Systems*. 107:1, pp. 75-82.

Baumes, L. A., A. Blansché, P. Serna, A. Tchougang, N. Lachinche, P. Collet and A. Corma (2009) Using Genetic Programming for an Advanced Performance Assessment of Industrially Relevant Heterogeneous Catalysts. *Journal of Materials and Manufacturing Processes*. 24:3, pp. 282-292.

Chipperfield, A., P.J. Fleming, H. Pohlheim and C.M. Fonseca. (1994) *Genetic Algorithm Toolbox User's Guide*. Research Report 512. Dept. Automatic Control and Systems Engineering, University of Sheffield, U.K.

Fujiwara, Y. and H. Sawai (1999) Evolutionary Computation Applied to Mesh Optimization of a 3-D Facial Image. *IEEE Transactions on Evolutionary Computation*. 32, pp. 113-123.

Gálvez, A., A. Iglesias, A. Cobo, J. Puig-Pey and J. Espinola (2007) Bézier Curve and Surface fitting of 3D Point Clouds Through Genetic Algorithms, Functional Networks and Least-Square Approximation. *ICCSA Proceedings of The 2007 International Conference on Computational Science and Its Applications. Lecture Notes in Computer Science*. 4706/2007. pp. 680-693.

Goinski, A. (2008) Evolutionary Surface Reconstructions. *Conference on Human System Interactions*. pp. 464-469.

Goldberg, D.E. (1989) *Genetic Algorithms in Search, Optimization and Machine Learning.* Addison-Wesley.

Holland, J. H. (1975) *Adaptation in Natural and Artificial Systems.* The University of Michigan Press.

Huang, H. L. and S. Y. Ho (2003) Mesh Optimization for Surface Approximation Using an Efficient Coarse-to-Fine Evolutionary Algorithm. *Pattern Recognition.* Elsevier Science. 36(5), pp. 1065-1081.

Iba, H. and N. Nikolaev (2000) Genetic Programming Polynomial Models of Financial Data Series. *Proc. Congress on Evolutionary Computation CEC 2000.* IEEE Press, pp. 1459-1466.

Keijzer, M. (2003) Improving Symbolic Regression with Interval Arithmetic and Linear Scaling. *6th European Conference on Genetic Programming EuroGP 200.* LNCS 2610. (Ryan *et al.*, Eds.). Springer-Verlag, pp. 70-82.

Keller, R.E., W. Banzhaf, J. Mehnen and K. Weinert (1999) CAD Surface Reconstruction from Digitized 3D Point Data with a Genetic Programming/Evolution Strategy Hybrid. *Advances in Genetic Programming 3,* (Spector *et al.*, Eds.), chapter 3. MIT Press., pp. 41-66.

Kodama, T., X. Li, K. Nakahira and D. Ito (2005) Evolutionary Computation Applied to the Reconstruction of 3-D Surface Topography in the SEM. *Journal of Electron Microscopy,* 54, Oxford University Press, pp. 429-435.

Koza, J.R. (1990) *Genetic Programming: A Paradigm for Genetically Breeding Populations of Computer Programs to Solve Problems.* Stanford University, Computer Science Dept. Technical Report STAN-CS-90-1314.

Mendoza, R., P. Alarcón and M. Berezowsky (1996) Cálculo del Campo de Velocidades en Cuerpos de Agua con Modelo Matemático Bidimensional en Coordenadas Curvilíneas Adaptables. *Informe Final Proyecto CONACYT 0641P-A9506,* Vol. 2, Instituto de Ingeniería, UNAM, México, D.F.

Mendoza, R. (2002) *Aplicación de la computación evolutiva en la estimación de cotas topográficas.* Tesis de maestría: Programa de Posgrado en Ciencia e Ingeniería de la Computación, Universidad Nacional Autónoma de México, México, D.F.

Miller, J. F. and S. L. Harding (2008) Cartesian Genetic Programming. *Proc. of the 11th Annual Conference Companion on Genetic and Evolutionary Computation Conference: Late Breaking Papers.* ACM, New York, NY, USA, p. 2701.

Parasuraman, K., A. Elshorbagy, S. K. Carey (2007) Modelling The Dynamic of The Evaporation Process using Genetic Programming. *Hydrological Sciences Journal.* 52:3. pp. 563-578.

Paszkowicz, w. (2009) Genetic Algorithms, a Nature-Inspired Tool: survey of Applications in Material Science and Related Fields. *Materials and Manufacturing Processes.* 24:2. pp. 174-197.

Periaux, J., D. S. Lee, L. F. González and K. Srinivas (2009) Fast Reconstruction of Aerodynamic Shapes Using Evolutionary Algorithms And Virtual Nash Strategies in a CFD Design Environment. *Journal of Computational and Applied Mathematics.* 232-1, pp. 61-71.

Streeter, M. and L.E. Becker (2001) Automated Discovery of Numerical Approximation Formulae Via Genetic Programming. *Proc. Genetic and Evolutionary Computation Conference GECCO 2001* (Spector *et al.*, editors). Morgan Kaufmann, pp. 147-154.

The Mathworks (1999) *Matlab Reference Guide*. The MathWorks Inc.

Wagner, T., T. Michelitsch and A. Sacharow (2007) On The Design of Optimisers for Surface Reconstruction. *Proc. of The 9th Annual Conference on Genetic and Evolutionary Computation (GECCO 2009)*. London, U.K., ACM, New York, pp. 2195-2202.

19

Matlab Solutions of Chaotic Fractional Order Circuits

Trzaska Zdzislaw W.
Warsaw University of Ecology and Management
Poland

1. Introduction

In the last two decades, integral and differential calculus of an arbitrary (or fractional) order has become a subject of great interest in different areas of physics, biology, economics and other sciences. It is accepted today as a new tool that extends the descriptive power of the conventional calculus, supporting mathematical models that, in many cases, describe more accurately the dynamic response of actual systems in various applications. While the theoretical and practical interest of these fractional order operators is nowadays well established, its applicability to science and engineering can be considered as an emerging topic. Among other, the need to numerically compute the fractional order derivatives and integrals arises frequently in many fields, especially in electronics, telecommunications, automatic control and digital signal processing.

The purpose of this chapter is to introduce the fractional calculus and its applications to solutions of fractional order circuits. Systematic methods and MATLAB-based computer routines are given. The next section provides a brief review of fractional calculus followed by useful approximations for these fractional operators (Section 2). In Section 3 we briefly present fundamental issues of the fractional order circuits in relation to nonlinear dynamical phenomena together with its fractional-order vector space representation - a generalization of the state space concept - and the modified Chua's circuit of fractional order as an example. Brief summary and conclusions follow in Section 4.

2. Fractional calculus

2.1 Fundamentals

The recent increased interest in the study of dynamic systems of non-integer orders (Baleanu et al., 2010, Caponeto et al., 2010, Das, 2008) stems from the premise that most of the processes associated with complex systems have non-local dynamics involving long-memory in time, and that fractional integral and fractional derivative operators share some of those characteristics. Many originally considered systems with lumped and/or distributed parameters can be more exactly described by fractional order systems (Dorčák et al. 2007; Kilbas et al., 2006; Monje et al., 2010; Nonnenmacher & Metzler, 2000; Sheu Long-Jye et al. 2007; Trzaska, 2010).

Extending derivatives and integrals from integer orders to non-integer orders has a firm and long standing theoretical foundation. For example, Leibniz mentioned this concept in a letter to L'Hospital over three hundred years ago and the earliest more or less systematic studies have been made in the beginning and middle of the 19th century by Liouville, Riemann and Holmgren. In the literature, people often use the term "*fractional* order (FO) calculus", or "*fractional* order dynamic system" where "*fractional*" actually means "*non-integer*" (Oldham, 1974; Petras, 2006; Podlubny, 1999; Tavazoei et al., 2008; Zhao & Xue, 2008).

The definitions most commonly used in the literature are the Riemann-Liouville definition, the Grünwald-Letnikov definition, and the Caputo definition, as given below:

$$ {}_aD_t^{\alpha}[f(t)] = \frac{1}{\Gamma(n-\alpha)}\left(\frac{d^n}{dt^n}\int_a^t \frac{f(\tau)}{(t-\tau)^{1-(n-\alpha)}}d\tau\right) \tag{1} $$

$$ {}_aD_t^{\alpha}\left[f(t)\right] = \lim_{h\to 0}\frac{1}{\Gamma(\alpha)h^{\alpha}}\sum_{k=0}^{\left\lceil \frac{t-a}{h}\right\rceil}\frac{\Gamma(\alpha+k)}{\Gamma(k+1)}f(t-kh) \tag{2} $$

$$ {}_aD_t^{\alpha}[f(t)] = \frac{1}{\Gamma(\alpha-n)}\int_a^t \frac{f^{(n)}(\tau)}{(t-\tau)^{\alpha-n+1}}d\tau \tag{3} $$

for $n-1 < a < n$ and where $\Gamma(\cdot)$ is the *Gamma* function, and $\lceil z \rceil$ means the integer part of z.

The "memory" effect of these operators is demonstrated by (1) and (2), where the convolution integral in (1) and the infinite series in (2) reveal the unlimited memory of these operators, ideal for modeling hereditary and memory properties in physical systems and materials. The initial conditions for the fractional order differential equations with the Caputo derivative (3) are of the same form as the initial conditions for the integer-order differential equations (Baleanu et al., 2010; Kilbas et al., 2006; Tavazoei & Haeri, 2008).

Two general properties of the fractional-order derivative are of major interest here. The first is the composition of fractional with integer-order derivative and the second is the property of linearity. Similar to integer-order differentiation, fractional-order differentiation fulfils the relations

$$ {}_aD_t^{\alpha}({}_aD_t^{\beta}f(t)) = {}_aD_t^{\alpha+\beta}f(t) - \sum_{k=0}^{n}[{}_aD_t^{\beta-k}]_{t=a}\frac{(t-a)^{-\alpha-k}}{\Gamma(1-\alpha-k)} \tag{4} $$

$$ {}_aD_t^{\alpha}[\eta f(t) + \lambda g(t)] = \eta[{}_aD_t^{\alpha}f(t)] + \lambda[{}_aD_t^{\alpha}g(t)] \tag{5} $$

In addition, fractional order systems may have other features that make them more suitable for the study of electronic circuits when most of the desired specifications are not readily achieved by traditional models (Petras, 2006; Trzaska, 2009).

2.2 Fractional order differential equations

A fractional order linear time invariant system can be represented in the form of a scalar differential equation of fractional order as follows:

$$ \begin{aligned} a_nD^{\alpha_n}y(t) + a_{n-1}D^{\alpha_{n-1}}y(t) + a_{n-2}D^{\alpha_{n-2}}y(t) + \cdots + a_0D^{\alpha_0}y(t) = b_mD^{\beta_m}u(t) + b_{m-1}D^{\beta_{m-1}}u(t) \\ + b_{m-2}D^{\beta_{m-1}}u(t) + \cdots + b_0D^{\beta_0}u(t) \end{aligned} \tag{6} $$

where $y(t)$ is the system response and $u(t)$ the excitation signal, D the derivative operator and $a_n > a_{n-1} > \ldots > a_0$ and $\beta_m > \beta_{m-1} > \ldots > \beta_0$ non-integer positive numbers. Coefficients a_k, $k = 0, 1, 2, \ldots, n$ and b_h, $h = 0, 1, 2, \ldots, m$ are constants.
An alternative representation of (6), more useful for the analysis of fractional-order systems, is given in the following state space form:

$$\frac{d^{\alpha}\mathbf{x}(t)}{dt^{\alpha}} + \boldsymbol{\varphi}(\mathbf{x},\alpha,\mathbf{A},\beta,t) = \mathbf{A}\mathbf{x}(t) + \mathbf{B}\mathbf{u}(t), \quad \mathbf{y}(t) = \mathbf{C}\mathbf{x}(t) + \mathbf{D}\mathbf{u}(t), \quad \varphi(\mathbf{x},\alpha,\mathbf{A},\beta,t) \text{ given for } t > \beta \quad (7)$$

where $x(t) \in R^n$, $u(t) \in R^m$, $y(t) \in R^p$ are states, inputs, and outputs vectors of the system and $A \in R^{n\times n}$, $B \in R^{n\times m}$, $C \in R^{p\times n}$, $D \in R^{p\times m}$ denote constant element matrices, and a is the fractional commensurate order (Das, 2008; Kilbas et al., 2006).
The fractional dynamic variables in the system of equations (7) are not states in the true sense of the 'state' space. Consequently, as the initialization function vector is generally required, the set of elements of the vector $x(t)$, evaluated at any point in time, does not specify the entire 'state' of the system. Thus, for fractional-order systems, the ability to predict the future response of a system requires the set of fractional differential equations along with their initialization functions, that is, equation (7).

3. Fractional order circuits

Today, micro- and nanoelectronic products are wide-spread in all kinds of industries and in commonly used household devices and the needs of microelectronic industry often drive science and technology research. One of such needs, and the primary task in modeling of micro- and nanoelectronic devices, is the prediction of circuits' behavior in various situations. This means, on the one hand, the estimation of the effective (or overall) properties of a circuit from its structural composition, commonly referred to as homogenization and, on the other hand, allowing for localization, i.e. estimation of the local load state within the individual constituents as response to an overall applied (far field) load. In an effort to better understand dynamical properties of electronic circuits, their stability features and the impact of various parameters, the fractional order approach seems to be very promising (see for example Das, 2008; Dorčák et al., 2007; Petras, 2006; Santhiah et al., 2011; Trzaska, 2008; Marszałek & Trzaska, 2011): many real dynamical circuits are better characterized by using non-integer order models based on fractional order differential or integral calculations. However, the newly produced nano-devices need superior accuracies and possibilities of correlating their hierarchies to models of the fractional order a (Baleanu et al., 2010). While stepping from micro- to nanoelectronics one is faced with heterogeneous multi-order models which couple mathematical descriptions using integer order and fractional order differential equations.
This approach requires the theoretical understanding and numerical modeling of the fundamental fractional order phenomena that underlie integrated devices. As a first step understanding the possible dynamic behavior of linear fractional order circuits (FOCs) is fundamental as most properties and conclusions of integer order circuits (IOCs) cannot be simply extended to that of the FOCs (Caponetto, 2010). The models of the FOCs exhibit more degrees of freedom and they contain unlimited memory that make the circuit behave in more complicated manner.

3.1 Basic properties of fractional order circuits

Generally, the descriptions of the components of electronic circuits need not to be limited to the separate characteristics of ideal resistors, capacitors or inductors: a component may have characteristics somewhere between the characteristics of standard components such as fractional order electrical impedance, that is between the characteristics of a resistor and a capacitor. For instance, a supercapacitor also known as ultracapacitor shows the constant phase behavior or capacitance dispersion, and thus simple RC circuit does not give an adequate description of the AC response of such elements. Its simplest model can be based on Curie's empirical law (Westerlund, 2002) which states that under DC voltage excitation U_0 applied at $t=0$ the current through a supercapacitor is

$$i(t) = \frac{U_0}{h_1 t^m} \tag{8}$$

where h_1 and m are constants.
However, for a general excitation voltage $u(t)$ we have the current

$$i(t) = C_f \frac{d^m u(t)}{dt^m} \tag{9}$$

where C_f is fractional capacitance of the supercapacitor depending on the kind of dielectric and rate of development of the electrode surfaces (Baleanu et al., 2010; Petras, 2006).
For a real coil with proximity and skin effects the relation between its voltage and current takes the form

$$u(t) = L_f \frac{d^n i(t)}{dt^n} \tag{10}$$

where L_f is the fractional inductance and $n \in (0, 1)$ depends on the coil form and its materials.
The importance of (9) and (10) lies mainly in the fact that they can easily be used to describe many other practical electronic and electrical devices because there is a large number of electric and magnetic phenomena where the fractional order models appear to be the most appropriate (M. Trzaska & Trzaska, 2007). It should be emphasized however that, although the real microelectronic objects are generally fractional (Dorčák et al., 2007), for many of them the fractionality is very low. To demonstrate these facts we shall consider some selected cases of FOCs.
Let us begin with a brief description of the application of fractional order calculus to analysis of a linear circuit shown in Fig. 1a which contains fractors L_f and C_f. The fractors represent a real coil and a supercapacitor, respectively, and are described by

$$u(t) = L_f \frac{d^{3/2} i_L(t)}{dt^{3/2}}, \quad i_C(t) = C_f \frac{d^{1/2} u(t)}{dt^{1/2}} \tag{11}$$

Denoting $x(t) = i_L(t)$ and then applying the Kirchhoff laws and taking into account (11) we obtain the following mathematical model of the fractional order

$$A_f \frac{d^2 x(t)}{dt^2} + B_f \frac{d^{3/2} x(t)}{dt^{3/2}} + x(t) = i_z(t) \tag{12}$$

where $A_f = C_f L_f$, $B_f = GL_f$ denote constant coefficients and $i_z(t)$ is a time varying right hand side term.

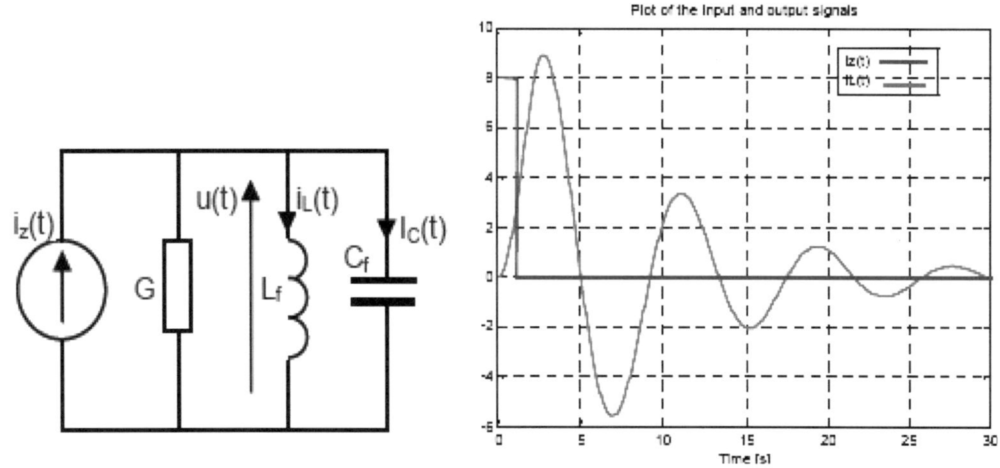

(a) (b)

Fig. 1. Linear circuit containing fractors L_f and C_f: a) structure, b) input and output signals

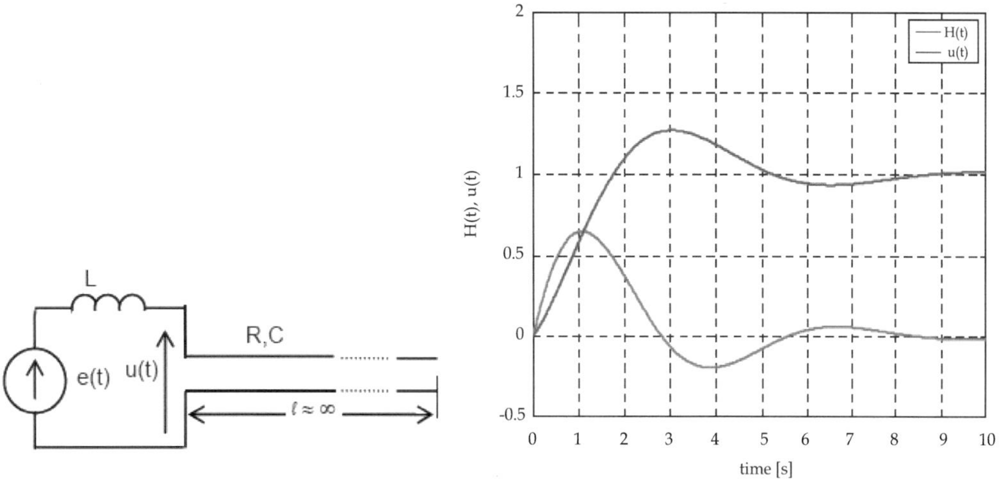

(a) (b)

Fig. 2. Voltage source connected to uniform RC line: a) scheme of the circuit, b) impulse $H(t)$ and unit-step $u(t)$ responses

To determine the solution of (12) we have used a special numerical procedure based on the Bagley-Torvik scheme (Trzaska, 2010). Taking into account $A_f = 1.25s^2$, $B_f = 0.5s^{3/2}$ and $i_z(t) = 8A$ for $0 < t < 1s$ with $i_z(t) = 0$ for $t > 1s$ and applying the mentioned numerical procedure implemented in MATLAB (Attia, 1999; Redfern & Campbell, 1998) we obtain the solution shown in Fig. 1b. It is easily seen that the circuit displays comprehensive dynamical behavior, such that the transient output signal varies very slowly in respect to the excitation.

Next, let us consider a fractional order circuit shown in Fig. 2a. It represents the connection of a voltage source *e(t)* exhibiting internal conventional inductance L=1H with a very long ($l \approx \infty$) uniform *RC* transmission line. The transmission line can be represented by a circuit with uniformly distributed constant parameters and the whole circuit considered at the line's input is described by the following fractional order model

$$L\sqrt{\frac{C}{R}}\frac{d^{3/2}u(t)}{dt^{3/2}} + u(t) = e(t) \tag{13}$$

where *u(t)* denotes the voltage at the line's input.
However, in order to effectively analyze such systems, it is necessary to develop approximations to the fractional operators using the standard integer order operators. In the work that follows, the approximations are effected in the Laplace variable $s = a + j\omega$. It should be pointed out that the resulting approximations provide sufficient accuracy for the time domain hardware implementations (Faleiros et al., 2006).
For the sake of simplicity of notations without any loss of generality we assume in what follows that $L\sqrt{CR^{-1}} = 1s^{3/2}$ and zero initial conditions are taken into consideration. Thus, applying Kirchhoff laws and relations describing circuit elements in the Laplace transform domain leads to the following fractional order model

$$U(s) = \frac{1}{s^{3/2}+1}E(s) \tag{14}$$

where *U(s)* and *E(s)* denote the Laplace transforms of $u(t)$ and $e(t)$, respectively. Now taking into account the inverse Laplace transforms of both sides of (14) yields

$$u(t) = \mathcal{L}^{1}[U(s)] = \int_0^t H_{3/2}(-1,\tau)e(t-\tau)d\tau \tag{15}$$

where the function $H_{3/2}(-1,t)$ is determined by

$$H_{3/2}(-1,t) = \sqrt{t}\sum_{n=0}^{\infty}\frac{t^{3n/2}}{\Gamma(\frac{3}{2}(n+1))} \tag{16}$$

and represents the impulse response of the circuit. In the case of the source voltage $e(t) = E_0\eta(t)$ with $E_0 = const$ and $\eta(t)$ denoting Heaviside function the voltage at the line's input is determined as follows

$$u_\eta(t) = [\eta(t) - E_{3/2}(t^{3/2})]E_0 \tag{17}$$

where $E_{3/2}(t)$ denotes the Mittag-Leffler function for $a = 3/2$ and $b = 1$. Taking into account (16) and (17) we can plot the circuit response for the inputs in the form of Dirac impulse and unit-step functions ($E_0 = 1$) separately. The computed responses are presented in Fig. 2b. It has to be noted that in almost all cases the impulse responses of fractional order circuits are related to the Mittag-Leffler function (Podlubny, 1999), which is effectively the fractional order analog of the exponential function. With this knowledge, it has been possible to better clarify the time responses associated with fractional order circuits.

Interestingly, an alternative approach to the solution of the above circuit can be sought by applying *Symbolic Math Toolbox*. On the base of (14) we can determine the fractance (fractional transfer function) of the circuit, namely

$$\mathcal{F}(s) = \frac{1}{s^{3/2} + 1} \tag{18}$$

Considering $s^{1/2}$ as basic complex variable we can expand right hand side of (18) in the following partial fractions

$$\mathcal{F}(s) = \frac{1}{3}\left(\frac{1}{s^{1/2}+1} - \frac{e^{j\pi/3}}{s^{1/2} - e^{j\pi/3}} - \frac{e^{-j\pi/3}}{s^{1/2} - e^{-j\pi/3}}\right) \tag{19}$$

Observe, that first term in (19) with pole at -1 on the complex plane with variable $s^{1/2}$ introduces an important damping of the impulse response and the remaining terms with poles at $e^{\pm j2\pi/3}$ are responsible on the damping oscillations and all terms taken in the whole give the circuit response which oscillates at an over damped rate. This is easily seen from the time-variations of $H(t)$ presented in Fig. 2b. The diagram corresponds to the expression

$$\mathcal{L}^{1}F(s) = H_{3/2}(-1,t) = \frac{1}{3}\Big[\frac{1}{\sqrt{\pi t}} - e^{\sqrt{t}} - \frac{e^{j2\pi/3}}{\sqrt{\pi t}} + e^{-j2\pi/3}e^{-j(4\pi/3)t}\operatorname{erfc}(e^{-j2\pi/3}\sqrt{t}) - \frac{e^{-j2\pi/3}}{\sqrt{\pi t}} + e^{j2\pi/3}e^{j(4\pi/3)t}\operatorname{erfc}(e^{j2\pi/3}\sqrt{t})\Big] \tag{20}$$

which has been determined by applying the inverse Laplace commands from the *Symbolic Math Toolbox*. It is worth noting that the form of (20) is an alternative form of (16).

Now, to highlight numerous benefits from the application of suitable procedures contained in the MATLAB package we consider the circuit shown in Fig. 3a. It is composed of a real coil L_f and a supercapacitor C_f, both elements considered as fractors and a zero order voltage

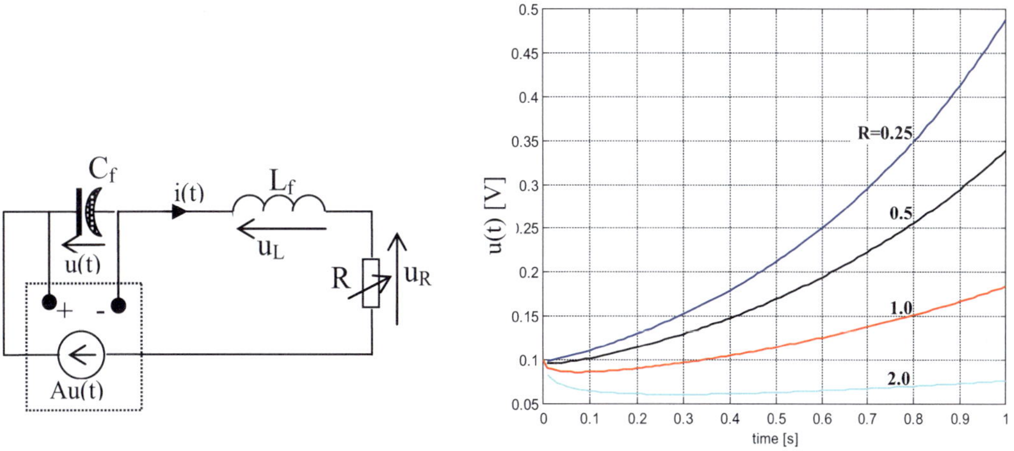

Fig. 3. Fractional order circuit with controlled source and resistor: a) circuit scheme, b) capacitor's voltage for various resistances

source controlled by the supercapacitor's voltage $v_C(t) = Au(t)$. Applying circuit laws we obtain the following set of expression in terms of fractional order derivatives

$$L_f \frac{d^{\alpha_1} i(t)}{dt^{\alpha_1}} = u_L(t), \quad C_f \frac{d^{\alpha_2} u(t)}{dt^{\alpha_2}} = i(t), \quad Ri(t) = u_R(t), \quad Au(t) = v_C(t) \tag{21}$$

with the same symbol meanings as in Fig. 3a. Applying the voltage Kirchhoff law and taking into account (21) and rearranging the terms we obtain the following fractional order equation

$$L_f C_f \frac{d^{\alpha_1+\alpha_2} i(t)}{dt^{\alpha_1+\alpha_2}} + RC_f \frac{d^{\alpha_2} u(t)}{dt^{\alpha_2}} + u(t) = Au(t) \tag{22}$$

If we assume that $L_f C_f \equiv 1$, $A = 3$, $R = var$, and $C_f = const$ then equation (22) takes the form

$$\frac{d^{\alpha_1+\alpha_2} u(t)}{dt^{\alpha_1+\alpha_2}} + R_\tau \frac{d^{\alpha_2} u(t)}{dt^{\alpha_2}} - 2u(t) = 0 \tag{23}$$

where $R_\tau = RC_f$ denotes the time constant of the R, C_f series connection. In order to analyze effectively the above equation it is convenient to apply the standard procedures supplied by the MATLAB programs package and particularly those from the *Symbolic Math Toolbox*. In this regard, the Laplace transform of the initialized fractional-order differential equation (23) with $\alpha_1 = \alpha_2 = ½$ takes the form

$$sU(s) - u(0) + \sqrt{s} R_\tau U(s) - \frac{d^{-1/2}}{dt^{-1/2}} u(0) - 2U(s) = 0 \tag{24}$$

where $U(s) = L\,[u(t)]$ denotes the Laplace transform of the capacitor voltage $u(t)$. Solving (24) with respect to $U(s)$ yields

$$U(s) = \frac{B}{s + R_\tau \sqrt{s} - 2} \tag{25}$$

where $B = u(0) + d^{-1/2}/dt^{-1/2}\, u(0)$ is a constant depending on circuit initial conditions. Because (25) contains the fundamental 'fractional' poles it can be rewritten, using partial fractions, in a more simple form as follows

$$U(s) = \frac{B}{p_2 - p_1} \left(\frac{1}{\sqrt{s} - p_1} - \frac{1}{\sqrt{s} - p_2} \right) \tag{26}$$

where $p_1 = \frac{1}{2}(-a + \sqrt{a^2 + 8})$ and $p_2 = \frac{1}{2}(-a - \sqrt{a^2 + 8})$ denote the fractional poles of $U(s)$ with $a = R_\tau$. The above result indicates that the response of the initialized fractional order circuit can be determined by inverse transforming of each term of (26) separately. To accomplish these tasks, it is convenient rewrite (26) in an equivalent form as follows

$$U(s) = U_1(s) + U_2(s) \tag{27}$$

with

$$U_1(s) = B / ((p_2 - p_1)(\sqrt{s} - p_1)), \quad U_2(s) = -B / ((p_2 - p_1)(\sqrt{s} - p_2)) \tag{28}$$

To obtain the inverse Laplace transform of (28) we have used quite simple procedure of symbolic computing, namely

```
syms a s t B;
p1=-a/2+0.5*sqrt(a^2+8);
p2=-a/2-0.5*sqrt(a^2+8);
U1=B/(p2-p1)/(sqrt(s)-p1);
U2=-B/(p2-p1)/(sqrt(s)-p2);
u1=ilaplace(U1),
u2=ilaplace(U2)
```

The symbolically computed expressions take the form

```
u1=-B/(a^2+8)^(1/2)*(1/(pi*t)^(1/2)-(-/2*(a^2+8)^(1/2)+1/2*a)*exp((-1/2*(a^2+8)^(1/2)
        +1/2*a)^2*t)*erfc((2*(a^2+8)^(1/2)+1/2*a)*t^(1/2)));

u2=B/(a^2+8)^(1/2)*(1/(pi*t)^(1/2)-(1/2*(a^2+8)^(1/2)
        +1/2*a)*exp((1/2*(a^2+8)^(1/2)
   +1/2*a)^2*t)*erfc((1/2*(a^2+8)^(1/2)+1/2*a)*t^(1/2)))          (29)
```

Thus, following (25) - (29) we can represent the desired response as

$$u(t) = u_1 + u_2 \tag{30}$$

The above expressions are useful for determining the influence of the resistance's control on the circuit response. Plots of the *u*-function versus time for $B = -0.1$ and various values of R_T are given in Fig. 3b. Looking at the values of the poles p_1 and p_2 we conclude that they correspond to a saddle node equilibrium point which involves instability of the circuit response for the whole range of possible values of the resistance R_T (Das, 2008).

The above results can be used in many possible applications of FOCs and help assessing whether the latter are capable of addressing the industry's problems. They can serve as an overall introduction to fractional order methods and approaches as well as hands on exercises using state-of-the art software capabilities.

3.2 Chaotic fractional order circuits

Although chaotic phenomena have been studied extensively for a few dozen of years, the chaos theory still remains a fascinating area for exploration and there always seems to be some new aspects that can be revealed. Chaotic behaviors have been observed in different areas of science and engineering and various mathematical definitions of chaos have been proposed, resulting in a lack of a commonly accepted definition for it (Awrejcewicz & Lamarque, 2003; Chua, 1994; Ogorzałek, 1997). Thus, instead of selecting a definition for 'chaos', it is much easier to list properties of chaotic systems: it is accepted that the chaotic behavior is a recurrent, bounded, nonperiodic, long-time evolution of a system leading to a strange attractor in phase space. Also, chaotic systems present an extreme sensitivity to initial conditions i.e. small differences in the initial states can lead to extraordinary differences in the system states (Marszalek & Trzaska, 2009; Tadeusiewicz & Halgas, 2005). Chaos can be a desirable feature in many applications. For example in electronics and telecommunications chaos could be induced to spread modal energy at resonance or to achieve optimal spatial emission of electromagnetic waves.

In this subsection the effects of fractional dynamics in chaotic circuits are studied. In particular, Chua's circuit is modified to include fractional order elements. It is worth mentioning that fractional order Chua's circuit has proven to be an excellent paradigm for generation of a multitude of different dynamical phenomena and can thus obviate the need to consider many different models to simulate those phenomena. One of the main reasons behind Chua's circuits' popularity is their flexibility and generality for representing virtually many practical structures, including those undergoing dynamic changes of topology. Varying the total circuit order incrementally demonstrates that systems of "order" less than three can exhibit chaos as well as other nonlinear behavior. This effectively forces a clarification of the definition of order which can no longer be considered only by the total number of differentiations or by the highest power of the Laplace variable s.

3.2.1 Analysis of oscillations in the modified Chua's circuit

Let us consider the fractional order circuit shown in Fig. 4a which represents a modified Chua's circuit (Marszalek & Trzaska, 2010). Standard Chua's circuit is well known and has been extensively studied in (Brown et al, 2001; Chua, 1994; Trzaska, 2005). The particular form to be considered here was presented by Trzaska (2008) and used further in Marszalek and Trzaska (2009). This circuit is different from the usual Chua's circuit in that the piecewise-linear nonlinearity is replaced by an appropriate cubic nonlinearity which leads to a very similar behavior. In a general case, this nonlinear oscillator comprises a nonlinear resistor with a cubic characteristic $I_n(V_1)$, three fractors represented by an inductor and two supercapacitors, a current controlled current source I and a biasing constant current source a. Its behavior depends on all six constants (parameters) involved. It can exhibit a wide spectrum of dynamical behaviors such as the relaxation, multi-mode oscillation, bifurcation and chaos. The mathematical description of dynamical components is based on expressions (16) and (17) and the studied circuit can be described as follows

$$\begin{aligned} C_1 \frac{d^{q_1} x_1}{dt^{q_1}} &= -x_2 + \alpha x_1^2 + \beta x_1^3, \\ L \frac{d^{q_2} x_2}{dt^{q_2}} &= x_1 - R x_2 - x_3, \\ C_3 \frac{d^{q_3} x_3}{dt^{q_3}} &= a - b x_2 \end{aligned} \tag{31}$$

where q_1, q_3 and q_2 denote fractional orders of the supercapacitors C_1, C_3 and of the real coil L, respectively. Constant resistance is denoted by R. It is worth mentioning that even in the case of integer orders $q_1 = q_2 = q_3 = 1$ the above circuit can exhibit a number of exceptional behaviors depending on circuit linear element parameters, the form of the nonlinear resistor characteristic as well as on initial conditions. Of particular interest here are the mixed-mode oscillations (MMOs) which consist of a series of small-amplitude oscillations (also called the subthreshold oscillations, or STOs) and large-amplitude oscillations, or relaxations, occurring in various patterns. For instance, assuming C_1 = 0.01F, L = 1H, C_3 = 1F and a = 0.0005A, b = 0.0035, α =1.5 and β = -1 with $q_1 = q_2 = q_3 = 1$ we get the MMOs illustrated in Fig. 4b with respect to the state variable $x_1(t)$. The solution of the circuit equations and the illustration figure have been obtained by applying standard MATLAB's procedure ODE45 and plot commands, respectively. A series of numerical computations when various parameters of the circuits bifurcate have been performed and the one showed is typical for MMOs. The importance of MMOs lies mainly in the fact that during bifurcations the circuits' dynamics undergoes complex transitions between various stable and chaotic modes, including the mixed mode oscillations, period doubling bifurcations and chaotic responses. In most cases the solutions pertain to canard phenomenon. The most accepted and popular approach to explain the MMOs phenomenon in $\boldsymbol{R}^3$ is that they result from a combination of canard solutions around a fold singularity and relaxation spikes coupled together by a special ***global return mechanism*** (Trzaska & Marszalek, 2011).

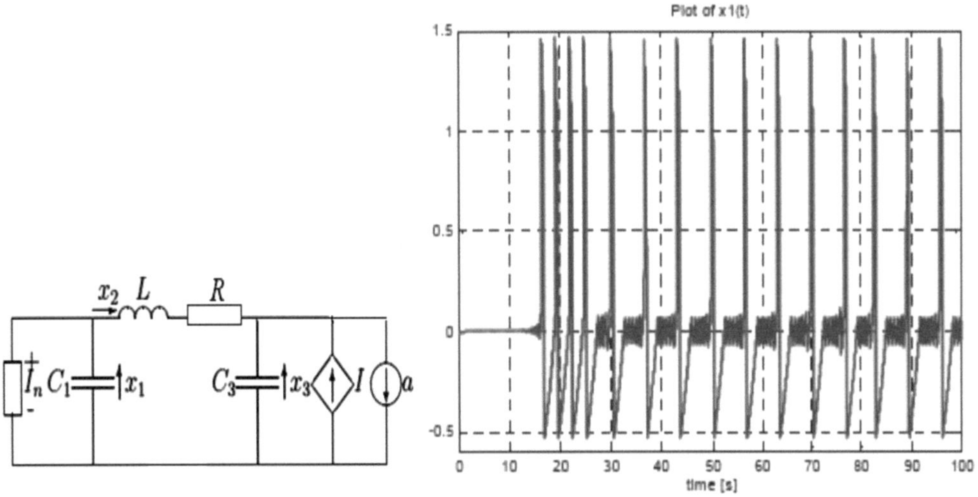

(a) (b)

Fig. 4. Modified Chua's circuit: a) scheme with fractors C_1, L, C_3 and $I = (1 + b)x_2$, $I_n = \alpha x_1^2 + \beta x_1^3$, a = const > 0, b = const > 0, $\alpha < 0$ and $\beta > 0$, b) MMOs in an integer order case

Using the same element parameters values as the ones assumed above and changing only the form of the nonlinear characteristic to $0.88 \leq \alpha \leq 1$ with step size 0.0005 we obtain the solutions exhibiting bifurcations between MMOs and chaotic oscillations. In this chapter, we use two no-chaos criteria for a fractional order circuit represented by state variable equation $d^q x(t)/dt^q = f(x(t))$. Those criteria are: (*i*) x(t) approaches a fixed point; (*ii*) x(t) is bounded. It is clear that if a circuit contravenes both of the above conditions, it has necessary, albeit not sufficient, condition to demonstrate chaotic behavior (Marszalek & Trzaska, 2010).
The code presented below computes bifurcation diagram shown in Fig. 5a. The same code can be used to compute diagrams for other parameters provided that appropriate changes are made in the lines with parameters in bold-face.

Main code:

```
Clear
M = [1 0 0
  0 1 0
  0 0 1];
x0=[-0.5; 0.2; 0.5];
options = odeset('Mass',M,'RelTol',1e-12,'AbsTol',[1e-14 1e-14 1e-14], 'Vectorized','on');
```

```
global t x y z dt alpha
dt=0.01;
for alpha=0.8800:0.0005:1.6000
alpha
clear n
clear m
[t,x]=ode15s(@equations,0:dt:500,x0);
n=length(x(:,1));
m=floor(n/2);
y=diff(x(m,n,1))/dt;
z=diff(y)/dt;
k=1;
clear aa
for i=m:n
t0=t(i); %Comp. local max. pts for m<t<n
option=optimset('display','off');
zer=fsolve(@differ,t0,option);
if interp1(t(m:n-2),z,zer)>0
aa(k)=interp1(t(m:n),x(m:n,1),zer);
k=k+1;
end
end
kmax=k-1;
h=plot(alpha.*ones(1,kmax),aa,'r.');
hold on
set(h,'MarkerSize',0.1);
end
```

Function equations.m:

```
function xdot=equations(t,x)
global alpha
a=0.0005; b=0.01; eps=0.01; beta=-1; R=0.3;
xdot(1) = (-x(2) + alpha*x(1)^2 + beta*x(1)^3)/eps;
xdot(2) = x(1) - x(3) - R*x(2);
xdot(3) = a - b*x(2);
xdot = xdot';
end
```

Function differ.m:

```
function f=differ(a)
global t x dt
s=diff(x(m:n,1))/dt;
f=interp1(t(m:n-1),s,aa);
end
```

Fig. 5 shows the solutions obtained with local maximum values of $x_1(t)$ as a function of α. In all the integrations the initial conditions were zero for all three variables in (31). Note that the number of local maximum points at the level 0.2 − 0.3 (on the lower fold of the surface $x_2 = \alpha x^2_1 + \beta x^3_1$) increases if α increases. The number of upper local maximum points (at the

0.7−0.9 level) increases, too. There are, however, sudden drops in the numbers of both lower and upper maximum points. This happens, for example, around α = 0.945 in Fig. 5a where we observe pure periodic MMOs of type 2-1. Thus, it is clear from Fig. 5a that by selecting α = 0.94 one may expect a chaotic response of the circuit. Similar diagram appears in the case of changing parameter b with α =1 and holding other parameters the same as above. The result is shown in Fig. 5b for $0.005 \le b \le 0.035$. The intervals of b leading to chaotic states are marked by $S_0, S_1, \ldots, S_9$ and the total range of b equals S_T.

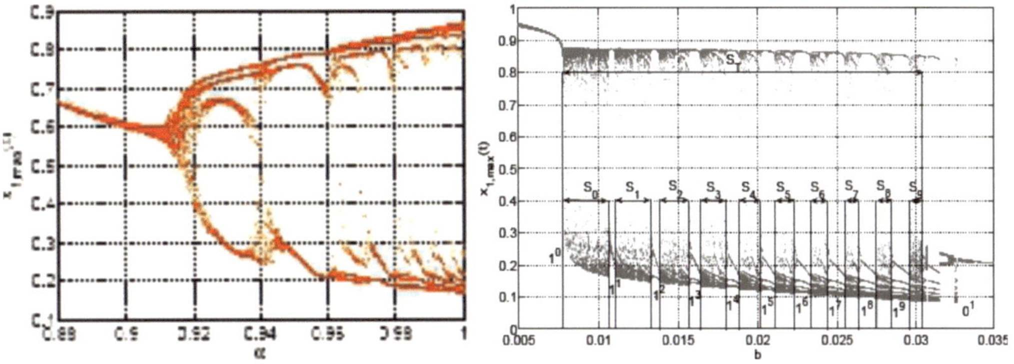

(a) (b)

Fig. 5. Local maximum values of $x_1(t)$: a) as a function of a , b) as function of b

The intervals S_i can be used to determine the fractal dimensions of the circuits, since a detailed analysis of the large-small (L_s) amplitude patterns clearly indicates that they are directly linked to the Farey sequence of the pairs of co-prime integers. Starting from the bifurcation diagram shown in Fig. 5b and using the values of S_k and S_T one can solve the following equation to compute the fractal dimension, denoted by D, namely

```
syms D

solve('(21/167)^D+(17/167)^D+(15/167)^D+(12/167)^D+(10/167)^D+(9/167)^D ...
    +2*(7/167)^D+ (8/167)^D+(6/167)^D-1')
```

In results we have

```
ans =
.84815781317251170768166648997506
```

On the basis of similar series of computations with respect to the remaining state variables x_2(t) and x_3(t) we can conclude that all three variables yield the counting box fractal dimension, denoted by D_c, of the circuits at $D_c = 2.5446$. As a consequence, we shall conjecture that the dynamics of the circuits presented in Fig. 4a is in fact of fractal type. Note that it is well known that chaos cannot occur in conventional continuous systems of total integer order less than three.

As mentioned above, determination of proper parameter range for which a dynamical circuit exhibits chaotic behavior is not always simple and sometimes needs a large amount of numerical simulations. Although more than three decades have passed from the birth of chaos theory, our knowledge about conditions for chaos existence in dynamical systems is still incomplete. Nowadays, it is commonly accepted that the chaotic behavior of nonlinear systems exhibits highly organized shapes leading to a strange attractor in phase space. Moreover, even if a system is characterized by the geometrical form of the corresponding attractor with a defined shape, the modified Chua's circuit can generate both an unusual complexity and an astonishing unpredictability. Noteworthy, up to date no analytical solution has been found for studies of chaotic systems.

3.2.2 Numerical solution of the fractional-order Chua's circuit

In what follows the effects of fractional dynamics in chaotic modified Chua circuits with the structure shown in Fig. 4a are studied. Taking into account the circuit state variable equation (31) we can approximate its solution by applying the discretization procedure and numerical calculation of fractional-order derivation using an explicit relation derived from the Grunwald-Letnikov definition (2). Using the following relation for the explicit numerical approximation of q-*th* derivative at the points kh, (k = 1, 2, . . .) (Kilbas et al., 2006):

$$_{(k-Q_m)}D^q_{kh}x(t) = \lim_{h\to 0} h^{-q} \sum_{n=0}^{k} (-1)^n \binom{q}{n} x((k-n)h) \tag{32}$$

where Q_m is the "memory length", h is the time step size of the calculation and $(-1)^n \binom{q}{n}$ are binomial coefficients $b_n^{(q)}$, (n = 0, 1, 2, …, k) which are calculated as follows

$$b_0^{(q)} = 1, \quad b_n^{(q)} = (1 - \frac{1+q}{n}) b_{n-1}^{(q)} \tag{33}$$

For discretized evaluation purposes it is convenient to simplify notation and introduce the following substitutions

$$x(i) = x_1(ih); \quad y(i) = x_2(ih); \quad z(i) = x_3(ih); \quad i = 0, 1, 2, ..., \tag{34}$$

Initial conditions are taken in the form

$$x(1) = x_1(0); \; y(1) = x_2(0); \; z(1) = x_3(0); \tag{35}$$

Introducing the solution approximation in the polynomial form we obtain the following discrete mathematical model of the circuit for state variables x(i), y(i) and z(i), namely

$$\begin{aligned} &x(i) = (alpha * (-y(i) + f1(a0, a1, x(i-1))) * h \,\hat{}\, q1 - back(x, b1, i), \\ &y(i) = (beta * (x(i) - R * y(i-1) - z(i-1)) * h \,\hat{}\, q2 - back(y, b2, i), \\ &z(i) = (gamma * (a - b * y(i)) * h \,\hat{}\, q3 - back(z, b3, i) \end{aligned} \tag{36}$$

where

$$alpha = C_1^{-1}; \quad beta = L^{-1}; \quad gamma = C_3^{-1}; \quad i = 2, 3, ..., n. \tag{37}$$

and for nonlinear characteristic f1(x)= αx^2 +βx^3 we have

$$a0 = \alpha; \; a1 = \beta; \tag{38}$$

To compute discrete state variable (36) and to plot their diagrams the code presented below can be used. The same code can be used for other parameters provided that appropriate changes are made in the lines with parameters in bold-face (Petras, 2010)

Main code:

```
Clc
clear
% Numerical Solution of the Fractional-Order Modified Chua's Circuit
% with cubic nonlinearity defined in function fm()
function [h, xdisc]=MOChua(parameters, orders, tfin, x0)
%
% time step
h=0.001; tfin=200;
% number of discrete points
n=round(tfin/h);
%orders of derivatives
q1=0.9; q2=0.9; q3=0.9;
%parameters
alpha=100.0; beta=1.0;gamma=1.0;R=0.1;a=0.0005; b=0.001;a0=1.5; a1=-1;
%initial conditions
x0=0;y0=0;z0=0;
% binomial coefficients
bp1=1; bp2=1; bp3=1;
for j=1:n
  b1(j)=(1-(1+q1)/j)*bp1;
  b2(j)=(1-(1+q2)/j)*bp2;
  b3(j)=(1-(1+q3)/j)*bp3;
  bp1=b1(j); bp2=b2(j); bp3=b3(j);
end
% initial conditions setting
x(1)=x0; y(1)=y0; z(1)=z0;
% discretized solution
for i=2:n
  x(i)=(alpha*(-y(i-1)+f1(a0,a1,x(i-1))))*h^q1 - back(x, b1, i);
  y(i)=(beta*(x(i)-R*y(i-1)-z(i-1)))*h^q2 - back(y, b2, i);
  z(i)=(gamma*(a-b*y(i)))*h^q3 - back(z, b3, i);
  f(i)=f1(a0,a1,x(i));
end
%plots
t=h:h:tfin;
plot(t,x),grid,pause
plot(x,y),grid,pause
plot(t,x,t,y,t,z),grid,pause
plot3(x,y,z),grid,pause
plot(x,f),grid
%
```

The codes *f1*(a0,a1,x) for the characteristic of a nonlinear resistor and back(x,b,i) are as follows

```
function [fn]=f1(a0, a1, un);
a0=1.5;a1=-1.;
fn=a0*un.^2 + a1*un.^3;
%
function [vo] =back(r, b, k)
%
temp = 0;
for j=1:k-1
  temp = temp + b(j)*r(k-j);
end
vo = temp;
%
```

Simulations were then performed using various q_k, k =1, 2, 3, from the value interval 0.8 ÷ 1.1. In all cases the Lyapunov exponents were computed and one of them at least exhibited positive value which indicates that the circuit is behaving chaotically. Moreover, the numerical simulations also indicated that the lower limit of the fractional derivative q of all state vector components leading to generating chaos takes values from the interval (0.8 ÷0.9). Therefore, using q = 0.9 as fractional state vector derivative yields the lowest value at 2.7 for circuit order generating chaos in the modified Chua circuit. The simulation results obtained for these circuits are presented in Fig. 6 for alpha =100.0, beta = gamma = 1.0, a = 0.0005, b = 0.005, a_0 = 1.5, a_1 = -1.

3.2.3 Fractional-order Chua's circuit with piecewise-linear resistor

Let us explore now the fractional-order modified Chua's circuit of Fig. 4a but with the nonlinear resistor exhibiting piecewise-linear current-voltage characteristic. In order to appreciate the richness of the dynamics of the present variant circuit we involve the resistor's piecewise-linear characteristic composed of three linear segments leading to the form quite similar to that shown in Fig. 6d. It can be described by the formula

$$I_n = \mathrm{abs}(u_1) + H_1 \cdot (u_2 - u_1) \tag{39}$$

where u_1 and u_2 determine successive segments of the piecewise-linear characteristic depending on the voltage at the nonlinear resistor terminals. These segments can be represented as follows

$$u_1 = a_1 x_1, \quad u_2 = a_2 x_1 + a_0, \tag{40}$$

where constant coefficients a_1 and a_2 determine the slopes of particular characteristic segments, and a_0 is the free term. To get a continuous piecewise-linear characteristic the segments are exactly matched as a result of the concatenation given by the shifted Heaviside function

$$H_1 = \frac{1}{2}\left(1 + \frac{\mathrm{abs}(x_1 - x_c)}{x_1 - x_c}\right) \tag{41}$$

with x_c fixed at the point of coordinate x_1 corresponding to characteristic folding of neighboring segments.

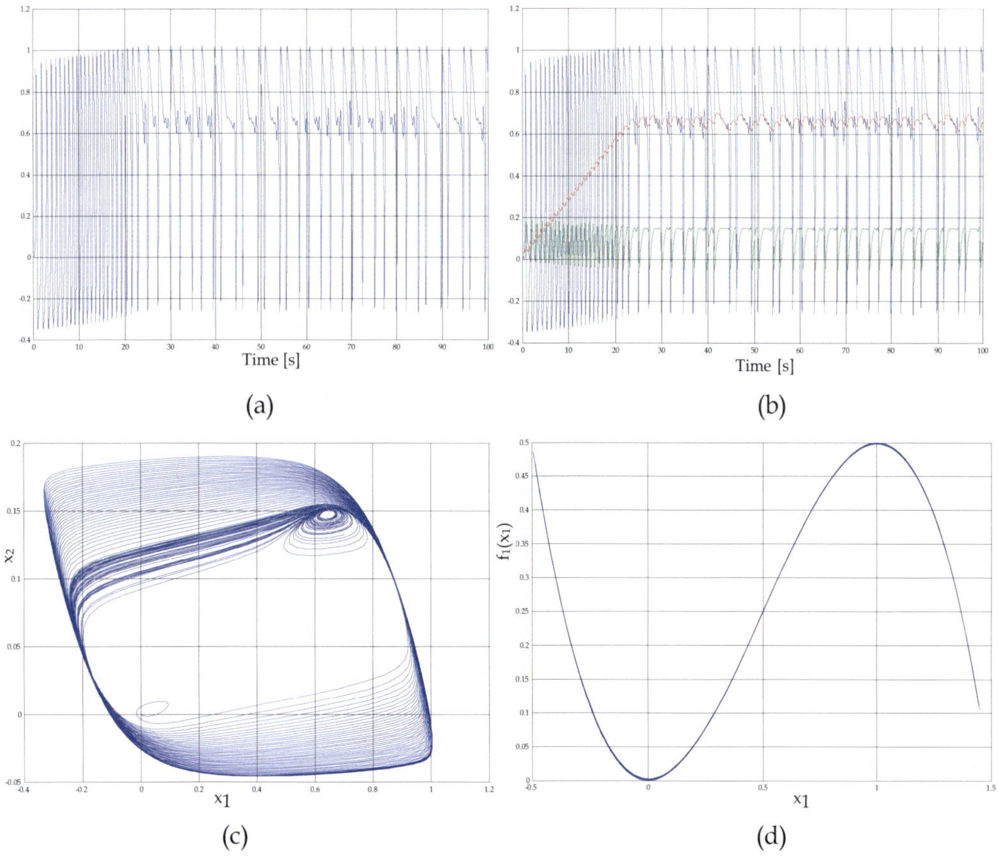

Fig. 6. Simulation results for a modified Chua's circuit of fractional orders $q_1 = q_2 = q_3 = 0.9$: a) state variable $x_1(t)$, b) all state variables: $x_1(t)$ - in blue, $x_2(t)$ - in green, $x_3(t)$ – in red, c) $x_2(t)$ versus $x_1(t)$, d) nonlinear resistor's characteristic $f_1(x_1)= 1.5x_1^2 - x_1^3$

To perform simulations of the fractional-order modified Chua's circuit with nonlinear resistor characteristic determined by (39) we can use the above presented MATLAB code after changing only the code corresponding to the nonlinear term by the following one

```
function [fn]=f2(a0, a1, a2, u0, un);
a0=1.0; a1=1.5; a2=-0.75; u0=1.0;
J1=abs(un-u0)./(un-u0);H1=0.5*(1+J1);
u1=a1*un;u2=a2*un+a0;
fn=abs(u1)+H1.*(u2-u1);
```

where appropriate changes can be made in parameters in bold-face, similarly to the main code. The resulting characteristic for a range of parameters assumed as above are shown in Fig. 7a.
A slight modification of arguments of the code above enables to generate other forms of piecewise-linear characteristics of the nonlinear resistor. For instance, the case of 5-segment characteristic obtained by such modified code is presented in Fig. 7b.
It is worth noticing that the piecewise-linear models are an attractive alternative to continuous nonlinear ones because they are both efficient in memory use and economical in computation time, despite the fact that the derivation of a model usually requires two steps:

first, the piecewise-linear approximation of nonlinear elements' characteristics, and second, their algebraic representations. Applying such an approach to studies of nonlinear circuits leads to piecewise-linear differential equations yielding a pervasively better understanding of various problems in applications. For instance, the piecewise-linear models for operational amplifiers (op amps) and operational transconductance amplifiers (OTA's) are both simple and frequently used. Another way of approximating dynamic circuits with semiconductor diodes can be obtained by replacing the real characteristic by piecewise-linear functions between diode current and voltage.

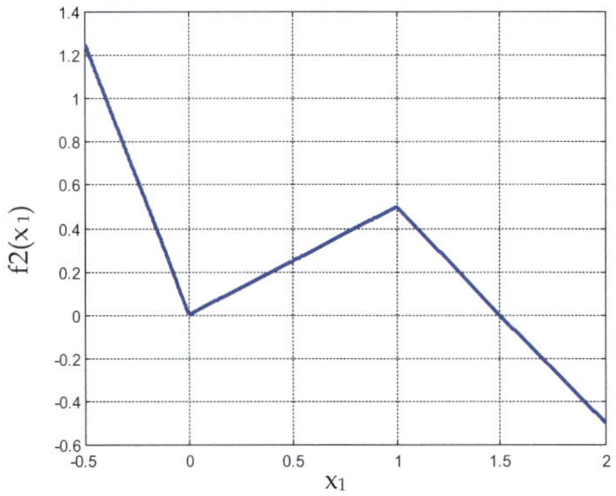

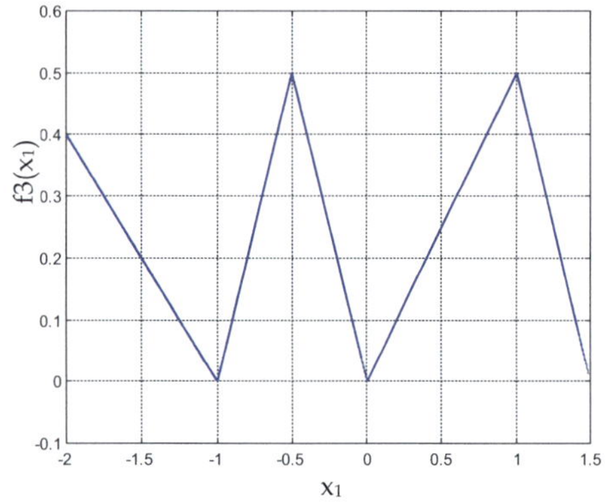

Fig. 7. Piecewise-linear characteristics of the nonlinear resistor: a) 3- segments, b) 5-segments

As it is well known nonlinear devices are already present in a great variety of applications in both power-electronic engineering and signal processing, and in many electrical networks controlling elements like thyristors. To reduce the simulation time of the transient behavior of such circuits and for analysis purposes (e.g., stability or chaos (Tang & Wang, 2005; Trzaska, 2007)), these circuit components are often modeled using piecewise-linear characteristics. Piecewise-linear circuits exhibit most of the phenomena of fractional order nonlinear circuits being yet weakly penetrating. Computer simulations of the suggested discrete maps with memory prove that the nonlinear dynamical circuits, which are described by the equations with fractional derivatives, exhibit a new type of chaotic behavior. This type of behavior demonstrates a fractional generalization of attractors. The subsequent numerical simulation results demonstrate this claim.

3.2.4 Chaotic oscillations in the circuit with piecewise-linear resistor

For the modified Chua's circuit of different fractional orders $\mathbf{q} = [q_1, q_2, q_3]'$ we have chosen function f(x) and the circuit parameters R, L, C_1, C_3, a, b, and h to satisfy the conditions of numerical stability, convergence and accuracy, so that the model (36) with appropriately adapted piecewise-linear characteristic (code for f2(a0, a1, a2, u0, un)) generates regular oscillations or demonstrates chaotic behaviors. For one of the chaotic circuits given in Fig. 4a with alpha = 1.5, beta = 0.85, gamma=1.0, R=0.0, a=0.005, b= 0.05, and piecewise-linear characteristic shown in Fig. 7a we have numerically investigated the sensitivity of the circuit states to the fractional orders q_1, q_2 and q_3. In all computations performed we have fixed initial conditions to be zero. The obtained numerical simulations demonstrated that the non-regular oscillations specified by chaotic attractors can be generated for the components of the vector fractional derivative **q** taking values from the set (0.8 ÷1.0). The chaotic dynamics was identified in two fractional order modified Chua's circuits with 3-segments and 5-segments piecewise-linearity.

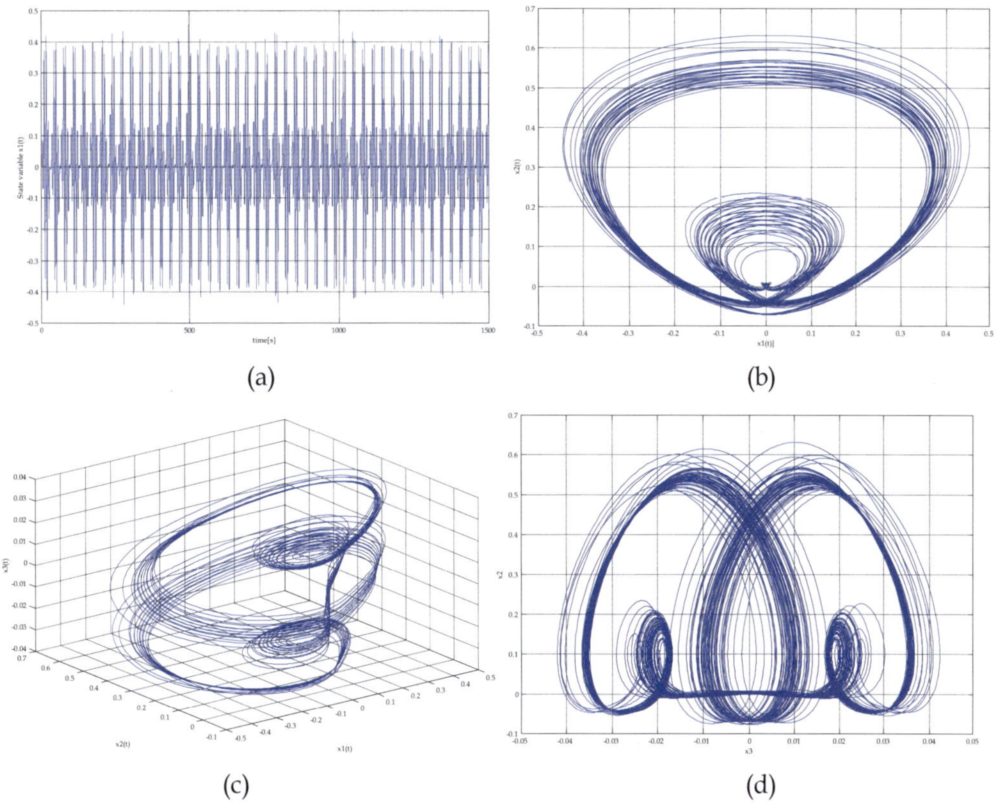

(a) (b)

(c) (d)

Fig. 8. Results of simulations for modified Chua circuits with three segments of piecewise-linear characteristic: a) state variable x1(t), b) phase trajectory x2(t) versus x1(t), c) 3D phase trajectory, d) phase trajectory x2(t) versus x3(t)

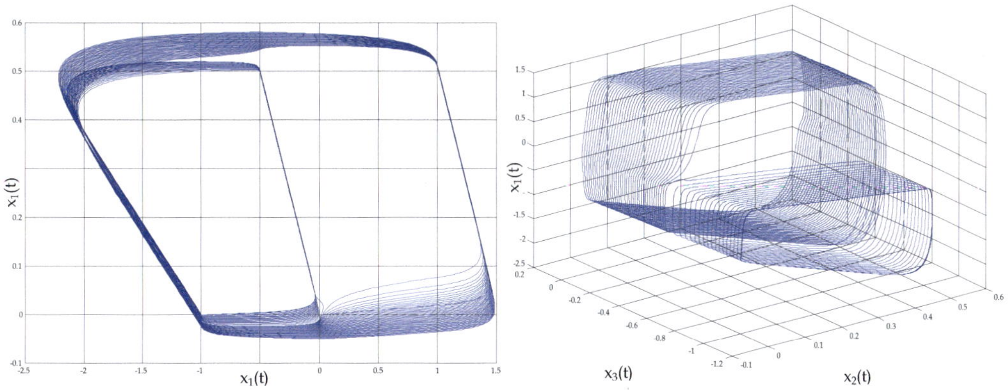

Fig. 9. Chaotic attractors for modified Chua circuits with quintuple segments of piecewise-linear characteristic: a) phase trajectory x2(t) versus x1(t), b) 3D phase trajectory

Examples of numerical simulation results confirming the existence of chaos in circuits with components described by piecewise-linear characteristics are presented in Figs. 8 and 9. It should be noted that the qualitative features of the studied circuits are very well predicted using sufficiently small step h of integrations in such a way that the quantitative results are reasonably close to the ones obtained for continuous relations representing cubic and quintuple nonlinearities.
As mentioned in the previous paragraph, determination of proper parameter range for which a dynamical system exhibits chaotic behavior is not always simple and sometimes needs a large amount of numerical simulations. Unfortunately, outside of numerical simulation, there is currently no other method to distinguish between regular and chaotic oscillations.

4. Conclusion

Most properties and conclusions of integer order circuits cannot be simply extended to that of the fractional order circuits. The models of the fractional order circuits contain unlimited memory and they exhibit more degrees of freedom. Due to the lack of appropriate mathematical tools, chaos analysis in fractional order circuits is more complicated than that in integer order systems. However, it is possible to design a circuit with moderate characteristics, which behavior is not properly represented using conventional methods. In that case the fractional calculus provides a framework for more efficient circuit modeling and control. For instance, the microstructures containing such components as supercapacitors with nano- and microcrystalline surface deposited electrodes can be modeled more successfully by fractional order equations than by traditional models. However, many challenges in the field of fractional order nonlinear circuits remain, notably the ones related to regularity and chaoticity of oscillations. In the case of the modified Chua's circuit the degree of chaoticity can be determined by a measure D_c expressing the counting box fractal dimension of chaotic flows. In the context of the emerging field of computational nanoscience, and in particular in the area of algorithms devoted to numerically explore the electronic circuits, the reported examples reinforce the suitability of the modified Chua's circuits for emulating fractional emergent phenomena.
In this Chapter different circuit dynamics have been described. The wide range of oscillation forms and their combination reflect the complexity of fractional-order nonlinear circuits. Numerical investigations of the behavior of the modified Chua's circuit for different forms of the nonlinear resistor characteristic can be realized with appropriate procedures from the standard MATLAB program package and from the *Symbolic Math Tools* box. It should be pointed out that the use of discretized form of the Grünvald-Letnikov fractional derivative provides a very important tool in the study of the dynamics of fractional order nonlinear circuits. Additionally, examples of program codes by which fractional order nonlinear circuits can be effectively simulated have been provided for studies of circuits with continuous nonlinear and/or piecewise-linear output-input characteristics of respective elements. This approach seems very promising for predicting chaos in fractional order systems studied in domains such as electrical science, diffusion process, electrochemistry, control science, viscoelasticity, material science, etc.

5. References

Attia, J. O. (1999). *Electronics and Circuit Analysis Using MATLAB*. CRC Press, ISBN 0-8493-1892-09, Boca Raton, USA.

Awrejcewicz, J. & Lamarque, C.-H. (2003). *Bifurcation and chaos in nonsmooth mechanical systems*. World Scientific, ISBN 981-238-459-6, Singapore, Republic of Singapore.

Baleanu, D.; Guvenc, Z. B. & Machado, J. A. T. (2010). *New Trends in Nanotechnology and Fractional Calculus Applications*. Springer, ISBN 978-90-481-3292-8, Berlin, Germany.

Basiński, R. & Trzaska, Z. (2008). Bifurcations and chaos in dynamical systems. *Elektronika*, Vol. 23, No. 2, (February 2008), pp. 7-14, ISSN 35722.

Brown, R.; Berezdivin, R. & Chua, L.O. (2001). Chaos and complexity. *International Journal of Bifurcation and Chaos in Applied Sciences and Engineering*, Vol. 11, No. 1, pp. 19-26, ISSN 0218-1274.

Caponetto, R. ; Dongola, G.; Fortuna, L. & Petras, I. (2010). *Fractional Order Systems: Modeling and Control Applications*. World Scientific Company, ISBN 9814304190, Singapore, Republic of Singapore.

Chua, L.O. (1994). Chua's circuit 10 years later. *International Journal of Circuit Theory and Applications*, Vol. 22, No. 4, pp. 279-305, ISSN 1097-007X.

Das, S. (2008). *Functional Fractional Calculus for System Identification and Control*. Springer, ISBN 978-3-540-72702-6, Berlin, Germany.

Dorčák, Ľ.; Terpák, J.; Petráš I. & Dorčáková, F. (2007). Electronic realization of the fractional-order systems. *Acta Montanistica Slovaca*, Vol. 12, No. 3, pp. 231- 237, ISSN 1335-1788.

Faleiros,A.G.; Percella, W.J.; Rabello T.N.; Santos, A.S. & Sonia N.Y. (2006). Chaotic Signal Generation and Transmission. In: *Chaos Applications in Telecommunications*. P. Stavroulakis, (ed), CRC Press, ISBN-10: 0-8443-3832-8, Boca Raton, USA.

Harris, S. T. (2009). *Circuit Analysis I with MATLAB Computing and Simulink/Sim Power Systems Modeling*. Orchard Publications, ISBN 978-1-934404-17-1, Fremont, USA.

Kilbas, A.A.; Srivastava, H.M. & Trujillo, J.J. (2006). *Theory and Applications of Fractional Differential Equations*, Elsevier Science, ISBN-10: 0-444-51832-0, Amsterdam, The Netherlands.

Marszalek, W. & Trzaska Z. (2009). Nonlinear electrical circuits with mixed mode oscillations. *Elektronika*, Vol. 24, No. 9, ISSN 35722.

Marszalek, W. & Trzaska, Z. W. (2010). Mixed-Mode Oscillations in a Modified Chua's Circuit. *Circuits, Systems and Signal Processing*, Vol. 29, No. 2 (February 2010), pp. 1075–1087, ISSN 0278-081X.

Monje, C. A.; Chen, Y. Q; Vinagre, B. M.; Xue, D. & Feliu V. (2010). *Fractional-Order Systems and Controls: Fundamentals and Applications*. Springer, ISBN 978-1-84996-334-3, Berlin, Germany.

Nonnenmacher, T. F.& Metzler, R. (2000). Applications of Fractional Calculus Techniques to Problems in Biophysics. In: *Applications of Fractional Calculus in Physics*. R. Hilfer (ed.), World Scientific, ISBN 978-981-02-3457-7, Singapore, Republic of Singapore.

Ogorzałek, M. (1997). *Chaos and Complexity in Nonlinear Electronic Circuits*. World Scientific, ISBN-13: 9789810228736, Singapore, Republic of Singapore.

Oldham, K.B. & Spanier J. (1974). *The Fractional Calculus*. Academic Press, ISBN 0125255500, San Diego, USA.

Petras, I. (2006). Method for simulation of the fractional order chaotic systems. *Acta Montanistica Slovaca*, Vol. 11, No. 4, pp. 273- 277, ISSN 1335-1788.

Petras I., (2010), Fractional Order Chaotic Systems, Matlab Central File Exchange, MathWorks, Inc., web:
http://www.mathworks.com/matlabcentral/fileexchange/27336

Podlubny, I. (1999). *Fractional Differential Equations*. Academic Press, ISBN 0125588402, San Diego, USA.

Redfern, D. & Campbell, C. (1998). *The Matlab®5 Handbook*. Springer, ISBN 0-387-94200-9, New York, USA.

Santhiah, M.; Philominath, P.; Raja, M. I. & Murali, K.(2011). Ordered and Chaotic Phenomena in Two Coupled Forced LCR Oscillators Sharing a Common Nonlinearity. *International Journal of Bifurcation and Chaos in Applied Sciences and Engineering,* Vol. 21, No. 1, pp. 161-175, ISSN 0218-1274.

Sheu Long-Jye; Chen Hsien-Keng; Chen Juhn-Horng & Tam Lap-Mou.(2007). Chaos in a new system with fractional order. *Chaos, Solitons and Fractals,* Vol. 31, No. 6, (June 2007), pp. 1203–1212, ISSN 0960-0779.

Tadeusiewicz, M. & Halgas, S. (2005). Transient analysis of nonlinear dynamic circuits using a numerical-integration method. *COMPEL: The International Journal for Computation and Mathematics in Electrical and Electronic Engineering,* Vol. 24, No. 2, pp. 707-719, ISSN 0332-1649.

Tang, F. & Wang, L. (2005). An adaptive active control for the modified Chua's circuit. *Physics Letters A,* Vol. 346, No. 2, pp. 342–346, ISSN 0375-9601.

Tavazoei, M. S.; Haeri, M. & Nazari N. (2008). Analysis of undamped oscillations generated by marginally stable fractional order systems. *Signal Processing,* Vol. 88, No. 12, (December 2008), pp. 2971–2978, ISNN 0165-1684.

Tavazoei, M. S. & Haeri, M. (2008). Chaos control via a simple fractional-order controller, *Physics Letters A*, Vol. 372, No. 6, (December 2008), pp. 798-800, ISSN 0375-9601.

Trzaska, Z. (2005). Oscillations in Chua's Circuit as Compendium of Chaotic Phenomena. *Electrotechnical Review,* Vol. 81, No. 2, pp. 25-32, ISSN 0033-2097.

Trzaska, Z. (2007). Characterization of Particular Circuit Elements Requisite for Studying the Electrochemical Processes. *Electrotechnical Review,* Vol. 83, No. 2, pp. 48-52, ISSN 0033-2097.

Trzaska, Z. (2008). Fractional-order systems: their properties and applications. *Elektronika,* Vol.23, No. 10, (October 2008). pp. 31-42, ISSN 35722.

Trzaska, Z. (2010). Chaos in fractional order circuits. *Electrotechnical Review,* Vol. 86, No. 1, (January 2010), pp. 109 -111, ISSN 0033-2097.

Trzaska, Z.(2009). Fractional order model of Wien bridge oscillators containing CPEs. *Proceedings of The MATHMOD Conference,* pp. 128-130, ISBN Wien, Austria, February 11-14, 2009.

Trzaska, Z. (2011). *Symbolic Computational Methods in Automatics and Robotics.* Publishing Office of Warsaw University of Ecology and Management, ISBN 978-83-62057-40-5, Warsaw, Poland.

Trzaska, Z. W. & Marszałek, W. (2011). Mixed Mode Oscillations and Chaos in Nonlinear Circuits. *Acta Technica,* Vol. No. 2, (February 2011), pp. 78-92, ISSN 0001-7043.

Trzaska, M. & Trzaska, Z. (2007). Straightforward energetic approach to studies of the corrosion behaviour of nano-copper thin-layer coatings. *Journal of Applied Electrochemistry,* Vol. 37, No. 2, pp. 1009-1014 , ISSN 0021-891X.

Westerlund, S. (2002). *Dead Mater Has Memory!* Causal Consulting, ISBN/ISSN 91-631-2332-0, Kalmar, Sweden.

Zhao, Ch. & Xue, D. (2008). Closed-form solutions to fractional-order linear differential equations. *Frontiers of Electrical and Electronic Engineering in China,* Vol. 3, No. 2, pp. 214–217, ISSN 1673-3460.

Digital Watermarking Using MATLAB

Pooya Monshizadeh Naini
University of Tehran
Iran

1. Introduction

Embedding a hidden stream of bits in a file is called Digital Watermarking. The file could be an image, audio, video or text. Nowadays, digital watermarking has many applications such as broadcast monitoring, owner identification, proof of ownership, transaction tracking, content authentication, copy control, device control, and file reconstruction (Cox et. al., 2008).
In literature, the host file is called the "asset", and the bit stream is called the "message". The main specifications of a watermarking system are: Robustness (Against intentional attacks or unintentional ones such as compression), Imperceptibility, and Capacity. Importance of each depends on the application. As a matter of fact there is a trade-off between these factors (Barni & Bartolini, 2004). Although watermarking in some literature includes visible imprints, here we only mean the invisible embedding of the data.
In this chapter, we will introduce how to use MATLAB to implement image watermarking algorithms. These algorithms include the most famous ones which are widely used in current literature or more complicated approaches are based upon. These are commonly divided into three categories (Barni & Bartolini, 2004)

1. Watermarking in Spatial Domain
2. Watermarking in Spectral Domain
3. Watermarking in Hybrid Domain

In section 2 we will go through some basic image processing commands in MATLAB. Section 3 provides information about different fundamental watermarking methods. Evaluating the algorithms is discussed in Section 4, and finally section 5 brings a conclusion.

2. Basic image processing commands in MATLAB

Digital Image, like many other files, is known as a matrix in MATLAB. Here, we go through several basic image processing commands.

2.1 Loading an image

For loading an image, it is better to put the image in the same folder with the m-file. This way, the image can be easily loaded through "imread" command:

```
A = imread('lena.tif');
```

Else if the image is in a different folder, it should be fully addressed:

```
A = imread('C:\Users\User1\Desktop\lena.tif');
```

The supported formats by MATLAB are: bmp, cur, fts(fits), gif, hdf, ico, j2c(j2k), jp2, jpf(jpx), jpg(jpeg), pbm, pcx, pgm, png, pnm, ppm, ras, tif(tiff), and xwd. 'A' is now a matrix of pixels brightness values. If the image is in black and white, the matrix is 2-dimmensional. However, if there is a color image, we will have a 3-dimmensional matrix, which has three planes of main colors: Red, Green, and Blue. The number of bits that are needed to preserve the value of every pixel is called "bit depth" of the image. The output class of "imread" command is "logical" for depth of one bit, "uint8" for bit depth between 2-8, and "uint16" for higher bit depths.

2.2 Displaying an image

The most common command for displaying an image(matrix) is "imshow":

```
imshow(A);
```

This command can also depict matrices with double values. If the values are not between 0-255, it is better to map them to this region. This can be simply done by adding an empty matrix to the command. This way, the lowest value of the matrix is considered '0', and the highest is considered 255:

```
imshow(A, [ ] );
```

2.3 Creating an image

"imwrite" is used for creating an image file out of a matrix. The image file is created in the same folder with the m-file if no address is given. This command has some useful parameters such as JPEG image compression ratio:

```
imwrite(A,'wm_lena.jpg','Mode','lossy','Quality',65,'Bitdepth',8);
```

3. Watermarking methods

As mentioned in Introduction there are 3 main categories for digital watermarking methods.

3.1 Watermarking in spatial domain

The message can be any coded or straight arrange of bits. Furthermore, the message can be another image. Consider the asset and the message as shown in Fig. 1.

Fig. 2 shows different bit-planes of the asset with a depth of 8 bits. Bit-plane is the plane that one specific bit of every pixel create.

The command "bitget" can be used here to create the bit-plane splitter function as depicted below:

```
function [B8,B7,B6,B5,B4,B3,B2,B1] = bitplane (pic)
  B1 = bitget(pic,1)*2^0;
  B2 = bitget(pic,2)*2^1 ;
  B3 = bitget(pic,3)*2^2 ;
  B4 = bitget(pic,4)*2^3 ;
  B5 = bitget(pic,5)*2^4 ;
  B6 = bitget(pic,6)*2^5 ;
  B7 = bitget(pic,7)*2^6 ;
  B8 = bitget(pic,8)*2^7 ;
end
```

Fig. 1. Examples of asset and message

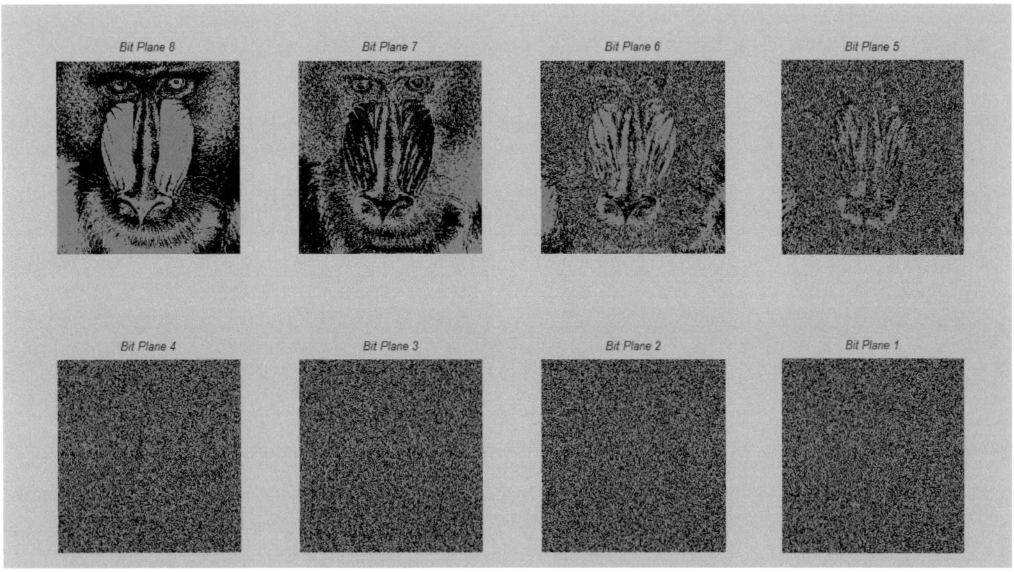

Fig. 2. Bit-planes of the asset image

The first bit-plane is the least significant one (LSB) and most of the time is hardly related to the main shapes of the picture. On the other hand, the last bit-plane is the most significant one (MSB) and contains the main lines and edges of the picture. We consider this image as the asset file. The message also, as shown in Fig. 3, contains 8 bit-planes. Note that the same story is true about lower bit-planes.

Now, as depicted in Fig. 4, we put the significant message bit-planes instead of insignificant bit-planes of the asset, and reconstruct the mandrill image.

As clear in Fig. 5, the resulting watermarked image has a good quality and the watermark message is imperceptible.

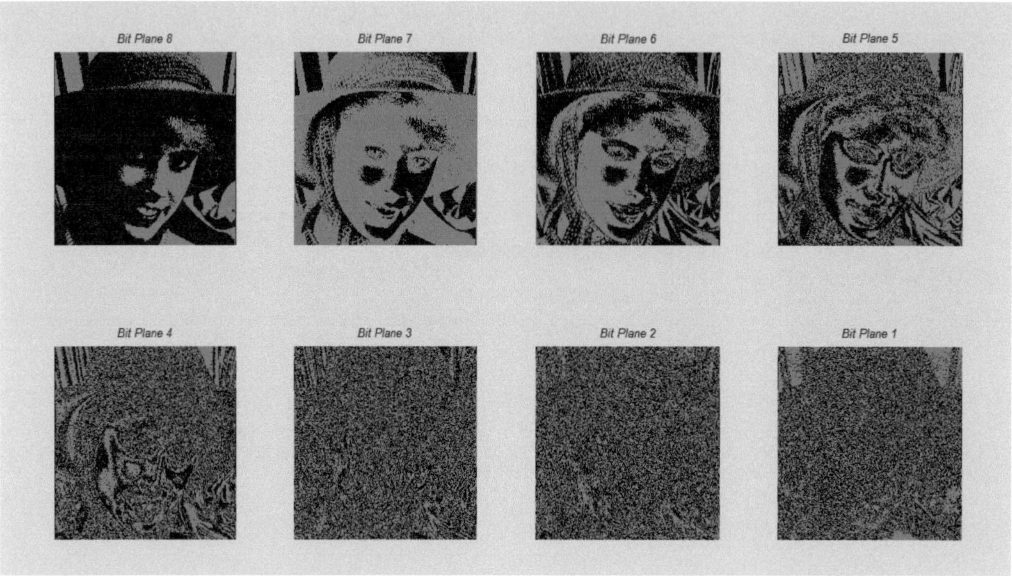

Fig. 3. Bit-planes of the message image

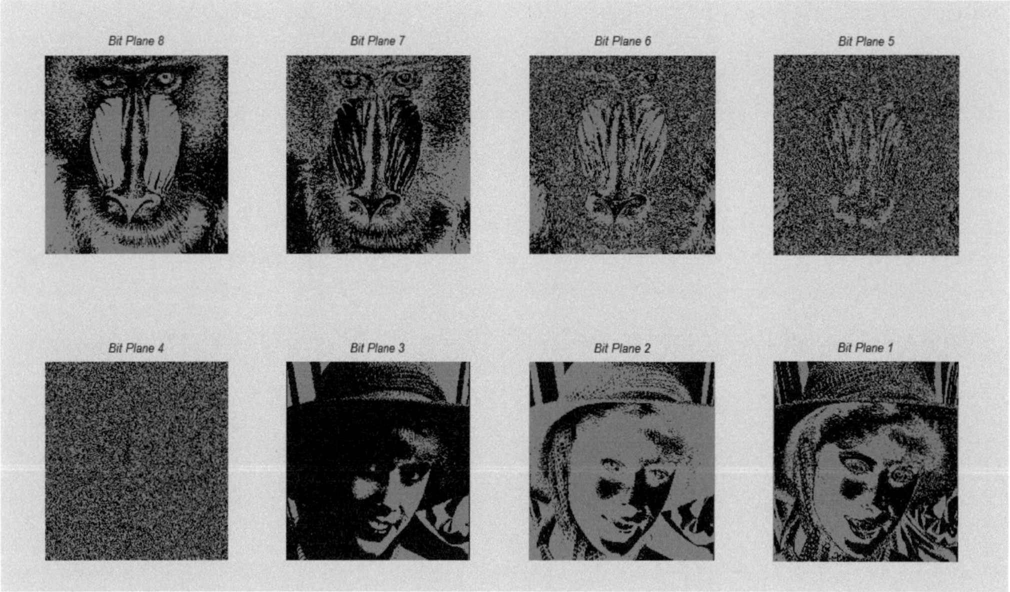

Fig. 4. Substituting the LSB(s) of the asset with MSB(s) of the message

The extraction process simply contains another bit-planes extraction and reconstruction of the message using insignificant bit-planes:

```
message = B3_w * 2^7 + B2_w * 2^6 + B1_w * 2^5;
```

Fig. 6 depicts the extracted message. Note that the main shape of the message is preserved by its highest bit-planes.

Fig. 5. Watermarked image

3.2 Watermarking in spectral domain

There are several transforms that brings an image into frequency domain. Among most common of those, we can mention are: Discrete Cosines Transform (DCT) and Fast Fourier Transform (FFT).

In frequency domain, coefficients are slightly modified. This will make some unnoticeable changes in the whole image and makes it more robust to attack compared to what we have in spatial methods. One of the most popular approaches in this category is the one proposed by Cox et al which is cited by 4166 articles so far according to Google Scholar[1]. In this method, discrete cosines transform (DCT) is applied on the asset image as shown in Fig. 7. Fortunately, there is a direct command for obtaining DCT coefficients of images:

```
B = dct2(A);
```

Note that the output is a matrix of the same size, but with values of "double" class. As illustrated in Fig. 7, the absolute values of the coefficients corresponding to the low

[1] http://scholar.google.com/scholar?cites=11123322177815572712&as_sdt=2005&sciodt=0, 5&hl=en

frequencies are higher and appear in the up-left corner of the square, while high frequency coefficients appear in down-right with lower absolute values.

Fig. 6. Extracted message

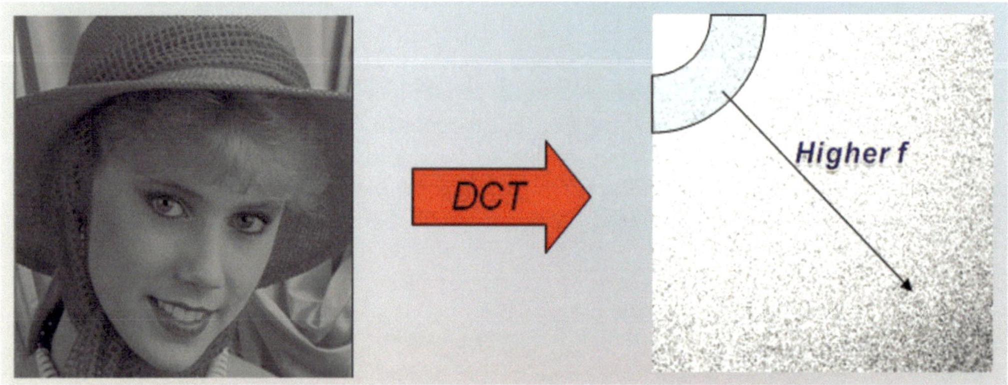

Fig. 7. Bringing an image into DCT domain

To have a better concept of values it is worth to mention that the largest value (51,614) is corresponding to the DC value of the image placed in position (0,0) of the square. "imshow" is used for displaying the DCT coefficients. The message is also coded into an spread spectrum sequence. This step makes the watermarking message robust against many attacks such as JPEG compression which aims to omit the unnoticeable details in high frequencies. Now how the message is added to the asset? Fig. 8 describes the process.

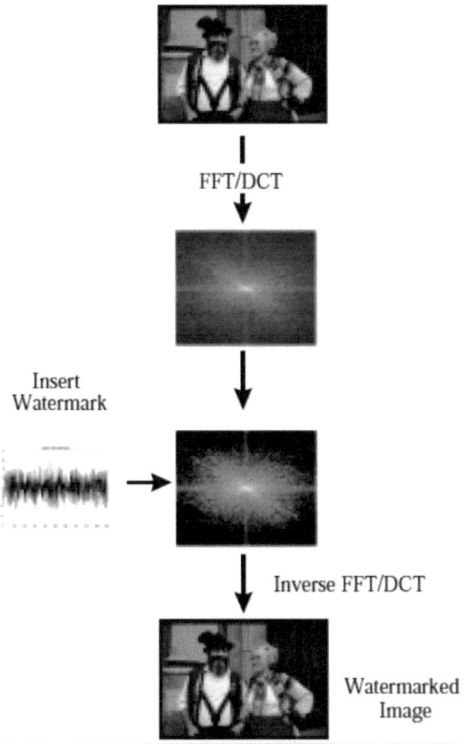

Fig. 8. Watermark embedding in spectral domain (Cox et. al. ,1997)

The question still remains that which coefficients are going to change and how. Cox et. al. use 1000 largest coefficients to embed a watermark sequence of length 1000. The only exception is the DC term, located in (0,0) of the DCT matrix, that should not be changed due to its perceptible change in the whole brightness of the picture. On the other hand, high frequencies are easily changed under common attacks such as compression. Nevertheless, the author suggests not to change some coefficients near to DC term due to their noticeable change. The suggested area is approximately depicted in Fig. 7 .Coefficients are modified according to the stream bits of the message using to the equation 1 (Cox et al., 1997):

$$C_{AW} = C_A \cdot (1 + \alpha \cdot W_i) \tag{1}$$

In which C_{AW} is the watermarked coefficient, C_A is the original one, α represents watermarking strength (e.g. 0.3), and W_i is the corresponding bit of the message data. The formula easily suggests that if a coefficient is larger, it should be modified to a greater extent. We can write the code for the method so far as follows (α=0.1):

```
[fname pthname]=uigetfile('*.jpg;*.png;*.tif;*bmp','Select the Asset Image'); %select image
I=imread([pthname fname]);
wmsz=1000; %watermark size
I=I(:,:,1);%get the first color in case of RGB image
[r,c]=size(I);
D=dct2(I);%get DCT of the Asset
D_vec=reshape(D,1,r*c);%putting all DCT values in a vector
[D_vec_srt,Idx]=sort(abs(D_vec),'descend');%re-ordering all the absolute values
W=randn(1,wmsz);%generate a Gaussian spread spectrum noise to use as watermark signal
Idx2=Idx(2:wmsz+1);%choosing 1000 biggest values other than the DC value
%finding associated row-column order for vector values
IND=zeros(wmsz,2);
for k=1:wmsz
   x=floor(Idx2(k)/r)+1;%associated culomn in the image
   y=mod(Idx2(k),r);%associated row in the image
   IND(k,1)=y;
   IND(k,2)=x;
end
D_w=D;
for k=1:wmsz
   %insert the WM signal into the DCT values
D_w(IND(k,1),IND(k,2))=D_w(IND(k,1),IND(k,2))+.1*D_w(IND(k,1),IND(k,2)).*W(k);
end
I2=idct2(D_w);%inverse DCT to produce the watermarked asset
```

The extraction process is simply subtracting the original DCT coefficients from the watermarked image ones. The code can be written like below:

```
W2=[];%will contain watermark signal extracted from the image
for k=1:wmsz
  W2=[W2(D_w(IND(k,1),IND(k,2))/D(IND(k,1),IND(k,2))-1)*10];%watermark extraction
end
```

Fig. 9 illustrates the process.
Cox et. al. provide equation (2) to check the similarity between the extracted watermark and the original sequence.

$$\mathrm{sim}\left(X,X^*\right)=\frac{X^*\cdot X}{\sqrt{X^*\cdot X^*}} \tag{2}$$

In which "X" is the original and "X*" is the extracted message. Creating a function for this equation would be useful:

```
function SIM=WM_detect(Wstar,Worig)
SIM=sum(Wstar.*Worig)/sqrt(sum(Wstar.*Wstar));
end
```

If the extracted message similarity is checked with 1000 random sequences including the original, a result such as what can be seen in Fig. 10 is obtained. Regarding this plot, a suitable value of threshold can be set to detect the original watermark.

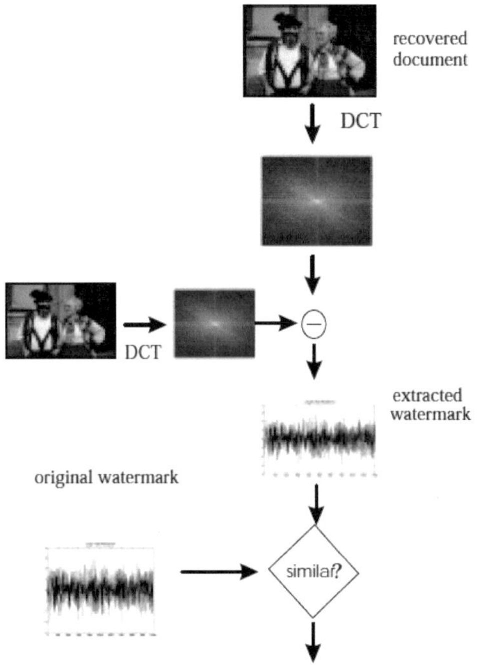

Fig. 9. Watermark extraction (Cox et. al., 1997)

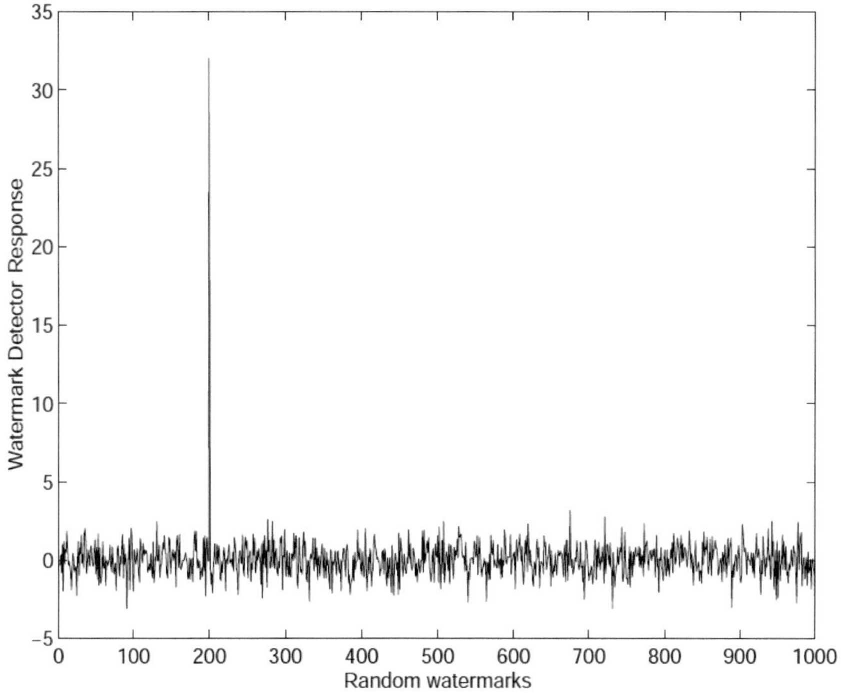

Fig. 10. Detector response to 1000 random sequences including the original (Cox et. al., 1997)

This algorithm, despite the previous in spatial domain, needs the original asset for extraction. Methods like these are called "non-blind detection" (LSB was a sample of "blind detection"). A solution for this can be setting fix mid-frequency coefficients for preserving the watermark message (Barni & Bartolini, 2004).

3.3 Watermarking in hybrid domain

Watermarking in hybrid domain means modifying the image regarding both spatial and spectral specifications. One popular algorithm in this domain is performing the previous method in small blocks of the image. This could happen in 8×8 blocks which ideally match JPEG compression to provide least distort to the message facing with JPEG compression attack (Barni & Bartolini, 2004). Fig. 11 illustrates this method. Pixels in blue represent intensity of middle frequencies in the image and are most suitable for carrying message data. The code has not been brought here because it is simply performing spread spectrum algorithm in separate smaller blocks.

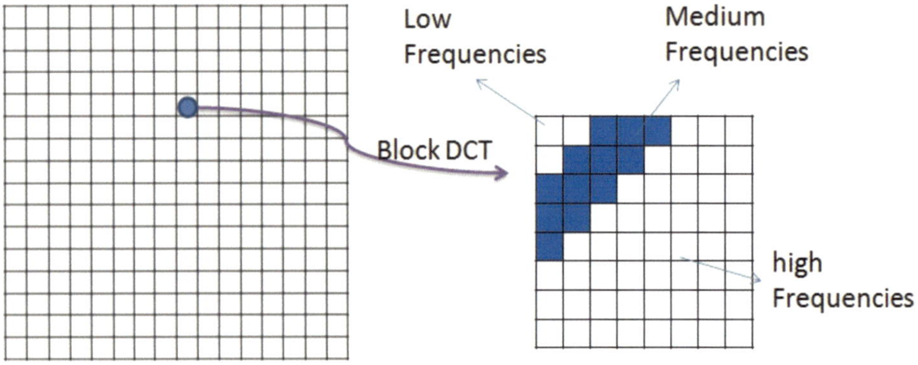

Fig. 11. Block-based hybrid method (recreated from Barni & Bartolini, 2004)

Another famous example of this is "Discrete Wavelet Transform" abbreviated as DWT. For bringing an image to the wavelet domain one can easily use the "dwt2" command:

```
[bA,bH,bV,bD] = dwt2(A, 'wname');
```

In which "wname" is the type of the filter you prefer to use as wavelet decomposition and reconstruction filters. This can be among the filter families of Daubechies ('db1'), Coiflets ('coif1'), Symlets ('sym2'), Discrete Meyer ('dmey'), Biorthogonal ('bior1.1'), and Reverse Biorthogonal (rbio1.1). The option is also provided that you can use your own defined filters:

```
Lo_D = [1 2 1]/4;    % LP Decomposition Filter
Hi_D = [1 -2 1]/4;   % HP Decomposition Filter
[bA,bH,bV,bD] = dwt2(A, Lo_D, Hi_D);
```

The same story is true about the inverse transform:

```
A = idwt2(bA,bH,bV,bD, 'wname')
```

Or

```
Lo_R = [-1 2 6 2 -1]/8;    % LP Reconstruction Filter
Hi_R = [1 2 -6 2 1]/8;   % HP Reconstruction Filter
B = idwt2(bA,bH,bV,bD, Lo_R, Hi_R);
```

The output decomposed matrices of "dwt2" are of class "double" and contain negative or above 255 values. Hence, there should be some mappings if you tend to display them. The result is provided in Fig. 12. In the code, the maximum value for sub-bands is set to 60 which is mapped to 255. This is because they have tiny values comparing the LL image.

```
[bA,bH,bV,bD] = dwt2(A,'bior1.1');
B=[bA,bH;bV,bD];
subplot(2,2,1);
imshow(abs(bA),[]);
subplot(2,2,2);
imshow(abs(bH),[0 60]);
subplot(2,2,3);
imshow(abs(bV),[0 60]);
subplot(2,2,4);
imshow(abs(bD),[0 60]);
```

Fig. 12. Single level wavelet decomposition

Watermarking usually takes place in sub-bands. Just like the spread spectrum method, largest coefficients can be modified according to a similar equation to (1). Another solution is to change LSBs of these values (Vatsa et. al., 2006).

4. Evaluation of watermarking methods

Several Functions are used to qualify the watermarking algorithm, examining tests on the resulted watermarked image.

4.1 Imperceptibility

The imperceptibility of the watermark is tested through comparing the watermarked image with the original one. Several tests are usually used in this regard.

4.1.1 MSE

Mean Squared Error (MSE) is one of the earliest tests that were performed to test if two pictures are similar. A function could be simply written according to equation (3).

$$M.S.E = \frac{1}{n}\sum_{i=1}^{n}\left(X_i - X_i^*\right)^2 \tag{3}$$

```
function out = MSE (pic1, pic2)
e=0;
[m,n]=size(pic1);
for i=1:m
   for j=1:n
      e = e + double((pic1(i,j)-pic2(i,j))^2);
   end
end
out = e / (m*n);
end
```

4.1.2 PSNR

Pick Signal to Noise Ratio (PSNR) is a better test since it takes the signal strength into consideration (not only the error). Equation (4) describes how this value is obtained.

$$PSNR = 10.\log_{10}\left(\frac{MAX_I^2}{MSE}\right) \tag{4}$$

```
function out=PSNR(pic1, pic2)
e=MSE(pic1, pic2);
m=max(max(pic1));
out=10*log(double(m)^2/e);
end
```

4.1.3 SSIM

The main problem about the previous two criteria is that they are not similar to what similarity means to human visual system (HVS). Structural Similarity (SSIM) is a function defined as equation (5) by Wang et. al. in 2004 which overcame this problem to a great extent.

$$SSIM = \frac{(2\mu_x\mu_y + c_1)(2\sigma_{xy} + c_2)}{(\mu_x^2 + \mu_y^2 + c_1)(\sigma_x^2 + \sigma_y^2 + c_2)} \quad (5)$$

Where "μ", "σ", & "σ_{xy}" are mean, variance, and covariance of the images, and "c1, c2" are the stabilizing constants. SSIM has a value between 0-1. Similar images have SSIM near to 1. Fig. 13 illustrates the magnificent advantages of SSIM over MSE.

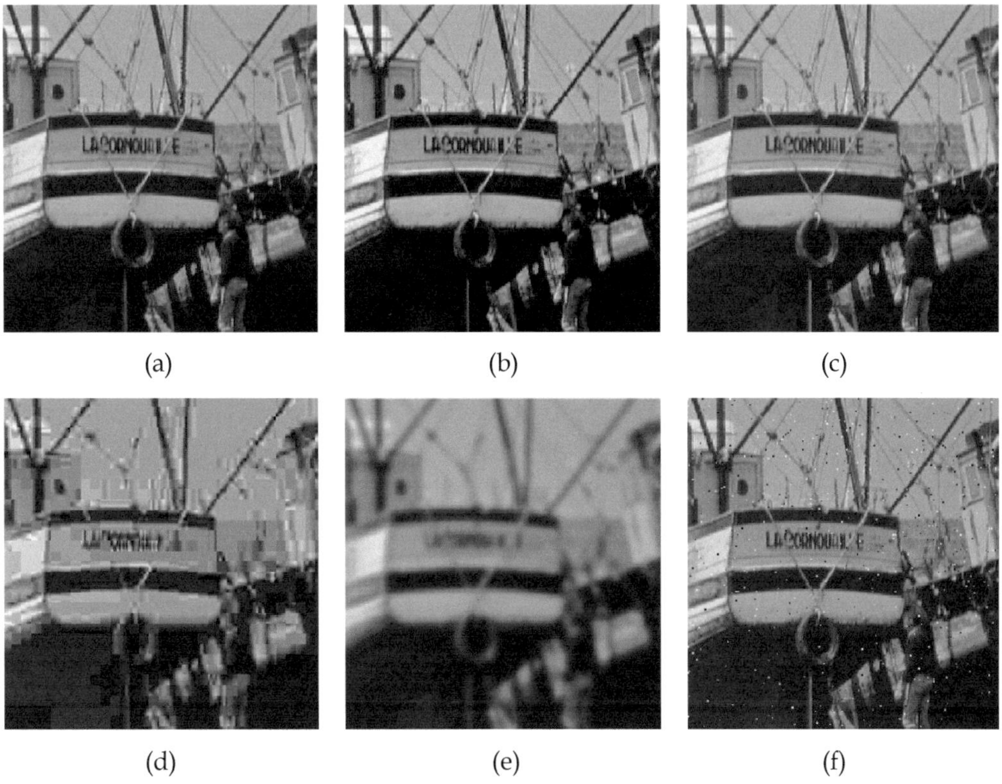

Fig. 13. Comparison of MSE and SSIM. All altered images have the same MSE=210 (a) Original image (b) SSIM=0.9168 (c) SSIM=0.9900 (d) SSIM=0.6949 (e) SSIM=0.7052 (f) SSIM=0.7748. (Wang et. al., 2004)

The MATLAB code is available on authors' webpage.[2]

4.2 Robustness

The robustness of a watermark method can be evaluated by performing attacks on the watermarked image and evaluating the similarity of the extracted message to the original one.

---

[2] http://www.cns.nyu.edu/~lcv/ssim/ssim_index.m

4.2.1 Compression attack

The most used image compression is definitely JPEG. In MATLAB, for compressing an image to different quality factors, the image should be created from a matrix and be reread:

```
imwrite(A,'wm_lena.jpg','Mode','lossy','Quality',75);
A = imread ('wm_lena.jpg');
```

4.2.2 Noise attack

Adding noise in MATLAB is simply done by "imnoise" command. Gaussian, Poisson, Salt & Pepper, and Speckle are among the noises that could be used here. Fig. 14 shows the result of the code:

```
Lena = imread('lena.tif');
Lena = imnoise(Lena,'salt & pepper',0.02);
imshow(Lena);
```

Fig. 14. Salt & Pepper noise

4.2.3 Croppinga

Cropping attack is simply cutting off parts of the image. If the algorithm is non-blind, it is better to bring back those parts from the original image for a better recovery of the message, as depicted in Fig. 15.

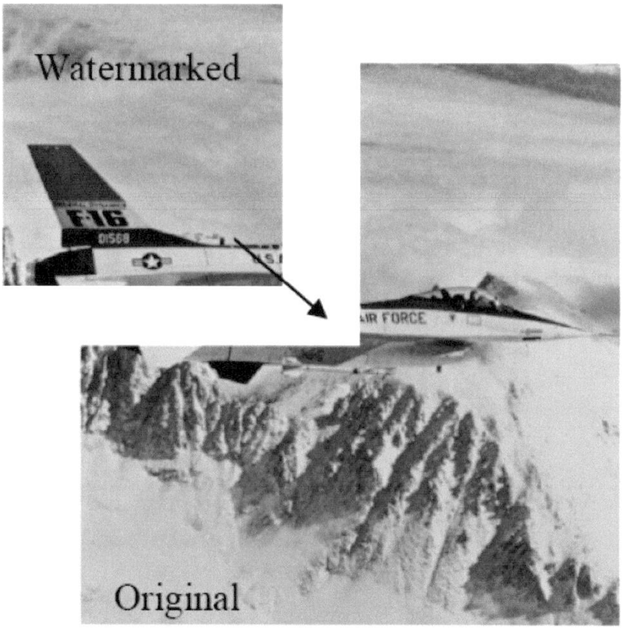

Fig. 15. Recovery from a cropping attack

4.3 Capacity

The capacity of the watermark method can be easily tested by increasing the length of the watermarking message. Any watermarking method is not capable of holding more than a certain length of message or it will endanger its imperceptibility.

5. Conclusion

In this chapter, implementation of basic digital watermarking methods in MATLAB is described. Fundamental methods in spatial, spectral, and hybrid domains are described and sample codes are given. Finally, some solutions for qualifying the watermarking method are described.

6. Acknowledgment

The author wants to thank Prof. Nasiri Avanaki who introduced the world of watermarking to students in University of Tehran.

7. References

Cox, J.; Miller, M. L.; Bloom, J. A.; Fridrich J. & Kalker T. (2008). *Digital Watermarking and Steganography*, Morgan Kaufmann Pub., Elsevier Inc.

Barni M. & Bartolini F. (2004). *Watermarking Systems Engineering*, Marcel Dekker Inc., Italy

Cox, J.; Kilian, J.; Leighton F. T. & Shamoon T. (1997). Secure spread spectrum watermarking for multimedia. *IEEE Transactions on Image Processing*, Vol. 6, No. 12,(December 1997), pp. 1673-1687

Vatsa, M.; Singh, R.; Noore, A.; Houck M. M. & Morris K. (2006). Robust biometric image watermarking fingerprint and face template protection. *IEICE Electronics Express, Vol. 3, No. 2, pp. 23-28*

Wang, Z.; Bovik, A. C.; Sheikh, H. R. & Simoncelli E. P. (2004).Image quality assessment: From error visibility to structural similarity. *IEEE Trans. Image Processing*, vol. 13, no. 4, pp. 600-612.

Made in the USA
Columbia, SC
01 July 2026

007357bb-5aa2-472b-b6ad-542beadc5ff1R01